EIGHTH EDITION

A Short History of Western Civilization

Volume One: To 1776

RICHARD E. SULLIVAN
Michigan State University

DENNIS SHERMAN
John Jay College of Criminal Justice
City University of New York

JOHN B. HARRISON
Late Professor Emeritus of History
Michigan State University

McGraw-Hill, Inc.

New York   St. Louis   San Francisco   Auckland   Bogotá
Caracas   Lisbon   London   Madrid   Mexico City   Milan
Montreal   New Delhi   San Juan   Singapore   Sydney   Tokyo   Toronto

to Mary, Vivian, and Pat

The present overwhelms our forgotten selves;
but we are what we were,
with only a frosting of changes
—D.S.

A Short History of Western Civilization
Volume One: To 1776

Copyright © 1994, 1990, 1985, 1980, 1975, 1971 by McGraw-Hill, Inc. All rights reserved. Copyright © 1966, 1960 by John B. Harrison and Richard E. Sullivan. All rights reserved. Printed in the United States of America. Except as permitted under the United States Copyright Act of 1976, no part of this publication may be reproduced or distributed in any form or by any means, or stored in a data base or retrieval system, without the prior written permission of the publisher.

This book is printed on acid-free paper.

3 4 5 6 7 8 9 0 **DOC/DOC** 9 0 9 8 7 6

ISBN 0-07-026899-1

This book was set in Palatino by Ruttle, Shaw & Wetherill, Inc.
The editors were Pamela Gordon and Larry Goldberg;
the production supervisor was Richard A. Ausburn.
The cover was designed by Katherine Hulse.
The photo researcher was Elsa Peterson.
R. R. Donnelley & Sons Company was printer and binder.

Credits
COVER: Limbourg Brothers, ''Les Très Riches Heures du Duc de Berry, June,'' 1416, Musée Condé, Chantilly. Giraudon/Art Resource. *PART OPENING PHOTOS: Part One*, Ralph Mandol/DPI; *Part Two*, National Archaeological Museum, Athens; *Part Three*, Phototheque Armand-Colin; *Part Four*, The Pierpont Morgan Library, New York. M.705, f.38v.; *Part Five*, The Granger Collection.

Library of Congress Cataloging-in-Publication Data

Sullivan, Richard Eugene, (date).
  A short history of Western civilization / Richard E. Sullivan,
Dennis Sherman, John B. Harrison.—8th ed.
      p.   cm.
  Rev. ed. of: A short history of Western civilization / John B.
Harrison, 7th ed. c1990.
  Includes bibliographical references and indexes.
  Contents: v. 1. To 1776—v. 2. Since 1600.
  ISBN 0-07-026899-1 (v. 1).—ISBN 0-07-026900-9 (v. 2)
  1. Civilization, Western—History.   I. Sherman, Dennis.
II. Harrison, John Baugham.   III. Harrison, John Baugham.
Short history of Western civilization.   IV. Title.
CB245.S9415   1994
909'.09812—dc20   93-42015

ABOUT THE AUTHORS

Richard E. Sullivan was born and raised near Doniphan, Nebraska. He received a B. A. degree from the University of Nebraska in 1942, and an M.A. degree and a Ph.D. degree from the University of Illinois in 1947 and 1949 respectively. His doctorate was earned in the field of medieval history. He has taught history at Northeast Missouri State Teachers' College (1949–1954) and at Michigan State University (1954 until his retirement in 1989). While at Michigan State University he has served as chairman of the Department of History (1967–1970), Dean of the College of Arts and Letters (1970–1979), and Associate Provost (1984–1987). Professor Sullivan held a Fulbright Research Fellowship and a John Simon Guggenheim Fellowship to Belgium in 1961–1962. He is a Fellow in the Medieval Academy of America. He is the author of *The Coronation of Charlemagne* (1959), *Heirs of the Roman Empire* (1960); *Aix-La-Chapelle in the Age of Charlemagne* (1963), *Speaking for Clio* (1991), and *Christian Missionary Activity in the Early Middle Ages* (forthcoming). His articles have appeared in many scholarly journals.

Dennis Sherman is Professor of History at John Jay College of Criminal Justice, the City University of New York. He received his B.A. (1962) and J.D. (1965) from the University of California at Berkeley and his Ph.D. (1970) from the University of Michigan. He was Visiting Professor at the University of Paris (1978–1979, and 1985). He received the Ford Foundation Prize Fellowship

(1968–1969, 1969–1970), a fellowship from the Council for Research on Economic History (1971–1972), and fellowships from the National Endowment for the Humanities (1973–1976). His publications include *Western Civilization: Images and Interpretations* (1991), *World Civilizations: Sources, Images, and Interpretations* (co-author), a series of introductions in the Garland Library of War and Peace, several articles and reviews on nineteenth-century French economic and social history in American and European journals, and short fiction in literary journals.

John B. Harrison was born in Lawrenceville, Virginia, and grew up in Rich Square, North Carolina. He received his B.A. and M.A. at the University of North Carolina, and his Ph.D. at the University of Wisconsin. He also studied at the Sorbonne. He taught history at Lees Junior College, Jackson, Kentucky, the University of Wisconsin extension, Ohio Northern University, and Michigan State University, where he was Professor Emeritus of History. He was Visiting Professor at the University of North Carolina, 1963–1964. Professor Harrison was a member of the American Historical Association and the Society for French Historical Studies. During seven trips to Europe he visited twenty-one countries. He had also traveled in the Far and the Middle East, Africa, and Latin America. He is the author of *This Age of Global Strife* (1952), and of a number of articles and book reviews.

CONTENTS

PREFACE

[Publisher's Note: *In order to provide an alternative to the hardcover edition,* A Short History of Western Civilization *is being made available in a three-volume paperbound edition. Volume One includes Chapters 1–36; Volume Two, Chapters 31–59; and Renaissance to the Present volume, Chapters 25–59. The page numbering and cross-references in these chapters remain the same as in the hardcover text.*]

In this eighth edition of *A Short History of Western Civilization,* we have attempted to achieve the right mix of continuity and change. Those features that made the seventh and previous editions so successful have been retained. We have kept our account brief enough so it offers readers a realistic opportunity to absorb a meaningful overview of the essentials of the history of Western civilization. The scope of the book is not limited to European history; brief treatments of other parts of the world, such as the United States, and non-Western civilizations as they have come to interact with the Western world, are included to put Western civilization into a broader context. Introductory and retrospective essays at the beginning and end of each of the units of the book provide a broad summarizing perspective on major historical eras. Primary documents introduce readers to the sources historians use to investigate a subject. The interpretative essays featuring points on which historians disagree are designed to encourage readers to develop a healthy skepticism toward accepted generalizations about the past and to learn to ask questions about the meaning of historical investigation. The large number of maps and illustrations highlights and complements the written text. The suggested reading lists offer alternatives for deeper study of topics. The student and instructor's guides are available to assist in making full use of this book.

Several important changes have been made in this edition to improve the quality and appeal of the book. There has been an additional infusion of social history and women's history into the text, continuing the changes already made in this direction in the seventh and sixth editions. The addition of this material reflects a growing consensus in modern scholarship that such matters need greater attention in order to portray past human experience fully and accurately. Several parts of the book have been reorganized to better integrate our understanding of the past. There have been extensive revisions of the text to include the most recent historical scholarship, and in some cases new sections have been written. A number of illustrations are new to this edition. Most of the maps have been revised and clarified. Seven "Historians' Sources" sections have been created for this edition, providing a balance to the "Where Historians Disagree" essays and the introductory "History and the Historian" essay. A new chapter covering the extraordinarily important developments of the past few years has been written. The suggested readings have been completely revised and updated.

As in previous editions, our goal is to produce a high-quality, clearly written, useful, and flexible account of Western civilization. We are indebted to numerous teachers and students who have aided us in this effort. We hope this book can serve as the basis for an effective survey of the history of Western civilization, a subject that remains essential for any understanding of who we are and what of significance is happening in the present.

We would like to thank the following reviewers: Janet Cornelius, Danville Area Community College; Kenneth E. Cutler, Indiana University; John C. Moore, Hofstra University; James Parry, Seattle University; and Carl Pohlhammer, Monterey Peninsula College.

RICHARD E. SULLIVAN
DENNIS SHERMAN

HISTORY AND THE HISTORIAN

This book seeks to expand and enrich our readers' connections with the past. Before each of you becomes engaged in that adventure, we ask you to reflect for a moment on some of the challenges involved in discovering, understanding, and retelling what has already happened.

Why should we turn our faces from the present and the future to explore what has already happened? Despite the inclination of many in our time to take seriously Henry Ford's pronouncement that "History is bunk," most of us find looking backward irresistible, as did our forebears. Many have found and still find the past inherently interesting, chiefly because a venture into that realm offers us an opportunity to relive in our minds all kinds of experiences otherwise closed to us by limitations imposed by the cultural environment in which we live. Others have been and still are convinced that learning about the past has an important social function. It can inform us about who and what we are as human beings. It can shed light on contemporary conditions, either by providing an understanding of how things came to be what they are or by supplying analogies that help us to comprehend our situation and formulate solutions to issues that face our society. Societies have especially prized history as an instrument for socializing their members (particularly their young), that is, for teaching them how and how not to behave and to think in ways that are appropriate to the cultural milieu in which they find themselves. As you begin your venture into the past, we urge each of you to reflect on why you are making the journey. Whatever your answer, it will make a difference in what you find and how you interpret your discoveries.

Also, we urge each of you to be mindful that the past is a unique territory. It involves an infinite number of "happenings," each of which is finished and therefore cannot be experienced directly. We can gain access to these already completed events only by reconstructing them in our minds and putting those constructs into words.

Thus, there is always a distance between what actually happened in the past and what those who try to reconstruct the past can discover and make understandable. As a consequence, the exploration of the past goes on continuously, and its reconstruction incessantly changes as those who explore it discover more information and bring new perspectives to bear on their interpretations of their findings.

Although any person is capable of reconstructing the past and often does so with respect to his or her personal or family past, most societies have entrusted that task of discovering the past to specialists, called historians. Most of them agree that there is a basic methodology suited to the task of reconstructing what happened. A first step involves formulating a question about past happenings. For example, this book was shaped by the question of what happened in the past that made the present world what it is. Or, on a smaller scale, suppose you asked yourself what happened to you between the ages of six and eight that relates to what you are now. The range of such questions is obviously infinite; as a result, historical inquiry is richly and unpredictably varied. In many ways the vitality of inquiry about the past depends on the imagination and ingenuity of historians in formulating problems they wish to study.

Once having defined a "subject," the historian starts searching for empirical, verifiable evidence that might provide an answer to his or her question. In the case of your interest in your earlier years, you might begin to look for letters and diaries, school records, picture albums, old clothing in the attic, toys in the basement, oral accounts of those who knew you then, and anything else possibly connected with your activities during that period in your life. What you would be looking for are "traces" left behind that provide evidence that something happened in the past involving you. These traces are what historians call primary sources, which are pieces of evidence produced by human beings who were directly involved in the past activity under investigation or by those in a position to know what happened. Primary sources exist in many forms. Most important are written documents in which observers of past events recorded what they thought happened; this book contains some examples of primary documents. But other kinds of primary sources can help historians find out what happened, including buildings, artworks, maps, pottery, tools, clothing, and oral traditions. Primary sources seldom speak to the historian in clear terms. Historians must subject them to rigorous criticism in order to assess their value as witnesses to what actually happened and to extract information from them that has a bearing on what the historian wants to know. In addition to primary sources, historians must also take into account and critically evaluate what are called secondary sources, which consist of the works of other historians who have examined the same general subject and the same segment of time. You will find examples of how secondary sources are used in the "Where Historians Disagree" sections of this book.

The search for, criticism of, and extraction of data from sources by no means finishes the historian's work. In our hypothetical cases involving your earlier years, when you had gathered and evaluated all the sources you could find, you would still not be able to say what had happened to you; all you would have is a collection of raw data. You, like all historians, would have to put your data together into some form that would approximate the realities in which you were involved then. This is a formidable task. In oversimplified terms it involves a series of choices: what sources deserve the greatest weight; what data are not relevant; how the sources relate to one another; how to organize the data contained in the sources in a way that would convey a meaningful and believable account of what happened; what literary devices to use in order to permit others to experience vicariously and to understand what happened. The process of converting data into history can never be totally objective, for historians inevitably decide these issues in terms of their own perspective and their own values. For this reason, many prefer to call the reconstruction of the past an art rather than a science.

In a rough way historians tend to reflect one of two perspectives in organizing their data to provide a comprehensible reconstruction of past reality. Some, representing a humanistic orientation, see the past in terms of unique actions and events that provide insights into the human situation in a particular setting. These historians tend to present the past as a narrative, telling a story that unfolds in a chronological order with each succeeding episode having its own significance but somehow related to and conditioned by what went before. If you were to choose this model in reconstructing your early life, you would proceed day by day, focusing attention on unique events in your experience that had a particular meaning to you then and something to do with what happened to you the next day or month or year. Other historians, reflecting a social science orientation, look for generalized patterns emerging from the record of the past. They tend to focus on repetitive commonalities rather than on the uniqueness of each happening, on thematic rather than chronological arrangement of evidence, on analysis rather than description, and on causal relationship linking data rather than linear connections. Sometimes they even seek to extract from their reading of the past generalized statements about human behavior that suggest how the future may unfold. Your own history written in this mode might highlight common occurrences in your life, an analysis of the relative weight of different experiences in making you what you are now, and what your experiences tell about what might happen to other children in the future. Quite clearly, each perspective produces a different history. Perhaps a combination of the two allows the fullest and most meaningful reconstruction of the past. We have tried to achieve that end in our reconstruction of the past.

Given the vastness and the complexity of the past, historians have been forced to adopt strategies that allow them to segment the past into manageable entities. One means to this end is to divide the past into discrete segments of time, each of which has common features that allow it to be treated as an entity. Another is to treat the past in terms of major topics around which data can be clustered to create meaning. Still another way of segmenting the past is to focus on geographical areas. As each of you proceeds through this book, you will become aware that we have employed all of these strategies as a means of making the past more understandable. Be aware that these are artificial devices, imposed on the record by historians. Choices have been made in defining periodization schemes, significant topics, and geographical partitions. Obviously, those choices have an important bearing on how the past is reconstructed. We urge each of you to be alert to the uses we have made of these conventions and to think about what the consequences might have been had other periodization systems, topical approaches, and geographical divisions been chosen.

Historical research and writing are decisively affected by judgments made by historians as to what facet of human activity is most important in shaping the destinies of individuals and collectivies in the past. For example, in reconstructing your personal history, you might conclude that private reading was more significant to you than formal schooling or that your family's economic status was more important in shaping your life than its political affiliation. Such choices would obviously affect how you reconstructed your past. In viewing the past from a broader perspective, historians are influenced by similar considerations. Some argue that political factors are crucial in forming societies, while others insist that economic conditions are decisive. Such formulations have produced several widely recognized categories or branches of history: political history, economic history, social history, intellectual history, religious history, and cultural history. The marks of this compartmentalization of past events will be evident in this book, calling on each of you to think about what facet of human activity was most crucial in determining the course of events at any particular stage in human development. Perhaps the supreme challenge for historians is achieving a synthesis that will produce a version of the past embracing all aspects of human activity. In presenting our reconstruction of the past we have sought to meet that challenge, and we urge each of you to try to grasp the whole picture that undergirds the diverse activities into which the human experience can be categorized.

Each passing generation brings changes in approaches to the past that provide particular stimulation to the historical consciousness and a special thrust to historical inquiry. In recent years three broad developments have been particularly influential. We have tried to integrate some of the results of these developments into our reconstruction of the past.

First, there has been a broadening of the approach to social history. Social historians increasingly emphasize looking at the past "from the bottom up" by studying the everyday experiences and attitudes of "ordinary" people, including especially subordinated groups, rather than concentrating on political leaders, elite groups, and "high culture" produced by great thinkers, writers, and artists. To recount the history of these heretofore "silent" people and to assess its significance in the total picture of the past, social historians have had to ask new questions and to make innovative use of sources often overlooked by traditional historians. Their efforts have greatly expanded the stage that we call the past, increased the number of actors on that stage, and changed the theme of the drama played out there in ways that have radically altered our understanding of the dynamic forces that gave shape to the past.

The second development has been the emergence of what is often termed "the new history" (although, like many elements of social history, its roots go back several decades). The new history has been shaped by the marriage of history and the social sciences. By applying the techniques and concepts formulated by demographers, psychologists, anthropologists, geographers, physiologists, linguists, and biologists derived from their study of the present, historians have been able to open immense new vistas on the past pertaining to matters of vital importance to the human condition. Just to cite a few examples, we are learning much more about past birth and death rates, marriage patterns, fertility rates, family size, child rearing, sexuality, death, disease, environmental conditions, patterns of popular belief, the impact of technology, ethnic stereotypes, insanity, and criminality. Many historians practicing the new history rely on comparative and statistical analyses of quantitative data to expand their knowledge of what happened in the past, a methodological technique that has been greatly facilitated by the use of computers. The result of the new history is unmistakable: the past looks different than it once did.

A third development has been the growing interest in women's history. Traditionally history was written from a male perspective and was focused primarily on the thoughts and behavior of men. Women's history attempts to correct this neglect of women in history and the distortions that inevitably result. It focuses on women's experiences and on the roles women played in a variety of developments in the past. It seeks to discern and clarify what has been unique and distinctive in the past experiences of women. And it tries to alert us to gender bias in the way historical questions are posed, evidence is evaluated, and history is written. Once again, the past has been enlarged and a different view of what mattered has taken shape.

Perhaps all of these considerations relative to reconstructing the past lead to one final and all-important point: Establishing a relationship with the past presents a real challenge to our intellectual faculties. Access to the past is possible only to those willing to perform a diverse range of mental activities: posing questions about what is essential in human existence; searching out evidence; evaluating the worth of that evidence; making judgments about the relative weight of different kinds of data; establishing causal relationships; organizing information into intelligible patterns; interpreting the meaning of newly acquired knowledge; communicating new knowledge and insight to others in ways that are intelligible and relevant to their situation. All of these are essential mental powers that each of us must exercise if we are to live usefully in the present. It follows, then, that the greatest value to come from the effort to connect with the past stems from the way that enterprise stretches our minds and hones our intellectual powers along lines that equip us to respond more effectively to challenges that face us and our society now and in the future. We hope that your venture into the past that we have reconstructed in the pages that follow turns out to be a great intellectual experience. Indeed, the writing of this book was that for us, not the least because we had to stretch our minds in order to cope with new evidence about what happened, changing views about how to judge things past, and new questions about what really matters in the human experience.

PART ONE

THE ANCIENT NEAR EAST, 4000–300 B.C.

This book will seek to explain the evolution of Western civilization by describing the numerous ingredients that combined over a long period of time to shape its basic features. While the emergence of civilized life on this planet occurred over immense ages, the crucial "roots" from which Western civilization developed began to grow about six thousand years ago in a particular area of the world known as the Near East.

This first section of the book will concentrate on developments occurring in the Near East over a long era stretching from about 4000 B.C. to 300 B.C. After a few introductory remarks concerning the long era of human history that preceded the emergence of civilization in the Near East, we shall focus on the amazing activity that unfolded in two river valley systems in the Near East: the Tigris-Euphrates in Mesopotamia and the Nile in Egypt. For it was in the challenging environment of these river valleys that human communities developed the first complex patterns of institutions, techniques, and ideas that can be called "civilizations." What was achieved in this setting established the foundations upon which Western civilization was to grow. Beyond characterizing the main features of the early civilizations of Mesopotamia and Egypt, we must consider the beginnings of a process as important to the history of the Western world as was the original creation of civilized life— namely, the beginning of the expansion of the river valley civilizations into a large area of northeast Africa and southwest Asia. Not only did this process permit new peoples to raise the level of their existence, but it also created a cultural setting in which they made their own unique contributions to the broadening stream of civilization. Until at least 500 B.C. the peoples of the Near East were in the forefront of the civilized world. This creative population fashioned a priceless heritage that was later exploited by other peoples participating in the shaping of Western civilization.

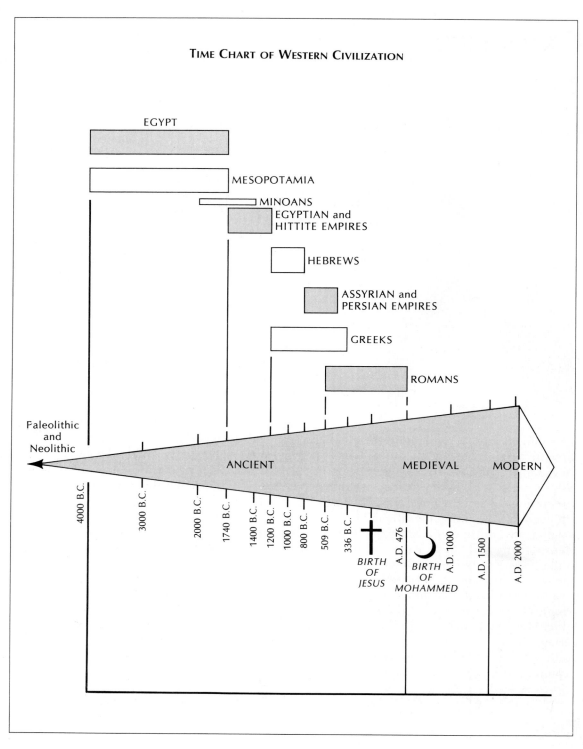

TIME CHART OF WESTERN CIVILIZATION

CHAPTER 1

The River Valley Civilizations: Mesopotamia and Egypt, 4000–1750 B.C.

FIGURE 1.1 A Divine Ruler The statue of Menkure (an Egyptian pharaoh of the Fourth Dynasty) and his queen conveys the majesty and power that surrounded the rulers of the early river valley societies of the Near East. The ability of such rulers to organize human effort on a large scale was crucial in establishing control over the rich river valleys that provided the material base for the first civilizations. This statue also illustrates the basic characteristics of Egyptian sculpture—rigid posture, stylized clothing, a personal touch revealed in the faces of even the majestic god-kings and their consorts. (Museum of Fine Arts, Boston)

Western civilization had its origins in what is known today as the Near East, a somewhat imprecise area embracing southwest Asia and northeast Africa. There diverse peoples utilized their creative talents and accumulated experiences to exploit a unique physical environment in ways that allowed them to create the first higher civilizations. An understanding of what these people did to achieve this end and how they did it is essential if we are to know anything about western Europe's cultural roots.

1. THE PREHISTORIC BACKGROUND

The emergence of higher civilizations in the Near East was made possible by complex developments during an immensely long prehistoric period of preparation—at least five or six hundred times longer than the time span shown on the chart on page 2. Our knowledge of what happened during this prehistoric period is fragmentary, and there is disagreement on how to interpret what is known. In simple terms these vast ages involved three interrelated processes: geological developments, which created the topography and the climate of the planet earth; biological developments, which produced the human species as well as other creatures and plants; and cultural developments, through which human beings created techniques and practices that allowed them to enhance their capabilities to survive and improve in a constantly changing physical and biological environment.

On the basis of meager skeletal remains found scattered over the earth, it appears that the existence of humanlike creatures (hominids) must be extended back at least 3 million years. It was only about forty thousand years ago that the human species (conventionally designated *homo sapiens,* meaning "thinking man") assumed its present physical form, perhaps first in East Africa or southwest Asia. During the long period separating primitive hominids from *homo sapiens,* most of it dominated by conditions created by four successive ice ages, something happened biologically to create unique creatures endowed with special physical traits that prepared them for a unique role in the earth's history. Especially important was the large and complex brain structure that *homo sapiens* possessed.

As a consequence of their superior brain, these evolving human beings developed a special capacity that was crucial in preparing for the emergence of higher civilization. They were able to create and transmit *culture* in the form of objects, techniques, and behavioral patterns that increased their ability to control the environment in ways beneficial to them. The reconstruction of prehistoric cultural development, derived chiefly from artifacts discovered and interpreted by archaeologists, is as complex and as open to debate as is the biological history of the human species. Despite these difficulties, certain broad lines of cultural development are generally agreed upon by specialists in the study of prehistory.

The cultural activity of prehistoric peoples is most fully recorded in the stone tools these creatures left scattered across the face of the earth. For this reason the prehistoric age has been called the Stone Age. Surviving stone tools indicate that during 99 percent of all human prehistory men and women lived as hunters and food gatherers. Although this culture varied in detail from place to place around the globe, it involved certain basic features that permit us to give it a common name—*Paleolithic* (Old Stone Age) culture. Paleolithic peoples lived in small groups dispersed at considerable distances from one another. These packs were made up of several nuclear families, probably related to one another by kinship ties, who cooperated in their quest for sustenance. They were perpetual wanderers, their lives controlled by the movements of animals and the growth patterns of plants upon which survival depended. They sheltered themselves temporarily in caves or fragile tents made of skins and branches. At best their existence was precarious, and improvement in the human condition was slow.

No matter how slowly and painfully, Paleolithic peoples did enrich their culture. They developed increasingly complex and effective techniques for making a greater variety of stone tools, eventually complemented by implements made from bone, horn, and wood. These improved tools made them more efficient killers of even the largest and fiercest animals. They learned how to use fire to warm themselves and prepare their food more easily. They developed spoken languages, a powerful instrument not only in facilitating group action in hunting and food-gathering activities but also in passing on to succeeding generations their cumulative knowledge about animals and plants. Specialized economic and social functions began to emerge within the hunting pack, perhaps based originally on gender. The efforts of male hunters and toolmakers were complemented by equally vital activities carried out by female plant gatherers, fire keepers, garment makers, and child raisers. These specialized functions probably played a prime role in defining the mental attitudes that controlled the relationships between males and females and between parents and children. Scanty bits of evidence indicate the existence of religious life centered on a belief in the existence of spirits in all things that had power to control the destiny of both the living and the dead, but that were also susceptible to human manipulation through the efforts of humans with special powers that allowed them to reach into the spirit world. The cave paintings found at Altamira in Spain and Lascaux in France, as well as crudely shaped human figures, decorated hunting weapons, and jewelry scattered wherever Paleolithic groups passed, suggest both an urge and the capacity to express ideas and feelings about the world and to enhance life by creating beauty.

A culture based on hunting and food gathering had limitations, perhaps too narrow to contain expanding human capabilities. Ultimately, Paleolithic culture gave way to a new pattern of life that changed the human condition in a fundamental way. This great transformation, which marked an essential step toward higher civilization, involved the domestication of plants and animals, which allowed human societies to rely on agriculture to provide the material basis for society. The results of recent archaeological research into human cultural development on a worldwide scale make it almost certain that the change from a hunting and food-gathering to a farming culture first occurred in a relatively limited area of southwest Asia lying along the western, northern, and eastern boundaries of what is called the Fertile Crescent (see Map 1.1). Not too much later, as time is measured on the scale of human prehistory, agricultural life appeared in most other areas of the world, sometimes borrowed from the original inventors and other times "invented" anew.

Archaeological evidence suggests that the "agricultural revolution" came gradually in southwest Asia and was accompanied by much experimentation. The transition period, extending from about 9000 to 6000 B.C. and coinciding in a rough way with the end of the last period of glaciation, has been called the *Mesolithic* (Middle Stone) age. The experimentation occurred in an ecosystem that had a unique combination of features: moderate but regular rainfall; large numbers of wild sheep, goats, cattle, and swine; rich stands of wild cereals, legumes, and plants with oil-bearing seeds; a substantial population sustained by a well-established Paleolithic culture. Perhaps modest changes in the climate and population pressure played a part in the change, but the main impetus most likely came from the capacity of human beings long accustomed to hunting and food gathering to take advantage of the resources offered by the ecosystem. In any case, behavior patterns began to change in Mesolithic times. People stayed longer in one place and gave increasing attention to the control and selective killing of animal herds and to management of wild plants. As these practices continued, certain wild animals—sheep, goats, cattle, and pigs—and certain wild plants—especially wheat and barley—were modified genetically to the point where they flourished best under human care. When that happened, human beings were in a position to abandon hunting and food gathering in favor of agriculture.

The emergence of agriculture as the basis of life opened what is called the *Neolithic* (New Stone) age. Its revolutionary impact is evident in the remains of many settlement sites excavated in recent years, including Jericho in Palestine, Halicar and Catal Hüyük in modern Turkey, and Jarmo and Tepe Gawra in modern Iraq (see Map 1.1). People settled permanently in villages, some of which supported populations of several hundred. They built substantial baked-mud houses featuring not only living quarters but also storage facilities, household shrines, and even burial places. Facilities serving communal functions, such as temples, protective walls, and wells, appeared. Human activity, shared by men and women alike, focused on regular planting and harvesting of wheat, barley, legumes, and fruits and on the care of domesticated animals, valuable not only for meat but also for milk, cheese, hides, and wool. This new mode of life called for a new kit of stone tools, especially hoes and sickles. Before Neolithic culture progressed far, people were beginning to complement stone tools

Map 1.1 CENTERS OF THE FIRST HIGHER CIVILIZATIONS: MESOPOTAMIA AND EGYPT This map locates the two centers where higher civilization originated. It dramatically highlights the limited geographical areas initially affected by the transition from Neolithic agricultural cultures to urban-based patterns of civilization. The revolutionary changes that occurred in the small areas nourished by the waters of the Tigris-Euphrates and the Nile rivers soon began to assert a powerful influence on the lives of the peoples inhabiting the vast stretches of territory surrounding the river valleys.

with copper instruments, heralding the age of metals that would make stone tools obsolete. Pottery making and basket weaving developed to provide storage for food, and the weaving of fibers emerged to create a new range of clothing.

Besides its new technological features, Neolithic culture had significant new social characteristics. Settled agricultural life demanded greater specialization of labor, which allowed for more highly developed skills and better products and made possible the accumulation of wealth in the form of stored grain and animal herds. This wealth provided the basis of exchange for products that a particular village was unable to provide for itself, thus creating trade; the development of trade is evident in the spread of pottery made in a specific area to widely scattered places across the Near East. Increased wealth also made the successful peasant village the target of outsiders, requiring collective action to defend the village. And wealth based on land and animal ownership generated quarrels that posed a threat to the internal order in the village. A major consequence of problems related to trade, defense, and adjudication of quarrels was the development of a more complex system of village governance. This system usually took the form of a tribal structure in which several kinship groups or clans acting through family heads selected a village chief who joined the family elders in making and carrying out collective decisions to meet common problems.

Neolithic villagers also had to expand their mental skills to cope with their new situation. The demands of farming called for more complex calculations, extended planning, and disciplined behavior than did hunting and food gathering. Different moral standards were required to fit situations arising from closer contacts with larger numbers of people and from ownership of things. Religion, increasingly centered on the worship of the forces of nature believed to control the fertility of plants and animals, challenged Neolithic villagers with concepts far more complex than those associated with animal spirits. The increasing complexities surrounding religion also led villagers to place greater trust in religious experts—priests—and to dedicate more energy and wealth to winning the favor of the spirits who nourished the crops and animal herds and protected the village. The responsibilities of directing the government of the village and of conducting religious life began to bestow on those involved in these functions a special place of prominence and power in village life, creating the basis for social stratification. Although women continued to play a key role in the economic life of farming villages, the evidence strongly suggests that males monopolized leadership roles as well as family life. Perhaps the emergence of agricultural life created a social system and a set of values that cast women into a position of dependence and inferiority that would be difficult to eradicate. However, it is worth noting that the female figure was a prime symbol used in Neolithic religious cults to represent the regenerative powers of nature. This symbolism suggests a high respect, perhaps even awe, for femininity as a potent force in shaping and controlling human destiny.

2. MESOPOTAMIAN CIVILIZATION: POLITICAL, ECONOMIC, AND SOCIAL LIFE

From a global perspective the emergence of agriculture put the peoples practicing dryland farming on the fringes of the Fertile Crescent in the forefront of human activity by about 6000 B.C. Recent archaeological explorations of the development of some of the area's peasant villages between 6000 and 4000 B.C. suggest a potential for further evolution, but nothing indicates that any of them was capable of developing the complex urban life that marked the advent of higher civilization. Urban civilization was created by farmers who mastered the more demanding environment of a particular region called Mesopotamia (from a Greek term meaning "between the rivers") whose character was defined by the Tigris and Euphrates rivers (see Map 1.1).

From their sources in the Caucasus Mountains these rivers flow southward through the semiarid steppes of northern Mesopotamia, cutting valleys too deep to allow the use of their waters for irrigation of the adjacent lands. Roughly three hundred miles northwest of where they flow into the Persian Gulf, the rivers enter a flat alluvial plain created by the silt deposited by the floodwaters that annually spilled over their low banks. This relatively small territory presented both opportunities and challenges to the Neolithic peoples on its fringes. The silt deposited by the annual floods made the soil immensely fertile. Those same floods provided a dependable water supply to an area almost devoid of rainfall. However, the potential gifts of lower Mesopotamia were not easily possessed. The somewhat irregular floods were destructive unless they were controlled, and the rich soil was useless unless it was cleared of swamp vegetation and properly drained to avoid salination. And even then the soil was nonproductive unless it could be watered during the arid growing season. Most of Mesopotamia was lacking in natural resources, especially stone, timber, and minerals. Unless its occupants could organize trading ventures extending over considerable distances, only the most primitive level of culture could be sustained. Finally, Mesopotamia lacked any natural barriers to restrain the incursions of neighboring peoples.

While agriculture slowly evolved around the fringes of Mesopotamia during the Mesolithic age, lower Mesopotamia remained relatively backward. Eventually, perhaps just before 4000 B.C., small peasant villages did appear that depended on primitive techniques of irrigation for survival in this arid region. Sometime after about 3500 B.C., larger and more complex communities began to develop, fed perhaps by immigrants from the area to the east between the river valleys and the Zagros Mountains, where Neolithic farming villages had existed for a long time. The evolution of these settlements was accompanied by the development of carefully planned artificial irrigation systems that permitted the cultivation of larger areas at greater distances from the riverbeds. Perhaps that achievement was the work of the Sumerians, a people of mysterious origin from whom south Mesopotamia took its name: Sumer. By 3100 B.C. several rich and populous city-states had developed in Sumer, including Ur, Lagash, Uruk, and Umma. Each consisted of a densely populated urban center surrounded by an island of irrigated farmland carved out of the chaotic river valley environment by an elaborate system of dikes, canals, and reservoirs and systematically cultivated under direction from the urban center. The Sumerian

accomplishment soon served as a model for another group of intruders who occupied the area just north of Sumer. These were Semitic-speaking seminomads originally from the northern Arabian Desert, who developed several thriving city-states in an area called Akkad. For at least seven centuries, from about 3100 to 2400 B.C., these city-states, each jealously guarding its independence, enjoyed remarkable stability and prosperity that produced a common pattern of culture marked by brilliant accomplishments in all aspects of life.

Of fundamental importance to the development of urban civilization was the creation of an effective system of government capable of controlling a large population engaged in a variety of mutually supportive activities. From an early date responsibility for decision making in each Sumerian city-state rested in the hands of a single human leader. Perhaps initially that power was held by a high priest, but eventually a secular king (called *lugal* in Sumerian) came to dominate. In either case authority was grounded primarily in religious belief. The Sumerians believed that each city-state had been created originally by a god or goddess who owned the city and its surrounding lands and who required all members to serve the divine will. The earthly ruler was the agent through whom the will of the divine owner was made known and carried out. Each city developed an elaborate temple-palace complex that served as the center of political life. From there flowed divine orders coordinating the numerous activities required to exploit the resources belonging to the patron deity. The efforts of the rulers to control the population were greatly aided by the development of writing, which allowed the keeping of records of what was produced and what was due. Back to the temple-palace came a huge income, much of it in the form of agricultural produce, that was used to sustain the divine city. A key function of government was the distribution of this income. Part of it went as rations to sustain those who tilled the soil and kept the irrigation system in repair. Another part provided for the support of a wide array of specialists who clustered around the temple-palace complex to serve the ruler and the community in a variety of ways: record keepers, scribes, engineers, architects, artists, traders, artisans, soldiers, and tax collectors. The combined efforts of these specialists, whose activities were made possible by the surplus agricultural production, created the essential features that elevated civilized urban life to a plane far beyond life in Neolithic villages. As part of his effort to carry out the will of the city's divine patron, the ruler developed instrumentalities that became permanent features of civilized polity: laws to define the relationships among citizens; courts to adjudicate disputes; a police force to maintain civic order; armies to protect the city-state from hostile outsiders; and public ceremonies to honor and placate the deities.

Although the independent city-state pattern of government dominated Mesopotamia between 3100 and 2400 B.C., tensions emerged that eventually modified its basic forms. Constant attacks from outsiders attracted by the wealth of Mesopotamia's urban centers, conflicts among city-states seeking to expand their territories, and the quest for vital raw materials lacking in Sumer and Akkad increasingly required that effective rulers look beyond the walls of their own city-states. These pressures led them to undertake conquests aimed at creating larger political entities. The establishment and maintenance of these *empires* required new political techniques for keeping peace and order among peoples of diverse backgrounds and loyalties.

The first attempts at shaping empires were made by strong kings from prominent Sumerian cities, but their "empires" were short-lived. Ultimately, the Semitic-speaking peoples from north of Sumer were more successful in uniting Mesopotamia. The first great empire builder was Sargon I (ca. 2370–2315 B.C.) from Akkad. He conducted military campaigns that not only subdued the city-states of Sumer but also extended Akkadian dominance into the foothills of the Zagros Mountains, Assyria, and Syria. Sargon's empire was sustained by his descendants until about 2200 B.C., but then it collapsed under the combined pressure of internal resistance and external attacks. For a brief interval the Sumerian city-states regained their independence, and one of them, Ur, even managed to assert dominance over much of Mesopotamia between about 2100 and 2000 B.C. However, the long history of the independent city-state as the prime political institution in Mesopotamia was drawing to an end in favor of larger political entities. Toward 1800 B.C. a new Semitic-speaking people, the Amo-

rites, began to assert dominance. Their day of glory came with the reign of Hammurabi (ca. 1792–1750 B.C.), who from his city of Babylon organized a series of military campaigns that once again created a large empire stretching in a great arc from the Persian Gulf to the Mediterranean Sea and imposed on diverse peoples a single political order. For all its brilliance, the Amorite Empire was relatively short-lived. Shortly after 1700 B.C., outside attackers began to batter its frontiers, until eventually the Kassites established control over Mesopotamia. As we shall see later (Chapter 2), the power structure prevailing in the Near East had undergone significant changes which redefined Mesopotamia's position in that area.

Hammurabi's career exemplifies the new ideas and practices of government introduced by the empire builders who dominated Mesopotamia between 2400 and 1700 B.C. These contributions, aimed chiefly at using political power to create common bonds among diverse peoples, proved to be among the most important of all Mesopotamian contributions to civilization. One technique used by Hammurabi to unify the peoples over which he ruled was to impress on them their total dependence on the power of their one ruler. This technique called for a conscious effort to exalt the person of the king as the sole source of earthly power. To heighten his visibility, Hammurabi made his court at Babylon the setting for a vast display of wealth toward which his subjects from "the Four Quarters of the World" could turn for their well-being. He sought to create a common religion in his empire, based on the worship of Marduk, once the patron god of the city of Babylon but now presented as the divine lord of all the other deities and of the earth. Hammurabi proclaimed himself as Marduk's sole agent, alone capable of bringing divine favor to his subjects. But his power was more than appearance. He maintained a well-organized army ready to curb threats to peace in the empire, a centralized bureaucracy based at the court in Babylon that was devoted to administration, and a network of governors sent out to the local units into which the empire was divided to collect taxes, raise troops, and administer justice.

One of Hammurabi's most significant measures to solidify and unify his empire was his law code. He claimed it was handed down to him from the deities ''to destroy the wicked and the evil, so that the strong may not oppress the weak'' (see Figure 1.2). Although a modern reader of Hammurabi's law code is taken aback by the brutal punishments imposed on lawbreakers, the code is better characterized by its commonsense, humane approach to basic human problems: protection for women, children, and slaves; fairness in commercial exchanges; protection of property; standard procedures for adjudicating disputes; debt relief for victims of flood and drought. It reflected an enlightened concept of justice that encouraged people of all kinds to accept the authority of a king trying to provide common rules to govern the behavior of his subjects.

The material base undergirding Mesopotamian civilization remained remarkably stable during the long period from about 3100 to 1750 B.C. Of crucial importance was a carefully organized and controlled agricultural system. Although there were some technological advances in agriculture, especially the introduction of bronze tools and wheeled plows, farming depended chiefly on the traditional crops and animals of Neolithic times. The chief difference was the larger productive capacity of the fertile, irrigated fields of Mesopotamia. The prime agricultural unit was a large farm, usually owned by the king, the temple priests, or a member of the aristocracy and tilled by tenants and slaves working under careful supervision of the owner or his agents. The rulers of each city or empire sought to develop and control extensive trade networks designed to make basic resources available. Every city supported a large number of skilled artisans who made a variety of fine products consumed in the city or distributed across the Near East by enterprising merchants in exchange for raw materials lacking in Mesopotamia. The urban civilization of Mesopotamia both required and permitted the development of a more complex and structured social system than was typical of Neolithic peasant villages. At the summit of society stood an aristocracy made up of priests, landowners, and royal officials who derived their high status from their close association with the ruler and their involvement in the governance of society. This aristocracy benefited most from Mesopotamia's material wealth. Merchants and artisans enjoyed a prosperous

FIGURE 1.2 An Ancient Lawgiver This relief, showing Hammurabi receiving a code of laws from a deity, was carved at the top of a stone cylinder upon which were inscribed the provisions of the law written in cuneiform script. Sumerian artists were especially adept in relief carving, an art form that would have an illustrious history. (Giraudon)

and relatively free life, often closely attached to the court, the temple, or aristocratic households. Each city-state had a large population of urban laborers who performed the menial tasks required to run the city and the households of the powerful. The bulk of the population consisted of farmers living in villages outside the urban center and devoting themselves to agricultural routines from which they derived meager rewards. Slavery existed but was not a dominant feature of Mesopotamian life. The relationships among various social classes, as well as the rights and responsibilities of each, were carefully defined by law.

At all levels of Mesopotamian society the family was a basic institution. Marriages were arranged by family agreements, and the husband and father exercised almost absolute control over his wife and children. As a consequence, women played a limited role in societal decision making. However, the law did recognize that they had certain rights. Surviving records indicate that women often inherited their husbands' property and were engaged in economic ventures of many kinds. Aristocratic women certainly shared in the luxuries that accompanied their husbands' social status. The wives and children of artisans and farmers were actively engaged in the work of the heads of households—and they shared the meager returns for their efforts. As a whole, Mesopotamian society was stable and seldom troubled by social strife and tension.

3. MESOPOTAMIAN BELIEF, THOUGHT, AND EXPRESSION

The advent of higher civilization in Mesopotamia was marked by impressive developments in religion, literature, and the arts which had a major influence on the later history of cultural life in the Western world. By and large, the Sumerians created the basic elements of Mesopotamian culture which Semitic-speaking peoples readily assimilated and sustained. The result of this relationship was a common culture based on Sumerian models that ultimately embraced all of Mesopotamia.

Religion was the prime force shaping all aspects of Mesopotamian life. The Mesopotamian religion was *polytheistic*, based on a worship of many deities who were believed to possess powers that allowed them to control all that happened. Especially awesome were the spirits that controlled the forces of nature: gods and goddesses of the sky, air, water, sun, moon, storms. One or another of these deities was usually accepted as the founder and ruler of each city-state. Particularly appealing to ordinary people who lived close to the soil was the goddess of fertility, called Inanna by the Sumerians and Ishtar by the Semites, whose munificent power renewed nature every spring, usually with the help of a male lover. Sharing the universe with these great gods and goddesses were legions of lesser spirits, each of whom could bring blessings or misfortunes, great or small, to men and women in all stations of life. The Mesopotamians spent considerable intellectual energy trying to define the powers of these deities, determine their origins, and clarify their relationships to one another and to the human community. The result was a rich and intriguing mythology that had a powerful influence on later religious thinking.

The lot assigned to human beings in the god-dominated universe was not an easy one. They were viewed as slaves of the deities, bound to suffer whatever the angry, vengeful, unpredictable gods and goddesses wished. Especially heavy was the burden of trying to please the deities. To do so required building splendid temples and countless shrines where the deities could live, supporting priests and priestesses who attended to divine needs, offering prayers and gifts, organizing expensive public festivals, and expending endless effort to discover the intentions of the gods and goddesses as these might be revealed in the movement of the stars, dreams, and the shapes of the entrails of animals. In return for their services to the deities, Mesopotamians expected the material gifts the deities had to offer—the safety and material prosperity of the city-state, the family, and the individual. Most men and women were never sure that the all-powerful gods and goddesses would smile on them. A tone of pessimism and fatalism permeated their view of life. Their religion was lacking in any ethical dimensions that taught that good behavior and good deeds were pleasing to the divine powers. Nor did the Mesopotamians entertain any hope for a happy life after death; the dead passed on to a "land of no return" somewhere underground "where dust is their feed, clay their substance; where they see no light and dwell in darkness." Without a chance to please the deities through good behavior or a hope for a happy afterlife, perhaps there was little choice but fear of the deities and pessimism about the human lot.

The urge to know and to please the gods and goddesses inspired an impressive literature, the recording of which was made possible by the development of a writing system—one of the great inventions in history. The Sumerians were the first to develop writing. In its earliest form their writing consisted of pictures (pictograms) used primarily to record what was due to the deities and the rulers. Gradually pictograms evolved into symbols representing sounds that could be combined into words expressing chains of thought of various kinds. To record such thoughts, these symbols were pressed onto soft clay tablets with a wedge-shaped stylus and then the tablets were baked; thus the writing is called *cuneiform* (from a Latin word meaning "wedge"). Eventually the Sumerian system of writing was adapted by Semitic-speaking Akkadians, whose language had by Sargon I's time begun to replace Sumerian in Mesopotamia. However, for centuries learned people continued to study Sumerian texts much as modern scholars learn ancient Greek, Latin, and Hebrew. Thus, much Sumerian literature survived as a model to be followed by peoples speaking and writing in other languages.

While writing in Mesopotamia served a major function in keeping records of a large array of ordinary activities, talented individuals learned to use it for creative purposes. Their most impressive literary productions were religious epics, of which the *Creation Epic* and the *Epic of Gilgamesh* are the most notable examples. The *Creation Epic* describes how Marduk won supremacy over the spirit world and created earth and human beings, a feat that earned him universal worship in the time of Hammurabi. The *Epic of Gilgamesh* recounts the adventures of a semilegendary king of Uruk, Gilgamesh, in his quest to learn from the deities how to gain immortality. The Mesopotamians also wrote hymns glorifying the deities and chronicles recounting the deeds of great rulers. The literary forms, themes, and styles developed by Mesopotamian writers not only enriched their own culture but also had an important influence on the literature of later peoples, as is evident in the ideas and stories of Mesopotamian origin imbedded in the Bible of the Hebrews, put into writing many centuries later.

From the beginning of their civilization, the Mesopotamians showed impressive skills and creativity in the visual arts. The need to provide their deities with suitable dwellings was the prime stimulant to monumental architecture and produced impressive mud brick temple complexes that were the central feature of every city. In its most fully developed form the temple complex featured a tower, called a *ziggurat*, designed as a series of terraces one on top of another, each successive layer smaller than the one below. A sanctuary dedicated to the patron deity of each city was placed atop the final terrace. Around the ziggurat there usually developed an elaborate array of lesser shrines, offices, priestly dwellings, storehouses, and workshops, all comprising a sacred precinct where the deities could be served. Hardly less elaborate were the palaces where the kings and their courts lived. The palace at Mari, an important city in the Amorite Empire, covered six acres and contained more than two hundred fifty rooms. Mesopotamian architects knew how to use columns, domes, arches, and vaults, but the lack of stone as a building material limited their ability to exploit these forms fully.

The Mesopotamians were also skilled sculptors. Most three-dimensional statues portrayed the deities and famous kings. Sculptors took some pains to give a distinctive character to the faces of their subjects but concerned themselves little with a realistic rendering of the human body. Their work, strongly influenced by geometrical forms, is solid, stiff, and motionless (see Color Plate 1). More realistic and animated scenes were created by sculptors working in low relief to depict historic events or divine exploits (see Figure 1.2). The most exquisite carving was done by seal makers, who wrought miniaturized scenes carved in stone that were used to press an identifying mark onto documents written in clay. The same deft skill is illustrated in jewelry, metalwork, and decorated pottery.

Chiefly as a result of their efforts to cope with the divine forces and the rivers, the Mesopotamians produced a body of knowledge that can be called science. They devised a system of time reckoning based on cycles of the sun and the moon. They developed a standard system of weights and measures almost universally used by Hammurabi's time. Their numbering system combined a decimal system with units of sixty. They were able to perform the basic functions of arithmetic and geometry. A body of medical knowledge, mixing observations and religious lore, was developed. As a result of the travels of merchants and soldiers, the Mesopotamians amassed a considerable store of geographical information. Inspired by an urge to foretell the future, the Mesopotamians gathered accurate information about the movement of the stars. Although the Mesopotamians were seldom concerned with gathering knowledge about the physical world for its own sake, the information they did compile in the course of meeting practical problems was stored up for the use of later peoples, particularly the Greeks, as the basis for theoretical science.

4. EGYPTIAN CIVILIZATION: POLITICAL, ECONOMIC, AND SOCIAL LIFE

Not long after urban civilization took shape in Mesopotamia, a similar leap forward occurred in Egypt. Although bits of archaeological evidence found in Egypt suggest the presence of Mesopotamian influences there at the moment of transition to higher civilization, the basic developments in northeast Africa were native and the resultant pattern of civilization was unique.

Just as in Mesopotamia, the advent of higher civilization in Egypt hinged on meeting the challenges posed by a river valley environment. The Nile has its sources in the mountains of equatorial Africa (see Map 1.1). From there it flows northward past a series of rapids (cataracts) to trace a narrow trough through bleak deserts almost devoid of rainfall. As it nears the Mediterranean, the river fans out into a series of channels to create the Delta, a triangle of rich land about one hundred twenty miles on each side. The annual floods of the Nile come with predictable regularity to create what the Egyptians called the "black land" of the narrow valley and the Delta, which they contrasted with the dreaded "red land" of the desert. However, the Nile floods had to be controlled and their waters distributed across the "black land" during the rainless growing season before the productive potential of the valley could be realized.

During many centuries prior to the emergence of higher civilization in the Nile Valley, Neolithic agricultural life existed across much of North Africa. However, only somewhere between 5000 and 4500 B.C. did some of these farmers begin to move from the west and south to establish villages on the fringes of the Nile Valley. During the next thousand years these peoples developed the technical and organizational skills that permitted them to establish irrigation systems capable of controlling the floods and utilizing the immensely rich soil as a basis of village life. By a process that is ill understood, these villages in time were joined together to form small kingdoms.

The era dominated by these small kingdoms, called the Predynastic Age, ended suddenly about 3100 B.C., when Egypt was united under a single ruler, later given the title *pharaoh*. Egyptian tradition ascribed this feat to Menes, who founded the first dynasty of pharaohs (a dynasty was a group of rulers from a single family who followed one another as pharaoh) and opened an era called the Old Kingdom (3100–2200 B.C.). Six dynasties ruled during this long era, the most glorious being the Third and Fourth dynasties. From their capital at Memphis, these pharaohs asserted a beneficial authority that brought prosperity and peace to the valley. Egypt benefited especially from freedom from outside attacks, a boon afforded by the formidable natural barriers guarding the Nile Valley: the cataracts, the deserts, the Mediterranean Sea. The massive pyramids built at Gizeh by the powerful pharaohs of the Fourth Dynasty—Menkure, Kephren, and Khufu (Cheops)—mirror the immense wealth of a society unified in exploiting the Nile and the great power of the rulers who directed this collective effort. During the period of the Old Kingdom basic political, economic, and social structures, religious concepts and practices, and modes of thought and expression were shaped that would dominate Egyptian civilization for the next two millennia.

The key to this remarkable civilization was the political system that had been put into place by the time of the Third Dynasty. Its central feature was the absolute power of the pharaoh, who was considered to be a god. The pharaoh literally owned Egypt and its people. Every person was his servant, subject to his unchallengeable orders. Despite their divine status, most of the pharaohs of the Old Kingdom were active leaders occupied in overseeing the irrigation system, giving justice, directing building programs, and sponsoring trade. They exercised their power through a highly developed administrative system centered at Memphis. Egypt was divided into smaller administrative units, called *nomes*, each controlled by royal officials held closely accountable for carrying out the pharaoh's orders in the villages making up each nome.

During the Sixth Dynasty this highly effective system faltered. Egypt entered a period of disorder called the First Intermediate Period (2200–2050 B.C.), marked by ineffectual pharaohs whose authority was challenged by local potentates. About 2050 B.C. political unity was restored by the princes of Thebes to begin what is known as the Middle Kingdom (2050–1750 B.C.). These rulers of the Eleventh and Twelfth dynasties consciously restored the basic political institutions and practices characteristic of the Old Kingdom—the divine power of the pharaoh, the centralized bureaucracy, the provincial administration—and labored successfully to revive and even to expand the economic system. A major concern of the pharaohs was to ensure that *ma'at* prevailed. In Egyptian thought *ma'at* was the principle of right order, justice, and harmony that should prevail throughout the universe, including the human community. Out of respect for this principle the pharaohs of the Middle Kingdom sought actively to provide justice, protection, and respect for all of their subjects, including the poor and the powerless, who had been badly abused by the powerful during the First Intermediate Period. The concern that *ma'at* should prevail for all society gave the government of the Middle Kingdom a quality not often seen in the history of the ancient Near East.

The Middle Kingdom came to an end about 1750 B.C., chiefly as a consequence of a threat that Egypt had not heretofore faced: outside invasion. A people called the Hyksos who came from Asia succeeded in taking control of part of the Nile Valley. Their presence led to divisions within Egypt and to violence and lawlessness. This interlude, called the Second Intermediate Period (1750–1580 B.C.), set the stage for another recovery and a new era of glory in Egypt to be discussed later (see Chapter 2).

The establishment of a unified political regime by the divine pharaohs was accompanied by the development of a remarkably stable economic and social order. A carefully controlled agricultural system provided the prime source of wealth in Egypt. This system was sustained by a numerous peasant population, living in small villages and devoting their lives to the endless round of labor required to maintain the irrigation system, to plant and harvest the crops of wheat, barley, flax, vegetables, and fruit, and to care for herds of animals. To these responsibilities was added the burden of extra labor on the immense building programs organized by the pharaohs and their agents and friends. The economy was enriched by the efforts of artisans and merchants who produced or acquired by exchange the luxury goods desired by the powerful and rich in society. Both artisans and traders often worked directly for the pharaohs, the rich officials of his court, the numerous priests, and the powerful provincial nobility.

Egyptian society was dominated by a relatively small aristocracy. At its summit stood the pharaoh and his family, who enjoyed command over all elements of society and control over the total wealth of the state. The rest of the aristocracy consisted of those to whom the pharaoh chose to extend high status and reward with wealth. Especially influential were the priests, who managed the religious system, and the officials, who assisted the pharaoh in governing Egypt. Despite the efforts of the good pharaohs the lower classes were sometimes exploited and oppressed; their laments constitute a major theme in literature. Yet the surviving evidence, much of it in the form of pictorial representations of the lower classes adorning the tombs of the pharaohs and their nobles, suggests social harmony. The scenes depicting peasants and artisans at work and play convey a sense of contentment and even joy. Slavery played only a minor role in Egypt during the Old and Middle kingdoms, and although women were subjected to control by fathers and husbands, they enjoyed an important place in society. The consorts of the mighty pharaohs were extended high respect by their divine husbands (see Figure 1.1) and by society in general. Noblewomen shared most aspects of aristocratic life, especially its material wealth. They owned property and played an important role as priestesses serving the chief deities of Egypt. Lower-class women joined their husbands in working in the fields and played a key role in sustaining the economy. In general, Egyptian society was stable and secure. Most people apparently felt that *ma'at* prevailed to reward a happy, confident society.

5. EGYPTIAN BELIEF, THOUGHT, AND EXPRESSION

The cultural achievement of ancient Egypt was an outgrowth of the same powerful religious forces that shaped political and social life. The fifth-century B.C. Greek historian Herodotus concluded that the Egyptians were the most religious of all peoples. From at least some perspectives that seems to be true. Certainly few peoples honored more gods and goddesses; the deities worshiped by the Egyptians numbered in the thousands. These spirits were portrayed in a confusing array of forms—as humans, animals, birds, plants, abstractions, and mixtures of any of these forms. They lived everywhere and were always present wherever and whenever humans were at work or at play. The deities were generally conceived as benevolent toward humans, easy to live with, and not to be feared. Over time the Egyptians did come to agree that certain deities possessed special powers and deserved universal worship. This mythology accorded special prominence to deities associated with pharaohs victorious in earthly wars, such as the falcon god Horus worshiped by Menes, the unifier of Egypt, and Amon, a minor deity at Thebes who became a powerful national god after the princes of Thebes rose to power as pharaohs of the Middle Kingdom. Two deities ultimately emerged as the most powerful divine forces in Egyptian religion: Ra, the sun god, whose worship reflected the power of nature in shaping the good life of the Nile Valley; and Osiris, the god who had the power to grant a happy life after death.

The Egyptians expended enormous energy and resources in an effort to please their deities and win their favor. An elaborate set of ritual practices was established early in Egyptian history and changed little over the centuries. To the pharaoh belonged prime responsibility for bringing the favor of his fellow gods and goddesses upon his land and people; no small part of the activities of a typical pharaoh was devoted to religious worship. He was aided by numerous priests and priestesses, who conducted an elaborate round of rituals to please the deities with food, gifts, song, prayer, and dance. A considerable portion of public income was devoted to these activities. Acts of worship and sacrifice took place not only in great public temples but also in simple shrines in homes and villages. A rich array of magical practices evolved to attract the attention of the deities and to drive away evil spirits.

Much of this religious activity was intended to win the material rewards that the gods and goddesses had to offer—abundant harvests, good health, security, happy times. Besides earthly benefits, the divine powers held another precious gift for deserving Egyptians—a happy life after death. From early times, Egyptians believed that every person had a *ka*, a spiritual double for the material body that lived on after death in close association with the divine spirits. The *ka* had to be supplied with what it needed for a happy afterlife. In early Egyptian history a key to caring for the *ka* centered on mummification of the body and its burial in a tomb where its spirit could continue to live in it. Elaborate arrangements were made to ensure that the spirit would have food, drink, luxuries, company—everything it had enjoyed during life—to make immortal life tolerable. Perhaps initially only the pharaoh could afford such equipment, as evidenced by the pyramids built to house his spirit eternally. But pharaohs were willing to build and provide tombs for their wives, children, officials, and friends so that they could continue to be their companions in the enjoyment of eternal life.

Although the fate of the spirits of ordinary people in early Egypt is not clear, the expectation of gaining immortality was gradually democratized and universalized. The concept of immortality found its focus in the worship of Osiris, which by the Middle Kingdom had assumed a central place in religious life and was embodied in a touching myth. Osiris, a god associated with life forces and the Nile, was murdered by his wicked brother, Seth, who dismembered his body and scattered it over the earth. Isis, the wife of Osiris, patiently gathered the pieces, whereupon Osiris returned to life. Thereafter, Osiris had the power to grant a happy afterlife in a paradise much like the earthly Nile Valley to those who could meet his test for goodness (see Figure 1.3). Implicit in this concept of immortal life was the idea of moral worth attached to each person, a concept that would have a rich history. One must be cautious, however, in assessing the impact of moral concerns on Egyptian society. People continued to provide for the material welfare of the dead, although from the Middle Kingdom onward the emphasis was not so much on the grandeur of the tomb as on its decoration with texts and pictures seeking to convince Osiris that its occupant had lived a "good" life; in time, many busied themselves devising clever formulas to conceal their moral shortcomings.

The immense effort to understand, please, and thank the divine forces produced vigorous literary activity. Egyptian literature proper was preceded by the development of a system of writing, called *hieroglyphic*, which made its appearance about 3200 B.C. Like cuneiform writing, it began as pictograms out of which evolved symbols representing sounds that could be combined into words. The first use of writing was probably in record keeping and letter writing connected with the pharaoh's court, but it was not long before more artistic uses were found. Much early writing has survived on pyramid walls in the form of hymns, prayers, magical incantations, mythology, and accounts of the deeds of the occupant of the pyramid, all intended to send a message to the divine forces. Besides the pyramid texts other forms of literature survive, set down on either stone or papyrus (a writing material made from the pulp of the papyrus plant pressed into flat sheets). The Egyptians apparently enjoyed poetry, collections of maxims and wise sayings, often presented in the form of instructions given by father to son or teacher to pupil, and tales of fancy and romance recounting the adventures of travelers, sailors, and soldiers. On the whole Egyptian literature was confident in mood but perhaps not as profound in content as Mesopotamian literature.

The visual arts reflect the character and quality of the Egyptian genius most clearly. In all its forms, Egyptian art mirrors what may be the keystone of Egyptian civilization: the ability of a creative people to work for long ages with set forms and subjects without loss of freshness and vitality. Egyptian artists created for eternity with confidence that the existing order was right and worth sustaining.

Architecture was the queen of all the arts, most of the other forms serving to adorn great buildings. Architects worked with bricks, reeds, and timber, but the most monumental work was in stone, of which there was a plentiful supply in Egypt. The first flowering of architecture came early in the Old Kingdom and was devoted chiefly to tomb building, which reached its apogee with the construction of the pyramids. The pyramid of Khufu, built about 2600 B.C., still stands as one of the major construction feats of all time. Built on a cliff overlooking the Nile, it measured 755 feet on each side and was 480 feet high. It contained over 2 million blocks of stone, each of which was precut in quarries many miles away and floated down the Nile to the building site, a procedure that required careful planning, skilled engineering, and a huge expenditure of labor. Surrounding the pyramid was a complex of temples and tombs for Khufu's dead family and friends. A roadway led down to the valley, where there was another building complex intended to house the priests, officials, and laborers who carried on the many services required to care for the spirit living in the pyramid tomb. Pyramid building continued for many centuries, but later architects never equaled those of the Old Kingdom. By the end of the Old Kingdom temples and palaces commanded more attention. The basic temple style, established very early, was the hypostyle hall, consisting of a high-ceilinged central hall flanked by side halls, each covered with a roof set on columns shorter than those of the central hall. Builders achieved splendid artistic effects by modeling their columns after plants—the palm tree, the lotus plant, the papyrus plant, the reed. Within the temple, numerous chambers were grouped to create a sanctuary where the god or goddess to whom the temple was dedicated could live (see Color Plate 2). Before the temple was an open court surrounded by a columned portico and entered by a massive gate. Scanty surviving evidence indicates that the palaces built for pharaohs and nobles were as splendid as the temples and probably utilized the same basic architectural forms.

FIGURE 1.3 Judgment Day This Egyptian funerary papyrus from the tomb of a princess shows some of the steps in the transition to afterlife. In the center, the gods weigh her heart in a balance against the figure of the Goddess of Truth. Any flaw in her life would result in a loss of eternal happiness. (The Metropolitan Museum of Art)

Egypt's sculptors matched architects in skill. At a very early date sculptural styles became fixed and changed little over most of Egypt's history. The chief subjects of three-dimensional sculpture were the deities, the pharaohs, their families, and their companions, most such statues being intended to adorn tombs and temples. Human forms were usually massive, stiff, unemotional portrayals following fixed proportions. But the faces were another matter; here the sculptor tried to project a quality embodied in or exemplified by the subject: the power of a god or goddess, the majesty of a pharaoh, the devotion of a royal servant (see Figure 1.1). Sculptors were also skilled at relief work, most of which was carved on the walls of tombs and temples and intended to record the deeds of those commemorated (see Figures 2.1 and 2.2). As a consequence, Egyptian reliefs contain a remarkably rich record of everyday life at all levels of society. However, sculptors seldom tried to be realistic. They let the space available determine the size and shape of their figures, and they often used conventional designs to represent objects. Human figures are distorted, the feet and faces usually shown in profile while the main trunk of the body faces the viewer. Many of the reliefs were painted to heighten the effect. Painting, most of which also survives in tombs, bears striking similarity to relief work in terms of subject and form.

The Egyptians made advances in technology and science that rivaled the work of the Mesopotamians. They recorded information about the movement of the stars, from which they developed an accurate time-reckoning system and a calendar of twelve thirty-day months plus five days added at the end of each year. They developed a system of numbers that permitted them to perform basic arithmetic functions and to calculate areas and volumes. They accumulated considerable information about the properties of metals and about plant and animal life. In medicine they developed surgical techniques and learned to use a wide range of drugs. Their understanding of anatomy was extensive, undoubtedly a result of observations made in the process of mummifying the dead. However, like the Mesopotamians, the Egyptians had little interest in pursuing knowledge about nature for its own sake. Once they found a practical solution for a problem of engineering, metallurgy, medicine, or discovering the intention of the deities, they sought no further.

SUGGESTED READING

Overview of the Ancient Near East to ca. 330 B.C.

H. W. F. Saggs, *Civilization before Greece and Rome* (1989).

Arthur Bernard Knapp, *The History and Culture of Ancient Western Asia and Egypt* (1988).

Either of these two books will provide an excellent overview.

Prehistory

Frank E. Poirier, *Understanding Human Evolution* (1987).

Richard E. Leakey, *The Making of Mankind* (1981).

John E. Pfeiffer, *The Emergence of Humankind*, 4th ed. (1985).

Robert J. Wenke, *Patterns in Prehistory: Humankind's First Three Million Years* (1990).

Each of these four works provides a provocative treatment of the much-disputed problem of human origins.

Brian M. Fagan, *People of the Earth: An Introduction to World Prehistory*, 4th ed. (1983). An excellent treatment of prehistoric culture.

Margaret Ehrenberg, *Women in Prehistory* (1989). An informative survey.

Mesopotamia

Hans J. Nissen, *The Early History of the Ancient Near East, 9000–2000 B.C.*, trans. Elizabeth Lutzeier and Kenneth J. Northcott (1988). A good survey taking archaeological data into account.

H. W. F. Saggs, *Everyday Life in Babylonia and Assyria*, rev. ed. (1987). Rich in material on how people lived in ancient Mesopotamia.

Thorkild Jacobsen, *The Treasures of Darkness: A History of Mesopotamian Religion* (1976). An excellent introduction.

Anton Moortgat, *The Art of Ancient Mesopotamia: The Classical Art of the Near East*, trans. Judith Filson (1969).

André Parrot, *Sumer: The Dawn of Art*, trans. Stuart Gilbert and James Emmons (1961).

Either of these beautifully illustrated volumes will provide a good introduction to Mesopotamian art.

Egypt

Cyril Aldred, *The Egyptians*, rev. and enl. ed. (1984).

T. G. H. James, *An Introduction to Ancient Egypt* (1990).

Micahel Rice, *Egypt's Making. The Origins of Ancient Egypt, 5000-2000 B.C.* (1990).

Any of these three works will provide an excellent guide to the development of Egyptian civilization.

Barbara Mertz, *Red Land, Black Land: Daily Life in Ancient Egypt*, rev. ed. (1978).

John Romer, *People of the Nile: Everyday Life in Ancient Egypt* (1982).

These two works are rich in details about how people lived in ancient Egypt.

Barbara Watterson, *Women in Ancient Egypt* (1991).

Wolfgang Decker, *Sports and Games in Ancient Egypt*, trans. Allen Guttmann (1992).

Erik Hornung, *Conceptions of the Gods in Ancient Egypt: The One and the Many*, trans. John Baines (1982).

A. Rosalie David, *The Ancient Egyptians: Religious Beliefs and Practices* (1982).

Either of these works will help the reader understand the complexities of ancient Egyptian religion.

Kurt Lange and Max Hirmer, *Egypt: Architecture, Sculpture, Painting in Three Thousand Years*, trans. Judith Filson and Barbara Taylor, 4th ed. (1968).

W. Stevenson Smith and William Kelly Simpson, *Art and Architecture of Ancient Egypt*, 2nd ed. (1981).

Either of these two works, both well illustrated, will provide a sense of the basic characteristics of Egyptian art.

CHAPTER 2

The Diffusion of Near Eastern Civilization, 1750–800 B.C.

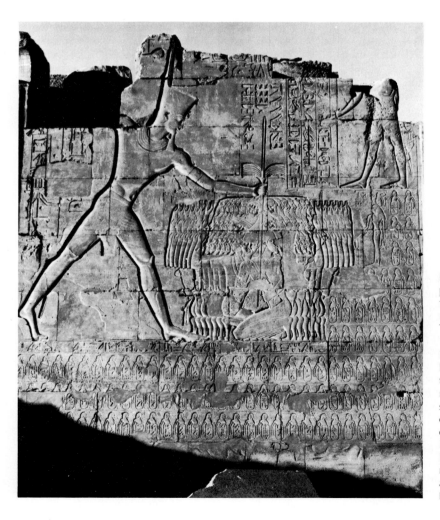

FIGURE 2.1 Egyptian Imperialism This scene, from the temple of Karnak, shows the pharaoh Thutmose III (1504–1450 B.C.) grasping Egypt's enemies by the hair prior to striking them to show Egypt's mastery over them. This scene captures the spirit of Egyptian imperialism during the period of the New Kingdom. Such relief carvings occupied a major place in Egyptian artistic activity. (Hirmer Fotoarchiv)

By about 1750 B.C. the history of the Afro-Asian zone of civilization entered a new phase with a new focus. The higher civilizations produced in the unique environment of the river valleys had matured fully. Well before 1750 B.C. the influence of the Mesopotamian and Egyptian civilizations had begun to spread beyond their original settings. During the period 1750-800 B.C. the process of cultural diffusion quickened and became a central theme of Near Eastern history. Not only did new peoples come to share higher civilization, many of them also made important contributions that enriched the basic patterns of civilized life.

1. DIFFUSION AND THE MOVEMENT OF PEOPLES

Cultural diffusion in this period was a complex process. Ideas, products, and techniques were carried out from the established centers of civilization by traders, soldiers, and diplomats. Imitation of the superior ways of the river valley civilizations by people long settled on their fringes was common. As cultural patterns spread, they were adapted and modified to fit new settings and situations. Especially important as a catalytic force was the movement of peoples into and around the civilized zones to create new political entities eager to share the benefits of civilized life.

Two peoples were especially significant in creating conditions that encouraged cultural diffusion. The Semitic-speaking seminomads of the Arabian Desert, with whom we are already familiar as intruders into Mesopotamia, continued their migrations after 1800 B.C. to play a prime role in the history of northern Mesopotamia, Syria, Palestine, and Egypt.

No less important were some newcomers, the Indo-Europeans, so named because they spoke a language that was new to the Near East and from which later evolved Sanskrit, Latin, Greek, Persian, and most modern European languages. Beginning about 2000 B.C., they fanned outward from their ancient homeland, perhaps north of the Caspian Sea, to make their impact felt over a broad area embracing central Europe, Italy, Greece, the Aegean area, the Near East, Iran, and India. At the time of their intrusion into the Near East, the Indo-Europeans had not reached the level of culture prevailing there. However, their superior weapons and military organization allowed them to play an important political role. And they proved adept at assimilating established patterns of civlization, especially the Mesopotamian, which they combined with their native culture to create cultural patterns with unique features.

2. THE EGYPTIAN AND HITTITE EMPIRES, 1750–1200 B.C.

The millennium under review in this chapter began with a series of disturbances that led to a major rearrangement of the power structure across the Near East (see Map 2.1). The Amorite Empire founded by Hammurabi suffered attacks which led to its destruction shortly after 1600 B.C. by the Kassites, immigrants from east of Mesopotamia, who were able to establish political domination over Mesopotamia. They ruled there for nearly four centuries, a period during which Mesopotamia played a secondary role in Near Eastern political life but continued to assert a major cultural influence over many peoples beyond Mesopotamia. To the north of Mesopotamia, Hurrian warlords established dominance over an area embracing the upper Tigris-Euphrates valleys and northern Syria to create the kingdom of the Mitanni, which flourished from about 1550 to 1350 B.C. As we shall see in the next section, a new power, the Indo-European Hittite kingdom, was emerging in Asia Minor. Also about 1750 B.C. the Hyksos, predominantly Semitic wanderers from the Palestine area, intruded into Egypt, contributing to a new era of internal disorder called the Second Intermediate Period (ca. 1750–1580 B.C.).

The Hyksos' presence in Egypt generated a powerful reaction against foreigners that led not only to the restoration of internal order but also to a new role for the Egyptians in the Near East. An effort to expel the Hyksos, led by local princes from Thebes, was finally achieved by Ahmose I (1558–1533 B.C.), the founder of the Eighteenth Dynasty. His victory opened the third period of glory in Egyptian history, the New Kingdom or Empire (1558–1200 B.C.). During the first century of the Eighteenth Dynasty, Egypt

Map 2.1 **THE ANCIENT NEAR EAST, CA. 1450 B.C.** This map illustrates the main centers of political power during the period 1600–1200 B.C. The ambitions of the rulers of the major states led to considerable conflict, especially in Syria and Palestine, where Egyptian and Hittite interests clashed. The map also indicates how extensively the ways of civilized life had spread beyond the original centers of civilization in the river valleys shown on Map 1.1.

was ruled by a succession of able pharaohs, one of whom was a woman, Hatshepsut. Her extraordinary career epitomized the policy of the restorers of Egyptian greatness: the exaltation of the divine ruler; "cleansing" the land of the taint of foreigners; the return to the traditional order in administration, economy, religion, and artistic and intellectual life. In a real sense, the "New" Kingdom was but the rebirth of the Old and Middle kingdoms.

However, a new factor played an increasingly important role: a more aggressive posture toward the outside world that ripened into full-scale imperialism. The first pharaohs of the Eighteenth Dynasty initiated expansionism by conducting raids against Nubia to the south and into Palestine and Syria, the original homeland of the Hyksos. These raids not only built Egypt's confidence in its military strength but also created elements in society that had a vested interest in expansionism. Eventually, during the reign of Thutmose III (1504–1450 B.C.), raiding turned into outright conquest (see Figure 2.1). Thutmose led a series of campaigns into Nubia, Libya, and Syria-Palestine that established Egyptian dominance. This expansion brought the Egyptians into contact with other Near Eastern powers, especially the Mitanni, who were rivals for control of Syria-Palestine (see Map 2.1). These confrontations resulted in active diplomatic efforts that made Egypt's might felt beyond the areas of actual conquest. The Mitanni, the Kassites, and the Assyrians all sought peace with Egypt. For a century Thutmose's successors pursued his policy and made Egypt the dominant power in the Near East.

Successful imperialism brought Egypt a new period of magnificence. Added to the wealth produced by the carefully managed agricultural system was a vast income from tribute exacted from foreign subjects and from greatly expanded trading connections embracing the Sudan, Mesopotamia, Asia Minor, Crete, and the Aegean world. Artistic life again blossomed, expressing itself with special brilliance in the magnificent temples built at Luxor and Karnak in honor of Amon-Ra, the chief national god (see Color Plate 2). The influences of Egyptian art styles, literary models, pottery and metalworking techniques, and religious practices were felt throughout the Near East with a force unknown prior to the New Kingdom.

But imperialism also brought problems. The burden of controlling conquered peoples required a standing army, the maintenance of garrisons abroad, periodic campaigns to display strength, and complex diplomatic efforts. All of this put a heavy demand on Egypt's resources. Major consequences were an increasing regimentation of Egypt's native populace and a growing reliance on slavery in the service of the state. The concerns of empire distracted the pharaohs' attention from the welfare of their subjects and created opportunities for oppression by grasping officials, especially the powerful priests of Amon-Ra. New ideas brought to Egypt by foreigners raised questions about the validity of traditional beliefs and practices.

Beginning about 1400 B.C., these problems, complicated by developments outside Egypt, put the New Kingdom to a severe test. The emerging crisis found its focus in the increasing rebelliousness of the dependent princes of Syria-Palestine, whose loyalty was a keystone of Egypt's imperial structure. These princes were encouraged to resist Egypt by a formidable external foe, the Hittites. Of Indo-European origins, the Hittites began to settle in central and eastern Asia Minor at least as early as 2000 B.C. and to impose their rule on the natives to form a series of small kingdoms. By about 1600 B.C. the ruler of one of these kingdoms imposed his power on the others to form a single Hittite kingdom with its capital at Hattusas (modern Boghazköy). The Hittites developed an advanced culture, derived in large part from their borrowing and adaptation of Mesopotamian models in politics, law, literature, art, and technology but also marked by distinctive features that displayed the creative powers of this "new" people. Their dominance in Asia Minor marked a significant expansion of the area of higher civilization.

Once firmly established in Asia Minor and fortified by their expanding level of material wealth and culture, the Hittites were able to expand eastward and southward to create their own empire (see Map 2.1). By 1400 B.C. they were actively engaged in encouraging and supporting rebellion among Egypt's client principalities in Syria and Palestine. Hittite power reached its zenith under King Suppiluliumas (1375–1355 B.C.), who threatened to oust Egypt from its Asian holdings.

In the face of the mounting threat to its empire, Egypt was distracted by an internal crisis brought on by a religious reform instituted by Amenhotep IV (1379–1362 B.C.) with the help of his queen, Nefertiti. Although his motives have been much debated, it appears that this enigmatic pharaoh acted for both political and religious reasons: to reestablish the pharaoh's absolute supremacy in the face of threats offered by such powerfully entrenched groups as the military establishment, the royal officials, and especially the priests of Amon-Ra and to revitalize a traditional religious system that had become encrusted with contradictory beliefs and overelaborate rituals based on crude materialism. In any case, Amenhotep IV proclaimed a new religion based on the worship of the god Aton, depicted as the source of all life, who was represented to humanity in the form of the sun disc giving off rays that sustained all existence (see Figure 2.2). To dramatize his break with the old order, Amenhotep IV changed his name to Akhnaton ("It pleases Aton") and abandoned the old capital at Thebes for a new one named Akhetaton (modern Tell el Amarna). Worship of the old deities was forbidden, their temples destroyed, their priests demoted. New rituals and a new art style, fresh and naturalistic, developed to honor and portray Aton. Many uncertainties surround what kind of religious system Akhnaton intended. Some have argued that he sought to establish monotheism, that is, a religion based on the worship of one god, a concept heretofore unknown. However, close scrutiny of the record does not support this view, for Akhnaton continued to present himself as a god. Perhaps he envisaged a religion that would rid Egyptian society of its restrictive traditionalism rooted in the old religious order and equip the Egyptians to take the lead in exploiting the cosmopolitan currents circulating in the Near East in this era of the mixing and mingling of cultures.

However, such questions are moot. Akhnaton's proclamation of a new religion raised a storm of protest, led by the priests of Amon-Ra, which for a decade consumed the energy of society. Even before his death Akhnaton's foes had forced him to abandon his reforms. Under his successor, his son-in-law Tutankhamon, the forces of reaction rapidly restored the cult of Amon-Ra and made a concerted effort to eradicate Aton worship and the memory of its chief proponent. The restoration of the traditional or-

FIGURE 2.2 An Egyptian Religious Reformer This scene shows Akhnaton with his wife, Nefertiti, and one of their daughters making an offering to the new deity, Aton, promoted by Akhnaton. The new deity is represented by the sun disc pouring its fruitful rays on the worshipers, who in turn would bestow such benefits on the pharaoh's subjects. The artistic style reflected in this carving is more naturalistic than the traditional Egyptian artistic canon (compare with Figures 1.1, 1.3, and 2.1). (The Metropolitan Museum of Art)

der is dramatically reflected in the objects found in "King Tut's" tomb; first excavated in 1922, its contents provide one of the most magnificent reflections of traditional Egyptian art and thought that has survived.

The disturbances caused by Akhnaton's attempted reform and the efforts to undo it weakened Egypt's capability to defend its empire. Hittite aggression in Syria and Palestine, accompanied by defections of local princes, temporarily ended Egyptian control in that area. Eventually, under the early rulers of the Nineteenth Dynasty, especially Seti and Rameses II, the Egyptians were able to regroup their military forces and to redress the balance in Syria and Palestine after a bitter and costly struggle with the Hittites which finally ended about 1270 B.C. with a settlement that assigned each a sphere of influence in that embattled area.

For an interval both Egyptians and Hittites regained their former vitality as the leading powers of the era. However, both empires were approaching the end of their greatness. Decisive in determining their fate was a new wave of Indo-European invaders, especially formidable because they possessed iron weapons, who spilled over Asia Minor, the Aegean Sea area, and the waterways of the eastern Mediterranean. The Hittite Empire was completely destroyed about 1200 B.C. Attacks by Nubians, Libyans, and the mysterious "People of the Sea," seafaring marauders probably from Asia Minor, forced the Egyptians back within their old boundaries and for a time established foreigners from Libya and sub-Saharan Africa as pharaohs. These setbacks greatly reduced Egypt's capacity to influence developments in the Asiatic Near East but opened opportunities for cultural interaction between Egypt and large areas of northeast Africa.

3. THE MINOAN WORLD, 2000–1400 B.C.

The age of diffusion witnessed the development of a vital new civilization on the island of Crete, named Minoan by modern historians after Minos, a legendary Cretan king. Although the development of Minoan civilization was affected by borrowings from other civilizations of the Near East, the Cretans demonstrated a capacity to create a pattern of culture that had a unique character. Their accomplishment was especially important because of the influence it asserted over the world to the north and west—especially Greece.

Minoan civilization had its roots in a Neolithic farming culture that took shape on Crete about 6000 B.C. For many centuries thereafter Neolithic farmers shared a simple pattern of culture with other people living in Greece, the Aegean Islands, and Asia Minor. Gradually, the Cretans developed skills in pottery making and metalwork; especially important was the introduction of bronze technology from Asia Minor about 3000 B.C. Moreover, the Cretans learned to sail the seas to establish contacts with the advanced civilizations of Egypt and Asia and to enrich themselves by gaining access to markets and raw materials in the area around the Aegean. By about 2000 B.C. their developing technical skills, increasing wealth, and expanding contacts resulted in the emergence of several full-fledged urban centers, including Knossos, Phaistos, and Mallia. Each was ruled by a king whose magnificent palace was the center of civilized life. Minoan civilization reached its peak between about 1700 and 1450 B.C. During this period Knossos outstripped the other cities of Crete, asserting a cultural leadership that provided a common pattern of life on the island and extending Cretan influences over much of the Aegean world, chiefly through trading ventures. Then, between 1500 and 1450 B.C., a disaster struck the Minoan world, destroying many cities. Perhaps this catastrophe was a consequence of a devastating volcano on the island of Thera, north of Crete. At about the same time Crete suffered at the hands of invaders from Greece called Mycenaeans (see Chapter 4). Knossos continued for an interval as a center from which the invaders ruled the island, but shortly after 1400 B.C. it too was destroyed, perhaps as a result of a revolt against the outsiders. Minoan civilization had run its course.

Our knowledge of the major features of Minoan civilization is derived chiefly from archaeological evidence produced by excavations of palace sites, especially Knossos. The Minoans did develop their own writing system, called Linear A by modern scholars, but it has not yet been deciphered. About 1450 B.C. that system was replaced by another, called Linear B, which has been deciphered and proved to be based on an early form of the Greek language. It probably represents an adaptation of Minoan writing by the Mycenaean invaders from Greece. The surviving documents in Linear B are chiefly economic records and provide only limited information about many facets of Minoan society.

At the height of Minoan civilization Crete was governed by several kings, each controlling a particular city and its surrounding territory. Perhaps the king of Knossos exercised some form of authority over the other kingdoms, but that overlordship was based on consent rather than force. The fact that Minoan cities were unwalled indicates that the kingdoms lived without serious conflict and great expenditure for arms. The power of Minoan kings rested on strong religious sanctions and on wealth derived from control of the agricultural system and from overseas trade. Royal administration was conducted by a highly developed bureaucracy especially skilled at orderly record keeping. A wealthy and influential nobility made up chiefly of landowners grouped itself around the kings to uphold royal authority.

The Minoan economy was based on a productive agricultural system devoted to the cultivation of grain, olives, grapes, and vegetables and to the raising of livestock, especially sheep. But trade and industry produced the additional wealth necessary to support an advanced civilization. Highly skilled artisans laboring in the workshops of the royal palace or in their own shops produced a wide variety of goods that adorned the lives of the rulers, their officials, and the wealthy landowners and merchants. Especially skilled were Minoan potters and metalworkers. Enterprising merchants, sometimes serving the kings and sometimes working on their own, carried Minoan manufactured products over the seas to a wide area around the Mediterranean, including not only the major Near Eastern centers of civilization but also the less developed peoples of the Aegean world. These merchants brought back a variety of raw materials and manufactured goods. The wealth produced by this vigorous economy allowed the Minoan upper class to live in well-furnished houses and enjoy fine clothing and abundant jewelry. Upper-class women shared freely in the social life of the palaces and aristocratic households. Every royal city had a considerable population of laborers who performed all kinds of work needed to sustain city life. The rural population clustered in villages, where they labored under the supervision of royal officials and pow-

FIGURE 2.3 Minoan Sports This bronze figure dating from the sixteenth century B.C. portrays a favorite Minoan sporting activity—vaulting over a charging bull. Both young men and young women participated in this dangerous game. The artist's ability to convey a feeling of movement on the part of both the leaper and the animal is reflective of much of Minoan art. (The British Museum)

erful landowners. There was little slavery in Minoan society.

The Minoans worshiped a variety of gods and goddesses, most of them representing the forces of nature and especially the goddess of fertility, whose life-giving powers were invoked by all classes of people. Religious practices were less elaborate than those of Mesopotamia and Egypt. The Minoans built no great temples; they worshiped at simple shrines in private houses, on hills, in groves and caves, and near springs. Priests and priestesses were maintained at the palace to serve the deities, but they played only a limited role in shaping Minoan life and culture. Prominent place in religious ceremonies was given to animal sacrifice, gift giving, dancing, and athletic events (see Figure 2.3). The pictorial representations of these rituals suggest an outlook that was joyful and lighthearted, little marked by fear or gloom. There was a belief in afterlife, and some attention was given to the care of the dead, but never on the scale that occurred in Egypt.

The spirit of Minoan civilization emerges most forcefully in the visual arts. Minoan architecture, devoted chiefly to building palaces and private dwellings such as those revealed by the ruins of Knossos rather than temples and tombs, reflected a technical mastery of a variety of materials and forms and a fine sense of scale. Many of the multistoried structures were equipped with a piped water supply, skillfully constructed drainage systems, and indoor toilets. Palaces and houses were decorated with paintings and carvings that focused on nature and human activity. Especially skilled were elaborate frescoes portraying processions of young men and women bearing gifts to the gods and goddesses. Animals, fish, and birds were also favorite subjects of carvers and painters. Minoan decorated pottery reflects a fine sense of form and a love of color. In all its forms Minoan art is mobile, free of stylization, intense, and energetic. It reflects a civilization focused on worldly concerns, lacking in fear, open to experimentation, and pleasure loving. In many ways the mentality shaping Minoan civilization contrasts sharply with that of Mesopotamia and Egypt, heralding a world yet to come.

4. THE ERA OF SMALL STATES, 1200–800 B.C.: PHOENICIANS AND ARAMEANS

The collapse of the Hittite and Egyptian empires about 1200 B.C., coupled with the decline of Minoan power, left the Near East without a dominant power center for about four centuries. Several small groups located in Syria and Palestine, the crossroad of the Near East, seized the opportunity to carve a place in and to make their unique contributions to the increasingly homogeneous world of the Near East.

Two peoples stand out especially as creative adapters and disseminators of established cultural patterns: the Phoenicians and the Arameans. Both were Semitic seminomads in origin, the products of the numerous migrations from the Arabian Desert that had been in progress for many centuries. These migrants were repeatedly conquered and strongly influenced by the Mesopotamians, Egyptians, and Hittites. Consequently, by 1200 B.C. they were already highly civilized peoples. The Phoenicians, located in the narrow coastal area between the Mediterranean

Sea and the mountains of Lebanon, developed a number of independent city-states, chief of which were Byblos, Tyre, and Sidon. The Arameans were located east of the Lebanon Mountains between the northern fringes of the Arabian Desert and the Euphrates River. They were organized into a number of small kingdoms centered around Damascus, Kadesh, and Palmyra (see Map 2.1). For about four centuries these city-states and kingdoms enjoyed independent existence until they were finally absorbed into the Assyrian Empire (see Chapter 3).

The Phoenicians and the Arameans derived most of their wealth from trade. The Phoenicians took to the seas and established a virtual monopoly on trade in the Mediterranean, chiefly as successors to the Minoan traders. Their merchants carried manufactured goods from the entire Near East to the less developed peoples of Greece, Italy, North Africa, Spain, and southern France and brought back the raw materials of these areas. From these traders many peoples to the west got their first taste of higher civilization. The Phoenicians not only traded but also established colonies, notably the North African city of Carthage, destined to become an important center of civilization after 800 B.C. The Arameans were overland traders, exploiting the trade routes that linked Egypt, Mesopotamia, Asia Minor, and points beyond. Both Phoenicians and Arameans reaped a rich reward from their commerce, which allowed them to live well and to support a wide range of cultural activities. Neither people was particularly creative in learning and the arts. However, the Phoenicians did perfect an alphabet that later served as a model for the written languages of the Mediterranean basin, and the Aramean language was widely adopted in the Near East.

5. THE ERA OF SMALL STATES, 1200–800 B.C.: THE HEBREWS

One people emerging into prominence during the Era of Small States had a particularly enduring impact on the spiritual and moral history of Western civilization. These were the Hebrews, who left a magnificent literary record of their version of their history in their Bible, now generally referred to as the Old Testament. The interpretation of this complex document, composed over many centuries by many authors drawing on a mixture of historical traditions, folklore, legal enactments, moral exhortations, and prophecies, confronts the modern historian with formidable problems. However, the main lines of the story it tells, coupled with supporting evidence from non-Hebrew literary sources and from archaeology, provide a fairly accurate account of the history of the Hebrews during the age of diffusion.

The surviving evidence suggests that the Hebrews were originally nomads searching for a place in which to settle, part of the extensive migration of Semitic-speaking peoples that played a crucial role in the age of diffusion. During what the Hebrew Bible called the age of the patriarchs, tribal groups based on kinship ties left their settlements on the fringes of Mesopotamia and, under the leadership of family heads such as Abraham, Isaac, and Jacob, migrated around the southern fringes of the Fertile Crescent to the area of Palestine. Perhaps this migration began about 1800 B.C., roughly in the time of Hammurabi, and took place over a relatively long period. In the Palestinian region the nomadic Hebrew herders encountered and began to clash with more advanced agricultural societies, especially the Canaanites. As a result of this interaction the Hebrews began a slow transition to settled agricultural life. An important feature of Hebrew tribal life was a religion rooted in a fierce allegiance by tribal members to a deity who gave special protection to the tribe and interacted with it through its patriarch. Among such deities was Yahweh, the god of Abraham.

Not all of the wandering Hebrews remained in the Palestine area. Some made their way to Egypt and settled in the Delta region (the biblical land of Goshen), where they prospered for a time, and some, like Joseph, even found favor at the pharaoh's court, suggesting that the Hebrews accommodated to the higher civilization of the Egyptians. Eventually, however, there arose a pharaoh "who knew not Joseph" and whose mistreatment led to a decisive event in Hebrew history—the Exodus from Egypt, which probably occurred during the reign of Pharaoh Rameses II (1292–1235 B.C.).

During a period of wandering in the desert of the Sinai Peninsula that followed the Exodus,

there occurred a religious experience that gave fundamental shape to the religious consciousness of the Hebrews. Under the leadership of Moses, the Hebrews of the Exodus came to believe that they as a people had become special partners of Yahweh, whom at least some had worshiped during the age of the patriarchs. Master of history and of nature, as he had demonstrated through the events of the Exodus, Yahweh made a *covenant*, or mutual contract, with Moses' people: He selected them as his people and promised to care for them. In return, they pledged to honor him as their only god and to follow his law, revealed to Moses as the Ten Commandments, in the conduct of their individual and collective existences. These fundamental concepts, which thereafter remained central to the Hebrew religion, became the basis for the transformation of Moses' "mixed multitude" of tribal groups into "a holy nation," the Israelites, whose identity was rooted in their unique relationship with their god.

Fortified by their pact with Yahweh, Moses' followers joined forces with other Hebrew tribes in search of the Promised Land. Their object became Palestine, an area where considerable instability existed in the wake of the collapse of the Egyptian and Hittite empires (see Map 2.1). The biblical version of this quest presents a relatively simple account of a succession of military triumphs, beginning with Joshua's dramatic capture of Jericho and forged by the collaboration of the twelve tribes into which the Hebrews were organized. In reality, the Hebrew struggle for Palestine was a drawn-out process involving more than military engagements. To be sure, the Canaanites were formidable foes, but they were not the only ones. Repeatedly the Hebrews had to contend with other outsiders equally intent on occupying Palestine, a threat that often necessitated cooperation between Hebrews and Canaanites and led to gradual assimilation of the two peoples in a way that hastened the transformation of the Hebrews into farmers and city dwellers. This process challenged traditional values in ways that caused tensions within Hebrew society. The Hebrew effort was impeded by tribal jealousies, intensified as a result of the attempts of each tribe to establish its identity on the basis of its claim to a particular territory won in the struggle for Palestine. These complex stresses produced crisis after crisis, sometimes dramatically resolved by charismatic figures such as Gideon, Samson, and Samuel, collectively designated in the Bible as "judges," who often employed religious arguments to persuade the Hebrews to act in unity—at least temporarily.

After about a hundred and fifty years of struggle and change, the Hebrews were close to winning the Promised Land. Then they were almost destroyed by the Philistines, warlike newcomers armed with iron weapons who settled along the south Palestine coast after being rebuffed in their attempt to enter Egypt. By about 1050 B.C. the Philistines had made major inroads into Palestine and seemed to be on the verge of overpowering the Hebrews. The threat of disaster led to a momentous step: an agreement among the Hebrew tribes—forged in large part through the efforts of a famous judge, Samuel—to place themselves under a single king, thereby creating a political "nation."

The unified Hebrew nation survived for about a century (1020–930 B.C.), embracing the reigns of Saul, David, and Solomon, who collectively brought the Hebrews to the high point of their history in ancient times. These kings were able to organize military resources that expelled the Philistines from Palestine and then subdued not only the Canaanites but also many small principalities on the borders of Palestine, allowing the unified Hebrew kingdom to assume a place as an important power in the Syria-Palestine area. A centralized government was established at Jerusalem, which, especially under Solomon, took on many characteristics of a typical Near Eastern monarchy. The kingdom was greatly enriched by royal economic policies that helped Hebrew traders take advantage of Palestine's strategic location on international trade routes. Solomon was particularly effective in creating an extensive network of diplomatic ties in the Near East that enhanced the prestige of the kingdom and brought its ruling elements into contact with the increasingly cosmopolitan world of the Near East; evidence of these contacts was provided not only by Solomon's many foreign wives but also by foreign influences on the arts and on lifestyles increasingly prevalent among the Hebrews.

As the Hebrews' political fortunes advanced

between 1200 and 930 B.C., their religion—Judaism—continued to develop. The struggles to occupy Palestine brought constant reminders to the Hebrews, especially from the aforementioned judges, to remain loyal to the covenant with Yahweh. The success under the early monarchs appeared to vindicate Yahweh's concern for his people and thus to keep his worship central to Hebrew life. In fact, the institution of a monarchy, which was believed to be sanctioned by Yahweh in a special way, marked an important step in creating a truly national religion. A prime symbol of this national religion was the establishment by David and Solomon of Jerusalem as the cult center as well as the political capital of the Hebrew people; the city's jewel was the splendid temple built by Solomon to house the Ark of the Covenant, a wooden chest containing sacred objects associated with the worship of Yahweh. The system of law originally set forth in the Ten Commandments was greatly expanded to serve as a common bond among the Hebrews and to relate their new lives as farmers and urban dwellers to basic religious principles rooted in the covenant. A more complex set of religious practices shaped by an emerging priesthood took on increasing importance in the collective lives of the Hebrews. The changes in law and worship involved the absorption into Judaism of elements from non-Hebrew sources, especially Canaanite cult practices associated with the agricultural seasons. This process of assimilation generated constant tension in Hebrew religious life but ultimately resulted in an enriched and flexible common religion attuned to the more advanced level of civilization that the Hebrews had attained by the time of Solomon.

Even while Solomon reigned in all his glory, deep-seated discontents within the Hebrew community threatened the unity of the kingdom. Among the major causes of this discontent were the autocratic methods of the kings, growing economic and social inequality, rural-urban rivalry, and concerns over foreign religious practices in the rituals of the temple and the royal court. Immediately after Solomon's death these discontents resulted in a division of the unified state into two kingdoms: Israel in the north, with its center at Samaria, and Judah in the south, with its capital at Jerusalem ruled by kings descended from the house of David (see Map 2.1). Each of these nations had a stormy internal history, marked by social and religious conflict. Ultimately, neither was able to survive outside aggression. In 722 B.C. Israel was conquered by the Assyrians and many of its people were carried off into captivity, to be enshrined in Hebrew memory as the Ten Lost Tribes. Judah survived until 586 B.C., when the Chaldeans captured Jerusalem, destroyed the Temple, and took large numbers of Hebrews to Babylon as captives. The Persian ruler Cyrus (ca. 560–530 B.C.) allowed those victims of the Babylonian captivity who wished to do so to return to Jerusalem and to rebuild the Temple, which again became the center of a vital religious community. However, the Hebrews remained politically subject to the Persians and then were absorbed into the empire of Alexander the Great when he destroyed the Persian Empire in 330 B.C. An important consequence of this troubled course of events was the beginnings of the Diaspora, the scattering of many Hebrews across the map of the Near East into new settings where their religion would undergo new challenges and where they would assert an important influence on the non-Hebrews among whom they lived.

In these times of almost constant tribulation Judaism took on new dimensions. During the period of the divided kingdoms and foreign conquests, religion became the sole force that sustained a sense of commonality and uniqueness among the Hebrews. Thrust into a position of leadership of a community ruled by foreign potentates, the Hebrew priesthood fashioned a sober, austere cult that cut away much of the magic and superstition surrounding other Near Eastern religions; observance of these practices became a mark of belonging to Yahweh's special community. Much more significant was the reformulation of the traditional concepts of Judaism by a series of powerful religious leaders known as *prophets*. Several of them rank among the world's greatest spiritual leaders: Elijah, Amos, Isaiah, Jeremiah, Ezekiel, the anonymous second Isaiah. And occasionally a female voice sounded among them: Esther, Ruth, and Judith. Although their careers spanned several centuries and each spoke a unique message appropriate to his or her own time, these remarkable figures

collectively explored with deep spiritual insight and articulated with great force many of the elements essential to all religious experience. Usually individuals of modest social status, little concerned with wealth and power or office, they presented themselves as messengers of Yahweh driven by an urge to put back on the right course all who claimed to be followers of Yahweh, including especially the rich and the powerful. The religious message of all of them was rooted in a shared conviction, based on their reading of history and their interpretation of their own times, that the Hebrews were guilty of abandoning their covenant with Yahweh. Their prophetic mission was to call Yahweh's errant and hard-hearted people back to that covenant. In the course of reinterpreting the essence of that covenant, they expanded and clarified certain fundamental concepts that became the essence of Judaism and the source of its powerful impact on the future course of Western civilization.

First, the prophets insisted that the Hebrews worship only one god; to give any sign of recognition to any other deity except Yahweh was the greatest of all sacrileges. In fixing this point at the center of religious life, the prophets ensured that Judaism became the first truly monotheistic religion.

Second, the prophets gave ultimate shape to a radically new concept of Yahweh's nature, a concept set forth in terms that demanded that he alone be worshiped. Yahweh, whose name means "he causes to be," was the creator of all things. He was omnipotent, ruling the entire universe and causing everything in the past, present, and future to happen. Unlike other gods worshiped in the Near East, he was not in nature and could not be depicted in any natural form; he created and controlled natural forces which were to be seen as reflections of his divine power but not as objects to be worshiped. Likewise, he was outside time, which was a created dimension of the universe within which would be worked his plan for the universe and for humanity, a plan in which all created things were destined to participate; each event along the trajectory of time was a meaningful manifestation of his unfolding plan. He was a god of justice, acting according to law instead of whim. He was a god of righteousness, pleased by those who did good according to his commands but offended to the point of vengeance by those who did evil. He was a caring god, "merciful and gracious, long-suffering, and abundant in goodness and truth," always watchful over his entire creation.

Third, the prophets projected a new vision of the essence of human nature. As Yahweh's special creatures, human beings were created to play a special role in the working out of the divine plan. This role could be achieved only by the realization by humans of their capacity for moral perfection, which involved a choice by each individual between good and evil. Human beings were basically moral beings, each endowed with the freedom and capacity to choose the good. They were not Yahweh's slaves, for whom he cared not and upon whom he might vent his wrath at his whim; rather, each was his child who could earn divine mercy and love and favor by righteousness. This moral freedom, allowing human beings to determine what they wished to be, imposed an awesome responsibility on each person, but it opened avenues of human aspiration and endeavor largely absent from the other religious systems in the ancient Near East.

Fourth, in what historically was probably their most provocative insight into the human condition, the prophets proclaimed a new basis for defining the behavior of each individual toward others and of a community toward the individuals who were its members. Just as Yahweh treated men and women with righteousness and justice, so also must moral human beings treat all others according to these same principles. Likewise, the community of Yahweh's followers must conduct its collective actions to promote righteousness and justice. The principles of responsible social behavior were set forth in a code of law (Torah, defined in the first five books of the Hebrew Bible) that provided detailed regulations for all aspects of individual and communal life that all were obliged to observe if they were to be counted among those faithful to Yahweh. The Hebraic law was firm in its insistence that every individual was worthy of respect and compassionate treatment. But beyond the letter of the law the prophets projected a vision of individual and collective social responsibility with radical implications for the conduct of human affairs. Their reflections on the relationships which interlinked the divine, society, and the individual led them to postulate certain fundamental principles that must undergird a righteous social order: an egalitarian social system; the responsibility of those with authority to abide by the law; the obligation of their subjects to challenge them if they do not do so; the right of each to keep what he or she possesses as long as those possessions have not been gained by unjust actions; and above all else the obligation of each individual and of the community to show mercy, charity, and compassion to the weak and unfortunate. To the prophets these principles undergirding the right social order seemed self-evident in terms of their understanding of Yahweh's nature and what he expected of his special creatures.

Finally, the prophets reaffirmed that the Hebrews—the followers of Yahweh—were the people chosen to carry out Yahweh's plan for his creation. No matter what disasters might befall them, they would ultimately serve as the instrument through which the world would come to know and to serve the true god according to his commands. In the face of the disasters that befell the Hebrews after Solomon, the prophets put special emphasis on Yahweh's intention eventually to send a messiah to lead the Hebrews to victory. While awaiting their deliverer, the Hebrews must remain steadfast in their allegiance to Yahweh, maintain their religious ties with one another, abide by the law in their social and individual behavior, and resist the temptation to follow false gods. Their role as the chosen people and their expectation of a messiah instilled in the adherents of Judaism a forward-looking attitude which made every moment in history pregnant with meaning of things to come and rich in challenges to serve Yahweh in ways that would ensure the day of deliverance.

As the last centuries of Near Eastern leadership in shaping the foundations upon which Western civilization would be built unfolded, Yahweh's promise to his chosen people seemed unlikely to be realized. By about 300 B.C. Yahweh's followers were few in number: a small community living around Jerusalem and tiny cells of Jews scattered around the Near East. All were dominated by non-Jewish overlords. Their situation generated disagreement among the faithful over how they should conduct their lives and relate to the foreign cultures of their masters.

The bulk of the population of the Near East remained untouched by the religion shaped by the Hebrews; these people preferred their traditional nature deities, their elaborate mythologies, their powerful priesthoods, and their complex rituals devoted to winning divine favor. Despite their religion's modest impact on the ancient Near East, the Hebrews had shaped one of the great chapters in the spiritual and moral history of humanity. Neither the message of Judaism nor those who proclaimed it would go unnoticed as the history of Western civilization unfolded.

SUGGESTED READING

Egyptian and Hittite Empires

P. H. Newby, *Warrior Pharaohs. The Rise and Fall of the Egyptian Empire* (1980). A full treatment of the history of the New Kingdom.

Donald B. Redford, *Egypt, Canaan, and Israel in Ancient Times* (1992). Helps understand the nature of Egyptian imperialism.

Donald B. Redford, *Akhenaton: The Heretic King* (1984). An excellent study of an enigmatic figure.

T. G. H. James, *Pharaoh's People: Scenes from Life in Imperial Egypt* (1984). An excellent social history of the New Kingdom.

J. P. Mallory, *In Search of the Indo-Europeans: Language, Archaeology and Myth* (1989). A balanced picture of the early Indo-Europeans and their culture.

J. G. Macqueen, *The Hittites and Their Contemporaries in Asia Minor*, rev. and enl. ed. (1986). An excellent survey.

Ekrem Akurgal, *The Art of the Hittites*, trans. Constance McNab (1962). A well-illustrated study.

Minoans and Phoenicians

Arthur Cotterell, *The Minoan World* (1979). A good introduction.

Reynold Higgins, *Minoan and Mycenaean Art*, rev. ed. (1981). A sound study that is well illustrated.

Raymond Weill, *Phoenicia and Western Asia to the Macedonian Conquest*, trans. Ernest F. Row (1980). A clear account of the role of the Phoenicians in the ancient world.

Hebrews

John Bright, *A History of Israel*, 3rd ed. (1981).

J. Maxwell Miller and John H. Hayes, *A History of Ancient Israel and Judah* (1986).

H. Jagersma, *A History of Israel in the Old Testament Period*, trans. John Bowden (1983).

Three fine histories of ancient Israel; the Miller and Hayes book provides the fullest treatment.

Bernhard W. Anderson, *Understanding the Old Testament*, 4th ed. (1986). A well-done attempt to weave together history, literary criticism, archaeology, and biblical theology in order to show how Judaism developed.

G. W. Anderson, *The History and Religion of Israel* (1966). A helpful treatment of the evolution of ancient Judaism.

Irving M. Zeitlin, *Ancient Judaism* (1984). Written from a sociological perspective.

Roland de Vaux, *Ancient Israel: Its Life and Institutions*, 2 vols. (1961). Rich in details about ancient Hebrew society.

CHAPTER 3

The Great Empires: Assyria and Persia, 800–300 B.C.

FIGURE 3.1 A Near Eastern Empire Builder This portrayal of the Assyrian ruler Sargon II (721–705 B.C.) conveys a sense of power—even arrogant power—that was typical of the rulers of the great Near Eastern empires from ca. 800 to 300 B.C. One can well believe that this man was capable of dominating "the four rims of the world," as Assyrian and Persian empire builders claimed to do. (Hirmer Fotoarchiv)

During the ninth century B.C. a new era began in the Near East that featured the formation of vast empires unifying almost the entire area which enjoyed the benefits of higher civilization under a single political regime. The ground for this development had been prepared during the previous millennium, when the diffusion of the river valley cultures had provided diverse peoples with common technologies, religious practices, and literary and art styles. Expanding trade connections had drawn distant communities into economic interdependency. Shared cultural, religious, and economic interests invited attempts at political consolidation, and adventuresome leaders arose to respond to the opportunity.

1. THE ASSYRIAN EMPIRE, 800–612 B.C.

The first people to unify almost the entire Near East were the Assyrians. They were a Semitic-speaking people who as early as 3000 B.C. had established a homeland on the plateau astride the upper Tigris River, a land that lacked natural barriers and was open to repeated attacks. During the ensuing centuries the Assyrians were so powerfully influenced by Mesopotamian civilization that their history is sometimes treated as an extension of Mesopotamian history. Although repeatedly assaulted by Akkadians, Amorites, Kassites, Hittites, Mitanni, nomads from the Arabian desert, and mountaineers from the east and north, the hardy farmers of Assyria maintained their political identity. A major factor in their survival was their success in developing a potent military force, especially after they adopted the new iron weapons and the horse-drawn war chariots introduced into the Near East shortly before 1000 B.C.

Eventually the absence of any major political powers in the Near East during the Era of Small States allowed the Assyrians to assert themselves more aggressively. During the ninth century several surrounding peoples began to feel the force of Assyrian raids. None was able to resist the well-armed Assyrian infantrymen, archers, and charioteers, ably backed by siege equipment and skilled engineers. The effectiveness of the military machine was increased by deliberate terrorism waged against those defeated by the Assyrians. So awesome did the Assyrians become that many people preferred to "embrace the feet" of the attackers rather than resist (see Figure 3.2).

FIGURE 3.2 Embracing the Feet of an Assyrian King This carving from an Assyrian royal palace represents Jehu, King of Israel, bowing before his Assyrian conqueror, King Shalmaneser III. It conveys the awe that Assyrian rulers struck into the victims of their conquest. (The British Museum)

These raids showed the Assyrians that they could enrich themselves by exacting tribute from their victims, a prospect that prompted them to undertake outright conquest and the establishment of permanent control over Assyria's enemies. Under the leadership of Tiglath-Pileser III (745–727 B.C.) and a successor, Sargon II (721–705 B.C.), Assyrian armies launched a series of expeditions that destroyed the chief political powers from Mesopotamia northward and westward to Syria and Palestine. Assyrian governors were imposed on most of the conquered peoples, although a few minor kingdoms, such as Judah, were allowed to exist as tribute-paying clients of Assyria. The central administration of Assyria was enlarged to supervise tribute collection, and effective means of communication were devised to keep the royal court informed of affairs throughout the empire. The army stood ready to crush all signs of resistence; it continued its policy of terrorism, even resorting to the large-scale deportation of conquered peoples, as was the case with a large part of the population of the kingdom of Israel. Once this power base was established, rulers such as Sennacherib (705–681 B.C.), Esarhaddon (681–669 B.C.), and Ashurbanipal (669–626 B.C.) devoted their energies to dealing with outsiders who insisted on interfering with Assyrian rule. Egypt was forced to accept Assyrian overlordship, and Assyrian influence was extended into Asia Minor, the Zagros Mountains region, Iran, the northern Arabian Desert, and the highland region north of the Assyrian homeland. By 650 B.C. almost the entire civilized Near East stood subject to a single master, the great king of Assyria, "ruler of the four rims of the world" (see Map 3.1). The arrogant visages of these conquerors still stare out at us in the remarkable stone busts and reliefs wrought by Assyrian artists to celebrate their deeds (see Figure 3.1); all of them left boastful written accounts of their exploits in building the first ecumenical empire in the Near East.

However, the Assyrian Empire was not as strong as its size and heavy-handed rule suggested. Its brutal treatment of subject peoples aroused their undying hatred, nowhere better reflected than in the writings of some of the Hebrew prophets. Constant warfare depleted Assyria's human resources and eventually forced its rulers to rely on less efficient levies from con-

quered subjects. Internal discontent, often stemming from dissatisfaction over the distribution of tribute, arose. Worst of all, the Assyrians encountered the plague of all empire builders—enemies beyond the frontiers, aroused by the threat of absorption and greed for the riches of the empire. During the reign of Ashurbanipal these problems began to weaken Assyrian power, and troubles mounted rapidly after his death in 626 B.C. The Egyptians successfully revolted and then stirred up trouble among Assyrian subjects in Syria and Palestine. A Semitic group, the Chaldeans, raised the standard of revolt in southern Mesopotamia, a threat so serious that the Assyrians were forced to commit most of their resources to quelling it. Then the Medes, a people living east of the Zagros Mountains who had learned a great deal by imitating Assyrian military techniques, struck out of the east. In 612 B.C. they and the Chaldeans destroyed the Assyrian capital at Nineveh. Assyrian power collapsed almost immediately, leaving the empire to be partitioned by its many foes.

No one in the Near East lamented Assyria's passing. The Hebrew prophet Nahum spoke for all the world: "All who hear the news of you clap their hands at your downfall." However, the Assyrians' bad reputation should not conceal their contributions to history. Their attempt to erect a centralized monarchy was to be imitated by others. They wiped out many artificial political boundaries that kept small groups at sword's point. At least briefly they imposed a beneficial, albeit burdensome, peace on the Near East, protecting it for nearly three centuries against barbarians who might have destroyed its civilization had they not been rebuffed. Even though their regime funneled vast amounts of wealth to the Assyrian homeland at the expense of their subjects, they promoted trade by breaking down barriers impeding the movement of goods, and they encouraged the spread of a common spoken language, Aramaic, across their empire, greatly facilitating the exchange of goods and ideas and the dissemination of technical skills.

The Assyrians also made a notable contribution to cultural history. Although their culture was derived primarily from Mesopotamian models, Assyrian leaders were active patrons of artistic and literary activities, chiefly as a means of glorifying their political accomplishments.

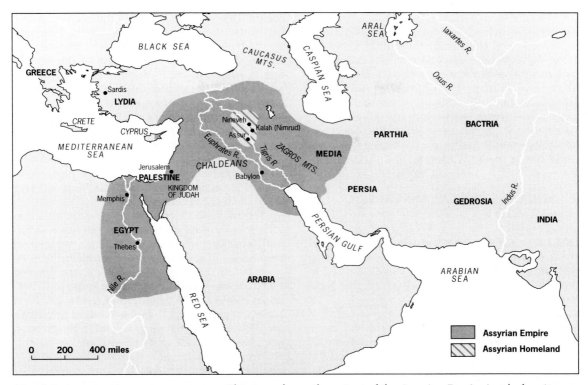

Map 3.1 THE ASSYRIAN EMPIRE, CA. 662 B.C. This map shows the extent of the Assyrian Empire just before its collapse. Some idea of its size is illustrated by the fact that it was more than one thousand miles from its capital at Nineveh to Thebes in Egypt—roughly as far as Washington, D.C., is from Omaha, Nebraska. Its size should be compared with that of the earlier empires of the Egyptians and the Hittites (see Map 2.1). A better appreciation of the Assyrian Empire can be gained by making an effort to account for the different peoples we have studied who were included in it.

Their kings were avid builders, constructing the great cities of Assur, Kalah (modern Nimrud), and Nineveh as monuments of their power and glory. In these cities earlier Mesopotamian architectural styles were followed closely and thus kept alive. Temples and palaces were decorated with massive sculptured pieces and excellent stone reliefs. To the tradition they honored, Assyrian artists often gave a unique quality. Especially impressive were the carved friezes done in relief to decorate the walls of royal palaces. This narrative art put together a succession of carved panels to tell in realistic detail the story of a military campaign or a hunting expedition (see Figure 3.2). The Assyrians were avid collectors and copiers of the literary treasure left behind by the Sumerians and the Akkadians. King Ashurbanipal built a huge library at Nineveh as a repository for thousands of cuneiform tablets containing copies of what was revered as "classical" literary works, especially the religious epics and creation stories so dear to the Mesopotamians. The Assyrians did show some originality in compiling annals vividly recounting the innumerable military campaigns of the kings, thereby making a contribution to the art of historical writing.

Assyrian religion was likewise strongly colored by borrowings from Mesopotamia. The great state god of Assyria, Assur, resembled the Amorite Marduk. Assyrian rituals, prayers, and priesthoods were almost indistinguishable from those of the earlier Mesopotamians. Assyrian religious life was colored by the militarism of society; perhaps their imperialism was motivated by a compulsion to assert Assur's dominion over other gods. In many reliefs Assur is shown hovering over the field of battle, ready to take up arms to assure the victory of the king serving Assur's cause. In all these ways the Assyrians kept alive some of the most precious cultural traditions in the Near East.

2. SUCCESSORS OF ASSYRIA, 612–550 B.C.

In the wake of Assyria's sudden collapse several states entered a spirited competition to carve up the empire. Some of these rivals even aspired to replace the Assyrians as masters of the Near East.

One of the competitors was Egypt. After a long period of weakness following the end of the New Kingdom about 1200 B.C. (see Chapter 2), foreign rule by the Assyrians again goaded the Egyptians to unify under a single pharaoh, Psammetichus (663–609 B.C.), founder of the Twenty-sixth Dynasty. Egypt again enjoyed a brief period of internal order, prosperity, and international prestige, especially in the Syria-Palestine area. But the Egyptians were incapable of sustaining the role of great power. The pharaohs had to rely on foreign mercenaries (chiefly Greeks) to provide a military force; these forces were a constant source of internal trouble. A backward-looking spirit, nourished especially by a reactionary priesthood, dominated thought and expression. Old age had gripped Egyptian society. In 525 B.C. the Persians were able to conquer Egypt without much difficulty.

In Asia Minor the small kingdom of Lydia, which first emerged after the fall of the Hittities, benefited from the fall of Assyria. Its rulers, the most famous of whom was Croesus (560–546 B.C.), fabled by the Greeks for his wealth, were able to establish control over most of Asia Minor, including several important Greet city-states on the Aegean seacost. Despite the considerable prosperity of Lydia, it was no match for the Persians, who conquered the kingdom in 546 B.C.

Another rival for succession to Assyria was Media. Descendants of Indo-European-speaking migrants who had overrun Iran about 1000 B.C., the Medes established a kingdom in northern Iran which eventually fell victim to the Assyrians. Under Assyrian domination the Medes raised their level of life considerably by borrowing from their oppressors. Eventually they played a major military role in destroying Assyria. After Assyria's fall, they laid claim to a vast area extending from Iran westward toward Asia Minor. However, the Median kingdom was badly organized. Eventually a vassal prince, Cyrus of Persia, deposed the Median king and laid claim to the Median realm.

The most spectacular of all Assyria's successors was the kingdom of the Chaldeans, a Semitic-speaking people who had established themselves in southern Mesopotamia prior to its conquest by the Assyrians. After playing a major role in destroying the Assyrian Empire, the Chaldeans established a kingdom based in southern Mesopotamia that consciously sought to restore the glory of old Babylonia. Under its greatest king, Nebuchadnezzar II (605–562 B.C.), Syria and Palestine were conquered. Among the victims of Chaldean expansion was the tiny kingdom of Judah. Jerusalem and its Temple were destroyed, and many Hebrews were deported to Babylon as captives. In their efforts to reclaim Mesopotamia's past glory Nebuchadnezzar and his successors promoted a notable cultural and religious renaissance. The jewel of this revival was the rebuilding of the city of Babylon. Its massive walls, its temples, its towering ziggurat (the legendary Tower of Babel), its royal palace featuring fabulous hanging gardens, its impressive sculpture and painting made it one of the most splendid of ancient cities. Even the redoubtable Hebrew prophet Jeremiah, amid his lamentations over the Babylonian captivity of his people, had to admit that "Babylon was a golden cup in the hands of Yahweh." A religious revival in this period restored the worship of ancient Mesopotamian deities, above all Marduk, and the authority of the traditional priesthood. Chaldean scribes and scholars were renowned for their mastery of ancient literature and their knowledge of astronomy. However, despite its outward brilliance, "New Babylonia" lacked military and economic strength and eventually proved an easy victim of the Persians in 539 B.C.

3. THE PERSIAN EMPIRE, 550–330 B.C.

The final victory in the competition for the Assyrian Emire belonged to the Persians. They were a people of Indo-European origin who about 1000 B.C. settled in the barren southern part of Iran as simple farmers and herders. For centuries they maintained their political independence. However, during this period civilizing influences, especially from Assyria, penetrated Persia, so that the Persians were slowly drawn into the orbit of the higher civilization of the Near East.

They did retain significant aspects of their old Indo-European culture, especially in religion and language. In the late seventh century they were forced to accept the overlordship of the Medes, who were closely akin to them in language and culture. About 560 B.C. a Persian prince, Cyrus, overthrew the Median king and proclaimed himself "king of the Medes and the Persians."

Cyrus (ca. 560–530 B.C.) and his two successors, Cambyses (530–522 B.C.) and Darius I (522–486 B.C.), launched a series of spectacular military campaigns that created one of the largest empires that ever existed (see Map 3.2). Victories over the

Map 3.2 THE PERSIAN EMPIRE, CA. 500 B.C. At its peak the Persian Empire embraced a vast territory, varied in terrain and climate and occupied by a complex mixture of peoples. In area the Persian Empire was approximately the size of the continental United States. The Persians were able to overcome some of these vast distances by building an excellent road system that fanned out from the capital cities of Susa and Persepolis to key cities across the empire. One of the most famous was the Royal Road, which extended from Susa to Sardis, a distance of about sixteen hundred miles. The Persians developed a system of regular outposts along this road and teams of mounted couriers who, by working in relays, could carry a message from Susa to Sardis in as little as a week.

Median Empire, the Lydian kingdom, the Chaldean kingdom, and Egypt gave them control over the heartland of the Near Eastern civilized world. Persian armies swept across vast stretches east of the Persian homeland to embrace the highly civilized Indian society of the Indus River Valley. Persian forces occupied Thrace to establish a foothold in Europe, but the thrust in that direction met a stubborn obstacle in the Greeks, whose dramatic encounter with the Persians had far-reaching consequences for the history of Western civilization (see Chapter 5).

The first Persian rulers were not only successful conquerors but also skilled, enlightened statesmen whose decisions in the face of the complex problems involved in ruling their huge and diverse empire laid the basis for sound government. Eschewing the brutal policy of the hated Assyrians, they ruled in a spirit of tolerance of and respect for the diverse cultural traditions and values of conquered peoples as long as those people accepted Persian political overlordship peaceably. That policy was dramatically illustrated by Cyrus' treatment of the Hebrews. He freed them from their Babylonian captivity, allowed them to return to Jerusalem, helped them to rebuild the Temple, and encouraged them to reconstitute their religious community. For this generous act the Hebrews hailed Cyrus as Yahweh's "shepherd." Many others enjoyed comparable treatment. Such treatment played a major role in making Persian domination more acceptable.

Committed to maintaining peace within their vast empire, the Persians were highly resourceful in developing effective political institutions fashioned by the creative adaptation of old ideas and practices in statecraft. Reaching its most mature form during the reign of Darius I, "the Great," that system was often imitated by later empire builders. Like his Near Eastern predecessors, Darius claimed absolute power with authority to make laws, to judge, and to command obedience and service from his subjects. Court life at his capital cities of Ecbatana, Susa, and Persepolis involved an elaborate etiquette designed to impress the constant stream of dignitaries who came there from throughout the vast empire and beyond that the ruler was indeed the "King of Kings" (see Figure 3.3). The ruler was served by a highly skilled bureaucracy staffed by officials, usually of Persian or Median origin, who represented an elite fanatically devoted to maintaining Persian power. Royal power was supported by an effective military establishment built around the Immortals, a loyal disciplined corps of about ten thousand professional warriors recruited from the Persians and the Medes. When occasion

FIGURE 3.3 The "King of Kings" at Work This relief from the royal palace at Persepolis shows Darius receiving a commander of the royal guard. Behind the king stands his son, Xerxes. (Oriental Institute, University of Chicago)

demanded, this elite force was reinforced by contingents mobilized in awe-inspiring numbers from the subject population of the empire. The Persians also commanded impressive naval forces, composed largely of Phoenician and Greek ships and crews.

Perhaps the most innovative feature of the Persian governmental system was the techniques devised for extending central authority to the component parts of the vast empire. By Darius' reign the empire was divided into twenty large districts, called *satrapies*, some of which were defined to respect ancient political, ethnic, and cultural entities. Over each the "King of Kings" appointed a governor, called a *satrap*, usually a Persian and often a member of the royal family, who was given sufficient power to control local affairs. The satraps were removable at the will of the king and were held strictly accountable for the effective administration of their districts. Periodically, the king sent out inspectors to investigate local administration and report to the central court. Contingents of the imperial army under trusted commanders were garrisoned in strategic spots both to support the satraps and to curb their ambitions. An excellent road system and a postal service were developed, permitting rapid communications between the satrapies and the central government. Careful records were maintained by the central government as a means of holding each satrap accountable. By these methods the great kings managed to create twenty semi-independent governments, each capable of reacting to situations that were unique to each locality by means that respected local customs and concerns but all guided by common policies shaped by the "King of Kings" and his high officials in an effort to maintain peaceful unity amid diversity.

The political regime fashioned by the Persians created an environment that was beneficial to economic, social, religious, and cultural life throughout the empire. For the most part farmers, artisans, and traders continued their traditional practices to sustain a prosperous economy. Trade and the transfer of technology were promoted by the abolition of restrictive political barriers, an improved system of communication, and the encouragement of the royal government. A rich and powerful nobility continued to dominate the social order. At its summit stood the Persian families who served the great king, but many local nobles gained status by involvement in the affairs of their local satrapy and by exploiting opportunities to serve the imperial regime. The climate of tolerance prevailing in the Persian Empire nurtured the development of a common cosmopolitan lifestyle that defined aristocratic attitudes and behavior throughout the empire. While the Persian government was concerned with protecting and affording justice to all subjects, the nonnoble elements of society remained in a position of social subservience that left them open to exploitation.

Assessing the intellectual and artistic life of the Persian Empire is a difficult task, chiefly because much important activity in these realms occurred in local settings as a result of the tolerant attitude of the Persian regime toward the different cultural traditions long established across the vast expanse of the empire. Preoccupied with administrative, military, and diplomatic affairs, the Persians were not innovators in cultural life. Like the Assyrians, they were primarily borrowers from the rich cultural resources that already existed in their vast empire. But they created an open, tolerant cultural environment that encouraged the synthesizing of the rich treasures of diverse cultures into common patterns of thought and expression that were increasingly meaningful and appealing to a variety of peoples. In this complex process the royal court played a key role. The great kings were active patrons of art and learning, in part as a means of exalting their authority. Their patronage centered primarily on the royal palaces built at Ecbatana, Susa, and Persepolis. These massive complexes reflect an eclectic blending of architectural and sculptural themes and techniques drawn from the artistic traditions of the entire Near Eastern world, perhaps best reflected in the stone reliefs recording royal exploits. Not only the great kings but also their satraps welcomed to their courts individuals from all over the empire who were schooled in the literary, religious, and scientific traditions of the past. As a result, the Persians helped substantially to keep these traditions alive to serve the cause of learning and expression among later peoples, especially the Greeks.

The Persians did make one significant contribution to Near Eastern civilization in the form of a new religion called Zoroastrianism, named for its founder, Zoroaster (Zarathustra in Persian). Although the details of Zoroaster's life are clouded by legend, it appears that he lived about 600 B.C., before the Perians established their empire. During his lifetime he played the role of reformer, seeking to purify the traditional religion of the Persians on the basis of revelations that came to him after long contemplation. The old religion of the Persians centered around the worship of many deities who represented forces of nature, especially a god of the sky and a god of fire. A complicated ritual, including sacrifices, magic, and prayer, developed as a means of winning the favors of the deities. Priests, called magi, played a prominent role in directing religious life among the early Persians.

Zoroaster's exact teachings are as elusive as the details of his life. His message was eventually set forth in a sacred book called *Zend-Avesta*, a work compiled over many centuries that contains a confusing array of interpretations and refinements of Zoroaster's original teachings. As a consequence, it is difficult to reconstruct what Zoroaster thought and said. Aside from his protest against many aspects of the prevailing Persian religious system, especially its polytheism and its ritualistic formalism, Zoroaster set forth a unique concept of the nature of the cosmic order based on a principle of dualism. On the one hand, there is the god Ahura Mazda (Lord of Wisdom), the all-powerful, all-pervading lord of creation. This good and benevolent spirit presides over all creation, emanating and personifying such qualities as justice, pure thought, integrity, good intentions, and virtue. But the good Ahura Mazda is opposed by the diabolical Ahriman, an evil force seeking to blot out justice, light, wisdom, and good. The warfare between Ahura Mazda and Ahriman, good and evil, which has been going on since the beginning of the world, provides the dynamic force in the universe. Eventually, in a final day of judgment, Ahura Mazda will prevail; but in the meantime, the conflict will rage, extending into every soul and demanding that each individual elect whether to serve good or evil. On the final day of reckoning, those who have chosen good will be rewarded with eternal happiness, while those who have elected the way of Ahriman will be condemned to eternal misery.

By postulating the struggle between good and evil as fundamental in the cosmic order, Zoroaster made the basic obligation of each human being clear. Only good conduct would win favor in the eyes of Ahura Mazda. The worship of old deities, magic, sacrifices, and priestly ministrations were irrelevant and even constituted a surrender to evil because they diverted attention from doing good. Zoroaster defined a vigorous moral code for his followers, derived in its particulars from the qualities of goodness surrounding Ahura Mazda. Obversely, he set forth a clear concept of sin, rooted in the evil nature of Ahriman. Certainly none of the religions in the world that the Persians were soon to rule, except Judaism, gave such emphasis to ethical issues—and not even Judaism placed the burden of goodness so squarely on each individual. Zoroaster did not associate goodness and righteousness with the history of a chosen people, adherence to a system of law, or the observance of a set of ritual practices. His message called all humankind to seek moral perfection by thinking and acting according to right.

Although Zoroaster's ideas initially met resistance, they took firm hold after the master's death. Accepted by the Persian rulers, Zoroastrianism became the official religion of the Achaemenid dynasty. However, its acceptance was not universal in the Persian Empire. The general policy of tolerance in the empire permitted other religions to maintain their hold. As time passed, Zoroaster's original message lost its uniqueness. Ritual practices aimed at pleasing Ahura Mazda and warding off Ahriman's evil powers grew increasingly prominent. Polytheistic concepts crept back into Zoroastriansim. Old Persian deities and hosts of angels and devils reappeared as combatants in the eternal war between light and dark. The concept of the struggle between good and evil tended to associate good with purely spiritual forces and evil with material things. This interpretation of dualism had the effect of belittling the practice of virtue in everyday life and of exalting withdrawal from the world. After the collapse of the Persian Empire, Zoroastrianism declined as a major religious force in the Near East. However, it has survived to the present among its modern adherents, called Parsees, who are concentrated chiefly in Iran and India. The Zoroastrian concept of dualism long provided a rich source of spiritual speculation for later religions, especially Christianity.

The generally benevolent regime of the Persians lasted more than two centuries. The imperial administrative and military system maintained internal peace and rebuffed numerous enemies along the empire's immensely long frontiers. The Persians played a major role in the diplomacy of the period, often using their money to build alliances with foreign powers and to manipulate relations among these outsiders; Persian diplomacy was especially significant in the Greek world during the fifth and fourth centuries B.C. Gradually, however, the Persian strength began to erode. Some of the later kings were deficient in political ability. Their courts became corrupt and torn by intrigue involving royal wives and children, officials, and friends. Ambitious satraps constantly attempted to overthrow the rulers, often putting themselves forward as champions of subject peoples and usually generous in their promises of rewards for those who joined them against the great king. A gradual decline in the efficiency and loyalty of the royal bureaucracy and the armed forces impeded the ability of the kings to control the satraps. By the middle of the fourth century B.C. all that was needed to destroy the Persian Empire was a strong attack from the outside. That attack was soon forthcoming from a powerful Greek-Macedonian army led by Alexander the Great, who was driven in part by an urge to destroy the Persian menace that had haunted the Greek world since the time of Darius the Great. After a brief, brilliant military campaign culminating in a decisive victory in 330 B.C., Alexander was able to destroy the Persian power and to claim possession of its territory.

Neither the dramatic end of the Persian Empire nor the negative attitude of its accomplishments bequeathed to the Western consciousness by the anti-Persian bias of the Greeks should detract from the importance of the Persians in history. The enlightened, tolerant rule of the Achaemenids built a universal empire in the ancient Near East in which all kinds of people at many levels of civilization were brought together into a viable community. The cosmopolitan environment in that empire permitted local cultures to persist and grow while providing instruments through which all could mix and fertilize one another. In a sense, the resulting amalgam reflected the best the ancient Near East had produced during the thirty-five centuries in which its people stood in the forefront of civilized life.

SUGGESTED READING

Assyrians

H. W. F. Saggs, *The Might That Was Assyria* (1984).
Georges Roux, *Ancient Iraq*, 2nd ed. (1980).
Two well-written treatments of Assyrian history and civilization.
André Parrot, *Arts of Assyria*, trans. Stuart Gilbert and James Emmons (1961). An excellent introduction to all aspects of Assyrian art.

Persians

J. M. Cook, *The Persian Empire* (1983). An effective treatment of Persian history and institutions.
Richard N. Frye, *The History of Ancient Iran* (1983). Surveys Persian history down to the Moslem conquest in the eighth century A.D.

Richard N. Frye, *The Heritage of Persia* (1963). Excellent survey of Persian cultural influence on the larger world.
Mary Boyce, *Zoroastrians: Their Religious Beliefs and Practices* (1984). A brief treatment covering the entire history of Zoroastrianism.
Mary Boyce, *A History of Zoroastrianism*, 2 vols. (1975-1982). A detailed history of early Zoroastrianism.
Roman Ghirshman, *Persia from the Origins to Alexander the Great*, trans. Stuart Gilbert and James Emmons (1964).
Edith Porada, *The Art of Ancient Iran. Pre-Islamic Cultures* (1965).
This and the preceding work provide a full treatment of all aspects of Persian art.

RETROSPECT

When in 330 B.C. Alexander the Great stood in triumph over the body of Darius III, a chapter in world history had ended. The Persians, symbolizing the old order, had given way to a youthful conqueror who represented a vital new order emerging on the western periphery of the Near East. That old order deserves a brief epitaph that will fix its accomplishments in our minds.

For the purposes of this epitaph, let us view the Persians as the last scions of a great family whose origins were rooted in simple Neolithic villages and whose members included all the peoples from southwestern Asia and northeastern Africa whose histories have been reviewed in the preceding pages. Over several millennia, especially after 4000 B.C., that family had put together a rich and varied patrimony. Its various members had devised effective techniques of agriculture, manufacturing, and trading for extracting sustenance from nature. They had made crucial advances in developing the technology by which humans exploited the world of nature, a leap forward epitomized by the transition from Stone Age technology through the Bronze Age to the Iron Age. They had developed impressive techniques of government and social control that allowed creative interactions among large numbers of people playing a variety of economic and social roles. Their religions provided an integrative, unifying, direction-giving dimension to their collective and individual existences. Their efforts to comprehend the mysterious cosmos generated a rich written literature, magnificent works of art, and a large store of knowledge about the natural world. In all these ways the African-Asian peoples of the ancient Near East created a priceless storehouse from which future peoples could draw without having to invent higher civilization over again. In one sense, Western history—indeed, world history—is a story of the diffusion of ancient Near Eastern achievements to future generations living in different geographical settings.

Yet, for all the splendid achievements of the peoples of the ancient Near East, the patterns of civilization that eventuated in the Persian imperial order ultimately proved incapable of generating additional creative forces capable of advancing the human condition. Historians have advanced various explanations for this seeming irony. Some have argued that the creative capacities of the peoples of the Near East were stifled by the fateful turn of political events which almost continuously from the time of Alexander the Great to the present has imposed foreign political masters on that area. Others have suggested that the physical environment imposed serious constraints, arguing that aside from the river valleys the Near East had limited potential in terms of material resources. Still others have argued that the Near Eastern world was limited by a constrictive political and social order based on control of power, wealth, and thought by numerically small elites who were unable and unwilling to tap wider sources of human talent. A persuasive case has been made that the mentality undergirding Near Eastern civilization became entrapped by one of its most striking creations, the rich array of myths explaining the cosmic order in terms of deified forces of nature. That mythic world view provided limited scope for reflection on human capacities, especially the potential of the human mind to seek, to discover, and to organize knowledge that would empower human beings to new levels of achievement.

Here, then, is the epitaph of the peoples of the ancient Near East: Their wondrous accomplishments created an enduring base—an unfinished pyramid or ziggurat, as it were—upon which new levels of achievement could be built by peoples bold enough to seek and inventive enough to unleash a wider range of human capacities.

PART TWO

GRECO-ROMAN CIVILIZATION, 1200 B.C.–A.D. 500

While the patterns of civilization established in the ancient Near East were assuming their most mature forms, a different pattern of life began to take shape to the west. It is called Greco-Roman civilization after the two peoples who played a central role in its development. Centered first around the Aegean Sea, the fundamental outlines of this civilization were established by the Greeks between about 1200 and 400 B.C. Well before 400 B.C., its institutional patterns and cultural values began to spread both eastward and westward. In the fourth century, the Greek world fell under the political domination of the Macedonians, who immediately combined forces with the Greeks to conquer the Persian Empire. That victory resulted in the spread of Greek civilization over that empire's huge expanse and its enrichment by borrowings from the ancient Near Eastern cultural heritage. In the third century B.C. the Romans began to be drawn into the orb of Hellenic civilization and soon became its prime imitators and disseminators. In addition to enriching what they took from the Greeks, the Romans forged a huge empire which until its collapse in the fifth century A.D. provided the setting for a further extension of the Greco-Roman pattern of life over much of western Europe and North Africa.

Since what the Greeks and Romans wrought has been fundamental in shaping modern Western civilization, it is essential to trace the main stages of the development of Greco-Roman civilization in search of a fuller understanding of what the Western world's debt to the Greeks and the Romans is. That debt is perhaps greatest as regards the Greco-Roman world's vision of the potential of human beings. Much of the Greco-Roman accomplishment focused on an effort to explore the implications of a statement made by the Athenian dramatist Sophocles: "Many are the wonders of the world, and none so wonderful as Man."

CHAPTER 4

The Origins and Development of the Greek City-State Polity

FIGURE 4.1 The Heart of a *Polis* The fact that the rocky promontory shown in this photo features the surviving ruins of one of the great artistic achievements in all history should not hide another important consideration: Such physical settings played a prime role all over ancient Greece as focal points that drew people together to form a unique community—the *polis*. That the Athenians chose to invest their wealth and talent in adorning the Acropolis is a reflection of the role that this modest hill played over many centuries as a center of their collective activities. (Alison Frantz)

Greco-Roman civilization initially took form in a group of small, independent communities located around the Aegean Sea. Their formation was a slow process involving experimentation and creativity. Only by tracing that evolution is it possible to understand what was history-making about these communities.

The development of the early Greek communities was conditioned by the physical environment of the Aegean basin. The area is blessed with a benevolent climate marked by mild winters and long, dry summers which allow comfortable living without great expenditure on clothing and housing. The topography, especially of the Greek mainland, is dominated by mountains, valleys, bays, and peninsulas that cut the land into small pockets of farmland and grazing areas defining settlement patterns that made unified political control extremely difficult. But such is the lay of the land that few communities are far from the sea. The area's resources are not abundant. Tillable soil is limited, poor in quality, subject to erosion, and ill suited to cereal production. Tin, copper, iron, and timber are in short supply. As a Greek historian said, "Greece has always poverty as her companion." But there was an avenue of escape: the sea. The Aegean provides excellent harbors and good sailing winds during the summer. It served as a roadway allowing access by sea to a wider world of raw materials and markets and stimulating contacts with other peoples. The challenges posed by a hard land and far-reaching seaways placed a premium on human resourcefulness.

1. THE MYCENAEAN AND DARK AGES, 2000–800 B.C.: GREEK ORIGINS

Except for fanciful accounts imbedded in Greek mythology, the distant origins of Greek civilization remained a mystery until the advent of systematic archaeological explorations of the Aegean world in the late nineteenth century. The evidence unearthed since then reveals that Neolithic culture was introduced to the Aegean area about 6000 B.C. During many ensuing centuries life centered around simple agricultural villages and typical Neolithic institutions. About 2000 B.C. this primitive order was profoundly affected by the intrusion of Indo-Europeans into the area, part of the same movement that disturbed much of the Near East. The newcomers in Greece imposed their overlordship and their language on the natives, but they adopted from their victims the basic features of agricultural life. For the next four or five centuries, Aegean history centered on the activities of a number of small principalities dominated by aggressive warlords and their armed retainers. The power and wealth of these rulers are reflected in the ruins of their huge fortress-palaces, the most impressive of which was located at Mycenae, which has given its name to this first phase of Greek history. The archaeological finds at Mycenae and other important centers provide clear proof that Mycenaean society was powerfully influenced by expanding contacts with more advanced societies of the Near East, especially the Minoan world. Not only the magnificence of Mycenaean palaces but also the records surviving in a written form of the Greek language, called Linear B, indicate that Mycenaean rulers had devised highly effective ways of asserting political and economic control over the populations living in the areas surrounding their fortress cities.

Mycenaean culture reached its zenith about 1300 B.C. As it matured, its political structures, religious usages, technology, and art increasingly reflected features that suggest that the first Greeks were on the way to being absorbed into the larger pattern of civilization developing across the Near East during the age of cultural diffusion described earlier (see Chapter 2). However, that process was cut short about 1200 B.C. by the decline and then collapse of Mycenaean culture. While the reasons for that collapse are not entirely clear, perhaps the rupture of trade connections accompanying the collapse of Minoan civilization and the disruption of the Hittite and Egyptian empires resulted in economic constraints that caused the warlike Mycenaean kings to turn on each other in search of a means to sustain their expensive way of life. It was during these troubled times, for instance, that warriors from several Mycenaean kingdoms joined hands to destroy Troy in Asia Minor, a venture immortalized in the poetry of Homer. Whatever the cause, between about 1200 and 1100 B.C. most of the mighty Mycenaean citadels, including Mycenae, were violently destroyed, bringing to an end the first chapter in Greek history.

Following the collapse of Mycenaean culture, the Aegean world began an era lasting about four centuries that modern historians have called a "Dark Age." Information about this period depends largely on scarce and enigmatic archaeological remains. The scanty evidence leaves no doubt that many aspects of Mycenaean civilization disappeared: the dominant royal courts, the great palaces, Linear B writing, trading, art, technical expertise. Many settled locations disappeared, suggesting a population decline. Life was simpler than during the Mycenaean Age, depending on simple farming carried on by the inhabitants of small communities with limited contacts with the larger world. But this simple world was not stagnant, as is evident in two literary masterpieces, the *Iliad* and the *Odyssey*, attributed to the poet Homer, who lived during the eighth century B.C. at the end of the Dark Age. Although his epics claim to recount the adventures of heroes living more than four centuries earlier during the Trojan War, Homer describes the feats of his legendary figures in terms that reveal much about the world in which he lived.

Homer's testimony combined with archaeological evidence indicates that during the Dark Age developments fundamental to the future course of Greco-Roman civilization occurred. Although the Greek world remained economically poor, its potential for growth was enhanced by technological advances, especially the adoption of Iron Age technology and advancing skills in pottery making. Between about 1200 and 800 B.C. there was considerable shifting of peoples from mainland Greece to the Aegean Islands and the coast of Asia Minor, where important contacts with the Near Eastern world were again established. The population of this entire area, whose people were linked by common cultural traits, established the demographic base for future Greek development. The peoples occupying the Aegean basin came to share a common Greek language, although that language had several different dialects. A new writing system, based on the adaptation of the Phoenician alphabet to

accommodate the Greek spoken language, was developed to a level that made possible the magnificent Homeric epics. A common pattern of religious belief and practice spread among the Greeks, nurturing a unique set of values forcefully delineated by Homer's literary masterpieces and in artistic forms which found expression especially in pottery decoration. Much of the future of Greek intellectual, literary, and artistic history involved working out the implications of these early forms of thought and expression. In a word, the Dark Age was marked by complex processes converging to define a people participating in a common pattern of life; these people would soon call themselves "Hellenes," a term that for them indicated an awareness of shared values that both transcended the localism dictated by political realities and made those who were Hellenes different from those who were not.

As the Homeric poems make clear, the Dark Age was especially important in shaping a form of community life of crucial importance to Greco-Roman civilization. The Greek world of the Dark Age remained politically divided into many petty kingdoms, each identified with a particular territory. Over each presided a chieftain who led his people in war, judged their disputes, and represented them before their deities. In marked contrast to the power enjoyed by kings during the Mycenaean Age, the power of these kings was limited by a politically active nobility whose authority was based on patriarchal family ties, loyal personal retainers, and control of the best lands and herds. The nobles in each kingdom met regularly to share with the king decision making on matters of common interest. The nobles' power was enhanced by the dominant role aristocrats played in warfare, an activity that contributed in an important way to defining the nobles' values. Peasants and artisans were considered to be free and even participated to a degree in political life through attendance at assemblies, where they shouted their approval or disapproval of decisions made by kings and nobles. By the end of the Dark Age each of these small political entities—its members united by kinship and personal ties, shared religious life, and active involvement in political decision making—constituted a base from which would emerge the key institution shaping Greek civilization: the city-state, called the *polis* by the Greeks.

2. THE GREEK ARCHAIC AGE, 800–500 B.C.: DEVELOPMENT OF THE *POLIS*

The crucial steps in the evolution of the *polis* occurred during what modern historians call the Archaic Age, which extended from about 800 to 500 B.C. The shaping of that institution fundamental to Greek civilization involved a complex process, proceeding at a different pace and in different ways from one place to another. However, among the nearly seven hundred city-states that established an independent identity during the Archaic Age (see Map 4.1 for the location of the major city-states) there were certain common patterns of development that provide the key to the basic nature of the *polis*.

Central to the emergence of each *polis* were processes that created powerful bonds linking the inhabitants of a relatively small geographical area into a community and that expanded the involvement of the "citizens" of each community in civic life. These communal bonds found their focus at a physical center, an urban center. Already at the beginning of the Archaic Age the rudiments of such urban centers were emerging in the petty kingdoms that had been established during the Dark Age. At such centers were the king's residence and often a hilltop fortress, called an *acropolis*, where those from the surrounding countryside could find protection. There temples were built where members of the community could gather to honor their shared deities. The same center served as a meeting place for the noble clan leaders when they gathered from their rural estates to counsel with the king; some even established residences there. A market, called an *agora*, developed in connection with the fortress. As the Archaic Age progressed, the range of activities affecting group life expanded in each urban center, and increasingly the members of each community developed a sense of attachment to and dependence on that special place. At the same time there emerged institutional forms that gave structure to the

shared experiences of those belonging to the community. Involvement and participation in the political, economic, religious, and cultural activities unfolding at each urban center became the central focus in the lives of those belonging to each *polis*.

A major step in shaping the political and social structure of the typical *polis* occurred in all but a few communities during the eighth century B.C. In a radical departure from the political order typical of both the ancient Near East and early Greece, monarchy was replaced with what the Greeks called *oligarchy*. Ultimate authority was entrusted to a council of nobles whose decisions were executed by elected officials drawn from that same noble class. Noble status, which qualified individuals for a political role, was based on landed wealth, control over the clan structure that undergirded early Greek society, and domination of the legal system. Although they were often greedy and always jealous of their authority, the nobles felt a strong attachment to their *polis* and were willing to take political action to resolve basic problems affecting the entire community.

One such step involved reshaping the military system in a way that broadened the base of participation in this key civic activity. As reflected in the Homeric epics, warfare during the Dark Age had been monopolized by nobles, who alone could afford the horses and equipment needed for cavalry and chariot combat. That system was replaced by a military organization based on the *phalanx*, a massed formation of infantry soldiers, called *hoplites*, armed with shields, breastplates, helmets, swords, and spears. This change brought larger numbers of citizens with modest means into the service of the *polis*, placed a premium on disciplined action in a common cause, and increased the civic importance of the new soldiers upon whom the safety of the *polis* now depended. Before long these *hoplites* were demanding a share in making the decisions that determined the course of affairs in the *polis*.

Even more significant in expanding the bonds that attached people to the *polis* were actions taken by oligarchies to cope with the major economic and social problems that began to afflict much of the Greek world during the Archaic

Map 4.1 **THE WORLD OF THE GREEKS** This map identifies the major geographical regions of the Aegean world and locates the most important Greek city-states—but by no means all of them. It highlights the extent to which the mountainous terrain of the Aegean Basin encouraged political localism in the Greek world and limited the agricultural resources available to most city-states. At the same time, it shows the near proximity of most Greek city-states to seaways that provided access to a larger world.

Age. The nature and impact of the crisis are reflected in a poem entitled *Works and Days*, written about 700 B.C. by Hesiod, a wealthy farmer embittered by the growing poverty and injustice of his time. The causes of the crisis were deep-seated: growing population, competition for limited land, and the greediness of what Hesiod called "the land-devouring lords" who controlled each *polis*. The chief victims were small landholders, who were forced into debt, economic dependence on noble landlords, and even slavery, thereby losing their status as citizens of their *polis*.

One response to this crisis was the resettle-

Map 4.2 GREEK COLONIES, CA. 500 B.C. This map shows the major areas colonized by the Greeks during the period 800–500 B.C. By 500 B.C. their major rival for dominance of trade in the Mediterranean Basin was the North African city of Carthage, originally a Phoenician colony but not a major power in control of most of the areas originally colonized by the Phoenicians. Wherever the Greeks colonized, they took with them the main elements of Hellenic civilization; as a result, their geographical expansion marked the spread of the Greek way of life beyond the confines of its Aegean homeland.

ment of Greeks outside Greece. In many city-states oligarchical regimes encouraged or even ordered colonizing ventures, usually led by enterprising nobles who recruited impoverished compatriots to follow them in search of new homes. A prime target for such ventures was southern Italy and Sicily, an area that was eventually so completely Hellenized that it became known as Magna Graecia (Greater Greece). Other Greek settlements were established on the northern shores of the Aegean, around the Black Sea, in southern France, in Spain, in Egypt, and in modern Libya (see Map 4.2). In all of these areas the Greeks carved out territorial enclaves where they established themselves as farmers, traders, and artisans. Although its objective was not usually conquest, successful colonization often allowed the Greeks to assert control over native populations or at least to assert a powerful cul-

tural impact on them. The new communities were not colonies in the modern sense. Rather, each was an independent *polis* with its own government, laws, and civic pride. Many such new city-states maintained contact with the Aegean city-states from which the settlers had originally emigrated. As a consequence, they became prime channels for a massive extension of Hellas—the area dominated by Greeks and their culture.

Economic pressures were also relieved by developments that created a more diverse economy in each *polis*. Especially important was the growth of trade and industry. The increasing number of Greek settlements around the Aegean, Mediterranean, and Black seas provided access to raw materials and markets. Greek traders exploited these opportunities vigorously, and by 500 B.C. they had become the leading traders in the Mediterranean world, rivaled only by Carthage, originally established as a colony by the Phoenicians. Trade spurred manufacturing in many city-states, and Greek artisans proved skillful at making products that were in high demand, especially pottery. The traditional agricultural system changed as a consequence of expanding trade. Enterprising farmers abandoned the raising of grain in favor of grapes, olives, and livestock, from which were derived products that found profitable markets throughout the Mediterranean area. Increasingly, Greek city-states imported grain, especially from the Black Sea area. For merchants, artisans, and commercial farmers, the center of economic life shifted to the urban marketplace, creating new ties between citizens and the *polis*.

The social structure in many city-states grew more diverse and complex amid economic change. Some aristocrats became involved in trade and industry and developed interests different from those of their peers whose status and wealth depended on landownership. Diverging economic interests among the aristocrats bred factionalism and intensified competition for control of public decision making. Enterprising individuals from the lower ranks of society were able to amass sufficient wealth through trade and industry to become rivals of the landowning aristocracy for power. Small farmers, lacking the resources needed to engage in the new forms of agriculture and unwilling to become dependents of great landowners, moved to the urban centers to become traders, artisans, or hired laborers. This change dissolved ancient family ties, weakened the control of aristocratic clan leaders over the populace, and thrust upon public authorities new burdens of providing for and controlling the socially displaced.

In this environment of economic and social change new mental attitudes began to emerge. They were mirrored in new religious concepts, innovative forms of literary and artistic expression, and the beginning of philosophical speculation. We shall return to the particulars of Archaic cultural developments later (see Chapter 6). Suffice it to say here that the new modes of thought and expression revealed increasing concern about the nature of individual human beings and their place in the cosmic order, their potential for independent action, and rational explanations of the natural world. The *polis* increas-

ingly provided a forum where new ideas and values could be articulated and tested against the views of others. And as this new mentality took form, it generated consciously formulated concepts for reshaping the *polis* to accommodate new views of human beings and to deal with changes in the human condition.

The tensions generated by economic, social, and mental changes necessitated and helped shape political change. In general, the oligarchic regimes in each *polis* tried to relieve mounting tensions by instituting "reforms" that did not require surrender of the monopoly of power held by nobles. They enacted written codes of law that defined more precisely the rights and responsibilities of all citizens and that limited aristocratic dominance over the administration of justice. They granted relief to debtors and protection to small farmers. They devised policies that sought to gain trading advantages for their city-state. They sponsored public projects that improved the facilities of the *polis*, often in ways that promoted changing religious, literary, and artistic trends. In these "reforms" the aristocrats were motivated in part by self-interest, but they were also moved by a realization that steps must be taken to retain the allegiance and services of artisans, soldiers, sailors, shopkeepers, farmers, writers, artists, and intellectuals, who increasingly made vital contributions to the welfare of the *polis*.

In many city-states these "reforms" were not sufficient to maintain stability. Continued economic, social, and cultural turmoil coupled with the growing attachment of individuals of all social levels to the city-state generated demands for broader political participation than the aristocratic masters were willing to grant. Usually force was required to break the nobles' monopoly on power. In many city-states the assault on entrenched power was spearheaded by individual leaders called *tyrants* (from a Greek word meaning "those who rule illegally"). Often of noble origin and ambitious for personal power, these charismatic figures seized control over the *polis* by force, sometimes with support from the *hoplites*, who dominated the military establishment in many city-states. The typical tyrant made no effort to change the existing political structure; rather, each sought to dominate it by filling the council and elective offices with loyal followers. Once in power, the tyrant launched policies aimed at currying popular support. Measures were taken to depose wealthy, highborn nobles from power, to tax their wealth, and to deprive them of their land, which was redistributed to small farmers. Policies pleasing to non-aristocratic elements of society were pursued, including measures to increase trade and industry, expenditures on city beautification, and efforts to assure more equitable administration of justice.

The duration of tyranny was relatively brief in most city-states, often little more than the tyrant's lifetime. Since tyrants had seized power illegally, their regimes depended on their individual talents and popularity. Eventually, the aristocrats who had been their chief victims took the lead in unseating them and in restoring "legitimate" government. But these aristocrats were seldom able to reestablish their traditional monopoly based on landownership and kinship ties. In those city-states where oligarchical control continued after the overthrow of tyranny, the ruling element was greatly expanded to include men of wealth but without noble heritage. In some city-states that had avoided tyranny, leaders of the old nobility understood the course of affairs well enough to open noble ranks and political power to a wider circle. In many city-states the end of tyranny led to radical political changes which established a *democracy* that allowed the total citizen body to take control of civic affairs. With all citizens entitled to participate in government, the last knot binding them to the *polis* was tied. For some Greeks as well as many in the modern world, the democratic *polis* represented the ideal form of government.

3. ATHENS

The history of Athens during the Archaic Age provides a case study illustrating the evolution of a democratic *polis*. During the Mycenaean Age, Athens was a prominent fortress center exercising control over the surrounding area, called Attica. The general decline occurring over most of the Aegean world during the Dark Age resulted in the emergence in Attica of a number of small agricultural villages led by local tribal leaders. Sometime early in the Archaic Age, under circumstances still not well understood, these vil-

lages coalesced into a single political entity centering on Athens and its *acropolis* to constitute an embryo *polis* (see Figure 4.1) embracing about a thousand square miles—the largest city-state in ancient Greece except for Sparta. The emerging *polis* was ruled by a hereditary king assisted by a council of clan heads called the *Areopagus* and a popular assembly called the *ecclesia*. For political and military purposes, the citizen body was grouped into four tribes, each composed of brotherhoods (called *phratries*, from which is derived our word "fraternity") made up of several clans. Citizenship was established by admission to a brotherhood and depended on an individual's ties to a clan. As a consequence, kinship ties provided the fundamental bond in the social order.

About 700 B.C. the monarchy was abolished and officials called *archons* (eventually nine in number) were elected annually by the *ecclesia* to provide collective leadership of the *polis*. Only wealthy men of noble birth were eligible for this high office. The real power rested in the Areopagus, composed of ex-archons who, upon completion of their terms as elected officials, automatically entered into lifetime membership in the Areopagus. Combining their political position with their control over the clan structure, this narrow circle of aristocrats completely dominated Athenian life for two centuries after 700 B.C. During those centuries Athens experienced mounting tensions, rooted primarily in the deterioration of the economic and social position of free small farmers. Under the pressures of a growing population, competition for limited land, and increasing emphasis on the production of olives, grapes, and livestock, many of them became debtors obligated to turn over a sizable portion of their crops to their noble creditors as debt payment; some were eventually enslaved because they could not pay what they owed. Athens was slow to seek overseas colonies but ultimately directed its efforts toward the grain-rich Hellespont and Black Sea areas, suggesting that the city suffered a serious food shortage. Toward the end of the seventh century B.C. trade and industry began to expand, creating a sector of the populace whose economic interests were not always satisfied with the policies of the dominant aristocrats, whose concerns were primarily agricultural.

Ultimately, the ruling aristocracy responded to these pressures by introducing reforms. During the seventh century Athens developed a *hoplite* army that brought a wider circle of citizens into a key role in society. In 621 B.C. a reformer named Draco drew up the first Athenian written code of law, harsh in its details (whence the modern term "draconian") but significant because it curtailed the power of aristocratic judges and family heads to administer justice in their own interests.

Shortly after, there appeared a more significant reformer, Solon, who was elected archon about 594 B.C. Although an aristocrat, Solon was a man of broad vision and strong patriotism whose concern for injustice in Athens is reflected in surviving fragments of his poetry. Central to Solon's program was his effort to aid the poor and oppressed by a "shaking off of burdens." He struck down the ancient debt laws that permitted landlords to extract exorbitant rents from small farmers who fell into debt and to enslave them. Many who had fallen into bondage were freed. However, while Solon ensured personal freedom to those victimized by debt, he did not return their lost land. He apparently realized that Athens could not remain a city-state totally dependent on an agricultural system devoted to grain growing. Thus, he took steps to promote new forms of agriculture, notably olive oil production, which would provide products for export. He was especially concerned with encouraging the growth of trade and industry as a means of providing new opportunities for displaced farmers. Particularly important was his encouragement of the immigration of foreign artisans with skills that would upgrade the quality of Athenian manufactured goods and the ability to teach those skills to Athenians.

Solon introduced political changes designed to curb the aristocratic abuse of power but not to deprive the oligarchy of control of political life. He reorganized the entire citizen population into four classes, each defined in terms of income derived from land. This classification system greatly diminished the power exercised by aristocratic families through their domination of the brotherhoods that had previously defined the tribal structure. Eligibility for the chief elective offices—from which individuals passed to life membership in the Areopagus—was confined to the two upper wealth groups, but under the new system involvement in the direction of the *polis* was no longer restricted solely to the highborn. Solon extensively revised Draco's law code to broaden public control over the administration of justice. He also sought to curb abuses in the administration of justice by making the *Heliaea* instead of the Areopagus the final court of appeal. The Heliaea was a large panel of citizens drawn by lot from the membership of the *ecclesia* for the specific purpose of hearing judicial appeals. Its operation permitted the citizen body to correct judicial inequities perpetrated in the tribal and brotherhood courts dominated by noble family heads. While Solon was certainly no democrat, taken together, the changes he introduced marked an important step in limiting the aristocratic monopoly of power and expanding the role of the citizen body in public affairs.

Despite Solon's reforms Athens continued to be torn by tensions caused chiefly by the competition among aristocratic factions for dominance of the *polis* and the continued unrest of depressed small farmers. Increasing civic turmoil paved the way for tyranny. Athens' first tyrant was an ambitious nobleman, Pisistratus, who after two unsuccessful attempts finally seized control in 546 B.C. with the help of mercenary troops paid for out of his own wealth and the contributions of foreign city-states hostile toward Athens. He held power until his death in 527 B.C., and his sons continued his regime until 510 B.C. Pisistratus and his sons made no changes in the constitutional structure of Athens. They sustained their power by controlling the election of archons, which in turn gave them a powerful hold on the Areopagus. They used harsh means, including confiscation of property and exile, to cow the powerful aristocratic families. Like most Greek tyrants, their major policy was directed toward building a popular following, chiefly among the small farmers and the emerging merchant and artisan groups. They provided jobs by sponsoring public works projects, promoted Athenian commercial and manufacturing interests through an aggressive foreign policy, tried to ensure an equitable administration of justice, and promoted civic, religious, and cultural life (see Figure 4.2). Their policies increased Athens'

FIGURE 4.2 Greek Civic Religion An important part of Greek civic life involved public religious ceremonies, the chief of which was the sacrifice of animals. This pottery painting shows Athenians sacrificing to Apollo, whose statue is shown on the right. The priest is placing the animal parts due the god on the blood-stained altar, while the good meat from the sacrificial animal is held on a spit by a youth; it will be cooked and enjoyed by the sacrificers. The scene reflects the familiarity felt by the Greeks toward their deities. (Museum für Vor und Frühgeschichte, Frankfurt)

wealth and expanded the number of citizens whose welfare depended on the well-being of the entire *polis*.

Despite its broad appeal and its role in promoting the advance of Athens as a leading city-state, tyranny marked only a temporary chapter in Athenian history. Under Pisistratus' sons the regime grew more arbitrary and oppressive. Finally, a coalition of aristocratic families with the support of Spartan military forces drove Hippias into exile in Persia in 510 B.C. Although some of the noble victors hoped to reestablish an aristocratic monopoly on power, their dreams were dashed by another noble faction, led by Cleisthenes, which turned to the citizenry for support

of reforms aimed at broadening citizen participation in political life as a means of restoring order.

Assuming leadership in 508 B.C., Cleisthenes instituted basic structural changes in the political system that allowed control by the citizen body. He abolished the political functions of the ancient clans, brotherhoods, and tribes, although he left them certain religious and social roles. To replace the kinship-dominated system, he divided Attica into territorial units, called *demes*. All free males living in each *deme* were registered as citizens, a right that passed to their descendants. The *demes*, perhaps totaling about a hundred and fifty, were grouped together to form thirty second-level organizations called *trittyes*. Three *trittyes* were then combined to create a *tribe*, of which there was a total of ten. In arranging this basic structure, Cleisthenes utilized an ingenious tactic aimed at overcoming regionalism and reconciling clashing economic interests. During the sixth century Attica had become divided into three distinct geographical regions, each with special economic and social concerns: the hill or interior country, dominated by poor farmers; the plain, where the land was most fertile and the great noble families were entrenched; and the shore or city, where merchants, artisans, and urban laborers predominated. Cleisthenes created ten *trittyes* in each of these regions. In shaping the ten tribes, he included one *trittyes* from each region in each tribe. As a consequence, each tribe contained a cross section of the entire population, requiring that conflicting interests be conciliated before each tribe could determine its position on major issues affecting the entire polis. Each *deme* and tribe was a political entity in its own right, with elected officials, courts, taxes, and military forces. Each offered wide opportunity for direct participation in local affairs by its citizen members.

Cleisthenes then rearranged the organs of government that controlled the entire *polis* to fit the new tribal organization. A Council of Five Hundred, composed of fifty citizens selected by lot from each tribe for an annual term, was created as a prime agency in shaping the political life of the *polis*. No one could serve on this council more than twice in a lifetime, thus ensuring that many citizens had an opportunity to participate in this all-important body. The Council of Five Hundred was in essence a steering committee for the citizen body, meeting frequently to supervise many aspects of the administration of the city and to prepare agenda of issues to be presented to the *ecclesia*, which had the ultimate authority in the government. Made up of all male citizens over eighteen years of age voting by tribe, this body met at least once a month to hear debate on issues presented by the Council of Five Hundred and to vote on courses of action. The citizens were further involved in governing the city by their participation in the popular court, the Heliaea, which played an increasing role in the administration of justice. Cleisthenes did not change the Areopagus, although it now lacked the authority to guide crucial decisions, and the elected archons remained the executive officers of the *polis*. These magistrates were elected by the *ecclesia* and were still usually from the wealthy, aristocratic segment of the population, but now aristocratic candidates for high office had to win the support of the entire citizen body. Perhaps it was Cleisthenes who introduced a powerful instrument for controlling elective officials and overly ambitious aristocrats by establishing the practice of *ostracism*, through which a majority of the *ecclesia* could declare an individual dangerous to the state and order that person into exile for ten years.

Although Cleisthenes' reforms created the framework for democratic government in Athens, not until the time of Pericles, the chief political figure from 461 to 429 B.C., did Athenian democracy reach full bloom. During that interval changes were made to encourage greater participation. The chief executive offices were increasingly filled by lot, expanding the chances of ordinary citizens to hold high office. The number of magistrates increased steadily, again allowing a larger number of citizens to take part in public life. Especially significant was the establishment shortly after 500 B.C. of a new elective official, called general (*strategos*), from each tribe to constitute a group of ten military leaders who quickly assumed a key role in directing public affairs. In contrast with the archons, who were eligible for only a one-year term, the generals could be elected year after year if they could command sufficient votes in their tribes. Property qualifications for officeholding tended to disappear. A crucial step in the development of democracy came when Pericles introduced public payment for service in the Council of Five Hundred, the Heliaea, the elected magistracies, and the army and navy. This step enabled ordinary citizens to serve the *polis* without sacrificing their livelihood. Increasingly, Athenian citizens were encouraged to exercise their power by leaders such as Pericles, an aristocrat by birth and wealth who felt no fear in entrusting the final political decisions of Athens to the citizens and who sought to convince them that public life was a dignified, responsible, and rewarding activity owed by all who enjoyed the benefit of living in Athens.

Never before in history had ordinary individuals enjoyed a greater role in determining their own political fate than did the citizens of Periclean Athens. However, Athenian democracy had its limits. Participation in political life was confined to males descended from those enrolled as citizens in the time of Cleisthenes. Women, foreigners (called *metics*), and slaves did not qualify for participation in the political life of the *polis*. In the fifth century B.C. the citizen population of Athens was about forty-five thousand; the total population of Attica was probably about three hundred fifty thousand. Thus, a male minority ruled the democratic Athenian *polis*.

4. SPARTA

The history of another important city-state, Sparta, illustrates a different pattern of development of the *polis* in the Greek world. Sparta emerged as a city-state during the ninth century B.C. as a result of the coalition of several small agricultural villages clustered around the site of the city. After this union the Spartans slowly established control over an area in the southern Peloponnesus known as Laconia, creating a base for future Spartan prominence. Until about 750 B.C. Sparta's development followed a pattern that differed little from most other city-states during the Archaic Age. But then Spartan society diverged from the common pattern. When the Spartans began to feel the economic stresses that gripped most of the Aegean world during the Archaic Age, their solution was to conquer a neighboring territory, Messenia, a fertile agricultural region west of Laconia, and to make the Messenian population servile dependents of Sparta, forced to labor as tillers of the soil to support their conquerors. In about 640 B.C. the Messenians revolted and were suppressed only after a desperate struggle lasting twenty years. That struggle led to a radical restructuring of Spartan society aimed at ensuring sufficient military strength to maintain control of the city-state's subject population. These reforms were attributed to a single lawgiver, Lycurgus, but probably were carried out by several leaders during the decades just before and after 600 B.C.—at roughly the same time that Solon was reshaping Athenian history.

A fundamental feature of the new order was the division of the population into rigidly defined classes, each with specific responsibilities in the service of the *polis*. Most important were the Spartans, a relatively small portion of the total population who alone enjoyed full citizenship. Numbering about ten thousand males considered to be social equals, the Spartans were required to devote their lives to military service in the interest of exerting control over other elements in the population and defending Sparta against outside enemies. The Lycurgan system prescribed a strict regimen for this group. At birth each male child of a Spartan citizen was inspected for physical fitness. If he was defective, the state ordered death by exposure. If allowed to live, the child remained with his mother until he was seven. Then he joined other males in barracks life, where all were subjected to rigorous military training until they were twenty. At twenty the Spartan became a regular soldier. He was assigned a piece of state land along with laborers to farm it as a source of his livelihood, thus freeing him from economic concerns so that he could serve the state. He could marry after the age of twenty, but he was not permitted to establish his own household until the age of thirty, when he became an "equal" with full rights to participate in the political life of the *polis*. During these long formative years the social life of each Spartan found its focus in a mess group, a small circle of military companions who shared barracks life and contributed payments derived from their state-assigned land allocations to provide common meals. The values molded in this environment dominated the life of each male Spartan: loyalty, obedience, devotion to the community, conformity, disdain for wealth and luxury. All Spartans were required to perform military service until they were sixty years of age. Spartan females were likewise rigorously trained to become wives and mothers. Their training emphasized physical fitness and the development of skills in the household arts. As wives, they often played an important role in managing the family economic resources, but there was no place for them in political life.

A second element of the population of Sparta was made of *perioeci* ("those who live around" the city of Sparta), most of whom were descendants of peoples subjected by the Spartans when they asserted mastery over Laconia. Although they were required to render military service and pay taxes, they were not subjected to the training regimen required of full Spartans. They served the state chiefly as artisans and traders. They enjoyed some degree of control over local affairs in the towns they inhabited but were not permitted to take part in the processes of government which made decisions affecting the entire *polis.*

Finally, there were the *helots,* state slaves required to spend their lives as agricultural laborers or household servants toiling to support the full Spartan citizens who had no occupation except soldiering. The *helots* were allowed to maintain family life and were permitted to keep enough of what they produced to maintain a simple level of life. However, they were treated brutally by the Spartans, who were intent on ensuring their service as the mainstay of the Spartan economy. The fear of *helot* revolt remained a constant factor in Spartan life, so much so that the Spartan state declared war on the *helots* every year, permitting the killing of a suspected *helot* troublemaker on the spot. Part of the military training of Spartan youths involved seeking out and murdering allegedly dangerous *helots.*

This rigid social order was held in place by a governmental system that Lycurgus was credited with shaping but that was derived in large part from earlier political institutions. The government was formally headed by two kings, but the actual power of the co-kings was slight unless they were able to distinguish themselves as military leaders. Real power rested with the *gerousia,* a council made up of the two kings and twenty-eight other men over sixty elected to serve for life. This body formulated all legislation, judged the most important cases, and acted as an advisory body in the administration of the state. Its decisions were subject to approval by an assembly made up of all male Spartans over thirty. Theoretically, the assembly could repudiate any proposed policy, but usually its members, trained from childhood to obey orders, were inclined to accept direction from superiors. The execution of laws was entrusted to a board of five *ephors,* elected annually by the assembly, which conducted foreign affairs, supervised military training, policed the *helots,* controlled state finances, and organized military operations. When supported by the *gerousia,* the *ephors* were

able to exercise almost complete control over Spartan political life, despite the fact that the male citizens possessed the power to check them. In essence, Sparta was ruled by an oligarchy of military commanders.

Although the Spartan political and social system has often been judged harshly for its restrictive militaristic features, its brutal treatment of its slaves, and its stress on conformity (a later Greek historian, Plutarch, described the Spartans as bees, "every individual an extension of the hive"), it worked. Sparta enjoyed an internal stability that was envied by many other Greeks. The dedication of Spartan citizens to the service of their *polis* was often praised. While the system was not conducive to intellectual and cultural activities, it made Sparta a dominant force in Greek intercity affairs. Proof of the effectiveness of the Spartan system was the ability of Sparta to persuade or compel most of the other city-states in the Peloponnesus to become members of the Peloponnesian League, whose members followed Spartan leadership in foreign affairs. Its control over this League allowed Sparta to play a major role in Greek history in the critical times after 500 B.C.

5. THE CHARACTER OF THE *POLIS*

A complete understanding of the nature of the Greek *polis* would require the study of the institutions of several hundred other city-states that had been formed by 500 B.C., each of which believed its institutions to be as typically "Greek" as those of Athens and Sparta. Such a wide-ranging study would certainly highlight diversity in the structure of Greek city-states, but it would also reveal certain shared characteristics of the *polis.*

Greek city-states were all small entities within which residents could interact intimately. In each *polis* life focused on an urban center, where there were concentrated political, economic, religious, and cultural activities bearing directly on the lives of all. Each city-state made citizenship a distinctive and precious condition of life. In some fashion or other, citizenship involved those who held it—almost exclusively males with the proper family pedigree—directly and actively in civic life. Such involvement was at once a great privilege and a grave responsibility. As Pericles allegedly put it, "We alone regard a man who takes no interest in public affairs, not as harmless, but as a useless character." The giving of one's talent in the service of the *polis* made one a complete human, drawing each out of self, clan, calling, and class into participation in a community enterprise. Active involvement nourished patriotism, a fierce pride in and love for the *polis*. Every *polis* was thus a pressure chamber compelling citizens to discover and exercise their individual capabilities in the interests of something larger, more enduring, and more splendid than themselves. As such, the *polis* nourished an intensity of life that produced a level of achievement seldom witnessed in the historical record.

SUGGESTED READING

General Surveys of Greek History

Michael Grant and Rachel Kitzinger, eds., *Civilization of the Ancient Mediterranean: Greece and Rome*, 3 vols. (1988). A stimulating collection of essays touching on many facets of Greco-Roman civilization.

John V. A. Fine, *The Ancient Greeks: A Critical History* (1983).

M. G. L. Hammond, *A History of Greece to 322 B.C.*, 3rd ed. (1986).

Hermann Bengston, *History of Greece: From the Beginnings to the Byzantine Era*, trans. Edmund F. Bloedow (1988).

Any of these three works will provide a full treatment of Greek history down to the time of the Macedonian conquest.

Early Greece to 500 B.C.

John Chadwick, *The Mycenaean World* (1976). An excellent treatment that reflects the best of recent scholarship.

R. J. Hopper, *The Early Greeks* (1976).

Oswyn Murray, *Early Greece* (1980).

Anthony Snodgrass, *Archaic Greece. The Age of Experiment* (1980).

M. I. Finley, *Early Greece: The Bronze and Archaic Ages*, new ed. (1981).

Any of the above four titles will provide an excellent treatment of a period in Greek history that has received significant new interpretations in recent times.

L. H. Jeffery, *Archaic Greece: The City States c. 700-500* (1976). Valuable for the attention paid to city-states other than Athens and Sparta.

Chester G. Starr, *Individual and Community. The Rise of the Polis 800-500 B.C.* (1986). A masterful treatment of the forces that produced the *polis.*

R. Osborne, *Demos* (1985). A clear discussion of early Athens.

W. G. Forrest, *History of Sparta, 950-192 B.C.*, 2nd ed. (1980).

J. T. Hooker, *The Ancient Spartans* (1980).

Two very perceptive treatments of Spartan history.

Economic and Social History

Chester G. Starr, *The Economic and Social Growth of Early Greece, 800-500 B.C.* (1977).

M. M. Austin and P. Vidal-Naquet, *Economic and Social History of Ancient Greece: An Interpretation* (1977).

Either of these two works will provide invaluable information on all aspects of Greek economy.

John Boardman, *The Greeks Overseas*, rev. ed. (1982). An excellent treatment of a crucial aspect of Greek development.

Sources

Homer, *Iliad* and *Odyssey* (many translations; among the best are those by Richmond Lattimore). Two works that played an essential role in shaping the Greek civic mentality.

Hesiod, *Theogeny and Works and Days*, trans. M. L. West (1988). A picture by a contemporary of the problems that caused stress in the Greek world about 700 B.C.

CHAPTER 5
The Greek Golden Age, 500–336 B.C.: Life, War, and Politics

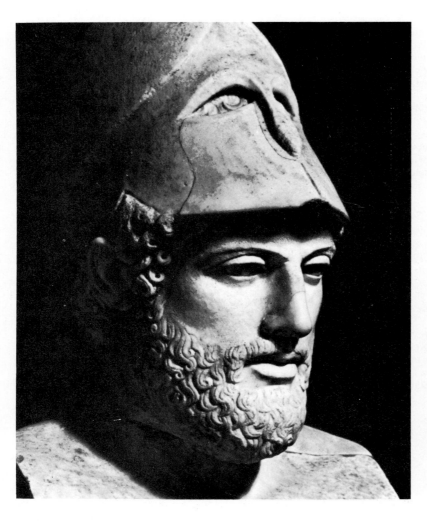

FIGURE 5.1 Pericles This statue portrays Pericles, under whose leadership the city-state of Athens reached the peak of its power politically, economically and culturally. The key to Pericles' fame rests largely in the faith he had in the Athenian citizen body to decide its own destiny democratically. The artist captures the intelligence, dignity, and political sagacity for which Pericles was honored. (Museo Vaticano/ Alinari)

Driven by the energies unleashed in its many city-states, the Greek world enjoyed a golden age during the fifth and early fourth centuries B.C. Shaped within the framework created by the *polis,* a pattern of daily life prevailed which engaged the energies and satisfied the needs of most Greeks. Central to the Greek way of life were ongoing political engagements, through which the citizen body reached decisions defining the rules governing collective behavior in each *polis.* Those engagements provided powerful stimuli to creative activity in artistic, literary, and intellectual life. However, the Golden Age had a darker side involving another issue that grew ever more critical: the problem of relationships among the fiercely patriotic communities, each struggling to strengthen and enrich itself. At the beginning of the fifth century, a threat from the outside demonstrated the need for cooperation, but progressively the city-states surrendered to their parochialism and became embroiled in destructive intercity struggles whose burdens created increasing instability within each *polis.* Their failure to resolve the dilemma posed by their dedication to self-determination and their need for cooperation left the Greek city-states easy prey for a powerful external foe.

1. DAILY LIFE IN GREECE

The triumphs and tribulations of the Golden Age were shaped by the conditions that surrounded the daily lives of men and women. Rooted in the long history that had produced each *polis,* the economic and social patterns defining life in ancient Greece constituted an essential aspect of Greek civilization.

Most Greeks devoted a part of every day to some kind of work related to Greece's diversified economy. In every *polis* the bulk of the people earned their living in agriculture. Most farms were small, producing barely enough cereal grains and animal products to sustain a household. The most productive agricultural enterprises, devoted to raising olives, grapes, and livestock, took place on larger farms managed by aristocratic owners and tilled by tenants and slaves. In the urban center, which was the focal point of each *polis,* large numbers of people worked as traders, artisans, and hired laborers.

The scale of operations of retail shops and artisan workshops was small, usually involving a family household with the help of a slave or two. Only a few enterprises, such as overseas trading, mining, and arms making, were large-scale, often utilizing slaves as laborers. As illustrated by the cases of Athens and Sparta, in every *polis* a considerable portion of the population lived as public employees or as recipients of state-allocated land. Compared to both earlier and later societies, the Greek economic system did not produce abundant wealth, an important factor in creating economic rivalry among city-states and social tensions within each.

By the fifth century B.C. the social structure in most city-states lacked sharp class distinctions among the citizen population. Leading families enjoying wealth and prestige did exist, but their status depended less on birth and legal sanctions than on their ability to persuade other citizens to follow their leadership in political life and on their willingness to use their wealth to support civic activities. Citizens of lesser means were treated with respect, perhaps because their voices counted in shaping public life. There was a strong tendency in Greek society to afford greater status to those who owned land, even in small amounts, than to those who worked as artisans and traders. This attitude not only bred a disdain for labor but also opened a place in most city-states for foreign noncitizens willing to fill economic roles demanding labor without enjoying the benefits of citizenship. Slavery was pervasive in Greek society and viewed by those who enjoyed freedom, including most political and intellectual leaders, as a necessary part of a viable society. These "man-footed animals"—both male and female—bore a heavy burden on farms, in households, in artisan and trading establishments, in mines, in building projects, and even in public service activities, but they enjoyed minimal legal protection against whatever their masters chose to do to them.

Although most Greeks worked to earn a livelihood, those who considered themselves free placed a high value on leisure. Free time was possible in part because slavery played an important role in the Greek economy. Equally important was the willingness of the Greeks to live simple lives, made easier by Greece's good climate. Their diet was plain: Bread, olive oil, vegetables and fruit, cheese, fish, and wine were the staple items. Even among the wealthy, houses were modest in size and sparsely furnished. Most men and women dressed in rough-spun tunics and sandals, although the more affluent favored linen garments and at least some jewelry. However, this simplicity of tastes and needs was confined chiefly to private life. The Greeks spent lavishly to adorn their city-states with costly temples and public buildings, sculpture, and paintings and to support festivals, games, and dramas at whatever price.

The family was the fundamental unit of Greek society. The nuclear family—husband, wife, children—living in a single household and perhaps served by a slave or two stood at the base of the family structure. But kinship bonds extending to a larger circle of relatives played an important role in determining citizenship, defining social status, controlling property, and deciding associations. Marriage contracts were arranged by families. The bride's father provided a dowry, which was returned to the bride if the marriage ended. Actual cohabitation of the contracted couple, an occasion for much celebration, usually began when the girl was fifteen or sixteen; the husband was usually older. Children were important in marriage, but a constant concern with the problems resulting from too many mouths to feed resulted in modest-sized families. The Greeks practiced various methods of birth control, and they were not averse to exposing unwanted children to death or giving them up for adoption. Husbands could divorce their wives easily, but it was much more difficult for a woman to end a marriage.

Greek women had a limited place in society. Although powerful and active women were enshrined in Greek legends (for example, Helen of Troy and Penelope as portrayed by Homer) and celebrated in poetry and drama (including Clytemnestra, Antigone, and Medea) and although powerful goddesses (such as Athena) figured significantly in Greek religion, the lives of most women were severely restricted. Greek literature and philosophical writing, most of it produced by men, are filled with portrayals of women as inferior in intelligence and self-control. That view found expression in legal terms. Although wives and daughters of male citizens were recognized and protected under the law, they were always subject to a male. Women could not own property (except, ironically, in Sparta) or engage in legal transactions and were excluded from political life. The prime role of respectable women was to direct the household, care for young children, and train their daughters for the same role. Women rarely participated in any aspect of public life, except for religious festivals, and they were usually excluded from the social activities of their husbands. Women of poor households did help their husbands run their farms and shops, thus involving themselves at least to some degree in the affairs of the larger society. But most women were literally out of sight, exerting whatever influence they had within the walls of their home. Some evidence suggests that in that private sphere wives enjoyed the respect and the genuine love of their husbands. A few rare women of beauty, intelligence, and social grace became the sexual companions of important citizens and shared their social lives with them; the most notable example was Aspasia, the sophisticated and widely admired mistress of Pericles. Prostitution was common in the Greek world.

While the household was the center of life for most Greek women, men appear to have spent as little time there as possible. Shortly after the break of day they were out of the house to occupy themselves with their jobs or with the bustling life of the *polis*. Almost from birth males found their lives enmeshed in a variety of social groups whose activities consumed much of their energy. When boys were seven or eight, they went forth daily from their homes to begin their education in reading, writing, speaking, and physical education under the guidance of private teachers. By the fifth century B.C. in a city such as Athens, that education might continue for years, focusing on skills suitable to political activity, especially rhetoric. The sisters of these young men remained at home to be educated in household arts by their mothers or household slaves. At an early age males were enrolled in a *phratry*, a kinship group that sponsored a variety of religious and social activities. As young men grew older, they gravitated to the *gymnasia*, male gathering places devoted to physical education, athletic competition, and endless talk. It was not unusual for a youth to attract the attention of an adult male who served as a role model in introducing young men to the full range of activities of the *polis*. These relationships, forged in a setting that provided little female influence and that often involved homosexuality, played an important role in shaping male values. No less intriguing to the maturing youth were the marketplace, the theater, and the bordello. Often his adult mentor began to involve him in private gatherings, called *symposia*, where males met in private houses to eat, drink, and talk—free from wives and mothers, who withdrew to the special female quarters featured in the typical house. By the time his teenage days were ending, a male entered into the responsibilities of citizenship: military service, participation in the popular assembly, officeholding. For the rest of his life these political activities would command an important part of his time and energies. Perhaps shortly after becoming a full-fledged citizen, the typical Greek male married, but already his life was so involved in the affairs of the *polis* and in the social associations to which he was attached that marriage was incidental to his life. Indeed, involvement in the *polis* was more than a political matter; it defined a broad range of activities that engaged its male members completely. And the Greeks were scornful of any man who did not involve himself in that life.

Even a brief look at the essentials of Greek daily life suggests that Greek citizens enjoyed considerable freedom to do what they wished and that many chose to use that freedom to involve themselves intensely in the varied activities of the *polis*. This environment posed challenges that unleashed powerful creative forces that played a prime role in shaping the political and cultural destiny of the Greek world in the Golden Age. It was especially on the political scene that the challenge to serve the *polis* was posed during the fifth and fourth centuries; the response of the citizens in many city-states was decisive in shaping the course of political history during that period.

2. THE PERSIAN WARS, 490–479 B.C.

The Golden Age began with a defining event in Greek history, a war against the Persians. Its outcome affirmed in the mentality of the Greeks the uniqueness and the superiority of their way of life, an attitude that played an important role in sustaining it in the future. And the threat posed by the Persians demonstrated the need for cooperation among the independent city-states, a lesson the Greeks learned less well.

During the Archaic Age intercity cooperation was not a major issue in the Greek world. No major outside power threatened the city-states, and their not infrequent clashes with one another were on a limited scale. In fact, there were significant developments encouraging interdependence among the Greeks. Their common language promoted a shared culture. Expanding commerce linked the city-states together. Religion was an especially important force promoting pan-Hellenism. It provided a common set of deities, pan-Hellenic festivals—such as the Olympic Games, which drew Greeks together for worship, athletic competitions, and cultural performances honoring their gods and goddesses—and shared shrines, such as the Delphic oracle, to which all Greeks went to seek divine guidance. Some progress had even been made in establishing political federations allowing city-states to collaborate without surrendering their autonomy; a prime example was the already noted Peloponnesian League led by Sparta.

The dramatic expansion of the Persians after about 550 B.C. created a frightening challenge for the Greek world, brought home by the Persian subjugation of Greek city-states along the Aegean coast of Asia Minor and the establishment in 512 B.C. of a Persian outpost in Thrace (see Map 4.1). Although Persian rule over the Ionian city-states was not particularly harsh, their inhabitants hated paying tribute and submitting to "tyrants" imposed on them by that "evil empire" and eventually rebelled in 499 B.C. The rebels appealed to their fellow Greeks on the mainland and received support from Athens and Eritrea. The Persian ruler, Darius the Great, eventually crushed the revolt. Moved probably by fear of future Greek intervention in Persian affairs and by ambition to expand his already huge empire, he apparently decided that Greece must be conquered. Political scheming among factions within many Greek city-states that saw the Persians as potential allies in the struggles for power and the neutrality proclaimed by several key city-states encouraged Darius to think that the Greek world was ready for conquest.

Map 5.1 THE PERSIAN WARS The map shows the location of the crucial engagements between the Greeks and the Persians in the campaigns of 490 B.C. and 480–479 B.C. The inset, showing the long route taken by Xerxes in 480 B.C., may suggest the challenge faced by the Persians in their bid to conquer the Greeks, for they had to engage the Greeks in a constricted setting where the Greeks could make the best use of their resources.

In 490 B.C. Darius made his move (see Map 5.1 for the Persian campaigns). He sent a fleet and a substantial army across the Aegean, ostensibly to punish Athens and Eritrea for their involvement in the rebellion of the Ionians. After destroying Eritrea, the Persian army landed in eastern Attica, near Marathon. The Greek world had made almost no preparations for the Persian onslaught. Standing alone, the Athenians seemed doomed. But they chose to resist, sending an army to challenge the Persians. Although outnumbered, the Athenian *hoplites,* brilliantly led by Miltiades, defeated the Persians and forced the survivors back to their ships. Miltiades then marched his victorious army back to Athens and stood ready to defend the city when the Persian fleet from Marathon appeared there. The Persians elected to return to Asia Minor. Athens celebrated a new breed of heroes whose feats at Marathon rivaled those of the heroes extolled by Homer.

The Persians were not ready to admit defeat, although a new attack was delayed ten years by internal troubles. That interval allowed the Greeks to prepare more adequately. Sparta took the leadership in organizing a Hellenic League made up of thirty-one city-states willing to pool their forces under Spartan commanders. Greek armed strength, based on the superb Spartan army, was greatly enhanced by a crucial decision made by Athens. A farsighted leader named Themistocles persuaded the Athenian citizenry to use the income from silver mines recently discovered in Attica to fund a major increase in the Athenian navy, which the Athenians pledged to the support of the Hellenic League. Despite this show of unity, many city-states remained neutral.

Early in 480 B.C. Xerxes, Darius' successor, launched a new attack spearheaded by a huge army and navy. Xerxes sent his army over a pontoon bridge crossing the Hellespont into Europe. Supplied by a huge fleet, it advanced slowly around the northern Aegean coast and then southward. The Hellenic League made its first stand at Thermopylae. Despite their success in defeating the Persian fleet and the heroic resistance of a Spartan detachment led by King Leonidas, the Greeks suffered a defeat that allowed the Persians to flood into central Greece, capturing Athens and striking terror into the Greek alliance.

At this critical point, Themistocles exercised a decisive influence on the course of the war. Despite strong pressure in the council of the Hellenic League to withdraw the armies to the Peloponnesus and the fleet to the Gulf of Corinth, Themistocles combined persuasion with threats of Athens' withdrawal to convince the League to trust the Greek fate to a naval showdown. In late September 480 B.C., he enticed the Persian fleet into a disadvantageous position in the narrow waters between Attica and the island of Salamis, where the Athenian fleet delivered a crushing defeat on the Persians. Xerxes was forced to order the surviving remnants of his fleet back to its bases in Asia Minor and the withdrawal of his army to northern Greece.

In 479 B.C. Xerxes again ordered his army southward. The Hellenic League put a major army into the field, anchored by Spartan troops. This force met the Persians at Plataea. Once again the Greeks imposed a major defeat on the larger Persian army. While these events were unfolding, the fleet of the Hellenic League sailed boldly across the Aegean and destroyed the main Persian fleet at Mycale, a victory that triggered a revolt among the Greek city-states of Asia Minor. Xerxes had no choice but to recall his armies from Europe. By their willingness to sacrifice in the service of their city-states, the jubilant Greeks had won a victory that not only saved their independence but also filled them with a sense of superiority.

While the Greeks of the Aegean world were throwing back the Persian threat, their fellow Greeks in the west were winning a victory hardly less significant. The struggle here centered on Sicily, where Carthage, a powerful maritime state, was attempting to expand its commercial empire by subduing the Sicilian Greeks. A coalition of Greek city-states led by Gelon, tyrant of Syracuse, inflicted a decisive defeat on the Carthaginians at the battle of Himera in 480 B.C., ensuring the continued independence of the Greek city-states in Magna Graecia.

3. THE DELIAN LEAGUE AND THE ATHENIAN EMPIRE, 479–431 B.C.

Although the Greeks had won a victory of mythic proportions to them, the Persian Empire remained a major power and a real threat which many felt must be countered by a cooperative offensive against the Persians. Leadership in this undertaking passed from Sparta to Athens, which took the initiative in 478 B.C. in persuading several cities to form the Delian League, so named because its treasury was to be kept on the island of Delos, the site of a temple venerated throughout the Greek world. Dedicated to the continuation of the war against Persia, the League's policy decisions were to be made by an assembly of representatives meeting annually with each member city-state having one vote. Each member pledged to contribute ships and money according to its abilities. Athens was charged with making the initial assessments and with commanding the League's forces. No member city-state would be required to surrender sovereign control over its internal affairs, thus protecting the principle of autonomy.

The League quickly swung into action. An Athenian, Cimon, was placed in command of its joint forces, which enjoyed impressive success. Within fifteen years, all the Greek city-states in Asia Minor were freed of Persian rule, while the Aegean and the Hellespont areas were cleared of Persian naval power. Athens was obviously the most powerful member of the League, but its leaders conducted themselves with marked restraint in dealing with other members and even toward nonmembers, such as Sparta.

This situation was not destined to last, and Athens was largely responsible for the change. As the danger from Persia receded, some members of the Delian League sought to reduce their contributions and even to withdraw. Athens was unwilling to allow the dissolution of the League. Increasingly, Athenian leaders and citizens came to realize that dominance over the League could be turned to commercial ends that would enrich Athens. The emergence of Athenian imperialist ambitions coincided with the final establishment of democracy in Athens under the leadership of Pericles (see Figure 5.1), who from 461 to 429 B.C. was the dominant force in Athenian political affairs. He placed the destiny of the city into the hands of his fellow citizens and constantly urged their support of policies designed to ensure Athenian preeminence in Greece. They responded with enthusiasm, partly because that course enriched the city-state and partly because imperialism fed the Athenians' pride in the greatness of their *polis*, by now the self-acclaimed savior of Hellas.

Emboldened by such support, Pericles launched a two-pronged drive to expand Athenian influence. One was aimed at aggressive actions against "foreign enemies," real or invented. The assault against the Persians, who constantly enhanced their already established reputation as a threat to the Greek world by subversive efforts aimed at disrupting political life in almost every Greek city-state, was expanded beyond the Aegean into the eastern Mediterranean. On the Greek mainland Pericles employed every device possible to draw more city-states into the Delian League. Athens supported revolts against non-democratic governments, tried to entice the members of the Peloponnesian League to abandon Sparta, and used Athenian sea power to bottle up rival trading powers, such as Corinth. This aggressive policy enjoyed considerable success, but eventually Pericles realized that Athens was overextending its power. In 454 B.C. an unsuccessful Athenian effort to liberate Egypt led to an understanding with the Persians that each would respect the other's sphere of influence: Athens' control of the Aegean and the Greek city-states in Asia Minor and Persia's dominance of the eastern Mediterranean coastal area. In the face of mounting threats of Spartan retaliation against Athenian expansionism on the Greek mainland, Pericles finally agreed to the Thirty Years' Truce of 445 B.C. Athens agreed to halt its aggression against mainland Greek city-states, especially those belonging to the Peloponnesian League, and Sparta promised to recognize Athenian hegemony over the Delian League.

In the years following 445 B.C. Pericles skillfully pursued the second aspect of his imperial policy: imposing control over the nearly three hundred city-states constituting the Delian League. Although the Persian danger no longer existed, Athens continued to collect funds from these cities. This "tribute" was used as Athens wished, chiefly to support the system of pay Pericles introduced for the vastly increased number of citizens who performed public service in Athens and to support the artists and writers who made Athens the "school of Hellas." Athens forced many League members to institute democratic governments. The subject cities were compelled to accept the Athenian money system and Athenian weights and measures, thus ensuring that their economies would be subservient to that of Athens. Athenians were settled on lands confiscated from residents of subject city-states, a policy that relieved Athens of excess population and provided a convenient means of influencing internal affairs in dependent members of what had become an Athenian Empire.

Although the subject city-states benefited from increased commerce and the security re-

Map 5.2 THE GREEK WORLD, 431 B.C. This map identifies the members of the two camps into which the Greek world was divided at the beginning of the Peloponnesian War. It highlights why its naval forces were so vital to Athens in the struggle that lasted until 404 B.C. and why an alliance with Persia eventually played a crucial role in the success of Sparta and its allies in dismembering the Athenian Empire.

sulting from enforced peace, their hatred for Athens grew steadily. Athens had usurped their most prized possession, their right to exist as independent city-states. The mighty, enlightened democratic gem of Greek civilization had, in the eyes of most Greeks, become an oppressor. The proud, arrogant Athenians made no attempt to compensate for depriving their subjects of their independence. They were not permitted to become citizens of Athens, and they were denied any representation in the Athenian government. Some Athenians raised concerns about the destruction of the liberty of any *polis*, but the Athenian citizenry, aware that the economic welfare of Athens and its citizens depended on imperial power and proud of Athens' glory, overrode

these voices. Mounting anti-Athenian feeling throughout much of the Greek world caused many to look toward Sparta as the champion of city-state independence. Such sentiments pointed toward a major clash engaging Greek against Greek.

4. THE PELOPONNESIAN WAR, 431–404 B.C.

The conflict pitting two hostile camps—the Spartan-led Peloponnesian League and the Athenian-led Delian League—against each other began in 431 B.C. (see Map 5.2). At the very beginning of the struggle, known as the Peloponnesian War, a Spartan envoy warned the Athenians that "This day will be the beginning of great evil for the Greeks." Implicit in this admonition was the widely shared view, then and now, that responsibility for the war belonged to Athens for threatening the independence of other city-states. That charge had ominous implications; for a generation the clash inflicted a terrible material and psychological cost on the entire Greek world which perhaps doomed the fundamental institution at stake, the independent *polis*.

The first years of the war were indecisive. Confident that the Spartan alliance would crumble, Pericles persuaded the Athenians to avoid land war against the superior Spartan armies; its populace withdrew within Athens' impregnable walls, depending on its superior fleet to hold the empire together and supply the beleaguered city. The Spartans responded by ravaging the Attic countryside, but they were unable to strike a decisive blow. This strategy put too great a burden on the Athenians, who were increasingly impatient as they watched their beloved land ravaged; to their rage was added the suffering caused by a terrible plague which between 430 and 427 B.C. killed at least one-third of the cooped-up population, including Pericles. The cry for bolder military action mounted. A militant democratic and imperialistic leader, Cleon, responded by leading Athenian armies outside Attica, especially into central Greece and western Peloponnesus, in an effort to wean away crucial Spartan allies. A resourceful Spartan leader, Brasidas, persuaded Sparta to send its military forces farther afield to encourage revolt among the subject cities of the Athenian Empire, especially in the northern Aegean area. However, in 422 B.C., before this new phase of the struggle reached a decisive point, both Cleon and Brasidas were killed. Powerful supporters of peace in both camps took advantage of their deaths to end the war. In 421 B.C. Athens and Sparta agreed to a Fifty-Year Truce, which restored the situation to what it had been when the struggle began.

The uneasy peace settlement, which addressed none of the basic issues, lasted only until 415 B.C. Again the Athenians were responsible for the renewal of hostilities. After the death of Pericles, Athenian political life became faction-ridden and unstable. Afflicted by the burdens of war, the citizens were increasingly swayed by ambitious demagogues willing to promise anything in return for power. Such a figure was the flashy, unscrupulous Alcibiades. Playing upon the imperialistic sentiments and the civic pride so strong in Athens, he persuaded the citizenry to undertake a major expedition against the powerful Greek city of Syracuse in Sicily, an important commercial rival of Athens. This ill-conceived venture, badly led by rival politicians, including Alcibiades, who deserted to Sparta to avoid criminal charges brought by his enemies in Athens, ended in a disastrous defeat for Athens in 413 B.C. Worse, the attack on Syracuse provoked Sparta and its allies to renew all-out war against Athens.

After 413 B.C. the fortunes of Athens declined steadily. Internal dissension, pitting prodemocratic forces against a growing faction fearful of the consequences of unbridled democracy, hindered decisive action. The Spartans, brilliantly led by Lysander, mounted a powerful attack on Athenian sea power and a skillful campaign to encourage revolt among the city-states of the Athenian Empire. A decisive step in this campaign was the Spartan success in forming an alliance with Persia which provided Sparta with naval forces sufficient to challenge the Athenian fleet that had so long provided the glue holding the Athenian Empire together. Athens occasionally won an isolated victory, but the net continued to close around the doomed city-state. Finally, in 404 B.C., Athens had to surrender. The victors forced Athens to tear down its walls, destroy all but twelve ships of its once-invincible fleet, and submit to a government of oligarchs backed by a Spartan army stationed in Athens. Although these Thirty Tyrants, as the Athenians called them, were ousted in 403 B.C. and democratic government was restored, Athens would never recover its former power.

Athens was not the only victim of the Peloponnesian War. Its ravages impoverished many Greek city-states, deepened and embittered the rivalries among them, bred internal dissension and violence within many city-states, caused widespread pessimism and disillusionment, and renewed the threat of Persian domination. Its impact unleashed forces that would soon drastically reduce the role of the Greek city-states in shaping the destiny of Greco-Roman civilization.

HISTORIANS' SOURCES

Thucydides: *The Peloponnesian War*

In his Peloponnesian War *the Greek historian Thucydides recorded a speech made by Pericles eulogizing the Athenians who died during the first year of that war. The following passage from that speech provides the historian with an insight into what the Athenians thought of themselves but raises questions about Pericles as an objective reporter of reality.*

"But before I praise the dead, I should like to point out by what principles of action we rose to power, and under what institutions and through what manner of life our empire became great. . . .

"Our form of government does not enter into rivalry with the institutions of others. We do not copy our neighbours, but are an example to them. It is true that we are called a democracy, for the administration is in the hands of the many and not of the few. But while the law secures equal justice to all alike in their private disputes, the claim of excellence is also recognised; and when a citizen is in any way distinguished, he is preferred to the public service, not as a matter of privilege, but as the reward of merit. Neither is poverty a bar, but a man may benefit his country whatever be the obscurity of his condition. There is no exclusiveness in our public life, and in our private intercourse we are not suspicious of one another, nor angry with our neighbour if he does what he likes. . . . While we are thus unconstrained in our private intercourse, a spirit of reverence pervades our public acts; we are prevented from doing wrong by respect for authority and for the laws, having an especial regard to those which are ordained for the protection of the injured as well as to those unwritten laws which bring upon the transgressor of them the reprobation of the general sentiment.

"And we have not forgotten to provide for our weary spirits many relaxations from toil; we have regular games and sacrifices throughout the year; at home the style of our life is refined; and the delight which we daily feel in all these things helps to banish melancholy. Because of the greatness of our city the fruits of the whole earth flow in upon us. . . .

"Then, again, our military training is in many respects superior to that of our adversaries. . . . We rely not upon management or trickery but upon our own hearts and hands. And in the matter of education, whereas they from early youth are always undergoing laborious exercises which are to make them brave, we live at ease, and yet are equally ready to face the perils which they face. . . .

"If then we prefer to meet danger with a light heart but without laborious training, and with a courage which is gained by habit and not enforced by law, are we not greatly the gainers? Since we do not anticipate the pain, although, when the hour comes, we can be as brave as those who never allow themselves to rest; and thus too our city is equally admirable in peace and in war.

"For we are lovers of the beautiful, yet with economy, and we cultivate the mind without loss of manliness. Wealth we employ, not for talk and ostentation, but when there is a real use for it. To avow poverty with us is no disgrace; the true disgrace is in doing nothing to avoid it. An Athenian citizen does not neglect the state because he takes care of his own household; and even those of us who are engaged in business have a very fair idea of politics. We alone regard a man who takes no interest in public affairs, not as a harmless, but as a useless character; and if few of us are originators, we are all sound judges of a policy. . . . For we have a peculiar power of thinking before we act and of acting too, whereas other men are courageous from ignorance but hesitate upon reflection. . . .

"To sum up: I say that Athens is the school of Hellas, and that the individual Athenian in his own person seems to have the power of adapting himself to the most varied forms of action with the utmost versatility and grace."

SOURCE: Francis R. B. Godolphin, ed., *The Greek Historians*, Vol. I (New York: Random House, 1942), pp. 648–650.

5. THE TWILIGHT OF THE WORLD OF THE GREEK CITY-STATES, 404–336 B.C.

Although one Greek historian proclaimed the end of the Peloponnesian War "the beginning of freedom for Greece," in fact the defeat of Athens marked the beginning of even greater trouble in the Greek world. Two interlocking issues dominated the next sixty years: the effort of a succession of leading city-states to establish hegemony over the Greeks and the struggle to sustain internal order and vitality within each *polis*. These issues combined to produce constantly shifting alliances, almost incessant intercity warfare, and bitter civil strife, all of which combined to weaken the Greeks.

At the end of the Peloponnesian War Sparta was the predominant power in the Greek world. For the next thirty years it devoted its energies to asserting its hegemony. The key to Spartan policy was the imposition of an oligarchic government on any city-state that could be bullied into submission, a policy that badly undermined Sparta's claim to be the defender of city-state independence. In fact, Sparta did not have the strength to control the Greek world. Its narrowly restricted citizen body was declining in numbers and in dedication to the Lycurgan regime. Its rigid social system prevented Sparta from replenishing its citizens from the ranks of the *perioeci* and *helots*. Ultimately, Sparta was forced to depend on Persian assistance to maintain its hegemony at the cost of allowing the Persians to reestablish dominance over the Ionian Greeks. Growing fear and resentment against Sparta led to the formation of an alliance led by Thebes. Under the brilliant generalship of Thebes' one great statesman, Epaminandos, this alliance smashed Sparta in a single battle in 371 B.C., a defeat that marked the end of Sparta's long history as a major Greek power. This victory allowed Thebes to play a central role in Greek affairs for a decade, but even with Persian help it was unable to dominate; its power was smashed in a decisive battle in 362 B.C. by an alliance formed by Athens.

In the generation after Thebes' defeat Athens sought to reestablish a dominant position, but its efforts were constantly thwarted by rival city-states and by internal dissension. The result was a succession of petty wars that wasted human and material resources and placed a constant strain on internal affairs in each *polis*. These internal struggles, centered on rivalry between democratic and aristocratic factions for control of political life and on issues pitting poor against rich over the distribution of declining wealth in each city-state, were often marked by a blatant abuse of power by ambitious power seekers and by violence. Increasingly, mercenary forces led by ruthless and adventuresome commanders replaced citizen armies and navies; these professionals much preferred war to peace. Some Greek leaders, aware of the destructive cost of intercity war, formulated a variety of plans aimed at forming some kind of voluntary union among city-states that would provide a peaceful setting in which each *polis* could restore internal stability. However, political pan-Hellenism was a lost cause. No Greek *polis* was willing to surrender any of its sovereignty to a superior organization—even in the interest of peace. Even great philosophers such as Plato and Aristotle, both of whom lived during the fourth century, vigorously insisted that only the traditional self-defining *polis* was fit for the Greeks.

6. THE MACEDONIAN CONQUEST OF GREECE

Incessant warfare and civic strife gradually deprived the Greek city-states of the ability to determine their own destiny. That role was snatched by the kingdom of Macedonia, suddenly elevated from relative obscurity to the rank of a major power under the leadership of King Philip II (359–336 B.C.). A gifted, ambitious ruler, Philip II was able to create a disciplined army and to impose an effective internal organization on his previously diverse, unruly subjects. Assured of a strong power base, Philip II turned his attention toward the turbulent Greek world, driven by an urge to gain access to the Aegean Sea and to bring his backward kingdom into closer contact with the Greek civilization he greatly admired.

Macedonian intrusion into Greece involved a complex play of political forces. The warring Greek city-states and the rival factions within many city-states could not resist seeking Philip's support. Philip encouraged them to do so, often intriguing in Greek affairs to create opportunities for his involvement. His skilled diplomacy and his adroit use of military force increasingly allowed him to manipulate political life over an ever-expanding area of the Aegean world. Although many warned of the Macedonian "menace," the Greeks were seldom able to join forces to resist. In fact, some Greeks favored Macedonian dominance as a solution for incessant warfare. Eventually Athens, moved both by fear of Macedonian power and by dreams of using the Macedonian threat to re-create Athenian hegemony in Greece, became the focal point of resistance. Under the leadership of the eloquent Demosthenes, always ready to use his oratorical skills to warn his fellow Athenian citizens of the Macedonian danger and to damn those in Athens and elsewhere who advocated peace with Macedonia, Athens was able to form a fragile league dedicated to resistance to Macedonian advances. Despite this effort at collective action, the Macedonian advance was irresistible. Philip finally maneuvered the Athenian alliance into committing itself to battle at Chaeronea in 338 B.C., which ended in a crushing defeat that left all of Greece at Philip's mercy.

While treating his vanquished enemies with mildness unusual for the era, Philip quickly demonstrated that he intended to end the old order. Soon after his victory and at his insistence all the Greek city-states except Sparta agreed to join the League of Corinth, dedicated to the establishment of a common peace. Members of the League were theoretically entitled to independence, but crucial restrictions were imposed on their power to make war or change their form of government. Such prohibitions obviously greatly restricted the ancient freedom of the *polis*. The League was to be governed by a council of representatives from each city-state, which would meet regularly and decide League actions to keep peace. Each member was obliged to contribute according to its means to a common military force charged with imposing peace. Macedonia was not a member of the League, but Philip did require that the League sign a treaty of alliance with Macedonia. Philip was also designated as military commander (*hegemon*) of the League, thus putting himself into a position to control its activities. At a meeting of the League council in 337 B.C. Philip proposed that its first undertaking should be joining its forces with Macedonia in a war against Persia; it was difficult for any city-state to protest against such a noble cause. But his assassination in 336 B.C. denied him an opportunity to direct this campaign against an ancient foe of the Greeks. Nevertheless, Philip's statesmanship had achieved a notable end: In the League of Corinth he provided an instrument that would allow the warring city-states to impose peace on themselves while enjoying internal autonomy and the protection of the potent Macedonian army against outsiders. Within this framework the *polis* survived as a key element in Greco-Roman civilization but never again in the same way that that institution had dominated the Greek world during the Golden Age.

SUGGESTED READING

Fifth- and Fourth-Century Greece

Simon Hornblower, *The Greek World, 479–323 B.C.* (1983). A good general survey.
A. R. Burn, *Persia and the Greeks: The Defence of the West, c. 546–478 B.C.*, 2nd ed. (1984). A full treatment of the clash between the Greeks and the Persians.
P. J. Rhodes, *The Athenian Empire* (1985).
Malcolm F. McGregor, *The Athenians and Their Empire* (1987).

Either of these works will help the reader understand Athenian imperialism.
Anton Powell, *Athens and Sparta: Constructing Greek Political and Social History from 478 B.C.* (1988). Helpful in assessing the impact of the Peloponnesian War.
Andrew Lintott, *Violence, Civil Strife, and Revolution in the Classical City, 750–330 B.C.* (1982).
G. E. M. de Ste. Croix, *The Class Struggle in the Ancient Greek World from the Archaic Age to the Arab Conquest* (1981).

Two provocative treatments of a facet of Greek life that was destructive of the *polis*.

J. W. Roberts, *City of Sokrates: An Introduction to Classical Athens* (1984).

R. K. Sinclair, *Democracy and Participation in Athens* (1988).

Josiah Ober, *Mass and Elite in Democratic Athens: Rhetoric, Ideology, and the Power of the People* (1989).

Chester G. Starr, *The Birth of Athenian Democracy: The Assembly in the Fifth Century B.C.* (1990).

These four works are useful in understanding how Athenian democracy worked.

J. R. Ellis, *Phillip II and Macedonian Imperialism* (1976).

George Cawkwell, *Philip of Macedon* (1978).

Two excellent studies explaining the Macedonian victory over the Greeks.

Social Life

In addition to the social and economic histories cited in Chapter 4, the following works treat selected aspects of Greek social life, as indicated by their titles.

R. J. Hopper, *Trade and Industry in Classical Greece* (1979).

Maurice Pope, *The Ancient Greeks. How They Lived and Worked* (1976).

Robert Garland, *The Greek Way of Life from Conception to Old Age* (1990).

M. T. W. Arnheim, *Aristocracy in Greek Society* (1977).

W. K. Lacey, *The Family in Classical Greece* (1984).

Sarah B. Pomeroy, *Goddesses, Whores, Wives, and Slaves: Women in Classical Antiquity* (1975).

Eva Cantarella, *Pandora's Daughters: The Role and Status of Women in Greek and Roman Antiquity*, trans. Maureen B. Fant (1987).

Roger Just, *Women in Athenian Law and Life* (1988).

Mark Golden, *Children and Childhood in Classical Athens* (1990).

Yvon Garlan, *Slavery in Ancient Greece*, trans. Janet Lloyd (1988).

K. J. Dover, *Greek Homosexuality* (1978).

Donald G. Kyle, *Athletics in Ancient Athens* (1987).

Sources

Herodotus, *The Histories*, trans. Aubrey de Selincourt (1955).

Thucydides, *The Peloponnesian War*, trans. Rex Warner (1954).

Most of what we know about the fifth century comes from these two great historians; they are essential reading.

CHAPTER 6
Greek Thought and Expression

FIGURE 6.1 A Greek Goddess This portrayal of the goddess Athena in mourning suggests the capability of the Greek sculptors to render the human form in an idealized fashion while still injecting feeling into an artistic composition. As the divine protector and patron of the city of Athens, Athena was constantly celebrated in art and literature by the city's artists and writers. She and other deities provided a constant source of inspiration for all forms of cultural creativity. (Acropolis Museum, Athens)

From the time of Homer at the beginning of the Archaic Age in the eighth century B.C. until the end of the Golden Age in the middle of the fourth century B.C., the *polis* provided an environment that in a unique way stimulated thought and expression. The result was a cultural achievement that for a thousand years after 500 B.C. provided the dominant force in shaping what people living around the Mediterranean Sea believed and said and thought. No less important, long after that millennium ended the Greek cultural legacy left an indelible mark on the cultural history of much of the world, but especially the western European world. The creations of Greek writers, artists, and thinkers have a quality that still makes them attractive for what they are in their own right—creations to read, to look at, and to think about for the pleasure and mental stimulation they provide. Beyond that these works opened vistas onto the human condition and onto the potential of human beings that have never ceased to challenge anyone concerned with what humanity means. Without coming to grips with the Greek cultural achievement, it is impossible to arrive at a full understanding of the course of Western civilization.

1. RELIGION

Religion played a powerful role in shaping all aspects of Greek life, but it was especially important in providing a seedbed out of which intellectual and artistic life emerged. The foundations of Greek religion were shaped during the earliest stages of Greek history, based on a complex mixture of beliefs and practices drawn from Indo-European, Asian, African, and Minoan sources. By the time the first systematic statements describing Greek religious beliefs were made—in the writings of Homer and Hesiod early in the Archaic Age—a set of beliefs and values expressed in an elaborate mythology and in complex rituals was widely shared in the Greek world. These beliefs and practices provided a framework which gave shape and meaning to individual and collective life and which played an important role in governing the behavioral patterns of the Greeks.

Greek religion was polytheistic. Among the divine agents were certain remote and abstracted forces—such as fate (*nemesis*) and justice—that provided the basic order governing the universe; anyone who defied these forces was sure to suffer. But most Greek deities were conceived of as having human forms and as conducting themselves much as earthly creatures did, except that the gods and goddesses were immortal and more powerful than humans. The most conspicuous and attractive deities were those who made up the tumultuous family of major gods and goddesses living on Mount Olympus under the authority of Zeus, whose position resembled that of an earthly father of a noble household. To each of these Olympian deities was ascribed a special role: Zeus was the father of the divine family, controller of the forces of nature; Hera, his wife, was the protectress of marriage and the family; Athena was the goddess of wisdom; Apollo was the bringer of light and patron of the arts; Ares was the god of war; Aphrodite was the goddess of beauty and love; and so on. One of these deities was often protector of an individual *polis*, so that the worship of the Olympian pantheon provided the basis for civic religion. Aside from the Olympian deities, the Greeks believed that the universe was filled with lesser spirits—nymphs, satyrs, demons, spirits of departed heroes and ancestors—who meddled constantly for good and bad in human affairs. A rich body of mythology developed to recount the activities of the deities and to describe their relationships with the human community. Learning that mythology was a fundamental aspect of the life of every Greek.

At least in the early centuries of their collective history, Greeks believed that the deities controlled human affairs. Therefore, individuals, families, and city-states had to attune their activities to divine will. There were fear-inspiring aspects of Greek religion, especially the inexorable working of fate and the taint of blood pollution that could fall on individuals, families, and even entire communities as divine retribution for such offenses as murder or incest. On the whole, however, the Greeks viewed their deities as benevolent, approachable, and concerned with human well-being. Although the gods and goddesses could be angry and unpredictable, they were too "human" to inflict a burden of terror on human beings. If humans learned the ways of the deities, bent to their will, and refrained from a prideful usurpation of their powers, they could expect divine support in gaining good fortune, long life, honor on earth, and success for their *polis*.

The Greeks devoted considerable energy and talent to pleasing their deities. In general, the gods and goddesses were not much concerned with moral behavior; they expected men and women to approach them in tangible ways. Prayers, sacrifices, and gifts were offered according to carefully defined rituals in shrines maintained in each home and by each clan. More impressive were the splendid civic cults, for which great temples were built and maintained at considerable expense to the city-states. Large numbers of people from all walks of life participated in these civic religious activities (see Figure 4.2). On occasion, the entire Greek world joined in honoring the Olympian pantheon; the Olympic Games, held every four years from 776 B.C. on, represented a pan-Hellenic celebration honoring Zeus. Almost every kind of human activity was acceptable as a way of praising the deities—athletic contests, poetry readings, songs, dances, dramatic presentations, and gift offerings. As a consequence, religious ceremonies were also cultural and social events. There were no elaborate priesthoods in Greece; fathers conducted rituals in households and clan centers, and public officials served as priests for civic ceremonies. Almost everyone depended heavily on the interpretation of dreams, the movement of the stars, and the entrails of animals to provide clues about divine intentions. But most of all, they relied on *oracles*, sacred places where the deities spoke through special agents to deliver responses to requests. The most famous oracle was at Delphi, where innumerable Greeks went to implore Apollo to tell them, usually through the mouth of a simple girl, how to solve problems ranging from personal matters to great political issues.

Alongside the religious life embodied in the cult of the Olympian deities was a more turbulent current involving cults which placed greater emphasis on personal and emotional needs. Rooted in the ancient worship of the regenerative forces of nature and deeply influenced by ideas and practices long familiar to peoples of the ancient Near East, these cults centered on a belief in a god or goddess who died and then came back to life to possess believers in a way that provided a mystical experience. The youthful wine god Dionysus was the center of such a cult. His worship, based on a belief that he had been torn to pieces by evil gods and then reborn (see pages 15–16 for a comparable concept in the Egyptian religion), involved his devotees in a highly emotional initiation ceremony and in ecstatic rites involving wild dancing, drinking, and the eating of raw flesh. A comparable cult, with its center at Eleusis near Athens, developed around the worship of the fertility goddess Demeter and her daughter Persephone, raised from the dead by her mother's efforts. Over time, the mystery cults became more subdued and respectable, as illustrated by the poorly understood movement called Orphism, which modified Dionysus worship by emphasizing the need for austere, ethical conduct as a way of pleasing Dionysus and winning escape from the material world into a happy hereafter.

In providing answers to many fundamental questions about the universe, religion fulfilled spiritual, psychological, and social functions that powerfully affected the way the Greeks lived. Its basic beliefs and practices asserted a significant influence on the religious history of later ages. Beyond that, religion provided both a framework and a stimulant for intellectual and artistic growth. Religious beliefs and values deeply rooted in the fabric of society constantly needed to be explained and clarified by writers and artists, a process that established a link between Greek daily life and cultural activity. Religion posed questions about the cosmos and about human nature that invited constant rethinking and reformulation of concepts common to all Greeks. Religion supplied writers, artists, and philosophers with themes and motifs that allowed them to communicate with the public in familiar terms. Although Greek thought and expression developed along paths that transcended the worldview defined by Greek religion, Greek culture never completely lost contact with its religious roots.

2. LITERATURE

Greek literature represented a magnificent outburst of creativity emerging from a substratum of religious themes and evolving along lines that reshaped religious consciousness. It was born in glory with two epic poems attributed to Homer, the *Iliad* and the *Odyssey*, probably set down in the eighth century B.C. Behind them lay a long tradition of oral poetry sung by bards for aristocratic audiences who loved to hear of the deeds of Mycenaean heroes. Homer, who remains a shadowy figure, drew these oral threads together into unified compositions of great artistry and dramatic power. The *Iliad* recounts the feats of a circle of heroes during a brief period in the war which the Mycenaean Greeks waged against Troy to avenge the theft of a Greek woman, Helen, by Paris, the prince of Troy. Although filled with an array of striking characters, the poem's central figure is Achilles, whose inflated pride (*hubris*) and misdirected anger cause many warriors to die and threaten to destroy the Greeks before he is brought to his senses and takes his place as a great warrior able to turn the tide of battle. The *Odyssey* is an adventure story celebrating the clever talents of one of the heroes at Troy, Odysseus, who needs ten years to overcome a variety of obstacles preventing his return from Troy to his homeland and his patient, long-suffering wife, Penelope. Not a little of the appeal of these epics lies in their gripping plots; but they have other dimensions. They create a heroic picture of men and women—but particularly men—who assume responsibility for their actions by virtue of their courage, their sense of honor, and their urge to prove their excellence. Homer's heroes served as models for noble character and action for all Greeks and for many people in later ages.

For all its richness, the epic genre could not contain the Greek literary genius. In about 700 B.C. the poet Hesiod wrote *Works and Days*, a guide to the ways of farming into which is woven a bitter lament about injustice heaped on simple farmers by the greed of the rich and powerful, and *Theogony*, a summary of Greek mythology that played an important role in defining the nature and the role of the Greek deities. The forces unleashed in the city-states evolving during the Archaic Age encouraged writers to formulate their individual reactions to life and to give vent to their personal feelings, producing an outburst of lyric poetry that gave new dimensions to literary expression. Among the best lyricists were Archilochus of Paros, Alcaeus of Mytilene, and above all the poetess Sappho of Lesbos. A

woman of aristocratic origins who ran a school for young women, Sappho composed lyrics celebrating the beauties of nature and the joys of everyday life and expressing her erotic feelings toward young women placed in her charge (later ages coined a word for female homosexuality—lesbianism—from the name of Sappho's native island). The nobility and force of Greek lyric poetry were perhaps best exemplified by Pindar of Thebes (ca. 518–441 B.C.), most of whose works took the form of choral songs in honor of athletes victorious in the competitions held at religious festivals. His poems set forth the classic view of aristocratic (in the Greek sense of "the best") qualities.

The burgeoning poetic talent reflected in epic and lyric poetry reached full fruition with the development of tragic drama, perhaps the greatest literary achievement of the Greeks. Tragedy originated in the dramatic choruses and hymns developed in connection with the worship of the god Dionysus. By the late sixth century B.C., the dramatic element in these rituals was greatly expanded to allow poets to create parts for actors who retold the deeds of the deities and heroes enshrined in Greek mythology and provided comments on the meaning of these deeds through choral interludes. This developing dramatic art suddenly burst forth in full maturity during the fifth century in the works of three of the world's greatest tragedians, all living in Athens amid the flowering of democracy and the rise and fall of the Athenian Empire. Taken together, their dramas probe deeply into the forces at work in the cosmic order and in human nature to draw human beings into tragic situations and provide profound insights into the resources that human beings possess that allow them to face their tragic fate with courage and determination.

The first was Aeschylus (525–456 B.C.). He wrote about ninety plays, only seven of which survive. His tragedies spell out with great power the consequences that result from prideful human transgressions of the dictates of the divine powers. His most impressive surviving work is a cycle of three plays called the *Orestia*, which employs the well-known legend of the family of Agamemnon to portray the tragic fate resulting from violation of the divine order against spilling the blood of one's own kin. Aeschylus had a genius for making his suffering characters noble and admirable, capable of bearing their burden of punishment with dignity and even with understanding. Implicit in his plays is a warning to his audience to curb pride (*hubris*) and to respect the deities who control the cosmic order.

Sophocles (495–405 B.C.), a citizen active in Athenian political life, produced a large number of plays, all but seven now lost. His dramas remained closely bound to the traditional themes provided by religion, but his interest is more human, more intent on searching out the psychological effects of suffering on humans who ran afoul of the gods and goddesses. He portrays suffering as an uplifting and purifying experience. Many would argue that Sophocles' *King Oedipus* is the greatest tragedy ever written. Essentially it is a drama that reveals the measure of the human spirit by showing the response of a heroic individual to a situation not of his making. Oedipus' fateful act was unknowingly killing his father and marrying his own mother (from whence Sigmund Freud's Oedipus complex), vile deeds that violated nature's order and for which he had to atone. In presenting Oedipus' discovery of his crime and his acceptance of his fate, Sophocles evokes a powerful celebration of the greatness of human beings. No less noble is the heroine of *Antigone*, a woman destroyed because she obeyed divine law in the face of the demands of human authority.

Euripides (480–406 B.C.) was a dramatist profoundly touched by the growing disillusionment, skepticism, and pessimism of the later fifth century—the generation of the Peloponnesian War. He utilized tragedy as a vehicle for posing profound questions about human values and problems in a way that arouses the suspicion that human powers are limited. His plays represent a search for some understanding of the dark and frightening passions that overpower reason with tragic consequences. That theme is explored with special force in his *Medea*, which portrays the ordeal of a woman whose desertion by her husband so fills her with rage and a desire for vengeance that she kills her children. Again and again Euripides casts doubt on conventional moral values and accepted religious beliefs. But from his incessant probing emerges a picture of humanity that is fuller and subtler—if not nobler—than the portraits drawn by Aeschylus and Sophocles.

Rivaling tragedy in public appeal was comic drama. Like tragedy, it developed out of religious ceremony, especially the ribald songs associated with the worship of Dionysus. By the fifth century, comedy had evolved into a distinct art form intended to inform and entertain audiences by satirical treatment of current politics and social affairs. The master of this form was Aristophanes (ca. 445–385 B.C.), a conservative Athenian whose comedies held up for scorn democratic politicians and institutions, artists and philosophers, and Athenian social mores. Typical is his play *Lysistrata*, in which Aristophanes voiced his own strong feeling about the folly of the Peloponnesian War by describing the plan of Athenian women to deny their husbands any sexual pleasures until they end the war; the audience is told, "We'll soon get Peace, be sure of that."

Prose literature long lingered in the shadow of poetry, but during the fifth century B.C. two historians produced works that demonstrated the Greek genius in that mode of expression. The first was Herodotus (ca. 484–425 B.C.), who wrote a history of the wars between the Greeks and Persians. His work is based on information he gathered through his travels and his search of written records. The result is a dramatic, colorful account of the events tracing the struggle between Greeks and Persians that Herodotus believed not only decided the fate of the Greek world but also revealed the superiority of the Greek way of life. The second major Greek historian was Thucydides (ca. 460–400 B.C.), whose *History of the Peloponnesian War* is one of the great works of historical literature. With unflagging energy he searched out information related to the details of the military campaigns and the political maneuvers associated with the war in which he was personally involved. On the basis of that evidence he compiled a moving narrative account that not only described the course of the war but also provided a critical analysis of the human motives and social forces that stoked that destructive struggle. His study lays bare a compelling picture of the folly, nobility, chicanery, and bravery of which human beings under stress are capable. His astute analysis of the evidence leads one to the conclusion that the Athenians caused that terrible struggle because of their *hubris* and lost it because of their contempt for moral principles and their cynical pursuit of power. Not only did Herodotus and Thucydides produce great literary works; they also pioneered a method of rational inquiry about past human activity based on the objective search for and verification of evidence about what had happened upon which could be based a rational reconstruction and explanation of the past in human terms free of the mythical elements that had governed the approach to the past up to their time. To this day their histories represent an ideal toward which all historians strive: to find the truth about the past and to let it enrich the understanding of the present.

3. ART

The fundamental characteristics of the Greek visual arts were shaped during the Archaic Age through a complex process involving adaptation of Near Eastern models and experimentation with new ideas and techniques. During that period pottery painters established basic themes and conventions for representing humans and animals in action. Sculptors slowly perfected a unique style of portraying the nude male and draped female figures. Although drawing heavily on mythology for their subject matter, these artists increasingly relied on what they saw in their own world to shape their treatment of mythological figures and themes. Out of these observations emerged concepts defining proportion, balance, and movement in new and unique ways. Also during the Archaic Age, architects developed a basic style for temples and other public buildings, which were increasingly built in stone: a rectangular ground plan whose elevation featured columns surrounding an inner temple chamber and low-pitched roofs. In all these art forms artists showed an increasing concern with proportion and balance, reflecting the impact of rational thought on artistic expression. Painters, sculptors, and architects received increasing support from the city-state, whose leaders and citizens were interested in beautifying their *polis* and in elaborating civic religions.

By the beginning of the fifth century, the long apprenticeship was over; a burst of creativity produced a golden age in art. Athens became the focal point of artistic excellence. The city's crowning glory was the complex of buildings constructed on the Acropolis, the hill dominating the *polis*. Under the sponsorship of Pericles and with funds derived from gifts by wealthy citizens and increasingly from tribute paid by the subject city-states of the Athenian Empire, three major temples were built there during the fifth century: the Parthenon, the Erectheum, and the temple to Victorious Athena. A splendid stairway and gate called the Propylaea gave access to the Acropolis, now the center of Athenian civic religion (see Figure 4.1). The Parthenon, portions of which still stand, embodied the basic features of classical Greek architecture (see Figure 6.2). Built in honor of Athena, it is modest in size (228 by 101 feet). Its two inner chambers, serving as shrines, are surrounded by simple, unadorned columns (in a style called Doric), seventeen on each side and eight on each end, which support the roof and create covered colonnades and entry vestibules. Its majesty stems chiefly from its simplicity, its proportions, its unity, and its balance. The total effect derives not only from the logic of its conception but also from subtle technical touches. For example, the middle of every long horizontal line is slightly higher than the ends to avoid the impression of sagging. The other Acropolis temples and the Propylaea incorporate the same features as the Parthenon, all adjusted to the size of each structure. The only basic departure was the utilization of slightly more slender and ornate columns (in the Ionic style), which add grace and lightness. The same basic principles were applied to a variety of other public buildings—theaters, gymnasia, marketplaces, meeting halls—constructed in Athens and other city-states.

The Greek style of architecture provided ample spaces for sculptors and painters to lend their talents in beautifying buildings. Their response brought Greek sculpture to its culmination, exemplified by the works of Phidias (ca. 500–432 B.C.), Polyclitus (ca. 452–412 B.C.), and Praxiteles (ca. 400–320 B.C.). Phidias was in charge of designing the sculptural program adorning the Parthenon. Unfortunately, his statues in the round, especially the famed statue of Athena in the inner chamber of the Parthenon, have been lost and are known only through copies and literary texts; that evidence suggests his skill in portraying divine figures in terms that captured both their majesty and their human qualities. His talents

FIGURE 6.2 The Parthenon This magnificent example of Greek architecture was the chief structure among a complex of temples adorning the Athenian Acropolis (see Figure 4.1). Begun in the Golden Age of Pericles and dedicated to Athena, its distinctive horizontal lines, stately Doric columns, and measured proportions typify the classical Greek architectural style. The pediments above the columns and the triangular space created by the roof were filled with sculpture celebrating Greek deities and portraying themes from Greek mythology. (Marburg)

are also reflected in the surviving remnants of a continuous frieze of carved reliefs extending around the walls of that same inner chamber to depict a procession in honor of Athena. These scenes, which portray ordinary people engaged in various pursuits relating to everyday life, reflect the power of Greek artists to represent the human scene in realistic terms. The external entablature (that part of the structure built atop the columns to support the roof) and pediments (the triangular structures filling the spaces created by the roof gables at each end of the temple) were covered with powerful representations of divine activities drawn from mythology. Polyclitus devoted his talents chiefly to shaping bronze statues of young men (see Color Plate 3—left). Praxiteles created splendid versions of gods and goddesses in human form (see Figure 6.3 and Color Plate 3—right). All of this sculpture focuses on the portrayal of the idealized human body; the figures are dignified, restrained, beautifully proportioned, filled with the potential for action. The effect of viewing them is to catch a vision of the nobility and the power of human beings extracted from the real world in which human beings lived and acted (see Figure 6.1). Little has survived of Greek painting, except for pottery painting (see Figure 4.2). There is evidence, however, from literary sources that large-scale paintings decorated temples and public buildings. For example, Polygnotus (mid–fifth century B.C.) decorated a colonnade in the Athenian *agora*, the area where political meetings and market activities took place, with painted scenes depicting episodes from the Trojan War. It is highly likely that Greek painting reflected the same traits as the sculpture: idealization of the human figure, balance, restraint, and dignity.

FIGURE 6.3 Hermes with the Infant Dionysus Most likely the work of the famed sculptor Praxiteles, this statue is an excellent example of Greek artistic canons; the gods are taken as subject matter and portrayed in an idealized human form that emphasizes physical perfection rather than spiritual qualities. (Alinari/Art Resource)

4. PHILOSOPHY AND SCIENCE

The feature that most sharply distinguished Greek thought from that of earlier civilizations found expression in philosophy and science, areas of inquiry the Greeks considered to be interdependent. Thinkers in these realms explored a new way of describing and explaining the cosmic order, the natural world, and human society that depended on rational interpretation of phenomena open to human observation. This rationalistic approach eventually touched almost every sphere of Greek political, social, and cultural life in some way and became one of the most enduring bequests left by the Greeks to later history.

Why the Greeks made this revolutionary intellectual leap escapes easy explanation. Until the sixth century B.C., most Greeks, like their Near Eastern predecessors, were content to accept the explanations provided by mythology to describe the nature of the universe and the place of human beings in it. Then, during the sixth century, some thinkers began to move beyond the mythological world view in search of rational explanations of the cosmos. Perhaps such inquiries were prompted by the ferment surrounding the efforts in the late Archaic Age to reshape the structure of many city-states to cope with pressing economic and social problems. The first speculative thinkers came from Greek city-states in Asia Minor and southern Italy, suggesting that perhaps interactions with foreign ways of looking at the universe posed questions to which only reason could provide answers.

The prime concern of these early speculative thinkers was to find a simple, unifying principle that would describe and explain rationally what constituted the universe and what made it work. This quest gave rise to diverse, contradictory answers, often based on imaginative interpretations of physical evidence but also marked by bold insights that have long fascinated those concerned with *cosmology*, that is, inquiry into the origins and nature of the universe. In general terms, the speculations of the Greek cosmologists fell into two broad schools of thought. One such school, originally centered in Ionia, developed a materialistic explanation that argued that some form of matter, such as air or water or fire, was the basic substance out of which all other things emerged through processes inherent in the nature of that substance. This materialistic approach reached its culmination with Democritus (ca. 460–370 B.C.), who propounded an atomic theory according to which the universe is composed of indivisible particles floating at random in empty space; by mere chance these atoms combined into beings and objects and by the same chance decomposed to end existing things. Another school of thought rejected materialism and sought the key to the universe in some nonmaterial force. Perhaps the source of this approach was the sixth-century B.C. thinker Pythagoras, whose career combined scientific interest with a strong religious bent. He argued that the basis of cosmic order lay in a numerical relationship among its many parts. Equally influential in shaping this school was Heraclitus (flourished ca. 500 B.C.), who insisted that change was the essence of the material world and therefore no simplistic physical explanation of the universe could have meaning. This whole school of thinkers ultimately concluded that a nonmaterial, changeless being, endowed with perfect intelligence, supplied the creative force of order in the universe. Despite their divergent views, the early thinkers shared one thing: Their explanations of the universe challenged the traditional mythological explanations based on arbitrary, irrational divine powers. Their thinking posited an ordered universe which could be understood through the power of human reason.

Although Greek thinkers continued to seek an explanation of the fundamental nature of the universe, about the middle of the fifth century B.C. rational inquiry increasingly focused on the human condition. A diverse group of thinkers, collectively called the Sophists, led the way into this new realm. The Sophists were primarily professional teachers interested in preparing their pupils for roles in public life. They rejected speculative philosophy on the grounds that objective truth was nonexistent, as demonstrated by the contradictory schemes put forward by prior thinkers. In the words of one of the chief Sophists, Protagoras (485–410 B.C.), a famous teacher in Periclean Athens, men and women were the measure of all things. Human reason should be dedicated to a search for the kind of knowledge that would be useful to humans in their quest for happy, useful lives. Since most Sophists believed that institutions and standards of behavior were human creations, not the results of an unchangeable natural order, they felt justified in criticizing traditional religious ideas, moral values, and laws and in urging their disciples to seek rules of life that were workable and beneficial. Their attacks led to widespread condemnation of the Sophists as skeptics and destroyers of morality and order. But their arguments deepened the awareness of fundamental ethical issues and encouraged their disciples to trust the power of reason, honed by rigorous training, as an instrument for improving the human condition. The intellectual ferment resulting from their philosophical relativism led to a new search for absolute truth that produced the greatest Greek philosophers.

One of these was Socrates (ca. 469–399 B.C.), an Athenian famous in his own time as a provocative teacher. He left no writings; he set forth his ideas orally in the Athenian *agora*, where he engaged all comers in debate about philosophical issues. From what his pupils remembered about his teaching, it appears that Socrates sought to counter the relativism of the Sophists by insisting on the existence of universal truths which provide objective standards defining moral excellence. Human beings were prevented from discovering these truths by their own ignorance. That ignorance could be dispelled only by active mental endeavor involving rigorous, logical self-examination of beliefs. The Socratic method consisted of asking questions until the error of someone who claimed to know something was exposed and then leading the mind through further questioning to the truth by way of precise definition and exact logic. Socrates' goal was to get people to understand themselves and to conduct their lives by the light of their reason. Although he attracted an eager following for many years, his gadfly tactics eventually led to trouble. In 399 B.C., amid the bitterness surrounding the Athenian defeat in the Peloponnesian War, he was accused of corrupting youth and sentenced to die. Refusing to compromise his principles in order to gain a lighter sentence from the jury of his fellow citizens, he accepted their verdict of guilt and drank the fatal poison.

Plato (427–347 B.C.) carried on the work of Socrates, his master. He spent most of his career as a teacher in a school which he founded in

Athens called the Academy. His voluminous works, elegantly written in dialogue form, provide a sometimes confusing but always challenging record of his thought. Plato was a philosophical idealist; his work brought to full maturity the nonmaterialist philosophical tradition dating back to the sixth century B.C.. He argued that the fundamental realities in the universe are ideas, or abstract forms, which define eternal and absolute standards of good, truth, and justice. The so-called realities that humans perceive with their senses are but imperfect reflections of the perfect universal forms. He likened sense perceptions gained from the material world to shadows cast on the wall of a cave by those moving about in front of a fire; neither is more than a dim, fuzzy, constantly changing image of ultimate reality. For example, the justice practiced in Athens was only a shadowy reflection of perfect justice; a man or a woman is but a pale image of a higher reality, humanity. Plato argued that by pure reasoning the human mind could reach beyond the level of comprehension provided by the senses to an understanding of the higher reality of forms. Only such wisdom could define truth and provide the basis for the good life.

Plato's dialogues center on an attempt to define by rational means the ideas or forms that constitute ultimate reality and to make that wisdom applicable to the problems of human existence. His best-known dialogue, *The Republic*, illustrates his idealism, his method, and his earnest concern for the human condition. This work, undoubtedly shaped in part by Plato's disillusionment with political life in fourth-century B.C. Athens, seeks to define the model *polis* that would provide the ideal setting in which the social nature of human beings could be realized. Plato assumes that the purpose of the state is to achieve justice, the ideal state being an earthly embodiment of the perfect idea of justice. Arguing that justice consists of each individual doing that for which he or she is best fitted, Plato defined the ideal state as one in which every person holds that station and does that job for which he or she is best qualified by nature. Since Plato defined human nature in terms of a hierarchy of capacities, his ideal state would be hierarchically structured. Most humans are suited to work; a lesser number are endowed with qualities that suit them for defending the community; and a

very few have the rational power that enables them to grasp truth and act with virtue. To these philosopher-kings must be entrusted the power to rule. Capable of shunning power and wealth by virtue of their wisdom, they alone have the capacity to formulate the laws that would establish a harmonious order in which everyone else would serve the community by doing what each is best qualified to do. Philosopher-kings alone have the ability to convince their subjects to accept what is best for them, even if that sometimes requires a "noble lie." In short, for Plato the perfect society requires an authoritarian political order in which those who are wise by virtue of their rational powers have the obligation to direct the lives of their less-well-endowed subjects in the interest of achieving ideal justice.

In his other dialogues Plato conducts a comparable search for an understanding of the nature of love, friendship, courage, the soul—in fact, virtually the whole range of those elements that constitute the ultimate reality lying behind the appearance of things. In distinguishing between the realm of pure ideas and the material world of the senses, Plato posed issues about what reality is and how it can be comprehended that since his time have been a major stimulant to philosophical inquiry.

The challenge of the Platonic system was central to the career of Aristotle (384–322 B.C.), Plato's most brilliant and productive pupil. As a youth, he came to Athens from northern Greece to study at the Academy. After Plato's death, he spent some time in Macedonia, perhaps as tutor to young Alexander the Great. He then returned to Athens and founded his own school, the Lyceum. His followers were called the Peripatetics (from the Greek for "to walk up and down") because Aristotle often walked about while lecturing. Aristotle produced a massive body of philosophical work dealing with such diverse topics as the physical sciences, political theory, psychology, ethics, and literary theory. Perhaps typical of effective teachers in all ages, he had a passion for systematizing and organizing knowledge, so that his works constitute a kind of encyclopedia of the total learning of the ancient world.

Aristotle's thought was undergirded by an original concept of ultimate being. Although influenced by Platonic idealism, Aristotle arrived at a different position. In his seminal *Metaphysics*, he argues that reality consists of a combination of matter and form (or idea). The form gives each object its shape, but it has no reality separate from the matter in which it exists and can be discerned only by studying things existing and happening in the material world. Every object has some purpose in a larger universal order; its perfection consists in serving that purpose. Behind the wilderness of individual objects lies an ultimate "cause," a higher force that animates everything. The philosopher's path is from the study of material objects toward an understanding of that higher force; such a quest would result in the formulation of concepts that would allow a comprehension of the nature of the entire universe and its operation.

In most of his works Aristotle pursued the course laid down in his *Metaphysics*. His *Politics* provides an illustration of his method. Starting with the assumption that human beings are political animals who cannot fulfill their true nature unless they are members of a state devoted to the promotion of virtue, he seeks to define possible political systems. On the basis of a study of the history and organization of more than a hundred and fifty Greek city-states, he concludes that the state as a "form" manifests itself in three basic systems: monarchy, aristocracy, and limited democracy, each of which is legitimate if it serves the general welfare. However, each form can be perverted when the ruling element—king, aristocrats, or people—seeks power to serve its own ends; monarchy becomes tyranny, aristocracy becomes oligarchy, and limited democracy becomes anarchy (the worst of all governments). Aristotle's analysis of these forms clarifies the unique consequences for human beings of each type of state, thus providing the rational basis for selecting the type of government best suited to the particular situation in which any community finds itself. In his *Ethics* Aristotle asks how men and women should conduct their individual lives and argues that happiness is the proper goal of every human action. Men and women can be happy and good only if they use reason to control the passionate elements in their nature and if they behave with moderation, seeking always to avoid doing anything in excess.

Aristotle's writings made an important contribution to epistemology, that branch of philosophy which seeks to define how human knowledge is acquired. In some cases, such as in his *Politics*, his method of seeking truth was inductive—that is, formulating generalizations on the basis of particular pieces of evidence gained by observing phenomena occurring in the world. Inductive thinking would play a crucial role in the advancement of science. However, he also used deduction, a mode of thinking that employs the rules of formal logic to extract the truth about particular things from premises defining general truths. Aristotle's treatment of the rules of formal logic provided a tool that shaped philosophical inquiry for centuries to come.

Aristotle's works dealing with the physical and biological sciences mark the culmination and provide a summary of what had been accomplished by a sustained interest in natural science among the Greeks extending back at least two centuries before his time. That interest resulted in significant work in astronomy, physics, botany, zoology, physiology, and geography. Although Greek scientists relied heavily on data about the natural world compiled by Mesopotamians and Egyptians, they made significant additions to scientific knowledge by their own observations of natural phenomena. Illustrative of this approach is the work of Hippocrates (460–377 B.C.), a practicing physician to whom is attributed the famous oath still used today to define the responsibilities of a physician. He insisted that nothing could be known about sickness except through observation of sick people and through a search for the natural causes of illness. He repudiated the traditional belief that sickness was due to evil spirits; it was a result of natural causes, and the cure for sickness was a natural process that could be controlled. He collected information about the curative power of drugs and about the effects of diet on health. The collective efforts of Greek scientists allow us to credit the Greeks with the invention of the scientific method, which relies on observation as the source of knowledge about nature. Lacking precision instruments, their observations were often imprecise and their interpretations of data erroneous. Moreover, few were interested in using their knowledge for practical purposes. Scientific knowledge was employed chiefly by philosophers seeking to explain the workings of the universe.

5. THE GREEK SPIRIT

In reflecting on the whole range of Greek achievements in literature, art, philosophy, and science, some common themes emerge that, taken together, give Greek culture its distinctive quality. Greek thought was intensely *humanistic*, concerned with defining the position of humans in the cosmic order, measuring human potential, and finding ways to enlarge human capabilities. Greek culture was *rationalistic*; its creators placed trust in the ability of human beings to understand nature and themselves through human intelligence and to act on the basis of rational decisions to resolve human problems. Rationalism emphasized the need to seek *order* and *symmetry* in all things and to act with *restraint* and *balance* in individual and collective life. Greek culture was animated by a *spirit of inquiry* that constantly pushed thinkers and artists toward new knowledge and new ways of expressing themselves. Greek thought began to map out a realm of *freedom*, where human beings could make responsible decisions shaping their political and moral destinies. These values combined to constitute a cultural ideal that asserted a powerful formative influence on later societies; we shall encounter these ideas again and again in tracing Western history.

It is difficult to ascertain the extent to which these basic values impacted on the lives of ordinary Greeks. Probably most Greeks, engaged in the routine of daily life, seldom paused to think about what their cultural values were or meant, just as most modern men and women seldom dwell on this question. But one thing does seem certain: An ordinary Greek would have had trouble escaping contact with the cultural achievements just described. The best of Greek thought on the human condition was made available to all citizens as an intimate dimension of civic life. Poetry readings accompanied religious ceremonies and athletic contests. The best drama was played out in public theaters. Philosophers wrangled in the streets, joined their fellow citizens in *symposia*, and taught in schools. Architects and sculptors devoted their best efforts to civic art. It seems inconceivable that any citizen could have escaped being touched by some of the values reflected in the most notable cultural artifacts created in the Greek world.

However, we must be cautious in assuming that all Greeks prized the values that modern historians have discerned as setting Greek culture apart from that of their predecessors. There were other facets of Greek cultural life that defined alternative and conflicting values. Many cultured Greeks, including leading intellectuals, were not prepared to ascribe to *all* humans the qualities noted above—among lesser creatures were women, slaves, "barbarians" (defined as those who did not speak Greek), and even some citizens. Greek culture was elitist, aristocratic in spirit, exclusive. Those who articulated the values so much admired by later generations were openly challenged by their intellectual peers and repudiated by public opinion; the fate of Socrates is a case in point. Anyone who follows Greek political history in detail or reads Greek drama or grapples with the discourse of Greek philosophers soon becomes aware of powerful currents shaping the Greek mentality other than those noted above. Political issues were often decided by oracles and omens sought out by "enlightened" leaders rather than by reasoned deliberation and votes. Belief in the power of some transcendental force—be it the Olympian deities or fate or supreme reason—to control human destiny remained a central feature of the worldview not only of common citizens but also of dramatists and philosophers. The mythical heroes that philosophers sought to debunk remained as models for human behavior. Traditional mores defined standards of individual and social behavior despite the efforts of moralists and social critics to point out their irrational features. The Greek spirit was multifaceted, not monolithic. Perhaps those aspects of Greek culture singled out above made a greater difference in the history of Western civilization than others did, but they by no means define the Greek spirit in its entirety.

SUGGESTED READING

General Cultural History

François Chamoux, *The Civilization of Greece*, trans. W. S. Maguinness (1965). A perceptive overview, well illustrated.

John Boardman et al., eds., *The Oxford History of the Classical World* (1986). Excellent studies of varied aspects of Greek civilization.

Religion

Robert Graves, *The Greek Myths* (1955; illustrated edition, 1981). A full description of the myths undergirding Greek religion.

Walter Burkert, *Greek Religion: Archaic and Classical*, trans. John Raffan (1985). A masterful treatment.

Walter Burkert, *Ancient Mystery Cults* (1987). A well-done guide.

Literature

Jacqueline de Romilly, *A Short History of Greek Literature*, trans. Lillian Doherty (1985).

Peter Levi, *A History of Greek Literature* (1985).

Either of these recent works will provide invaluable guides to the main currents of Greek literary history.

Charles Rowan Beye, *Ancient Greek Literature and Society*, 2nd rev. ed. (1988). A stimulating effort to put Greek literature into its social context.

Art

John Boardman, *Greek Art*, new and rev. ed. (1985). An excellent brief treatment.

Richard Brilliant, *Arts of Ancient Greece* (1973).

Jean Charbonneaux et al., *Classical Greek Art (480–330 B.C.)*, trans. James Emmons (1972).

These longer treatments, both illustrated, provide a rich appreciation of the Greek artistic accomplishment.

J. J. Pollitt, *Art and Experience in Classical Greece* (1972).

Jeffrey M. Hurwit, *The Art and Culture of Early Greece, 1100–400 B.C.* (1985).

Two challenging treatments of the social and intellectual foundations of Greek art.

Philosophy and Science

Rex Warner, *Greek Philosophers* (1958).

W. K. C. Guthrie, *Greek Philosophers: From Thales to Aristotle* (1960).

Although old, either of these two works will provide a good introduction to the Greek accomplishment in philosophy.

Jean-Pierre Vernant, *The Origins of Greek Thought* (1982). A challenging study stressing the uniqueness of Greek thought.

H. D. Rankin, *Sophists, Socratics, and Cynics* (1983). A balanced treatment of the major schools of philosophy in Greece.

G. B. Kerferd, *The Sophistic Movement* (1981). A full treatment.

G. E. R. Lloyd, *Early Greek Science: Thales to Aristotle* (1970). A thorough assessment of the Greek accomplishments in science.

K. D. White, *Greek and Roman Technology* (1984). A well-done assessment of Greek accomplishments in technology.

Sources

Michael Grant, ed., *Greek Literature: An Anthology in Translation* (1973). A rich sampling that will tempt a reader to read Greek writers in their entirety. Good translations of the works of all the authors mentioned in this chapter are easily available.

CHAPTER 7

Greek Imperialism: The Hellenistic World, 336–31 B.C.

FIGURE 7.1 Alexander the Great
This Roman copy of an original bust of Alexander the Great (perhaps done by the fourth-century B.C. sculptor Lycippus) attempts to capture the strength and idealism of a great hero of the ancient world. (Giraudon/Art Resource)

Although many Greeks feared that the coming of the "barbarian" Macedonians spelled doom for Hellenism, the Macedonian conquest set the stage for a new chapter in the history of the Greeks. Under Macedonian leadership, they exploded out of their Aegean-centered world to establish mastery over a wide area of Asia and Africa. Their genius and their traditions began to mix with those of the Near Eastern civilizations to produce a new culture that historians have called "Hellenistic."

1. ALEXANDER THE GREAT

The Greek-Macedonian world was launched into this new phase in its history under the charismatic leadership of Alexander the Great (see Figure 7.1). Imbued with a deep admiration for Greek culture absorbed at the court of his father, Philip II, Alexander drew on his towering ambition, restless energy, iron will, and military genius to achieve feats in the cause of Hellenism that have never ceased to fascinate students of history.

Only twenty when his father died in 336 B.C., Alexander turned to a project that Philip had already planned, the crusade against the hated enemy of the Greeks, the Persians (see Map 7.1). Although Persia possessed a huge empire, a rich treasury, and a large army and navy, Alexander was victorious from the beginning. His initial campaigns, begun in 334 B.C., were aimed at depriving the Persians of control of the coastal cities of Asia Minor and Phoenicia, the chief source of Persian naval power. Shortly after entering Asia Minor, Alexander overpowered a major Persian force at a battle on the Granicus River; this victory ensured control of the Greek cities along the east coast of the Aegean Sea. From there he moved into Syria and in 333 B.C. won a brilliant victory at Issus. This victory solidified Alexander's control of Asia Minor and opened the way for his conquest of Syria, Palestine, and Egypt. Then he marched on the center of Persian power in Mesopotamia and in the spring of 331 B.C. destroyed the last major military strength of the Persians at the battle of Gaugamela (Arbela). Following this victory, he occupied the major centers of Persian political power and hunted down the fugitive King Darius III, who was finally murdered in 330 B.C. by his own officials as Alexander closed in on him.

The conquest of the Persian Empire did not satisfy Alexander's ambition. During the next five years he drove on eastward. Battling vast distances, native resistance, and defection among his own troops, he relentlessly destroyed pockets of resistance led by Persian satraps in the regions of Parthia and Bactria. Then he pushed across the Hindu Kush Mountains into the Indus River Valley, a venture that brought the Greeks into direct contact with Indian civilization. Beyond the Indus Valley his troops refused to go. Alexander therefore turned back westward through southern Persia and into Mesopotamia, where he fell ill and died in June 323 B.C. at the age of thirty-three.

A career so short and so completely occupied with military campaigns left Alexander little time to face the problems of ruling his vast conquests. Probably he had no definite plans when he launched his campaign, but before he died he had made decisions establishing certain broad policies that guided his successors. He moved toward creating a style of rulership that cast him in the role of divinely sanctioned autocrat, a kind of rulership foreign to both Greeks and Macedonians. He at least toyed with the idea of combining the talents of conquered peoples, especially Persians, with those of the conquerors to create a cosmopolitan elite to control his empire. However, his followers found this policy unacceptable, forcing him to take steps to ensure that Greeks and Macedonians would dominate his empire. This plan required their migration to Asia and Africa, a move that Alexander sought to make attractive by establishing city-states in which the newcomers would have a special place. However, aside from his conquests, Alexander's accomplishments were few. His main influence on the course of history lay in his legend: what later generations believed he was trying to do.

2. HELLENISTIC POLITICAL DEVELOPMENTS

In the three centuries following his death, the political history of the vast area that Alexander conquered was not a simple one. Its complexity

Map 7.1 ALEXANDER'S EMPIRE AND ITS SUCCESSOR KINGDOMS This map dramatically depicts the magnitude of Alexander the Great's military accomplishment between 336 and 323 B.C. to create an empire even larger than those of the Assyrians and Persians. His success shaped a vast realm over which Greeks and Macedonians established their political, economic, and cultural mastery in a way that decisively changed the history of the entire area. The most intensive Hellenization occurred around the eastern end of the Mediterranean from Egypt through Palestine, Phoenicia, and Syria into Asia Minor. But the powerful force of Greek culture was also felt in Mesopotamia and still farther east.

stemmed primarily from the division of the empire. Immediately after Alexander's death a council of his generals tried to maintain a united empire ruled jointly by Alexander's son and half brother, but that plan failed amid mounting rivalry among the generals. Within a generation their rivalry had produced a hodgepodge of political entities of various sizes, strengths, and internal structures. By far the most prominent were the major kingdoms established by three of Al-

exander's companions: Antigonus in Macedonia and the Aegean world; Ptolemy in Egypt; and Seleucus in the vast area stretching from Asia Minor to India (see Map 7.1).

Only the briefest summary of the complex histories of these kingdoms can be undertaken here. The Macedonian kings sustained a fairly effective government during most of the third century B.C. Although the Antigonid dynasty always had ambitions to play a major role in the larger Hellenistic world, Macedonian political history centered chiefly on the efforts of the rulers to maintain hegemony over the Greek city-states and to hold back the attackers who were constantly pressing on the northern frontier of Macedonia. These were major burdens, testing the limited human and material resources of Macedonia. Control of the Greek city-states was particularly difficult. Claiming to act in the name of "freedom" for the *polis*, the Greeks constantly intrigued against their masters, often seeking help from outsiders. Macedonian efforts to defuse this resistance by interfering in local city-state political processes and establishing military garrisons in Greece only sharpened the resistance. Ultimately, the Macedonian kingdom was incapable of bearing the burden. Shortly before 200 B.C. some of the Greek city-states appealed to Rome for help against what they claimed was Macedonian interference with their freedom. In the ensuing wars, Roman armies conquered both Macedonia and Greece and absorbed them into Rome's expanding empire.

The kingdom established in Egypt by Ptolemy was the most stable Hellenistic state. The Ptolemaic dynasty quickly organized an autocratic regime modeled on the ancient Egyptian system of the pharaohs. The key to Ptolemaic power was a bureaucracy and a military force dominated by Greek-Macedonian immigrants. This regime skillfully exploited the native population and the agricultural and commercial resources of Egypt to sustain its power. Internal stability and wealth permitted the Ptolemies to play an active role in the larger Hellenistic world. They concentrated chiefly on extending their sphere of influence in Syria-Palestine, Asia Minor, and the Aegean world. These ambitions involved them in almost constant conflict, especially the Seleucid kingdom. By the second century B.C. the grip of the Ptolemies on Egypt began to weaken, chiefly because they were forced to rely increasingly on native Egyptians in the army and the bureaucracy and to make concessions limiting their own royal income. Growing internal unrest ultimately forced the rulers to seek support from the Romans. Eventually, in 30 B.C., Rome annexed Egypt to its empire.

The Seleucid kingdom had the most troubled history. Its huge size and mixed population provided little basis for unity except what its kings and their Greek-Macedonian followers could impose. Rather quickly the Seleucid rulers lost control over the area east of the Tigris-Euphrates Valley, where kingdoms of considerable importance to the future, including Bactria and Parthia, went their separate ways. In northern and western Asia Minor local rulers established small but virile kingdoms. Most of the Seleucid political energy was devoted to creating a viable state embracing Mesopotamia, Syria-Palestine, and southeastern Asia Minor. Royal authority was based chiefly on the military service provided by Greeks and Macedonians established in cities from which they dominated the native population. Attacks by outsiders, especially the Ptolemies, and internal native uprisings constantly threatened the Seleucids. Ultimately, the Seleucid kingdom was torn to pieces by internal strife and squeezed to death by Parthian pressure from the east and Roman intrusions from the west.

Numerous smaller states shared the political scene with the three major kingdoms. Chief among them were many old Greek city-states that remained independent and sought to continue their traditional pattern of governance. A good deal of the political energies of these city-states was devoted to internal affairs, which were often marked by bitter partisanship and class rivalry. But each also had to concern itself with the ambitions of other city-states and the threat of the great powers, especially Macedonia. Their fragile independence encouraged many city-states to develop techniques aimed at reducing intercity rivalry and strengthening the religious and cultural ties shared by all Greeks. Especially innovative was the development of effective leagues or federations based on some compromise of total autonomy in the interest of common action decided upon through shared political processes. Two particularly important leagues were the Aetolian League, which embraced several city-states in central Greece, and the Achaean League in northern Peloponnesus. Despite their continued existence, the old Greek city-states lost much of their power of self-determination during the Hellenistic Age. Among the smaller states of the era, the most successful were the Kingdom of Pergamum in western Asia Minor and the Republic of Rhodes, both of which fared well by capitalizing on commercial activity.

In this world of competing "successor" states into which Alexander's empire was divided, the conduct of interstate relations took on new intensity and sophistication. Great and small states developed techniques designed to ensure safety and to gain advantage over others: military force, diplomacy, psychological warfare, internal subversion, economic penetration, arrangements extending privileges to citizens of other states. In a general way, these techniques tended to promote a balance of power in the Hellenistic world. While that balance was constantly in the process of readjustment, it provided a degree of stability and security until the machinations sustaining it began to draw an emerging external power, Rome, into the scene.

The Hellenistic Age witnessed significant developments in terms of political ideology and institutions that had an important impact on the future, especially in providing models for the Romans. Despite their long enchantment with the small, autonomous *polis* as the ideal political entity, the Greeks' political vision expanded after Alexander. The experiences of the Hellenistic Age put into the Greek vocabulary and mentality a vision of a world state in which peoples of many kinds would share a common citizenship and a common destiny—a concept long familiar to the peoples they had conquered and most effectively manifested in the Persian Empire. Even more significant was the Greek acceptance of the concept of monarchy—an institution that had disappeared from the world of the *polis* as early as the eighth century B.C. During the Hellenistic Age monarchy became the standard form of government among the most successful Greek rulers who succeeded Alexander.

The system of monarchy practiced by the Greeks was shaped by the traditions of the Near East, but it reflected uniquely Greek qualities. In the Hellenistic monarchies the king's power was personal, deriving from his feats at arms, his intelligence, his will, and his favor with the deities. By virtue of his personal abilities, he could bestow blessings on his subjects. No constitution, entrenched nobility, or popular vote acted to limit his power. No law other than what he decreed was recognized. Such a concept of royal

power clearly reflected the Greek confidence in human ability. To exercise his vast powers effectively, the king of each Hellenistic kingdom relied on the advice of a circle of "friends" selected because of the king's confidence in their talents and loyalty. Each ruler developed a well-organized central government featuring a strong army, an elaborate bureaucracy, and an efficient taxation system. Greeks and Macedonians filled the chief positions in royal governments and controlled the old structures of local government, which were usually left intact.

Yet in this world tending toward larger political groupings, the idea and the reality of the *polis* lived on. We have already noted the survival of many of the old city-states in the Aegean basin during the Hellenistic Age. The large numbers of Greek and Macedonians who migrated across the Near East to serve Hellenistic kings congregated in cities—some ancient and many newly founded. Into their new settings the newcomers brought political institutions and practices from their native city-states. Assemblies, councils, popular courts, and elected magistrates were established to give the elite outsiders considerable control over local affairs. The Greeks and Macedonians in the Near East thus retained their ancient allegiance to the ideal of the small, intimate *polis*, as did their compatriots still living in old Greece. This continued attachment to the ideal of the *polis* detracted from a complete commitment to monarchy. Generally, the Hellenistic kings encouraged and supported the development of such nearly autonomous communities, chiefly because royal power depended on support from Greeks and Macedonians. At the same time concerns about retaining their ethnic identity and their elite position in political, social, and cultural life forced all Greeks in the Hellenistic world to seek the support of monarchs. As a result, strong, mutually beneficial bonds developed between the monarchs and the city-states of the Near East dominated by Greeks and Macedonians. The kings could usually count on the support of the local communities and, given their superior resources, were able to impose their will on these communities. Slowly but surely, monarchy overshadowed the *polis* as the decisive political force in the Hellenistic world. But the idea of the semiautonomous *polis* as a key component of a larger political entity took deep roots across a wide sweep of the eastern Mediterranean world.

3. HELLENISTIC ECONOMIC AND SOCIAL LIFE

Although the Hellenistic era brought prosperity to some areas and to particular groups, on the whole the economic impact of Greek-Macedonian expansion was modest, chiefly because it was not accompanied by changes in the basic structures of production. Agriculture remained the basic source of wealth in the Hellenistic world, but the new masters did not fundamentally change the established system. The conquerors claimed possession of a considerable portion of the agricultural land in their vast empire and imposed on native tenants and slaves the obligation to till the soil for their benefit. Some Greek owners, including especially the kings seeking revenue, undertook land clearance, new irrigation projects, crop rotation, and the introduction of new crops and equipment; but the resultant increase in production was modest and beneficial to only a few.

An increase in trading activity, promoted by the Hellenistic kings, provided a significant element of prosperity in some areas of the Hellenistic world, especially in a zone embracing the great cities of Egypt, Syria, and Asia Minor. Greek entrepreneurs played a significant role in exploiting the commercial potential of this area and in extending trade connections toward old Greece, Mesopotamia, India, China, the western Mediterranean, and sub-Saharan Africa. Extensive new capital was made available to these entrepreneurs when Alexander confiscated and put into circulation the vast treasury of the Persian kings and the wealth controlled by the Persian aristocracy. At least some of this wealth was invested in activities beneficial to commerce: harbors, roads, market facilities, ships, coinage systems, credit and banking operations. A variety of luxury items, often originating outside the Hellenistic world, as well as foodstuffs, metals, and timber products, moved through the commercial network crisscrossing the Hellenistic world. Industrial activity, carried on chiefly by

native artisans operating small establishments devoted to products needed by the populace of each city, constituted a significant element of the Hellenistic economy. The surviving evidence suggests that there was no great increase in industrial production and no fundamental change in the organization of manufacturing. Especially noteworthy was the lack of technical progress. Despite some remarkable advances in the level of scientific knowledge, almost no effort was made in applying that knowledge to manufacturing, probably because of the vast supply of cheap native labor and slavery.

Whatever economic expansion there was during the Hellenistic period benefited only a few in society—chiefly the newly established Greek-Macedonian rulers and the immigrants who followed them. With the exception of a few natives who adopted Greek ways, most natives were economically exploited. As the Hellenistic era progressed, the gap between the wealthy "foreign" masters and the poor native farmers, city laborers, and slaves widened. Moreover, economic prosperity was not evenly distributed geographically; its effects were felt chiefly in the belt extending from Egypt around the eastern end of the Mediterranean into Asia Minor. Increasingly impoverished were the old Greek city-states in the Aegean area, where depopulation and even starvation were not uncommon.

In both the old Greek world and the vast area conquered by Alexander, established social patterns persisted during the Hellenistic period. In the old Greek city-states family structures and social practices governing daily life remained much as they had been in the fifth century. The chief change involved growing disparities in wealth, which hardened class lines, and social tensions, which bred conflict and even violence. In "new Hellas" native life was little disturbed by the coming of the Greeks; for most people Greek masters merely replaced Persians. Perhaps the chief new social phenomenon of the period was the implantation amid the native population of colonies of Greeks and Macedonians who sought to re-create and perpetuate the social order they brought from their native city-states. But that proved impossible. Wherever Greek migrants settled, they found themselves living among other Greeks from many different cities and were constantly confronted by uprooted Greek intellectuals, athletes, soldiers, merchants, and assorted adventurers seeking their fortunes, a situation that eroded commitment to local customs based on place of origin. All kinds of opportunities existed to abandon old social ties in order to take advantage of new ways of winning wealth, favor, and high status. Despite their commitment to "Greekness," the newcomers could not avoid interactions with the natives of the Near East, an encounter which modified their traditional patterns of behavior and social values. All of these factors combined to nurture individualism, social mobility, and cosmopolitan values within the elite group that dominated the Hellenistic world. One aspect of social life so affected involved the status of women. Although still surrounded by legal constraints, many women in the Hellenistic cities of the Near East enjoyed greatly expanded opportunities for education, involvement in cultural and economic life, and even political life—opportunities not available to their ancestors in old Greece.

As the Hellenistic era progressed, some of these social and economic trends produced increasing instability in Hellenistic society. Deepening differences in wealth, native resentment against Greek exploitation, retreat of the members of the ruling elite from civic-mindedness toward individualistic concerns, and an abiding sense of Greek superiority generated explosive tensions. Unlike their predecessors in the Archaic Age, the Greek leaders of the Hellenistic world were unable to shed their role as exploiters in order to come to grips with economic and social problems in ways that would strengthen the entire fabric of society. That failure, repeated by the Romans, would have serious consequences for the fate of Greco-Roman civilization.

4. HELLENISTIC THOUGHT AND EXPRESSION

The three centuries following Alexander's death marked a highly significant era in cultural history distinguished by two interdependent developments: the spread of the classical Greek culture into an immense area theretofore little touched by it and the recasting of that culture in

ways that enriched it. The spread of Greek culture across much of Alexander's empire was a consequence of the migration of numerous Greeks who left their old city-states to serve Alexander and his successors as a ruling elite in the Hellenistic world. Unable to imagine a civilized existence without their accustomed cultural life, these migrants consciously implanted and sought to sustain Greek literary, artistic, philosophical, and scientific concepts and forms wherever they settled. But sustaining classical Greek culture in a foreign setting was not simple. The culturally dominant Greeks found themselves in a political, economic and social milieu in which some aspects of their old culture, originally shaped in the intimate, tightly knit environment of the *polis*, appeared to have little relevance. Moreover, the Greeks soon discovered that the "barbarian" Egyptians, Syrians, Mesopotamians, Persians, and Indians possessed knowledge, techniques, and ideas that were both new and attractive to the conquerors. Inevitably, these conditions set into motion processes that transformed the old modes of thought and expression in ways that broadened and enriched the classical Hellenic culture. The result was the shaping of a distinctive culture deserving its own name: Hellenistic culture.

While many of the old city-states of the Aegean area, particularly Athens, remained important cultural centers, the most intense cultural activity of the Hellenistic Age was generated in the new Greek centers in the Near East, especially Alexandria, Antioch, and Pergamum. The population of these cities was cosmopolitan, mixing Greeks from throughout the Hellenistic world with the native peoples. The royal governments that controlled these cities and the affluent Greeks who dominated social and economic life were generous patrons, anxious to attract artists, writers, and thinkers in order to enhance the prestige of their city and to sustain the main features of civilized life. In Alexandria, for example, the Ptolemaic kings built a large library that contained about seven hundred thousand books (actually handwritten papyrus scrolls) and created a research center, called the Museum, where scholars were supported so that they could pursue scientific studies. The best talent flocked to these centers and devoted their skills to satisfying the cultural interests of those who patronized them. The cultural activities generated in these "new" cities addressed a much broader world, a different set of interests, and a new range of problems than had the Greek cultural efforts within the small, independent *polis* of the Aegean world.

The Hellenistic Age witnessed a massive outpouring of literature written in Greek. This literary activity was due in part to an expanded patronage system supported by wealthy monarchs, their officials, and private individuals, all eager to fortify their status in a world where individual recognition was prized over collective identity. More significantly, there was an increased demand for literature by a growing number of literate people, a demand fostered by the emergence of a simplified version of Greek (*koine* Greek) that became the common tongue of government, commerce, and learning. Many natives learned the language and became readers of Greek literature. While the writers of the Hellenistic Age were prolific, they were not especially inventive. Mainly they devoted their energies to imitations of the epic and lyric poems, the tragedies and comedies, and the histories of classical Greece. Most writers, especially poets, were chiefly concerned with style, often reworking old subject matter in an attempt to achieve stylistic perfection. There were some authors, however, who produced literature that dealt with current situations and appealed to broader audiences than did the "classics"; such literature included digests of scientific and philosophical knowledge, romantic and adventure novels, histories, and biographies.

During the Hellenistic Age creative writers had to share the literary scene with literary critics, scholars concerned with reconstructing earlier Greek literary masterpieces, writing commentaries on their meaning, analyzing their grammar, and discussing their stylistic features. Their scholarly labor played an important role in establishing and preserving the texts of the Greek classics and in elaborating the rules that governed grammar, rhetoric, and literary form. Their work was important in defining an expanding educational system whose substance was increasingly literary. Education played a major role in preparing the Greek ruling elite to discharge

its duties and to sustain the cultural brand that was its mark of superiority.

The artists of the Hellenistic period were no less active than the literary figures. Again classical Greek models exerted a powerful influence, almost completely overshadowing the artistic traditions of the Near East. Architecture enjoyed a great boom because of the numerous new cities built by the Greeks and filled with the traditional Greek buildings—temples, *gymnasia,* theaters, and halls for the conduct of public business. Although the basic forms remained classic, there was a tendency to stress size and ornateness in these buildings. Most Hellenistic cities were much better planned than the older Greek cities, with emphasis on a rectangular grid layout, wide streets, adequate water supplies, commercial conveniences, and parks.

Hellenistic sculpture likewise sought to imitate the masters of the Classical Age; in fact, most sculptors did little more than copy classical models, often for sale to private collectors. They remained fascinated by mythological subjects and the human figure. Sometimes they were able to capture the full spirit of classical style, as is illustrated by the well-known *Winged Victory of Samothrace,* with its idealized, well-proportioned portrayal of the human form. Hellenistic sculptors showed a greater interest in the nude female than had sculptors of classical Greece; their best work in this respect reflected a pleasing combination of idealization of the body and sensuousness, as is evident in the famous *Aphrodite of Melos* (more commonly known as the *Venus de Milo*). Hellenistic sculptors produced impressive relief carvings as a part of temple decoration. Although little evidence has survived, it is clear that the classical tradition in painting was continued during the Hellenistic period. Despite the powerful appeal of classical Greek subjects and models in the visual arts, Hellenistic art did develop its own unique characteristics. Perhaps the most striking development was the increasing realism and emotionalism reflected in sculpture and painting. In place of the classic quest to create idealized perfection, Hellenistic sculptors often came down into the streets—the world of children, old people, laborers, barbarians—for their subjects. In portraying these figures they sought to capture the passions, sorrow, suffering, and emotions that are part of real life (see Figure 7.2).

The most original cultural contributions of the Hellenistic Age were made in science and philosophy, where investigators and thinkers often moved beyond their Hellenic predecessors. The moment was especially ripe for scientific advance. Earlier Greek philosophers had postulated challenging theories about the natural world and had argued that nature could best be understood by observing its workings. These concerns continued during the Hellenistic Age and were stimulated when the Greeks gained access to a huge body of data about the natural world compiled over many centuries by learned individuals in the Near East. Hellenistic kings and wealthy Greeks were eager to patronize scientists and to provide facilities to make research possible. The result was active scientific inquiry, centered especially at Alexandria, which led to a more systematic, rational organization of inherited scientific data, an impressive accumulation of new knowledge, and fresh interpretations of its meaning.

Introduced to a much larger world by Alexander's conquests and by commercial expansion, Hellenistic scientists made noteworthy progress in compiling and organizing geographical information. From this data emerged challenging geographical speculation, illustrated by the work of Eratosthenes (ca. 275–200 B.C.). He calculated the circumference of the earth to be 24,662 miles, about 200 miles less than the actual figure. On the basis of his study of tides, he insisted that the Atlantic and Indian oceans were joined and that India could be reached from Spain by sailing south around Africa or directly west. He made maps using lines of longitude and latitude and divided the earth into climatic zones still used by geographers. Seleucus (second century B.C.), along with others, studied the tides and came close to relating them to the gravitational force of the moon.

Two names reflect the widespread interest in astronomy: Aristarchus (ca. 310–230 B.C.) and Hipparchus (ca. 185–120 B.C.). On the basis of geometrical calculations Aristarchus put forward a heliocentric theory of the universe which argued that the earth and the planets rotated around the sun. Hipparchus denied this theory, working out a geocentric version of the cosmos

FIGURE 7.2 An Old Woman of the Hellenistic Age
This portrayal of an old market woman of the third or second century B.C. reflects the concern of Hellenistic artists with portraying the real world about them. The work suggests a world that had its share of suffering and hardship. The contrast with the serene, idealized figures portrayed in the sculpture of the Classical Age in Greece is striking. (The Metropolitan Museum of Art, Rogers Fund, 1909)

that involved an intricate pattern of movements of the sun, moon, and stars around the earth. His system, which took into account what astronomers were then able to observe, won the day and would survive for centuries. He compiled an extensive atlas of the stars and from observation of their movements arrived at an extremely accurate calculation of the solar year. Both these great astronomers tried to calculate the size of the sun and its distance from the earth, but with little success.

Much was also done to advance mathematics. Euclid (323–285 B.C.) compiled a textbook containing hundreds of rationally demonstrated proofs of propositions pertaining to flat surfaces that remained the standard work on plane geometry until the twentieth century. Archimedes (287–212 B.C.) calculated the value of *pi* (the ratio between the circumference and the diameter of a circle), devised a system for expressing large numbers, solved the problem of the relative volumes of a cylinder and a sphere, and laid the foundations for calculus. Trigonometry was developed by Hipparchus, and a fundamental work on conic sections was done by Apollonius of Perga (third century B.C.).

Medicine was of great interest to the scholars of this period. Following the lead of Hippocrates, Hellenistic physicians made important progress in anatomy and physiology, chiefly on the basis of careful and systematic observation. Surgery advanced considerably; so did the use of medicines. Alexandria was especially prominent as a center of medical study, an activity that the Ptolemaic rulers supported even to the extent of supplying physicians with the cadavers of prisoners for dissection.

Hellenistic scientists were also interested in physics, zoology, chemistry, and botany, devoting most of their energies to collecting and classifying data in these areas. Illustrative was the work of Theophrastus (ca. 372–287 B.C.), who compiled descriptive works on botany based on his own observations of plants and their habits. New advances in these fields were limited. However, Archimedes did discover the laws governing floating bodies and developed the theory of the lever.

Although the evidence is scanty, it is clear that the Hellenistic era witnessed noteworthy advances in technology. Archimedes developed the windlass, the double pulley, the endless screw for pumping water, and a variety of devices useful in the defense of besieged cities. Other less famous engineers devised machines operated by water, air pressure, and weights, cranes capable of moving huge weights, surgical instruments, and water clocks. However, Hellenistic scientists, like their Hellenic predecessors, had little interest in the practical applications of scientific knowledge. In fact, virtually the only area where applied technology developed was in the military field. As a consequence, daily life during the Hellenistic era was little affected by the notable advances in science.

Hellenistic philosophy rivaled science in vigor and creativity. The old philosophical interests lived on, as evidenced by the continued activity of Plato's Academy and Aristotle's Lyceum in Athens. However, Hellenistic philosophy was primarily concerned with problems of human conduct and individual destiny, interests that had already attracted the Sophists of the fifth century B.C.. This emphasis reflected the stresses felt by Greeks living in a cosmopolitan, impersonal, changing world, which left them seeking escape from alienation, reassurance against uncertainty, personal identity, and peace of mind.

The search for individual identity and peace of mind produced several schools of thought that competed vigorously for public attention. Some attracted popular fancy and aroused ire for their eccentricity and excess. A school called Skeptics called into question all systems of truth, arguing that peace of mind could come only when people accepted their inability to discover truth by rational means and lived on the basis of practical experience. The Cynics were more spectacular; they advocated that individuals should reject the conventions and material trappings of civilized society in order to gain individual freedom. These disciples of a counterculture refused gainful employment, abandoned family life, took to the streets in filthy rags to deliver diatribes against the establishment, and generally conducted themselves in ways offensive to civilized society.

More appealing was the teaching of Epicurus (ca. 341–270 B.C.), who founded a school at Athens which developed a set of ethical concepts derived from the atomic theory propounded by Democritus. Epicurus argued that the universe consisted of atoms, which by chance formed themselves into beings and things. Given this materialistic cosmos, human beings could put aside troubling fears of the deities, who, if they existed, had nothing to do with the processes that controlled all being, as well as concerns about death, which was nothing more than the dissolution of atoms that had come together by accident to bring living creatures into being. Rather, humans should occupy themselves only with happiness and pleasure. Contrary to some of his disciples, Epicurus argued that happiness did not result from mere physical pleasure but rather from pursuits that avoid physical pain and promote a peaceful mind undisturbed by any anxiety. He urged his disciples to withdraw into a small circle of intimate friends and to avoid excessive wealth, political involvement, and too great contact with the world; "to live in hiding" would shield one from much that could disturb the mind. Many educated and refined Greeks found in Epicureanism justification to escape the uncertainties of a hostile world, but in doing so they turned their backs on the active, involved life that had once been the ideal for the Greek citizen.

The most powerful movement shaping the moral atmosphere of the Hellenistic Age was Stoicism, whose founder, Zeno (336–264 B.C.), taught in Athens while Epicurus was there. Stoicism was based on Zeno's conviction that the universe was governed by an unchanging law of nature ordained by a Divine Reason to establish harmony and order in the universe. By nature every individual, regardless of status or place of origin, shared in the universal order established by the Divine Reason, making them members of the common community of humankind. The course of human beings emerged clearly from such a universal order: They must use their reason to define a pattern of behavior that would attune their lives to the laws of nature. Such a course would compel all humans to accept the inevitable dictates of the natural order. They must bear all misfortunes with patience and accept good fortune without pride, since everything that happens has been ordained by an all-knowing providence. Such harmony with the natural order brings tranquillity and peace of mind. It ends concern for material things and allows the soul to reach the ideal state—*apatheia* (apathy, or absence of feeling). Although in its

early stage Stoicism was primarily an individualistic philosophy, it did in time develop a larger dimension that stressed the community of all humans under one law, the need for involvement in public life in order to sustain order and civility, and concern for other members of the single human community.

As the second century B.C. progressed, Hellenistic cultural activity began to lose momentum, chiefly in the face of ideas and values embodied in religious systems that had roots in the traditions of the ancient Near East. But by that time Hellenic-Hellenistic culture had won the admiration of the conquering Romans, who would continue the diffusion and enrichment of the Greek way that had progressed so remarkably during the Hellenistic Age.

5. HELLENISTIC RELIGION

Religious developments during the Hellenistic Age took an unexpected turn destined to be of major importance for the future. In contrast to Greek dominance in most aspects of life, the religions of the conquered peoples gradually asserted a powerful influence in shaping Hellenistic thought and values. As the Greeks migrated across the Near East, they took with them and sought to sustain their old civic religions as a part of their "superior" culture. Although this effort put the trappings of Greek religion into place everywhere across the Hellenistic world, the old deities and the rites in their honor increasingly ceased to answer the basic spiritual needs generated by the changed environment of the Hellenistic world and consequently suffered eclipse.

In the face of the insecurity and alienation of the Hellenistic world, more and more Greeks found spiritual satisfaction in what are called *mystery religions*. Although pre-Hellenistic Greeks were familiar with such religions in the form of the cults of Dionysus and Demeter, they encountered among their Near Eastern subjects a variety of flourishing mystery cults of diverse origins centering on the worship of different deities: Serapis, Isis, Mithra, the Earth Mother. All shared certain fundamental ideas with wide appeal. They centered around the worship of a savior deity, usually identified with the forces of renewal in nature, whose death and resurrection provided eternal life for each individual believer. Those yearning for assurance drew close to that deity by trusting in the deity's saving power, by submitting to a special initiation ceremony, and by participating in emotional rituals, often involving a reenactment of the deity's death and rebirth. Favor with the saving god or goddess depended heavily on the moral conduct of each believer. Since faith in a savior deity, ritual participation, and upright behavior were tests everyone could meet, the mystery religions appealed to men and women of all classes, all levels of wealth, and all ethnic groups. In the cosmopolitan, mobile environment of the Hellenistic world, ideas from various mystery religions constantly mingled. This process, called *syncretism* (see Figure 7.3), pointed toward the emergence of a common faith that not only tended to link Hellenes and native Near Easterners but also created a seedbed out of which would emerge such universal religions as Christianity and Islam.

As the Hellenistic period unfolded, the religious attitudes exemplified by the mystery religions increasingly asserted a powerful influence over literary and artistic expression and philosophical and scientific thought. This "religionizing" of thought and expression initiated a subtle redirection of Hellenistic cultural life that highlighted a dimension of Hellenistic civilization that was destined to be an important heritage. The Hellenistic mentality was marked by an inner tension. On the one hand, there was a thrust, most evident in science, art, and creative writing, to know and to understand rationally the world of people and nature. On the other, there was an equally powerful impetus, reflected best by philosophers and priests, to retreat from the material world into the spirit world, to abandon thinking in favor of quietude of mind sustained by faith in an all-powerful deity. Perhaps the emergence of this polarity was the most potent consequence of the encounter between the civilizations of the ancient Near East and the Greeks. In any case, the juxtaposition of reason and faith, realism and mysticism, activism and withdrawal that was at the heart of Hellenistic culture would recur in later chapters of the history of Western civilization as a stimulant to creativity.

Even as the Hellenistic world was swept along a course pointing to a common religion, note must be taken of one religion that stood apart from, although not untouched by, the ma-

FIGURE 7.3 Religious Syncretism This Hellenistic relief illustrates the mixing of religions that was an important aspect of Hellenistic civilization. The seated deity reflects a mixture of Greek and Near Eastern concepts of deity. The priest burning incense in honor of the god is Near Eastern, while the garment of the figure on the right crowning the god is clearly Greek/Macedonian. (Yale University Art Gallery, Duro-Europas Collection)

jor religious currents: Judaism. The political status of the adherents of Judaism remained much the same under Hellenistic rule as it had been under the Persians; Jews were subjects of Hellenistic monarchs who granted them special privileges that allowed them to observe their religion and to control many aspects of life in their own community. At the center of the people of Israel was the community in Palestine centered around the Temple in Jerusalem, a community held together and set apart not by nationhood but by adherence to Judaic law as set forth in the Torah and by time-sanctioned cult practices in honor of Yahweh. In addition to the Jerusalem community there were Yahweh's followers dispersed widely across the Hellenistic world, where they were allowed to maintain quasi-autonomous communities in which they too could live and worship according to Judaic law. In this general setting Judaism continued to mature along the basic lines defined prior to the Hellenistic Age (see Chapter 3). The Hebrew Bible assumed the basic form in which it is now known, scribes studied the law and taught its letter and its spirit to the faithful in synogogues, teachers of wisdom scrutinized and refined the ethical dimensions of Judaism, and speculative minds injected concepts of such matters as sin, the afterlife, and divine providence into traditional Judaism. Although sometimes at odds over such issues as the meaning of the law, the standards of right living, the appropriateness of new theological concepts, and the future of Yahweh's chosen people, the adherents of Judaism remained a remarkably coherent group.

As the Hellenistic Age progressed, perhaps the most disruptive force in the Jewish community was the question of Hellenization. Many Jews, especially those dispersed in the great cities of the Hellenistic world, were deeply attracted to and influenced by Greek thought and lifestyle; for example, so many Jews living in Egypt spoke Greek that it was necessary to prepare a Greek translation of the Bible, called the Septuagint, to serve their religious needs. This intrusion of Hellenistic ideas and values seemed to other Jews to be a grave threat to Judaism. That issue was at the heart of the most dramatic event in Jewish history during the Hellenistic Age, the Maccabean revolt, which began in 167 B.C. It was provoked by the efforts of the Seleucid ruler, Antiochus IV, abetted by Hellenizing Jews in Palestine, to force Hellenization on the community in Palestine as a means of unifying the shaky Seleucid kingdom against the threat of Rome. Antiochus' policy led to persecution of the Jews, a suspension of Jewish religious worship, and the desecration of the Temple with a pagan altar. Outraged Jews, led by Judas Maccabaeus, took up arms to wage a successful guerrilla war that culminated with the recapture of Jerusalem, the purification of the Temple (the first Hanukkah), the cessation of Seleucid persecution, and the establishment of a virtually independent Jewish state under Roman auspices. However, the issue surrounding the problem of Hellenization—the relationship of the community made up of adherents of Judaism to the larger world—was by no means settled. It would continue to agitate Judaism and lead to consequences of decisive importance in shaping the future not only of Judaism but also of the non-Jewish world.

SUGGESTED READING

Political History

Peter Green, *Alexander to Actium. The Historical Evolution of the Hellenistic Age* (1990).
F. W. Walbank, *The Hellenistic World* (1982).
Two syntheses covering all aspects of Hellenistic life.
Peter Green, *Alexander of Macedon, 356–323. A Historical Biography* (1991).
Robin Lane Fox, *Alexander the Great* (1973).
Either of these biographies will help understand Alexander.

Cultural Life

John Ferguson, *The Heritage of Hellenism. The Greek World from 323 B.C. to 31 B.C.* (1973). An excellent overview of the main features of Hellenistic culture.
G. E. R. Lloyd, *Greek Science after Aristotle* (1973). A balanced description of the accomplishments of Hellenistic science.
A. A. Long, *Hellenistic Philosophers: Stoics, Epicureans, Sceptics* (1986). A clear presentation of the teachings of the major Hellenistic schools of philosophy.

Jean Charbonneaux et al., *Hellenistic Art (330–50 B.C.)*, trans. Peter Green (1973).
J. J. Pollitt, *Art in the Hellenistic Age* (1986).
Two excellent treatments with good illustrations.
John Onions, *Art and Thought in the Hellenistic Age: The Greek World View, 350–50 B.C.* (1979). A challenging effort to interrelate art and thought.
Arnaldo Momigliano, *Alien Wisdom: The Limits of Hellenization* (1975). Discusses how the Greeks dealt with other cultures, especially during the Hellenistic period.
Walter Burkert, *Ancient Mystery Cults* (1987). A good picture of the most powerful religious forces in the Hellenistic world.

Sources

M. M. Austin, *The Hellenistic World from Alexander to the Roman Conquest. A Selection of Ancient Sources in Translation* (1981). A well-selected collection of documents that will help the reader understand many aspects of Hellenistic life as seen and felt by those who lived in that world.

CHAPTER 8

The Rise of Rome to Domination of the Mediterranean World, 800 B.C.–133 B.C.

FIGURE 8.1 A Roman Patrician Honoring His Ancestors This portrayal of a Roman patrician bearing busts of his ancestors conveys the sobriety, seriousness, and respect for family that characterized the aristocratic citizens who acted through the Senate to lead the Roman Republic to ascendancy in the Mediterranean world. (Art Resource)

The powerful impulse toward the establishment of a common culture in the Mediterranean basin, initiated by the Greek city-states and continued by the Hellenistic kingdoms, was continued toward the end of the third century B.C. by a new power emerging from the West: Rome. The major accomplishment of the Romans was to create a universal political order which allowed the major features of Hellenic civilization to spread over a much larger geographical area, where it affected peoples to whom higher civilization had heretofore been unknown, especially the peoples inhabiting the area around the western Mediterranean. But Rome's political achievement was not done in a day; the shaping of the Roman imperial order required several centuries.

1. THE ORIGINS OF ROME TO 509 B.C.

The emergence of Rome as the dominant force in the Mediterranean world owed much to a combination of geographical factors and the human resources of the Italian peninsula. Aside from its strategic location in the Mediterranean basin, Italy had considerable productive farmland, important mineral deposits, and good timber. Its climate was generally mild and conducive to agricultural production. The Italian population was formed over a long period out of several different elements whose diverse patterns of culture fragmented the peninsula into a bewildering array of political entities and institutional systems. Perhaps as early as 4000 B.C., a native population developed a Neolithic farming culture. Beginning about 2000 B.C., Italy experienced successive waves of Indo-European invaders, who established political dominance over the long-established native Neolithic farmers. Their language eventually prevailed over much of Italy, creating the base from which classical Latin emerged.

The still-backward Italian population was decisively influenced after about 800 B.C. by the settlement in Italy of two outside peoples bringing with them the more advanced civilization of the eastern Mediterranean world. As we have already seen, the Greeks founded numerous city-states in southern Italy and Sicily from which flowed powerful cultural forces affecting the entire Italian population. Even more important

were the Etruscans, probably immigrants from Asia Minor, who established a series of cities along the western coast of Italy in a region called Etruria (see Map 8.1). Although each of these cities remained politically independent, between about 700 and 500 B.C. they collectively dominated western Italy from the Po Valley to Naples. They transmitted to the native population technical skills, agricultural and commercial practices, political techniques, religious usages, and art forms that provided many Italians with their first taste of advanced urban civilization.

Among the most precocious pupils of the Etruscans were the inhabitants of several tiny villages built on a cluster of seven hills lying on the south bank of the Tiber River about fifteen miles from the sea. These first "Romans" later created a colorful legend recounting the founding of their city in 753 B.C. by Romulus and Remus, allegedly descendants of a hero of the Trojan Wars, Aeneas. Legend aside, the evidence suggests that Rome began as a settling place for herder-farmers from an area just south of the Tiber known as Latium, who perhaps were attracted to the site by an important ford which controlled traffic across the Tiber.

Shortly after 600 B.C., these villages coalesced into a single city-state, a unification probably forced on them by Etruscan warlords. Within a century Rome was transformed into a thriving urban center focused around a marketplace called the Forum. Etruscan techniques of trade and industry were adopted, greatly strengthening the city's primitive economy. An alphabet was derived from Etruscan models, resulting in the rapid development of written Latin. Etruscan architecture and decoration served as models for the temples and public buildings in the burgeoning city. Primitive Latin religious practices took on more sophisticated patterns reflecting Etruscan usages.

In this urban setting political and social structures emerged that would exercise a powerful influence over Roman society for centuries. The unified city was ruled by a king who was advised by a council, called the Senate, composed of about three hundred men of wealth who drew their authority from their headship of families. Freemen, who constituted the bulk of the citizen body, were given a limited voice in political affairs by membership in two assemblies, the most

Map 8.1 ITALY, 265 B.C. This map shows the main geographical regions into which early Italy was divided and indicates the date at which each was brought under Roman domination. As noted in the text, Roman domination did not mean total loss of independence for the peoples of Italy. Many in central Italy became citizens, as is indicated on the map; most of the rest were allies who retained considerable rights of local control as long as they supported Rome's foreign policy and kept the peace.

important of which was the Assembly of Centuries. This body emerged from a military reorganization, probably instituted during the sixth century B.C., that grouped the population on the basis of wealth into miliary units called *centuries*. The centuries were composed in such a way as to give predominant voice to Rome's wealthiest citizens. The city-state populace was divided into two distinct classes, *patricians* and *plebeians*. The patricians, consisting of a small number of land-owning families each rigidly controlled by the father of the family (*pater familias*), exercised the predominant influence over society. Custom prohibited intermarriage between the two classes. A powerful force of social stability and patrician domination was the institution of *clientage*. Under this system many plebeians were closely tied to patrician families as *clients*, with their noble *patrons* providing legal protection and material assistance in return for various services, including following political orders.

Despite their debt to the Etruscans, the Romans chafed under their domination. Shortly before 500 B.C., Etruscan power began to be contested by the dependent subjects everywhere in western Italy. In Rome the patricians took the lead in a revolution that dethroned the Etruscan king and established in his place two *consuls* elected annually from patrician ranks to wield the *imperium*, that is, the highest executive authority of the state. This revolution of 509 B.C. marked the beginning of the Roman Republic, an episode long celebrated by the Romans as the greatest event in their history.

2. THE EARLY REPUBLIC, 509–265 B.C.

Two themes dominate the first two and one-half centuries of the history of the Roman Republic: Roman conquest of the Italian peninsula (see Map 8.1) and the shaping of an effective political and social order. Given the fact that in 509 B.C. Rome was only a tiny city-state lost among many other political entities, Roman expansion in Italy represented a remarkable feat. In a larger sense, Roman success created the human and material resources that would soon permit Rome to become a world power.

For a century after the expulsion of the Etrus-

cans in 509 B.C., Rome's survival depended on cooperation with neighboring cities in Latium, which joined Rome to form the Latin League. This league fought a long succession of wars against the Etruscans, the tough mountain peoples trying to gain a foothold in the rich agricultural lands of Latium and Campania, and the Gauls, a Celtic people who raided central Italy from their base in the Po Valley and captured and sacked Rome in 390 B.C. Rome survived these threats with sufficient strength to take the offensive against the other members of the Latin League, whose attempts to resist led to the dissolution of the League in 338 B.C., leaving Rome in control of Latium.

From this base, the Romans proceeded to expand their sphere of influence. Between 326 and 290 B.C. they subdued the Samnites, a formidable mountain people living south and east of Rome, who provoked the Romans by challenging them for control of Campania. While engaged in the bitter Samnite Wars, the Romans were attacked from the north by Gauls, Etruscans, and other mountain peoples from north-central Italy, but these attacks were thrown back and Roman dominance was gradually established over most of northern Italy lying south of the Po Valley. Hardly had the Samnite Wars ended than Rome was drawn into the affairs of the Greek city-states of southern Italy, chiefly to arbitrate their quarrels. Despite assistance from military adventurers from "old" Greece, the badly divided Italian-Greek city-states could not hold off the Romans. By 265 B.C. Rome had established mastery over all of Italy south of the Po Valley.

Many forces combined to explain Rome's triumph. Later Romans constantly retold the stories of these wars as proof of their superior civic virtues and divine favor. Beneath these legends there was a core of truth: In these arduous wars the Roman citizens demonstrated bravery, persistence, and self-sacrifice. However, other, more tangible factors also played a decisive part in Roman success.

First, the Romans developed a superior military organization based upon a citizen army in which most of the city's male population served at each soldier's own expense. The effectiveness of this army was greatly enhanced by the development of the *legion* as the basic military formation. The legion was essentially a massed formation of well-armed infantry soldiers, not unlike the Greek phalanx. During the long wars against mountain peoples, the legion formation developed greater flexibility by the creation within it of small subunits capable of independent action.

A second, more important factor contributing to Rome's victory in Italy was the innovative policy devised for the treatment of conquered peoples. In essence this system encouraged conquered peoples to identify their well-being with Roman success. Rome achieved this end through a series of treaties with conquered subjects which provided a flexible definition of "belonging" to Rome's spreading network of power. To some conquered peoples, especially those in Latium, Rome extended full rights of citizenship. The residents of other communities became "citizens without vote." These people could not participate in the Roman political process, but they were permitted to trade in Rome and to intermarry with Romans. These cities continued to govern themselves in most matters except foreign affairs, but their half citizens owed to the Roman state the same financial and military obligations as Roman citizens did. Still other communities were made "allies" (*socii*) of Rome, each enjoying independence in local affairs but required to provide military contingents to serve in Rome's wars. Implicit in these arrangements was the possibility that partial citizenship and ally status would eventually result in full citizenship, especially for those who became Romanized. In many communities that were granted powers of local self-government, the Romans gave strong support to ruling aristocracies who found it in their best interests to support Rome. Roman colonists were settled across Italy to become important agents in the Romanization of the peninsula. This complex set of arrangements, contrasting so sharply with the way in which other conquerors treated their victims, meant that by 265 B.C. Rome ruled over a loose confederation of Italians, most of whom enjoyed a considerable degree of independence but all of whom were tied to Rome by virtue of an obligation to serve in its armies, by the hope of achieving full citizenship, and by an increasing identification with Roman culture in all its facets. From the Roman point of view this system provided a pool of military resources that ensured

the security of Italy and made possible further expansion.

A third element contributing to Rome's success was the ability of its leaders to reshape internal political and social structures in a way that promoted loyalty among its citizens. Those adjustments were painfully worked out during a protracted internal conflict, called the "struggle of the orders," which went on almost continually for over two centuries after the founding of the republic in 509 B.C. On one side stood the patricians, who were determined to maintain their monopoly on power and their exclusive social position. Challenging them were the plebeians, a diverse group ranging from affluent, ambitious figures eager for a share in political decision making to poor, humble farmers and artisans concerned chiefly with escaping economic oppression, gaining more equitable treatment under the law, and finding more land. Aside from the sometimes brilliant tactics of plebeian leaders, occasionally supported by individual patricians, perhaps the decisive factor in the struggle was the fear of the ruling patricians that the plebeian soldiers would refuse to serve the state unless their demands were met. In fact, at certain critical moments in the struggles the plebeians did secede from the state to make their point.

Whatever the motives and however bitter the struggle, the significant fact was that the dominant patricians did give sufficient ground to prevent civil strife and to avoid alienation of any major segment of the citizen body. Certain of their concessions mark crucial stages in shaping the republican constitution. As early as 494 B.C., the plebeians gained the right to elect special plebeian officials, called *tribunes*, who were given the power to veto any act of the regularly elected officials that threatened plebeian interests. A new plebeian assembly, originally called the Council of the Plebs and later the Assembly of Tribes, was instituted to provide a forum where the plebeians could enact resolutions (called *plebiscites*) indicating their will to the tribunes. In about 450 B.C. plebeian pressure led to a written codification of ancient legal customs, called the Twelve Tables, that protected citizens from arbitrary decisions by patrician judges. A succession of laws approved by the Senate and the Assembly of Centuries gave protection to debtors, permitted marriage between patricians and plebeians, limited patrician monopoly on the use of public lands, and provided land grants to poor plebeians. One by one the major elective offices were opened to plebeians; particularly important was a law of 367 B.C. that required that one consul be a plebeian. Since election to the consulship automatically qualified a Roman citizen for membership in the Senate, plebeians had finally gained access to that powerful body. Finally, in 287 B.C., plebiscites enacted by the Assembly of Tribes were recognized as the ultimate law binding on the entire state, a concession that gave the citizen body final authority.

On the surface the struggle of the orders had created a constitution for the republic that placed the control of the state in the hands of Rome's citizen body—the Senate and the people, as the Romans put it. By 265 B.C. the citizen body, acting through the Assembly of Centuries and the Assembly of Tribes, theoretically had the final power to decide public policy. Aside from the power to enact laws binding on all, the citizens elected the various magistrates who executed the decisions of the citizens enacted in the assemblies. The Roman executive system was collegiate in form. With minor exceptions, every administrative function was carried out by a board of at least two members of equal rank, each of whom had the power to veto the acts of his colleagues, a system that both constrained rash action by elected officials and led to intricate bargaining in order to achieve any results. The highest executive authority in the state—the *imperium*—was exercised by two consuls charged with the joint management of all civil and military affairs. Below them were the *praetors*, who were elected primarily to administer justice but under special circumstances were capable of exercising the *imperium*. In time other administrative offices with specialized functions were created to assist in running the increasingly complicated affairs of the expanding republic. Most elective officials were elected for one-year terms. An important exception was the *censor*, chosen every five years to classify citizens for military service and to judge their moral fitness public functions, particularly membership in the Senate. In times of grave crisis, a *dictator* with unlimited power to run the state could be elected for a term of six months. By law any citizen was

eligible for election to these offices, but since there was no pay for service and since electioneering was expensive, few men of humble means aspired to high office and even fewer gained it.

Especially potent in the republican system of government was the Senate. It was composed of about three hundred men who qualified for membership by virtue of service as consul or praetor, a selection process that ensured that the Senate was dominated by the wealthy and the socially prominent. In theory the Senate was an advisory body, counseling the magistrates and the assemblies in making decisions that best served the interests of the state. In fact, its decisions were almost invariably accepted by the assemblies and the magistrates because of the prestige, wealth, and experience of the senators.

Despite appearances, at the conclusion of the struggle of the orders real power in the Roman Republic remained in the hands of a small circle of wealthy landowners, descendants of a few ancient families. The members of this circle were convinced that right order in society depended on their collective political wisdom, and thus they acted consciously to control the machinery of government; involvement in the governance of Rome was their career. From the ranks of this circle came most of the elected magistrates, who passed from elected office into the Senate. That body, with its extensive role in decision making, was the bastion of aristocratic control. The power wielders worked as a group to manage the election process and to control the assemblies. Especially effective in achieving these ends was their ability to maintain and manage their plebeian clients, whose support was usually forthcoming in return for public policies that provided economic concessions and protection from oppression under the law. The chief threat to the political power of the patrician families came from enterprising, increasingly wealthy plebeians who sought a share in power. The patricians met this challenge by absorbing these "new men" into their circle, chiefly by opening public offices and Senate membership to them and by linking them to patrician families through marriage. This process in no way weakened the control over political life by a small circle of wealthy families, which the Romans increasingly called the *nobiles*, the ruling nobility (see Figure 8.1). Most Romans were content to entrust the destiny of the city to these *nobiles*. That trust was based on the deep-seated respect on the part of the Roman citizen body for traditional ways of doing things (what the Romans called "customs of our forefathers"), on a sense that the leadership of the *nobiles* had been effective in enhancing Rome's power and wealth, and on the assurance that citizens had the means to curb abuses of power. By 265 B.C. this oligarchic system was so powerfully entrenched and so widely accepted that it seemed to many Romans that the ideal form of government had been fashioned. Perhaps the only issues for the future were whether the ruling *nobiles* could remain united in their collective exercise of power and whether they would remain sensitive and responsive to the needs of the citizen body as a whole.

The experiences surrounding expansion in Italy and the struggle of the orders played a decisive role in shaping a collective mentality among the Romans that was destined to cast a long shadow over Roman political, social, and cultural life. During the first centuries of the republic the Romans were basically a simple people whose outlook on life was shaped by four major forces—family life, an agricultural economy, warfare, and religion. The family structure was predominantly patriarchal. The authority of the male head of a household (*pater familias*) over his wife and children was total and absolute. Fathers impressed on the other members of their tightly knit families a sense of discipline, obedience, and respect for authority and tradition. Farm life made the early Romans a practical, realistic people, content to live simply and frugally. Constant warfare in defense of hearth and city deepened the sense of duty owed to the larger community and strengthened societal discipline.

Religion had an especially profound effect on early Roman life and thought. Romans believed that all things in existence were animated by powerful spirits, a view that instilled in them a deep awe of the unseen; the Romans called such awe "piety" and lauded it as a prime virtue. In the early stages of Rome's history the chief objects of this piety were household and agricultural deities: Janus, the protective god of the doorway of each household; Vesta, the goddess of the hearth; the *lares* and *penates*, spirits guarding the productive powers of the family and its lands and flocks. As the city grew, it too developed its divine protectors. Roman civic religion centered especially on a trio of deities, perhaps derived from Etruscan models: Jupiter, the god of lightning, thunder and power; Juno, the goddess of women, family, and procreation; and Minerva, the goddess of arts, sciences, and wisdom. In time, other deities, derived chiefly from the Greek pantheon, were added to this trio as major civic deities. Eventually this divine circle protecting the expanding city became the object of an elaborate mythology, much of it borrowed from the Greeks, that accounted for the behavior of each of its members. The approach to all the gods and goddesses, whether civic or household, was highly formal and unemotional. From very early times the Romans developed set patterns for offering sacrifices and prayers to their many deities. They also had well-defined expectations of what the gods and goddesses would return to families and the city. Close observance of these customary rituals became a part of responsible citizenship; any deviation threatened to earn the wrath of the deities and misfortune for men and women. Responsibility for proper worship rested with the heads of families and with priests elected to represent the city-state community before the civic gods.

The values defined by home, farm, battlefield, and altar combined to exalt sobriety, industry, discipline, piety, civic responsibility, respect for tradition, and honor of the family. Less prized were originality, creativity, and individuality. As time passed, the Roman mentality tended to idealize the values of these early times and to project them onto political and cultural life as norms governing political and social behavior and shaping thought and expression. As a result, the traits ingrained in Roman society during its early history cast a long shadow over all facets of Roman history.

3. OVERSEAS EXPANSION: THE PUNIC WARS, 264–201 B.C.

By 265 B.C. the Romans had completed the unification of Italy and had put into place an effective system of government. Perhaps without yet knowing it, Rome had become a major power because of these developments. During the next

Map 8.2 THE ROMAN EMPIRE, 265–44 B.C. As this map shows, Rome's expansion around the Mediterranean came a bit at a time. By the beginning of the second century B.C. the Romans had established their supremacy in the western Mediterranean, chiefly as a consequence of territory annexed following the Punic Wars. Between about 200 and 125 B.C., the Romans established dominance over Macedonia, Greece, and the west coast of Asia Minor. With that power base it was only a matter of time until further expansion occurred in both the east and west. The circumstances surrounding Rome's expansion after 133 B.C. will be discussed in later chapters.

century and a half, Roman history was shaped by an expanding involvement in the complex affairs of the entire Mediterranean world, which resulted in a series of victories that made the Romans the rulers of a large empire spanning three continents (see Map 8.2).

Rome's first encounter with a major Mediterranean power was with Carthage. Originally a Phoenician colony, Carthage had established its independence about 800 B.C. In the succeeding centuries, the Carthaginians built a thriving commercial empire based on colonies located at stra-

tegic places around the western Mediterranean. During much of this period, their main rivals for commercial supremacy were the Greek city-states of Sicily and southern Italy. Carthaginian relationships with Rome during this period were generally friendly. Eventually their interests clashed over control of Sicily. In 265 B.C. the Carthaginians, who had established a foothold in western Sicily, took steps to protect the Greek city-state of Messana against the aggression of another Greek city-state, Syracuse. After some hesitation, the Romans decided to intervene, perhaps persuaded by fears that Carthaginian control of Messana would result in intervention by a major power in the affairs of Rome's recently conquered allies in southern Italy. The prospect of booty made the choice easier. Rome's decision meant war with Carthage.

The First Punic War (264–241 B.C.) was a struggle for Sicily. The Romans soon realized that they would need a navy to dislodge the Carthaginians from their seaport strongholds. With great resolve coupled with help from their Greek allies, they soon achieved that end. There then ensued a long series of engagements for control of the waters around Sicily. Although the fledgling Roman navy suffered several defeats and an army sent to attack Carthage in Africa was crushed, the Romans persevered until Carthage sued for peace in 241 B.C. By the treaty ending the war, Rome gained Sicily as its first tribute-paying overseas province as well as a sizable monetary payment to cover war expenses.

However, the issue between the two powers was far from settled. In the years following the peace of 241 B.C., the Carthaginians turned their attention to rebuilding their strength, which had been seriously threatened by the loss of Sicily and the Roman challenge to their sea power. Under the leadership of Hamilcar Barca and his son Hannibal Carthage undertook to create a new power base in Spain by subduing the native population, recruiting and training a potent army of Spaniards, and collecting a huge war chest derived from Spain's rich mines. The Romans were much too involved in other matters to pay attention to Carthage's recovery: organizing Corsica and Sardinia, which had been treacherously seized from Carthage; extending Roman control into the Po Valley; coping with plebeian agitation for fairer distribution of public land; and curbing piracy in the Adriatic Sea. When they did finally turn their attention to the rising power of Carthage in Spain, their efforts to intervene there soon led to a new war with Carthage.

The Second Punic War (218–201 B.C.) was Rome's sternest military test, due in large part to the genius of Hannibal. Rome's initial plan to attack the Carthaginians in Spain and Africa was totally negated by Hannibal's bold counterstroke: the dispatch of a major army on a thousand-mile march from Spain to invade Italy. His strategy centered on depriving Rome of the manpower provided by its Italian allies, who, Hannibal presumed, would be glad to rid themselves of the Roman yoke. On three different occasions between 218 and 216 B.C. the Romans challenged him with large armies, only to be crushed each time. The last and most disastrous of these battles, at Cannae, convinced the Romans that they could not match Hannibal in open battle. They adopted a policy of harassing his army, otherwise leaving him free to do as he pleased in Italy. Until 203 B.C.—a total of fifteen years—Hannibal maintained an army in Italy and spread destruction up and down the peninsula; this was a remarkable feat in view of the fact that he received almost no reinforcements or supplies from Carthage or Spain. But he failed to achieve what he had counted on to defeat Rome: He never persuaded a decisive number of Rome's Italian allies to desert.

While holding Hannibal at bay in Italy, Rome mounted an offensive on many fronts and actually won the war outside Italy. Large armies sent to Spain slowly crushed Carthaginian power and cut off Hannibal's reinforcements. Another Roman force was dispatched to Sicily to choke off a rebellion of Greek city-states led by Syracuse in support of Carthage. Roman naval forces patrolled the western Mediterranean and the Adriatic, preventing Hannibal from getting help from Carthage or its chief ally, the kingdom of Macedon. The Romans encouraged African peoples to attack Carthaginian territories. Rome's counteroffensive culminated in 205 B.C., when a large army under Scipio Africanus was sent to Africa. In him, Rome had found a military talent equal to that of Hannibal, who was recalled from Italy in 203 B.C. to save Carthage. But even he could no longer stem the tide: He met Scipio in a battle in 202 B.C. at Zama and suffered a complete defeat.

After Zama, the Carthaginians sued for peace. They were forced to surrender Spain to Rome, to destroy their navy, to accept a heavy fine to be paid over the next fifty years, and to agree never again to wage war outside Africa and within Africa only with Rome's permission. Part of Carthage's African territory was turned over to Numidia, a state Rome hoped would balance Carthaginian power in Africa. Carthage was reduced to a minor power; victorious Rome was dominant in the western Mediterranean.

4. OVERSEAS EXPANSION: THE EASTERN MEDITERRANEAN, 200–133 B.C.

Even before the victory over Carthage had been sealed, Rome was being drawn into the turbulent world of the eastern Mediterranean (see Map 8.2). Although Roman leaders stoutly protested that Rome's engagement there was a "just" cause undertaken to ensure Rome's safety and to protect Roman allies, powerful forces were at work to generate an expansionist policy in the east. As we shall see later, aristocratic Roman society was increasingly enchanted by Greek culture, causing many to feel deeply the need to protect the Greek city-states in which it had originated. The Punic Wars had demonstrated to Roman politicians that leadership in victorious wars was an assurance of fame and power, as illustrated by the career of the immensely popular Scipio Africanus. Equally obvious to all Romans was the fact that successful warfare brought vast riches to Rome in the form of indemnities, tribute, and booty. Developments in the east encouraged many there to turn to "the rising cloud in the west" for help. By 200 B.C. the fragile balance of power that had existed in the Hellenistic world since the partition of Alexander's empire in the early third century was breaking down. Aggressive leaders, such as Philip V of Macedon and Antiochus III of the Seleucid Empire, sought to capitalize on the progressively unstable situation by enlarging their spheres of influence. To many in the east Rome's intervention seemed the only hope for safety against these aggresssors.

Rome's first involvement in the east came during the trying times of the Second Punic War. Seeking to deny the Carthaginians access to the Adriatic Sea, the Romans took steps that challenged the interests of the Illyrians, who controlled the eastern Adriatic coast. Led by an able and ambitious queen, Teuta, the Illyrians resisted and forced Rome to establish a protectorate over the coastal areas. A little later, a new threat arose when Philip V of Macedon formed an alliance with Carthage. As a counterbalance, Rome entered into alliances of friendship with several Greek city-states, especially the Aetolian League. These ventures increased the Roman awareness of possible dangers from the East and led to more serious involvement. In 201 B.C. Pergamum, Rhodes, and several Greek city-states appealed to Rome for help against what they argued was Philip V's threat to their freedom. Although the war-weary Roman populace opposed involvement, the ruling oligarchy, led by the pro-Greek Scipio Africanus, declared war on Philip V in 200 B.C. and within three years defeated his forces. Philip was then required to refrain from further involvement in Greek affairs. Amid considerable fanfare and with understandable praise from the Greeks, the Romans reaffirmed the autonomy of each Greek city-state, which henceforth would be a Roman ally. The "liberators" of Greece then withdrew without annexing any territory or demanding any tribute.

Peace in the east was brief. In 192 B.C. Antiochus III invaded the Greek peninsula at the urging of the Aetolian League, the members of which were angry at their Roman ally for not rewarding them sufficiently for their assistance in the recent war against Philip V. Rome again sent its armies east, moved in part by the fact that Hannibal was serving as military adviser to the Seleucid army. The Roman legions drove Antiochus out of Greece and in 189 B.C. inflicted a crushing defeat on him at the battle of Magnesia in Asia Minor. He was required to keep out of Asia Minor, his fleet was destroyed, and a staggering indemnity was imposed. Rome turned over large areas of Asia Minor to Pergamum and Rhodes and sanctioned them as Roman-backed peacekeepers. Most of the Greek city-states were restored to independence, although those that had aided Antiochus were fined and forced to surrender some territory to Greek city-states that had remained loyal to Rome. Again the victors annexed no lands.

Rome's peacekeeping efforts in the east led only to further frustration. The reduction of the kingdom of Macedon and the Seleucid state to secondary importance finally destroyed the balance of power in the east and opened the way to rivalry, intrigue, and strife among the petty states of the area. Even the Greeks, whom the Romans had "saved," proved treacherous and unreliable. As the chaos mounted, so did the appeals to Rome for intervention. The lure of imperialistic ventures coupled with growing impatience with their fickle allies in the east slowly pushed the Romans toward a more drastic solution: direct Roman rule in the east.

The Kingdom of Macedon was the first to experience the new policy. Macedonian efforts to curry favor among the Greek city-states led to another Macedonian war from 171–167 B.C. In the settlement following Rome's victory the Macedonian monarchy was abolished and the kingdom divided into four weak republics. A few years later a minor disturbance in Macedon led the Romans to annex the entire territory as a tribute-paying province under a Roman governor. Persistent intrigue and disturbances among the Greek city-states resulted in increasingly stern Roman reprisals, culminating in 146 B.C. with the savage destruction of Corinth as an example to all Greeks. By that date Rome had forced pro-Roman governments on most of the Greek city-states. Now the governor of the Macedonian province was charged with supervising the affairs of the Greek city-states, thus ending their freedom. Rome's chief allies in Asia Minor, Pergamum and Rhodes, proved equally unreliable and troublesome, resulting in harsh measures against them by Rome that greatly weakened them. Finally, in 133 B.C., the king of Pergamum willed his weakened kingdom to the Romans, who accepted it as a province. Once established in Asia, rich prizes tempted Rome: Ptolemaic Egypt and the Seleucid kingom, both too weak to offer effective resistance to the Romans.

While concentrating its attention chiefly on the east between 200 and 133 B.C., Rome continued to solidify its power in the west. The occupation of Spain and its organization into two provinces required a long and testing struggle against native resistance. The area of northern Italy between the Alps and the Apennines, called Cisalpine Gaul, was organized into a province. And the Romans finally settled the score with their ancient enemy, Carthage. Although Carthage was no longer a serious threat, fear of it continued to haunt Rome and prompted actions to humiliate what was now a minor state. The final step occurred in 149 B.C., when Rome declared war on Carthage on the pretext that the Carthaginians had violated the terms of the treaty ending the Second Punic War; Carthage's crime was taking up arms to protect itself against incessant harassment by the Kingdom of Numidia, a North African ally of Rome. After a heroic defense Carthage was captured and destroyed in 146 B.C., and its territory was annexed as a Roman province. The destruction of Carthage was a fitting symbol of Rome's position in the Mediterranean world as the second century B.C. drew to a close. With provinces on three continents and with unbeatable military forces, the city-state on the Tiber could speak of the Mediterranean as "our sea." The fate of civilization was now in Roman hands.

SUGGESTED READING

Overview of Roman History

Karl Christ, *The Romans: An Introduction to Their History and Civilization*, trans. Christopher Holme (1984). A fine survey.

Early Italy

Jorgen C. Meyer, *Pre-Republican Rome: An Analysis of the Cultural and Chronological Relations, 1000–500 B.C.* (1983). Relying on archaeological evidence, this challenging work throws important light on the origins of Rome.

Massimo Pallotino, *A History of Earliest Italy* (1991). A good up-to-date synthesis.

R. M. Ogilivie, *Early Rome and the Etruscans* (1976).

Michael Grant, *The Etruscans* (1980).

Ellen MacNamara, *The Etruscans* (1991).

Maja Sprenger, *The Etruscans: Their History, Art, and Architecture* (1983).

Any of the above works will provide a clear picture of Etruscan society and its impact on Rome.

The Republic to 133 B.C.

H. H. Scullard, *History of the Roman World from 753 B.C. to 146 B.C.*, 4th ed. (1980). A detailed account.

Michael Crawford, *The Roman Republic* (1978). A challenging account of political developments with interesting interpretations.

Arthur Keaveney, *Rome and the Unification of Italy* (1987). Treats how Italy was forged into a single community.

R. Develin, *The Practice of Politics at Rome, 366–167 B.C.* (1985).

Richard E. Mitchell, *Patricians and Plebeians: The Origin of the Roman State* (1990).

These two works treat the formation of the republican regime.

R. M. Errington, *The Dawn of Empire: Rome's Rise to World Power* (1972).

William V. Harris, *War and Imperialism in Republican Rome, 327–70 B.C.* (1979).

These two titles deal with the forces that led to Roman expansion and with its effects on Roman society.

Erich S. Gruen, *The Hellenistic World and the Coming of Rome*, 2 vols. (1984). A detailed study explaining how and why the Hellenistic world came under Roman sway.

B. H. Warmington, *Carthage*, 2nd rev. ed. (1969). A fine treatment of the history of Rome's greatest foe.

Nigel Bagnall, *The Punic Wars* (1990). An excellent treatment of the military history of the Punic Wars.

Biographies

Ernle Bradford, *Hannibal* (1981).

H. H. Scullard, *Scipio Africanus: Soldier and Politician* (1970).

CHAPTER 9

The Failure of the Roman Republic, 133–31 B.C.

FIGURE 9.1 A Roman Warship Warships such as the one shown in this relief, created to celebrate Octavian's victory over Antony and Cleopatra at Actium in 31 B.C., played a major role in establishing Roman dominance over the Mediterranean world during the era of the republic. Control over fleets of such ships and the soldiers they carried was also a prime factor in the rise of the military strongmen—such as Sulla, Pompey, Julius Caesar, and Octavian—to positions that allowed them to end the republic. (Alinari/Art Resource)

Rome's rise to dominance in the Mediterranean world during the period 265–133 B.C. had understandably generated confidence among the Roman citizenry, especially the ruling oligarchy, that the political and social system of the republic was not only successful but also capable of meeting any situation. Developments after 133 B.C. proved that such confidence was misplaced. During the next century a series of crises tested that system beyond its capabilities and ultimately left the long-established system of the Roman Republic in ruins.

1. THE BURDENS OF A WORLD POWER

At the root of the crises that afflicted Rome after 133 B.C. were complex problems, some rooted in the nature of the republican order but most a result of Rome's expansion from a small city-state to a large empire. Many of them were neglected during the heady era of triumphant expansion prior to 133 B.C., but eventually they surfaced to create a succession of crises that dominated the history of the last century of the republic.

First, Rome's conquests had by 133 B.C. created a long and ill-defined frontier which faced out toward potentially dangerous enemies, as well as inviting territories still open for conquest (see Map 8.2). While a part-time army composed of Roman citizens and Italian allies had conquered this vast empire, the problem of establishing a military system to defend the empire's boundaries had not been faced.

Second, there was the problem of how the several million conquered subjects would be governed and treated. In contrast to the enlightened policy originally applied to the Italian population, the Romans increasingly viewed conquered non-Italians as subjects to be exploited. Annexed territories were organized into provinces. Control over each province was entrusted to a Roman governor invested with absolute military and civil power; little attention was given to holding these governors accountable. The residents of each province were subject to heavy tribute, the collection of which was entrusted to tax farmers (called *publicans*) who paid the Roman government what it expected from each province and then extorted all they could from the provincials, often in collusion with the governors. The voiceless victims had virtually no way of protecting themselves against their masters. This abusive system disrupted order among the provincials and bred discontent, resistance, and hatred.

Third, Rome's Italian allies, whose military service played a key role in Rome's conquests, were increasingly disregarded. Not only did they benefit little from the fruits of conquest, but the prospect of citizenship implicit in Rome's earlier arrangements also grew increasingly remote. As a consequence, the allies became restless and rebellious.

Fourth, ominous trends began to emerge during the third and second centuries B.C. that pointed toward a significant transformation of the traditional economic system. Rome was greatly enriched by the influx of tribute exacted from conquered peoples. Most of that wealth fell into the hands of a small segment of the population. The beneficiaries not only developed a taste for luxurious living but also sought new opportunities for investment. Trade and manufacturing investments absorbed some of this wealth, but not enough to expand manufacturing production in Italy significantly. Although Roman aristocrats generally disdained trading as unworthy of their status, other Romans began to involve themselves in the extensive commercial activity existing in territories conquered by Rome. Their involvement slowly began to reveal that Rome's continuing prosperity was becoming dependent on the economic well-being of the entire Mediterranean world. Little mindful of this development, most rich aristocrats preferred to invest their new wealth in land and money lending.

Changes affecting agriculture offered them ample opportunity. The traditional Italian agricultural system, based on the small, independent farm tilled by a freeholder and his family and devoted to cereal crops, was eroding. Competition from cheaper grain imported as tribute from more productive provinces debased the income of cereal farmers. Many small farms were ruined as a result of the devastation caused by Hannibal's wars in Italy and the long absence of their owners in military service in far-off places. Often these citizen-soldiers borrowed to save their land, only to find themselves dispossessed for failure to repay their loans. Enterprising Romans with capital began to create large estates (called *latifundia*) by buying or seizing the land of impoverished small farmers and by using political influence to lay claim to public land. These new agricultural units concentrated on the production of cash crops such as grapes, olives, and livestock. Increasingly the labor supply on the *latifundia* was provided by slaves, most of whom were victims of Rome's wars of conquest, or by formerly independent farmers forced to become tenant farmers or hired laborers. The real victims of this transformation of agricultural life were Roman citizens and Roman allies whose loyal service as soldiers had won Rome's empire.

These trends, which heralded a fundamental transformation of the economic system of the Roman Republic, contributed to a fifth set of problems of a social nature. Down to the mid–third century B.C. the Roman social order had been relatively simple. Atop the social structure stood a small circle of nobles of both patrician and plebeian origin whose authority was based on family connections, control of political life, and landed wealth. Below them was the rest of the citizen body, chiefly freeholding farmers, whose economic and social status made them equals. But changing times slowly introduced complexity and tensions into that simple order. As already noted, the aristocrats became richer; their wealth allowed a style of life that distanced them from the rest of the population. Their virtually unchallenged monopoly over political life tended to focus their attention on competition with other members of their group for power and prestige and to dull their concern for the fate of the bulk of the population. Although these *nobiles* were firmly entrenched at the top of society, they were increasingly challenged by a new group known as *equites*. The members of this group were wealthy entrepreneurs who grew rich as military suppliers, organizers of large-scale trading ventures, building contractors, bankers, and provincial tax collectors. Their economic interests were intimately linked to public policies with respect to war, provincial administration, public works, and taxation. Consequently, the *equites* were increasingly anxious for a share of political power and for social recognition.

Changing economic conditions began to create social distinctions within the ranks of the plebeian population, once a fairly homogeneous group. Many rural plebeians survived as independent farmers but benefited little from Italy's growing prosperity. The inexorable changes affecting agriculture forced increasing numbers of the rural populace to become tenants or hired laborers, with a consequent lowering of their social status. Others in growing numbers left their farms for the cities, especially Rome, to seek a livelihood as artisans, shopkeepers, and laborers; their new condition changed their economic and social needs and concerns. Many citizens who flocked to Rome became members of what the Romans called the proletariat, a rootless, restless population endowed with rights of citizenship but victims of an unstable economic life and an uncertain social status. This volatile "mob," its members ever more dependent on the state or rich patrons for their livelihood, offered a tantalizing power base for ambitious political leaders. At the bottom of the social scale was an expanding slave population; its presence not only helped depress the economic condition of free citizen-farmers but also put a stigma on the menial labor required to sustain Roman society. The stresses building up in this increasingly complex social structure had the potential to disrupt the internal order of the Roman Republic.

Finally, by 133 B.C., there were significant signs that a transformation of the collective mentality of the Roman citizenry was in progress, pointing toward an erosion of confidence in ancient values and an opening of minds to the need for change. The expanding awareness of a world larger and more diverse than Rome not only undermined but even made ridiculous and senseless a narrow dedication to the traditions of a single city-state. As we shall see later in discussing Roman cultural life (Chapter 11), a significant segment of aristocratic society began to experience a broadening of their intellectual horizons as a result of their growing familiarity with Hellenistic culture and the style of life their new wealth permitted. Especially potent in reshaping their values was their encounter with classical Greek literature and Hellenistic philosophical systems such as Epicureanism and Stoicism. Many Romans were captivated by the emotional, individualistic mystery religions from the east. With good reason many groups—the peasantry, the urban population, the *equites*—began to lose faith in the ability of the republican political order to further their interests. Incessant military involvement engendered a disturbing tolerance for violence and arrogance. These currents made the Roman populace less willing to abide by traditional values and moral standards, the "customs of their forefathers" associated with the simpler, more rustic world of the early republic.

These problems created a dangerous situation that required innovative political action. The burden of meeting that challenge rested in the hands of a narrow oligarchy, which by 133 B.C. had established an unchallenged control over Roman political life. There were, however, ominous signs that the traditional consensus within the ranks of the *nobiles* was in danger of dissolving. Ambitious members of that group sought wealth, political and military honors, and cultural distinctions that would exalt them over their aristocratic peers. Although the ruling oligarchy sought to curb such tendencies, there remained the danger that rivalries among the *nobiles* would become another disruptive force. Could that caste utilize political institutions and processes originally shaped to govern a small city-state to find solutions to complex problems rooted in the realities dictated by Rome's rule over an extensive empire? The search for an answer led to a political upheaval that ultimately destroyed the Roman Republic.

2. ATTEMPTED REFORMS AND FACTIONAL STRUGGLES, 133–79 B.C.

The ordeal of the republic opened with an effort to institute reforms aimed at resolving some of the critical problems facing Rome. That effort quickly devolved into a struggle between two factions over how the political process should work in reaching decisions about critical issues. On one side was a group known as the *optimates* (the "best"), who represented the established ruling oligarchy and whose members believed that decision making should remain where it had always been—in the hands of the Senate and the elected magistrates drawn from the *nobiles*. Opposed was a faction known as the *populares* (the "people"), who sought to involve a broader range of the citizen body in political decisions, utilizing for that purpose the ancient political tools of the "people"—the tribunes and the Assembly of Tribes. The *populares* were usually led by men of noble origin, who often were motivated by a mixture of genuine concern for Rome and ambitions to advance their careers. To achieve these ends, they appealed to the plebeian citizens, especially those living in Rome, and the *equites* to use their votes to shape political decisions.

The initial engagement in the struggle for reform and power occurred between 133 and 121 B.C., when the brothers Tiberius and Gaius Gracchus took up the cause of the *populares*. Aristocratic, well educated, and ambitious, the Gracchi were deeply troubled by the threat posed to Rome's military resources and to the safety of the state by the declining numbers of citizen-farmers who could afford to perform military service. Elected tribune for 133 B.C., Tiberius proposed a land law aimed at enforcing an older law that limited the amount of public land any citizen could hold. Land recovered by the application of this law would be redistributed to landless citizens. Although Tiberius' measure had some support in the Senate, it threatened the wealth of many *nobiles,* who over many generations had blatantly disregarded the existing law to take possession of most of the public lands. In order to pass his proposal, Tiberius resorted to political tactics that were not unconstitutional but that ran counter to the way in which decisions were customarily made. He used his power as tribune to put the land law before the Assembly of Tribes, which approved the measure without senatorial approval. When Tiberius tried to apply his land law, the Senate attempted to thwart him by withholding funding. Tiberius responded by threatening to divert revenues from the provinces for this purpose, a measure that challenged the Senate's traditional control over public finances and foreign affairs. Finally, Tiberius sought reelection as tribune in order to complete his reform. Since such reelection ran contrary to the custom that forbade elected officials to hold office in successive years, the Senate raised the charge that Tiberius was seeking to become a dictator. This inflammatory accusation led to violence and the murder of Tiberius at the hands of those calling themselves "the best." After Tiberius' death the application of his land law went forward, suggesting that the substance of the law was not the real issue. Instead, at the heart of the struggle was the threat to the Senate's monopoly on political power posed by Tiberius' political tactics, especially his appeal to the "people" for support.

A decade after Tiberius' death the reform issue was raised again by his brother Gaius. Elected tribune for 122 B.C., Gaius put forward a much more comprehensive program than that of Tiberius. He persuaded the Assembly of Tribes to pass legislation providing for new land laws, cheap grain at public expense for Rome's urban populace, the establishment of colonies for the resettlement of poor Romans, expanded political privileges for the Italian allies, and greater control by the *equites* over provincial tax collection. These measures, which were aimed at creating broad popular support for Gaius, aroused bitter opposition from the *optimates,* who again resorted to violence, which this time claimed the lives of Gaius and three thousand of his followers.

Although the death of Gaius Gracchus left the *populares* leaderless for more than a decade, the Gracchi had formulated a broad reform program that in the future would provide ambitious leaders with a wide range of issues upon which to build popular support. A leader capable of exploiting this situation soon appeared: Marius (ca. 155–86 B.C.). A wealthy man of nonnoble origin with small prospects of a major political role, Marius took advantage of a military crisis to gain power. The occasion was a badly managed war undertaken by Rome against Jugurtha, a claimant to the throne of Numidia, a client kingdom of Rome in North Africa. Growing impatience with the failure of Roman armies to defeat Jugurtha and charges that this clever, unscrupulous king was holding his own through bribery of Roman officials generated widespread unrest in Rome. Playing upon suspicions of corruption in the Senate and proclaiming his support for *populares* reforms, Marius succeeded in winning the consulship for 107 B.C. He then persuaded the Assembly of Tribes to vote him command of the army in Numidia. In recruiting troops for his campaign, Marius took a bold and fateful step. Disregarding the traditional property qualifications for military service, he enlisted large numbers of propertyless volunteers attracted by promises of rewards from their general. The first step had been taken in the creation of private armies as a political tool.

Marius quickly justified the trust placed in him by defeating Jugurtha in 105 B.C. Then he was annually reelected as consul during the years between 104 and 101 B.C. to conduct campaigns against Germanic tribes threatening northern Italy and southern Gaul. Again Marius was successful, in no small part because of his skill in professionalizing his volunteer army; his efforts marked an important step toward resolving the problem of defending Rome's frontiers. While he earned fame as a general, Marius' *populares* allies asserted pressure on the Roman government to provide land allocations for his veterans. However, in 100 B.C., during his sixth term as consul, Marius was maneuvered by the Senate into using armed force to curb the increasingly violent actions of his own political allies. This action temporarily ended his grip on power.

The decade of the nineties was relatively quiet, perhaps because moderate elements in the Senate took measures to respond to critical problems. However, two issues defied these efforts and provided fuel for the next crisis. One was the festering problem of the Italian allies, long discontented over Rome's failure to expand their rights in recognition of their contribution to military conquests and increasingly impoverished by the decline of small-farm agriculture. To relieve their situation, the allies demanded full citizenship. Although Roman leaders from Gaius Gracchus onward had often proposed such a step, the Romans repeatedly refused to share the rewards of citizenship with their allies. When one more such proposal was voted down in 91 B.C., the allies joined in a great rebellion, sometimes called the Social War, which threatened Rome's very existence. Sulla (138–78 B.C.), a noble who had established a reputation while serving under Marius in the war against Jugurtha, was chosen to lead the army raised to suppress the uprising. By 89 B.C. Sulla defeated the rebels, whose cause was undermined when the Romans finally granted citizenship to the allies. For his success Sulla was elected consul for 88 B.C.

While the Social War was in progress, Rome faced another threat caused by the corruption-ridden, oppressive system of provincial administration. In 89 B.C. Mithradates VI, king of Pontus in Asia Minor, played on this discontent to launch a war of liberation in Asia Minor and Greece. Faced with the threat of loss of its empire in the east, the Senate charged Sulla with leading a campaign against Mithradates. However, a faction of *populares* leaders defied the Senate to vote the command to Marius. Sulla responded by marching his army to Rome, crushing the *populares*, and securing the command by force. His actions left little doubt where the real power lay.

Once in control, Sulla led his army to the east. He forced Mithradates to return to his old kingdom and reestablished Roman control over the eastern provinces. But he made no decisive settlement in the east; his eyes were on Rome, where developments threatening his career were unfolding. Immediately after his departure for the east, the *populares* under Marius forced their way back into power and imposed a reign of terror on the Senate. They dominated until 83 B.C., when Sulla returned to Italy, greatly enriched by booty seized in the east. His battle-tested soldiers routed the *populares*, whose leader had died in 86 B.C. To seal his victory, Sulla ordered the murder of thousands of citizens from all over Italy identified with the *populares* cause and the confiscation of their property, much of which was used to reward his soldiers and political supporters.

Having established dominance by force of arms, Sulla had himself appointed as dictator. Intent on restoring control of the republic to the Senate, he enacted legislation that severely limited the power of the tribunes and the Assembly of Tribes to initiate legislation. The size of the Senate was doubled, many of the new seats being granted to *equites* and upper-class Italians. Steps were taken to regularize the election procedures for the magistracies, to improve the administration of justice, and to organize provincial government more efficiently—all sources of political agitation. Confident that he had restored the ancient constitution with the Senate in control, Sulla retired from public life in 79 B.C. In fact, the Senate was in power only because a powerful military leader had decreed so. The bitter clash between *optimates* and *populares* had resolved few of Rome's basic problems. Rather, the struggle had created a situation that encouraged bold, ambitious individuals to exploit those problems to gain control of the real source of power: military forces and political followings. The republican form of government had suffered a mortal blow.

3. THE ERA OF MILITARY STRONGMEN, 79–31 B.C.

The Senate proved itself unable to bear the burden thrust upon it by Sulla. Its failures created successive opportunities for "strongmen" to control Roman political life during the half century following Sulla. The decade between 79 and 70 B.C. witnessed several serious crises: a revolt in Italy led by a disaffected consul seeking to undo Sulla's reforms; a rebellion in Spain organized by a disillusioned Roman governor who enjoyed widespread native support; a slave uprising in Italy led by a professional gladiator named Spartacus; a mounting threat from pirates to the grain supply for Rome; and a new war with Mithradates VI of Pontus. The Senate responded to these challenges with a singular lack of political imagination: It granted extraordinary powers to ambitious individuals in a fashion that left the Senate little opportunity to control their actions. A protégé of Sulla, Pompey (106–48 B.C.), was given command of forces to deal first with the Italian revolt and then with the insurrection in Spain (see Figure 9.2). Crassus (ca. 115–53 B.C.), a rich moneylender and real estate speculator ambitious for a political career, was charged with suppressing the slave revolt. Both were successful, and although neither was constitutionally eligible for office, they used their military followings to secure election to the consulship for 70 B.C.

During their co-consulship, Pompey and Crassus negated most of Sulla's settlement; their enactments, applauded by the remnants of the *populares*, restored the opportunity for ambitious leaders to exploit popular support as a path to power. But after their term ended neither Pompey nor Crassus was satisfied. Pompey was the first to move toward greater power. By manipulating Rome's political factions, he persuaded the Senate and the people to vote him two important military commands: In 67 B.C. he was granted sweeping powers to clear the Mediterranean of pirates, a task he completed in a matter of months. Then, in 66 B.C., he was voted com-

FIGURE 9.2 Pompey and Julius Caesar These two men, Pompey (left) and Julius Caesar (right), virtually controlled the destiny of the Roman Republic and the Mediterranean world between 79 and 44 B.C. Their busts reflect the talent of Roman sculptors in portraiture. (Pompey, Culver Pictures; Julius Caesar, Alinari/Art Resource)

mand of the army fighting against Mithradates, who since 74 B.C. had again challenged Rome's rule in Asia Minor. Pompey quickly defeated Mithradates. He then took it upon himself to reorganize Rome's position in the east. The territories that formerly had comprised the kingdoms of Bithynia and Pontus were annexed to Rome and combined to create a new province. Still another new province was established in Syria (see Map 8.2), a step that in effect ended the Seleucid kingdom. To protect the eastern provinces, he worked out a series of agreements with small kingdoms beyond Rome's new eastern frontier, making each a client of Rome charged with protecting the frontier in return for Roman support in maintaining each king's power over his subjects. One group cast roughly in that role was the

Jewish community in Judea, the governance of which was entrusted to a high priest expected to support Roman interests. Pompey also regulated tribute collecting in the east so as to greatly increase the return to the Roman government. His efforts represented a major step in solidifying provincial administration; they also won Pompey important support from Romans who had interests in the east, especially *equites* engaged in provincial tax collection and in trade in the east.

Pompey's success, reminiscent of Sulla's rise to power, drove other ambitious politicians to maneuver to check him. A key figure in this endeavor was Crassus, who found a skilled ally in Julius Caesar (100–44 B.C.), a man of patrician origins but with family connections that linked him with Marius and the *populares* cause (see

Figure 9.2). Crassus and Caesar promoted laws to attract popular support and spent huge sums in an attempt to secure extraordinary military commands such as those held by Pompey. Their maneuvers were resisted by the Senate, supported in its effort by Cicero (106–43 B.C.), a "new" man who clawed his way to the consulship for 63 B.C. by utilizing his skills as an orator and lawyer. His finest hour as consul came when he earned public acclaim for foiling an alleged conspiracy by Cataline, a frustrated power seeker and sometime agent of Crassus, to overthrow the system. While Cicero shared the ambition for power with most other political leaders of his time, he disdained one-man rule in favor of a "concord of orders" that would link the talents of the old aristocracy and the *equites* into a new ruling force capable of curbing demagogic rabble-rousers and strong-armed generals.

Finally, in 62 B.C., Pompey returned from the east. Contrary to expectations, his first act was to disband his army and request that the Senate reward his veterans and legalize the settlement he had made in the east. Under the leadership of intractable conservatives, the Senate chose a course that drove Pompey, Crassus, and Caesar into a political alliance. It not only refused to meet Pompey's requests but also acted to curb a major source of Crassus' wealth by restricting the activities of provincial tax farmers and to discredit Caesar by blocking his election to the consulship. Equally frustrated, the three joined in an informal secret agreement, called the First Triumvirate, designed to ensure that each obtained what he wished. Exploiting his growing popular appeal and with the support of Pompey and Crassus, Caesar won the consulship for 59 B.C. Once in office, he forced through measures that satisfied his fellow triumvirs. His reward was a five-year military command to look after Roman interests on its northern frontier in Gaul and Illyria.

During the decade after 59 B.C. Rome's political destiny hinged on the actions of the triumvirs. During the first years of the decade the triumvirate held together uneasily. It was renewed in 56 B.C. with the understanding that Pompey and Crassus would be consuls for 55 B.C. and then be granted governorships of important provinces under terms that would provide them command over armies. Caesar's command in Gaul was also extended for five years. But the arrangement was increasingly shaky. Caesar proved to be a brilliant military leader, exploiting local political conditions in Gaul to create opportunities for military campaigns that added Gaul as a Roman province and took Roman armies into Germany and Britain. Not only did these highly publicized victories enhance Caesar's reputation, they also allowed him to create a disciplined personal army totally devoted to his cause. Crassus' long search for fame came to an end in 53 B.C., when he was killed leading an unsuccessful campaign against a Roman foe in the east, the Parthians. An important link between Caesar and Pompey was broken in 54 B.C. with the death of Pompey's wife, Julia, the daughter of Caesar. Caesar's growing fame fed a familiar fear in Rome—that of a victorious general returning to impose his will. Pompey increasingly won the favor of the Senate as its protector against such an eventuality and was voted powers that made him virtual dictator. Amid the heightening tension fed by the fear of Caesar and by the violent mob actions fomented in Rome by his agents seeking to protect his interests, Pompey and the Senate moved to ruin Caesar. As his command in Gaul approached its legal end, Caesar sought to run in absentia for the consulship for 49 B.C. so that he could remain in public office and avoid prosecution for alleged illegal acts which his foes claimed he had committed during his service in Gaul. Early in 49 B.C. the Senate decreed that he must surrender his command in Gaul, and Pompey was empowered to take necessary action to protect the state. Rather than face political ruin, Caesar chose to defy the state. He led his legions across the Rubicon River separating Gaul from Italy and plunged Rome into a civil war.

Caesar quickly demonstrated his military genius in guiding his seasoned veterans against the larger forces of Pompey. In a succession of campaigns in Italy, Spain, and finally Greece, he battered Pompey's forces. The defeated Pompey finally fled to Egypt, where he was murdered. Caesar used this crime against a Roman citizen as a pretext to intervene in Egypt, where a struggle for control of the crown was in progress among members of the Ptolemaic family. Caesar supported the claims of Cleopatra against her brother-husband, Ptolemy XIV. Perhaps his decision was prompted by the fact that he had become Cleopatra's lover; but more likely he hoped that by putting the young princess on the throne, he could dominate the last independent Hellenistic kingdom and tap Egypt's fabulous wealth for Rome's benefit. His position secured in Egypt, Caesar continued his triumphant march through the empire—Asia, Africa, Spain—hunting down Pompey's allies and showing his own power. Finally, in 45 B.C., he returned to Rome as undisputed master of the Roman world.

Although Caesar's real power rested on his loyal army, he made an effort to legalize his authority. Despite being elected consul several times, he relied chiefly on the office of dictator as the basis for his actions. He allowed the traditional elective offices to be filled, but with men willing to bend to his command. The Senate was greatly enlarged, the new places being filled with Caesar's supporters. As a consequence, that venerable institution became little more than an advisory council to the dictator. On the basis of his dictatorial power, Caesar assumed control of crucial areas of government previously dominated by the Senate: public finances, provincial administration, command over the military forces. A grateful citizenry heaped a wide range of honors on him, creating around him the aura of superiority over other citizens. In many ways Caesar's position in Rome resembled that of a Hellenistic king; indeed, some of Caesar's contemporaries insisted that it was his intention to establish a monarchy in Rome.

In using these powers, Caesar demonstrated qualities of statesmanship to match his military genius. During his brief rule over Rome, he began shaping a reform program that addressed some of the major problems plaguing Rome: reduction of the number of citizens dependent on the dole by resettling them in the provinces; debt regulation; suppression of mob violence in Rome; aid to Italian farmers; improvement of provincial administration; extension of citizenship to some provincials; reorganization of local government in Italy to allow greater local autonomy. It is not clear, however, whether he planned to reshape the structure of the political system to meet Rome's responsibilities as ruler of the Mediterranean world. Perhaps given more time, Caesar would have faced this issue, but that was not to be. A hard core of conservatives, including such former supporters of Caesar as Cassius and Brutus, formed a conspiracy to end what they saw as a threat to the traditional order. These guardians of "right" order struck their blow for liberty on the Ides of March (March 15), 44 B.C., stabbing Caesar to death while he was attending a Senate meeting just prior to his departure for a major campaign against the Parthians.

Caesar's murder did not lead to the restoration of the old order; rather, it produced a new civil war among rivals seeking to replace Caesar. Two candidates emerged as the main contenders. One was Mark Antony (ca. 83–30 B.C.), an experienced politician who had served Caesar as a military commander. The other was eighteen-year-old Octavian, a distant relative whom Caesar had adopted as his son. Faced with efforts by the Senate to eliminate them from power, Antony and Octavian, along with another supporter of Caesar named Lepidus, joined forces in 43 B.C. to form the Second Triumvirate and to force the Senate and people to grant them joint absolute power in the state. Within a year the triumvirs brutally murdered most of the anti-Caesar senatorial forces, including Cicero, and conducted a military campaign in Greece that destroyed the armies raised by Caesar's assassins, two of whom—Cassius and Brutus—died at the decisive battle of Philippi in 42 B.C.

After 42 B.C. Antony, Octavian, and Lepidus continued to rule Rome jointly under the powers voted them in the legislation that had established the Second Triumvirate. Actually, each was making preparations to destroy the others. Antony spent most of these years in the east, seeking to strengthen Roman control there and to mount a war against the Parthians. Although he made some progress in these endeavors, his standing in the Roman world was increasingly tainted by his involvement with Cleopatra, for whom he eventually repudiated his Roman wife—none other than Octavian's sister—and by whom he had two sons. This liaison was cleverly exploited by Octavian to portray Antony as a mad traitor and the pitiful victim of a crafty eastern harlot intent on robbing Rome of its territories to advance her own power and reward her children.

Octavian proved more adept at building a power base. Under the arrangement agreed upon by the triumvirs, he was charged with the heavy responsibilities of providing land for the veterans from the large army that had defeated the forces of Caesar's assassins, of rooting out the powerful remnants of anti-Caesar forces in the west, and of coping with the official government still operating in Rome. He worked patiently to meet these challenges, doing so in a way that gave him a solid hold over Italy and the west. Along the way, he forced Lepidus to retire from the triumvirate. Gradually, Octavian came to be looked upon as the protector of Roman interests against Antony, increasingly portrayed by Octavian's clever propaganda as an enemy of Rome. By 32 B.C. Octavian felt strong enough to refuse to rule jointly with Antony and declared war on Cleopatra. The decisive engagement between the huge armies and navies of the protagonists was fought in 31 B.C. at Actium in Greece (see Figure 9.1). Octavian's forces won an easy victory. The triumphant leader pursued Antony and Cleopatra to Egypt, where Cleopatra made one final effort to entice a Roman to support her cause. When Octavian would have none of her favors, she committed suicide, as Antony had already done. Her kingdom was annexed as a Roman province. Again the Roman world had an undisputed ruler whose sword had raised him to a position comparable to that Caesar had enjoyed in 46 B.C. Rome's future depended on what victorious Octavian would decide to do.

4. THE FRUITS OF CIVIC STRIFE

In many ways the events transpiring between the attempted reforms by the Gracchi begun in 133 B.C. and Octavian's victory in 31 B.C. marked a terrible chapter in human history. Civil strife, fomented by ruthless power seekers and abetted by factions seeking to serve self-interests, cost countless lives, loss of property, disruption of livelihoods, dissolution of traditional social bonds, and constant insecurity in every rank of society and across the vast territory that Rome controlled. Nor did Octavian's victory offer his contemporaries any assurance that the ordeal was over. It had often happened earlier that the ascendancy of a strong man was merely a prelude to the emergence of challengers who sparked a new—and usually more destructive—round of civil strife.

One consequence of the long struggle that

had wracked the late republic provided a major source of uncertainty. The republican political system shaped prior to 133 B.C. and much revered by many Roman citizens lay in shambles by 31 B.C. Although still in existence, the key institutions marking the republican constitution—citizen assemblies, elected magistrates, the Senate—and the processes by which decisions were reached under the republican system had become totally ineffective. Power lay in the hands of a military dictator whose constitutional position lacked any clear definition beyond the fact that he possessed the brute force to impose his will. Rome's very survival hinged on fashioning a new political system to replace the discredited republican order.

Another ominous result of the turmoil marking the final century of the Roman Republic was the failure to resolve most of the basic problems that had been the cause of civil strife. The frontiers of Rome's empire remained fluid and ill defended. Between 133 and 31 B.C. new provinces were added in Asia, Africa, and Europe (see Map 8.1), chiefly as a result of conquests prompted by ambitious leaders seeking a means of advancing their political fortunes, but little attention had been given to the defense of Rome's ever-lengthening frontiers. Rome's conquered subjects continued to be exploited mercilessly by Roman armies, corrupt governors, and rapacious tax collectors. The economic and social lot of Italy's citizen-farmers deteriorated still further as more of them were deprived of their land, forcing them to become dependents serving noble owners of large estates (*latifundia*) or migrants to urban centers, especially Rome. Rome's population, by now approaching a million residents made up of a polyglot mixture of citizens, foreigners, slaves, and freedmen living in crowded tenements, spawned increasing numbers of impoverished, rootless citizens with little stake in the existing order. Increasingly manipulated by demagogues willing to utilize public resources to provide "bread and circuses" in return for votes and for service in gangs willing to commit acts of political violence, this undisciplined mob was a constant threat to order. And slavery grew apace during the last century of the republic, enlarging the number of people in the Roman world who were exploited mercilessly, breeding a false sense of superiority in the nonslave pop-

FIGURE 9.3 Aspects of Life During the Late Republic These two scenes reflect important aspects of life in the late republic. On the left laborers unload grain brought by ship from African provinces to feed Rome's growing numbers of unemployed citizens. On the right a Roman aristocrat and his wife are instructed by a Greek slave; to be educated in Greek ways was critical to social respectability in first-century B.C. Rome. (Alinari/Art Resource)

ulation, and demeaning many kinds of labor needed to sustain the economy of the Roman world. Unless solutions could be found for this whole range of problems, the prospects for a better future remained uncertain.

However, the political, social, and economic landscape created by a century of turmoil was not completely bleak. Amid the mounting chaos there were factors at work pointing toward recovery, some of them products of the civil strife. Despite the havoc wrought by political and social upheaval, the Roman citizen body still represented a potent human resource. At its center stood the old noble families, who showed a remarkable ability to survive political proscription, confiscation of their wealth, and political humiliation at the hands of military dictators and *populares* demagogues. Although insistent on its social superiority and little averse to accumulating an ever greater share of the wealth, this class became more aware of the wider world now embraced by Rome and more open to new ideas and values. Even aristocratic women, long completely under the domination of male heads of households, began to break the shackles of custom to become property owners, active participants in cultural and social life, and even political forces as key partners in political marriages (see Figure 9.3). The ranks of the old aristocracy were imperceptibly expanded, especially by the

addition to its ranks of the Italian aristocracy, which exercised an important role in shaping local affairs. This noble class represented a considerable political talent and social influence that could be tapped to reconstruct the Roman political order. While taking advantage of the disorder accompanying civil struggle to reap enormous rewards as provincial tax collectors, suppliers of private armies, moneylenders, and speculators in confiscated property, the *equites* gained experience related to provincial administration, military organization, and trade that could be invaluable in reshaping society. Especially significant was the potential of the plebeian citizens as a military resource. Although a source of massive disorder during the last century of the republic, the private armies recruited by Marius, Sulla, Pompey, Julius Caesar, and Octavian chiefly from the ranks of landless plebeians laid the foundation for a professional citizen army capable of defending Rome's huge empire.

In the outwardly destructive course of events unfolding between 133 and 31 B.C., there was some evidence that new directions in the shaping of Rome's public policy were being plotted. Alliances began to take shape that established a network of client states as a stabilizing force along Rome's extensive frontiers. Leaders such as Pompey and Caesar enacted measures pointing toward a regularization of provincial administration that took into account the needs and interests of Rome's huge subject population. Among other things, such arrangements often allowed local authorities in the provinces considerable control over local affairs. In a few instances provincial subjects, especially local aristocrats, were granted rights of citizenship as a reward for their willingness to support Roman interests. Some Romans began to show an awareness that Rome's material welfare depended not only on the exaction of tribute but also on expanding commercial relations that gave Rome access to grain, raw materials, and manufactured goods produced in the provinces (see Figure 9.3). Efforts were made to come to grips with Rome's urban problems, especially by resettling citizens in Italy and the provinces, where they became agents promoting Romanization; by initiating public works projects to provide employment; and by developing regularized administrative personnel to deal with such matters as law enforcement and food supply. Although such actions were usually taken by strongmen seeking to serve their quest for power, they suggested that, despite the violence and the abuse of power so prevalent during the last years of the republic, Roman leadership was not completely bankrupt politically.

Particularly notable about the tumultuous era marking the end of the Roman Republic was a quickening of intellectual and artistic life that heralded the assumption of cultural leadership by Latin-speaking Romans. As we shall see in greater detail later (see Chapter 11), the literary activities of such figures as Cicero, Lucretius, and Julius Caesar and the works of anonymous architects and sculptors signaled the dawn of a golden age in Roman cultural life. Although heavily influenced by Greek models, these figures produced works with a distinctive and unique Roman stamp that established Rome's claim to supremacy in the Mediterranean world beyond the realm of politics and military force. Cultural leadership provided a new focus around which Roman creative energies could rally and opened avenues through which Roman values could be reformulated and propagated to counter the moral confusion brought on by the disturbances accompanying the fall of the Roman Republic.

Viewed in its entirety, the century extending from 133 to 31 B.C. marked a decisive transition period in the history of Western civilization. It witnessed the dramatic, painful collapse of a time-sanctioned order that had permitted the residents of a small city-state to establish domination over an extensive empire surrounding the Mediterranean Sea. But even while that darker side of the era ran its course, there were signs of a regrouping of resources and talents heralding a new day for Rome.

SUGGESTED READING

Political Developments

H. H. Scullard, *From the Gracchi to Nero: A History of Rome from 133 B.C. to A.D. 68*, 5th ed. (1982). A detailed history.

Ronald Syme, *The Roman Revolution* (1952).

Richard E. Smith, *The Failure of the Roman Republic* (1955).

Erich S. Gruen, *The Last Generation of the Roman Republic* (1974).

Mary Beard and Michael Crawford, *Rome in the Late Republic: Problems and Interpretations* (1985).

These four works present significant but differing interpretations of the causes of the failure of the Roman Republic.

Claude Nicolet, *The World of the Citizen in Republican Rome*, trans. P. S. Falla (1980). A reconstruction of the civic life of the average citizen.

A. W. Lintott, *Violence in the Roman Republic* (1968).

Paul J. J. Vanderbroeck, *Popular Leadership and Collective Behavior in the Late Roman Republic (ca. 80–50 B.C.)* (1987).

A. M. Eckstein, *Senate and Generals* (1987).

David F. Epstein, *Personal Enmity and Roman Politics (218–43 B.C.)* (1987).

Keith R. Bradley, *Slavery and Rebellion in the Roman World, 140 B.C.–70 B.C.* (1989).

The preceding five titles all deal with aspects of political life that had a bearing on the decline of the republic.

A. N. Sherwin-White, *Roman Foreign Policy in the East, 168 B.C. to 1 A.D.* (1984). An excellent study.

Economic and Social Developments

Géza Alföldy, *The Social History of Rome*, trans. David Braund and Frank Pollock (1985). A challenging introduction.

P. A. Brunt, *Social Conflicts in the Roman Republic* (1971). A good description of social tensions affecting late republican society.

K. D. White, *Roman Farming* (1970). Clarifies the problems of Roman agriculture during the republican period.

Biographies

A. H. Bernstein, *Tiberius Sempronius Gracchus. Tradition and Apostasy* (1978).

Arthur Keaveney, *Sulla: The Last Republican* (1982).

Peter Greenhalgh, *Pompey: The Roman Alexander* (1980) and *Pompey: The Republican Prince* (1981).

B. A. Marshall, *Crassus: A Political Biography* (1976).

Elizabeth Rawson, *Cicero: A Portrait*, rev. ed. (1983).

Christian Habicht, *Cicero the Politician* (1990).

Matthias Gelzer, *Caesar: Politician and Statesman* (1968).

Arthur D. Kahn, *The Education of Julius Caesar: A Biography, a Reconstruction* (1986).

Sources

Cicero, *Selected Works*, trans. Michael Grant (1971).

War Commentaries of Caesar, trans. Rex Warner (1960). Contains two of Caesar's political works, *The Gallic Wars* and *The Civil Wars*.

CHAPTER 10
The Roman Empire and the *Pax Romana,* 31 B.C.–A.D. 180

FIGURE 10.1 Augustus, First Citizen of Rome This majestic statue of Octavian, or Augustus, as he came to be known soon after he seized power, was intended to idealize and exalt the man who had restored peace to the Roman world after the troubled times of the late republic. (Alinari/ Art Resource)

The year 31 B.C. marked a critical point in the history of the Mediterranean world. After suffering a profound internal crisis that ended with the collapse of their traditional political order, its Roman masters faced the challenge of restoring order in their own house if their dominance of the Mediterranean world was to continue in a fruitful way. During the following two centuries the Romans met that challenge by fashioning their most notable contribution to civilization—a system of government known as the Roman Empire. This system became a powerful force promoting peace, order, and cultural diffusion among millions of people living in a vast territory surrounding what the Romans called "our sea."

1. OCTAVIAN'S NEW POLITICAL ORDER, 31 B.C.–A.D. 14

The establishment of a new order was the work of Octavian (see Figure 10.1). His victory at Actium in 31 B.C. made him master of the Roman world by virtue of conquest. With an uncanny grasp of the mentality of his times, Octavian sensed that naked power would not suffice to restore order. In the minds of the Roman citizenry any form of military dictatorship or monarchy was unacceptable because it flaunted a five-century-old tradition that held that Rome's destiny could be determined only by the decisions of the Senate and the people acting through the institutions of the Roman Republic. Yet the experience of the previous century had shown that the only hope for the management of the vast, problem-ridden Roman world lay in the concentration of power in the hands of a single individual. Octavian's challenge was to reconcile the collective mind-set rooted in tradition with existing reality. His solution was masterful: He sought to preserve the outward forms of the republican constitution while obtaining, by legal means, sufficient power to permit him to rule the Roman world. Lacking the charisma of a Julius Caesar, Octavian proved to be a patient, realistic, cautious, pragmatic statesman who understood the deeper currents at work in his world and who was amazingly flexible in devising means to achieve his program. His forty-five-year rule

gave him time to experiment and shift direction as the occasion demanded.

As early as 27 B.C., Octavian made a decisive move toward defining his position when he proclaimed before the Senate "the transfer of the state to the free disposal of the Senate and the people." This apparent surrender of all the powers he then held was interpreted as a restoration of the republic. Impressed by this noble gesture, fearful of the recurrence of civil war, and skillfully guided by Octavian, the Senate and the people quickly took legal action to bestow on him a wide array of powers. Included were the power of tribune for life, full consular authority without need to hold that office, authority over most of the provinces, command of the armies, and the highest priestly office. To these legal powers the grateful citizenry added several honors: first senator; *augustus* ("most revered one"); *imperator* ("victorious general"); and *pater patriae* ("father of the country"). This array of legal powers and tradition-laden honors surrounded Octavian with an aura of authority so great that he began to be seen as *princeps*, the first citizen of Rome, trusted to do what he wished to rule the Roman world without a hint of illegal abuse of power or of violating tradition. What was crucial in Octavian's position was that he did not have to share the authority legally granted him and that his power need not be renewed regularly. Buttressing his position as *princeps* were his immense personal fortune and his wide circle of political dependents, both created during the period of his rise to power after Julius Caesar's death.

Octavian—or Augustus, as he came to be known by virtue of the title that vaguely suggested a semidivine status—sought to use his vast authority to resolve the major problems that had so long plagued Roman society. One concern was the revitalization of the citizen body—basically the population of Italy—on whose shoulders rested the responsibility for ruling the vast empire. Adhering to the ancient and widely held conviction that only a class-structured society could ensure right order, Augustus tried to redefine class divisions and to assign civic responsibilities to each group. Rigid standards of birth, wealth, and conduct were established to define senatorial ranking, resulting in a considerable reduction of those eligible for this rank. This elite was assigned a major role in political life. The

Senate, the traditional focus of political life for the *nobiles*, retained important powers in selecting magistrates, judging cases, enacting laws, and governing selected provinces. Members of the senatorial class were expected to fill the traditional elective offices, to serve as provincial governors, and to command armies. Augustus counted on the equestrian order (*equites*) to serve the state in critical administrative positions in the army, the tax system, and the judicial system. To the plebeians, Augustus offered order and economic security in return for their votes in support of his regime and service as citizen-soldiers in the army. While this arrangement was sensitive to traditional class roles, it effectively defined the responsibility of citizenship in terms of service to the state at the direction of the *princeps* rather than in terms of citizen formulation of basic policy.

Concerned by what many perceived to be low morale among the citizens, Augustus initiated sweeping measures to rebuild a sense of community and to revive a feeling of pride in Rome, ends he hoped to achieve by playing on tradition. He made a major effort to revive ancient civic religious practices as a central part of public life. He patronized writers such as Vergil, Horace, and Livy and artists (see Chapter 11) who were willing to celebrate Rome's ancient glory and present blessings. Laws were enacted to curb what Augustus believed to be vices that sapped civic virtue—luxury, sexual irregularities, divorce, childless marriages, gambling, drinking, idleness. Immense sums were spent to beautify Rome and provide better public services in the hope of eliciting pride in what was now "head of the world."

Aware of the need to protect Rome's extended frontiers and mindful of the disruptive role played by private armies during the last century of the republic, Augustus was particularly concerned with the military system. His response was the creation of a professional army consisting of twenty-five legions (about one hundred fifty thousand troops) made up chiefly of Roman citizens serving twenty-year terms. Each legion was complemented by an equal-sized auxiliary unit composed of noncitizens recruited in the provinces and granted citizenship upon completion of service. A command structure, employing carefully selected members of the senatorial and

equestrian orders but always subordinate to the *princeps*, was developed. Steps were taken to provide training, discipline, systematic provisioning, regular pay, and pensions to the soldiers. The bulk of this force was stationed in frontier provinces facing potential enemies. Only the Praetorian Guard, a select contingent of about nine thousand troops acting as a bodyguard for the *princeps*, was garrisoned in the vicinity of Rome. During Augustus' reign the army was used both to secure control over existing provinces and to attack external foes. The most important campaigns were waged in an effort to strengthen the empire's European frontier. As a result, the Roman hold on Illyricum was made secure and the new provinces of Raetia, Pannonia, and Moesia were added along the Danube frontier (see Map 10.1). An effort to expand into the Germanic world east of the Rhine ended in a crushing defeat in A.D. 9. Thereafter, Augustus gave up expansion, seeking instead to establish a fixed frontier between Romans and foreigners to be defended by the imperial army.

Aware of the disarray produced in the provinces by Rome's predatory conduct during the republican period, Augustus made a major effort to improve provincial governance. Provinces needing the presence of armed forces were administered directly by the *princeps*. He was represented in each by a *legate*, usually a senator, who directed provincial administration, and by a *procurator*, usually an equestrian, who was charged with collecting taxes. The provinces not needing armed forces were left under the jurisdiction of the Senate, which annually selected *proconsuls* to act as governors; their selection and conduct were carefully monitored by the *princeps*. This arrangement put an end to the rapacious governors and tax farmers who had for so long preyed on the helpless provincials. To complement this administrative system, Augustus encouraged the city-states scattered across the empire to take responsibility for many matters relating to life in each city-state and its dependent countryside: police regulation, justice, public works, charity, religion. Most city-states had or were encouraged to develop a working system of government based on elected magistrates, a local senate, and assemblies—a system similar to Rome's old republican order. Local aristocracies whose interests were served by cooperating with

Map 10.1 **THE ROMAN EMPIRE, 44 B.C.–A.D. 284** This map shows the expansion of the Roman Empire between the death of Julius Caesar in 44 B.C. and the accession of Emperor Diocletian in A.D. 284. The territories annexed during these three centuries brought the empire to its greatest size; all the peoples living within its vast expanse felt the influence of Greco-Roman civilization. However, by the beginning of the third century A.D. Roman domination of this territory was being threatened by increasing pressure along the frontiers facing the Germans and the Parthians.

the Roman government tended to dominate these governments. This new system, based on political authority shared by the central government and local authorities, almost immediately brought order and more equitable treatment to the provincials.

The expanding range of functions associated with the office of *princeps* generated the need for permanent civil servants skilled in administration. Although Augustus and a small circle of confidants managed to handle a huge range of administrative detail, there slowly emerged around the *princeps* a corps of helpers, composed chiefly of freed slaves, whose only political attachments were to the *princeps*. In Augustus' time one of the prime accomplishments of this embry-

onic bureaucracy was the establishment of a sound fiscal system to support the imperial regime, especially its army. The key element of that system was a land tax and a head tax equitably imposed on noncitizens on the basis of regular census taking. Roman citizens contributed to support of the state chiefly through a form of sales tax and an inheritance tax.

Concerned with perpetuating his system, Augustus was forced during most of his long reign to wrestle with the issue of succession to his position as *princeps*, a problem complicated by his perennial ill health. Aware that only the Senate and the people could legally bestow the powers upon which his veiled system of one-man rule depended, he sought to establish a successor in a position where the Senate and people would have no choice except to grant that person the same powers that Augustus wielded. To achieve that end, he tried to combine two principles: hereditary succession so that each future princeps would enjoy the prestige of descent from Julius Caesar and Augustus; and public visibility acquired by the future *princeps* through actual involvement in the governance under the tutelage of the present *princeps*. Augustus' problem turned out to be finding someone who could meet these criteria. Since he had no sons, his search for an heir focused on a series of arranged marriages of his only daughter, Julia. Augustus outlived two of her husbands as well as two grandsons considered as possible successors. Finally, chiefly through the connivance of his formidable wife, Livia, Augustus settled on her son (and his adopted stepson), Tiberius, as his successor. Tiberius was forced to divorce a beloved wife in order to become Julia's third husband and after A.D. 4 was granted ever-greater powers by Augustus with the concurrence of the Senate. When Augustus died in A.D. 14, Tiberius was in a position to claim and receive full authority as *princeps*.

2. TESTING THE AUGUSTAN ESTABLISHMENT, A.D. 14–96

During the century following Augustus' death, the Augustan system was severely tested but ultimately proved its viability. The testing took place primarily in a relatively narrow political circle involving each *princeps*, his family, his chief political agents, the senatorial class, and sometimes the army. Their activities, set forth in lurid detail by the historians Tacitus and Suetonius (see Chapter 11), leave the impression that this era was marked by monumental misrule and perpetual crisis. But more constructive developments beyond this circle provide indisputable evidence of the success of the Augustan principate.

A constant source of tension stemmed from the succession problem. The office of *princeps* as defined by Augustus required a leader descended from his family who had the ability to direct a vast empire while remaining respectful of the authority entrusted by Augustus to the

Senate and the people. Augustus' first four successors, called the Julio-Claudians, were related to him. But their selection bred intrigue, conspiracy, and violence and produced rulers of limited abilities whose actions provoked incessant opposition and obstructionism from the senatorial order. Augustus' handpicked successor, Tiberius (A.D. 14–37), was an able, experienced leader, but he was also cold, suspicious, distrustful, and easily provoked to brutal retaliation against those he suspected of undermining his power. Gaius (A.D. 37–41), nicknamed Caligula, a term meaning "little boots," given to him when he was a boy strutting about military camps in small boots, was an indolent pleasure seeker whose excesses earned him an assassin's knife. Claudius (A.D. 41–54) was a timid, scholarly man who suffered a physical handicap, was ill at ease in Roman high society, and was constantly victimized by his wives and advisers. Most notorious of all was Nero (A.D. 54–68), a cruel, vain degenerate who avoided assassination by killing himself, but only after he had murdered his mother and two wives, disposed of numerous senators, persecuted Christians, made a fool of himself by posing as an artist, and depleted public funds to satisfy his expensive whims. It is indeed easy to conclude that none of the Julio-Claudians was worthy of respect and trust as "first citizen."

Even during the era of the Julio-Claudians, there occurred a development with ominous implications for the future: the intervention of the army in the choice of the *princeps*. In a single year following Nero's death four different men were thrust into office by the Praetorian Guard in a climate of violence reminiscent of the late republic. Finally, a general named Vespasian seized the office and put an end to the bloody military competition for control of the political system. Between A.D. 69 and 96 he and his sons, Titus and Domitian, known as the Flavian dynasty, ruled effectively but in the face of repeated charges of tyranny. These charges were rooted in a constitutional problem implicit in the Augustan principate: the lack of precise definition of the powers belonging to the *princeps* and those belonging to the Senate and the people. While the Julio-Claudian and Flavian rulers tried to honor the role of the Senate and the people in directing the state, the fuzzy line between the two spheres prompted senators to charge repeatedly that the rulers were usurping authority and destroying the liberties of citizens. The rulers sometimes reacted by silencing their critics; more often, they simply did what had to be done, disregarding the alleged rights of the Senate and people. Either course led to a climate of mistrust so acute that it seemed at times that civil war would again erupt to ruin the Augustan settlement.

In reality, all this strife was little more than an intriguing sideshow detracting from the substantive advances made in achieving the peaceful order envisaged by Augustus. Several of the much-maligned rulers of this era—Tiberius, Claudius, Vespasian, Domitian—were able statesmen who worked patiently and effectively to resolve the problems facing the imperial regime. They maintained Rome's military capability and utilized it to defend the frontiers and to extend Rome's domain: Claudius conquered Britain and annexed Noricum to strengthen the Danube frontier, and Domitian won territory along the upper Rhine frontier that was crucial to the containment of the Germanic threat (see Map 10.1). They worked hard to sustain and improve equitable administration of the provinces, to develop a proficient professional bureaucracy, to sponsor public works in Rome, Italy, and the provinces, and to encourage trade, industry, and agriculture. For the most part, the Senate and people demonstrated little interest and less competence in dealing with these crucial matters. Despite their recurrent laments that their liberties were being usurped by rulers unworthy of such honor in terms of ancient standards, by the end of the first century A.D. most people had reached the conclusion that rule by a powerful *princeps* was the only guarantee of peace, security, and prosperity. The Augustan system had prevailed.

3. *PAX ROMANA:* THE "GOOD EMPERORS," A.D. 96–180

With the end of the Flavian dynasty in A.D. 96 much of the conflict that had marked the testing of the Augustan system ended. During the next century, the empire enjoyed a golden age, a time of *Pax Romana*—the Roman peace. Seldom has an era produced leaders more highly praised than the five "good emperors" who ruled from A.D. 96 to 180. Nerva (A.D. 96–98) was a respected aristocrat whose conciliatory actions calmed fears of military dictatorship. Trajan (A.D. 98–117), a native of Spain and the first emperor from the provinces, won the admiration of the entire Roman world by his respect for the Roman aristocracy, his brilliant military exploits, and his honest administration. Hadrian (A.D. 117–138), also of Spanish origin, was a cultured humanitarian who spent most of his reign traveling throughout the empire promoting the cause of peace, lawful administration, and material well-being. Antoninus (A.D. 138–161), by the excellence of his character and his humane legislation, earned the title "Pius" ("devoted to duty") from a grateful Senate. Most illustrious of all was Marcus Aurelius (A.D. 161–180), a noted Stoic philosopher who exemplified a sense of duty, a willingness to work, and a nobility of purpose in the service of the state.

The regime of the "good emperors" was one that produced little history of a conventional kind—battles, intrigues, scandals. These emperors were sometimes engaged in warfare, chiefly in defense of Rome's sprawling, lightly defended frontiers. Trajan pursued an aggressive policy that resulted in the annexation of a crucial area north of the Danube called Dacia and of extensive territories east of the Euphrates River at the expense of Parthia (see Map 10.1). However, Trajan's conquests in the east were soon abandoned. Hadrian replaced expansionism with a policy emphasizing strong defense of a fixed frontier and diplomacy. The problem of defense remained crucial, as was clear from the fact that peace-loving Marcus Aurelius had to spend most of his reign defending the northern frontier against Germans.

Less spectacular were other activities of the "good emperors" related to internal peace and stability. They resolved the succession problem by utilizing an adoptive system whereby each emperor early in his reign adopted as his son a man of ability who was then involved in imperial governance and vested with increasing legal powers to the point where he was able to take over when his "father" died. All these rulers were tactful and respectful toward the senators, who filled most of the high offices, were regularly consulted, and increasingly became staunch supporters of the imperial system. Citizenship was granted to ever-larger numbers of provincials, some of whom were elevated to senatorial rank; this policy facilitated the Romanization of the provincial population. The administrative system was steadily expanded and regularized. The rulers encouraged the development of a unified body of law for the whole empire. They championed humanitarian projects to aid the downtrodden. Every encouragement was given to city-states to determine their own course as long as that freedom did not threaten the imperial peace. The rulers worked tirelessly to establish a sound financial system to support the imperial structure. All these efforts slowly bound the diverse peoples of the empire—numbering perhaps 70 million—into a secure, peaceful commonwealth guided from Rome. By A.D. 180 a vision expressed nearly two centuries earlier by the poet Vergil in his *Aeneid* seemed fulfilled: "You, Roman, remember—these are your arts: To rule nations, and to impose the ways of peace."

4. THE NATURE OF THE IMPERIAL POLITICAL ORDER

In its mature form in the second century A.D. the imperial government was remarkably effective, but its operation is not easy to describe. One is tempted to oversimplify by stressing form without giving sufficient attention to process. The structure of the imperial government can be described in fairly simple terms. At the head of the Roman state stood a single figure, the *princeps* or *imperator*, who was vested with extensive executive, legislative, and judicial powers and with a variety of honors by the vote of the Senate and the people. Theoretically, the emperor exercised these powers by making decisions that were executed through a bureaucracy consisting of paid "civil servants" appointed by the ruler to serve the central government and of agents dispatched across the empire to carry out imperial orders. Backing the authority of the *princeps* was the army, a highly professionalized body of about three hundred thousand soldiers commanded by officers appointed by the emperor and capable of enforcing imperial orders if the need arose. The emperor's authority was represented in each of the forty-five provinces into which the empire was divided by a governor (usually called a *le-*

gatus) vested with authority to keep order and administer justice and a *procurator* charged with collecting taxes. An efficient tax system supported this complex apparatus and allowed the imperial government to provide a wide range of public services. Complementing the imperial government everywhere in the empire were active city-state governments that played a major role in directing local affairs; however, these local regimes were always open to intervention by agents of the emperor's government. When described in structural terms the imperial government seems best characterized as a highly centralized, bureaucratized regime capable of imposing on a vast population a uniform policy decided upon by one man.

However, an examination of the processes through which the Roman government impacted on the governed peoples in specific situations presents a more subtle, complex picture. The person of the *princeps* or emperor, elevated to semidivine status by a sustained and skillful propaganda effort, commanded a reverence from imperial subjects that inclined them toward obedience. That very reverence led to a widely shared expectation that the emperor could "do" all things. Since Greco-Roman political thought and practice made little allowance for delegation of power, the result was that second-century emperors were personally swamped with detailed administrative work: conducting military campaigns, arbitrating disputes, responding to petitions for favors, receiving embassies, making constant public appearances, and seeing to it that public property was properly exploited. Because the Roman record-keeping system was limited, all this detail had to be handled without much knowledge of specific situations. To assist in meeting this burden, the emperors relied more often on their household servants than on professional civil servants; members of the imperial household became real power wielders without holding official positions or being constrained by rules defining their conduct of public business. The emperors often entrusted public business to private contractors who acted according to their own lights once commissioned to perform a service for the state. Perhaps the only area in which there was anything like a regularized, empirewide administrative system was in revenue collecting, and even in this vital activity the procedures were haphazard and arbitrary.

Beyond the emperor and his circle, the political process was even less systematic and uniform. It is almost unbelievable to a modern observer to realize how few public officials in the Roman system actually had the *imperium*—the legal power to make final decisions. Those who did—army commanders, governors, procurators—held sway over extensive jurisdictions; as a result, they too were swamped with administrative details. Like the emperor, they too relied on their personal servants to assist with these details, and they too depended heavily on private contractors to get things done. All too often, things did not get done; like the famous case involving the Roman official Pontius Pilate, authorities simply "washed their hands" of problems confronting them. Far from being a mechanism through which uniform decisions were imposed upon the population through uniform procedures, the Roman imperial government operated through enclaves of power in which officials vested with the authority of Rome did what they wished in the way they wished.

The lives of most residents of the Roman empire were seldom touched directly by the imperial government—except in the pocketbook. For them the most important political force was the local city-state government, whose far-ranging activities were encouraged by the imperial government. Each urban center with its surrounding territory was ruled by a body of local aristocrats (called *decurions*) who formed a local senate (called a *curia*). These senates elected local magistrates, collected local taxes, administered justice, and assumed responsibility for keeping order and providing public facilities. Although the imperial government sometimes intervened in their activities, especially in fiscal matters, the city-state regimes were allowed wide latitude to govern those in their jurisdiction as they wished.

In view of these aspects of political reality, it is obviously impossible to think of the Roman imperial regime as one headed by a wise emperor who established general policies on the basis of extensive knowledge of conditions and with the advice of informed councilors and then issued orders that were enacted by a hierarchy of public officials capable of ensuring universal conformance to the emperor's law. Instead, governance depended on the decisions and actions of a wide array of individuals, some officeholders and some private parties, acting within a framework of overlapping jurisdictions where pragmatic concerns and individual judgment were more important than rules. To run a vast empire in such a manner would seem to be a formula for chaos. Yet during the second century A.D. the system worked.

One wonders how! The explanation may seem strange in terms of modern conceptions of statecraft. Rome was governed by a narrow, tightly knit elite. Reflecting an attitude deeply ingrained in the Greco-Roman mentality, that elite viewed public life as the highest form of human activity, to be taken seriously by those involved in the political sphere. The members of this elite also shared economic interests, social status, and cultural values that led them to think in a common pattern about the means through which power was exercised and the ends it was to serve. Whether they were public officials, senators, local decurions, army officers, or equestrian contractors, their shared perceptions of the right political order prompted each of them to decide on a course of action in a particular political situation in a way similar to the way all other power wielders would act in that same situation. Thus, without the guidance of clearly formulated policies or rigid rules regulating political behavior, the ruling elite quite unconsciously guided the Roman world in a common direction that especially prized peace and order. Perhaps the tone for this remarkable consensus was set by the "good emperors," whose conduct was shaped by a conviction that power imposed on its holders the duty to unite their subjects in a community where behavior was defined by the law of nature dictated by divine reason—a political philosophy based on Stoic ideas. Certainly from Augustus onward successive emperors acted to sanction the position of this elite and to replenish its ranks, especially by extending citizenship to provincials in a position to exercise power. But in the final analysis it was the political activism of this elite bound together by shared social values and a common culture that ruled the empire in its golden days. In a real sense the future of the empire depended on the continuation of this consensus among the members of this elite.

5. ECONOMIC AND SOCIAL LIFE IN THE ROMAN EMPIRE

A major consequence of the establishment of the imperial regime was a general improvement of material life in the Roman world to a level higher than ever before and not to be equaled again for many centuries. Not all shared that affluence equally; in fact, fewer and fewer of the population of the empire tended to enjoy more and more, a prime factor in making the imperial regime acceptable to the powerful in society. This prosperity was not the consequence of any basic change in the system of production or of a conscious economic policy fostered by the state. Rather, it stemmed from the favorable environment created by peace and order, from the security of property (including slaves) afforded by the imperial regime, from the closer integration of formerly isolated areas into the total economy, from the stimulus supplied by the expanding activities of the imperial political system, and from the entrepreneurial activities of nobles and equestrians eager to expand their family fortunes.

The Roman imperial economy remained basically agricultural. Although the organization of agricultural production varied from region to region, small farms cultivated by freeholders or renters flourished over wide reaches of the empire. The large estate system (*latifundia*), based on the labor of sharecroppers, hired workers, and slaves and devoted to the production of cash crops such as grapes, olives, and livestock, continued to spread in Italy and in the highly Romanized areas of southern Gaul, Spain, and North Africa. For the most part, these diverse forms of agricultural production provided sufficient returns to feed those who labored on them and a modest surplus to supply the needs of local urban centers. However, some areas, such as Egypt and North Africa, produced large surpluses of grain for export to the empire's great cities, especially Rome. Farming methods and technology changed little during the imperial era. Increased agricultural production resulted from better management and from the expansion

of land under cultivation, notably in Spain, Gaul, and along the Danube frontier, where urban growth and the presence of Roman army camps stimulated the demand for agricultural products and where retired army veterans provided a steady supply of new settlers.

An important key to prosperity during the first two centuries A.D. was the expansion of trade and industry. Most of the commercial activity involved the exchange of agricultural products and simple manufactured goods on a local level. However, there was a significant movement of luxury goods, raw materials, and foodstuffs on a scale embracing the whole empire and even extending beyond to Parthia, India, China, Africa, and the Germanic world. The Mediterranean became a busy commercial roadway linking its bordering lands into an interdependent economic community. The famed Roman road system encouraged the movement of goods inland to urban centers and army camps. Most manufactured goods were produced by artisans working in their own small shops; often they also marketed their products. In some cases such enterprises were financed by nobles or equestrians, whose slaves and freedmen produced goods and shared the returns with their masters. Large-scale industrial activity was rare, confined chiefly to ceramics, glassware, bricks, and mining. One of the most significant developments of this era was the remarkable expansion of industrial activity in Spain and Gaul as a result of the incorporation of these previously "backward" areas into the mainstream of Mediterranean life. A powerful stimulant to trade and industry was provided by a massive building boom that occurred throughout the empire. Funded by both public and private sources, this outburst filled numerous cities, Rome above all, with forums, basilicas for the conduct of public business, temples, theaters, stadiums, palaces, baths, and private dwellings. Across the countryside were built roads, bridges, aqueducts, villas, and army camps. This vast enterprise required capital, labor, the skilled services of artisans and suppliers, and managerial skills.

Most economic life in the first and second centuries was conducted by private individuals with little interference from the imperial government, which demonstrated a limited interest in economic matters except in tapping the system through taxation. However, what we would today call the public sector played an increasing role in the economy. Through its taxation system the Roman government drained off a portion of the wealth of the entire empire. That wealth was redistributed to pay officials' salaries, support the jobless in Rome, beautify the capital city, and maintain the army. As a consequence, most public expenditures tended to be concentrated in Rome and in frontier areas where the army was stationed. Such distribution of public funds stimulated nonproductive economic activity in these areas while depriving the most productive areas of the financial resources needed to sustain and expand economic activity. Moreover, the expanding role of the Roman government in distributing the wealth of the empire made the economy increasingly sensitive to public policy decisions involving taxation, the size of the army and the bureaucracy, and the frequency of war. This development introduced an element of instability into the economic system.

The basic social order prevailing in the Roman Empire was little changed from that of the late republican period. The distinction between citizens and noncitizens remained an important social fact; citizens had rights and privileges denied noncitizens. However, that division was increasingly blurred by the granting of citizenship to ever-larger numbers of provincials. The citizen population was divided into classes defined by law: *nobiles*, *equites*, plebeians, and slaves. Although the social status of the noncitizen population of the empire varied greatly, over most of the empire there prevailed a social structure roughly equivalent to that of the Roman citizenry.

At the summit of the social order stood the senatorial order, headed by the *princeps* and his family. Aside from its basis in law, the social status of this class was buttressed and enhanced by various factors: family origin, marriage connections, wealth based on land, education, involvement in the highest levels of political life, control over a circle of clients, and lifestyle. While small and keenly conscious of its status, the nobility was never totally exclusive. Its ranks were constantly replenished by those who could meet the standards for noble status; most often those who ascended socially were drawn from rich equestrians who served the state and provincial nobles who gained citizenship.

Although their wealth was based largely on landownership, Roman nobles were creatures of the city. Rome, of course, was the most attractive center for the *nobiles* of senatorial rank, but many other cities across the empire had their noble circles. In this urban setting noble life centered in the family household, where the *pater familias* (father of the family) ruled as he wished over his wife, children, slaves, and clients. He did not "work," as did the lower classes, but "managed" his estates, his investments, and often some segment of public life entrusted to him through selection for an office. Always uppermost in his mind were increasing the family patrimony and enhancing family prestige. These concerns prompted a keen interest in the education, careers, and marriages of his children, especially sons. Roman nobles participated in a constant round of social activities—banquets, festivals, races, gladiatorial contests, cultural events. Worthy nobles were expected to provide the major source of funding for many of these activities.

Although their lives were surrounded by constraints imposed by law and tradition that subjugated them first to their fathers and then to their husbands, women still played a prominent role in aristocratic life (see Figure 10.2). A long succession of talented wives of first- and second-century emperors helped shape decisions on such crucial matters as political patronage, succession, and the selection of advisers to each *princeps*. Noblewomen managed family households, an operation that involved large expenditures and the direction of numerous slaves (see Figure 10.3). They owned and managed property, defended their interests in court, and took part in many social activities. Not a few of them took lovers, just as their husbands did. Some evidence suggests that by the second century male nobles increasingly viewed wives as equal partners in marriage, worthy of respect and considerate treatment. This changing attitude was reflected in new marriage practices that allowed a bride to retain control over property she brought to the marriage and made divorce easier for a wife.

Although Roman moralists often painted the lives of noblemen and women in terms of gluttony, drunkenness, sexual excess, and frivolity, other evidence suggests that noble life was guided by a moral code that placed a high value

FIGURE 10.2 A Roman Lady This painting portrays a noble Roman lady of the imperial period. It suggests that Roman women were respected for their dignity, sobriety, and strength of character. Women such as this one played an important role in managing the affairs of aristocratic households and sometimes in promoting the political careers of their husbands and sons. (Courtesy of the Detroit Institute of Arts)

on sober, ordered, restrained conduct and required concern with and involvement in public affairs in the cause of creating a civilized order. The *equites* imitated the noble lifestyle, often with success, in terms of wealth, sumptuous living, and education; however, members of this order were not accepted as being real nobles and thus were excluded from the summit of the social order unless the nobles chose to co-opt them into the ranks of the real elite.

Rome and most other cities had a teeming lower-class population: shopkeepers, artisans, day laborers, the idle poor, slaves. In Rome and Italy the bulk of these people—slaves excepted—were plebeian citizens; in provincial cities they had some status as members of the community.

The political power of plebeian citizens, traditionally expressed through votes in assemblies, steadily eroded during the first and second centuries, leaving plebeians with few means of influencing their destiny. Tightly knit family units remained at the center of urban life. Most urban residents devoted their time and energy to ignoble "work" through which they earned a living, an enterprise that often occupied not only the heads of lower-class households but also their wives and children. Some shopkeepers and artisans enjoyed comfortable lives, but most urban dwellers lived near subsistence level in crowded tenements. Large numbers of poor people were dependent on the state or noble patrons for the bare essentials; it has been estimated, for instance, that an average of two hundred thousand Roman residents (perhaps a fourth of the city's population) lived off the public grain dole. The Roman imperial government as well as local city-state administrations in the provinces made serious efforts to provide police and fire protection, an adequate water supply, sanitary facilities, and cheap food. Nevertheless, life in the city was for many marred by poverty, violence, and insecurity. There were some avenues of escape from these conditions. Many residents of Rome were resettled in the provinces on their own farms. Especially attractive was service in the army, which provided regular pay, promotion opportunities, adequate pensions, and honor.

Despite its difficulties, city life had its compensations, even for the lowliest. Magnificent public buildings and parks provided an impressive setting for one's life. Holidays were numerous—perhaps as many as a hundred fifty a year by the second century A.D. Each was the occasion for splendid religious festivals featuring animal sacrifices that provided free meals, for the triumphs of victorious emperors, and for chariot races, gladiatorial contests, and bloody combats between wild animals and between animals and human beings. Numerous and sumptuous public baths provided attractive gathering places for everyone. Social clubs (called *collegia*), usually made up of individuals sharing a common occupation, provided opportunities for banqueting and help to members in time of need. Taverns abounded like oases where one could escape from the urban desert.

Those who received the least benefit from the

FIGURE 10.3 Scenes from a Roman Household These two panels done in relief illustrate some of the activities associated with household life in the Roman world: storing, preparing, and cooking food. The scenes suggest that such households were the setting for a secure and comfortable life. (Alinari)

Pax Romana were the peasants and the slaves. Isolated from city life, the rural population seldom felt the impact of the forces that gave the Roman world its vitality. Their existence centered around the family, hard work, and the simple social activities of the rural village. At best, the material return for their labor was small. Powerful trends were at work in the empire pushing many farmers into dependency on powerful absentee landlords; these dependent agricultural workers (called *coloni*) were increasingly victimized by heavy rents, an ever-heavier share of the tax burden, and loss of social status. To its discredit, the imperial government did little to check the exploitation of the peasantry; in fact, the aristocratic landowners who dominated the political process were quite happy to allow this drift toward peasant exploitation.

Slavery, an institution absolutely essential to the economy, remained a basic element of Roman imperial society. Slaves constituted a considerable portion of the population throughout the empire. It has been estimated that in the first century A.D. perhaps one-third of Italy's population of 7 to 8 million inhabitants were slaves. They served as household servants, agricultural laborers, workers in urban workshops and merchant stalls, teachers, miners, rowers, and gladiators; and their reward was minimal. The record is full of instances of brutal treatment by masters, whose rights over slaves were complete. There is some evidence that the condition of slaves improved. Many were freed by their masters, in some cases out of gratitude for faithful service. Funerary inscriptions and literary sources suggest amicable associations between masters and slaves. Slaves were allowed to marry and maintain families. Imperial legislation sought to curb physical abuse of slaves. However, no one—not even the most enlightened of the "good emperors"—thought of ending slavery. That institution continued to debase the lives of the victimized slaves and to poison the minds of their social superiors at all levels of society.

Our description of the Roman world in the second century A.D. points to a remarkable political achievement that established peace, order, and security for a huge population; undoubtedly these were blessings to all. However, the economic and social conditions suggest that the main beneficiaries of the *Pax Romana* were the members of a narrow, proud, self-satisfied circle with limited concern for millions of people less well positioned economically and socially. Many beyond the circle of the favored few—probably more than in earlier societies—appear to have managed fairly well. But it is clear that many suffered from poverty, injustice, and oppression. How these people perceived their existence is almost impossible to ascertain. Implicit in the structure of the Roman Empire at its height were economic and social conditions that meant that many of its members had only a limited stake in its existence. That situation would eventually test the empire's strength.

SUGGESTED READING

Political Developments

Chester G. Starr, *The Roman Empire, 27 B.C.–A.D. 476* (1982).
Colin Wells, *The Roman Empire* (1984).
J. S. Wacher, *The Roman Empire* (1987).
Any of these three works will provide an excellent survey.
Kurt A. Raaflaub and Mark Toher, *Between Republic and Empire: Interpretations of Augustus and His Principate* (1990). Helpful in assessing Augustus' accomplishments.
Fergus Millar, *The Emperor in the Roman World: 31 B.C.–A.D. 337* (1977). Although massive, this study is vital to understanding how the imperial political system worked.
Ronald Syme, *The Augustan Aristocracy* (1986). Rich in insights into how Augustus related to a key social group.
Graham Webster, *The Roman Imperial Army*, 3rd ed. (1986). A thorough treatment.

Economic and Social History

Peter Garnsey and Richard Saller, *The Roman Empire. Economy, Society, and Culture* (1987). An excellent survey.
Ramsay MacMullen, *Roman Social Relations, 50 B.C. to A.D. 284* (1974). Attempts to capture attitudes of major social groups.
Joan Liversidge, *Everyday Life in the Roman Empire* (1976). Excellent treatment of how the Romans lived.
The general picture of social conditions presented in the preceding titles can be supplemented by the following works.
Judith P. Hallett, *Fathers and Daughters in Roman Society: Women and the Elite Family* (1984).

Jane F. Gardner, *Women in Roman Law and Society* (1986).
John K. Evans, *War, Women and Children in Ancient Rome* (1991).
Suzanne Dixon, *The Roman Family* (1992).
Beryl Rawson, ed., *The Family in Ancient Rome: New Perspectives* (1986).
Suzanne Dixon, *The Roman Mother* (1988).
Thomas Wiedemann, *Adults and Children in the Roman Empire* (1989).
K. R. Bradley, *Slaves and Masters in the Roman Empire: A Study in Social Control* (1984).
L. A. Thompson, *Romans and Blacks* (1989).

Biographies

A. H. M. Jones, *Augustus* (1970).
Barbara Levick, *Tiberius the Politician* (1976).
Barbara Levick, *Claudius* (1990).
Miriam T. Griffin, *Nero: End of a Dynasty* (1984).
Steward Perowne, *Hadrian* (1960).
Anthony Birley, *Marcus Aurelius: A Biography*, rev. ed. (1987).

Sources

Moses Hadas, ed., *Complete Works of Tacitus* (1942).
Suetonius, *The Twelve Caesars*, trans. Robert Graves (1957).
Two lively treatments of the history of the first century A.D.

CHAPTER 11
Roman Thought and Expression

FIGURE 11.1 The Fruits of Peace This relief is from a larger composition decorating the Ara Pacis (Altar of Peace) built in Rome during the first century A.D. It glorifies the benefits bestowed by Augustus. The serene goddess of fertility and her happy children are surrounded by symbols of well-being. The work reflects how art was used to promote the greatness of Augustus. (Alinari)

While Roman statesmen and their citizen supporters were conquering and organizing a vast empire, writers, thinkers, and artists combined their creative efforts to make a major contribution to cultural history. Rome's prime cultural role was its assimilation and dissemination of Greek culture. But in the course of adapting the basic elements of Greek culture, the Romans put their distinctive mark onto its thought and expression, thereby creating a Latin cultural heritage destined to influence the future decisively, especially in western Europe.

1. ROME AND THE RECEPTION OF GREEK CULTURE

Before the third century B.C. the Romans displayed little interest in cultural pursuits. Although Etruscan cultural models, especially building techniques and religion, influenced early Roman society, the Romans long remained a simple people occupied chiefly with politics, war, and earning a living. As we have seen (see Chapter 8, Section 2), their early experiences in these pursuits ingrained in them deep-rooted values that influenced their cultural life throughout their history.

Beginning in the third century B.C., the simple mentality of the early republic experienced a cultural revolution, brought on largely by Roman expansion. As their armies absorbed first southern Italy and Sicily and then the Hellenistic Near East, Roman aristocrats became aware of Greek culture, especially in its Hellenistic forms. They were so impressed that they were, as the first-century poet Horace put it, taken captive by those they conquered. This encounter, which placed a high social value on becoming culturally Hellenized, was critical in determining Rome's role in the total stream of cultural history.

One of the major consequences of the "discovery" of Greek culture was the introduction into Rome of a new educational system. Down to the end of the third century B.C. young Romans were usually educated at home: males by their fathers, who taught them family customs, the principles of Roman law, civic duties, and religion; females by their mothers, who taught them the household arts. By the second century B.C. that traditional system began to be replaced by the Hellenistic pattern of education. In many aristocratic Roman households Greek slaves were employed to complement basic instruction in reading and writing Latin with instruction in the Greek language and the Greek "classics" of literature and philosophy. Bilingualism became a mark of social distinction, but those not able to master Greek could still gain access to Greek masterpieces through translations into Latin. Not only were young men introduced to this new education, young women were also often involved (see Figure 9.3). Private schools emerged to provide young men with an opportunity to extend their formal education over a longer period of time. They often went to the east, especially to Athens, to finish their education. Grammar (the study of language and literature) and rhetoric (the study of effective expression and argumentation) became the touchstones of the new education, providing invaluable skills for successful public careers and for acceptance into the ranks of the *nobiles* and the *equites*.

Their fascination with Greek culture soon spurred the Romans to imitate it. Borrowing heavily from the content and forms provided by Greek models, Latin writers produced epic poems, dramas, histories, and philosophical tracts. As a result, the Latin language was enriched as a vehicle of independent literary expression. Romans were equally captivated by Greek and Hellenistic art. During the wars in the east, numerous art pieces were "liberated" to decorate Roman residences, and eastern artists were imported to produce copies of Greek statues and paintings. The Greek style of architecture was employed for civic and private buildings so often that Rome began to resemble a Greek or Hellenistic city.

Even the Roman masses felt the impact of Greek influences, but they were touched chiefly through religion. The wars of conquest and the resultant economic and social dislocations left many people intellectually and emotionally lost. Traditional Roman religion offered little to meet these needs. The eastern religions did. New deities, myths, and rituals taken from the Greek civic religions were added to public religion in Rome, but even these additions did not satisfy many. From eastern slaves they learned about more exciting Hellenistic mystery religions such as the worship of Dionysus or Cybele or Isis.

These emotional, personal cults increasingly challenged the traditional religion for the allegiance of the Italian population and began to reshape the value system of the Roman populace.

This cultural revolution was fought by some conservative Romans, most notably Cato the Elder (234–149 B.C.), a prominent statesman who saw foreign culture as a threat to Rome's traditional values. He spent much of his public career railing against the Greek way, bemusing his contemporaries with dramatic exposures of cultural "subversives," and seeking to induce public authorities to curb their activities. But he was fighting a lost cause. Rome was destined by circumstance and choice to be heir to the magnificent patrimony of the Greeks. Many of Cato's contemporaries saw the perpetuation of Greek culture as a Roman responsibility and acted eagerly to fulfill that mission. For example, no less a person than the powerful Scipio Africanus, along with many of his descendants (including the Gracchi brothers), championed the Hellenization of Roman thought and expression.

By the first century B.C. the stimulus provided by the encounter with Greek culture had readied Roman writers, artists, and thinkers to put their own stamp on what they had borrowed. The result was a burst of creativity launching Rome's cultural "golden age"; the Augustan age marked its high point. After a brief slackening in the first century A.D., there followed a second period of considerable activity during the era of the "good emperors," often called the "silver age."

2. ROMAN LITERATURE

The Roman cultural genius is perhaps best reflected in literature. After a long apprenticeship under Greek influence during the third and second centuries B.C., a succession of writers living between about 100 B.C. and A.D. 150 produced a rich and varied body of Latin literature. Almost without exception, these works reflect strong Greek influences in content and form. But their authors demonstrated remarkable talent in adapting Greek modes to produce works in the Latin language that were marked by stylistic grace and force, depth of personal conviction, a powerful grasp of social reality, and a passion for instructing readers. That literature was es-pecially important to the intellectual history of western Europe because it served as the main vehicle through which Greek literary forms, ideas, and values were transmitted to the West.

Outstanding among all Roman writers was Vergil (70–19 B.C.). Born in rural Italy, he grew to manhood during the last years of the civil wars that ruined the republic, and he personally suffered their ravages. Eventually he attracted the attention of Augustus, whose patronage permitted him to devote the last years of his life to writing. Although much of his great talent was poured out in the service of the new Augustan order, it would be erroneous to overemphasize Vergil's role as a propagandist; he wrote in support of the Augustan system out of deep conviction and enthusiasm. His *Georgics* express a strong feeling for nature and for what involvement in pastoral life can mean—especially to those corrupted by the violence and greed surrounding the last days of the republic. Vergil's masterpiece was his *Aeneid*. An epic modeled after Homer's and filled with material drawn from Greek legend, this majestic work sought to show that Rome's rise to mastery of the world was divinely ordained. The plot centers on the adventures of a mythical Trojan hero, Aeneas, who after the fall of Troy was ordered by the gods to establish, in Italy, a new city destined to rule the world. Aeneas is portrayed as an ideal Roman whose virtue is constantly tested by such challenges as the spiteful behavior of the deities, a heartrending love affair with Dido, queen of Carthage, and a horror-filled journey to the underworld. But he persists in his mission to found a city whose decisive role in shaping the civilized world came to fruition with the accession of Augustus. Never was the Roman ideal of the dedicated patriot portrayed with more intensity and dignity; and never was the theme of Rome's predestination to shape a good world more dramatically stated.

Two other poets, Catullus and Horace, illustrate a more personal, internalized facet of the Roman literary genius. Catullus (ca. 85–54 B.C.) was a product of high society in the late republican period, living his life amid a dissolute, pleasure-seeking crowd of young nobles. Among his many adventures was a love affair with a noble lady who was already married and who eventually jilted him. The experience inspired him to pour forth powerful lyric poetry portraying with great intensity his feelings of love and of the pain and hatred caused by lost love. Horace (65–8 B.C.), a son of a freed slave, enjoyed the patronage of Augustus and was second in influence only to Vergil. His best work, the *Odes*, capture with telling effect his personal reactions to hundreds of situations he met in his lifetime; he was particularly eloquent in his praise of the Augustan peace. Although he lacked the fire of Catullus, Horace spoke to a wider circle, his lyric poems reflecting the reasoned, thoughtful reactions of an educated, humane Roman to life as a whole—a great spirit looking at the world about him with sanity, intelligence, and wit. He was and remains the ideal of a civilized person.

Lucretius (ca. 95–55 B.C.) demonstrated still another aspect of Roman poetic genius: moral seriousness. A contemporary of Catullus, he too was profoundly moved by events of the civil war era. He found his personal salvation in Epicurean philosophy, which he undertook to explain to his Latin-speaking contemporaries in a long poem called *On the Nature of Things*. With almost missionary zeal Lucretius put poetry to the service of instruction. He made a noble plea to educated Romans to seek in philosophy the bases of moral regeneration and personal fulfillment. Seldom has a poet shown greater moral earnestness.

Other notable Latin poets were Ovid, Martial, and Juvenal. Ovid (43 B.C.–A.D. 17) entertained Augustan high society with his *Art of Love*, a frivolous but amusing poem on the art of seduction, and his *Metamorphoses*, an entertaining, lively rendering of Greek mythological stories into Latin. Martial (ca. A.D. 38–102) and Juvenal (ca. A.D. 55–140) exercised their poetic talents as satirists painting in vivid colors the shortcomings of Roman aristocratic society during the post-Augustan age.

The talents of the Latin poets were matched by those of the prose writers. Perhaps Rome's most accomplished prose writer was Cicero (106–43 B.C.). Although an active lawyer and statesman, he produced a wide variety of writing in many forms. His masterful speeches, shaped by the Greek rhetorical tradition, his intimate knowledge of political life, and his personal ambitions, raised political argumentation to the level of art. Among his numerous tracts on various subjects were two important essays on po-

litical theory, *The Republic* and *The Laws*, which defended Roman republican institutions but pleaded for the establishment of a first citizen to guide the state. In other tracts he sought to make abstract Greek philosophical thought understandable to Roman readers and relative to their lives. His numerous *Letters* supply a brilliant picture of Roman politics and society in the first century B.C. Taken together, the works of this eloquent, learned Roman set a model for Latin prose writing that would be imitated for centuries.

The Romans also excelled in historical writing. Interest in the past was promoted by the deep respect for tradition ingrained in the Roman mentality from almost the beginning of Roman history and by the need to explain and justify Rome's rise to supremacy in the Mediterranean world. Those concerns were exemplified by the most influential Roman historian, Livy (59 B.C.–A.D. 17), another of those inspired to creative activity under the Augustan regime. His masterpiece, the immense *Roman History*, sought to treat developments extending from the foundation of Rome by the mythical Aeneas to the time of Augustus. Although a large part of the work has been lost, it is clear from what is left that Livy believed Rome had a great historical mission about which he wished to instruct his readers. To achieve that end, Livy put together in an artful fashion a mixture of truth and legend intended to teach a lesson. The work presented with great dramatic impact the people and events that made Rome great and highlighted the traditional virtues—in Livy's view now restored by Augustus—undergirding that success.

Less monumental but equally artistic was the work of Tacitus (ca. A.D. 55–117), who wrote about Roman history during the century after Augustus. Together his two major works, *Histories* and *Annals*, cover the period A.D. 14–96. Although Tacitus was a man of senatorial and republic sentiments prejudiced against the successors of Augustus, he described the activities of Rome's ruling circle with brilliance and deep moral sense. Another of his works, *Germania*, gives important information about the Germanic peoples, who were soon to play a major part in Roman life. Suetonius (ca. A.D. 75–150) also treated the rulers from Julius Caesar to Domitian in his *Lives of the Twelve Caesars*, a spicy account mixing fact with gossip and especially stressing scandal and sexual excesses. Several Romans produced personal memoirs that were historical in character. Probably the best examples were Julius Caesar's *Commentaries on the Gallic Wars* and Marcus Aurelius' *Meditations*.

In their initial encounters with Hellenic culture, some Latin writers sought to imitate the magnificent dramatic art of the Greeks. The most notable Roman dramatists were Plautus (ca. 254–184 B.C.) and Terence (ca. 195–159 B.C.), both writers of comedies. But drama failed to take root among the Romans. Moreover, only occasionally did a fiction writer grace the Roman literary scene. These gaps in the repertory of genres cultivated by Roman writers suggest that the creation of highly imaginative literature was foreign to the Romans, whose concerns focused on reality—on history, current moral problems, personal experience.

While our concern here is primarily with assessing the achievements of Latin writers, it is important to note that throughout the golden and silver ages of Latin literature (that is, from about 100 B.C. to A.D. 150) Greek writers continued to produce a significant body of literature in a variety of genres. For example, one of the greatest historians of antiquity was a Greek, Polybius (ca. 200–118 B.C.). While living in Rome from 167 to 151 B.C. as a hostage, he became an intimate of the pro-Hellenic Scipionic circle and produced a superb work chronicling Rome's rise to world power. Another Greek author, Plutarch (ca. A.D. 46–120), wrote of a series of biographies of illustrious Greeks and Romans entitled *Parallel Lives* that sought to provide readers with a guide to moral excellence. But these are only a few of the many Greek authors whose efforts enriched the cultural scene under Roman rule. That Greek literature continued to flourish is an indication of the cosmopolitan, tolerant cultural environment resulting from the *Pax Romana*.

3. ROMAN ART

Like literature, the visual arts developed slowly in the Roman world. After an initial impetus derived from Etruscan models, artistic tastes among the Romans were decisively affected after about 250 B.C. by their growing familiarity with Greek forms, motifs, and techniques. Not until the first century B.C. did the unique artistic genius of the Romans begin to manifest itself; it reached its full maturity during the first two centuries A.D. During that "golden age" the imperial government provided a powerful impetus to artistic creativity, partly as a means of glorifying the imperial regime and its rulers but also because members of the ruling elite in Rome enjoyed beauty and refinement. This imperial art never lost its Greek imprint, but it had qualities that gave it a distinctive character.

Rome's most impressive artistic achievements were in architecture, where important elements were added to what was borrowed. The Romans invented concrete, which provided a cheap, durable, adaptable building material. This material allowed architects to exploit the arch, the dome, and various forms of vaulting more effectively than had been done before and to create imaginative exteriors by the use of marble and brick facings over concrete. These technical advances permitted larger structures and innovative variations on the rectangular ground plans and predominantly horizontal elevation lines characteristic of the typical Greek structure.

Although they were avid temple builders, the Romans were generally content to imitate the Greek temple style, as is illustrated by the famous Maison Carrée still standing in Nîmes, France. However, they were capable of innovation. The Pantheon, built in Rome in the second century A.D., is one of the most imposing round temples ever built. Its domed roof, 142 feet in diameter and supported by niche-filled concrete walls, covers a vast internal space that evokes a sense of awe. A rectangular porch, its gabled roof supported by Greek columns, leads into this inner sanctum, supplying a pleasing mixture of Greek and Roman architectural ideas.

Much more distinctly Roman in style, technique, and spirit were the public buildings: forums, baths, amphitheaters, aqueducts, bridges, meeting halls (basilicas), and palaces, built in abundance not only in Rome but also in provincial cities throughout the empire (see Figures 11.2 and 11.3). The Roman Forum, a huge complex of meeting halls, market facilities, and shrines laid out on an axial plan, reflects the Roman genius for planning and adapting architectural forms to

FIGURE 11.2 A Roman Aqueduct The Pont du Gard, built across the River Gard to bring water to the Gallo-Roman city of Nîmes, is an impressive monument to Roman engineering skill. The structure rises 160 feet above the river bed and is about 900 feet in length; each of the large arches is about 80 feet across at its base. Roman architects and engineers have seldom been matched in the application of the arch to utilitarian ends. (Art Resource)

a variety of uses. The Colosseum, a massive sports facility begun during Vespasian's reign, accommodated fifty thousand spectators and provided special boxes for the emperors and other dignitaries. It featured an elliptical ground plan above which were elevated four levels of arch-covered passageways giving access to the seats looking down on the arena where the bloody gladiatorial combats so beloved by the Romans occurred. The most common Roman building was the basilica, essentially a long hall flanked by side aisles and often featuring a rounded apse at one end. The walls of the main hall extended above the roofs of the side aisles, allowing windows to be cut high in the walls. Arches and columns were skillfully used to permit access from the side aisles into the main hall and to support its roof; in the Basilica of Maxentius (early fourth century A.D.) a concrete roof was put over a main aisle eighty feet wide. Roman baths, which consisted of a great central court surrounded by numerous smaller rooms, demonstrated the Roman talents for organizing interior space for utilitarian purposes and creating internal plumbing and heating systems. The Romans also built huge imperial palaces (the most famous are those of Nero and Domitian) and rural villas characterized by multistoried layouts featuring different-sized and -shaped rooms and sumptuous internal decor (see Color Plate 4). Not the least accomplishment of Roman architects was the development of living quarters suited to the needs of crowded cities: multistoried concrete structures containing standardized small apartment units suited to the needs of low-income residents.

Roman sculptors were less innovative than the architects were. Greek and Hellenistic models were constantly and even slavishly imitated. The best Roman sculpture was devoted to portraiture and to relief work treating historical incidents, both art forms especially useful in serving the purposes of patrons who wished to keep their images before the public for political and social reasons or to commemorate their deeds for posterity. The artists who rendered portrait sculptures were remarkably adept at realistic portrayal, but always their work accentuated the

FIGURE 11.3 Roman Architecture
This photo of an arena and a theater built in Arles in southern France near the end of the first century B.C. illustrates the Roman talent for constructing impressive public buildings to serve as the focus of civic life. Arenas provided the settings for such popular activities as races, gladiatorial combats, and wild animal hunts. The close proximity of a spacious theater suited for drama, dance, song, and poetry reading suggests a wide range of interests among the citizens of a Roman provincial city. (French Government Tourist Office, New York)

dignity of their subjects (see Figures 8.1, 9.2, and 10.1). Roman relief carvings—featured especially on the walls of public buildings, arches and columns celebrating the deeds of emperors, and coffins honoring the dead—were remarkably effective in capturing scenes from everyday life in a way that conveyed a powerful message lauding the feats of those honored and reinforcing the virtues exemplified by their careers (see Figures 9.1, 9.3, 10.3, 11.1, and 12.2). Perhaps the most remarkable example of Roman relief work is the freestanding column erected to celebrate Trajan's military triumph in Dacia. Around the column spirals a continuous scene seven hundred feet long that depicts in almost photographic detail the activities of about twenty-five hundred figures engaged in various activities associated with a military campaign. Surviving examples of Roman painting (see Figure 10.2 and Color Plate 5) and mosaic work (Color Plate 6) are rare; examples found in the ruins of Pompeii and Her-

culaneum, two cities buried by an eruption of Mt. Vesuvius in A.D. 79., suggest that Greek and Hellenistic influences remained strong and that these arts played an important role in decorating interiors, thus being strongly shaped by architectural plans. Painters and their patrons were especially fond of mythological subjects and portrayals of nature.

4. ROMAN PHILOSOPHY, SCIENCE, AND RELIGION

Philosophical interests in the Roman world were shaped by patterns of thought established during the Hellenistic period, focusing chiefly on applying classical Greek philosophical principles to ethical issues facing individuals and society. While many of the most significant philosophers in the Roman world were Greek speakers, educated Romans absorbed their ideas and sought to utilize those ideas to formulate answers to problems facing the Roman world. The most significant accomplishment of these Roman thinkers lay not in advancing philosophical speculation but in recasting Greek philosophy into a Roman idiom and transmitting that wisdom in the Latin language to later western European society.

Six individuals will illustrate the main currents of philosophical development during the period of Roman domination; most of them were not philosophers in the strict sense but writers, statesmen, or educated citizens seeking personal and social guidance from philosophy. The extensive writings of Cicero (106–43 B.C.) are filled with philosophical reflections which illustrate a powerful tendency in Roman philosophical thought to intermingle the viewpoints of various schools into an eclectic response to moral issues. However, the major Roman philosophers usually became advocates of one or another of the Hellenistic schools of thought. In his *On the Nature of Things* the poet Lucretius (ca. 95–55 B.C.) used his talent to entreat his Roman readers to follow the Epicurean ideal of seeking pleasure and peace of mind in a materialistic universe through contemplation and withdrawal from the world. Particularly attractive to many Romans was the sober philosophy of Stoicism, certainly the most influential philosophical movement of the first two centuries A.D. Three individuals were its noted advocates: Seneca (ca. 4 B.C.–A.D. 65), an essayist who served Nero; Epictetus (ca. A.D. 55–135), a freedman who, after being exiled from Rome, spent most of his life teaching his ideas to ordinary people; and Emperor Marcus Aurelius (A.D. 121–180), whose famous *Meditations* summarized the Roman version of the Stoic worldview, emphasizing acceptance of duty and resignation to whatever fate brings. The Roman Stoics did not neglect the emphasis of Hellenistic Stoicism on personal peace of mind, but they gave greater attention to social responsibility and public morality. Especially influential was their expansion of the idea of an all-pervading, unchangeable law of nature governing the universe to provide a justification for a single human community governed by a system of law that conformed to the law of nature. Perhaps the thinker most important for the future was Plotinus (A.D. 204–270), an Egyptian who spent much of his career in Rome teaching a system called Neoplatonism. Derived from Plato's thought, Plotinus' system, as set forth in his *Enneads*, posited the superiority of the spiritual world over the material, the existence of a perfect being at the summit of spiritual reality, and the possibility of human participation in spiritual reality through a mystical experience that involved the penetration of the supreme spiritual being into the human spirit properly prepared by contemplation. Neoplatonism represented a fundamental aspect of the development of thought during the Roman period: the merging of philosophy and religion, a trend that perhaps best met the needs of people in what was increasingly becoming an "age of anxiety" who were seeking some higher order of truth beyond the worldly realm.

The Roman period was not marked by significant advances in science. Romans were little interested in speculation about the natural world or in systematic investigation of natural phenomena. Perhaps the most significant scientific achievement resulted from the effort of scholars to compile great encyclopedias intended to summarize in systematic fashion all the scientific knowledge contained in Greek and Hellenistic sources. Notable examples included Strabo (ca. 63 B.C.–A.D. 21) in geography, Pliny the Elder (ca. A.D. 23–79) in natural history, Ptolemy (ca. A.D. 121–151) in astronomy, and Galen (A.D. 131–201) in medicine. These compilations would long remain the chief guides to understanding nature. The Romans excelled in practical science: the engineering of monumental structures; the construction of roads, bridges, aqueducts; more effective farming techniques. The technical skills developed by engineers, artisans, and farmers formed a precious heritage perhaps as important to the West as the literary, artistic, and philosophical tradition nurtured and transmitted by Rome.

While a relatively narrow circle of the educated upper class of the Roman world absorbed Greek and Hellenistic philosophy and science and derived from it new values and patterns of behavior, religion remained a powerful force shaping the basic outlook of the great bulk of society, including many nobles. The ancient Roman family and civic religious beliefs and practices continued to play a prominent role in private and public life. In fact, traditional Roman religion took on new vigor during the first and second centuries A.D. as a result of efforts by rulers from Augustus onward to utilize religion as an official instrument for the renewal of Roman civic life. An important consequence of this overt linkage of imperial politics and religion was the gradual emergence of emperor worship, especially in the eastern provinces of the empire, as a powerful dimension of imperial government. Perhaps the most momentous religious development between about 100 B.C. and A.D. 180 was the spread of Hellenistic mystery religions over the entire world ruled by the Romans. Their diffusion was facilitated by Roman tolerance of any religion that did not threaten to disturb public order or challenge imperial authority. Particularly appealing were the cults of the Great Mother goddess associated with Cybele, of the Egyptian goddess Isis, and above all of the Persian deity Mithra, which took deep root in the Roman army. The ideas and practices associated with these religions emphasized personal identification with a deity through highly emotional rituals and life after death earned for good behavior. Such concepts tended to weaken the appeal of traditional Roman religions, which stressed highly formalized rituals performed by groups in return for material rewards. The trend already under way during the Hellenistic Age toward religious syncretism—the mingling of beliefs and practices—continued everywhere in the Roman world. The ground was being prepared for the acceptance of a common religion. The advocates of the religion that eventually filled that role—Christianity—were already spreading their "good news" during the Golden Age of the Roman Empire (see Chapter 12).

5. ROMAN LAW

One of Rome's most enduring cultural monuments was its law, which was vital not only as a force promoting orderly life throughout Rome's history but also as a legacy handed on to later societies to guide them in establishing effective societal relations. As early as about 450 B.C., the principle was set forth in the famous Twelve Tables that citizens had rights that could be claimed and defended in courts. From then on these rights of citizens, which collectively constituted the law of citizens (*ius civile*), were explored, tested, and expanded in the context of changing times. During the republican period the enactments of assemblies enriched the substance of the law. Even more important, the magistrates charged with administering the law, the *praetors*, were allowed to pronounce their interpretation of the law at the beginning of their term; this practice resulted in a constant reinterpretation of the law within a framework that highlighted principles that should govern the *ius civile*. During this same period, the decisions of the judges who actually conducted cases in court shaped an ever-growing body of precedent that had the weight of law. In reaching their decision judges were advised by *jurisconsults*, specialists whose study of the law allowed them to assert a significant role in shaping the precedents that were applied in court as law. Roman expansion across the Mediterranean world not only witnessed the spread of Roman civil law to new geographical areas but also presented judicial officials with the problem of settling cases involving noncitizens. The result was the development of a law of nations (*ius gentium*), which represented a mixture of the laws of subject peoples, Roman practices, and the commonsense decisions of judges. With the institution of the Roman Empire the content of the law was further expanded by a vast outpouring of decrees and instructions issued by each *princeps* in an attempt to ensure that the huge empire would be ruled uniformly and equitably.

As the body of the law expanded and the society to which it was applied grew more complex, there was increasing pressure to codify the law into a single, systematic body. This concern had become central to the study of law by the second century A.D., when a series of brilliant *jurisconsults*, working under the patronage of the emperors, focused their attention on defining the principles undergirding sound law and its application. Their efforts were spurred by their realization of the importance of unified law as a tool for governing the empire and by their awareness that the distinction between citizens and noncitizens was disappearing. In addition, their thinking was decisively influenced by Stoic philosophy, which argued that there existed a law of nature (*ius naturale*) governing the universe to which human law must conform. The concept of natural law was a fruitful source of principles according to which all aspects of human law could be arranged and interrelated into a consistent, logical body. The codification of Roman law was not completed until the reign of Emperor Justinian (A.D. 527–565) (see Chapter 14). But as imperial legislators, judges, and students of law moved toward that end, their efforts shaped an immense body of law that became a storehouse to which many people would turn in the future for guidance in the humane, equitable conduct of human affairs.

6. THE ROMANS AND CULTURAL DIFFUSION

When assessing the role of the Romans in cultural history, one must give them due credit for raising the level of culture in large areas previously little affected by higher civilization. Since the main ingredients of Roman culture were derived from Greece and the Hellenistic east, the Roman's role as disseminators of culture in that part of the empire was limited. However, it must be noted that the establishment of the *Pax Romana* in that area encouraged the continued maturing of Greek cultural life and promoted the Hellenization of non-Greek natives of the eastern provinces. The case was different in the west, where the impact of Roman culture was widespread and of decisive importance in the lives of non-Romans. The Romans were much less exclusive in their attitude toward non-Romans than the classical Greeks were, chiefly because they understood from early in their history the importance of Romanization in establishing and maintaining their domination over their culturally diverse subjects. The marks of their success as disseminators of culture are still visible. For example, modern "Romance" languages—Ital-

ian, French, and Spanish—are direct descendants of the Latin spread into those areas when the Romans conquered them. A modern traveler in Western Europe and North Africa will repeatedly encounter the remains of Roman baths, aqueducts, temples, theaters, and roads—all evidence of the presence of the Romans as a creative force in enriching life in these areas.

The processes through which Romanization was achieved were complex. Roman soldiers, officials, merchants, and colonizers were important agents in carrying Roman culture outward across the empire. The Roman government actively promoted the creation of cities and encouraged those settling in them to imitate Roman ways. Provincial aristocracies were encouraged to become Romanized as a test of their eligibility for citizenship and for Roman approval of their leadership of local government. In these provincial urban centers, schools were established to teach Latin and Greek grammar and rhetoric and to promote the study of literature and philosophy; as a result, a common store of ideas and set of tastes spread to the far corners of the empire. The imperial government promoted extensive building activities, which led to the spread of a common style in architecture, sculpture, and painting. Scholars, religious missionaries, philosophers, artists, and teachers circulated freely throughout the empire to spread a common culture. From the third century B.C. onward, the government and aristocracy of the city of Rome welcomed artistic and intellectual talent from all over the empire, making the capital of the empire the center of a cosmopolitan culture from which flowed influences affecting life throughout the empire. All of these factors combined to bring large numbers of people under the sway of a common culture that would decisively affect their histories for many centuries to come.

SUGGESTED READING

General Overviews

Pierre Grimal, *The Civilization of Rome*, trans. W. S. Maquinness (1963).

John Boardman et al., eds., *The Oxford History of the Classical World* (1986).
Two insightful surveys of Roman cultural life.

Religion

Margaret Lyttelton and Werner Forman, *The Romans: Their Gods and Their Beliefs* (1984).

John Ferguson, *The Religions of the Roman Empire* (1970).

Either of these two titles will provide rich material on religious life in the Roman world.

Stewart Perowne, *Roman Mythology*, new rev. ed. (1984). A splendidly illustrated description of Roman myths.

Alan Wardman, *Religion and Statecraft among the Romans* (1982).

Alan Watson, *The State, Law, and Religion: Pagan Rome* (1992).

These two works explore the role of religion in political life.

Thought and Expression

Stanley F. Bonner, *Education in Ancient Rome: From Cato the Elder to the Younger Pliny* (1977). A full treatment.

Elizabeth Rawson, *Intellectual Life in the Late Roman Republic* (1985). A landmark study dispelling stereotypes about the lack of Roman intellectual creativity.

E. J. Kennedy, ed., *Cambridge History of Classical Literature*, Vol. 2 (1982). A thorough, scholarly survey.

R. M. Ogilivie, *Roman Literature and Society* (1980). Seeks to relate literature to social conditions.

F. H. Sandbach, *The Stoics* (1975). Describes the basic ideas of the Stoics.

H. F. Jolowicz and Barry Nicholas, *Historical Introduction to the Study of Roman Law*, 3rd ed. (1972). A massive survey.

Nancy H. Ramage and Andrew Ramage, *Roman Art: Romulus to Constantine* (1991).

Susan Walker, *Roman Art* (1991).

Two excellent surveys touching all phases of artistic life.

Niels Hannestad, *Roman Art and Imperial Policy* (1986). Relates art and political life.

Sources

Kevin Guinagh and Alfred P. Darjahn, eds., *Latin Literature in Translation*, 2nd ed. (1952). A good sample of Latin literature. Better still would be to read the complete works of the major Latin authors mentioned in this chapter; their works are readily available in good translations.

CHAPTER 12

Crisis in the Roman World, A.D. 180–284: Conflict, Change, and Christianity

FIGURE 12.1 The Ascension of Christ This ivory carving from about A.D. 400 portrays Christ's ascension into the hand of God while an angel speaks to the three Marys and soldiers cower in terror. It illustrates how Christian artists adapted classical art styles to Christian purposes; note especially the pagan sarcophagus, which certainly had no part in the scriptural account of this crucial event in Christian history. (Marburg/Art Resource)

As the second century A.D. progressed, many contemporaries—and many later historians—were persuaded that Greco-Roman civilization as embodied in the Roman Empire marked a high point in human history. A vast, peaceful community of diverse peoples had been joined together by powerful forces: an enlightened system of government fashioned by the Romans; a common culture derived chiefly from the Greeks that fostered a common basis of discourse and shared values; and expanding economic ties linking the far corners of the Roman Empire. However, like any human order, the *Pax Romana* was not immune to the forces of change. During the third century Roman society began to experience stresses which set in motion forces of disintegration so powerful that Greco-Roman civilization was unable to survive. In order to understand the long succession of events leading to the "fall" of Greco-Roman civilization, it is necessary to identify the sources of these tensions, many of which were rooted in the basic structures of the Roman imperial order.

1. CONSTITUTIONAL PROBLEMS

Although it proved remarkably effective during the two centuries after its foundation by Augustus, the governance system known as the principate had inherent limitations that came to the forefront during the third century. The result was a prolonged period of disorder that brought about subtle changes heralding a major transformation of the Roman governmental system.

One important problem centered on an old issue: the choice of a successor to the office of *princeps*. The adoptive principle utilized so successfully by the "good emperors" had been abandoned by Marcus Aurelius, who returned to hereditary succession by designating his incapable son Commodus (A.D. 180–192) as his successor. Commodus' misrule ended with his assassination and a savage struggle among segments of the army to decide on a successor. The victor was Septimus Severus (A.D. 192–211), a career army officer of African origin, whose dynasty controlled the imperial office by right of inheritance until A.D. 235. Following the advice of Septimus to favor the troops and forget the rest of the population, the Severi encouraged the soldiery to think that the state should be run to reward the army, a policy given impetus by the dangers mounting along Rome's frontier. The result was almost constant civil war from the end of the Severan dynasty until A.D. 284, bloody struggles instigated by army units that took up arms to elevate their generals to the imperial office in expectation of special favors. Successful leaders of these uprisings—often called "barracks emperors"—barely had time to eliminate the followers of their predecessor and reward their troops before new rebels violently removed them from office. Amid this civil strife the *Pax Romana* increasingly seemed a distant memory.

The army's involvement in the succession issue was not entirely due to ambition and greed. It stemmed from another unresolved problem: the defense of the frontier. After a long period of successful expansion extending from the third century B.C. to the early second century A.D. (see Maps 8.2 and 10.1), the Romans sought to establish a fixed frontier defended by a professional army of citizen-soldiers. Although temporarily effective, that defense system was insufficient to cope with a massive change destined to affect the geopolitical balance around the Mediterranean world for many centuries to come: For the first time since the Persian attack on the Greeks in the fifth century B.C., forces beyond the empire's control were taking shape that set into motion a massive movement of peoples toward the Mediterranean basin. During the third century the initial thrust of this movement brought a threat to Roman security that reached crisis levels. A new dynasty, the Sassanians, seized power in Parthia in A.D. 224. Its aggressive rulers, dedicated to the restoration of Persia's ancient glory and the repossession of its ancient territory—which included most of Rome's Asiatic provinces—began to assert constant pressure on Rome's eastern frontier. Along the European frontier the Germans became ever more threatening, chiefly because of developments within the Germanic world that prompted the migration of Germans southward under circumstances that led to the formation of larger groupings of tribes into warrior-led "nations" capable of more effective military actions. During the third century Parthian and German intrusions into Roman territory not only disrupted the peace but also posed the need for a stronger Roman military establishment.

The uncertainties surrounding succession and defense were complicated by continued confusion about the exact nature of the office of *princeps* or emperor. Although from its original establishment by Augustus that office had contained the seeds of one-man rule, that potential had been veiled for two centuries by conscious efforts to involve the aristocracy in the political process and by the style of leadership practiced by the "good emperors." That fiction began to dissolve during the third century. The Severan dynasty and the "barracks emperors" were a different breed from earlier rulers. Most were provincials whose entire careers had been spent in the army. They had little experience with the problems of civil administration, sensitivity to the needs of the civilian population, or understanding of the principles undergirding the Augustan principate. Their concern was the acquisition of power and its unrestrained exercise. Rule by a *princeps*, a first citizen on the model of Augustus or Trajan or Hadrian, was being replaced with rule by a *dominus*, an absolute lord over all citizens, who increasingly were viewed as mere subjects.

The emergence of autocratic leadership based on military power led to the dislocation of other basic elements of the imperial political order. To meet the threat to Rome's frontier, the army was steadily enlarged, its ranks increasingly filled by noncitizen recruits, a process that diminished the importance of citizen-soldiers. Increasingly, the chief administrative posts were filled from the army, reducing the crucial role of the senatorial aristocracy in political life. The emperors intruded more decisively into the affairs of local city-state governments to limit local self-determination and to threaten the delicate relationships that had long given local authorities a vital share in the governance of the empire. The thrust of public policy shifted toward administrative centralization and the regimentation of society pursued in the interests of buttressing the power of military autocrats and serving the needs of defense.

Taken together, this array of political problems not only disturbed the internal order to which the Roman populace had grown accustomed but also pointed up the need for a restructuring of the political system.

2. ECONOMIC, SOCIAL, AND CULTURAL STRESSES

During the third century stress and transformation were not confined to the political realm. Faced with the need for greater resources for defense, the Roman world was unable to expand its economic bases; in fact, economic production decreased during the third century. In part this decline was due to the ravages caused by civil strife and invasions, but more ominous were the structural limitations inherent in the traditional economic system.

Most serious was a decline in agricultural production. The Roman world began to be plagued by a shortage of agricultural labor resulting from a variety of factors: a population decline in the entire Mediterranean world caused by a serious plague in the late second century; the ongoing flight of farmers to urban centers; and a decline in the number of slaves. Farmland was increasingly abandoned despite efforts of the state to encourage resettlement. Agricultural technology did not advance to offset soil depletion and erosion. The spread of the large estate system (*latifundia*) continued, displacing independent small farmers with dependent *coloni* and slaves whose status provided little incentive for them to increase production. In the face of political and economic instability the owners of large estates sought economic security in self-sufficiency rather than production for a market.

Trade and industry were also depressed. The disturbances accompanying civil strife impeded the movement of goods. In their search for funds to reward the army the emperors of the third century not only confiscated urban wealth but regularly debased the currency, leading to massive inflation. Increasing regimentation of the economy in the interest of supplying the enlarged army impeded new commercial and industrial ventures. New investment capital was scarce because the directive elements in Roman society continued to invest their wealth in land and luxurious living and because wealth was diverted into nonproductive military expenditures. The aristocratic ethos dominating society continued to preclude any thought of generating economic growth by elevating the standard of living of lower-class members of society. All of these signs pointed toward an impending, perhaps irreversible decline in the real wealth of the Roman world, a development with ominous implications for the poor and the powerless and for the sense of well-being that had prevailed among the elite in the times of the "good emperors."

The highly stratified social structure put into place by Augustus and nurtured by the imperial government during the first and second centuries A.D. began to unravel during the third century. The long-standing and socially important distinction between citizens and noncitizens was finally obliterated in A.D. 212, when Emperor Caracalla decreed that all free residents of the empire were citizens. The ascending military autocrats systematically diminished the role of the old senatorial aristocracy in political life, thereby depriving that group of involvement in an activity that had long been a mark of its social preeminence. In cities throughout the empire local aristocracies had new burdens heaped on them to provide money and supplies for the armies and were deprived of control over local affairs by the bureaucrats representing the central authority; this treatment persuaded many of them to seek escape from what had once been a privileged status. Ever-larger numbers of the equestrian order gave their allegiance to the military emperors in return for opportunities to profit from supplying the expanding military establishment. This realignment of social positions began to undermine the shared values and interests that had once allowed the upper stratum of Roman society to play a vital role in controlling the social order. Artisans and merchants were increasingly forced into compulsory associations (*collegia*) through which their wages and production were controlled in the interests of the state. The peasants were steadily being driven toward hereditary tenancy and dependency on landowners, conditions that made their already depressed condition even worse. Sporadic peasant revolts, usually brutally suppressed, suggested a growing discontent in the peasant ranks.

Two elements in this changing social scene were advantaged by the social flux of the era: great landowners and soldiers. The owners of large estates were able to tighten their control over agricultural production and the labor force. The imperial government, interested chiefly in

FIGURE 12.2 Roman Aristocratic Life This scene decorating a third-century A.D. mausoleum reflects important aspects of the daily life of a typical Roman noble—returning from the hunt (top) and settling accounts with his tenants and his financial agent (bottom). (Landesmuseum, Trier)

securing revenue and produce from the land to support the army and the bureaucracy, gave the landowners greater freedom to exploit the peasantry and to pass the burden of taxation on to them. As their control over the *coloni* expanded, the great estateholders moved inexorably toward independence of action and the satisfaction of their own self-interest (see Figure 12.2). At the same time, soldiers enjoyed ever-greater status. Men of ability from nonnoble elements of society found the army the chief avenue for social advancement; many rose to key positions in public life—even to the emperorship—to challenge the old aristocracy for social dominance. Even the lowest ranks of the army enjoyed favors not open to other citizens. Because the army was increasingly composed of recruits from the least developed areas of the empire or from "barbarian" outsiders, people little acquainted with or committed to traditional Roman ideas and institutions now moved to leadership roles in society. Perhaps already in the third century the foundations of a future social order dominated by landowners and warriors were being laid.

These transformations of the social order combined to disrupt the traditional patterns of social relationships, to cause widespread discontent and alienation, and to drive many to seek new social ties that would give them moorings in a hostile world. All of these factors pointed toward a restructuring of the social order and a redefinition of social values along lines not yet clear.

In the face of the crisis of the third century the Roman world seemed paralyzed intellectually. Culturally, the third century was one of the least productive periods of the entire classical era. Writers, artists, thinkers seemed to have lost their ability to address the problems of their time creatively and their faith in the humanistic, rationalistic values of the Greco-Roman tradition. The vaunted powers once attributed to human beings to control their own destinies at last seemed inadequate in the face of the realities of a troubled world.

In fact, the troubled society of the third century increasingly sought and found refuge in another realm—religion. The era was alive with powerful religious currents that seriously threatened the classical worldview and undermined allegiance to the state in favor of trust in the divine. Although the ancient civic deities of Greece and Rome still had their adherents, the eastern mystery religions, with their personal deities, emotional rituals, and promises of eternal salvation, won increasing numbers of adherents at all levels of society. There was a vast resurgence of interest in astrology and magic. Even philosophy was permeated by mystical elements. Everyone seemed in search of escape from a meaningless world through mystical contact with the divine. In this quest many Greco-Roman values, including confidence in human reason, seemed irrelevant.

3. CHRISTIANITY: ORIGINS

Among the diverse spiritual movements contending for attention during the third century was Christianity, soon to play a decisive role in transforming Greco-Roman civilization. That role was conditioned in part by what had happened to Christianity since its origin at almost the same moment that Augustus had laid the foundations of the Roman imperial order.

Christianity originated early in the first century A.D. as a splinter movement within the world of Judaism, a world charged with tensions deeply rooted in two fundamental and interconnected elements of Judaism: the hope of recovering lost national independence and the expectation of the moral redemption of all humanity that God had promised to realize through his Chosen People. Particularly incendiary was the political situation of the Jewish community in Palestine following the Maccabean revolt in 168 B.C. against the Seleucid regime (see Chapter 7). That revolt, ending with the establishment of an independent Jewish kingdom, raised high hopes of Jewish independence. However, those hopes were increasingly frustrated both by the misrule by the kingdom's rulers and by the intrusion of Roman power into Asia, which ended in 63 B.C. with Rome's annexation of Palestine. The Romans were willing to concede special privileges allowing the Jews to practice their religion, but they were suspicious of Jewish visions of independence. At first the Romans established a client king in Judea to keep the peace in Rome's name. The autocratic conduct of these kings, typified by the hated Herod (40–4 B.C.), and the burdens imposed by Roman taxation goaded the Jews to constant agitation. In response Augustus abolished the client kingdom and imposed direct Roman rule exercised by a prefect charged with keeping order and collecting tribute.

Faced with an aggressive alien power on its own sacred soil, the unity of the Jewish community was severely tested. Although still joined by the fundamental beliefs defined earlier in their history, the Jews increasingly disagreed on how to act in the immediate historic setting in order to realize what they all agreed was their collective mission. Some of their differences were reflected in various sects prominent at the beginning of the Christian era. The Sadducees, an aristocratic group who as high priests controlled the Temple operation, were primarily concerned with shaping community life and cult practices in strict accord with the letter of the written law. Since their position cast them as the intermediaries between the Jewish community and the Roman authorities, they were anxious to maintain a good relationship with the Romans. The Pharisees, along with the learned *scribes,* were lay interpreters of Jewish law (Torah) who asserted a powerful influence on most Jews as a result of their teaching activities in the synagogues where most Jews met for prayer and scripture reading. Convinced that adherence to the law was the key to fulfillment of the promise established by the Covenant, the Pharisees sought to exercise prudence in political affairs so as to avoid measures that would disrupt life according to the law. Interpreting the law in the light of oral tradition rather than according to its strict letter, they introduced a certain flexibility into Judaism that allowed not only for adjustment of the law to fit changing conditions but also for an enrichment of the moral and social values guiding spiritual life. Their position lay at the roots of rabbinic Judaism that by the end of the first century A.D. began to assert a decisive influence on Jewish history. More inflammatory were the Zealots, who followed the Maccabean tradition by urging their compatriots to take up arms in the cause of political independence and who showed their militancy by repeated acts of terrorism against the Romans and against fellow Jews who made any accommodation with foreign culture. The Essenes, whose views have become better known since the discovery nearly a half century ago of a collection of documents known as the Dead Sea Scrolls, represented a community which withdrew from association with other Jews to pursue a collective life of prayer and asceticism in preparation for the deliverance promised by God. Added to these diverse groups were numerous individuals uttering prophecies that the hour of decision for the Jews was at hand and advocating various courses of action. Complicating the situation surrounding the Palestinian Jewish community were the Jews of the Diaspora—those dispersed by accident or choice across the entire Mediterranean world. Pursuing their traditional

religion primarily in numerous synagogues while living their daily lives in a setting dominated by "Gentiles" (a term designating non-Jews), these Jews were strongly influenced by Greco-Roman ideas and practices, which they tended to incorporate into their version of Judaism, a process that raised suspicions of compromise in the minds of Palestinian Jews but that also created links between the Jewish and non-Jewish worlds that raised prospects of conversions to Judaism.

To the turmoil created by these diverse responses to what was widely perceived as a crisis in Judaism must be added another ingredient that asserted a powerful influence on Jewish thought and practice during the two centuries following the Maccabean revolt. The times were alive with revelations about the approaching end that touched almost all segments of Judaism to a greater or lesser degree. Rooted firmly in Jews' interpretation of their own history and in the pattern of discerning God's intentions shaped by the ancient prophets, this line of thought focused on a central point: The time was at hand when God would intervene dramatically and decisively in history through a messiah to institute the promised kingdom where oppression, sin, injustice, and idolatry would end and all humanity would be embraced in the true Israel where justice under God's true law would prevail. This apocalyptic vision of the impending end of time raised questions of terrible urgency that agitated and divided the entire Jewish community: How, when, where, by whom, with what consequences would the new age come? Jews who heard the mounting chorus of revelations in this vein were led to act in strange ways that unsettled collective Jewish life. No less important, these apocalyptic prophecies heightened Roman suspicions of political subversion and potential rebellion. They reacted with savage reprisals against suspected insurrectionists, a policy that many Jews interpreted as evidence that Rome epitomized the force of evil impeding the fulfillment of God's promise. The growing climate of hatred and distrust, exacerbated by a succession of incompetent Roman governors little sensitive to the nuances of Judaism, finally provoked a major Jewish rebellion in A.D. 66 that ended four years later with Rome's capture of Jerusalem and the destruction of the Temple. With the end of the temple state at Jerusalem, religious leadership of the Jews passed into the hands of rabbis who sought to rally the faithful to observance of the Torah as the basis for Judaism.

Into this complex and highly charged scene came Jesus, probably born about 6 B.C. at almost that fateful moment when Augustus was taking steps to bring the Jews under direct Roman rule. Any reconstruction of his career upon which everyone can agree presents almost insurmountable obstacles that from Jesus' own time to the present have led to disagreements about his life and teachings. The problem lies in the nature of the evidence relating to his career. The earliest surviving written evidence, the writings of Paul, was recorded a generation after Jesus' death by a writer who admitted that he had not known Jesus in person. The other major sources, the gospels of Mark, Matthew, Luke, and John and the Acts of the Apostles, were all set down later, during the last half of the first century. All of these accounts were written in Greek on the basis of oral memories originally recounted in Aramaic, the language Jesus spoke; how their authors understood and interpreted this material was understandably influenced by their awareness of what had happened to the Christian movement after Jesus' time. But perhaps a few points can be ventured about the historical Jesus.

Jesus was born into a modest Jewish household and raised as a member of the Jewish community. When he was about thirty, he began a public ministry, perhaps influenced by John the Baptist, one of many proclaiming the apocalyptic message that the Kingdom of God was at hand and calling all who would listen to demonstrate repentance by accepting a washing by water symbolizing their cleansing of sin. Jesus' public ministry, lasting about three years, focused primarily on a fervent call to those who would listen to prepare themselves for the imminent coming of God's kingdom. Although some of the later gospel accounts gave a central place in Jesus' teaching to his repudiation of the empty formalism of contemporary observance of Judaic law and cult practices advocated by "the scribes and the Pharisees," there is little to support an interpretation of his ministry as a protest against the establishment, be it Jewish or Roman. As best it can be reconstructed, his message was firmly anchored in the Judaic religious tradition, reflecting acceptance of a wide range of fundamental beliefs shared by most Jews. Jesus himself observed the Jewish law and taught his followers that they must do likewise. His vision of the new order that was close at hand—as reflected, for example, in his Sermon on the Mount—echoed themes central to the Jewish prophetic tradition, especially the idea that the poor, the weak, the humble, and the peacemakers would receive justice while the rich, the powerful, and the prideful would be brought low. Perhaps the key element in his message was his insistence that fitness for membership in the coming kingdom required a radical spiritual transformation of all who would be children of God. By a self-willed conversion, each must go beyond observance of the law and performance of accustomed rituals to live a life defined by love, forgiveness, turning the other cheek to violence, abandonment of concerns for property and even family. Acceptance of these values would purge from the inner self of every person the demonic forces that were the source of all evil offensive to God and humanity. Repentance cast in these terms meant preparation for a radically different world; in that "kingdom come" such things as rendering unto Caesar what was Caesar's or departure from strict observance of the Judaic law lost all relevance.

Any assessment of how Jesus was viewed by his contemporaries and how his message was interpreted is likewise fraught with immense difficulties. It seems certain that he gained some kind of status as an authority figure. In contrast with John the Baptist, who cried out in the desert to draw those who had repented to come to him, Jesus actively went into the villages and towns of Palestine to seek out and convert sinners. His preaching attracted a diverse, enthsiastic following, including many women to whom he gave a place of equality seldom accorded them in other contemporary religions. Early in his ministry, he gathered around him a small circle of disciples who assisted him in proclaiming his message, a step that suggests the emergence of a distinct sect. Later tradition portrayed his role in many ways: miracle worker, prophet, messiah, Son of God. While it is possible that tradition reflects elements of truth concerning how Jesus' followers viewed him while he was still in their midst, there is no way to speak with absolute certainty on that matter. During his ministry Jesus also made enemies. Again, tradition singled out certain opposition forces: the power establishment in the Jewish community, especially the Sadducees, who were frightened by his appeal to the poor and oppressed; "the scribes and the Pharisees," who were disturbed by his alleged attacks on their formalistic interpretation of the law; political radicals,who were disappointed by his disavowal of a messianic role seeking to restore an earthly Jewish state. But it is no easier to make a definitive statement on how his opponents saw Jesus than it is to establish how his followers viewed him.

However one resolves these uncertainties surrounding Jesus' career, the end of his ministry was decisive. Probably in A.D. 27 during the reign of Tiberius, Jesus and some of his followers went to Jerusalem to fulfill the traditional religious obligations associated with Passover. His appearance and subsequent activities created a situation in which many of the sources of discontent and expectation rife in the Jewish community came into play in a fashion that threatened to produce violence. Faced with the possibility of an insurrection, Pontius Pilate, the Roman prefect representing imperial authority, took action, perhaps encouraged by Jewish leaders anxious to avert Roman reprisal against all Jews. Jesus was arrested by Roman soldiers, tried before Pontius Pilate, convicted of a crime against Rome, and crucified—a form of punishment reserved by the Romans for rebels and slaves. This sequence of events profoundly shocked his followers and created disarray in their ranks, perhaps symbolized by his disciples' denial that they knew him at the decisive moment in his life.

However, the story was not finished. Jesus' death triggered a crucial development. Some of his followers were convinced that he had arisen from the dead, proving to them that he was the Christ ("the anointed"), the Messiah, the Savior sacrificed in accordance with divine plan to bring about the salvation of all humanity. This belief set the little band apart; in the words of Paul, "We preach Christ crucified, a stumbling block to Jews and folly to the Gentiles . . ." (I Cor. 1:23).

The cornerstone of a new religion was put into place.

4. THE SPREAD OF CHRISTIANITY

During the first generation after Jesus' death his followers carried on in Palestine as a sect of Judaism. While observing Judaic law and cult practices, these "Jewish Christians" were sustained by their expectation of the imminent return of the crucified Christ to establish the Kingdom of God. Guided in their community life by Jesus' disciples, they sought to live in a manner that would conform to Jesus' teaching concerning preparation for membership in the kingdom. Among other things, this preparation involved sharing wealth, acts of charity, group prayer, and partaking of a common meal of bread and wine in Jesus' memory. Although the larger Jewish community continued to regard the members of the Christian community with suspicion and sometimes hostility, the flock did grow, not only in Palestine but beyond. Followers of Jesus, called apostles, carried Christian ideas to many cities, particularly in Syria and Asia Minor, where they attracted the attention of Diaspora Jews and of non-Jews, or Gentiles. Before long many Gentiles were asking to join the new community and were being received. This development posed a grave question for the foundling movement: whether or not new converts were to be held to strict observance of Judaic law and practices. There were those in the primitive Christian community who took a conservative position, but others, typified by Peter, leader of the disciples, increasingly insisted on universalizing Jesus' message so that it would be acceptable to Jew and Gentile alike.

A major figure in shaping the Christian mission to the Gentiles was Saul of Tarsus. Saul (soon renamed Paul) was a representative of the Jews of the Diaspora—an ardent adherent of orthodox Judaism in the tradition of the Pharisees but also a Roman citizen who was familiar with the Greco-Roman cultural life. Early in his adult life he took an active part in resisting the spread of Christianity in the Jewish community, even to the point of persecuting Christians. But then he underwent a powerful personal experience that

Map 12.1 THE SPREAD OF CHRISTIANITY TO A.D. 311 This map shows how extensively Christianity had spread across the Roman empire during the first three centuries A.D. In an important way the journeys of Paul provided a crucial beginning step in this expansion. In general, Christian life was still confined largely to cities by A.D. 311. The heavier concentration of Christians in the east is worth noting; it is perhaps understandable why the newly converted emperor, Constantine, chose to move the capital of the empire from Rome to Constantinople.

convinced him that salvation hinged on faith in Christ. Then followed a long missionary career, extending from about A.D. 46 until his martyrdom during the reign of Nero in about A.D. 67, which took him to many cities in Asia Minor, Greece, Macedonia, Palestine, and eventually Rome (see Map 12.1). Central to his missionary effort was his determination to win non-Jews to Christianity. As set forth in letters written to sustain or correct the faith of those he had converted, his message emphasized what he understood to be the precepts of Jesus that were applicable to all humanity: Jesus as the messiah sent to fulfill God's promise; the redemption of sinners ef-

fected by the Son of God through his death; the need for moral regeneration through faith and love of God and humanity; salvation as a reward for belief in Christ and acceptance of God's grace; purity of moral life. These teachings, soon to be elaborated by the Gentile authors of the synoptic Gospels and the Acts of the Apostles, marked a crucial step in establishing the basic formal doctrines of Christianity as a religion distinct from Judaism.

Forces other than the demands of the Gentile mission hastened the separation of the Christian and Jewish communities. The delay in the coming of the kingdom proclaimed by Jesus led

Christians to reformulate traditional Jewish concepts concerning the Covenant, the Chosen People, the messiah, the nature of God's ultimate kingdom, the validity of Judaic law, and the meaning of history in ways that were unacceptable to many Jews. Often these emerging Christian views were validated by interpretations of Jewish scripture that violated Jewish understanding of these sacred text. Quite understandably, such views made Jews increasingly reluctant to recognize Christianity as a sect of Judaism and led them to resist the progress of Christianity, which prompted Christians to portray Jews as enemies of God's truth. The defeat of the Jewish revolt of A.D. 66–70 not only encouraged the Christians to distance themselves from the Jews out of fear of bringing Roman wrath onto themselves but also reinforced the growing conviction in Christian circles that the Jews were not God's Chosen People. Under the guidance of the rabbinical leadership that emerged in the wake of the blasted hopes for a restored Jewish nation after the destruction of the Temple by the Romans in A.D. 70, Judaism sustained a proselytizing effort that put it into competition with Christianity for converts. All of these developments deepened Jewish antipathy toward Christians and imbedded in Christianity a vein of anti-Semitism that would bear evil fruits in the future.

Once launched in the Pauline direction, Christianity spread slowly but steadily over most parts of the Roman world; the pace of conversion quickened, especially in the third century, a development certainly linked with the crisis gripping the Roman world. That expansion was facilitated by the atmosphere of religious toleration prevailing in the Roman Empire, the increasingly intense search for individual spiritual satisfaction in the Greco-Roman world, and the powerful forces of religious syncretism at work in Hellenistic and Roman society that were preparing the ground for a common religious life. Of critical importance to Christian expansion was the existence of the Hellenized Jewish communities of the Diaspora and their synagogues, which often provided the setting for the initial planting of the seeds of the new faith and which served as a model for adapting a religion rooted in Judaism to the needs of the Greco-Roman world. During at least the first century after Jesus' death, a series of dedicated missionary preachers working under all kinds of conditions were the chief agents of expansion. They concentrated their efforts in the major cities of the empire, so that early Christianity developed chiefly as an urban religion. The efforts of these missionary preachers usually won a small group of adherents who formed themselves into self-sustaining cells. The members of these "churches," who increasingly came from the ranks of the Gentiles, then took up the burden of spreading the faith, working in local communities to increase the flock through methods that are not easily discerned in the surviving historical record.

But the results are clear enough. By the end of the third century, vigorous and expanding Christian communities existed in urban centers everywhere in the empire (see Map 12.1). The heaviest Christian population was in the cities of Egypt, Syria, Palestine, Asia Minor, Greece, and Italy. Christians certainly formed only a small minority of the total population by A.D. 300, but they had become a potent factor in the Roman world, far exceeding what might have been expected in view of Christianity's inauspicious beginning and early struggles.

The progress of Christianity was not, however, unopposed. From time to time the Roman government persecuted Christians because of their refusal to discharge any civic responsibility—including military service—that involved recognition of the Roman deities. The Christians who suffered were viewed by their fellow believers as martyrs whose heroic example strengthened the resolve of most Christians to remain steadfast. Anti-Christian feelings developed in many elements of the Roman populace. Among the masses of people there circulated rumors about strange beliefs and immoral, bestial practices of this "third race," rumors fed by the Christian refusal to participate in public religious rites and by their private worship services. Roman intellectuals scorned Christianity, holding up for ridicule its simplistic, illogical beliefs derived from faith in a crucified criminal. The leaders of the state religion and of the Jewish synagogues sometimes charged the Christians with false beliefs and debased practices. Not only Judaism but also several mystery religions featuring ideas and practices similar to those of Christianity proved worthy rivals in the competition for souls.

The Christians made difficulties for themselves as well. From the very beginning there were divisions in their ranks as to what constituted right belief and proper usage. The early communities disagreed on the nature of the relationship between Christianity and Judaism. The proper moral posture for a Christian was often a subject for debate, especially because some insisted on a puritanical denial of the world and its pleasures. By the second century and increasingly in the third, Christians disagreed violently on certain fundamental doctrines, especially those relating to the nature of Jesus' relationship to God, thus generating what may be called the first heresies. These conflicts inevitably set Christian against Christian, diverted the faithful from proselytizing, and discredited the movement in the eyes of nonbelievers.

5. THE TRANSFORMATION OF EARLY CHRISTIANITY

It is not sufficient to discuss the growth of early Christianity simply in terms of geographical and numerical expansion. Christianity proved to be a movement rich in inner resources which allowed it to grow in substance and structure in ways that increased its impact on the Greco-Roman world. That capacity for constant transformation goes far to account for its increasing appeal to the Roman world.

Of central importance in early Christian history was the ongoing reexamination and rearticulation of the new religion's fundamental beliefs. A crucial stage in that process occurred during the first century after Jesus' death, called the Apostolic Age, which produced a collection of writings that came to be called the New Testament, accepted as the divinely inspired "good news" proclaimed by Jesus. Concerned primarily with explaining the meaning of Jesus' career, the authors of the New Testament texts appropriated the Jewish Bible, which became for them the Old Testament, interpreted chiefly as a sacred text prefiguring the coming of Jesus and the new kingdom. Although rich in its many levels of meaning, the New Testament set forth dramatically and simply certain key concepts defining the essence of the new religion: a single, almighty, merciful, loving God; a universe given

order and purpose by God's plan for its ultimate destiny; an explantion of the evil and suffering in the world rooted in human sin; a divine savior, made man in the person of Jesus, son of God, sacrificed by his loving father to atone for the sins of all humans; a new covenant established by the coming of Jesus the messiah that assured eternal salvation to all men and women who earned God's grace through faith in Jesus the savior; a hope for a peaceful, just earthly community made up of the faithful who awaited the Kingdom of God by living according to the precepts of Jesus counseling love, forgiveness, nonviolence, and mutual concern for one another.

Originally shaped by believers seeking to explain Jesus' life and ministry within the framework of the Judaic tradition, Christian religious teachings soon began to take on new dimensions as a result of borrowings from Greco-Roman culture. This development marked a rather dramatic departure from primitive Christianity. Jesus had preached in Aramaic to followers who were largely apart from the mainstream of Greco-Roman intellectual and literary life. The early leaders of the new religion were quite open in their rejection of this culture, which would have no place in the new kingdom; for example, Paul could ask: "Has not God made foolish the wisdom of the world?" (I Cor. 1:20). Although there long remained a strain of antipathy toward Greco-Roman culture in Christian thought, another view began to take precedence. As is clearly evident even in Paul's writings and in the rest of the New Testament, as soon as the Christians began their effort to convert Gentiles, they had to employ the Greek and Latin languages and the modes of thought and expression prevailing in the Roman Empire in order to speak intelligibly to those they sought to convert.

During the second and third centuries two additional forces spurred the Christians to borrow increasingly from Greco-Roman culture to explain what they believed: the need to answer charges by non-Christian intellectuals that the new religion was irrational and the problem of resolving differences within Christian ranks on the meaning of basic doctrines. Both the "apologists" answering the critics of Christianity and the theologians defining the exact meaning of the faith relied heavily on various aspects of Greco-Roman intellectual life: the rational mode of

FIGURE 12.3 Honoring the Christian Dead Following an ancient Roman custom, early Christians sought to perpetuate the memory of the dead by decorating their sarcophagi with scenes from the life of the deceased. This third-century A.D. sarcophagus, which clearly reflects pagan art styles, shows the dead man (reading in the center while being prayed for) surrounded by representations of Christian history: the good shepherd, John baptizing Jesus (as a child), Jonah being washed ashore. (Alinari/Art Resource)

thought defined by logic; argumentation based on rhetoric; the content of philosophy, especially the Platonic tradition. The most influential figures in this movement wedding Christian religion and Greco-Roman culture were two scholars from Alexandria, Clement (ca. A.D. 150–216) and Origen (ca. A.D. 185–254). Their efforts not only expounded fundamental Christian ideas in rational, systematic terms but also increasingly persuaded Christians that classical learning, like Judaism, had been a preparation for the true revelation and was therefore useful in illuminating the meaning of God's word. The result of what has been called the Hellenization of Christianity was a more systematic, reasoned articulation of Christian beliefs that appealed especially to educated circles. In the process many fundamental Christian teachings, such as the nature of divinity, grace, sin, redemption, the relationship of God the Father to God the Son, and morality took on greater depth, new shades of meaning, and new complexity. Viewed in its entirety, the evolution of Christian belief provided the Christian community with an ever more persuasive armory of teachings that offered a resolution of the spiritual concerns troubling a wide range of people from all levels of society in the Greco-Roman world.

The early Christians strengthened the appeal of their religion by developing ritual practices that were attractive in a world accustomed to public pageantry, spectacles, and the highly charged rites associated with the mystery religions. Originally, Christian worship was simple. The faithful gathered in private houses to share a common meal, called the Eucharist, in commemoration of Jesus, to pray and sing, and to be instructed in Jesus' teachings. As time passed, this ritual life became more complex, marked by the adaptation of Jewish and pagan practices to Christian uses. Special places for worship were built and adorned with art inspired by Christian motifs but increasingly enriched by the adaptation of Greco-Roman art forms to Christian purposes (see Figures 12.1 and 12.3). The eucharistic ceremony became more elaborate, constituting what came to be called the Mass. Ceremonies were established for such events as baptism, marriage, and burial. Special holidays—"holy days" to the Christians—developed to commemorate highlights in Jesus' career and the death of the early martyrs. The end result was a Christian cult life that gave a religious dimension to almost any event in the life cycle of believers and that added an emotional dimension to every encounter with the Divine.

Of decisive importance to the spread of Christianity during the first three centuries of its history was the development of an organization unrivaled by any other religious movement. The first Christian communities consisted of small groups of converts lost in the non-Christian population of the cities of the Roman world. Leaders emerged in these cells to direct worship services, teach, and oversee charitable activities; women often played an important role in these functions. Eventually, these leaders were given titles: bishop (*episcopus*), elder (*presbyter*, later translated as priest), and deacon (*diaconus*). With the passage of time problems emerged that called for firmer organization: larger numbers of Christians, expanding relationships with non-Christians, increasing wealth available to the community, disagreement over what constituted right beliefs and practices. Authority over all the affairs of the entire Christian community in each city began to settle on the bishop. In cases where the number of Christians required additional places of worship within any given city or its surrounding countryside, direction of each new establishment was entrusted to a priest. However, the bishop of the city retained final authority over these new priests and their flocks. The authority of the episcopal office was given ideological justification by the concept of *apostolic succession*, which argued that every bishop was a successor to the original apostles and heir to the spiritual authority that Jesus bestowed on those apostles to proclaim the faith and to forgive sinners. The evolution of the episcopal system resulted in tightly knit, self-governing local units that closely resembled a basic entity of the ancient world—the city-state.

While many congregations were being fashioned from city to city, the Christians never lost sight of their universal spiritual kinship, rooted in their belief in the one God who had given his son to ensure salvation for all his children. From this sense of kinship emerged efforts to forge bonds of unity that would link the many "churches" into one "Church." Jesus' disciples and the early missionaries such as Paul tried to keep in touch with as many Christian communities as possible by means of extensive travel and letter writing. By the second century, bishops met together on a regional basis in *councils* to discuss common problems and decide on common solutions that each could apply in his own church. Bishops of great cities such as Jerusalem, Antioch, Alexandria, and Rome exerted considerable influence over lesser bishops in the regions surrounding these centers. These influential bishops began to be called "patriarchs" to indicate their preeminence.

Eventually some Christians became concerned with vesting ultimate authority over all Christians in the hands of one of these great bishops. A prime candidate was the bishop of Rome, who gained special prestige not only from the fact that Rome was the capital of the world but also from an important doctrine, the *Petrine theory*. According to this doctrine, rooted in a particular scriptural passage (Matt. 16:18–19), Jesus had granted Peter a special place as his vicar on earth; Peter had chosen Rome as the seat of that power; and those who followed him as bishops of Rome after his martyrdom were believed to have succeeded to Peter's authority as head of the total Christian community. By the end of the third century Peter's successors as bishops of Rome, increasingly referred to as *popes* (a title derived from the late Latin word *papa*, meaning "father"), were turning this claim to spiritual supremacy into active leadership in defining doctrine and prescribing discipline for Christian communities over much of the Roman Empire. And many of these communities were seeking the pope's guidance, especially in doctrinal matters. In terms of organization the Christian community was assuming a shape that replicated the structure of the Roman Empire—an expanding structure subdivided into well-governed local units and headed by a spiritual "emperor."

As the Christian movement evolved during the first three centuries, one of its most notable achievements was its success in creating among its followers a sense of community, a feeling of belonging to a tangible, intimate collectivity that provided secure moorings in a world increasingly impersonal and insecure. That sense of community, initially rooted in the Jewish tradition of community and given shape by shared beliefs and cult practices and by organizational structures, was fortified by a strong social consciousness among the early Christians that impinged on the lives of those in each Christian congregation in tangible ways. The teachings and the example of Jesus concerning love for others, charity, and kindness received concrete expression in Christian practice almost from the beginning. Christians poured out their resources to help the sick, the poor, criminals, slaves, orphans, widows, and other unfortunates in society. They devoted their time and energy to actions that sought to console the mourning, counsel the troubled, help the disillusioned and alienated, and seek out the outcasts of society. Such social interactions gave substance to what it meant to be a brother or a sister in a way that forged bonds within each community that transcended wealth, status, education, and power. In a real sense, membership in a Christian community diminished the need for membership in any other community. Many were drawn to the new religion by an urge to share in a bonding that gave them a meaningful place in society.

6. CHRISTIANITY AND THE CRISIS IN THE ROMAN WORLD

Historians have long debated what the advance of Christianity had to do with the crisis that gripped the Roman Empire in the third century A.D. The evidence offers no clear answer. The record provides little evidence that the early Christians were subversives. They earned their living in much the same ways as did all other Romans. They performed their civic duties as long as they were not required to deny their god. They paid their taxes and obeyed the emperor. They tried their best to help the unfortunate members of Roman society. Their minds were not completely closed to what was best in Greco-Roman intellectual, literary, and artistic life, from which they constantly borrowed to sustain their cause.

However, in other important ways, the early Christians were strangers in their world; as one critic put it, they were a people who "wall themselves off and break away from the rest of humanity." They served a god who would tolerate no rivals, including Roman emperors who claimed divinity. Believing that their god disapproved of the ways of non-Christians, they tended to avoid involvement in worldly affairs and to keep apart from social life outside their intimate communities. Their concept of sin led them to regard the world, including the Roman Empire, as a perpetual source of evil, hardly worth saving. Their beliefs in the omnipotence of God and human frailty caused them to distrust human reason and to put little faith in human ability to build a paradise on earth; the kingdom they expected to come with the return of their messiah would bear little resemblance to the powers and dominions of the past and present. They thus found little that appealed to them in the basic premise of Greco-Roman civilization: the conviction that enlightened human activity could create a perfect society on earth. The Christians were committed members of an organization that acted independently of the Roman state to focus attention on social issues defined in the interests of that organization. Through its evolving religious ceremonies, the Christian movement kept before its members a series of symbols that made them feel their separateness and uniqueness.

Perhaps in the final analysis, the growth of Christianity can best be understood as one more facet of a complex of political, economic, social, and cultural forces welling up within Roman imperial society that by the end of the third century A.D. had brought the Roman Empire to a critical juncture. Christianity's prime symbol, the sign of the cross, was an urgent reminder that at least to some there was good news amid all the bad, albeit a different kind of good news than what was usually associated with Greco-Roman civilization. The future of the empire and the entire civilization it sustained depended on what responses would be made to that sign—as well as many other signs—that an old order was passing.

SUGGESTED READING

The Decline of the Empire

Peter Brown, *The World of Late Antiquity from Marcus Aurelius to Muhammad* (1971). A thought-provoking overview.

The following works provide diverse interpretations of Rome's decline.

Joseph Vogt, *The Decline of Rome: The Metamorphosis of Ancient Civilization*, trans. Janet Sondheimer (1969).

Stewart Perowne, *The End of the Ancient World* (1966).

F. W. Walbank, *The Awful Revolution: The Decline of the Roman Empire in the West* (1969).

Michael Grant, *The Fall of the Roman Empire: A Reappraisal*, 2nd ed. (1990).

A. Ferrill, *The Fall of the Roman Empire: The Military Explanation* (1986).

Ramsay MacMullen, *Corruption and the Decline of Rome* (1988).

The Rise of Christianity

R. A. Markus, *Christianity in the Roman World* (1974). An excellent brief account of the rise of Christianity.

H. C. Frend, *The Rise of Christianity* (1984).

Robin Lane Fox, *Pagans and Christians* (1987).

Two masterful, detailed accounts of the rise of Christianity.

E. Mary Smallwood, *The Jews under Roman Rule* (1981).

Shaye J. D. Cohen, *From the Maccabees to the Mishnah* (1987).

These two works present a clear picture of Judaism at the beginning of the Christian era.

Richard A. Horsley and John S. Hanson, *Bandits, Prophets, and Messiahs: Popular Movements in the Time of Jesus* (1985). Provides a sense of the tensions in Jesus' world.

Paula Fredrikson, *From Jesus to Christ: The Origins of the New Testament Images of Jesus* (1988). A brilliant treatment of the problem of the historical Jesus.

Alan F. Segal, *Rebecca's Children: Judaism and Christianity in the Roman World* (1986). A challenging treatment of the interactions between the two religions.

Francis Watson, *Paul, Judaism, and the Gentiles* (1986). Good on the issues involved in Paul's Gentile mission.

John G. Gager, *Kingdom and Community: The Social World of Early Christianity* (1975). Excellent on the formation of the early Christian community.

Wayne A. Meeks, *The First Urban Christians: The Social World of the Apostle Paul* (1983). Excellent social history.

Ben Witherington III, *Women and the Genesis of Christianity* (1990). A provocative study.

Ramsay MacMullen, *Christianizing the Roman Empire, A.D. 100–400* (1984).

Steven Benko, *Pagan Rome and the Early Christians* (1984).

Marta Sordi, *The Christians and the Roman Empire*, trans. Annabel Bedini (1986).

These three works throw light on the spread of Christianity.

Jocelyn W. Godwin, *Mystery Religions in the Ancient World* (1981). A good treatment of religions competing with Christianity.

CHAPTER 13

Late Antiquity, A.D. 284–500: The End of Greco-Roman Civilization

FIGURE 13.1 Constantine the Great This photo shows the surviving pieces of a huge statue, nearly forty feet in height, that Constantine had placed in a magnificent basilica he built in the Roman Forum. The massive head retains some features of earlier Roman portrait sculpture (see Figure 9.2); however, its creator was more intent in conveying Constantine's lordship than in producing a realistic portrayal of the emperor. (Art Resource)

The mounting crisis that gripped the Roman world during the third century finally prompted action aimed at addressing its basic problems. Major reforms were instituted that restored the vitality of the Roman Empire during the fourth century. However, the respite was temporary. During the fifth century the empire was unable to contain Germanic invaders who seized control of the western part of the empire and ruptured the unity of the Mediterranean world. The sequence of events that disrupted the Roman Empire destroyed the framework within which Greco-Roman civilization had developed, thereby ending a distinctive era in history.

1. THE REFORMS OF DIOCLETIAN AND CONSTANTINE

The architect of the reforms that sought to end the third-century crisis was a general named Diocletian, who in A.D. 284 seized the imperial throne by force. Like so many third-century emperors, he was a man of provincial origin who worked his way to prominence in the military service and acquired many of the autocratic ways associated with military life. However, he did have a clear insight into the basic problems facing the Roman world and the will to take action which addressed these problems. The result was a restructuring of the imperial regime into a form that would prevail through late antiquity and even beyond.

Conscious of the chaos resulting from the rivalry within the army for control of the succession and of the impossible burden imposed on a single ruler by the mounting problems of the empire, Diocletian instituted a system of shared authority to ensure orderly succession and a division of administrative responsibility. He and an associate each assumed the title *augustus,* and to each was assigned a subordinate entitled *caesar.* When an augustus died, his caesar would succeed him as augustus and appoint another caesar. In theory the four co-rulers would jointly share the *imperium,* that is, the supreme power to command; in practice each was responsible for administering one of four newly established territorial units, called *prefectures,* into which the empire was divided. Although Diocletian in-

tended that co-rulers would follow a common policy, the ground was being laid for political division of the empire.

Diocletian sought to solidify and exalt the authority of the four co-rulers. Their pronouncements constituted the final law; no pretense was made of consulting with the Senate and the people. The official activities of each ruler were surrounded by elaborate symbols and rituals designed to exalt his position and associate him with divine powers. Few could escape the obvious: Rome was now ruled by an autocratic lord (*dominus*) whose position resembled that of a Persian or Hellenistic ruler more than it did the office of *princeps.*

A significant expansion and restructuring of the bureaucracy was undertaken to ensure that the autocratic rulers were able to exercise their power. At each imperial court greater numbers of professional civil servants were organized under a chief official, called the *praetorian prefect.* The number of provinces was nearly doubled by dividing old ones, and imperial officials were installed in each to carry out the orders of the central government. An intermediate level of administration was interposed between the provinces and imperial court in each prefecture by the grouping of provinces into thirteen administrative units called *dioceses;* each had its own bureaucratic apparatus responsible to the augustus or caesar or to his praetorian prefect. This elaborate hierarchy gave the central government the means to act directly in local affairs and effectively ended the independent political role of the once-active local city-state governments. Perhaps more significantly, the bureaucratic structure opened positions of power and status and opportunities for acquiring wealth to large numbers of people from all levels of life and from all over the empire who had previously been excluded from active political life by the dominance of a narrow circle of *nobiles.*

Administrative centralization was given urgency by the threat of external foes. One of Diocletian's major concerns was increasing the effectiveness of the army. Following initiatives introduced by his immediate predecessors, Diocletian sought to strengthen and regularize the permanent frontier garrisons and to develop a mobile strike force, strong in cavalry and capable of responding quickly to contain crises arising when the frontier forces were unable to cope with outside attackers. This reorganization increased the size of the army considerably—to about six hundred thousand troops—and raised monumental problems of recruitment and support.

The expansion of the bureaucracy and the army placed a massive financial burden on the imperial government. Diocletian tried to meet this challenge in various ways. The taxation system was restructured to provide for a regular census aimed at identifying units of land and human heads upon which uniform levies could be imposed. At the same time, the government imposed upon the key productive elements of society a requisition system aimed at extracting crucial produce in kind and services required to sustain the courts, the army, and the bureaucracy. To assure the labor force required to sustain production in these areas of the economy, steps were taken to freeze those in key occupations and their descendants in their positions. In an effort to stabilize the economy and curb inflation, decrees were issued to fix prices for a wide range of commodities and services. Taken together, these measures created the parameters of a regimented economy in which the state had first claim on all resources and all citizens were required to give first priority to service to the state.

Beyond claiming his subjects' labor and wealth for the service of the state, Diocletian insisted on ideological conformity. Even before his reign, the imperial government initiated steps to rally the citizenry around the worship of the traditional state deities and their agent, the semi-divine emperor. This policy led to conflict with the Christian community, many of whose members steadfastly refused to honor the pagan deities or to obey the state when it commanded them to do so. As had his immediate predecessors, Diocletian responded to Christian resistance with a series of punitive decrees in A.D. 303 and 304 that were aimed at destroying Christianity. His assault, the most serious ever mounted by the Roman state against Christians, took a heavy toll but failed in its prime objective and was soon abandoned. It did, however, demonstrate the close connection between religious conformity and political autocracy.

When Diocletian decided to abdicate in A.D. 305, his reforms had gone far to restore order in the empire. Only one of his initiatives was a signal failure—his elaborate plan for regulating the succession. Although lip service was temporarily given to its provisions, eventually there occurred a new round of armed conflict pitting various contenders and segments of the army against one another for control of the imperial office. The ultimate victor was Constantine (A.D. 306–337), who by force of arms finally won sole control of the entire empire. Constantine (see Figure 13.1) was a worthy successor of Diocletian. He vigorously pursued the main elements of Diocletian's reform program: strengthening the army; expanding and tightening bureaucratic control over imperial affairs; improving the fiscal machinery; enlarging the emperor's power; and imposing tighter control over the imperial population. Under his guidance the autocratic regime took permanent form.

Constantine added important elements to the new order. Most significant was a new religious policy officially proclaimed in A.D. 313, when he and his co-emperor issued the Edict of Milan, which granted religious freedom to all in the empire, including Christians. On the surface the state appeared to take a position of neutrality in religious affairs, but such was not the case. Associated with the grant of toleration was another event of immense psychological impact. According to the somewhat muddled surviving record, Constantine attributed victory in a battle won in A.D. 312 that was decisive in his rise to power to the intervention of the Christian God, who revealed to him in a vision prior to the battle that victory would be his if he displayed the cross as his battle emblem. To many contemporaries this event marked Constantine's conversion to Christianity. Although Constantine was not baptized until just before his death in A.D. 337 and although he took few overt actions against other religions, after the Edict of Milan he gave increasing indications that he favored the Christian cause. He poured out money to build churches, drew Christian clergymen into the councils of state, and extended them a variety of special privileges. His legislation affecting many social issues increasingly reflected Christian teachings. Every sign pointed in one direction: The empire was becoming a Christian state.

Many contemporary Christians hailed Constantine's conversion as a crucial step in the fulfillment of God's plan; in their enthusiasm they soon hailed him as Constantine "the Great," a divinely ordained agent who removed the final barrier to Christian victory. What motivated his decision has long been the subject of debate. Some evidence suggests that he was a man of his age who was powerfully drawn to religion and especially to Christianity, not the least as a result of the influence exercised over him by his Christian mother, Helen. And like so many of his contemporaries of various religious persuasions, he was convinced that the fate of the renewed empire depended on divine favor and on a people united in devotion and service to the imperial community. Perhaps his religious inclinations and political ideology led him to sense that by committing the state to the service of Christian ends, he could create a reliable nucleus of supporters whose obedience to a ruler who was God's agent would sustain a unified empire. Whatever his motives, Constantine's religious policy linked the destinies of the late Roman Empire and Christianity in ways decisive to both and to the history of the future.

Hardly less momentous was Constantine's decision to build a new capital at the ancient Greek city of Byzantium, located on the strait of Bosporus, now renamed Constantinople and officially dedicated in A.D. 330. The building of the "new" Rome was more than an autocratic whim. From the second century onward it was clear that "old" Rome was not the most advantageous physical center for the empire. With increasing frequency, emperors were chosen whose roots were outside Rome. The whole thrust of political development during the third century diminished the role of the *nobiles* of Rome and Italy as prime factors of political life. Because Rome was badly located strategically in terms of frontier defenses, the reorganization of the defense system resulted in the emergence of new political centers: Nicomedia in Asia Minor, Milan in Italy, Sirmium in the Balkans, and Trier in the Rhineland. Prompted by such considerations, Constantine's choice of a capital was well advised. The site was nearly impregnable against attacks by land or sea. It offered ready access to the most vulnerable frontiers—the lower Danube and Euphrates river frontiers. The new city was close to the great centers of wealth in the east, and it was situated where Christian strength was greatest.

It also offered its founder and his successors freedom from the restrictive traditions of republicanism and Roman civic religion, both deeply entrenched in old Rome. Although the full impact of the founding of Constantinople was not immediately obvious, the new city soon became the center of a wide range of activities that pointed toward a shift in the center of gravity of political, economic, religious, intellectual, and artistic life from Rome and Italy to the east. In fact, Constantine had created a bastion that in the not too distant future would serve as the center of a different but long-lasting Roman Empire (see Chapter 14).

2. AN UNEASY PEACE

For a time it appeared that the autocratic, bureaucratized, militarized regime shaped by Diocletian and Constantine had saved the empire. By contrast with the third century, the fourth century was one of relative stability. Succession to the imperial office was usually peaceful, there was little civil strife, the frontier defenses seemed secure, and in some places there was even a semblance of economic recovery. The era witnessed vigorous literary and artistic activity, much of it in the service of Christianity but some of it engendered by enthusiasm for traditional Greco-Roman culture. The eastern part of the empire, with its tradition of autocratic government, superior economic resources, more vital urban centers, and heavier concentration of Christian population, adjusted more easily to the new regime than did the western part with its more primitive economy and the strong commitment to traditional Roman values that was deeply entrenched in the mentality of its upper class. But everywhere there was a sense that the civilized world had been saved, a sentiment voiced by frequent references to "eternal Rome."

Despite the appearance of a restored order, there were ominous signs that the reforms of Diocletian and Constantine had not only failed to resolve but had also deepened the empire's problems. The new regime affected different parts of the empire in different ways, thereby accentuating regional differences that weakened the bonds of imperial unity. The adverse effects were especially apparent in the western part of the empire, while the east reaped greater benefits. The basic factors already present in the third century to cause declining economic production were not resolved; they were worsened by economic regimentation and by the diversion of an ever-greater proportion of wealth to support the army and the bureaucracy. The burden of taxation, requisition in kind, and compulsory labor fell chiefly on groups vital to economic well-being: peasants, artisans, merchants, and local urban aristocrats. The gap between the few rich and the many poor grew ever wider, leading to deepening social discontent. The autocratic imperial government itself became an instrument of economic and social oppression. The costly, ever-growing bureaucracy, unchecked by exalted emperors remote from practical affairs, became intrusive, corrupt, and arbitrary to the point where it was universally detested. The adequacy of the defense system remained uncertain, but the antipathy between the army and the civilian population deepened as a result of brutal, arbitrary actions by military leaders seeking to lay hands on needed supplies.

To manifest their discontent, many citizens from all walks of life sought to escape from civic responsibilities. The traditional senatorial class, once the pillar of civic virtue but now largely replaced in positions of power by nonsenatorial bureaucrats, turned its attention to accumulating land, creating self-sustaining estates, and living in luxury. Ensconced in their rural strongholds and often openly disdainful of "nonnoble" emperors and their lowly agents and army officers, these powerful figures defied the government's efforts to compel them to bear their share of the public burden. In ever-larger numbers peasants sought to escape taxation, compulsory labor service, and military duty by accepting dependent status under these landlords in return for protection and an assured livelihood. In city after city across the empire, members of local aristocracies fled to the countryside, took service in the imperial bureaucracy, or joined the clergy in order to escape the responsibilities thrust on them by the government to deliver the money and the services due from their localities. Such widespread disaffection boded ill for the future of the "new" empire.

Nor did Constantine's religious policy strengthen the bonds of unity. Christianity did continue its march to dominance during the fourth century, culminating when Emperor Theodosius (A.D. 379–395) made it the state religion and outlawed all others. The imperial policy of favoring Christianity alienated many Romans, especially aristocrats, who still placed trust in the ancient civic religions. That resentment surfaced with particular vigor during the reign of Julian (A.D. 361–363), called "the Apostate" by the Christians because he repudiated Christianity and sought to replace it with a restored pagan "church." His effort failed, but it kept alive a fundamental schism in imperial society. The Christian community itself was badly divided by a succession of bitter doctrinal disputes. Often partisans in these quarrels resisted the efforts of the imperial government and the Christian leaders who supported it to impose doctrinal unity, producing "heresies" that divided Christians and made many of them enemies of the state. Some Christian leaders even challenged the right of the imperial government to interfere in religious affairs, claiming that the Christian community constituted an independent authority when religious issues were at stake. In short, Christianity failed to supply a unifying force in the service of the "new" empire; it was a movement with its own ends and strengths, not easily bent to other purposes.

Taken together, these trends suggest that the renewal of the Roman world envisaged by Diocletian and Constantine was flawed. Faithful to a tradition deeply ingrained in the Greco-Roman mentality, they had sought to counter disarray by political means. They had taken action to create a political regime that would compel "citizens" to commit themselves to the service of the state in both body and mind. For reasons deeply imbedded in the very structure of Roman imperial society, the response was far from unanimous. Instead of heightened unity in action and purpose, society was increasingly afflicted by fundamental divisions that frustrated the state's ability to muster its material and human resources in the face of a major crisis that began to emerge at the end of the fourth century in the form of a decisive encounter between the Romans and the Germanic peoples facing each other across the Rhine-Danube frontier.

3. THE GERMANS

In describing the encounter between the Romans and the Germans during the fourth and fifth centuries, historians have traditionally referred to the Germans as "barbarians." The term is appropriate only if used to signify that the Germans differed from the Romans in terms of the basic features of the culture under which they lived. The Germans' pattern of life had been formed in their original homeland in north-central Europe and southern Scandinavia during many centuries before their first encounters with the Roman world in the late republican period. In reconstructing its main features modern historians must rely on limited information, coming chiefly from archaeological remains, the testimony of a few Roman authors, especially Tacitus' *Germania*, and Germanic law codes that were not written down until the sixth century A.D. or later under circumstances that resulted in their coloration by Roman and Christian influences. In its entirety that evidence suggests that there is a danger in assuming that the early Germans shared a uniform culture or any sense of ethnic identity. However, the record does reveal certain fundamental Germanic institutions that set them apart from the Greco-Roman world and that were destined to play a part in shaping life in western Europe in future centuries.

The basic Germanic political institution was the *tribe*, headed by a tribal chief who was chosen primarily because of his ability as a war leader. Each tribe was composed of a number of kinship groups, or *clans*. The elders of these clans, acting as a council, played a decisive role in shaping tribal decisions, but all free males capable of bearing arms were allowed to have some voice in determining collective action. Tribal government concerned itself with a limited range of affairs, chiefly war and religion. Other matters relating to group life were left largely in the hands of kinship groups; especially crucial was the responsibility of each kinship group to protect its members against injury from others. Each tribe had a body of customary law to regulate such relationships that was transmitted orally from one generation to another. Although it has survived only in written versions colored by Roman and Christian concepts, it is clear that in its substance Germanic law was primarily concerned with damages against persons. The law prescribed how much compensation could be demanded for various kinds of damage done to a person. That price, called *wergeld*, varied not only according to the nature of the crime but also according to the rank of the person in the kinship group. For example, any damage to a warrior commanded a higher *wergeld* than did the same offense against a woman of childbearing age; in turn, damage done to such a woman called for a higher *wergeld* than did a comparable crime against an aged person. It was the responsibility of those suffering damage or their kin group, not public authority, to initiate judicial processes to collect the *wergeld* defined by law. Customary law provided complex procedures for resolving disputes involving damages to persons. One such procedure, called *compurgation*, involved finding a certain number of individuals, depending on the nature of the crime and the status of the accused, who would swear under oath that the accused was innocent. Another, called *ordeal*, involved putting the accused to a test, such as holding a hot iron or being thrown into water, the results of which could be interpreted as a divine message indicating guilt or innocence. If the individual judged guilty of damage to another agreed to pay the *wergeld* prescribed by custom, the issue was settled. If not, the aggrieved kinship group often sought vengeance on the clan of the alleged criminal; the resultant feuds were a common feature of Germanic life.

By the first centuries of the Christian era the Germans practiced a mixed economy combining animal husbandry, foraging for natural products, and farming. Exchange activity played a limited role in economic life, and manufacturing focused chiefly on weapons, tools, and items for personal adornment. The basic unit of economic and social life was the family household, controlled by a male who usually but not always had a single wife. Although dependent on males in many ways, women enjoyed considerable status in Germanic society. Kinship ties within clans were established through both male and female lines. Women possessed wealth in their own right, derived chiefly from gifts conveyed to them at the time of marriage. They also played an important part in the economic pursuits that supported family life. In many ways all free males were considered to be equals. However, social gradations existed, evidenced not only by differing *wergelds* but also by a unique Germanic custom of gift exchange through which gift givers who were able to be generous earned prestige and placed recipients who were unable to reciprocate with gifts of equal value into a position of inferiority.

Germanic religion was polytheistic, based on the worship of personfied deities who embodied the forces of nature dominating the skies and the forests. An orally transmitted mythology existed to explain the nature and powers of these deities, who were usually portrayed as remote, terrible forces that must be placated constantly through prayer and offerings. Although the Germans did not develop writing until the fourth century A.D., they did possess a well-developed oral poetic tradition that dealt with the adventures of their deities and with the feats of warrior heroes. The early Germans produced no monumental architecture; their artistic talent expressed itself chiefly in skilled metalwork featuring animal forms and geometric patterns.

Although their pattern of culture differed from that of the Romans, the Germans were not locked into a pattern of "backwardness." By the fourth century their society was changing. Small tribal groups were being unified, often by force, into nations ruled over by elected kings enjoying considerable powers. Within Germanic society a warrior aristocracy was forming around a unique institution—the war band (*comitatus*), composed of individuals united by pledges made under oath to follow a military chief in return for a share of booty. The bonds linking these warriors increasingly took precedence over kinship and tribal ties to create a dominant caste in society that exalted a warrior ethos. The emergence of nations and of skilled war bands greatly increased the military capabilities of the Germans. As already noted, Germanic society was moving toward an agricultural economy that encouraged the development of an aristocracy of landowners at the expense of the older, more egalitarian social structure. These changing conditions made Germanic society dynamic, mobile, adaptable, and open to foreign influences.

Having faced each other across a more or less fixed frontier for nearly four centuries before A.D. 400, the Greco-Roman and Germanic worlds were by no means strangers to each other, divided by irreconcilable cultural and psychological barriers. The Germans had often demonstrated a desire to share the fruits of Greco-Roman civilization, especially its material wealth. Although the Romans saw the Germans as "barbarians," they often expressed admiration for their physical prowess, fighting skills, and moral excellence. They permitted and even encouraged large numbers of Germans to cross the frontier as soldiers and farmers; many even rose to high places in Roman society. Roman products, techniques, and ideas crossed the frontiers to affect many aspects of Germanic society. Such interactions suggested that the Germans might be absorbed into the mainstream of Greco-Roman civilization without causing any great disruption of its development. But that possibility depended on the ability of the Romans to control the interactions between themselves and the Germans, a matter that hinged on maintaining the frontier defenses.

4. THE GERMANIC MIGRATIONS: THE DISRUPTION OF THE ROMAN EMPIRE

Throughout the third and fourth centuries Germanic pressure on the Rhine-Danube frontier mounted steadily due to massive migrations of land-hungry Germans southward and westward and to the coalescence of Germanic tribes into nations led by warrior kings and their war bands. Beginning about A.D. 370, a sequence of events unfolded which resulted in Rome's losing control of the frontier. The crisis was triggered by a horde of nomads, the Huns, who swept out of central Asia westward toward the Germanic world. As they advanced, they encountered two Germanic nations settled along the north shores of the Black Sea: the Ostrogoths, who were overpowered, and the Visigoths, whom the Romans allowed to resettle as a nation within the empire in the area south of the Danube in return for military service. When the imperial government failed to provide for their needs, the Visigoths revolted and inflicted a crushing defeat on the Romans at the battle of Adrianople in A.D. 378. The Romans now had a hostile Germanic nation within their borders. For a time Theodosius (A.D. 379–395), the last ruler of a unified empire, was able to contain the Visigoths in the Balkan area by establishing them as allies (*foederati*) to whom lands were assigned in return for military service. Theodosius was succeeded by two sons, one ruling the west and the other the east. Almost immediately, the two courts became involved in a series of power struggles fomented by ambitious generals seeking not only personal advantage but also resources to support their Germanic soldiers. These struggles distracted attention from the defense of the frontiers, setting the stage for a political disaster.

As the fifth century opened, the Visigoths, led by a capable king named Alaric, skillfully manipulated the conflict between the two imperial courts to win permission from the eastern emperor to migrate from the Balkans to the west (see Map 13.1 for the movements of the Germans). The result was an attack on Italy that led to the capture and sack of Rome in A.D. 410, an event that deeply shocked the Roman world. In an effort to fend off the Visigothic attacks, the imperial court in the west recalled troops from the Rhine and Danube frontiers and from Britain. Other Germanic nations immediately broke through the weakened frontier defenses and overran most of the western provinces. The imperial government in the west sought desperately to control the Germans by assigning them areas where they could settle as allies, nominally subject to Roman authority, and by allocating them a share of public revenues. In fact, wherever the Germans settled and whatever the terms, their kings and warriors soon became the real rulers. As a consequence, during the fifth century a series of independent Germanic kingdoms emerged on Roman soil in the west to create a new political geography of major importance for the future.

After a brief stay in Italy the Visigoths moved on to southern Gaul, where they established a kingdom that soon began to extend into Spain. Already other Germanic nations that had broken across the Rhine—Vandals, Sueves, Alains—had made their destructive way across Gaul and into Spain. The Vandals, under the leadership of their one great king, Gaiseric, crossed into Africa in A.D. 429 and carved out a large kingdom that deprived Rome of access to its main grain supply. The Vandals then developed sufficient sea power to allow them to pillage Rome in A.D. 455.

The Burgundians created a kingdom in southeastern Gaul in the Rhône Valley, effectively blocking the routes linking Italy to Gaul and Spain. Beginning about A.D. 425, Angles, Saxons, and Jutes went by sea to wipe out the badly weakened Roman outposts in Britain and to establish several petty kingdoms; in the process the newcomers drove the native Celtic population into Wales and across the English Channel into Brittany.

Without abandoning their original homelands, Franks and Alemanni began the occupation of northern Gaul and the middle Rhine Valley. Late in the fifth century the Franks, led by a ruthless warrior king named Clovis (A.D. 481–511), seized most of Gaul as their base of power; in the process they drove the Gallic Visigoths into Spain and absorbed the Burgundian kingdom as well as much of the territory of the Alemanni. In A.D. 493 the Ostrogoths, led by King Theoderic, acting as an agent of the eastern emperor, established control over Italy. The confusion caused by the movements of these Germanic peoples was compounded by the presence of a powerful Hunnic kingdom established north of the Danube. Under their feared king, Attila, the Huns harassed the East and then, in A.D. 451–452, invaded Gaul and Italy, which were successfully defended by a coalition of Roman and Germanic troops. After Attila's death in 453, the Hunnic kingdom quickly broke up, leaving central Europe in a chaotic state.

While the boundaries of these new kingdoms remained fluid and their political institutions unstable, there could be no doubt that by A.D. 500 the Germans had won the West. The fate of the empire in the east during the critical fifth century was quite different. Although German forces repeatedly ravaged imperial territory in the Balkans and sought entry into the eastern provinces, their assaults were turned away. The imperial government in Constantinople mustered the superior resources of the East to sustain an effective defense system and mounted a diplomatic effort that successfully diverted Germanic attacks toward the west. The consequence was of immense significance: the Roman imperial regime as structured by Diocletian and Constantine survived virtually intact in the east.

By contrast, in the west the imperial political system slowly disintegrated under the impact of

Map 13.1 GERMANIC INVASIONS, FIFTH CENTURY The map shows the movements of the various Germanic nations in the course of their migrations into the Roman Empire in the fifth century. Most of them ended their wandering by establishing a kingdom on Roman soil. Especially important for the future was the kingdom established by the Franks in Gaul.

the Germanic migrations. Despite the efforts of some military leaders to stem the tide, the imperial government was unable to muster the resources required to contain the Germans militarily. The bulk of the Roman population showed little zeal for defending themselves; some even welcomed the Germans as liberators who ended the oppressive policies of the late empire (see Historians' Sources, p. 170). Although the Germans were settled under terms that gave the Roman government nominal lordship over them,

in fact they took over real power. As the settlement process advanced, the Roman bureaucracy broke down, imperial income dwindled, the imperial armies melted away, and the authority of the successors of Augustus vanished. By A.D. 476 the political realities in the west were officially recognized. A German general, Odoacer, deposed the last western emperor and turned the insignia of the imperial office over to the emperor in Constantinople. In theory, this act reunited the empire under a single ruler. In reality, the em-

Salvian: *On the Governance of God*

In a work entitled On the Governance of God, *written just before 450, the Christian priest Salvian set forth a catalogue of the evils of his day resulting from human sin. His observations about the lot of the poor perhaps give the historian an insight into why the Roman government failed to maintain the allegiance of its subjects, why the victory of Christianity did not solve all problems, and why the rule of the "barbarian" Germans was acceptable to many.*

But what else can these wretched people wish for, they who suffer the incessant and even continuous destruction of public tax levies. To them there is always imminent a heavy and relentless proscription. They desert their homes, lest they be tortured in their very homes. They seek exile, lest they suffer torture. The enemy is more lenient to them than the tax collectors. . . . This very tax levying, although hard and inhuman, would nevertheless be less heavy and harsh if all would bear it equally and in common. Taxation is made more shameful and burdensome because all do not bear the burden of all. They extort tribute from the poor man for the taxes of the rich, and the weaker carry the load for the stronger. There is no other reason that they cannot bear all the taxation except that the burden imposed on the wretched is greater than their resources. . . .

If you look at what they pay, you will think them abundant in riches, but if you look at what they actually possess, you will find them poverty stricken. Who can judge an affair of this wretchedness? They bear the payment of the rich and endure the poverty of beggars. . . .

Indeed, the most wretched poor thus pay all that I have mentioned, but for what cause or for what reason they pay, they are completely ignorant. For, to whom is it lawful to discuss why they pay; to whom is permitted to find out what is owed? . . .

But, surely, those who are wicked in one way are found moderate and just in another, and

compensate for their baseness in one thing by goodness in another. For, just as they weigh down the poor with the burden of new tax levies, so they sustain them by the assistance of new tax reliefs; just as the lower classes are oppressed by new taxes, so they are equally relieved by tax mitigations. Indeed, the injustice is equal in taxes and reliefs, for, as the poor are the first to be burdened, so they are the last to be relieved.

For when, as has happened lately, the highest powers thought it would be advisable that taxation should be lessened somewhat for the cities which were in arrears in their payments, the rich alone instantly divided among themselves the remedy given for all. Who, then, remembers the poor? Who calls the poor and needy to share in the common benefit? Who permits him who is first in bearing the burden even to stand in the last place for receiving redress? What more is there to say? . . .

Do we think we are unworthy of the punishment of divine severity, when we thus constantly punish the poor? Do we think, when we are constantly wicked, that God should not exercise His justice against all of us? Where or in whom are evils so great, except among the Romans? Whose injustice is so great except our own? The Franks are ignorant of this crime of injustice. The Huns are immune to these crimes. There are no wrongs among the Vandals and none among the Goths. So far are the barbarians from tolerating these injustices among the Goths, that not even the Romans who live among them suffer them.

Therefore, in the districts taken over by the barbarians, there is one desire among all the Romans, that they should never again find it necessary to pass under Roman jurisdiction. In those regions, it is the one and general prayer of the Roman people that they be allowed to carry on the life they lead with the barbarians. And we wonder why the Goths are not conquered by our portion of the population, when the Romans prefer to live among them rather than with us. Our brothers, therefore, are not only altogether unwilling to flee to us from them, but they even cast us aside in order to flee to them.

SOURCE: *The Writings of Salvian, the Presbyter*, trans. Jeremiah F. O'Sullivan (New York: Cima Publishing Co., Inc., 1947), pp. 138–141.

peror in the east had virtually no control over the west, where the Germans ruled by virtue of conquest but without the benefits of the splendid political system created by the Romans. The end of that system marked a turning point in the history of the Mediterranean world.

Beyond the disruption of the imperial political system in the west, the immediate impact of the Germanic migrations must not be overstated. The destruction of life and property was not excessive, and in most cases Germans and Romans soon settled side by side on peaceful terms. Except in Britain and along a thin stretch of the old empire facing the Rhine, the intruders were not sufficiently numerous to affect the ethnic composition or language of the native Roman population. Many aspects of Roman civilization survived the shock of the Germanic intrusion and continued to play a decisive role in the way people in the west lived and thought.

Of more fundamental significance was the fact that the migration of the Germans into the west helped to create a general environment that accelerated and made irreversible certain trends in economic and cultural life which had begun to undermine the fabric of Greco-Roman civilization long before the Germans arrived. The trend toward a predominantly agricultural economy continued during and beyond the fifth century, accentuated by the decline of trade and industry and by political instability. The result was a continued decline in the general level of material wealth. Agricultural life increasingly focused on self-contained large estates tilled by a peasantry dependent on their owners. Of both Roman and German descent, these landowners constituted a new ruling force whose interests were narrowly focused on family welfare, economic self-sufficiency, acquisition of land, and local political power. Most cities in the west shrank to a fraction of their former size and ceased to be active commercial, administrative, and cultural centers. Their decline meant the end of the urban aristocracy that had long sustained Greco-Roman civilization in the west. Deprived of an urban setting and the patronage of the Roman imperial government, Greco-Roman cultural activity stagnated despite the efforts of some rural aristocrats, both Roman and German, to support education, literature, and art. The growing irrelevance of many aspects of classical culture to the realities of a changing world made their efforts ineffectual and opened the way for a different culture defined in Christian terms. All of these aspects of change point to one conclusion: Greco-Roman civilization did not "fall" because of "barbarian" invasions; the arrival of the Germans simply reinforced the powerful forces already at work transforming long-standing patterns of civilization into a different kind of order to which the Germans would contribute in important ways.

5. CHRISTIANITY IN LATE ANTIQUITY

Christianity was inevitably involved in the events of the fourth and fifth centuries that transformed the Roman Empire; that involvement changed the nature of the Christian movement. From one perspective the fourth century was a time of triumph for Christians. Massive numbers of converts from all levels of society swelled the ranks of the Christian community to the point where Christians were the dominant religious force in the empire. Christian clergymen increasingly advanced to prominent leadership positions in society, using the organizational structures and the increasing wealth they commanded as instruments to shape life in imperial society. The imperial government gave powerful support to these developments, thereby intertwining the Christian establishment and the secular authority ever more closely. By about A.D. 400 the Roman Empire had become a Christian Roman Empire, a fact recognized by Theodosius when he proclaimed Christianity as the state religion. That action instilled into many Christians a triumphal, even arrogant sense that the kingdom promised by God had come.

However, success brought problems that troubled the souls of many Christians and prompted still further adaptations of their religion. The avalanche of converts diluted the spiritual fervor of pre-Constantinian Christianity and opened the way for an intrusion of pagan ideas and practices that threatened to obliterate the distinctiveness of Christianity. The massive influx of educated Romans into the Christian community accelerated the efforts to reformulate the essential Christian message in terms that reflected the Greco-Roman philosophical and literary tradition. Wealth and power turned the heads of Christian leaders from pastoral functions toward worldly pursuits. The insistence of Christian emperors on using Christianity to advance political ends that had little to do with the "good news" that Jesus had taught threatened the independence of the Christian community. Large numbers of people, from powerful aristocrats to lowly peasants, still adhered to their traditional religions; what to do with these "pagans" posed troublesome issues.

At the heart of all of these issues was a profound intellectual, moral, and even emotional dilemma posed by the very success of Christianity: How could a movement that had historically been distrustful of the powerful and of worldly things, committed to peace and justice, and expectant of the coming of a kingdom in which the corrupt ways of the world would be overturned suddenly become a willing handmaiden of an oppressive regime upon whose hands was the blood of Christian martyrs? How could a community that had been exclusive, highly selective of its membership, animated by deep moral fervor, and concerned with human interactions based on love and charity suddenly become a corporate entity flooded with members whose moral purity was untested, whose motives for "conversion" were unexamined, and whose subsequent behavior was little changed? These profound contradictions, which touched every aspect of Christianity during the fourth century, led to responses that hastened what one modern scholar has called "the conversion of Christianity." Some of those responses put a mark on the Christian movement that had an immense impact on the future.

One response, aimed primarily at resolving the disciplinary problems brought on by the huge increase in the number of Christians, involved steps to strengthen the organization of the Christian community. The distinctions between religious leaders, the clergy, and ordinary Christians, the laity, were drawn more sharply. The powers of the clergy, especially bishops, were expanded to allow them to define Christian behavior and modes of worship more precisely and to compel the laity to obey the evolving "law" of the Christian establishment, called *canon law*. Bishops were vested with judicial

powers, usually with the support of the imperial government, to punish those violating canon law, including the power of *excommunication*, that is, cutting offenders off from participation in the religious life through which salvation was gained. While the strengthening of a hierarchical system of governance promoted order in the Christian world, it also introduced an element of compulsion and authoritarianism into religious life that contrasted sharply with the voluntarism and self-discipline that had marked earlier Christian community life.

Another response to the new situation in which the Christian movement found itself was a search for new ways of finding and living a holy life, a quest most dramatically illustrated by the rise of monasticism. Although the movement involved elements of protest against political and economic oppression and against an increasingly formalized, legalistic, intellectualized religious establishment, monasticism in its essence represented a radical new way of seeking God defined by individuals lacking the qualifications generally required for positions of authority: wealth, family connections, office, education. This new breed of Christian, calling themselves "athletes of Christ," sought to follow Jesus' command to leave all worldly things behind by physically separating themselves from the civilized world to live in a setting apart where through prayer and mortification of the flesh they sought to purge themselves of temptation and sin. The monastic movement began in the late third and early fourth centuries in Egypt, where individuals of modest circumstances left everything behind to live in the desert. The first desert fathers, exemplified by Anthony, who soon became a hero as the father of monasticism, were hermits who sought perfection through individual ascetic actions; Anthony's model of individual (*eremetic*) spiritual quest was widely imitated outside of Egypt, especially in Syria and Palestine. In time hermits seeking guidance in their quest for perfection began to cluster around a father (*abba*) who had gained renown for his spiritual feats. This led to the formation of monasteries, groups of individuals living in isolated physical compounds where the pursuit of spiritual perfection was governed by rules that defined patterns of communal behavior for achieving perfection. Especially important in establishing models for communal (*cenobitic*) monastic life were the rules of the Egyptian monk Pachomius and the Greek monk and bishop Basil of Caesarea. Spread by word of mouth and by written biographical sketches and collections of sayings of the desert fathers, the spiritual heroics of the early monks soon electrified the Christian world. By A.D. 400 monasticism, especially in its cenobitic form, had spread across most of the Roman world. While the monastic ethos was excessive in its denial of worldly affairs and its obsession with the danger of sexuality as a source of sin, it did remind Christians of the need for inner struggle in order to win salvation. The monastic movement created a new type of hero to replace the martyrs of old and a new type of authority figure to challenge the official clergy. In the eyes of many ordinary Christians, the holy men and women forged in the austere, world-denying environment of the monastery became a special breed able to serve as agents through whom divine favors could flow to relieve the heavy burdens imposed by a troubled, uncaring world.

While some chose to flee the world, other Christians, especially ecclesiastical leaders, chose to become more closely identified with it, a response that likewise had momentous consequences. Operating within a long tradition of viewing religion as an instrument of political control, the religious hierarchy was put into a new position once the Roman imperial order accepted Christianity as the official religion. It came under strong pressure to use its expanding authority to define religious behavior in terms that supported political policy and to use its powers of enforcement in ways that promoted political conformity. For a variety of reasons ranging from pastoral concerns to an urge for power, most Christian officials of the fourth century were quite willing to cooperate fully with the state in the promotion of a Christian empire. That willingness hastened the intermingling of secular and religious affairs to a point where it was virtually impossible to distinguish between the two realms. Equally important, it led to the sacralization of the state and its rulers, whose office bestowed on them a divinely ordained right and duty to promote Christian welfare and to whom obedience became a Christian obligation. Nowhere was this process more dramatically demonstrated than in the case of Constantine. Although his actual conduct as emperor was far from exemplary by any standards, let alone Christian, even during his lifetime he came to be viewed as one touched by divinity, a new David upon whom God had bestowed powers that made him an agent in working out the divine plan for humankind and that allowed him to command Christians as he wished for their own good. A new dimension had been added to Christianity which gave a different meaning to rendering unto Caesar that which was his.

However, to some who were mindful of the earlier Christian tradition of hostility and suspicion toward the world and its ways, that development posed grave dangers. They began to articulate a case for limitation of state control over religion. Of particular importance for the future was the contention that Christian ends were different from and more important than secular ends and therefore must take precedence. That view was given dramatic visibility by the powerful bishop of Milan, Ambrose (ca. A.D. 340–397), who excommunicated Emperor Theodosius for massacring some of his subjects under circumstances that some thought exceeded the authority of worldly rulers. Ambrose justified his sentence on the grounds that the Christian community constituted a corporate body—a Church—which possessed a separate realm of jurisdiction that must take precedence over the state when spiritual issues were at stake. Implicit in this argument were fundamental issues involving the nature of the Christian community and how it should be governed that would long pose a challenge. As the concept of the separateness and independence of the "Church" took shape, it spurred discussion of where the locus of ultimate authority in the Christian community was. As the fourth century proceeded, more and more Christians agreed that the bishop of Rome, Peter's successor, was the spiritual head of the Christian community. The ascendancy of the bishop of Rome was promoted by the imperial government, which relied on the successors of Peter to formulate and lend support to definitions of dogma and discipline that would serve to unify the empire. The popes responded by expanding their claims to authority and by asserting that authority more vigorously over the Christian community, steps that gave added impetus to the evolving hierarchical structure of Christian organization. But not all were happy with the rising star of the bishop of Rome, least of all the patriarchs of the venerable Christian communities in Antioch, Alexandria, and Jerusalem, to which was added a newcomer, the patriarch of Constantinople, who was closely linked to the emperor of Constantinople. The stage was being set for a long, bitter, and sometimes unholy struggle for supremacy within the Christian community.

Fourth-century Christianity was given special shape by a growing concern with doctrinal uniformity. Although doctrinal disagreement had been present in the pre-Constantinian Christian community, the intensified urge to define and enforce "orthodoxy" and to suppress dissident "heresy" represented another response to Christian victory. The basic dilemmas posed by the sudden favorable turn of events for the Christians evoked diverse views that had doctrinal implications and that revealed the possibility of irreconcilable divisions that would make folly of Jesus' "good news" and the whole idea of a single Christian community. The complexity of the issues raised by divergent doctrinal positions is illustrated by two particular "heresies."

One was Donatism, a movement originating in North Africa, which centered on the fate of clergymen who had compromised their faith in the face of Diocletian's persecution but subsequently sought restoration to their offices. A party of zealous Christians, led by Bishop Donatus of Carthage, denied them this privilege, arguing that their apostasy barred them forever from Christian fellowship and that their impurity rendered invalid all the sacred rites they had performed—baptisms, marriages, ordinations, forgiveness of sins. Implicit in the Donatist position was a concept of the true Christian community as a small, elite, pure group led by bishops and priests untouched by sin. When theological arguments failed to dissuade these purists, Constantine used the power of the state to suppress them, but to no avail. Backed by popular support in North Africa which linked religious dissent with resistance to the Roman imperial regime, the Donatist movement survived for over a century, constituting what amounted to a separate Christian establishment that served to keep alive the issue of who qualified as a true Christian.

Even more disruptive was Arianism, a movement that emerged from the teachings of a priest from Alexandria named Arius concerning the Trinity. Disturbed with the blurring of monotheism that had resulted from the absorption of Greco-Roman religious and philosophical ideas into Christian teaching, Arius argued that God the Son was subordinate to God the Father, thereby denying the absolute divinity of Jesus. His position raised a storm of protest from bishops and theologians who supported a trinitarian position maintaining that the Son was coequal with the Father and that, together with the Holy Spirit, these three "persons" constituted a single deity. In an attempt to settle this dispute Constantine summoned bishops from all over the empire to the ecumenical Council of Nicaea in A.D. 325. This assemblage, presided over by the emperor in person, agreed upon the Nicene Creed, which defined "orthodox" teaching on several issues, included a strong affirmation of the trinitarian position. Despite official condemnation and punitive measures taken by the state against its adherents, Arianism survived for generations to divide Christendom. In later efforts to resolve the trinitarian issue, emperors and their supporting theologians demonstrated a tendency to cut doctrinal cloth in ways that would appeal to political factions and regional ecclesiastical rivalries, thereby politicizing the quest for doctrinal unity.

The upshot of the quest for orthodoxy was the hardening of doctrine into an official creed, deviation from which earned the charge of heresy and brought political and religious sanctions down on dissenters. The implications of this development toward a monolithic ideology in terms of personal religious experience were ominous. On the obverse side of this development were increasingly harsh sanctions against paganism and more strident assaults on Judaism; these manifestations of the narrowing of the limits of tolerance had widespread support at all levels of Christian society.

Still another response to the situation in which the Christian community found itself in the fourth century was a more aggressive involvement of Christians in intellectual and artistic life. The result was an outburst of cultural activity that resulted in their assumption of cultural leadership in late antiquity. That leadership was clearly demonstrated in the arts. Church building provided one of the chief outlets for the talents of architects, sculptors, and painters. They developed new modes of conveying the Christian message by creatively adapting the classical artistic tradition to Christian purposes (see Figures 12.1, 12.3, and 13.2). Some of the most inspired poetry of the age flowed from the pens of Christian writers seeking to express their thoughts and feelings about their faith. Christian writers such as Bishop Eusebius of Caesarea (ca. A.D. 260–340) recast the writing of history to incorporate the past of the non-Christian world into the Judeo-Christian version of sacred history as delineated in Scripture; in the process the Roman Empire and its rulers emerged as integral, preordained elements in the working out of God's plan for the cosmos. Inspired chiefly by the feats of the monks, Christian writers developed a new literary genre, hagiography, devoted to the lives of the saints.

But the most important intellectual achievement of the period was the theological writings of a remarkable group of intellectuals, known collectively as the *Church Fathers*. Among the most prominent were the Greeks Athanasius, Basil, Gregory of Nyssa, and Gregory Nazianus and the Latins Augustine, Jerome, and Ambrose. Although each was an individual intellectual in his own right, this potent group of thinkers collectively reshaped the basic thrust of intellectual life. The fruit of their labor was a massive body of literature destined to guide intellectual life for centuries to come. Their intellectual posture was rooted in their deep Christian faith as informed by the Old and New testaments, but they also borrowed boldly and creatively from the content

FIGURE 13.2 A Sixth-Century Christian Church This magnificent church was built in Ravenna in honor of S. Apollinare. Its architectural form represents an adaptation of the Roman basilica style (see p. 140) for Christian purposes. The central hall (the nave) served as a gathering place for the faithful. An altar often stood in the semicircular apse at the far end of the nave. Aisles flanked the nave on either side, set off by columns and arches supporting the walls of the nave. These walls rose above the roof over each side aisle. At their upper levels the walls were pierced by windows that lighted the structure's interior. This style of architecture was destined to assert a powerful influence on religious architecture in later western European history. (G. E. Kidder-Smith)

and methods of the Greco-Roman literary, philosophical, and scientific tradition to formulate a consistent, logical, persuasive statement of the Christian interpretation of the universe. In the process they not only provided reasoned and enduring positions on key elements of Christian doctrine but also literally redefined human values and the purpose of human existence in terms of a quest for salvation in another world, thereby overpowering the classical Greco-Roman worldview, which stressed the reasoned search for excellence in this world. In working out this transformation of values the church fathers selectively appropriated the Greco-Roman intellectual achievement as an indispensable tool for understanding what they perceived to be ultimate Christian wisdom, but in the process they reshaped that achievement in ways that deprived it of much of its original meaning.

As the Church Fathers progressed in formulating a Christian worldview, subtle differences began to emerge that distinguished the Greek Fathers from the Latin Fathers in terms of their basic religious concerns and their interpretation of classical culture. These differences marked an initial step in the emergence of distinctive eastern and western Christian establishments. Of particular importance in shaping the western intellectual tradition was Augustine (A.D. 354–430). Born in North Africa, the son of a pagan father and a Christian mother, Augustine received a good Latin education to prepare him as a teacher of rhetoric. As his education progressed, his searching mind experimented with a variety of pagan philosophical and religious systems, none of which satisfied his yearning for spiritual security. Neither did the mistress he took as a young man nor the child born to that union. Eventually he converted to Christianity and was chosen bishop of Hippo in Africa. As a bishop, Augustine's major concern was to be an effective pastor. In that role he worked tirelessly to guide his flock toward sound belief and spiritual perfection and ended his life trying to protect his city from the Germanic Vandals. But he also turned out a prodigious body of writing on a variety of theological and moral issues, much of it prompted by his efforts to combat heresy, especially Donatism and Arianism. In his own time his writings served many as guides to a fuller understanding of the faith; for centuries to come his thought provided the basis for the major positions adopted in the West on most doctrinal and moral issues.

Two of his many works were particularly significant. His *Confessions* recounts his own spiritual pilgrimage as an educated Roman through most of the philosophical and religious systems of the ancient world to his final realization that only Christianity could satisfy his spiritual hunger. The work presents not only a forceful critique revealing the failure of Greco-Roman philosophy and religion to satisfy many thinking people but also a compelling argument in support of the Christian faith as the only adequate response to life's problems. Even more influential was his *City of God*, written to answer charges that the Visigothic sack of Rome in A.D. 410 was a punishment imposed on the Romans by their ancient deities, who were angry at them for becoming Christians. Augustine sought to demonstrate that this "catastrophe" was only a step in the unfolding of God's plan for the universe. God, he argued, had ordained two cities, that of God and that of the world. The true City of God exists only in the other world; membership will be awarded to true believers who have been predestined for salvation by God. The worldly city, presently embodied in the Roman Empire, is tarnished by sin and due eventually to pass. The coming of Christ had established an earthly embodiment of the City of God in the form of the Christian community, into whose body all must now be enfolded. Not despair but joy should greet the passing of Rome, since that event was a preordained step toward a more perfect world planned by God from the beginning. Members of the human community, both those who are sinners and those destined for salvation, must accept their lot in this world, including submission to worldly government, whose function is restraining the forces of evil by whatever means possible. Augustine justified warfare, slavery, persecution of heretics, social inequality, and suffering as inevitable consequences of flawed human nature, for which there was no cure except God's grace, which would not be bestowed to perfect this world. In offering an explanation for the misery and evil of this world and a vision of redemption in another world that did not hinge on human accomplishment, Augustine's interpretation of both the cosmos and history provided an appealing answer to basic human concerns that had not been supplied by classical philosophy. In this sense, his intellectual achievement marked a watershed between the Classical Age and the future.

Other Christian intellectuals helped to ensure the victory of a Christian culture in the west. One was Ambrose (ca. A.D. 340–397), bishop of Milan and a key figure in guiding Augustine to his conversion. In his writings Ambrose not only helped to shape the rationale for the independence of the Church but also persuasively articulated the basic principles of Christian morality. He drew heavily on the moral principles developed by classical thinkers, but he skillfully recast their moral values to fit within the framework of Christian doctrine. Another influential figure was Jerome (A.D. 340–419), a man of immense learning and a formidable linguist who was drawn to monastic life despite the great appeal that classical literature had for him. His voluminous letters played a significant role in guiding the spiritual life of an important circle of Roman nobles, including many women. He employed his linguistic talents to produce a Latin translation of the Old and New testaments, basing his translation on both Hebrew and Greek versions of Scripture. Jerome's Bible, called the Vulgate, became the standard Latin Bible for centuries. Its existence ensured that Latin would survive as the language of the Christian religion in the West and that its readers would retain an ability to read the literature of classical Latin antiquity. Jerome's extensive commentaries on the Bible also guided later generations in their efforts to interpret the meaning of the Bible.

The traumatic events that befell the Roman Empire during the fifth century posed new problems for Christianity. The collapse of the Roman political system in the west deprived the Christian community there of a major protector and a prime source of material support. Churches were destroyed and Christians were killed by the Germans. Although the Germans converted to Christianity, almost all of them became adherents of Arian Christianity, which resulted in clashes with the main body of the Christian population in the west, which accepted the orthodox trinitarian position; this doctrinal schism impeded the assimilation of Romans and Germans. Moreover, the Germanic nations were usually con-

verted from the top down, their kings decreeing that their followers accept baptism but not having much concern for their instruction in their new faith. As a result, a large residue of Germanic religious ideas and practices continued to flourish in the Germanic population, often reinforcing the paganism still flourishing among non-Germans living in the rural areas of the west. Powerful theological disagreements still divided the Christian population, especially in the east, where heresy often became associated with regional political discontent to form separatist movements threatening the already fragile unity of the empire.

However, firmly in possession of its early traditions and fortified by the new organizational, intellectual, and spiritual vitality shaped during the fourth century, the Christian community survived the ordeal of the fifth century and became a more potent directive force in society. In the east a significant segment of Christian leaders rallied to the support of the imperial government and utilized their position and resources to solidify public acceptance of the imperial policy seeking to perpetuate a Christian Roman Empire as envisaged by Constantine. In many parts of the west, bishops replaced local aristocracies and bureaucrats as keepers of order, administrators of justice, and caretakers of the unfortunate. Pope Leo I (A.D. 440–461), for example, served as virtual governor of the city of Rome and as a forceful diplomat who defended the city against attacks by the Vandals and Huns. Many other bishops played a similar role in cities across the entire west. By A.D. 500 there were clear signs that the Arianism of the Germans was giving way to orthodoxy and that Germans and Romans were finding a common basis in a single faith. A key event in ensuring the victory of orthodoxy was the conversion of the pagan Frankish king Clovis to orthodoxy. Most Germanic kings, whatever their particular religious persuasion, began to lend their support to the Christian establishment and to draw on its personnel for assistance in ruling their kingdoms. As the focus of life shifted from the city to a rural setting, bishops began incorporating the neglected peasantry into the mainstream of Christian life. A sign of its concern with rural life was the emergence of a new organizational structure, the rural parish, which provided a local center from which to convert the nobles and peasants increasingly bound to a rural environment and guide their spiritual formation. As cultural life in the declining cities collapsed, monasteries increasingly provided havens for education and the preservation of culture. By A.D. 500 the Christian clergy had become a pillar of order and stability in all aspects of life in the west. It members had inherited the leadership role once held by the Roman imperial officials, a role that its earliest adherents would probably never have dreamed possible or perhaps even desirable. That leadership provided a clear indication that the old order was giving way to a new one.

SUGGESTED READING

Political, Economic, and Social Developments

The general history of the period covered in this chapter is treated in the works cited in Chapter 12 on the decline of the Roman Empire. The following works cover more specialized aspects of the period, as indicated by their titles.

Ramsay MacMullen, *The Roman Government's Response to Crisis, A.D.. 235–337* (1976).

Diana Bowder, *The Age of Constantine and Julian* (1978).

A. H. M. Jones, *Constantine and the Conversion of Europe* (1948; reprinted 1978).

History of Christianity

The developments in religious history are treated in the works of Markus, Frend, and Fox cited in Chapter 12. The following works treat particular aspects of religious history.

Jaroslav Pelikan, *The Christian Tradition: A History of the Development of Doctrine*, Vol. 1: *The Emergence of the Catholic Tradition (100–600)* (1971). A masterful treatment of the shaping of Christian doctrine.

Derwas J. Chitty, *The Desert a City* (1966).

Philip Rousseau, *Pachomius: The Making of a Community in Fourth-Century Egypt* (1985).

Two excellent studies on monastic origins.

Peter Brown, *Society and the Holy in Late Antiquity* (1982). A brilliant portrayal of the spiritual forces that transformed the late Roman world.

Peter Brown, *The Body and Society: Men, Women, and Sexual Renunciation in Early Christianity* (1988). A masterful treatment of Christian attitudes about sexuality.

John Holland Smith, *The Death of Classical Paganism* (1976). A good account of another side of religious life in the late empire—that of the losers.

The Germans and Their Migrations

Malcolm Todd, *The Northern Barbarians, 100 B.C.–A.D. 300* (1987).

E. A. Thompson, *The Early Germans* (1965).

Either of these works will help the reader understand the nature of early Germanic society.

Hans-Joachim Diesner, *The Great Migrations: The Movements of Peoples Across Europe, A.D. 300–700*, trans. C. S. V. Salt (1982). A brief account, beautifully illustrated.

Lucien Musset, *The Germanic Invasions: The Making of Europe, A.D. 400–600*, trans. Edward and Columba James (1975). A more detailed account of the Germanic migrations.

Justine D. Randers-Pehrson, *Barbarians and Romans: The Birth Struggle of Europe, A.D. 400–700* (1983). Especially good on the efforts of the Germans to establish themselves in the empire.

Biographies

Stephen Williams, *Diocletian and the Roman Recovery* (1985).

Ramsay MacMullen, *Constantine* (1988).

Peter Brown, *Augustine of Hippo: A Biography* (1967).

RETROSPECT

Few epochs in all history witnessed greater achievements than that extending from the Golden Age of Greece in the fifth century B.C. to the generation that saw the Roman imperial system reach its full maturity about A.D. 180—the epoch from Pericles to Marcus Aurelius. The

Greco-Roman accomplishment was driven by one fundamental idea—confidence in the ability of human beings to shape their own destiny by utilizing powers inherent in their own human nature. Trust in those powers, especially the power to reason, prompted a many-faceted search for more knowledge about the physical world in which human beings lived and a fuller understanding of the human condition. The fruits of that inquiry found expression in a rich literature, philosophy, science, and art. Viewed in its entirety, the Greco-Roman cultural achievement provided persuasive evidence that there was order in the universe, that men and women could know themselves, and that they could define and live by ethical standards capable of producing a good and full life. Out of this quest emerged a shared set of values which supplied intellectual, aesthetic, and emotional bonds that drew a wide circle of peoples into a cultural community that persisted across many centuries. The same trust in the human power to shape human destiny generated efforts to shape and reshape political communities in quest of a social environment that would foster the good life and the pursuit of human excellence, an effort that proceeded along a continuous trajectory from the Greek city-state polity to the Roman Empire. These developments not only greatly expanded the human vision but also brought to many—including those who had not heretofore tasted the fruits of higher civilization—peace, security, and even a better material life.

Yet the Greco-Roman achievement was somehow flawed. Not even its creators were completely convinced that their vision of humanity was true. They suspected that in human beings lurked an elusive element of the demonic and that beyond them existed forces they were powerless to control. Moreover, the kind of society that emerged from the centuries-long effort to create a world fit for reasonable, good, enlightened people had some features that were disturbing. The confidence that political action could achieve perfection had given the state a dangerous dominance over its peoples at the expense of other dimensions of existence. The majestic assumptions about human rationality and capacity for good had given undue power to those who managed to acquire the symbols of rationality and good: an education, offices, wealth, and manners. These aristocrats tended to be oblivious to those who had not been enlightened or blessed with power and prestige: women, slaves, even lower-class citizens. The politicized and intellectualized flavor of classical civilization bred in the elitists who wielded power and participated in the mainstream of cultural life a disdain for other kinds of activity and feelings. The rationalizing of human conduct and nature bred an intellectual posture that saw things in terms of absolute, fixed forms and found it difficult to accept or to initiate change.

This darker side of Greco-Roman civilization became more prominent from the third century A.D. onward. In an effort to control the forces threatening to destroy the traditional order, the Roman world was turned into a prison for the human spirit marked by autocratic government, regimented economic life, militarized society, and callous social elitism. Traditional Greco-Roman institutions and values increasingly became empty forms from which flowed no inspiration capable of mitigating what had become the burden of civilization. Into this troubled setting came the first of many "new" peoples—the Germans—who would intrude into the Mediterranean world to become doers, learners, and experimenters and a powerful religious movement—Christianity—that proclaimed a new vision of humanity which provided a new sense of direction. Working within the fabric of a declining civilization, these new forces began a transformation of Greco-Roman civilization that marked its "fall."

However, to speak of the fall of Greco-Roman civilization is to utter only a partial truth. That civilization left behind models of civilized existence that have served to shape human activity over a wide sweep of terrritory around the Mediterranean Sea since A.D. 500. Whatever its limitations, that civilization changed the course of history. Its legacy must occupy the attention of all who would understand the development of civilization during the next millennium and a half.

PART THREE

THE EARLY MIDDLE AGES, 500–1000: TOWARD A NEW ORDER

The dissolution of Greco-Roman civilization posed a challenge for the peoples living around the Mediterranean Sea: how to replace the old order with a new civilizational pattern. Despite false starts and confusion, they met the challenge with remarkable creativity. Between 500 and 1000, an era called the early Middle Ages by modern historians, three new cultural communities were defined, each based partly on old Roman soil but each extending into "new" territory. One was the Byzantine cultural world with its center in Constantinople, its heartland in Asia Minor and the Balkans south of the Danube, and its frontier in Slavic Europe. The second was the Islamic cultural world with its heartland in the ancient Fertile Crescent stretching from Mesopotamia to Egypt and its frontiers eastward to India and Central Asia, westward across North Africa to Spain, and southward toward sub-Saharan Africa. The third new civilization was created by the Germanic invaders of the western Roman Empire. Gaul and Italy formed its center; its frontiers included England, Germany, Scandinavia, Spain, and the western portions of the Slavic world in central Europe.

In each of these societies there were seminal forces at work generating new institutions and new ideas. In all three societies powerful vestiges of Greco-Roman civilization persisted to shape the essential features of each new civilization. In two of them—the Moslem and western European worlds—new peoples, Arabs and Germans, supplied a leavening agent. But perhaps it was religion that furnished the major animating force in this period. Two universal religions dominated the history of the period. Christianity, finally achieving its full power in the fifth century, provided that force in the Byzantine and western European cultural worlds. Islam, a new religion, asserted a powerful formative force over its Arab followers, called Moslems, as they established the foundations of Islamic civilization.

Modern historians have often dismissed this age as a "dark age." Before accepting that characterization, we must try to assess the creative aspects of the period.

CHAPTER 14

Heirs to the Roman Empire: The Byzantine and Moslem Empires

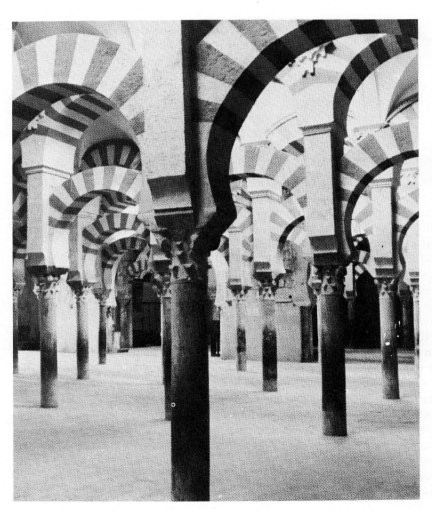

FIGURE 14.1 Moslem Mosque This view of the interior of the magnificent mosque built at Cordoba, Spain, in the eighth century illustrates key features of Moslem architecture, especially the skillful use of arches and pillars to create spaces for private worship and the employment of geometric decorative designs. Many features of Moslem art represent a creative synthesis of artistic traditions borrowed from earlier cultures embraced in the Moslem world. A comparison of this mosque with a typical Christian basilica (see Figure 13.2) will suggest differences between Moslem and Christian religious practices. (Georg Gerster/Comstock)

Two of the new civilizations emerging from the Greco-Roman world—Byzantine and Islamic—had their centers in the eastern territories of the old Roman Empire. These areas, comprising the most affluent and culturally sophisticated part of the Roman Empire, provided a richer seedbed for development than existed in the west. As a consequence, during the early Middle Ages the Byzantine and Islamic cultures were more precocious and vigorous than that of western Europe. Their very success in the early Middle Ages established their own special place in history, separate from the development of western European civilization. Given our focus on the western world, we can give them only limited attention—far less than their accomplishments deserve.

1. BYZANTINE CIVILIZATION: ORIGINS AND HISTORY, 395–1100

Byzantine civilization, so named by modern historians after the ancient Greek city-state of Byzantium where Constantine built his capital, began as a direct continuation of the old Roman Empire. After the division of the empire following the death of Theodosius in 395, a succession of rulers in Constantinople successfully resisted Germanic attacks and maintained the basic features of late imperial society. Their claim to be the heirs to old Rome was validated in 476, when the imperial title in the west was transferred to Constantinople and the eastern emperors assumed themselves to be legitimate rulers over the entire Roman world, including those parts seized by Germans. But that sequence of events aimed at maintaining the fiction of Rome's survival was marked by developments in the east that by the sixth century pointed toward the shaping of a new society.

The watershed between the old and new Rome can perhaps be placed in the reign of Justinian (527–565), often called the last Roman and the first Byzantine emperor. Justinian's talents and accomplishments have been variously judged across the ages, but few would dispute the fact that he made decisions of immense importance in redirecting the course of history. He was given invaluable assistance by Empress Theodora, one of the most gifted women in history (see Figure 14.2). The daughter of a circus bear trainer, she was an actress and courtesan before Justinian took her as his wife. Intelligent, beautiful, and courageous, she was instrumental in helping her often-indecisive husband make critical decisions. She was especially astute in reading the temper of the complex imperial court circle and the factious populace of Constantinople.

Justinian's claim to be called the last Roman stems from the central focus of his policy: a major effort to restore the unity of the old empire. To this end, he set out to reestablish imperial authority over the western provinces held by Germanic rulers. Although his effort was brilliant, his success was partial. The best his armies could do was to recapture North Africa from the Vandals, Italy from the Ostrogoths, and a small strip of southeastern Spain from the Visigoths. Gaul, most of Spain, England, and the upper Danube provinces remained in German hands. More significantly, the price for these limited conquests was great, for Justinian's western policy left the eastern frontiers exposed to the Sassanian Persians, who continued their efforts to recapture the territory held by the ancient Persians. By the end of his reign, it was clear that imperial resources must be concentrated in the east if areas crucial to the survival of the empire were to be held. The western part of the old Roman Empire would have to be abandoned to its German masters.

Justinian's reign was also significant in shaping a unique governmental system. He saw himself as the direct descendant of the Roman emperors, and he worked actively to perfect the system of absolute, sacred monarchy originated by Diocletian and Constantine. An important part of this effort led him to commission a corps of legal experts to organize into a single, consistent code the complex tradition of Roman law, which dated back at least a thousand years. That commission produced the *Corpus juris civilis*, which not only summarized the substance of Roman law as it had been defined in a long series of legislative acts and imperial edicts but also collected legal opinions that defined the principles on which the law rested. While the Code of Justinian was destined to influence the develop-

FIGURE 14.2 Justinian and Theodora These mosaic representations of Emperor Justinian and Empress Theodora were created as part of the decoration of the church of San Vitale in Ravenna (built about 574). They reflect the sense of sacred and solemn majesty that increasingly surrounded the Byzantine imperial office. Byzantine artists were highly skilled in creating mosaics to convey a message while adding color to interior spaces. (Justinian, The Granger Collection; Theodora, Scala/Art Resource)

ment of law considerably in the future, it served Justinian's age to legitimatize a highly centralized, absolutist government that became a distinctive feature of Byzantine civilization.

Justinian's reign was also marked by important religious developments. Following the pattern already established by Constantine and his successors, Justinian claimed as part of his imperial authority the right to play a major role as leader of the Christian religious establishment in his empire. Particularly troublesome in his time were several violent disputes over dogmatic issues concerning the relationship between Christ's human and divine nature. The emperor sought repeatedly to settle these quarrels by imperial edicts, often worked out after extensive discussions with prelates and theologians, which he hoped would curb the violence generated by religious passion and restore religious unity. His involvement did implant the idea of a Byzantine church whose organization and doctrines were dependent on the authority of the autocratic, semisacred emperor. But his actions also alienated large numbers of his subjects.

Justinian's reign witnessed the birth of a distinctive Byzantine culture. That culture assimilated the ancient Hellenic component of classical culture with Christian ideology. Into that basic mix were incorporated cultural influences from the Near East, especially from Persia. The symbol of this new culture was the church of Santa Sophia built by Justinian, a visible tribute to an earthly empire favored by God and to its exalted ruler.

Byzantine political history from the reign of Justinian until the First Crusade (1095) was dominated by one theme: the constant struggle to fend off attacks from aggressive outsiders, pressing in especially from the east and north. In a sense, the movement of peoples toward the Mediterranean basin left new Rome facing the same type of challenge that had been fatal to old Rome. These assaults reduced the Byzantine state in size, changed its ethnic composition, and caused modifications in its internal structure that accentuated its uniquenesss (see Map 14.1, p. 192).

Hardly was Justinian dead when the first blow was struck. In 568 the Lombards, a Germanic nation, invaded Italy and seized a considerable portion of the peninsula, leaving only Venice, a corridor of land from Rome to Ravenna, and southern Italy under Byzantine control. The partition of Italy was significant for two reasons: It left Rome, the seat of the papacy, in Byzantine hands, and it provided a setting in which the Byzantine and western European worlds would interact. Little could be done to stop the Lombard assault because the Byzantine Empire was facing a greater menace elsewhere. Late in the sixth century the Sassanid rulers of Persia mounted their greatest offensive on the Byzantine eastern frontier, seizing Syria, Palestine, and Egypt and advancing through Asia Minor to Constantinople. At the same time the Avars, an Asiatic nomadic people who established a state composed largely of Slavs north of the Danube, moved into the Balkans and toward Constantinople. In the first decades of the seventh century it appeared that the empire would perish in the Persian-Avar pincer. But a savior appeared in the person of Emperor Heraclius (610–641), who regrouped Byzantine resources and flung back the enemies in a war of liberation that permanently weakened both Persians and Avars.

The dynasty of Heraclius soon had to face an even greater challenge from another "new" people, the Arabs, who suddenly burst out of their homeland in the Arabian peninsula to become a major power in the Mediterranean world, as we shall see later. Within little more than a half century in the middle of the seventh century, Arab armies wrested Syria, Palestine, Egypt, and North Africa from Byzantine control. By the early 700s they occupied most of Asia Minor and in 717 placed Constantinople under siege. Again a savior appeared: Emperor Leo III, the Isaurian (717–741), who rescued the capital and eventually reclaimed Asia Minor. However, the eastern provinces were permanently lost, and the Byzantine Empire was reduced to a state comprising Asia Minor and the Balkan peninsula. This was a far cry from the Mediterranean-wide realm that Justinian claimed or even the eastern Roman Empire that he actually controlled. But it was defensible as a territorial state and would survive nearly intact until the middle of the fifteenth century.

Despite Leo III's remarkable success in rescuing the Byzantine Empire from what seemed certain destruction, his successors suffered renewed trials that plagued the empire for a century after his death. In part their difficulties stemmed from the internal strife brought on by their religious policy (see the next section). But outsiders again contributed to their problems. The Franks seriously undermined the Byzantine position in Italy (see Chapter 16). Even more dangerous was the emergence of a powerful state in the Balkans shaped by the Bulgars, another Asiatic migrant people who established dominance over Slavic peoples north of the Danube. The Bulgar threat eventually produced another series of strong rulers, the Macedonian dynasty (867–1057), under whose rule Byzantine society reached its high point. The greatest Macedonian emperor, Basil II, the Bulgar Slayer (976–1025), finally destroyed the Bulgar state and extended Byzantine influence deep into the Slavic world of central Europe and Russia. Byzantine power was also expanded in the east at the expense of the Moslem world, laying the groundwork for a Christian counterattack against Islam.

By the late eleventh century the Byzantine state began to decline, due in part to internal problems and in part to new assaults from the east by the Seljuk Turks and from the west by Italian cities seeking commercial advantages and Norman princes seeking territorial expansion (see Chapter 20). To save the empire from these threats, the emperors appealed to the West for help, an act that was instrumental in launching the crusading movement. But this policy also meant that the fate of the long self-reliant Byzantine Empire was increasingly dependent on outsiders.

2. BYZANTINE CIVILIZATION: INSTITUTIONAL AND CULTURAL PATTERNS

In response to the pressures caused by incessant attacks, the Byzantine world slowly evolved institutional and cultural patterns that not only permitted its survival but also made its civilization unique and distinctive.

A major source of Byzantine strength was its government, based on the absolute authority of the emperor. That authority was defined in terms that combined traditions drawn from the Roman imperial system and from Christian concepts of governance; Constantine served as the model. To the Byzantine populace the emperor was an agent ordained by God to ensure the material and spiritual well-being of God's people—the ''Romans,'' as the Byzantines called themselves. As an intermediary between God and his holy people, the emperor must be obeyed and served loyally. Without the imperial presence at the center of Byzantine life, God's favors would not be forthcoming and chaos would ensue. Although Byzantine court life was often filled with intrigues and violence and conspiracies and revolts deprived many emperors of their diadems and their lives, still the divinely sanctioned imperial office provided the prime directive force in Byzantine society.

The Byzantine emperors were served by a large, carefully structured bureaucracy. Each civil servant was assigned a specialized function, a rank, and a salary. Well educated and loyal, these bureaucrats efficiently kept the fundamental activities of the state in operation. The empire was divided into districts, called *themes,* where officials representing the emperor recruited troops, collected taxes, maintained order, judged cases, and enforced the emperor's edicts. The emperor's power was buttressed by a well-organized army and navy and an efficient system of taxation. Of crucial importance was the army.

During the crises brought on by Persian and then Arab attacks during the seventh and eighth centuries, the government developed an army recruited from the free small farmers of Asia Minor and Thrace, who were granted plots of land in return for their military service. The peasant contingents were organized by *themes,* each under the command of a local military governor. For centuries these loyal soldiers, their freedom and land carefully protected by the imperial government, provided the key to Byzantium's survival in the face of incessant attacks.

Byzantine society rested on a diversified economic system that produced a high level of prosperity. Agriculture formed the backbone of the Byzantine economy. Large estates, farmed by tenants, existed, but the key component of the agricultural system was the small farm operated by free landowners. The state took a vital interest in keeping agricultural production high so that taxes could be collected from the farmers, whether large or small. The empire also enjoyed tremendous commercial activity; for many centuries Constantinople was the world's chief trading and industrial center. Byzantium's resourceful traders were supplied with many valuable products by the numerous skilled artisans who practiced their crafts in Constantinople and other imperial cities. The imperial government exercised a powerful influence over economic activity through wage and price controls, supervision of the guilds into which merchants and artisans were organized, and a stable money system.

Christianity provided another fundamental force in shaping every aspect of Byzantine society. In terms of beliefs and practices the Christians of the Byzantine Empire were like Christians everywhere. However, with the passage of time Byzantine Christianity underwent changes that gave rise to a separate religious establishment, later called the Greek Orthodox church.

One area of distinctiveness in Byzantine religious life was the close alliance between the state and the religious establishment shaped along lines defined in the fourth-century Roman Empire. In contrast with the situation in the west, where the collapse of the Roman political order forced religious leaders to act independently, the Byzantine emperor claimed to be and was accepted as the divinely ordained director of both spiritual and secular life; in fact, any distinction between those two realms had little meaning in Byzantine society. This system, called *caesaropapism* by modern historians, allowed the emperor to play a decisive role in appointing church officials, defining dogma, settling theological disputes, imposing discipline on both clergy and laity, and using the wealth and the persuasive authority of the religious establishment to serve the state. In its pastoral role the episcopal establishment in Byzantium, headed by the patriarch of Constantinople, served as a crucial force in carrying out imperial policy and in shaping a powerful bond linking the populace to the imperial regime that created a strong and lasting loyalty among imperial subjects.

Byzantine religious life was given a distinctive quality by a widespread, intense interest in questions of dogma. Diverse opinions on such matters as the Trinity and the relationship between Christ's divine and human nature aroused strong feelings and fierce partisanship that produced serious political crises on many occasions, especially when the emperors tried to resolve such quarrels in the interests of unity. Greek Orthodoxy placed a strong emphasis on ritual practice as a key element of religious life, and over the centuries a rich liturgy featuring elaborate symbolism and unique musical forms evolved as a distinctive feature of piety. On occasion both emperors and religious leaders thought this emphasis on ritual life needed to be curbed. The chief such effort led to the bitter iconoclastic struggle that raged from 725 to 843. This quarrel began when Emperor Leo III, backed by part of the clergy, attempted to remove all visual representations of the deity (called icons) from churches and rites, insisting that Christians were worshiping the statues instead of God and thus were guilty of idolatry. But these iconoclasts (icon smashers) ultimately failed, and in 843 the use of icons was restored to ritual practices. Byzantine religious life gave a prominent place to mysticism—religious practices by which believers sought direct communion with God through prayer and contemplation. A powerful, resourceful monastic establishment played an important role in encouraging and shaping a popular spirituality based on ritual and mysticism.

These unique characteristics of the Byzantine religious establishment, coupled with equally unique developments shaping Christian life elsewhere, led to a separation of the Byzantine Christian community from the rest of Christendom. During the fifth and sixth centuries quarrels over dogma and the claims of the patriarch of Constantinople to precedence over the ancient patriarchs of Alexandria, Jerusalem, and Antioch encouraged the Christians of Egypt, Palestine, and Syria to separate themselves from the imperial religious establishment. The Moslem conquest of these areas severed religious contacts with Christians in the Byzantine Empire and the west. The result was the emergence of separate eastern churches, such as the Coptic church in Egypt and the Jacobite church in Syria. Differences also began to separate the Byzantine church from Christians in the west. Dogmatic disagreements (particularly iconoclasm), different ritual practices, and divergent disciplinary usages played a role in creating the rift. Especially divisive was the ever-deepening quarrel over whether the pope in Rome was superior to or coequal with the patriarch of Constantinople in defining dogma and exercising disciplinary jurisdiction over the entire Christian community. Although the Byzantine emperors often turned to the bishops of Rome to seek sanction for their religious policies, they more often supported the claims of their patriarch to authority equal to that of Rome. The slow drift toward separation between Rome and Constantinople finally culminated in 1054, when pope and patriarch excommunicated each other, creating a schism that to the present has proved irreparable.

The separation between Rome and Constantinople was promoted by rivalry in the missionary field. Early in Byzantine history, Greek missionaries began to penetrate the Slavic world of central and eastern Europe, where missionaries from the west were also active. Supported by the diplomatic, military, and material resources of the imperial government and willing to make concessions to local cultures, such as allowing rituals to be performed in native languages, Byzantine missionaries eventually converted most of the Slavs in the Balkan peninsula and Russia and attached them to the Greek Orthodox church. Not only did they give their converts a new religion, they also spread significant aspects of Byzantine political, economic, literary, and artistic life. As a consequence, at a crucial point in the development of Slavic institutions and culture, a large part of the Slavic world was permanently oriented toward Byzantium and set apart from western Europe.

The Byzantine world gradually developed its own cultural life, maintaining in its essence the thrust established in late antiquity toward turning classical thought and expression to the service of the Christian worldview. Within a short time after Justinian's death the use of Latin virtually ceased in the Byzantine world; as a consequence, Byzantine culture centered on the Greek tradition. A vigorous educational system flourished in the Byzantine world, especially in Constantinople, where imperial, episcopal, and monastic schools offered a curriculum based on the study of classical Greek literature and philosophy. In at least some aristocratic circles, women were often provided a literary education in their homes. The system produced not only a literate clergy but also an educated laity conversant with the literary, scientific, and philosophical masterpieces of ancient Greece and the Hellenistic world. This educated group, which was often associated with the imperial court, the prime patron of cultural life, also collected copies of the Greek classics, commented on them, and wrote in imitation of them. Their efforts ensured the survival of the Greek classics and their eventual dissemination to the Islamic and western European worlds to serve as the basis for cultural renaissances.

The all-pervasive influence of Greek models, however, tended to make Byzantine literature and thought imitative. Probably the most creative figures in Byzantine intellectual circles were the theologians, whose incessant quarrels over dogma produced a huge volume of writing in which philosophical concepts from the classical tradition were applied to Christian teachings. Byzantine historians, influenced by the models of Herodotus, Thucydides, and Polybius, also produced excellent works: Procopius (sixth century) described Justinian's wars and wrote a spicy *Secret History* describing court life; Michael Psellus (1018–1079), a high official in the imperial regime, chronicled the exploits of the Macedonian emperors; and Anna Comnenus (1083-1148), the daughter of Emperor Alexius I, celebrated the career of her father in *Alexiad*. Byzantine poets expressed themselves most originally in hymns, some of which can still be heard in the Greek Orthodox liturgy.

Byzantine art is perhaps the best mirror of the spirit of the culture. Architecture was the preeminent art. It represents a skillful fusion of classical Greek and Near Eastern traditions. The style was formed during the fourth and fifth centuries in Egypt, Syria, and Asia Minor. It was elevated to official status by Justinian's building program in sixth-century Constantinople. The great church of Santa Sophia was based on a floor plan derived from the Greco-Roman rectangular basilica upon which was imposed a great central dome after the Persian manner. The glory of this combination lies in the internal spaciousness it permits. The dome of Santa Sophia is more than one hundred feet across and rises about one hundred eighty feet above the floor of the church. Although it rests on four great arches springing from four massive pillars that form the central square of the nave, the dome indeed seems "to hang by a golden chain from heaven," as a contemporary put it. Justinian, upon viewing the completed church, exclaimed: "I have outdone you, O Solomon!"

The architectural style represented by Santa Sophia was widely imitated, and in the course of time a variation gained considerable popularity: A ground plan was based on the Greek cross with its four equal arms; each arm was crowned by a dome, as was the space where the arms cross. The famous church of St. Mark in Venice is an example of this five-domed structure. Byzantine architects also built huge and splendid palaces, most of which have unfortunately disappeared.

Byzantine architecture, for all its technical ingenuity, is incomplete without its decor. The churches and palaces were immense frames for sumptuous decoration. Santa Sophia's interior, for instance, blazed with precious metals, mosaics, paintings, jewels, and fine stone. Byzantine mosaics and frescoes centered primarily on portraying the great episodes of the Christian epic; the best surviving examples are seen in the churches built in Ravenna during the sixth century (see Figures 13.2 and 14.2). Byzantine artists made an immense contribution to the development and enrichment of Christian iconography, that is, the visual symbols through which religious ideas and feelings are expressed. They were never basically concerned with portraying the world realistically; rather, they sought to use human, natural, and abstract forms to evoke spiritual understanding. Color, created by glowing combinations of stones, metals, jewels, and paints, played a crucial role in enhancing the impact of every artistic creation (see Color Plate 7). Byzantine artists were also noted as skillful jewelers, goldsmiths, silversmiths, and manuscript illuminators. In every medium the same features predominated—the fusion of Greco-Roman and oriental motifs and styles, the love of elaborate decoration and color, and the preoccupation with symbolism.

3. ISLAMIC CIVILIZATION: ORIGINS AND EARLY HISTORY

A second new civilization emerged in the eastern Mediterranean world during the early Middle Ages to rival Byzantium as an heir of the Greco-Roman world: Islamic civilization, which originated among the nomadic inhabitants of the Arabian Desert. Although peoples from that desolate area had powerfully influenced the course of history in the ancient past (for example, the Akkadians, the Assyrians, and the Hebrews), no one living about 600 would have guessed that the desert-dwelling Bedouins would soon have a major impact on the course of history. Although Arabia's inhabitants shared a sense of ethnic community rooted in a common language, Arabic, and common historical experiences, the Bedouins were badly divided into numerous competing tribes led by warrior chieftains, called *sheiks*. The desert dwellers lived a poverty-stricken life that depended chiefly on the pasturage of animals—particularly camels—around oases. Raids on other tribes were common, so that Bedouin life was dominated by a warrior ethos. Tribal life was bound by rigid customs that governed most social relationships. Especially powerful were kinship ties, which created fierce family loyalties and prompted violent family feuds. Bedouin life was deeply influenced by a polytheistic religious system based on the worship of deities representing the forces of nature.

For the most part the Bedouins had been little influenced by the advanced civilizations lying in a great arc around the northern end of the vast desert. However, they were not completely isolated, which was a significant factor in the changes that thrust the Arabs into a new historical role during the seventh century. In the long struggle between the Romans (and their Byzantine successors) and the Persians, both parties had tried to win allies among the Bedouin tribes of northern Arabia; as a result, Roman-Byzantine and Persian influences touched the lives of some Arabs in that area. Southern Arabia felt significant cultural influences from Ethiopia. The major religions of these civilizations—Christianity, Judaism, Zoroastrianism—had made modest inroads into the Arab world. Much more significant in bringing outside influences into the world of the Arabs were the caravan routes along the western side of Arabia that linked the cities of Egypt, Syria, and Asia Minor to the Indian Ocean and the Far East. During the sixth century these routes became much more important because Byzantine-Persian rivalry disrupted the trade routes running from the eastern Mediterranean area through Persia to the Far East. Increased trade stimulated the growth and expanded the wealth of the Arabian cities along the caravan routes. Mecca, in particular, became a flourishing cosmopolitan center. Merchants from many places mingled with an ever-growing Arab population attracted to Mecca from the desert by the growing economic opportunities created by trade. Many Bedouin tribes came annually to Mecca to worship at a temple called the *Kaaba*, which contained a black stone that was a cult object for most Arabs. The sharp contrast between the affluent, cosmopolitan life in Mecca and the impoverished, tradition-bound Bedouin desert life began to pose disturbing questions about traditional Arabic values and the potential dangers of new ways.

The forces of change were suddenly unleashed in the Arab world early in the seventh century. The catalyst was a religious prophet, Muhammad, who galvanized the Arab world into unity and jolted it out of its isolation. Muhammad was born in Mecca about 570. Orphaned in his youth, he was brought up by an uncle as a trader. Eventually he entered the service of a rich widow, whom he married, thus ensuring himself a respectable and leisured career. As a trader, Muhammad came into contact with foreign merchants passing through Mecca. But there is reason to suspect that the decisive aspects of his life were shaped less by these extraneous conditions than by his own introspective, brooding, ascetic spirit, which caused him to spend much of his time in prayer and meditation, often in the solitude of the desert. While the question of his own salvation may have been central to his spiritual searching, it is likely that he was also troubled about the breakdown of traditional communal values and the moral laxity evident in Mecca.

When Muhammad was about forty, he suddenly claimed that God—*Allah* in Arabic—had spoken directly to him and named him his prophet. Throughout the rest of his life these revelations continued, gradually providing the key elements for a new religion. And they gave Muhammad his mission: He dedicated himself to convincing others that Allah had revealed through his prophet the way to righteousness, truth, and salvation.

What did Allah reveal to his prophet? The answer is contained in the Koran (*Qur'an* in Arabic), the sacred book of Islam, which was compiled shortly after the Prophet's death by his associates as a record of Allah's message delivered through his prophet. The central tenet of Muhammed's teaching was a rigorous monotheism: there is but one god, Allah, whose power is infinite and whose wrath against those who worship other deities is terrible. Muhammad taught that Allah had revealed himself bit by bit down through the ages, the Jewish prophets and Jesus all being accepted as his messengers. However, Muhammad was the last and greatest prophet, superseding all others, and his revelation—Allah's final message—was destined to conquer the world. Muhammad insisted that almighty Allah requires complete submission to his will; the religion is thus called *Islam*, which means "submission to God." Every true adherent of Islam, called a *Moslem*, must regulate his or her life so as to abide completely by the will of Allah as revealed to the Prophet and set down in the Koran. Those who believe in Allah and submit to his law will gain a happy life after death in a sensuous heaven; nonbelievers and the disobedient will be damned to eternal suffering in hell.

It is obvious that many of these fundamental teachings were closely akin to beliefs long held by Jews, Christians, Zoroastrians, and pre-Moslem Arabs, a fact that has led some to the conclusion that Muhammad was little more than a borrower of the religious ideas of others. However true this claim may be, it neglects the essential fact: The Prophet brought to the Arab world in which he lived a religious vision that not only was new to the Arabs but also gave them a historic mission of spreading the true religion revealed in God's final revelation. To the Arab world this message was as radical as early Judaism and primitive Christianity were to their worlds.

To these simple articles of faith Muhammad added a list of duties required of all believers. All must proclaim daily their belief that there is but one God, Allah, pray five times daily while facing Mecca, give of their wealth to support the poor, fast during the holy month of Ramadan, and, if possible, make a pilgrimage to Mecca once in a lifetime. Muhammad also laid down the foundations of a law code regulating diet and marriage, prohibiting drinking and gambling, and demanding honesty, fair play, and respect for others. This code of conduct, strongly reminiscent of that defined in the Jewish Bible, injected a strong ethical vein into the new religion. Each individual was personally responsible to Allah; there were no churches, no clergy, no sacraments to assist in gaining Allah's favor.

For several years, Muhammad's preaching netted only a few converts in Mecca; in fact, Muhammad won many more enemies than followers. By 622 these foes forced him to flee to Yathrib (later renamed Medina, which means "city of the Prophet"), north of Mecca. This flight, called the *Hegira*, marked a turning point in the history of the new religion, which the Moslems recognized by making 622 the first year of their calendar. At Mecca Muhammad—always speaking as Allah's prophet—gave increasing attention to the shaping of a religious-political community, a "people of Allah" dedicated to the advance of Allah's cause by force of arms and to the enforcement of right living on the faithful. Into this community were drawn increasing numbers of Arab converts who subordinated their ancient tribal allegiances to a new, egalitarian companionship based on total submission to Allah and obedience to his prophet. The focus of the new community was the mosque, the meeting place where the faithful gathered as equals to affirm their faith in Allah, pray, and demonstrate their unity in serving his cause. Reflecting the warrior ethos of the Arabic world, this holy community felt justified in living off the booty its warriors seized from nonbelievers, including the considerable Jewish community at Medina and especially the caravans of the rich Meccans. By 630 Muhammad's following was strong enough to recapture Mecca, a feat that persuaded many Arabs of the validity of his message and led them to join his community. During his last years the Prophet used his forces to compel other Arab tribes to accept his leadership, so that when he died in 632 he was the leader of a large and dedicated religious following.

Muhammad's success in uniting the Arab world was impressive enough, but even more astonishing developments were to come. Almost immediately the newly formed "people of Allah" burst out of Arabia and began a series of military conquests that affected most of the civilized world (see Map 14.1). Between 632 and 656, the Arabs destroyed the Persian Empire; wrested the prize provinces of Syria, Palestine, and Egypt from the Byzantine Empire; were probing toward India; and were challenging Byzantine sea power for control of the Mediterranean. After a brief interlude to settle internal problems over Moslem leadership, the advance resumed in the late seventh century. All of North Africa was conquered, and Arab forces pushed into the Indus Valley and the outer reaches of China. An offensive was mounted in Asia Minor that moved closer and closer to Constantinople. Before 700 Moslem naval forces were in virtual control of the Mediterranean. In 711 a Moslem army crossed from Africa into Europe and quickly overran the Visigothic kingdom in Spain. From there the Moslems began to raid Gaul to threaten the Frankish kingdom. But Arab expansion was weakening: In 718 Arab forces besieging Constantinople were defeated by Leo III and soon after were driven out of Asia Minor. The Byzantine victory, which was decisive in checking the Moslem advance into Europe, was complemented in 732 when the Frankish leader Charles Martel defeated a Moslem force at the battle of Tours in Gaul.

The conquest of this vast empire within a century after the Prophet's death represents one of the great military feats in all history. Several factors played a part in Arab expansion. The Arabs' opponents were weak. Both the Sassanid and the Byzantine empires were exhausted from their long struggle. Religious disaffection among the Christians in the eastern Byzantine provinces caused the residents to welcome the Arabs as liberators from religious tyranny and burdensome fiscal exactions. The conquerors interfered little with local affairs, making their overlordship easy to accept. They demonstrated great military prowess, especially in desert warfare, in siege tactics, and in adapting to naval warfare. Their enthusiasm for their cause was also a factor. Muhammad had said, "Fight and fear not; the gates of Paradise are under the shade of the swords." Their wars were thus holy wars (*jihad* in Arabic).

4. ISLAMIC CIVILIZATION: INSTITUTIONAL AND CULTURAL PATTERNS

The amazing victories of the Arabs presented the conquerors with a wide range of challenges: how to rule a huge empire inhabited by diverse peoples; how to support themselves in a strange environment; how to sustain their faith in a world where other religions dominated; how to interact with different cultures. Their responses and the reactions of their subjects to their dominance produced a new, uniquely Islamic pattern of civilization that would be of immense importance to the future of a large part of the world.

A major problem facing the victorious Arabs was establishing a political system that would permit them to control their numerous and diverse subjects. While Muhammad had established the basis for a primitive Islamic state, no one could succeed to his special place as Prophet. From his death in 632 down to 661, his close associates picked one from among themselves to serve as *caliph*—an Arabic term meaning "deputy"—to interpret and apply the law as revealed in the Koran. This office, bestowing on its holder a vast range of powers sanctioned by religion, became the key element in the Moslem political system. Whoever controlled it and used the authority surrounding it effectively could claim ab-

Map 14.1 **THE EXPANSION OF ISLAM TO 750** This map shows the amazing success of the Arabs as conquerors during the first century after Muhammad's death in 632; the dates indicate when each major conquest was completed. It indicates clearly that the Persian Sassanian Empire and the Byzantine Empire were the major victims of Arab expansionism. By 750 large numbers of peoples in the lands conquered by the Arabs had accepted Islam as their religion.

solute lordship over all Moslems and all who were their subjects. But a major problem of Moslem political life centered on deciding who had a legitimate claim to the caliphate.

As long as Muhammad's personal associates were available, they could legitimately claim the office. But with their passing, a struggle developed for succession. Finally, in 661, a military leader seized control and made the office of caliph hereditary. The dynasty he founded, known as the Omayyads, held power until 750. Its legitimacy was challenged from the beginning by Muhammad's nephew and son-in-law, Ali, and Ali's son Hussein, who claimed authority to in-

terpret the Prophet's word on the basis of their kinship with him. Their claims resulted in their assassinations, but their followers formed a powerful and dedicated religious-political faction called the Shiites, which for centuries challenged the authority of successive caliphs.

The Omayyads established their center of power at Damascus. Although totally committed to Arab supremacy in the expanding empire, they realized that ruling the lands and peoples conquered by the Arab armies of Allah demanded more complex political institutions than those that had characterized Muhammad's first Moslem community. Strongly influenced by Byzantine models, the Omayyads created a central-ized court, a bureaucracy, and an efficient tax system. The authority of the Omayyad caliphs was exercised primarily through garrisons of Arab troops established at strategic spots across the vast empire. Bound to the caliph by ethnic and religious ties, the commanders of these garrisons controlled local affairs; often they did so by utilizing already established native political structures. These garrisons were supported by allocations from the caliph's treasury, which was supplied by booty and by taxes paid by the conquered non-Moslem population. This system meant that the Moslem world was dominated by an Arab elite whose religious convictions legitimatized for its members their right to possess and exploit what they had won by the sword. For almost a century, this system worked. Arab military supremacy gave conquered subjects little choice. Generally, the isolated, exclusivist Arab garrisons interfered little in local affairs except to enforce peace and to collect the tribute that supported them.

But eventually the Omayyad regime faltered. The strength of the Arab elite was diluted by its dispersion over the huge empire. More important, as the number of non-Arab converts to Islam increased, resentment against Arab domination grew. Non-Arab Moslems could see no reason why their faith should not make them equal to Arab Moslems in the sight of Allah. That sentiment led to the overthrow of the Omayyads in 750—except in Spain—and the seizure of the caliphate by the Abbasid dynasty, a family of Persian origin claiming distant kinship with Muhammad. Abbasid rule meant the end of Arab domination. The capital was shifted from Damascus to Baghdad, and the political system was reshaped on the model of ancient Persia. The Abbasid caliphs reclaimed the absolute authority to interpret Allah's word for all the faithful, whatever their ethnic origin. Around their court there developed a professional bureaucracy made up of educated Moslems representing many ethnic groups. The caliph's authority was extended across the empire through an elaborate system of governorships over which officials representing the caliph administered justice and collected taxes. In this new political environment Arab militancy was greatly diminished and expansionism by force came to an end.

During the eighth and ninth centuries the Abbasid caliphs enjoyed immense power, exemplified by rulers like Harun al-Rashid (786–809), immortalized in the *Arabian Nights*. But by the end of the ninth century Abbasid power began to decline. Rival caliphs, challenging the legitimacy of the Abbasids to interpret Allah's will, were established in Spain, North Africa, Egypt, Syria, and India and began to compete with one another for dominance in the Moslem world. Seeking to protect themselves against these rivals, the Abbasids increasingly placed their trust in Seljuk Turkish mercenaries, nomads from Central Asia who by 1055 made the Abbasids their puppets. By that time, Moslem political unity had vanished forever. Disunity invited attacks from outsiders, especially Byzantine and western European Christians, whose memory of Arabic militarism and hostility toward the Islamic religion generated a crusading mentality against the Moslems.

More enduring than the unified Moslem political empire were the economic benefits that flowed from the Arabic conquests. Agriculture remained the basic element of economic life across the Moslem world. The early Arab conquerors were little interested in farming except as a source of tribute to support the military elite. As a consequence, the traditional village-farming structure of the Roman-Byzantine and Persian worlds persisted. Later, under Abbasid rule, fiscal policies were introduced that stimulated land clearance, production for urban markets, and the introduction of new crops and farming techniques, all of which combined to increase agricultural production. Economic growth was most marked in commerce and manufacturing. The emergence of Moslem civilization gave new impetus to urban life. Cities—new and old, large and small—became centers of life for the ruling elite and their dependents. Their needs, ranging from food to luxury items, stimulated trade and industry, which in turn filled cities with merchants and artisans. While much commerce and manufacturing filled local needs, long-distance trade routes stretching from Spain to India and from central Asia to sub-Saharan Africa developed, promoted by the removal of artificial trade barriers, a sound money system, and specialized manufacturing developing in many cities (for example, the steel weapons and textiles of Damascus and the leather goods of Córdoba in Spain). The Moslem political regime allowed merchants and artisans much greater freedom than had been the case in the Byzantine and Persian empires; as a consequence, these groups exercised their entrepreneurial talents to increase their wealth. On the whole, during the early Middle Ages, the Moslem economy was the most advanced and resourceful in the world.

The social structure of the Moslem world was immensely complex. Arab tradition and the teaching of the Koran emphasized the equality of all male Moslems. In fact, important social distinctions existed, initially between Arabs and non-Arabs and then between Moslems and non-Moslems. As time passed, a social elite emerged that was defined by officeholding, wealth, education, and lifestyle. This elite congregated in urban centers, where its ranks were constantly replenished by those whose talents as administrators, merchants, artisans, and scholars permitted them to accumulate the wealth and acquire the social graces required for elite status. The bulk of the agricultural population and urban laborers remained outside this elite circle and were considered to be inferior. Non-Moslems, although tolerated, were also treated as inferiors, subjected to special taxes and excluded from public life. The stratification of Moslem society was countered to some extent by the force of Moslem law, which considered all of Allah's followers to be equal and which sought to define a common standard of conduct binding on all Moslems.

The family was a basic institution in the regulation of social life. But it was an institution dominated by males. Severe restrictions were placed on women, forcing them into a secluded existence and isolating them from many aspects of social and economic life. Polygamy was legally recognized and widely practiced among the affluent, putting women in a position of competing with one another for a place in the family structure and control over children. Husbands were able to divorce their wives easily and exercised considerable control over the destinies of their children. However, Moslem law did permit women to share in inheritances and sought to protect their interests in their possessions.

The most important forces giving Moslem civilization cohesion and unity were religion and culture. The Islamic religion demonstrated an amazing power to win converts. Although there was forced conversion and although many accepted the faith to escape the special taxes imposed on non-Moslems and to gain access to the mainstream of Moslem political and social life, still Islam appealed to many. Christians and Jews were extended special privileges because they were, as Moslems put it, "people of the Book" who had received at least a portion of God's revelation. As the years passed, however, devotees of many religions—Christians, Jews, Zoroastrians, and Hindus—were converted in massive numbers, and the vast Moslem Empire became predominantly Islamic. Islam also expanded beyond the boundaries of the empire to win converts in southern Asia and sub-Saharan Africa. Important non-Moslem communities always remained in the empire, including Christian churches in Egypt, Syria, and Armenia and significant Jewish communities, especially in Spain.

Islam tended to grow more complex as the centuries passed. This enrichment resulted chiefly from the efforts of a long succession of theologians, philosophers, and lawyers, all of whom reflected on the nature of their religion and reinterpreted its meaning from different perspectives. The theologians developed a rich body of literature in the form of commentaries (called *sunnas*) on the Koran and on pronouncements attributed to Muhammad but not recorded in the Koran (called *hadiths*). The philosophers incorporated concepts derived from Greek thought into Islam in an effort to illuminate the meaning of the Koran. The lawyers constantly elaborated the body of law that governed Moslem life, seeking to make it consistent, complete, and relevant to the varied conditions of life among the faithful. The collective efforts of theologians, philosophers, and lawyers resulted in an orthodox faith that was much more complex than the message first proclaimed by the Prophet; yet Islam always remained firmly rooted in the basic doctrines set forth in the Koran. The adherents of this orthodox religion, called Sunnite Moslems, constituted the vast majority in the Islamic world. But there were dissenters, the chief of which were the Shiite Moslems, who insisted that the true faith was preserved by Muhammad's blood descendants. They rejected many of the ideas about Islam proclaimed by the Sunnites and often did battle with Sunnites on many issues—a conflict that still divides the Moslem world.

The Islamic world also sustained a long tradition of seeking to deepen spirituality. The quest was carried on primarily by *sufis*, religious mystics who, through contemplation and ascetic practices, sought to establish a direct communion with the Divine that would deepen their spiritual life as well as that of their followers. Despite these diverse movements, Islam as a common faith provided the prime basis of unity in the Moslem world.

The advent and expansion of Islam generated a tremendous cultural revival that brought together into a rich synthesis nearly all the world's great cultural traditions: Greco-Roman, Persian, Mesopotamian, Egyptian, Germanic, Jewish, Indian, and Arabic. Synthesis remained a central feature of Moslem culture throughout the Middle Ages. Religion provided the matrix and the inspiration for synthesis. Since Muhammad had forbidden the translation of the Koran into any other language, all Moslems had to learn Arabic and all foreign literature had to be translated into Arabic; and since the Koran contained the final truth, all facets of other cultures had to be reconciled with Islamic teachings. The response to these challenges was a brilliant outburst of scholarship that allowed the Moslems to claim with some justification to be the cultural heirs of the ages.

Many historians would agree that the greatest Moslem achievements were in philosophy and science. Moslem philosophers devoted their efforts chiefly to absorbing Greek philosophy and reconciling it with the teachings of the Koran. At the same time, they wrestled with the contradictions inherent in the Greek tradition, especially those separating Platonic and Aristotelian thought. The result was a huge body of philosophical literature that played an important role in sustaining Islam and in giving Moslem intellectual life a high level of sophistication. The efforts of Moslem philosophers are closely akin to those of the scholastic philosophers of medieval western Europe (see Chapter 22). In fact, the speculations of the greatest Moslem thinkers, Ibn Sina (980–1037) and the Spanish Ibn Rushd (1126–1198), known in the West as Avicenna and Averroës, exercised a direct influence on Western scholasticism.

In science the Moslem achievements were spectacular. The efforts of Moslem scholars as collectors resulted in a huge body of scientific information from Greek, Indian, Persian, Mesopotamian, and Egyptian sources—more than scientists anywhere in the world would possess until modern times. To this they added knowledge derived from their own investigations of the natural world, all of which became available to a large circle of people because it was recorded in a common language, Arabic. In mathematics, Moslems adopted the Indian numerical system, to which they added the use of the zero to create the Arabic system of numbers used almost universally today. A Moslem, al-Khwarizmi (ca. 780–850), combined Greek and Indian concepts to create algebra. By combining Greek, Persian, and Mesopotamian data on the movements of heavenly bodies, Moslem scientists made notable advances in astronomy. The works of medical writers such as al-Razi (865–925) and Avicenna represent compilations from numerous sources. Moslem doctors studied diseases, dissected bodies, and experimented with drugs, adding significantly to the existing body of medical knowledge. Geographers and physicists also made significant advances.

Moslem literature demonstrated great vigor and variety. Its poetry, familiar to Western readers chiefly through the works of Omar Khayyám, is marked by brilliant imagery and highly complex verse forms. Perhaps the most characteristic feature of Moslem literature was the ability of writers to recast subject matter borrowed from various non-Arabic sources into masterpieces attuned to the spirit of Moslem religion and the values of Moslem society. Nothing illustrates this feature better than the *Arabian Nights;* the adventures of Sinbad the Sailor and the feats of Aladdin are stories gleaned from the literary traditions of many non-Moslem peoples, but they are given a unique coloration by the genius of Arabic authors, who retell them in a mode reflecting the spirit and tastes of their own culture.

Like most of Moslem culture, Moslem art reflects a creative synthesis of many traditions. Architectural talents were devoted chiefly to building mosques and palaces. The mosques, primarily places for individual prayer rather than community worship, are simple structures whose inner space is often divided by rows of graceful columns creating aisles covered by arches. As a rule, the mosques are covered by domes similar to those of Byzantine churches; above them rise graceful towers (*minarets*) from which the call to prayer is issued. Before each mosque is an open court containing a purification fountain and surrounded by a covered passageway. The greatest mosques, such as those at Damascus and Córdoba, are beautiful structures marked by delicacy and grace (see Figure 14.1). Surviving palaces, such as the Alcazar at Seville and the Alhambra at Granada, reflect the same architectural style but are much more elaborate.

Most Moslem buildings are rather bare on the outside but brilliantly decorated inside, especially with paintings and mosaics in splendid colors. The representation of human and animal forms was discouraged lest the faithful be tempted to compromise their monotheism by worshiping graven images. Instead, the decorations accentuated floral designs and geometric patterns (*arabesques*). Exquisite artistry also manifested itself in the crafts; Moslem fabrics, tapestries, carpets, leatherwork, metalwork, weapons, and jewelry were the most prized articles in the medieval world.

The vitality and achievements of the early Byzantine and Islamic civilizations far excelled that emerging in western Europe, which lagged far behind them for centuries. As we shall see, during the medieval centuries no aspect of western European civilization escaped the subtle influences of the Byzantine and Moslem worlds. That immense debt was often forgotten in the West in later centuries—but not by the heirs of those who created the Byzantine and Islamic civilizations.

SUGGESTED READING

Overview of the Early Middle Ages

Robert Fossier et al., *The Cambridge History of the Middle Ages*, Vol. 1: *350–950*, trans. Janet Sondheimer (1989). Rich in insights, especially into social history.

Byzantine Civilization

Robert Browning, *The Byzantine Empire* (1980).
Cyril Mango, *Byzantium, the Empire of New Rome* (1980). Either of these works will provide a good general treatment of all aspects of Byzantine civilization.
J. J. Norwich, *Byzantium: The Early Centuries* (1989).
Warren Treadgold, *The Byzantine Renewal, 780–842* (1988).
Robert Browning, *Justinian and Theodora*, 2nd ed. (1987). These three works will provide fuller treatment of the period of Byzantine history covered in this chapter.
J. M. Hussey, *The Orthodox Church in the Byzantine Empire* (1986). An excellent treatment.
Jaroslav Pelikan, *The Christian Tradition: A History of the Development of Doctrine*, Vol. 2: *The Spirit of Eastern Christendom* (1974). A masterful but demanding treatment.
D. Talbot Rice, *Byzantine Art*, rev. ed. (1968). A brief treatment, effectively illustrated.
Tamara Talbot Rice, *Everyday Life in Byzantium* (1967). Provides a good feel for how people lived in the Byzantine world.

Moslem Civilization

M. A. Shaban, *Islamic History: A New Interpretation*, 2 vols. (1971–1976).

Hugh Kennedy, *The Prophet and the Age of the Caliphates: The Islamic Near East from the Sixth to the Eleventh Century* (1986).
Ira M. Lapidus, *A History of Islamic Societies* (1988). Any of these three works provides a challenging introduction to early Islamic history and civilization.
Patricia Crone and Martin Hinds, *God's Caliph: Religious Authority in the First Centuries of Islam* (1986). Good treatment of the way the caliphate worked.
Maurice Lombard, *The Golden Age of Islam*, trans. Joan Spencer (1975). Will help the reader to understand economic and social history.
Alfred Guillaume, *Islam*, 2nd rev. ed. (1956). A clear description of the major features of Islamic religion.
Dominique Sourdel, *Medieval Islam*, trans. J. Montgomery Watt (1983). Especially good on the role of religion in shaping Moslem society.
Martin Lings, *Muhammad: His Life Based on the Earliest Sources* (1983). A sound biography.
W. Montgomery Watt, *The Formative Period in Islamic Thought* (1973). A good introduction to early Moslem intellectual history.
C. A. Qadir, *Philosophy and Science in the Islamic World* (1988). An excellent assessment.
David T. Rice, *Islamic Art*, rev. ed. (1975). A well-illustrated treatment.

CHAPTER 15

Heirs to the Roman Empire: Latin Western Europe

FIGURE 15.1 Life in a Medieval Monastery This scene from an illuminated manuscript reflects the essential elements of the daily routine in a Benedictine monastery: the tolling of bells to summon the monks to worship services; studying and copying manuscripts; manual labor. The combination of these activities into a disciplined routine permitted monastic communities to make a major contribution to the shaping of all aspects of medieval civilization, despite the fact that monks sought to escape the world within the confines of their monasteries. (The Pierpont Morgan Library)

The third heir to the Roman Empire emerged in Latin western Europe. In contrast to developments in the Byzantine and Islamic worlds, western European civilization took shape amid the instability and disorder resulting from the collapse of the Roman political system in the West. Not until about 750 were the first dim outlines of a new order becoming evident in the form of new institutions and ideas destined to be crucial to the future of western Europe.

1. THE POLITICAL ORDER: GERMANIC KINGSHIP

A prime factor in the history of the Latin West between 500 and 750 was political instability stemming from two interrelated factors existing in 500. First, the boundaries of the various Germanic kingdoms established on Roman soil during the fifth century had not been fixed; as a result, there was fierce competition among these kingdoms—Visigothic, Vandal, Ostrogothic, Burgundian, Frankish, Anglo-Saxon—for territory. Second, all of these kingdoms lacked well-defined internal political structures capable of maintaining public order.

Between 500 and 750 there was considerable rearrangement of the fragile boundaries of the Germanic kingdoms (see Maps 13.1 and 14.1). Of prime importance was the emergence of the Franks as a major power. During the fifth century the Franks slowly penetrated northern Gaul but played only a minor role in partitioning the Roman Empire. Then suddenly, led by their first able king, Clovis (481–511), the Franks exploded into prominence. A ruthless warrior, Clovis unified the Franks and unleashed their military potential. He and his immediate successors wiped out the last remnants of Roman power in northern Gaul, absorbed the Burgundian kingdom, drove the Visigoths out of southern Gaul, and established dominance over Germanic peoples living immediately east of the Rhine in territories that had not been part of the Roman Empire. The Frankish cause was aided by the conversion of Clovis and his followers to Orthodox Christianity, which made their domination more acceptable to the population of Gaul than that of the Arian and pagan rulers they had defeated.

Byzantine and Moslem pressures also played a role in shaping the political map of the West. As already noted, Justinian's attempt to reconquer the West led to the destruction of the Vandal kingdom in North Africa and the Ostrogothic kingdom in Italy. However, his successors lost northern and central Italy to the Germanic Lombards; the Byzantines retained a band of land extending across central Italy from Ravenna to Rome, southern Italy, and Sicily. In 711 Moslem forces overran the Visigothic kingdom and established control over the Iberian peninsula except for small Christian enclaves in extreme northern Spain.

Meanwhile, other political entities began to take shape in the West. In England, where several competing petty kingdoms had been formed by Anglo-Saxon intruders, forces pointing in the direction of unification were at work. In central Europe Slavic groups moved westward and southward into lands vacated by the Germans and began to develop territorial principalities. In the Scandinavian world, new political groupings were taking shape, preparing the people of the north for an important role in western European history in the future.

Thus, by 750 the political map of the West had assumed a more settled shape (see Map 14.1). The heartland of western Europe—northern Italy, Gaul, western Germany, and England—was occupied by kingdoms shaped by three Germanic peoples: the Lombards, the Franks, and the Anglo-Saxons. Facing this German-dominated world on the south were the Byzantines in southern Italy and Sicily and the Moslems in Spain, North Africa, and the western Mediterranean. To the east and the north were the Slavs and the Scandinavians.

While the political boundaries of the West took shape, constant experimentation went on as the rulers of each Germanic kingdom searched for a workable system of government to replace the Roman imperial regime. That experimentation varied from kingdom to kingdom. As a result, significant regional differences in political institutions emerged in the West during the early Middle Ages, quite in contrast to the unitary political orders characteristic of the Byzantine and Moslem worlds. Out of this experimentation emerged two systems that would be especially important for the future: those of the Franks and

WHERE HISTORIANS DISAGREE

The Division of Times Past

In order to provide a framework into which random data can be arranged, historians divide past time into segments, each treated as a discrete unit that has its unique characteristics. Although necessary, attempts at *periodization* lead to basic disagreement among historians. Nowhere have such disagreements been more apparent than in the attempt to define the division between classical Greco-Roman civilization and what came after in western Europe.

The first widely accepted periodization system relating to the transition from the classical age to a new era was formulated in the early modern period. It was shaped by Renaissance humanists, Protestant religious reformers, and Enlightenment philosophers, whose various interests led them to agree that a major break occurred in the fifth century A.D. This break took the form of a "disaster" marked by the failure of the Roman political system, the triumph of Christianity, and the victory of the barbarian Germans. What followed was a "dark age." This interpretation found particularly persuasive expression in Edward Gibbon's classic *The History of the Decline and Fall of the Roman Empire* (1776), which argued that in the fifth century a new age began with the victory of "religion and barbarism" over the rational, enlightened civilization of classical Greece and Rome.

The periodization scheme defining a decisive break in the fifth century that separated the ancient world from a prolonged "dark age" dominated historical thinking well into the twentieth century. Then a new approach was developed, chiefly as a result of the work of the Belgian historian Henri Pirenne. In his seminal work, *Mohammed and Charlemagne* (1939), he argued that in western Europe the end of the classical world came not in the fifth but in the eighth century when Moslem expansion finally interrupted the economic unity of the Mediterranean basin. In Pirenne's words, "It is . . . strictly correct to say that without Mohammed Charlemagne would have been inconceivable." Thus, it is to the Carolingian era (ca. 750–900) that one must look for the shaping of the essential features of western European civilization, for the "first" Europe. All developments prior to 750 must be annexed to classical history.

Despite heated criticism from many quarters, the Pirenne "thesis" has enjoyed wide acceptance among historians for the past half century. However, there are signs that a new periodization scheme is emerging. It is being shaped by advocates of what is sometimes called the "new social history." They are convinced that the determinant forces shaping the historical process are basic social structures that dictate the activities and thoughts of common people, the "silent," neglected actors on the human stage. Their investigations of the medieval world have led them to conclude that somewhere around 1000 there occurred changes in the basic structure of western European society so fundamental that a new age was born. These changes had to do not with politics, war, and high culture but with demography, family structures, technology, social groupings, and popular religious mentalities. Compared with these changes, the Carolingian "revival" was a mere episode with little consequence. Before 1000 western Europe was a moribund society, dependent on remnants of the classical world. Only after 1000 did a unique and vibrantly creative civilization emerge in western Europe.

These brief remarks lead to two conclusions. Historians divide time past in terms of what interests them most deeply. And their periodization schemes make a difference in how historical data are organized and interpreted.

Anglo-Saxons. We shall return to the Anglo-Saxons (see Chapter 16); here we shall concentrate on the Frankish political system to illustrate the major features of the new political order in the West.

The Frankish kings sought to create a government based on strong monarchy. Clovis claimed a broad range of royal powers on the basis of his position as elected leader of his Germanic followers and as ruler over former Roman subjects by right of conquest. From these sources derived his right to command (the *bannum*) all his subjects to do the royal will. Although Frankish kingship had been elective, Clovis succeeded in establishing the concept that the power to command belonged to a single family whose royal blood was believed to be sacred, thus ensuring hereditary succession in Clovis' dynasty, called the Merovingians, down to 751. To execute the powers they claimed, Clovis and his successors created a central court of royal officials and established local units of government based on the old Roman administrative system. The kingdom was divided into territorial units, called *counties*, where *counts* appointed by the king were charged with collecting taxes, rendering justice, maintaining order, and mustering freemen to military duty.

However, the Merovingian kings were unable to exercise the power they claimed in a fashion leading to uniform administration and internal order. In fact, royal power steadily declined to the point where the last Merovingians were justifiably dubbed "do-nothing" kings. At the heart of their failure was a simple fact: They sought to build a political order on the Roman model without understanding it or having the political skills to direct it. Repeatedly they fell back on the tactics of Germanic warrior kings, resorting to force as the basis of authority. They had a very limited sense of the public good, so that their policies seldom served little more than the interests of the dynasty and their warrior followers. Most kings had little managerial ability; as a result, their administrative machinery degenerated into a household officialdom serving only to meet the king's personal needs. The Merovingians were unable to sustain an effective system of taxation; increasingly they were forced to depend on their own lands and on booty they could extract by force from their subjects. Following Germanic practice, they allowed each of their subjects to be judged by the law under which he or she was born, be it Frankish, Roman, Burgundian, or Visigothic; the result was chaos in the administration of justice. The Merovingians compounded their problems by treating the kingdom as private property, which in accord with Germanic custom was divided among all male heirs at the death of each king. By the early eighth century this practice had split the unified kingdom once ruled by Clovis into three distinct subkingdoms (Neustria, Austrasia, and Burgundy), each ruled by a branch of the Merovingian dynasty and each often at war with the others for control of territory. Disorder was compounded by constant private feuding among powerful Frankish families who followed Germanic custom in seeking to avenge wrongs to members of their families by other families.

Unable to maintain effective centralized government, the Merovingian kings were gradually forced to share power with lay and ecclesiastical landowners. The emergence of the landed nobility as possessors of political power was one of the major developments of the early Middle Ages. The strength of these nobles was rooted in possession of land, family connections, and control over dependents; some noble families could trace their exalted status back to late antiquity. Increasingly important in establishing their position were royal favors. In part those favors stemmed from Germanic custom, which demanded that warrior kings generously reward their loyal warrior followers. More significantly, they resulted from the kings' dependence on the nobles for vital political services. Lacking regular income and a professional bureaucracy, rulers were forced to rely on subjects who could and would serve the royal government at their own expense. Only the great noble families and high ecclesiastical officials could afford such services. In return they exacted from the kings grants of land and the right to govern those who lived on their possessions. A system of private government thus evolved with great nobles and religious officials controlling affairs in their localities as they wished. This trend was accentuated by the increasing willingness of the weak in an unstable society to seek the protection of the strong. Through a process known as *commendation* individuals from all levels of society pledged under oath to serve others willing to offer protection and material support. Although the specific terms of these arrangements varied considerably, the result was to allow the strong to build up private followings of dependents, often called *vassals*, over whom they exercised control and upon whose services they depended to extend their power. The expanding power of the nobles was a source of incessant strife, for the demarcation between royal authority and noble privilege was imprecise and the rules governing the relationship of one noble to another were chaotic.

Thus by 750 a unique political order had begun to take shape in western Europe. It involved several coexisting kingdoms, each ruled by a king. Surrounded by religious and military sanctions, the royal office was accepted as necessary to right order. Although kings claimed extensive powers, they were incapable of exercising them effectively. As a consequence, many public functions fell into the hands of private individuals. This diminution of the power of the state greatly reduced the role of government in society in western Europe, as is obvious when the West is compared to contemporary Byzantine and Moslem societies. What the role of government should be would become a major issue in western European society in the future, an issue that had seldom arisen in earlier civilizations.

2. ECONOMIC AND SOCIAL PATTERNS

When compared with the Byzantine and Moslem worlds, economic life in western Europe during the early Middle Ages was almost primitive. In many ways the low level of economic production was a consequence of recessionary trends that had begun in late antiquity and that were given impetus by the chaotic conditions surrounding the collapse of the Roman imperial order. However, changes did begin to take place in the organization of economic activity which provided a basis for future economic growth.

The western European economy was almost totally agricultural. Agricultural production was organized in a variety of ways. In some areas, especially around the Mediterranean, where Roman survivals were strongest, the *latifundia* system continued. These large estates, increasingly called *villas*, were owned by lay nobles or church officials who reserved part of the land for their own support. Although slavery persisted, the villas were tilled chiefly by tenants, each allotted a piece of land sufficient to maintain a household in return for which they performed labor on the soil reserved by the owner of the villa and rendered dues. Their status tended to become hereditary, but such status also assured them permanent use of a plot of land. The villa system offered certain advantages. It provided landowners with a permanent labor force, encouraged cooperative effort, and gave peasants not only security but some freedom of choice in how they exploited their tenancy. In other areas, farming was organized around village communities of free landowners; in such communities each family owned and cultivated its own land but also shared common rights in forest and pasture land. Also scattered across the landscape were numerous individual farms cultivated by free peasants. Tilled land was used chiefly for cereal grains and vegetables. Peasants showed considerable ingenuity in linking the exploitation of tilled land with the exploitation of forests, streams, and animal herds. In gross terms, this agricultural system produced barely enough to provide the basic needs of the population.

The shift of the center of economic life to a rural setting was accompanied by the decline of urban-based commerce and industry, again continuing a trend that had begun in late Roman times. Although urban centers survived, cities served chiefly as political and religious centers rather than as centers of economic production. Near the Mediterranean in southern Gaul, Italy, Spain, and North Africa, some commercial activity did continue, and contacts with the rich East were maintained. But on the whole the West experienced a diminishing exchange of goods, a declining flow of money, and the virtual disappearance of active merchants and artisans, except as they were supported by owners of large estates to provide for local consumption. What little long-distance trade did survive was increasingly conducted by foreigners, especially Syrians and Jews.

Amid this grim picture there were signs pointing toward a restructuring of economic life into patterns that promised greater productivity. The end of the voracious Roman taxation system opened opportunities for channeling surplus wealth toward productive ends. The formation of villas and villages created disciplined productive cells encouraging cooperation between landowners and peasants. The emergence of the family household permanently in possession of a piece of land provided a solid foundation for agricultural production. The resourcefulness of peasants in linking field and forest gave flexibility and variety to the agricultural system. Modest technological advances, especially the development of ox-drawn plows capable of turning over heavy soils, allowed full exploitation of the rich land north of the Alps for the first time. Isolated efforts at land clearance held out the promise of bringing forest and wasteland under the plow. Trading activity began to quicken in the North and Baltic seas and along the rivers flowing into them, opening new opportunities for commercial exchange.

The social structure in the West changed in response to new conditions. The direction of change was toward a simpler system than had been characteristic of the Roman world of late antiquity. The old Roman *nobiles*, whose status and social role were intimately linked to the Roman imperial regime and Greco-Roman culture, faded away. A new aristocracy emerged, composed of resourceful, aggressive, self-made individuals of both Roman and German descent who were capable of acquiring land, exercising private political power, and gathering dependents around them. As this new aristocracy (often referred to as the *potentes*, the powerful) took shape, the rest of the population, almost all peasants, tended to be grouped into a single lower class (often called *pauperes*, those without power). While many in this class retained legal status as free persons, increasingly peasants saw their freedom erode as a result of constraints placed on them by landowners that bound them to the soil of a large estate and imposed obligations on them in exchange for use of a piece of land. Slavery continued to exist, especially as a means of supplying household servants, but there was a tendency to attach slaves to the land in the same fashion as other peasant workers.

Social behavior and attitudes among the powerful increasingly reflected Germanic values and habits at the expense of the more refined standards of conduct of the old Roman world. Generally illiterate and often short-lived, aristocratic males were creatures of violence and passion, their lives centered on fighting, hunting, gaming, and sexual exploits. They loved ostentatious display, particularly in the form of personal adornments made of gold and jewels. Especially important to them were family connections, chiefly because the family circle offered security in an uncertain environment. It was not unusual for aristocrats to collect wives and concubines so as to assure themselves of many children who could be advantageously married to promote family interests. Feuds among competing noble families were a common feature of life. Although male heads of families exercised extensive power over females, aristocratic women played a significant role in society. Dowries and gifts associated with marriage gave them control over considerable property. High respect was paid and special protection was extended to them because of their procreative power, the key to family survival. Kinship ties established through female lines provided a basic link in constituting extended families. The social importance of women is illustrated by the prominent role played in public life by several Merovingian queens and by the influence asserted by several gifted leaders of Merovingian monasteries for women. Peasant life, anchored in the nuclear family and confined to a tiny rural community, was marked by poverty, drudgery, and ill-treatment.

3. RELIGIOUS LIFE

Of decisive importance in shaping western European life during the early Middle Ages was the Christian religious establishment, one of the main components of the world of late antiquity that carried over into the new age almost intact. Although Christians in the West shared a vague sense of belonging to a universal body, in reality the religious establishment was embodied in hundreds of individual "churches" led by bishops and priests whose offices bestowed on them considerable authority to direct the lives of their flocks.

Between 500 and 750 these Christian communities were sorely tested by a variety of disruptive forces. The replacement of the unified Roman imperial regime by several Germanic kingdoms meant the end of any agency concerned with Christendom as a whole. The new Germanic kingdoms lacked the material resources to support churches on the scale the Roman government had. Powerful forces were at work diverting the attention of religious leaders from spiritual concerns. Like all other power wielders in the West, influential ecclesiastical officials, especially bishops, paid increasing attention to gaining land and dependents. Not only did this quest detract them from their pastoral duties, it also made their offices a focus of wealth and power. These offices became the object of competition in which the worldly usually triumphed over the pious. Ecclesiastical offices were prizes that kings used to reward their followers and that self-seeking noble families sought to fill as a means of increasing their wealth and power. Discipline among the lower clergy suffered from the lack of spiritual concern among higher church officials; the result was increasing numbers of unlettered priests who were ignorant of basic Christian teaching and morally lax. Powerful nobles often controlled the appointments of local priests, especially those serving the increasing numbers of private churches established on local estates by nobles who viewed such churches as private property. Although the early Middle Ages was a period of intense religious fervor among all people, religious life in general reflected inferior spiritual direction. Pagan and Christian ideas and practices mingled to produce a religious mentality focused on gaining material ends and avoiding evil spirits through magic and the intervention of the saints rather than on learning basic Christian doctrines and practicing Christian morality.

The disruptive forces in spiritual life producing disunity, worldliness in leadership, debased religious consciousness, and moral laxness were still rampant in 750. However, the Christian establishment had begun to devise means of counteracting them in ways that gave western Christianity a distinctive quality.

Of particular significance was the expanded involvement of the Christian establishment in activities that were not strictly religious, filling an important social role to which the weak Germanic monarchs were unable to respond. Bishops played an important role in the councils of kings and royal administrations, allowing them to inject Christian ideas of justice and mercy into the harsh law codes of the era. Ecclesiastical leaders took on the burden of caring for the poor, maintaining schools and hospitals, and protecting the weak. Resources to support such activities were drawn from income derived from church lands and gifts from the faithful, who were prompted to give at least in part by some sense that charity was a Christian responsibility. Each time the religious establishment intervened in such matters, its prestige as a social agency and its influence over the social order increased. No less important, such actions added a social dimension to religious consciousness.

A major source of vitality in religious life was the quest to win new converts. We have already noted that most of the Germanic invaders accepted Christianity as soon as they entered the Roman Empire. In succeeding centuries the Christian frontier continued to advance. During the fifth century missionary forces, spearheaded by St. Patrick, converted Ireland. Missionaries from the Frankish kingdom, itself Christianized late in the fifth century under Clovis, pushed the Christian frontier to the Rhine and beyond during the sixth and seventh centuries. Beginning late in the sixth century, the Anglo-Saxons were converted by missionaries from Rome and Ireland. During the late seventh and eighth centuries, English and Irish missionaries crossed to the Continent to win new converts on the northern and eastern frontiers of the Frankish kingdom. Meanwhile, the work of converting the rural population of the West went forward. As new converts were won, a network of bishoprics, monasteries, rural churches, and private chapels was developed to ensure pastoral care for new Christians. In some cases conversions were imposed from the top down; as a result, acceptance of the new religion had only a superficial impact on most converts. However, the missionary establishment was often especially intent on imposing a high level of religious life, thus serving as a model of pastoral care and a source of reforming zeal.

Another significant development involved the emergence of religious agencies capable of attacking weaknesses within the body of the Christian establishment—corruptness and worldliness of the clergy, moral laxness, ignorance of religious precepts, lack of discipline.

Two agencies, neither new, were especially important: the papacy and the monastic establishment.

During late antiquity the papacy had utilized the Petrine theory (see Chapters 12 and 13) to establish its position as the guardian of true doctrine and right practice. That position was reinforced during the troubled fifth century. With the collapse of the Roman imperial government, the bishops of Rome assumed a larger role in governing the city of Rome, as was dramatically illustrated by the role played by Pope Leo I (440–461) in protecting St. Peter's city from the Huns and the Vandals and in fiercely defending the papal right to define Orthodox doctrine, especially against the claims of the emperors and the patriarchs of Constantinople. The expanding sense of papal authority was reflected by Pope Gelasius I (492–496), who argued that God had established two independent and separate realms of authority, the spiritual and the secular, to achieve different aspects of the divine plan, but when the two powers clashed, spiritual authority must prevail. However, many factors limited the ability of the popes to exert their claimed authority. The Arian Ostrogoths who ruled Italy from 493 to 554 were little inclined to respect papal authority. When Justinian reincorporated Rome into the Byzantine Empire, he treated its bishop as one of his religious agents whose authority was no greater than that of the patriarch of Constantinople. The installation of the hostile, aggressive Arian Lombards as rulers of northern Italy after 568 left the popes with no choice but to accept Byzantine protection and to acquiesce to imperial religious policy as defined by the emperor.

It was Pope Gregory I, the Great (590–604), who began to rechart the papal course (see Figure 15.2). A Roman noble by birth and education and a monk by personal choice, he accepted the papal office with reluctance, but once in control he moved in decisive directions. Convinced that the papacy must command material resources to survive on the troubled Italian scene, Gregory spent considerable energy in the management of the patrimony of St. Peter—that is, the property belonging to the papacy in Italy. He used the large income derived from this property chiefly to expand papal control over Rome, often with little consideration of the officials of the emperor

FIGURE 15.2 Pope Gregory the Great Gregory was one of the most influential figures of the formative period of medieval western European society. His varied activities as bishop of Rome put an important imprint on the office of the papacy as the leader of the Christian community in the West. Throughout the Middle Ages his successors looked back to his career as a model of Christian leadership and as a precedent for their actions. (Alinari/Art Resource)

in Constantinople, who claimed legal authority to rule the Eternal City. His increasingly powerful position in Rome allowed him to play the Lombards against the Byzantines in a way that not only prevented Lombard conquest of Rome but also undermined Byzantine power in the city. This effort marked an important step in laying the groundwork for a future papal state in Italy.

But Gregory was more than a hardheaded administrator and wily diplomat. He never forgot the pastoral responsibilities that tradition assigned to the successor of St. Peter and to all bishops. In this capacity he took significant steps toward reshaping the Christian message to fit the unique needs of the Germanic West and toward drawing the western Christian community to

Rome for spiritual guidance. He wrote important books on theology and ecclesiastical administration that circulated widely to guide the clergy in explaining the faith and shaping the moral lives of their flocks. His powerful sermons became models for preaching as a means of improving spiritual life. He sought to provide a model of liturgical practice that would be useful in all churches; tradition credited him with a role in developing Gregorian chant as an element of the liturgy. He wrote innumerable letters to kings and clergy throughout the West, offering them advice on religious matters and reminding them of Rome's authority in the religious sphere. His influence was crucial in converting the Lombards and Visigoths from Arianism to orthodoxy, thus ending a major cause of religious division in the West. He initiated the missionary effort that played a major role in converting the Anglo-Saxons of England, and he guided the religious organization of the new converts in a way that attached them to Rome. In short, Gregory enlarged the role of the papacy in the religious life of the West and began to direct papal efforts toward the resolution of religious problems unique to the West, thereby setting a model of papal leadership that would serve for centuries.

A second force crucial in shaping religious life in the early medieval West was monasticism. Monasticism had been imported from the east in the fourth century, but early western monasticism failed to sustain its initial vitality, perhaps because it was too imitative of eastern models to address the unique conditions in the West. Only when the West found its own style of monastic life did that instituition begin to assert a decisive force on religious life.

One distinctive form of western monasticism developed in Ireland, where the severe ascetic practices of the east took deep hold as the standard for monastic life. However, Irish monastic communities became thoroughly enmeshed in Irish tribal society, placing monks in a position to shape popular religious life. An example of this engagement was the unique system of penance developed in Irish monastic circles, involving private confession and the use of penitential books that—much like Germanic law codes—cataloged sins and instructed confessors on the appropriate punishment for each. Irish monasticism placed a strong emphasis on learning as a dimension of piety; as a result Irish monasteries became active centers of education and of the study of sacred literature. Finally, Irish monasteries generated a powerful missionary movement that spread Irish monks over England and the Continent, bringing with them deep piety, skill in uplifting the level of religious life, and great learning.

Another unique form of monastic life was introduced by Benedict of Nursia (ca. 480–543). Like Gregory I, he was an Italian of noble origin who abandoned the world to follow a monastic life. After experimenting with the hermit life, he eventually founded a monastic community at Monte Cassino and formulated a rule to guide the lives of its members. The *Benedictine Rule*, which combined features from several earlier rules, emphasized that a community of dedicated individuals could serve God and each other better than the individual hermit isolated from interaction with other humans could. However, such a "school for the service of God" must be made up of selected individuals willing to make a commitment to perfection. After a rigorous testing period, each new member was required to take vows to renounce all personal wealth, to remain chaste, to obey his superiors, and to remain permanently in the community he had entered. The rule entrusted absolute authority over the community to an abbot who was responsible before God to direct each monk toward holiness; thus discipline was a key feature of Benedictine communities. A major aspect of the rule was its provision for an orderly daily routine for all members of the community, consisting of specified periods of prayer, manual labor, contemplation, and reading (see Figure 15.1). This regimen ensured that each community would be self-sufficient economically and that its members would be engaged in varied activities rather than in endless ascetic practices aimed at suppressing the urges of the body and awareness of the world. Although Benedict had no intention of devising a rule for all monasteries, his rule—given powerful endorsement by Pope Gregory I in his popular biography of Benedict—was adopted by both male and female communities across western Europe.

By 750 monasteries, especially Benedictine and Irish houses, were asserting a powerful influence in society. Monks and nuns were the new holy people, "athletes of Christ" serving as models of piety and moral excellence for all elements of society. They were able to teach bewildered Christians the basic elements of the faith and the proper way to perform Christian worship. They were the chief preservers and transmitters of learning. They performed numerous acts of charity and goaded the rich and powerful to emulate them. As a result of their disciplined labors in the service of God, monks carved new estates out of Europe's wilderness and made them the best-managed economic institutions in the West, from which all could learn about farm management and artisanry. As a bulwark against both the Devil and barbarism, many found the monks and nuns worthy of emulation.

4. CULTURAL LIFE

Although the chaotic conditions prevailing in western Europe from 500 to 750 were hardly conducive to cultural activity, certain developments were significant in shaping a new culture. Of prime importance was the preservation of significant elements of classical and patristic literature and learning in Latin (the use of Greek virtually disappeared in the West). During the sixth century both secular society and the religious establishment played a role in this enterprise. In Italy, southern Gaul, and Spain lay aristocrats and bishops of Roman descent continued to read classical and patristic Latin authors, to write works imitating them, and to support schools where the young could study rhetoric and grammar. Germanic courts, especially that of the Ostrogoths, actively patronized learning and art.

As the sixth century progressed, the role of secular society in sustaining cultural life virtually ceased; the burden fell to the Christian establishment, especially the monasteries. Irish and Benedictine monasteries established schools to teach new members to read and write Latin, encouraged the copying of the works of classical and patristic authors, and promoted the writing of commentaries on old texts to make them understandable. Especially active in these enterprises were the Benedictine monasteries of England, where Irish and Continental influences merged to generate an important outburst of literary and

scholarly activity in the early eighth century. Monastic intellectual life placed an especially strong emphasis on mastery of the Bible as the prime source of wisdom. The concerns of monks tended to be narrow, governed by a passion to know God, to understand his revealed word, and to pray well. Thus, the monks were selective in their approach to the classical tradition. And they felt no compunction about turning the classical heritage to Christian purposes, sometimes distorting classical thought almost beyond recognition.

In a world dominated by the effort to maintain a tenuous contact with the Latin literary and theological heritage of classical Roman writers and the Church Fathers of late antiquity, there was little room for charting new directions in cultural life. However, a few figures were able to transcend mere preservation to produce works that revealed creative talent. One was Boethius (ca. 475–525), a luminary at the Ostrogothic court who set out to translate the works of Aristotle and Plato into Latin; although he made limited progress in that project, for centuries his translations provided the West with virtually its only access to the Greek philosophical tradition. His famous *Consolation of Philosophy*, written while he was in prison awaiting execution for treason, was a moving defense of philosophy as a guide to inner peace and happiness. In *Etymologies* a Visigothic bishop, Isidore of Seville (ca. 560–636), provided an encyclopedia of information about many subjects derived from ancient sources that encouraged the systematic organization of knowledge. Gregory the Great's writings set forth basic theological concepts in terms more suited to the intellectual capabilities of his age than were the sophisticated works of the Latin Fathers from whom he borrowed most of his ideas. Especially important in shaping western European intellectual life was Gregory's mode of interpreting Scripture, which sought to discover the hidden meaning behind the literal words of the Bible. A Frankish bishop, Gregory of Tours (ca. 538–594), in his *History of the Franks*, demonstrated skill at compiling historical material. The most outstanding intellectual figure of the age was the English monk Bede (673–735), whose theological, historical, and biographical writings set high standards of learning and style. His *Ec-*

clesiastical History of the English People is one of the best pieces of history written during the entire Middle Ages. The age was also rich in saints' lives celebrating the feats of holy men and women who had surrendered themselves to the service of God.

As a few struggled to preserve Latin education and learning, the lay world sank into illiteracy. That world was not without culture; its members kept alive the oral tradition of the Germanic world, as is evidenced by the magnificent epic entitled *Beowulf*, put into writing in about 800 in the Anglo-Saxon language to record oral tradition concerning the heroic struggles of warriors against the forces of evil. The illiteracy of the laity created a situation of immense importance for western European cultural history: The languages men and women spoke in their daily lives were different from the language of learning and literature. For centuries learning would remain the monopoly of an elite especially trained to use Latin, the language of the religious establishment. Under such circumstances, it remained a constant challenge to prevent the world of learning from becoming remote from and irrelevant to the realities of life.

The art of the early Middle Ages reflects a mixture of old and new. Greco-Roman forms and themes persisted in architecture, sculpture, and painting, but they were constantly modified to serve Christian ends. Many of the churches of the era followed the basilica plan characteristic of Roman structures. However, Byzantine architectural forms, shaped by Justinian's building program, asserted a strong influence on sixth-century Italy, especially in Ravenna (see Figure 13.2), and persisted there to affect building styles in other areas of the West. In sculpture and painting, classical and Byzantine influences merged to create a pictorial art emphasizing symbolical representation of religious motifs at the expense of realistic portrayal of humans and the world of nature (see Figures 12.1 and 15.3). Germanic and Celtic influences, especially their decorative style, which used animal and geometric forms to create abstract designs, asserted their effects on the pictorial arts. The vigor of this composite early medieval art is especially evident in the designs created to illustrate handwritten manuscripts; prime examples include the Irish Book of

FIGURE 15.3 Two Thieves Awaiting the Crucifixion This sculpture from the mausoleum of a seventh-century abbot from the Frankish city of Poitiers shows two unhappy thieves bound to crosses while awaiting their end with Christ. While classical art styles persist (e.g., the representation of a building), the portrayal of the human figures indicates that new influences were penetrating artistic expression in the German-dominated world. (Marburg/Art Resource)

Durrow (late seventh century), the English Lindisfarne Gospels (eighth century), and the Irish Book of Kells (early ninth century) (see Color Plate 8).

By 750 the western European world had by no means emerged from the time of troubles that followed the collapse of the Roman imperial regime. Habits of violence, ignorance, poverty, and moral laxness had been ingrained into people's lives and would long affect the western European world. However, out of the experiences of the early Middle Ages had emerged innovative institutions and patterns of life: a form of limited monarchy, a new nobility, a stabilized peasantry, an involved ecclesiastical organization, the papacy, monasticism, a store of Greco-Roman literature and learning, a new art style. Their potential had not yet been realized, but their existence pointed toward the emergence of a vigorous and unique civilization in the West that might in the future equal the level of civilized life already flourishing in the Byzantine and Moslem worlds.

SUGGESTED READING

Political, Economic, and Social History

J. M. Wallace-Haddrill, *The Barbarian West, 400–1000*, 5th rev. ed. (1988).

Roger Collins, *Early Medieval Europe, 300–1000* (1991). Two excellent general surveys of the early Middle Ages.

Henri Pirenne, *Mohammed and Charlemagne*, trans. Bernard Maill (1939). A classic expounding the thesis that the Islamic invasions of the eighth century brought a break with the classical world.

Patrick Geary, *Before France and Germany: The Creation and Transformation of the Merovingian World* (1988).

Edward James, *The Origins of France: From Clovis to the Capetians, 500–1000* (1982).

Katharine Scherman, *The Birth of France: Warriors, Bishops, and Long-Haired Kings* (1987).

Chris Wickham, *Early Medieval Italy: Central Power and Local Society, 400–1000* (1981).

Roger Collins, *Early Medieval Spain: Unity in Diversity, 400–1000* (1983).

Martyn J. Wittock, *The Origins of England 400–600* (1986). These six titles provide excellent treatments of the major Germanic kingdoms of the early Middle Ages.

Georges Duby, *The Early Growth of the European Economy: Warriors and Peasants from the Seventh to the Twelfth Century*, trans. Howard B. Clarke (1974).

Renée Doehaerd, *The Early Middle Ages in the West: Economy and Society*, trans. W. G. Deakin (1978). Two comprehensive treatments of economic and social history.

Richard Hodges, *Dark Age Economies: The Origins of Towns and Trade*, A.D. *600–1000* (1982). Uses archaeological evidence to revise views about the low level of trade and urban life.

Philippe Ariès and Georges Duby, *A History of Private Life*, Vol. 1: *From Pagan Rome to Byzantium*, ed. Paul Veyne, trans. Arthur Goldhammer (1987). The appropriate chapter in this study is rich in details about social life.

Suzanne Fonay Wemple, *Women in Frankish Society: Marriage and the Cloister, 500 to 900* (1981). A balanced treatment.

Religious and Cultural History

Judith Herrin, *The Formation of Christendom* (1987). Stresses the role of religion as a prime force in shaping the new civilizations of the early Middle Ages.

Hubert Jedin and John Dolan, eds., *Handbook of Church History*, Vol. 2: *The Imperial Church to the Early Middle Ages*, trans. Anselm Biggs (1980). Deals with all aspects of religious life.

J. M. Wallace-Haddrill, *The Frankish Church* (1983). A topical approach, rich in interpretations.

Jeffrey Richards, *The Popes and the Papacy in the Early Middle Ages, 476–752* (1979). An excellent treatment.

James C. Russell, *The Germanization of Early Medieval Christianity: A Sociohistorical Approach to Religious Transformation* (1992). New views on changes affecting Christianity during the early Middle Ages.

Pierre Riché, *Education and Culture in the Barbarian West: Sixth through Eighth Century*, trans. John J. Contreni (1976). A work rich in insights into the nature of early medieval culture.

Ludwig Bieler, *Ireland: Harbinger of the Middle Ages* (1963). A brilliant treatment of Ireland's contribution to cultural life.

J. Hubert et al., *Europe of the Invasions*, trans. Stuart Gilbert and James Emmons (1969). An excellent treatment of artistic development during the early Middle Ages.

Sources

Rule of Monasteries, trans. L. J. Boyle (1949). Benedict's rule.

Gregory of Tours, *The History of the Franks*, trans. Lewis Thorpe (1974).

Bede, *The History of the English Church and People*, rev. ed., trans. L. Sherley-Price (1968).

Beowulf, trans. D. Wright (1957).

PLATE 1. Gudea of Lagash (Ruled ca. 2150 B.C.) This is one of several surviving statues of Gudea, a very active ruler of the Sumerian city of Lagash. Represented in prayer, the ruler's expression reflects the spirit of resignation which characterized the Sumerian worldview. The stylized features and the immobility surrounding the human figure were characteristic of Mesopotamian sculpture. (The Metropolitan Museum of Art, Harris Brisbane Dick Fund, 1959)

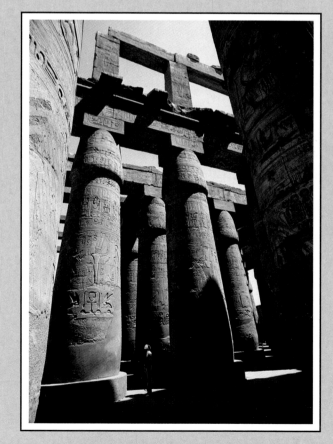

PLATE 2. Egyptian Temple This photo shows the remains of a massive temple built in honor of Amon-Ra at Karnak in the time of Rameses II (1299–1232 B.C.), when the Egyptian empire was at its height. The structure marked the culmination of a long tradition of temple building. The huge columns defined an inner hall which rose above side aisles also defined by columns. The columns contained numerous reliefs and hieroglyphic texts exalting Amon-Ra and the feats of the pharoah. (M. Timothy O'Keefe/Bruce Coleman)

PLATE 3 *(left and right).* **Ideal Greek Humans** These two statues, both Roman copies of Greek originals, reflect the search by Greek artists to represent ideal human beings. The male figure by Polyclitus (fl. ca. 450–420 B.C.) portrays a spearbearer. The female figure by Praxiteles (fl. ca. 350 B.C.) portrays Aphrodite, the goddess of love. These statues reflect the Greek genius for creating a calculated symmetry of the parts of the body without sacrificing the sense that one is observing a living human about to move. (Left, National Museum, Naples: Scala/Art Resource; right, Vatican: Scala/Art Resource)

PLATE 4. A Room in a Roman Villa
This photo shows a reconstructed room from an aristocrat's villa near Pompey. The decoration of such rooms occupied much of the attention of Roman artists. Paintings dealing with history and nature adorned wall spaces, while elaborate mosaics covered the floors. Examples of such paintings are shown below. (The Metropolitan Museum of Art, Rogers Fund, 1903)

PLATE 5. Aeneas at the Doctor Inspired by Vergil's *Aeneid*, this scene from a villa at Pompeii shows a doctor treating Aeneas; his weeping son stands by while Venus appears with healing herbs. (National Museum, Naples: Scala/Art Resource)

PLATE 6. The Countryside This scene formed part of the decoration of a magnificent villa built by Emperor Hadrian near Tivoli. The bucolic countryside was a favorite subject of Roman artists and writers. (Monumenti Musei e Gallerie Pontificie, Vatican)

PLATE 7. Christ, Ruler of the Universe This mosaic from the cathedral of Cefalu in Sicily portrays a theme often treated by Byzantine artists. It reflects the skill of Byzantine artists in conveying a spiritual message visually. (Scala/Art Resource)

PLATE 8 *(right)*. Christ Enthroned This manuscript illumination from the Irish Book of Kells represents one of the major art forms of the early Middle Ages. Churches and monasteries and their patrons prized sacred books decorated with such illuminations highly. (Trinity College Library, Dublin)

PLATE 9. A Medieval Battle As the Latin lettering says, this scene from the Bayeux Tapestry shows the English and French in battle. This remarkable weaving, nearly 240 feet long, portrays a series of episodes involved in William of Normandy's successful effort to conquer England in 1066. (Scala/Art Resource)

PLATE 10. Stained Glass One of the most stunning features of a Gothic church was its stained-glass windows. Although the effect such windows created is impossible to capture in a photograph, the one shown here from the cathedral at Laon in France shows how an artist could use different-colored pieces of glass to tell a story, usually from sacred history. This window treats the childhood of Jesus. (Archives Photographiques, Paris: Jean Feuillie © C.N.M.H.S./S.P.A.D.E.M.)

PLATE 11. A Winter Scene Very popular in the late Middle Ages were illustrated books of hours used for private devotions. A splendid example was one created for the duke of Berry. It contained a painting for each month of the year. The one below is for February. (Musée Condé/Chantilly: Giraudon/Art Resource)

PLATE 12. Giovanni Bellini, *Transfiguration of Christ*, Late 1480s Giovanni Bellini (1430–1516) was one of the leading painters of the Italian Renaissance. In the *Transfiguration of Christ,* the sacred figures, Peter, James, and John, crouch below Christ, who stands calmly between Moses and Elijah. In the background is a fifteenth-century town and the hills of northern Italy. The individualism of the figures, the depth and realism of the landscape, the immediacy of the scene, and the religiosity of the subject matter were characteristic of Renaissance art. (Museo di Capodimonte, Naples: Scala/Art Resource)

PLATE 13. Raphael, *Portrait of a Man,* ca. 1503 While Renaissance artists typically painted religious scenes, they also painted secular scenes—often reflecting the tastes and characters of their patrons. Raphael is considered the central painter of the High Renaissance. In portraits such as this, he conveyed the strength and individuality of important secular men without resorting to flattery or conventions. (Borghese Gallery, Rome: Scala/Art Resource)

PLATE 14. Peter Paul Rubens, *The Crucifixion of St. Peter*, 1642 Baroque paintings are often extraordinarily dynamic and rich. This is particularly so in the large paintings of Rubens. In this altarpiece, the subject matter is religious, but the feeling of the painting is not one of calmness or piety. The heroic, heavily muscled figures are caught in a moment of dramatic struggle; color and lines create a sense of movement; details are carefully rendered creating a sense of realism. (Church of St. Peter, Cologne. Fotografie Wim Cox)

PLATE 15. Claude Lorraine, *The Marriage of Isaac and Rebekah (The Mill)*, 1640 This painting, with foreground figures framed by trees under a radiant sky, reveals certain characteristics of the classical style: the geometrically balanced Italian landscape, the figures in classic dress, and the general calm and discipline of the scene. Compared to the dynamic, dramatic nature of Rubens' Baroque style, the classical style is logical and restrained. Claude Lorraine (1600–1682) and Nicolas Poussin (1594–1665) helped make classicism popular in France during the seventeenth century. (Reproduced by courtesy of the Trustees, The National Gallery, London)

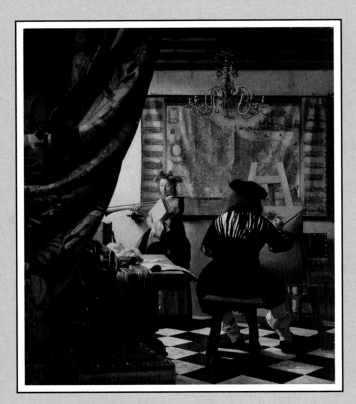

PLATE 16. Jan Vermeer, *The Painter's Studio*, ca. 1665 Dutch artists often painted interior scenes depicting popular and middle-class life. In this painting a woman poses as an allegorical figure of fame. Light spreads smoothly through a window in front of her, affecting everything in the studio. A map, something particularly crucial for the commercial Dutch, hangs below a geometrically precise candelabra. (Kunsthistorisches Museum, Vienna)

PLATE 17. Antoine Watteau, *A Pilgrimage to Cythera*, 1717 During the early modern period, painting often reflected the tastes of the dominant aristocracy. This was particularly so in eighteenth-century France. This theme is one of classical mythology, but the figures are like eighteenth-century aristocrats gracefully at play in an idyllic garden of nature. The line between life and the roles they are playing blurs in this lush scene. (The Louvre, Paris)

CHAPTER 16
The First Europe: The Carolingian Age, 750–900

FIGURE 16.1 Dispensing Justice in the Carolingian Age This drawing from a ninth-century manuscript shows Emperor Charlemagne and his son, Pépin, king of Italy, presiding over a court of law while a clerk is ready to record their judgment. Concern for justice was an important aspect of the Carolingian effort to provide better government. (Modena Cathedral Archives)

The pace of the slow, troubled struggle to create a new basis for society in western Europe suddenly quickened in the eighth century. Between about 750 and 900 a narrow but energetic segment of society, spearheaded by kings and clergy, devoted its talents to an effort to "renew" society both on the Continent and in England. Although their ambitions were by no means realized, their limited success had two important results: It made the West visible in the larger world as a coherent culture. And it gave the West an expanded awareness of its unique identity. In a sense, this renewal created the first "Europe."

1. THE RISE OF THE CAROLINGIANS

The central force promoting revival on the Continent was a new Frankish royal dynasty, the Carolingians, so named after its most famous king, Carolus, or Charles. The Carolingians originated as one of the many ambitious noble families whose power and wealth grew steadily under the Merovingians. In the middle of the seventh century, the family utilized its extensive landed possessions and its connections with the religious establishment to gain hereditary control over the office of mayor of the palace in the subkingdom of Austrasia, where the family wealth was concentrated (see Map 16.1). This key office allowed the family to control the weak Merovingian kings of Austrasia and to utilize royal lands to increase its wealth and its circle of dependents. As their family power expanded, the Carolingians sought to extend their influence to the other Merovingian subkingdoms—Neustria and Burgundy. That effort culminated in 687, when Pépin of Herstal, the Carolingian mayor of the palace of Austrasia, defeated the Neustrian mayor and claimed the mayoralty of the entire Frankish realm.

Once established as sole mayor of the palace, Pépin of Herstal and his son and grandson, Charles Martel (714–741) and Pépin the Short (741–751), became the most powerful men in the Frankish state, far overshadowing the "do-nothing" Merovingian kings they served. Their efforts were aimed chiefly at checking the forces of disintegration within the kingdom and defending its frontiers. Charles Martel gained undying fame by defeating a Moslem army at the battle of Tours in 732. Their military success was due in part to their ability to take advantage of a significant military innovation that began to spread in the eighth century: the heavily armored mounted warrior. This innovation was perhaps made possible by the invention of the stirrup, which permitted a mounted warrior to keep his mount while striking or receiving blows from sword or spear. The equipping and support of a force of mounted warriors involved costs beyond the means of the impoverished royal government; increasingly it was necessary to rely on men of wealth willing to arm themselves at their own expense. Charles Martel and Pépin rewarded such service by grants of land, called *benefices*, the income from which the recipients used on the condition that they would provide military service at their own expense. Although some of these benefices were derived from royal lands, Charles Martel and Pépin made a regular practice of utilizing ecclesiastical lands to provide military benefices.

Although condemned by some clergymen as pillagers of religious property, Charles Martel and Pépin used other means to court and win the ecclesiastical support that was vital to their growing power. Their support of missionary activity and religious reform was particularly welcome among many bishops and monks. A key figure in shaping their religious policy was Boniface, an Anglo-Saxon Benedictine monk who went to the Continent in 719 to convert the pagans living beyond the eastern frontier of the kingdom. Until his martyrdom by pagan Frisians in 755, Boniface not only won many converts but also organized bishoprics and monasteries in newly converted territories and guided the mayors of the palace in shaping a program to reform Frankish religious life. Soon after his arrival in Francia, Boniface sought and received the blessing of the papacy for his varied activities. As a result, papal influence expanded among the Franks, and the mayors of the palace gained increasing recognition as supporters of the successors of St. Peter.

Although the Carolingian mayors of the palace clearly exercised control over the Frankish kingdom, they legally remained agents of the powerless Merovingian kings. Finally, Pépin took the logical step to end this incongruous situation by transferring the crown to his own fam-

Map 16.1 THE EMPIRE OF CHARLEMAGNE One of Charlemagne's great achievements was his military victories, which greatly expanded the Frankish kingdom. This map shows his major conquests. The extent of his holdings indicates that he came close to dominating western Europe, an ambition that would spark the dreams of many later western European rulers. Not long after Charlemagne's death, his empire would suffer savage attacks on all its frontiers and would be divided by his heirs.

ily. Concerned about the potential hostility that might arise among the Franks by a forced deposition of the ancient dynasty, whose sacred blood was held in deep respect, Pépin sought to sanction his action in an unprecedented way. He sent an envoy to Rome to ask Pope Zachary whether the "right ordering of things" did not demand that he who held actual power should wear the crown. On the basis of the pope's affirmative answer, Pépin in 751 deposed the reigning Merovingian and had himself elected king by the Frankish nobles. On the occasion of his coronation, a clergyman (perhaps Boniface) gave him a special anointment never before bestowed on a Frankish king. This sequence of events indicated to many that Pépin's royal office was different from that held by his Merovingian predecessors. Although duly elected by the Franks according to Germanic tradition, papal consent to the dynastic change and anointment by a clergyman made Pépin an agent of God charged with caring for the material and spiritual needs of the Christian community according to God's will.

The papacy was especially anxious to strengthen its bonds with the Franks because of the significant changes taking place in Italy. Since Justinian's reconquest of Italy in the middle of the sixth century, the city of Rome had been under the jurisdiction of the emperor in Constantinople, and the popes had relied—sometimes reluctantly—on imperial protection. During the first half of the eighth century, however, the Moslem assault on Byzantium left the emperors increasingly unable to defend their position in Italy. Moreover, the iconoclastic policy of emperors Leo III and Constantine V had been condemned as heretical by the papacy. The decline of Byzantine power in Italy encouraged its longtime rivals, the Lombards, to expand their sphere of influence. Beginning early in the eighth century, a succession of able Lombard kings undertook military campaigns that increasingly threatened to engulf Rome and to impose a new master on the papacy. Bereft of help from the Byzantine emperors, now both weak and heretical, the popes desperately needed a new protector.

In the face of the mounting Lombard threat, Pope Stephen II (752–757) undertook a journey to Pépin's kingdom in 754, perhaps emboldened by the fact that his predecessor had extended an important favor to the new king. After long negotiations and despite resistance by some Frankish nobles, the king agreed to protect the pope from the Lombards. In return, the pope reanointed Pépin king of the Franks and bestowed on him the somewhat ambiguous title of "*patricius* of the Romans,*" implying Pépin's role as

protector of the people of Rome, including the papacy. Pépin undertook campaigns into Italy in 754 and 756 and forced the Lombards to surrender territories in central Italy that they had recently annexed. In a grant known as the Donation of Pépin, he bestowed these lands on the papacy, thereby establishing the basis for the papacy's claim to an independent state. Although the lands involved legally belonged to the Byzantine emperor, Pépin's action clearly recognized what was reality: Since the time of Pope Gregory I the bishops of Rome had established de facto control over Rome and its environs. There is some evidence that a document known as the Donation of Constantine may have played a part in these transactions. This document, which seems to have been composed in Rome at about this time, claimed to date from the time of Constantine and stated that the first Christian emperor, out of gratitude for being cured of leprosy, had granted Pope Sylvester I (314–335) the rights to the western empire, especially Rome and Italy. Pepin's donation was therefore only a confirmation of an earlier legal grant made by a universally renowned ruler whose mantle the contemporary emperor in Constantinople had inherited.

2. THE REIGN OF CHARLEMAGNE, 768–814

The foundations established by Pépin of Herstal, Charles Martel, and Pépin the Short were brilliantly exploited by Charlemagne. In the eyes of his contemporaries he possessed many qualities of greatness: imposing physical stature, prowess as a warrior, piety, generosity, intelligence, devotion to family and friends, joy for life. His actions made him a hero not only in his own time but for many future generations of Europeans.

As befitted a Frankish king, Charlemagne was above all else a successful warlord. Few years passed during his long reign without a military campaign; the cumulative result was a considerable expansion of his kingdom (see Map 16.1). His most severe test came from the pagan Saxons along the northeastern frontier of his kingdom; only after many campaigns extending over thirty years was he able to conquer and convert them. The northeast frontier was also advanced by the conquest of Frisia. In 774 he crushed the troublesome Lombards, assumed the title of king of the Lombards, and laid claim to all of Italy except the Byzantine territories in the south and the Papal State, over which he continued the protectorship assumed by Pépin. His armies drove down the Danube and annexed territories held by the Avars and Slavs. His attack on Moslem Spain resulted initially in a defeat at Roncesvalles, later immortalized in an epic poem called *The Song of Roland*. But persistent pressure in that direction led to the creation of the Spanish March, a Frankish bridgehead south of the Pyrenees that threatened Moslem power. Frankish military might also curbed the separatist aspirations of the people of Aquitaine, Bavaria, and Brittany. Beyond the new frontiers established by conquest, and especially in central Europe and Denmark, Charlemagne combined force and diplomacy to compel various Slavic and Scandinavian peoples into a tributary status observing respect for Frankish territory and interests. He was even able to assert military pressure on Byzantine holdings in southern Italy and the northern Adriatic.

A tribute to Charlemagne's skill as a military organizer, these victories yielded a rich harvest of booty, which Charlemagne dispersed liberally to sustain the services and the allegiance of the warriors who fought the many battles and to win the favor of the nobles and church officials upon whose support royal power depended. But Charlemagne succeeded in surrounding his military ventures with an aura transcending mere material considerations. They were struggles against barbarians, pagans, and infidels, fought to save the Christian world and to win converts for the true religion. For his efforts he won the plaudits of popes, poets, and nobles, who hailed him as "the strong right arm of God." And he caught the attention of the larger world, as is demonstrated by his diplomatic exchanges with the emperors of Constantinople, the caliphs of Baghdad, the emirs of Moslem Spain, and the kings of England.

Charlemagne's military successes were accompanied by a strenuous effort to expand royal authority and improve the effectiveness of the central government within his growing realm. Charlemagne's concept of kingship was rooted firmly in the Germanic concept of the *bannum*, which entitled a ruler to command his subjects to serve him and to punish those who disobeyed. That Germanic basis of royal authority was elevated and enriched by ideas drawn from Christian concepts of royal authority and responsibility and of the public well-being. The Christian view of the state, rooted in Old Testament precedents and especially in Augustine's *City of God*, which was Charlemagne's favorite book, envisioned the state as a society of Christians linked together by a common faith for the purpose of realizing God's plan for humanity, including the salvation of each individual soul. To achieve that end, society must strive for right order, harmony, and justice, each defined in Christian terms. The key to achieving the good Christian society was the king. Like the biblical David, the Christian king was God's anointed agent, who was charged with commanding his subjects to do good and restraining them from evil. He was, in effect, God's minister in the cause of righteousness. This concept of royal power, sometimes called ministerial kingship, provided norms for defining governmental action and political behavior that were much broader than those that had prevailed in the Frankish state during the Merovingian period.

In applying his expanded concept of royal authority, Charlemagne utilized the basic political structures inherited from the Merovingians. What especially marked his reign was his own vigorous action aimed at making those structures work more effectively to realize Christian right order. He was a tireless worker, traveling constantly across his realm, checking incessantly on the performance of his officials, administering justice (see Figure 16.1), and consulting frequently with those upon whom he depended to sustain political order. At the heart of his government was the royal court (called the *palatium*), made up of trusted clergy and lay nobles. Collectively, the court circle advised the king in shaping policies. In addition, each member of the court was assigned a political function as practical needs demanded: guarding the royal treasury, judging cases, keeping records, conducting diplomatic missions, commanding armies, providing for the material needs of the royal family. The royal court was supported chiefly by the products collected from royal lands; additional support, never very predictable, came from war booty, tolls on trade, fines, and gifts offered the king in return for favors. The court moved constantly, chiefly to expedite military campaigns and to gain access to the produce from royal estates. Only near the end of his reign did Charlemagne establish a semipermanent residence at Aachen.

To assert his authority on the local level, Charlemagne relied on the traditional system of counties, of which there were about three hundred. In each county the king was represented by a count who administered justice, enforced order, and mustered the freemen of the county to military service. The counts were rewarded by grants of land from which they could derive income as long as they held office. The counts were served by a small group of subofficials, most of them concerned with administering justice. Bishops and abbots were also assigned important responsibilities in local affairs. Charlemagne tried hard to select capable men for these offices and to supervise their activities. He developed a system of sending out special agents (*missi*) to investigate what was going on, to instruct local officials on what the king expected, and to report back to the court on local conditions. He issued a constant stream of royal orders (*capitularies*) to inform local officials of royal intent and to direct their actions on a wide range of matters relating to public order. Almost every year, Charlemagne also called his officials and other great men of the realm to an assembly at his court, where he heard their concerns and proclaimed new regulations designed to govern their actions.

The operation of this modest political apparatus, which involved only a few thousand officials, depended heavily on the loyalty not only of royal officials but also of all of the king's subjects, especially the *potentes*, the powerful ones. Charlemagne was constantly concerned with expanding the bonds of loyalty. His own feats as a warrior played an important role in this respect. On several occasions he required all of his free subjects to swear an oath of fidelity, binding them to refrain from activities contrary to public order. He regularly bestowed gifts, derived chiefly from war booty, on those whose loyalty he especially prized. Most important of all, he greatly expanded the use of commendation and benefices to bind royal officials, nobles, and churchmen to him. Those who were willing to commend themselves under oath to become royal vassals were granted benefices, usually in the form of land grants or offices, to be enjoyed as long as the recipients served the king faithfully. Unfaithfulness to these oaths was considered a major offense.

In defining the royal office in terms that assigned to the king a God-given duty to sustain the Christian establishment in its mission of saving souls, Charlemagne assumed a major responsibility for religious life in his realm. Religious reform became a prime focus of his program, a policy pursued in a way that made the royal government the directive force in religious affairs and left to the clergy a subordinate role in the service of the ministerial king. Charlemagne assumed a lead role in the spread of Christianity, even using force to compel reluctant pagans, such as the Saxons, to receive baptism. He strengthened church organization by issuing legislation aimed at reestablishing the authority of bishops and subordinating parish priests to them. He sought to improve the quality of the clergy by imposing higher moral and educational standards on those who assumed ecclesiastical office. Monastic establishments were encouraged to adopt the Benedictine rule as a means of upgrading discipline and spiritual life. Royal authority was used to protect ecclesiastical property and to provide material support for the religious establishment; especially important was the imposition of a tax of 10 percent of income, called the *tithe,* on all Christians to support religious life. Charlemagne made a major effort to establish uniform doctrines and ritual practices as a way of eliminating the diverse practices and bizarre beliefs that passed as Christianity. In formulating his religious program, Charlemagne relied heavily on guidance from the papacy; especially close was his relationship with Pope Hadrian I (772–795). As a result, a distinctly Roman stamp was imposed on religious life in his realm. Charlemagne must be counted as a major architect of the Roman Catholic church and as a major force in enhancing the authority of the papacy in the West.

All of these achievements played a part in shaping the culminating event of Charlemagne's career: his coronation as emperor. The stage was set for this event when a disturbance in Rome in 799 led to charges of misconduct against Pope

Leo III (795–816), who was forced to flee to Charlemagne's court. In his role as protector of the pope and the Romans, Charlemagne went to Rome in 800 and acted directly to exonerate the pope and restore him to full authority. Then, on Christmas Day in the year 800, while the king was attending Mass in St. Peter's Basilica, the pope placed a crown on his head, and the clergy and people in attendance hailed the king of the Franks as "Augustus, crowned by God, the great and peace-bringing Emperor of the Romans." For the first time since 476 a ruler from the West was emperor.

Ever since that momentous occasion, there has been a debate about who instigated the renewal of the imperial office and what it signified. Perhaps responsibility for the event was shared by the pope, Charlemagne, and his advisers as a means of realizing different aspirations. For Leo III the bestowal of the crown offered a way to restore papal prestige, recently tainted by Leo's need to depend on Charlemagne merely to hold his office. For Charlemagne the new title was a suitable recognition for his accomplishments as conqueror and protector of the Christian world. Some of Charlemagne's ecclesiastical advisers felt that such a title would exalt their ruler's authority as a new David and a new Constantine seeking to perfect Christian society. Almost everyone in the West shared the opinion that the emperors of the East had failed to serve the Christian cause, especially in view of the fact that a woman, Empress Irene, held the crown at the moment. It is probably also true that Charlemagne's assumption of the imperial title meant different things to different people. The Byzantine rulers saw it as an outrageous usurpation. The popes, at least in the long run, interpreted the event as a precedent for their right to designate the ruler of the Christian world; in the short run, it was now clear beyond doubt who had the legal power to rule Rome. For many church leaders the event was a signal to intensify the effort to create the ideal Christian commonwealth.

What Charlemagne thought of his new title is likewise an enigma. He ruled as emperor for fourteen years. Some of his actions suggest that he took the title seriously. He conducted a skillful military and diplomatic campaign that finally compelled the Byzantine emperor to recognize him as emperor. He pursued his religious reforms with renewed vigor, suggesting a responsiveness to the political Augustinianism of those advisers who had encouraged him to become emperor. However, he disdained the trappings of the imperial office, and he insisted on being called king of the Franks. Contrary to all that the imperial title implied about the unity of his realm, he made plans to divide his empire in order to provide a "kingdom" for each of his three sons; such a division was avoided because only a single son, Louis, outlived him. In 813 Charlemagne personally crowned Louis emperor without papal involvement. These actions suggest that Charlemagne viewed the imperial title as a personal honor that he had earned by his achievements and that he could dispose of as he pleased. Whatever the case, the event of 800, which translated an ancient title rich in political symbolism into a Germanic and Christian context, was of major significance in creating a western European political consciousness.

3. THE CAROLINGIAN RENAISSANCE

Perhaps the most enduring facet of the Carolingian Age was a reinvigoration of cultural life that owed much to the personal interest and effort of the indefatigable Charlemagne. This revival was based on pragmatic motives. Charlemagne was convinced that political and religious reform could be achieved only through the efforts of better-educated leaders, especially the clergy, who were equipped to extract from the learned tradition of the past what the Carolingians called the "norms of rectitude" that would provide guidance in shaping a Christian renewal of the present world. Because of its focus on the past, especially the Roman and patristic worlds, modern historians often speak of a Carolingian "renaissance." Whatever it is called, the movement represented a radical idea in a society that had almost lost sight of the connection between learning and public order.

A major factor in generating cultural revival was Charlemagne's ability to utilize the intellectual leadership produced by the modest cultural revivals that had occurred earlier in several parts of the West—Italy, Spain, Ireland, and especially England. The setting for the interaction of these leaders was what has been called the palace "school," which the king began to form in the 780s and which took on special vigor in the 790s, after Aachen was established as the permanent royal residence. To this somewhat informal circle came some of the most learned individuals from all over Christian Europe, often with Charlemagne's personal encouragement. The palace school served as a setting where individuals of varying cultural perspectives met to study, write, and reflect on intellectual issues. Because Charlemagne himself was an active and enthusiastic participant, the palace school became a highly visible symbol of the dedication of his regime to revitalizing cultural life; some even spoke grandly of Aachen as the "new Athens."

More significantly, the palace school became a kind of laboratory, generating ideas and techniques out of which emerged an educational system that was crucial to the Carolingian renaissance. A key figure in shaping this educational program was Alcuin (735–804), an English monk reared in the monastic cultural environment that had produced Bede and Boniface. Alcuin served at the royal court from 782 to 796 and then became abbot of an important monastery at Tours, where he continued to assert leadership in cultural life until his death in 804. His concepts of education decisively shaped the thinking and practices of cultural leaders across the entire ninth century and even beyond.

Alcuin, and with him most Carolingian cultural figures, saw education as a preparation for understanding the holy literature that contained God's message, from which must be drawn the norms of rectitude that alone could guide the revitalization of Christian life: the Bible, the writings of the Church Fathers, the liturgical books, canon law texts, saints' lives. To comprehend the message of salvation contained in these texts, people must master Latin and acquire a body of knowledge and intellectual skills that would allow them to grasp their meaning. These objectives could best be achieved by organizing education around the old Roman system of the seven liberal arts, which consisted of two basic groupings of "disciplines": the *trivium*, embracing grammar, rhetoric, and dialectic (logic); and the *quadrivium*, comprising arithmetic, geometry, astronomy, and music.

The realization of these educational goals in their culturally impoverished world confronted Carolingian leaders with major challenges. They needed to provide textbooks for each of the seven arts, but especially for the *trivium*, which emphasized language study, effective writing, and logical thinking. The material for such textbooks was to be drawn from classical Latin literature, but textbook compilers had to adapt such material to Christian purposes. Once learners had mastered the skills and knowledge embraced in the seven liberal arts, then they needed to apply their minds to the texts containing true wisdom. This objective raised the problem of the quality and availability of books. A major effort was devoted to establishing authentic versions of Scripture, liturgical books, texts defining ecclesiastical and secular laws, writings of the Church Fathers, and even pagan Latin texts and Germanic legends. Once scholars had established sound texts, accurate copies had to be made. This need encouraged the development of workshops, called *scriptoria*, where book copying was systematically pursued; such work was particularly appropriate for Benedictine monks and nuns seeking to meet their obligation to serve God by working. Concerned with making reading easier, Carolingian copyists developed a simple but effective system of handwriting called Carolingian *minuscule*, which replaced the almost illegible Merovingian cursive writing with separately formed lowercase letters. The formation of libraries was also encouraged so that good texts would be widely available.

As the tools of education were forged, Charlemagne and his successors employed royal authority to universalize their use. Bishops and abbots were commanded to organize schools and to adopt authentic texts as a basis of teaching. This effort resulted in a significant increase in the number of schools and a heightened concern for the quality of teaching. Many bishops and abbots became active collectors of libraries and organizers of *scriptoria*. Although the palace school had declined in importance by the end of Charlemagne's reign, his successors remained active patrons of culture. However, during the ninth century cultural leadership passed to new centers, especially monastic schools, which effectively sustained the thrust of cultural revival even in the face of political decline.

Although Carolingian educational reform

had only a limited impact on the massive illiteracy afflicting all levels of society, it did have significant consequences in shaping an environment more favorable to learning than had existed since late Roman imperial times. The concern with language instruction led to the development of a simplified, flexible form of Latin that became the standard means of literary expression over much of the West. The effort to establish authentic versions of a wide variety of texts created a substantial base of knowledge on which a common intellectual life could be erected. That effort also reestablished contacts with the learning and literature of classical Rome and the patristic age; almost all surviving versions of classical Latin literary works date from the Carolingian period. The capacity for clear thinking and effective writing was considerably improved. Taken together, these developments established the base on which a creative, independent western European intellectual and literary life would eventually develop.

A measure of the impact of the Carolingian renaissance can be found in the literary works produced by leading Carolingian writers and scholars. One court luminary and longtime confidant of Charlemagne, Einhard (ca. 770–840), produced an excellent biography of his master; many other writers tried their hands at biography, especially saints' lives. An Italian, Paul the Deacon (ca. 720–799), wrote a *History of the Lombards* which reflected the capacity of Carolingian writers to produce historical works. Alcuin, Bishop Hincmar of Reims (ca. 806–882), and many others produced lively letters reflecting the major concerns of the age. Theodulf (ca. 750–821), a Spaniard, was but one among many who composed poetry. Several clerics, including Bishop Jonas of Orléans (ca. 780–843), composed books intended to guide princes which reflect considerable sophistication in political thought. A succession of theologians prepared impressive commentaries on Scripture and compiled significant tracts on specific doctrinal points; especially notable as theologians were Hrabanus Maurus (ca. 780–856), abbot of Fulda, and John Scotus Erigena (ca. 810–877), an Irishman who lived in Francia from 850 to 875. Even lay society was affected by the cultural revival to the point where some nonclerics were able to produce literary works of some distinction; not the least was the noble lady Dhuoda, whose handbook prepared to provide moral guidance for her son reflects her good education, her considerable literary talent, and her excellent grasp of Christian precepts. Although most Carolingian scholarly work was derived from earlier works, it did reflect an ability to interpret tradition in terms applicable to contemporary issues. That dimension of Carolingian learning can be grasped only when one observes in detail how the light of learning played on and shaped the efforts of kings, bishops, abbots, scholars, and even lay nobles to cope with a myriad of problems facing the age.

The forces unleashed by the effort to renew Christian life and culture stimulated artistic activity. Carolingian art borrowed from diverse traditions: classical, Byzantine, Germanic, Celtic. The age produced several impressive churches; the most unique was the one built by Charlemagne at Aachen. That octagonal structure, strongly influenced by Byzantine churches in Ravenna, reflects an effort to make architecture a link between religion and the ideology of royalty. The mosaics and frescoes created to decorate churches and the miniature paintings used to illustrate manuscripts reflect skill in producing narrative art, especially in visually reconstructing episodes from sacred history. Carolingian artists produced fine ivory carvings, metalwork, and jewelry, much of which was employed for liturgical purposes. Underlying most Carolingian art was a powerful urge to deepen religious understanding and promote piety. In this respect, art shared the basic urge that sustained the entire Carolingian renaissance.

4. THE DISINTEGRATION OF THE CAROLINGIAN EMPIRE

The religious revival and the cultural renewal initiated by Charlemagne retained their momentum for most of the century after his death. However, his political achievements were less permanent, leaving many unresolved issues for his successors. His son, Louis the Pious (814–840), continued his father's policies with some success. His chief energies were devoted to realizing the ideal of a unified Christian society governed according to Christian principles. In pursuit of this end he formed a close alliance with powerful churchmen that was dedicated to solidifying the unity of the realm, extending religious reform, and deepening cultural renewal. But Louis's course, basically aimed at perfecting ministerial kingship in a direction that magnified the role of the clergy and the centrality of religious values in shaping political life, met resistance from important elements in society which saw political life primarily in terms of advancing the interests of the powerful. Consequent tensions laid bare the basic weaknesses of the Carolingian system.

The most disruptive problem during Louis's reign involved the question of succession. As we have already noted, ancient Frankish custom demanded that a ruler divide his realm among his surviving sons. With minor exceptions—which were resolved without major disturbances—the Carolingian rulers did not have to face the issue of multiple heirs until the reign of Louis. In the face of this problem, Louis's intention, expressed clearly in a document issued in 817, was to preserve the unity of the empire by entrusting the imperial title and authority over the entire empire to his eldest son, with the younger heirs receiving subkingdoms. Throughout the rest of his reign Louis was forced to compromise his plan in the face of intrigue, factionalism, and even civil war fomented by his younger sons, by their noble supporters, and especially by his second wife, Judith, who was anxious to protect the interests of her son by Louis against the claims of his half brothers. On Louis's death his oldest son, Lothair, did succeed to the imperial title but with only a very vague authority over his two younger brothers, each of whom received a kingdom. The pretext of imperial unity lasted only briefly. Shortly after Louis's death, the younger sons declared war on Emperor Lothair and in 843 forced him to sign the Treaty of Verdun. This document legalized the division of the empire into three independent entitites: the kingdom of the West Franks (roughly modern France), to be ruled by Charles the Bald; the kingdom of the East Franks (roughly modern Germany), assigned to Louis the German; and the kingdom of Lotharingia (Lothair's realm), a narrow band lying between the western and eastern kingdoms and stretching from the North Sea to Italy (see Map 16.2). The Treaty of Verdun provided that the ruler of the middle kingdom would hold the imperial title, but his authority over the other

Map 16.2 PARTITION OF THE CAROLINGIAN EMPIRE, 843 This map shows the divisions of the unified Carolingian Empire arranged by the sons of Louis the Pious at the Treaty of Verdun in 843. The kingdom of Louis the German (the Kingdom of the East Franks) and the kingdom of Charles the Bald (Kingdom of the West Franks) became the bases from which Germany and France would evolve. Lothar I's kingdom was later divided into three small kingdoms, the most important of which was the Kingdom of Italy.

kings was only nominal. Later in the ninth century the middle kingdom was further divided to create three kingdoms: Italy, Burgundy, and Lotharingia. With the passing of time the imperial office lost all meaning except to the papacy, which used it to reward anyone willing to protect papal interests in Rome.

The struggles surrounding the succession issue revealed another threat to imperial authority. Louis found many of his royal vassals ready to desert him and to align themselves with one or another of his sons in return for additional benefices. This situation revealed that Charlemagne's widespread use of vassalage and benefice to create bonds of loyalty to the ruler had its dangers. The granting of land and offices to vassals as a means of winning or holding their political support began to diminish royal property, the basic source of support for the government, and to weaken royal control over public admin-

FIGURE 16.2 The Viking Terror This representation of Viking ships filled with fierce warriors illustrates why they struck terror into those who witnessed the vessels approaching their undefended shores. One senses that the artist had witnessed such a scene. (Culver Pictures)

istration. Such benefices became the basis upon which recipients expanded their independence without concern for the obligations they owed. Their growing power allowed them to demand new grants in return for service, thus creating a vicious cycle that undermined royal authority and expanded the power of the landed nobility.

During Louis's reign another ominous danger emerged: mounting attacks from external foes. From bases in North Africa came assaults by sea by aggressive Moslems called Saracens, who ravaged the coasts of Italy and southern France. From the east the empire was attacked by still another wave of invaders from Asia, the Magyars or Hungarians, skilled at hit-and-run attacks by mounted warriors. Most formidable were the Vikings or Norsemen (Danes, Swedes, and Norwegians). Still barbarians and pagans,

the Vikings lived along the wild coasts of Scandinavia, surviving chiefly by fishing and piracy. Late in the eighth century, for reasons not entirely clear, they began to expand. Traveling by sea in small groups, they raided an immense area, touching Ireland, England, the Atlantic coast of Europe, the southern shores of the North and Baltic seas, Russia, Iceland, Greenland, and even North America (see Figure 16.2). Wherever they went, they pillaged for booty and struck terror into their victims. Gradually some of them began to settle permanently in the lands they had been raiding, especially Ireland, northern England, Iceland, a region in northwestern France called Normandy after them, and the area in Russia around Novgorod and Kiev. Slowly their piracy gave way to trade and they adopted the religion and culture of western Europeans. But that was too late to spare the Carolingian Empire from the destructive fury of this last wave of Germanic invaders.

The Carolingian military establishment, organized primarily for attack warfare on land and completely lacking in naval forces, was helpless against these highly mobile marauders. The only effective way to deal with them was to organize local defenses under local leaders willing to assume that responsibility and capable of acting on their own. By assuming this burden, nobles greatly expanded their control over local political affairs. From Louis the Pious onward, kings had no choice but to reward these individuals for their military role with additional grants of land and authority, a process that further undermined royal power.

During the last half of the ninth century royal authority in each of the Carolingian kingdoms steadily declined. The energies of their rulers were absorbed in rivalaries aimed at snatching territory from one another. They had no choice but to continue seeking the support of the powerful in society by granting new lands and conceding political power. As a consequence, the landed nobles tightened their control over local territories, creating increasing numbers of independent principalities and forcing the peasantry into dependence. Invaders continued to pillage western Europe almost at will. The most persistent defenders of royal power were ecclesiastical officials, but in the long run even ecclesiastical support worked against the interests of the Carolingian monarchs. Constantly mindful of the important role Charlemagne had attributed to religious leaders in creating Christian order, later Carolingian churchmen became bolder and bolder in their attempts to control the shape of public policy. Frankish bishops repeatedly challenged royal authority and criticized royal conduct. By the middle of the ninth century the pope was openly claiming superior authority over all Christians, including kings and emperors. Pope Nicholas I (858–867) actually tried to assert such claims by interfering in the private lives of Carolingian kings, negotiating to halt civil strife, legislating for the entire Church in the West, taking the lead in spreading Christianity, and doing battle with Byzantine emperors over dogma and jurisdiction—all activities that Charlemagne had claimed to control as ministerial king and em-

peror. And even while expressing lofty sentiments about their role as protectors of Christian order, high church officials joined lay nobles in increasing their landholdings and political power over local affairs at the expense of the royal government.

By 900 the Carolingian rulers had been reduced to impotence. The effort to create, in western Europe, a single Christian state where concord and justice prevailed had foundered. However, this failure must not hide the deeper significance of the Carolingian era. The redefinition of the nature of the state and of the role of the Christian ruler, the religious reform, the cultural renaissance, the revival of empire, the expanded role defined for the papacy, and the expansion of personal bonds as an element of public order would all affect the future shape of western European society. Much of later medieval history consisted of working out the concepts about civilized life given embryonic form in the "first" Europe shaped in Carolingian times.

5. ANGLO-SAXON ENGLAND

While the Carolingians were attempting to renew society on the Continent, active rulers and their followers were pursuing comparable ends in England. The Anglo-Saxon invasions of England in the fifth century had virtually wiped out Roman civilization. Latin culture, including the language, had been replaced by Germanic culture and religion. The newcomers established several small kingdoms whose political institutions were almost completely Germanic. These kingdoms constantly warred with one another to create a condition almost as chaotic as that prevailing on the Continent between 500 and 750.

The introduction of Christianity into this divided society provided an important impetus to the development of a common culture. Late in the sixth century missionaries from Ireland and Rome went to England and within a century had converted most of the land. For a brief period in the seventh century, Roman and Irish forces clashed over the right to dominate England. The Roman forces won, chiefly because of the support offered by the Anglo-Saxon kings. This victory ensured uniformity in ecclesiastical organization, ritual, and doctrine and put England into touch with the mainstream of Continental religious life. The encounter of Irish monasticism and Roman Benedictine monasticism generated a vigorous cultural revival in England, that reached its zenith in the age of Bede in the early eighth century. As already noted, that revival also produced leaders such as Boniface and Alcuin, who helped shape the Carolingian revival and who strengthened the ties between England and the Carolingian world.

During the eighth and ninth centuries, England suffered devastating blows from the Vikings. Some of these raiders occupied a large area in northeastern England known as the Danelaw (see Map 16.1). The Viking raids also destroyed several of the old Anglo-Saxon kingdoms. The kingdom of Wessex became the center of resistance and eventually of counterattack against the Vikings. The reign of Alfred the Great (871–899) was the decisive moment. He not only stopped Viking expansion but also laid the groundwork for the reconquest of the Danelaw. Under his leadership religious and cultural life was revitalized. During the tenth century, Alfred's successors rewon the Danelaw and in the process created a unified kingdom for England.

The unification of England led to a single political system that was heavily influenced by ancient Anglo-Saxon institutions. A king, claiming to be supreme judge, army leader, head of the religious establishment, and lawgiver, ruled over the kingdom. Royal authority was supported by the household officials who constituted the royal court. The king supported himself and his court chiefly from the income from royal estates. However, he could levy direct taxes on his subjects; for example, several kings collected the Danegeld, a tax first levied in 991 to buy off Viking raiders. The monarch retained the authority to summon all freemen to serve in the army (called the *fyrd*). He could also depend on the military services of his noble retainers, called *thegns*, whose support was won by grants of land. He was advised on matters of public interest by the *Witan*, an assembly of great nobles and churchmen that was held to represent all freemen. However, a strong king could act without this body's approval. This complex of institutions surrounding the king made the central government of England a significant force in public life, much more so than the late Carolingian monarchs were.

A crucial factor in the political order was the system of local government that had developed over a long period. The kingdom was divided into territorial units called *shires*, of which there were about forty in the tenth century. In each shire the king's interests were represented by three officials—the earl, the sheriff, and the bishop. The earl was the most notable in rank and prestige, but the sheriff conducted most of the royal business. A court was held in each shire twice a year, and all free individuals were expected to attend. Royal orders were proclaimed and all civil and criminal cases were adjudicated at this court. Although Anglo-Saxon kings could and did enact laws binding on their subjects, the law administered was primarily customary law, dating from far back in Anglo-Saxon history and "remembered" by the influential members of each shire. Each shire was subdivided into *hundreds*, where courts presided over by a royal official met monthly to settle minor cases; the hundreds also provided the basis for recruiting military forces for the *fyrd*. Agricultural villages also had their own courts, usually conducted by landowners. This network of local institutions, providing a means by which royal authority could be applied at the local level, acted as a buffer against the emergence of private political power and political fragmentation so characteristic of the Continent in the tenth century.

Although by the eleventh century the Anglo-Saxon political order began to falter, the pattern of institutions created in the ninth and tenth centuries provided a heritage that would play a major role in shaping a unique English constitutional system in the future.

SUGGESTED READING

The Carolingian World

The works of Wallace-Hadrill, James, Duby, Doehaerd, Hodges, and Herrin listed in Chapter 15 provide material on Carolingian history. The following titles treat special aspects.

Donald Bullough, *The Age of Charlemagne*, 2nd ed. (1973). An excellent general overview of Carolingian civilization.

Pierre Riché, *The Carolingians: A Family Who Forged Europe*, trans. Michael I. Allen (1993). A good political history.

Rosamond McKitterick, *The Frankish Kingdom under the Carolingians, 751–987* (1983). Especially helpful on the later Carolingians.

Pierre Riché, *Daily Life in the World of Charlemagne*, trans. Jo Ann McNamara (1978). Rich in details on Carolingian life.

Robert Folz, *The Coronation of Charlemagne: 25 December 800*, trans. J. E. Anderson (1974). A balanced treatment of a disputed subject.

Hubert Jedin and John Dolan, eds., *Handbook of Church History*, Vol. 3: *The Church in the Age of Feudalism*, trans. Anselm Biggs (1969). A detailed treatment of religious life.

Rosamond McKitterick, *The Frankish Church and the Carolingian Reforms, 789–895* (1977). A good assessment of Carolingian religious reform.

John Marenbon, *Early Medieval Philosophy (400–1150). An Introduction* (1983). Places the Carolingian intellectual achievement in a larger historical context.

J. Hubert et al., *The Carolingian Renaissance* (1970). A magnificent treatment of Carolingian art.

The Vikings

Gwyn Jones, *A History of the Vikings*, rev. ed. (1984).

P. H. Sawyer, *Kings and Vikings: Scandinavia and Europe, A.D. 700–1000* (1982).

Two excellent treatments of Viking history and the Viking impact on the European world.

Anglo-Saxon England

Peter Hunter Blair, *An Introduction to Anglo-Saxon England*, 2nd ed. (1977).

P. H. Sawyer, *From Roman Britain to Norman England* (1978).

Two concise, clearly written surveys of Anglo-Saxon history.

H. R. Loyn, *The Governance of Anglo-Saxon England, 500–1087* (1984). Excellent on Anglo-Saxon political institutions.

Sources

Two Lives of Charlemagne, trans. Lewis Thorpe (1969). Contains the famous biography by Einhard.

P. D. King, *Charlemagne: Translated Sources* (1987). A good sampling of the Carolingian cultural achievement.

CHAPTER 17
Lordship and Dependency: Feudalism and Manorialism

FIGURE 17.1 The Bastion of Local Lordship: The Medieval Castle Castles such as this one were built over much of western Europe during the eleventh and twelfth centuries as centers from which local potentates and their armed vassals could assert lordship over the surrounding countryside and its inhabitants. This castle, Château Gaillard, built in the late twelfth century on a cliff above the Seine River by King Richard of England to protect his Norman fiefdom from his feudal overlord, the king of France, was virtually impregnable. Outer walls (whose ruins are still visible) and a moat protected the inner fortress and its keep. Living quarters, a great meeting hall, and a chapel were built in the inner courtyard of this structure. (Roger-Viollet)

Chiefly as a result of the failure of the late Carolingians to sustain a strong central government and of the devastations caused by the Saracen, Magyar, and Viking assaults, western European society underwent a new era of instability during the late ninth, tenth, and early eleventh centuries. However, amid these difficulties new institutional patterns began to move to the forefront. This new order was the fruit of a complex process which since the end of the Roman imperial order had been transforming the basic relationships that defined political, social, and economic life. The result of this process became manifest about 1000 in the form of new human communities. The restructuring of society took a variety of forms across western Europe, thus making any attempt at generalization difficult and even misleading. But everywhere certain key patterns emerged that together would provide the basis for a remarkable revival of western European society after 1000.

1. LORDSHIP AND DEPENDENCY

As we have seen, one of the notable features of the western European world during the early Middle Ages was the inability of political leaders to establish effective central governments capable of exercising authority over large numbers of subjects in the interest of the public welfare. A major consequence of this failure was a slow drift toward the privatization of power in the hands of landholders. This trend was given final impetus in the late Carolingian period by the failure of the successors of Charlemagne to sustain his effort to create a strong state. The partition of the Carolingian Empire after 843 resulted in a diminution of royal resources in each of the Carolingian kingdoms. In their attempts to muster support, the late Carolingian kings slowly granted away their royal holdings to powerful nobles and great ecclesiastical officials; technically such grants were made in return for loyalty and service, but the recipients increasingly disregarded their obligations. The inability of the kings to defend their realms against invaders eroded their prestige and necessitated an increasing reliance for security on local power wielders. Although kingdoms and kingship survived this ordeal, by the tenth century public authority had become a limited force in the lives of most people in the West.

As public authority disintegrated, a new force emerged as the dominant feature of political life. *Private lordships* controlled by individual landholders replaced the state as the effective directive force in society. These lordships were formed in various ways. In some cases, Carolingian public officials, such as dukes, counts, and viscounts, simply arrogated to private use the public authority associated with their offices as well as the territory embraced in their jurisdictions. In other instances, aggressive landowners, with the support of armed followers, forcefully seized control of a territory and imposed their private rule on its inhabitants. Often the key to the success of such lords was their control of castles as the focal points of their military power (see Figure 17.1); thus, they are often referred to as *castellans*. In still other cases, enterprising nobles fashioned lordships out of lands they owned or gained through marriage alliances or received as benefices for services rendered to others under the terms of the feudal contract, which will be examined later. But whatever the means, the results were the same: the fragmentation of kingdoms into a mosaic of private lordships in which powerful individuals exercised control over those who lived within their principalities. Some of these lords occasionally paid a shadowy allegiance to the impotent kings within whose kingdoms their lordships lay, but in reality each was "king" in his own principality.

The development of lordship was accompanied by the spread of *dependency* in various forms. Since late Roman times a variety of forces had been at work to encourage or compel individuals to place themselves in a position of dependence on other individuals under conditions that regulated their political, economic, and social interactions on a private basis beyond the sphere of public authority. By the tenth century almost everyone, including many who exercised some kind of lordship, was a dependent in some form. The conditions of dependency varied enormously from place to place and from person to person. However, two broad categories existed to determine the status of most dependents.

First, some lived in a condition of noble dependency. A prime requirement for those who succeeded in creating and then sustaining independent lordships was military force. To provide this force, lords gathered around themselves armed followers who were willing to provide military service in return for material considerations sufficient to allow them to live a life befitting their warrior status. In some cases, lords supported their retainers as a part of their households, but more often military followers were given grants of land from which a living could be derived. As we shall see, the conditions governing the relationships between lords and followers came to be institutionalized in forms that defined a unique way of life for those involved. Although armed retainers were originally drawn from all levels of life, by the tenth century they along with their lords had come to claim a special status for themselves as nobles.

Second, the bulk of the population lived in a condition of servile dependency. In a world where almost everyone from the most powerful to the lowliest depended on agriculture for a livelihood, those who exercised lordship and their noble dependents required a peasant labor force to till the soil from which power and wealth were derived. They gained it by asserting their jurisdiction over the peasant population in a way that compelled peasants to perform a range of menial services related to agricultural production and to render dues to the lord. The reduction of the peasantry to dependency had been evolving over many centuries, powerfully abetted by the unsettled political conditions that had forced the peasants to seek security at whatever cost. By the tenth century the dominance of the powerful had become nearly complete, subject to almost no controls by public authority. In the process of establishing domination over their servile dependents, lords had in many cases congregated their peasants into village communities to expedite effective management of their labor and the exaction of dues. As was the case with noble dependency, by the tenth century the conditions governing servile dependency had assumed institutional forms that gave stability and permanence to the system.

2. THE COMMUNITY OF THE POWERFUL: THE FEUDAL ORDER

By the tenth century the relationships among the powerful—the lords and their noble dependents—were defined and controlled by a variety of interlocking forces whose impact varied from place to place and time to time. On rare occasions, the community of the powerful might be influenced by the commands of the king in whose realm they lived. Some whose lordships were derived from possession of a former royal office sought to employ the powers inherent in those public offices to define their authority over their noble dependents. All members of the community of the powerful shared the Christian religion, which set forth certain precepts about social behavior. Powerful kinship ties shaped the concerns and actions of all members of the community of the powerful. In short, by 1000 the community of the powerful drew its solidarity from a variety of forces.

In many places in western Europe—although not everywhere—relationships among the members of the dominant warrior class were given a special configuration by a set of institutions called *feudalism*. Over the centuries this term has been given so many ambiguous meanings that some historians question its usefulness in describing the medieval sociopolitical order. However, certain practices associated with it can serve to highlight certain concepts of fundamental importance to the order prevailing in the community of the powerful.

The essential practices associated with tenth-century feudalism grew out of the merger, over the course of many centuries, of two practices with roots in both the Roman and the Germanic worlds: personal dependence and shared rights in land tenure. The confusion and chaos in western Europe following the Germanic migrations encouraged the spread of these ancient institutions. In search of strong protectors, many were willing to enter a *commendation* agreement, which established a personal bond linking the two individuals—often called *lord* and *vassal*—to each other in a way that was mutually useful. Likewise, those in search of a livelihood or a way to enlarge their holdings were willing to accept the use of another's land in return for some kind of service. The lands involved in such grants, called *benefices*, remained the property of the grantor and could thus be made without diminishing one's basic holdings. The Carolingian rulers relied heavily on commendation and benefices to solidify control over their subjects and to support their military forces, thereby expanding these practices across a much broader spectrum of society and giving them status in public law. In many cases, kings also granted their vassals *immunities*, which forbade royal officials to interfere in the governance of their benefices, increasingly called *fiefs*. With the breakdown of royal power after about 850, those seeking to establish private lordships utilized these practices as a means of creating military followings. They gathered around them a circle of followers who agreed to serve as vassals in return for fiefs that gave to each vassal the use of land and a labor force that would provide the basis for status, wealth, and security. Feudal usages took deepest root in the heartland of the Carolingian empire—the land between the Loire and Rhine rivers; from there these practices spread in modified forms to southern France, England, Germany, Spain, southern Italy, and the Holy Land.

Central to the arrangements creating the lord-vassal bond was the establishment of a mutually binding contract between two free persons. The ritual that evolved to mark entrance into such a contract provides a convenient key to the nature of the feudal bond (see Figure 17.2). By a voluntary act called *homage* (after the Latin world *homo*, "man"), one man knelt before another, placed his hands between the other's, and declared himself willing to become his "man," that is, his vassal. Whereupon the second lifted up the first and gave him a kiss signifying that he as lord accepted the other as his man. To solidify the lord-vassal relationship thus established, the vassal then swore an oath of *fealty*, binding himself in the sight of God to be faithful to his lord. The lord then gave his new vassal a token material object symbolizing *investiture* with a fief, that is, something of value in the form of a piece of land, an office, or a money stipend which the vassal could use to support himself. By the acts of homage, fealty, and investiture, two individuals bound themselves together in a way that gave each rights and imposed on each obligations through which their political and social interactions were controlled. By the tenth century the lord-vassal relationship had become hereditary, ensuring that the bonds would continue within the same families for generations.

The specific rights and obligations of lords and vassals were slowly elaborated over time in a special legal system called feudal law. Although feudal law varied widely across western

FIGURE 17.2 The Feudal Contract: The Act of Homage This scene pictures the basic act creating the feudal contract—the act of homage by which the kneeling men became vassals of the seated lord. (Archive of the Crown of Aragon, Barcelona/MAS)

Europe, certain rights and obligations binding on each party in the contract were fairly standard.

The feudal contract established the lord's right to command his vassal's services and to expect obedience from his vassal; in this sense, the lord exercised authority over his vassal. He retained important rights over the fief he had granted to his vassal for the latter's use. The lord was obligated to protect his vassal and to provide him justice—to use his army to defend his vassal against attacks and to maintain a court where the vassal could receive a hearing for any grievances. Put briefly, the lord had the grave responsibility of running a small-scale government to serve the mutual needs of himself and his vassals.

The vassal also had important rights and obligations. He was entitled to the use of the fief and the respect of the lord. In return, he was expected to conduct himself honorably and loyally toward his lord. More specifically, a vassal owed his lord four basic obligations: first, *military service*, which required the vassal to serve at his own expense as an armed knight for a specified length of time each year, usually forty days; second, giving *counsel*, usually defined as compulsory attendance at the lord's court; third, payment of *aids* in the form of money payments in certain specific situations (ransoming the lord, the knighting of the lord's eldest son, the marriage dowry of the lord's eldest daughter); and fourth, *hospitality*, which involved entertainment of the lord and his entourage when the lord visited the fief that the vassal had received. In addition, the vassal was obliged to respect certain usages, called feudal *incidents*, reflecting the lord's rights in the fief and its transmission to the vassal's heirs.

The enforcement of the terms of these private contracts posed constant problems, especially in a society lacking effective public authority. In fact, lords and vassals had to settle disputes surrounding rights and obligations themselves. The chief instrument was the lord's court, where the custom governing the feudal contract was applied as law. A lord could summon to his court any of his vassals accused of infidelity to be judged by the vassal's "peers"—other vassals of the lord—and, if found guilty, to be punished as custom dictated. To this same court every vassal could bring complaints against his lord or his fellow vassals; again, his peers decided whether he had redress. Despite this machinery, force was always the final recourse, with the result that feudal society was plagued by constant petty wars fought to force fulfillment of obligations and to gain redress for violation of rights. It would be wrong, however, to picture lords and vassals as seeking any opportunity to start a brawl. In a society lacking effective means of keeping order, both lords and vassals were often willing and even anxious to observe the terms of the contract that served their mutual interests.

The elements involved in the feudal contract provided the basis for the formation of communities among the powerful. An individual with land at his disposal was able to form a circle of vassals made up of individuals willing to provide specified services to their common lord in return for fiefs that allowed them to meet their material needs on a basis befitting their status. By fulfilling the obligations implicit in the contract binding the lord and his vassals, all of the members of such groupings were able to provide defense and justice for themselves and security for their property and those who tilled it.

How large could such circles be? In theory, an entire kingdom might constitute a single feudal community. At the top of such a theoretical community stood the king as supreme lord, who could divide his kingdom into large fiefs he would then grant to nobles, who became royal vassals in return for services commensurate with the size of the fief. By a process known as *subinfeudation*, each royal vassal could then subdivide his fief to create a second layer of vassals, who in turn could repeat the process until the entire kingdom was subdivided into fiefs just large enough to support a single warrior vassal. From such a process would emerge an orderly hierarchy in which each successive layer of vassals owed allegiance and service to a lord standing one step higher in the hierarchy.

In reality, there were limits on how large communities based on feudal bonds could be. In trying to provide fiefs for too many vassals, a lord ran the danger of depleting his landed resources to the point where he deprived himself of the means of compelling his vassals to render the services they owed. The larger a community based on feudal usages, the more vulnerable it became to disruption by individual vassals who by attaching themselves to several lords acquired sufficient fiefs to create a resource base large enough to permit them to defy all of their lords. Communities of the powerful based on feudal ties were most effective when they involved limited numbers of mutually interdependent warrior nobles concentrated within a small geographical area and directed by competent lords who knew how to compel or persuade their vassals to meet their obligations. Historians are still engaged in trying to reconstruct the relationships governing the working of such communities. Their inquiries leave no doubt that the bonds of lordship and noble dependence did provide a basis for order among limited circles of powerful figures and their servile dependents that restored some semblance of stability to western European society.

Beyond shaping the compact circles of lords and vassals within which order could be maintained, the practices and concepts undergirding feudal arrangements brought into sharp focus a special ethos and style of life that gave distinction to the lords and their noble dependents as a social class. Although the evolution of the western European nobility involved factors reaching back to the Roman and Germanic worlds, the conditions that surrounded lordship and noble dependence finally brought into focus the functions that defined noble status. That group consisted of those capable of engaging in warfare at their own expense using the resources derived from land under their control. Collectively, that group claimed responsibility for protecting and governing society. Although those who enjoyed this distinctive status constitutued a small portion of the total population, the nobility was by no means a closed caste during the tenth and eleventh centuries. In their eagerness to build followings to support their power, lords were willing to accept as vassals free individuals from the lower levels of society who were willing and able to perform miltiary service; such individuals were even attractive as sons-in-law. Since vassalage brought material rewards and status, such individuals were eager to accept it.

The values associated with nobility, reflected with special force in medieval vernacular literature (see Chapter 22), stemmed chiefly from what was vital to sustaining the bonds of lordship and vassalage: loyalty, bravery, faithfulness, generosity. Above all else stood prowess—the ability to excel in warfare. The life of a noble centered on a career of fighting for his lord, his lands, his family, his dependent peasants—and his God. In early youth, he began to learn his craft as an apprentice in the service of someone who already knew the art of warfare, often his father's lord. The culmination of his education was his knighting, an elaborate ceremony surrounded by religious symbolism that climaxed with his receiving the tools of war; these were used often during his adult life. Of course, he had to sustain himself as a warrior, so the management of the lands received as a fief constituted a part of his vocation. And he had a political function stemming from his position as the vassal of another and probably as lord over still others.

The life of the tenth-century nobility was crude and rough, in part because of the primitive level of economic life and in part because of the habits and mentality of its members. The typical noble residence was a wooden fortress designed for defense rather than comfort. The living quarters were crowded, sparsely furnished, cold, without sanitary facilities, and lacking in privacy. The routine of life featured pursuits typical of male warriors: heavy eating, drinking, gambling, hunting, dancing, wenching, and warfare. Nobles were usually illiterate, "reading" by listening to tales of war sung by bards and to the simple preachings of the priests. Marriage was arranged with an eye toward gaining new lands, more vassals, and stronger lords; seldom was it marred by considerations of sentiment. But the family was another matter, for a household rich in strong sons and nubile daughters was a great asset in a world of war, land acquisition, and personal relationships. Most families shared inheritance with all members of the nuclear family and placed emphasis on maintaining ties with an extended kinship group. Nobles were religious in a simple way: They trusted God to take care of them if they met their obligations as warrior lords and vassals. Their way of expressing their faith was active, impelling them to do something visible to show their piety—build a church, give land to a monastery to ensure prayers for their souls, go on a pilgrimage, or fight for God.

The community of the powerful was dominated by males. Women were accorded inferior legal standing. They were usually excluded from the ranks of lords and vassals; their social status reflected that of their fathers and husbands. Their marriage, the crucial event in determining on whom they would be dependent most of their lives, was controlled by males seeking to enhance family status in a world dominated by warrior landholders. Unless they betook themselves to a convent, unmarried women were a liability to their families. Noble daughters were married young, often to men much older. This situation, coupled with the dangers of warfare, often resulted in widowhood and the burdens of protecting the interests of minor children. But despite their general subservience, women played important roles in sustaining noble society. In a world where concubinage was common, it was the legal wife of a noble male who bestowed legitimacy on those eligible to share the family wealth. Women took an active part in directing the household servants, who produced most of what was needed to sustain the noble household. On occasion, women managed fiefs when their husbands were absent and adjudicated disputes involving their husbands' vassals. Their dowries—over which they maintained control—were often crucially important in expanding the landholdings their husbands could exploit. Women were frequently called upon to witness legal transactions involving land transfers, suggesting an involvement in sustaining the family fortune and a knowledge of the substance of that fortune.

3. THE COMMUNITY OF THE SERVILE: MANORIALISM

The community of the powerful concerned chiefly with warfare and governance rested on an agricultural base. Members of the nobility exercised control over parcels of land of varying sizes that each noble had to exploit in order to sustain himself and his family and to fulfill the complex obligations implicit in noble status. To exploit those lands, the nobility imposed another order of dependency on the peasantry of western Europe. This system, sometimes called the *seigneurial* system, was shaped over a long period out of elements rooted in Germanic and Roman economic and social institutions. By the tenth century the essential features of the system were in place: Each noble had imposed on the peasant inhabitants of the land he controlled an organizational structure that allowed him to command their labor, take a portion of their produce, and govern them. Although agricultural structures varied from place to place, many lords, especially those living in the highly productive area stretching from southern England across northern France and western Germany into northern Italy, organized their land into one or more large estates called *manors*.

The manor was an economic unit organized to produce everything needed by its seigneur and his dependent peasants (see Map 17.1). It was also a political and social unit that provided for the governance of the peasants living there and defined their relationships with their seigneur and with one another. The typical manor's size was determined by the requirements of self-sufficiency. A workable manor required a balanced combination of arable land for raising cereal crops, meadowland for animal support, and woodland for fuel and building material. The seigneur usually reserved one-third to one-half of the arable land as his *demesne,* from which he took all of the produce for his own support. The rest was divided into tenancies, called *mansi* or *hides,* each large enough to support a peasant household. The products of meadows, pastures, wastelands, and woods were shared in common by the manorial community. Under the widely used *open-field* system, the tillable land was divided into large, unfenced plots whose cultivation required extensive cooperation among the peasants. Each open field was subdivided into strips. The seigneur reserved a third to a half of these strips in each large field as his demesne; the tenancy of each peasant was made up of strips located in each open field. To protect the fertility of the soil, part of the land was left idle each year. During the tenth century a *two-field system* of rotation was widely used, with half of the manor's tillable land seeded each year while the other half was left idle. Most peasants supplemented the return from their tenancies with vegetables grown in small, well-fertilized gardens near the huts in which they lived. Yields on most manors were small, discouraging the keeping of animals that could lighten human labor, such as horses and oxen, which were heavy consumers of grain and hay. However, pigs, poultry, and goats, which could live by scavenging in the woods and wastelands, were common.

Since there was little trade in the tenth century, most manufactured goods were made on the manor. Although specialized artisans such as blacksmiths and carpenters plied their trades on some manors, ordinary peasants generally made and repaired equipment, buildings, and furnishings. Women, including noble ladies, made clothing, preserved food, and concocted medicines. Only a few crucial items, such as metals, salt, and wine, came to most manors from out-

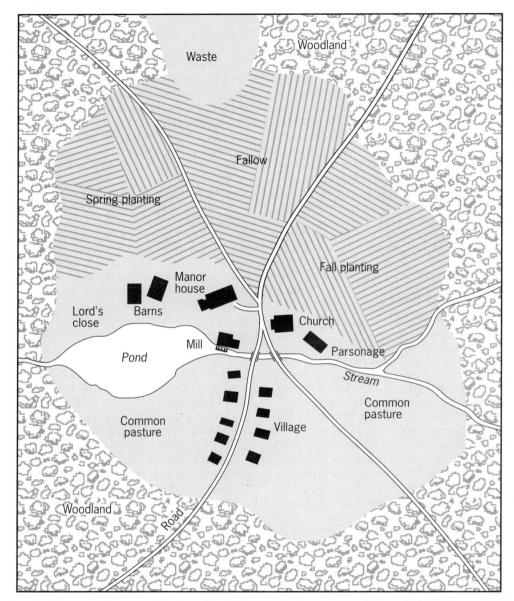

Map 17.1 A HYPOTHETICAL MEDIEVAL MANOR This drawing shows how a medieval manor might have been laid out. It will help identify the major components of a medieval manor as described in the text: the seigneur's manor house, the church, the village settlement, the three-field and strip systems, the commons, the woods, and wasteland. All of these components were required to make the manor self-sufficient.

side. Perhaps from time to time an itinerant merchant arrived offering to sell the seigneur or his lady such luxuries as spices, jewels, or fine cloth; so also did a peddler with trinkets for peasants and their wives.

The center of the manor was a village containing the seigneur's manor house, peasant huts, a church and cemetery, granaries, a mill, a bakery, and a brewery. Each village was more than a collection of buildings; it was a vital human community with a governing system and a social order. Its governor was the seigneur, who exercised the power to command, judge, and punish his dependent peasants with virtually no interference from any authority beyond the manor. If he lived on the manor, the seigneur exercised his lordship in person. If he lived elsewhere—as many nobles with numerous manors did—he entrusted control of the manor to *stewards* and *baillifs*, usually recruited from the peasantry. Although force provided the means of control of last resort, seigneurial overlordship was exercised chiefly through the manorial court. In this court the law of the manor, consisting of a body of custom defining every aspect of the relationships among those involved in manorial life, was applied to impose discipline on the peasantry and to allow individuals to gain recourse for damages done to them.

The peasant population of a typical manor included individuals whose legal status ranged from slave to free individual. But most were *serfs*, who were legally bound to the soil but who also held a tenancy from which they could not be dispossessed. Thus, a serf was legally unfree but possessed both a precious right in a piece of land that ensured his livelihood and a place in a community that provided protection and a court of law through which rights could be protected. Serf status was passed on by inheritance, as was the tenancy to which a serf was attached. Powerful forces were at work in the ninth and tenth centuries among both seigneurs and peasants to merge slaves and free individuals into serfdom.

More important to peasants than their precise legal status were the obligations they owed their seigneur. These obligations, defined by manorial custom, varied greatly over Europe, but everywhere certain dues were imposed on peasants. Their chief obligation was labor service. On most manors serfs were required to spend three days a week tilling the demesne of the seigneur. In addition, they might be required to do extra days of work during the planting and harvesting seasons and to maintain roads and buildings. Often these labor obligations extended to the serfs' wives, who were required to perform such duties as spinning, cleaning, and preparing food in the seigneur's household. In addition to labor services, most peasants owed their seigneur some portion of the produce of their tenancies, which provided the seigneur with an important supplement to the produce of his own demesne. Peasants had to pay a tithe to support the local church; often tithes found their way into the seigneur's hands. Fees were assessed for the use of the manorial mill, bakery, and brewery—facilities the seigneur alone could afford to build and over which he maintained a monopoly. The seigneur collected a death tax from each peasant household when the tenancy passed from father to son and a tax from any peasant whose daughter married outside the manor. There were also, of course, fees and fines to be paid by peasants involved in litigation in the manorial court.

This system obviously provided the seigneur with many opportunities to enrich himself at the expense of the peasantry, and many exploited these opportunities to the fullest. There were however, limits. The seigneur was wholly dependent on the peasants for the one prime ingredient of the manorial economy—labor. Without peasant labor the seigneur's land would go uncultivated and his wealth and status in the noble world would diminish. There was no other source of labor. The seigneur thus had to act with some restraint toward his laborers if he hoped to get efficient and constant work from them. Peasants were in a position to damage the interests of an oppressive seigneur by willful neglect of crops, buildings, and animals or by calculated mischief. Killing, maiming, or even irritating peasants in the interest of exacting more from them might be more costly than just treatment according to custom. The weight of custom, which tended to fix obligations over long periods, acted as a powerful brake on rapacious seigneurs.

Peasant life in the ninth and tenth centuries was brutally harsh. At best, the manorial system provided a livelihood at subsistence level. Crop failure, sickness, or warfare could erase the thin margin separating subsistence from famine and death. Too many children could overtax the meager supply of food that could be extracted from a tenancy of fixed size (see Figure 17.3). The seigneur or his agents were always at hand, seeking any spare wealth. The simple, one-room, scantily furnished huts offered little comfort. Nor did the monotonous diet of bread, soup, beer, cheese, and eggs, with an occasional bit of meat, fish, or fruit. Yet there were compensations. The religious establishment, represented by the local priest, was ever present, offering solace in the face of life's hardships, including charity at especially desperate moments, and the hope of a better life beyond this world. Its ministrations at life's crucial moments—birth, marriage, death—helped to give dignity and significance to human existence, even in the midst of squalor and poverty. Membership in the village community provided the psychological security that stems from living among people long and intimately known. That same community provided an array of simple pleasures, often occasioned by the numerous religious holy days—beer drinking, gaming, singing, dancing—all capable of easing the burden of a life of bare subsistence.

FIGURE 17.3 A Peasant Family This miniature shows a peasant, his wife, and their two infant children. The scene suggests both close and affectionate family ties and the burden of children in a world of poverty. (Photothèque Armand-Colin, from Bibliotheque Nationale, Paris)

4. THE CHRISTIAN COMMUNITY IN THE WORLD OF LORDSHIP AND DEPENDENCY

During the late ninth and tenth centuries the complex processes at work to put into place a system of lordship and dependency posed new kinds of problems for the religious establishment. These difficulties resulted largely from the entanglement of religious officials in the world of lordship and noble dependency. By the ninth and tenth centuries, the ecclesiastical system held an immense amount of landed property. Its holdings were attached to bishoprics, monasteries, and individual churches and administered by bishops, abbots, and priests. Part of its possessions had come from gifts from the faithful, but much had been acquired in the form of fiefs

granted by kings and other powerful laymen, who expected church officials so favored to render services as any other vassals did. In order to protect their holdings in a world where self-help was the key to survival, ecclesiastical officials acted like other lords. They granted church lands as fiefs in return for military and political services and thus became lords in their own rights. Like their lay counterparts, ecclesiastical property holders forced the peasants on their lands into a servile condition and gave full attention to asserting their seigneurial authority. They too had to concern themselves with protecting their vassals, holding courts, and collecting dues. Such necessary concerns directed their efforts away from their pastoral duties. Lay leaders refused to invest any bishop or abbot with a fief unless he had the qualities of a good vassal, including military prowess and loyalty to the lord rather than to the Church as an institution. In effect, this system meant that secular leaders gained control over elections to ecclesiastical offices, often filling them with loyal kinsmen or proven vassals with little interest in spiritual matters. Secular lords treated church land received as fiefs as if it were private property, diverting the income to uses that had little to do with spiritual needs. This thoroughly secularized officialdom in control of ecclesiastical offices and property neglected discipline, education, charity, and moral guidance. Members of the lower clergy, usually appointed and controlled by the lords of the manors where parish churches were located, were unlettered, undisciplined, and undersupported. They tended to live much like the peasant population with whom they associated, marrying, raising children, and sharing the pleasures of the manorial community. They were constantly tempted to traffic in religious services in return for money. The level of religious life in lay society deteriorated badly; superstition, moral laxity, and corruption of ritual practices abounded. To some contemporary pious souls, especially those who harbored some sense of the original Christian community or even those who remembered the Carolingian reform effort, religious life had become a scandal worse than had ever been seen. Mammon had seemingly triumphed over God!

While recognizing the abysmal condition into which the Christian community had sunk, it remains necessary to note another dimension of the position of the religious establishment in the world of lordship and dependence. Its involvement in that world drew it more directly than ever into contact with the basic institutions and dynamic elements of society. Its leadership shared the mentality and felt the needs of western Europe's warrior aristocracy and peasantry. Such involvement prepared that leadership to shape a religious order that was responsive to reality. Even in the midst of a genuine religious crisis, evidence of that response began to surface. Clerical writers began to explore the theoretical implications of a social structure based on three orders, each with a special social responsibility: those who prayed, those who fought, and those who labored. The religious establishment gave the feudal contract a religious dimension by making the oath of fealty a key element in establishing the relationship binding two men to-

gether. Christian moral concepts began to shape a code of behavior known as *chivalry* that befitted the warrior life (see Chapter 18). Ecclesiastical leaders instituted two practices aimed at curbing violence in feudal society. One, called the Peace of God, sought to restrain acts of war against certain categories of people (the clergy, women, children); the other, called the Truce of God, tried to prohibit warfare during certain periods holy to all Christians (Sundays, major holy days, Lent). A monastic reform beginning in the tenth century, known as Cluniac monasticism (see Chapter 21), encouraged certain practices of piety that appealed strongly to the warrior nobility. The grouping of the peasantry into organized villages provided a setting for the development of a parish structure through which the Christian population could be reached. Thus, despite the institutional and spiritual disarray caused by the worldliness of the Christian establishment, its immersion in the world of lordship and dependency provided new arenas where it could assert its influence over the development of European society.

The tenth-century world of lordship and dependency, of dominant warrior landlords and subservient peasant laborers, does not usually receive a sympathetic evaluation. The record affirms the potential of such a system for violence and oppression. Not nearly so clear except to those who investigate in detail what happened in tiny areas to tiny groups of people is the potential of that same system to create effective order. Taking all the evidence into account, it seems safe to conclude that the system of lordship and dependency played a fundamental role in preparing a backward society for a new outburst of creativity. That system shaped small communities of people capable of concerted, disciplined action. These new groupings created a situation requiring collaborative action among peoples of different social status and talents. These collectivities nurtured capabilities that were especially suited to attending to western Europe's porous frontiers and exploiting its chief resource, its underutilized lands, forests, and rivers. It is not coincidence that western European society began a spectacular period of growth *after* the system of lordship and dependency was established.

SUGGESTED READING

Lordship and Dependence

F. L. Ganshof, *Feudalism*, trans. Philip Grierson, 3rd ed. (1964). Stresses the legal aspects of feudalism.

Marc Bloch, *Feudal Society*, trans. L. A. Manyon (1961). A classic, approaching feudalism from a sociological perspective.

Perry Anderson, *Passages from Antiquity to Feudalism* (1978). A Marxist perspective on feudalism and its origins.

Guy Fourquin, *Lordship and Feudalism in the Middle Ages*, trans. Iris and A. L. Lytton Sells (1976). Provides insights into how power was exercised in the feudal world.

Jean-Pierre Poly and Eric Bournazel, *The Feudal Transformation, 900–1200* (1990). Good on the formation of lordships.

Timothy Reuter, ed. and trans., *The Medieval Nobility. Studies on the Ruling Classes of France and Germany from the Sixth to the Twelfth Century* (1978). These essays provide conflicting views on the origins and role of the medieval nobility.

Georges Duby, *Rural Economy and Country Life in the Medieval West*, trans. Cynthia Postan (1968). The best work on manorial economy; provides translations of medieval sources.

Robert Fossier, *Peasant Life in the Medieval West*, trans. J. Vale (1988). A balanced treatment.

Pierre Bonnassie, *From Slavery to Feudalism* (1991). Examines the end of slavery between 500 and 1200.

Philippe Contamine, *War in the Middle Ages*, trans. Michael James (1984). Treats an important aspect of feudal society.

RETROSPECT

In a letter written in 593 or 594, Pope Gregory I called his contemporaries' attention to the strife, suffering, destruction, and injustice seen everywhere. "See what has befallen Rome, once mistress of the world," he mourned. "What is there now, I ask, of delight in this world?" In a way, Gregory's lament reflected an element of truth about the history of the early Middle Ages if one limits his or her attention to western Europe. Much of what had characterized Greco-Roman civilization had been lost there, and society was poorer. One can easily write, as many have, the history of the early Middle Ages in terms of the destruction of classical civilization and the onset of a dark age.

However, from a larger perspective much happened between A.D. 500 and 1000 to replace what had been lost. Three new civilizations— Byzantine, Islamic, and western European—had been shaped within the confines of the classical world. Each retained precious elements of the old order. Each developed new institutions and ideas to suit its needs and situation. An inventory of what people had fashioned in these difficult centuries gives ample evidence that these "dark" years deserve a decisive place in the continuum of history. By 1000 there were still "things of delight" in the world.

The emergence of three new civilizations was not the only transformation that occurred during the early Middle Ages. In addition to the creative forces at work within each, a new dynamism had developed in the form of interactions among these civilizations. The Greco-Roman world had tended to absorb existing cultures into a unified pattern that stood counterposed to the barbarian world. By 1000 lines of interaction and points of tension existed among civilized societies rather than between the civilized and uncivilized orbits. This situation was of decisive importance in shaping the future of each new society.

The period just reviewed belonged to the East; Byzantium and Islam far surpassed western Europe in every respect. This little-appreciated fact demands attention, for the accomplishments of the Byzantine and Islamic worlds in these centuries gave their peoples a proud sense of contribution to the creation of civilized life that other societies later forgot. None benefited more from the achievements of these leaders than the struggling western Europeans, whose future glory would have been different had it not been for what they absorbed from the East.

PART FOUR

THE CENTRAL AND LATE MIDDLE AGES, 1000–1500: THE RESURGENCE OF EUROPE

As the end of the first millennium of Christian history approached, some predicted that in fulfillment of ancient prophecy the world would end. In fact, the passing of that date did mark the end of the old world, but not in the way apocalyptic visionaries anticipated. As a result of a revival in western Europe during the period 1000–1300, sometimes called the central Middle Ages, the underdeveloped society of the early medieval world was transformed to create a vibrant order that elevated western European civilization to a new position in a world setting.

The sudden upsurge of a formerly backward society is not easy to explain. But as our account of the effervescent, creative centuries from 1000 to 1300 unfolds, there can be no doubt that growth was rooted in the foundations established in the old world that was supposed to end. The institutions connected with lordship and dependence, the religious establishment, and the treasure of learning stored up by Carolingian scholars provided basic patterns of organization, social control, thought, and belief that permitted men and women to apply their energies toward new ends: producing greater wealth; constructing larger political entities; shaping more complex class structures; creating new forms of thought and expression; exploring new spiritual realms; thrusting outward from their beleaguered world into new geographical areas.

Although this sustained burst of creativity enriched western society in every respect, it eventually reached its limits. During the fourteenth and fifteenth centuries a succession of challenges for which existing institutions could not provide instant solutions temporarily disrupted the development of western European civilization. The eventual response to that crisis of the late Middle Ages provided the impetus to western Europe's continued advance in the early modern era.

CHAPTER 18
Economic and Social Revival, 1000–1300

FIGURE 18.1 Medieval Farming This miniature used to illustrate an English psalter shows peasants plowing their fields. It indicates that medieval agriculture was a cooperative effort: Peasants combined their labor, draft animals, and equipment to till the manor fields. The heavy moldboard plow was a major technological advance of the Middle Ages: It was especially efficient in cutting through and turning over heavy soils. Producing yields sufficient to feed both people and livestock was a major problem. (The British Museum)

Throughout the early Middle Ages a major deterrent to growth was the severely limited and constantly uncertain level of material resources available to western European society. Between 1000 and 1300 that situation was dramatically changed by a major economic expansion accompanied by significant adjustments in the social order. These changes had their source at the base of society. Their agents were modest seigneurs, toiling peasants, peddler merchants, and simple artisans, whose collective efforts provided the material means that made possible the more spectacular accomplishments of the central Middle Ages in politics, religion, and culture.

1. POPULATION GROWTH

The forces that generated economic growth after 1000 were complex. However, one contributing factor is evident: The population of western Europe increased substantially between about 900 and 1350. This demographic change, reversing a decline that had extended from late antiquity until the Carolingian age, resulted in a doubling of the population of western Europe; one generally accepted estimate suggests that the population grew from about 35 million in 900 to about 70 million in 1350. Modern demographers do not yet fully understand the causes of this growth. There is some evidence that during this period Eurasia was relatively free from killer diseases, especially bubonic plague. Perhaps the curbing of the more destructive aspects of warfare and the availability of more and better food contributed. Some have even suggested that the prospects of a better society encouraged people to have more children. Whatever the causes, the simple fact was that for three centuries a constantly expanding population put pressure on the agricultural system for greater productivity and provided a larger work force that could be turned to new enterprises.

There remains a whole series of fascinating and important problems associated with the effects of population growth on the structure of medieval society. For example, it is clear that the population growth was not uniform across western Europe, but the geographic pattern and the regional impact of growth have not yet been clearly established. Neither is it clear how growth affected different age groups and social classes. The impact of increasing population on life expectancy, marriage patterns, size of households, and child rearing is still poorly understood. Virtually all one can say is that population increase affected all these matters so vital to people's lives. A better understanding of these issues will undoubtedly make it more obvious that population growth was a major dynamic force changing western European society during the central Middle Ages.

2. AGRICULTURAL EXPANSION

The most important aspect of economic growth between 1000 and 1300 was expansion of agricultural production. The manorial system, with its reservoir of managerial ability, disciplined labor force, and technical skills, provided the base for growth. At least five factors were involved in expanding on that base.

First, western Europe's climate improved during this period, especially in northern Europe. Milder winters, longer growing seasons, better distribution of rainfall, and fewer violent storms and excessive variations in temperature all combined to create an improved setting for agricultural pursuits.

Second, a large amount of land was put under cultivation for the first time as a result of an immense effort devoted to land clearance and peasant resettlement. Much of this land clearance involved pushing out the boundaries of existing cultivated areas, which in the early Middle Ages stood as isolated, often overpopulated islands of cultivation in vast stretches of forest. Now the forests were cleared, swamps were drained, and land was even recovered from the sea. In addition to this internal expansion European cultivators, organized by enterprising landlords, moved great distances to settle on virgin or underutilized land on the frontiers of western Europe. The chief areas of colonization were the German frontier east of the Elbe River, the Spanish lands being wrested from Moslem control, and southern Italy. It appears that the cultivated acreage in western Europe nearly doubled between 1000 and 1300.

Third, technological advances greatly increased the efficiency of the labor force, especially by supplying new sources of power. The adoption of the horseshoe and the development of new harnesses, especially the shoulder collar, permitted the more efficient horse to replace the ox as a draft animal. Although known since Roman times, water mills and windmills finally came into common use and were improved by the development of complicated power trains which allowed the motion from these mills to be applied to such tasks as grinding grain, sawing timber, and processing wool for cloth production. Traditional agricultural tools—plows, spades, hoes, scythes—were improved by more effective practices of metallurgy. Especially important was the increasing use of the wheeled, moldboard plow, which could cut through and turn over the heavy soils of northern Europe (see Figure 18.1). One suspects that these advances owed much to the ingenuity and experience of simple peasants searching for ways to make their labor easier and more productive. Whatever the cause, the result was greater productivity and the freeing of human labor for other productive uses.

Fourth, agricultural production was increased in quantity and variety by improved methods of tillage and animal husbandry. Irrigation systems were developed in some parts of western Europe. Increasing opportunities for exchange encouraged agricultural specialization, as in the vineyards of Burgundy and the great sheep-raising granges in England; such specialization not only brought variety to the productive system but also allowed for a much more efficient use of diverse types of land than cereal production did. Greater attention was given to the use of animal waste for fertilization. Of special significance was the spread after 900 of the three-field system of crop rotation to replace the traditional two-field system. Under this new system the tillable land on a typical large estate was divided into three open fields. Every year and in rotation, one field was left fallow, a second was planted in the fall with wheat or rye, and a third was planted in the spring with barley, oats, or legumes (such as beans or peas). Not only did the three-field system put more land under cultivation each year, it also improved the human diet by making available high-protein foods, such as beans, to supplement the mostly carbohydrate diet of earlier times and provided oats

to feed the increasing number of horses used as prime beasts of burden. Better seeds were developed to take advantage of local soil and weather conditions. And improvements in animal breeds produced better animals and more animal products, such as meat and wool.

Finally, entrepreneurship played a part in expanding agricultural production. Planning was required to free labor to clear new lands, to organize peasant resettlement in distant places, to apply new tools and techniques, and to launch specialized production. Ingenuity was involved in finding ways to dispose profitably of excess production. Innovative thinking was required to develop new seeds and improved livestock strains. The surviving medieval record tells us little about such matters, but entrepreneurship, exercised in small and undramatic ways, must certainly have been a key to one of the great advances in the history of agriculture.

Inadequate evidence makes it difficult to quantify with any accuracy the overall magnitude of the growth of agricultural production between 1000 and 1300. However, in crude terms the consequences are beyond doubt. The increased amount of land under cultivation and higher yields permitted everyone to live better and produced a surplus of food, which left more people free to devote their energies to activities other than subsistence agriculture. That critical difference made possible significant changes in all aspects of the society of the central Middle Ages.

3. THE REVIVAL OF TRADE AND MANUFACTURING

The expansion of agricultural production after 1000 stimulated the revival of trade and manufacturing. Trade had never entirely vanished from the western European scene, but it had declined steadily from late Roman times, so that by 1000 it was a minor factor in the total economic life of western Europe. Neither had manufacturing totally disappeared, but during the early Middle Ages manufacturing was restricted to the manorial setting, where only a limited range of products needed for local self-sufficiency was produced. During the late tenth and early eleventh centuries, a revival began in both commerce and manufacturing; it continued until the mid-fourteenth century. During this era commerce became the catalytic force in European economy, and new forms of manufacturing emerged to provide an expanded range of products for exchange. Among the factors contributing to the commercial and industrial revival were population growth, agricultural expansion, greater political order, outside stimuli, and western European political, military, and religious expansion. But to these must be added the labors and enterprise of men and women whose activities are for the most part only vaguely known to us.

In considerable part, commercial expansion was a story of the ability of western Europeans to gain a share of the flourishing commercial activity in the Byzantine and Moslem worlds (see Map 18.1). Beginning in the tenth century, Italian cities took the lead in expanding trading endeavors in the Mediterranean area. The Venetians steadily enlarged their contacts by sea with Constantinople and brought an ever-increasing volume of goods to the West. In the eleventh century Pisa and Genoa used their navies to loosen Moslem control over the western Mediterranean, and their merchants established trade relations with the Moslems in Spain and North Africa. As a result of the success of the early crusading movement (see Chapter 20), Italian cities established important commercial footholds in the Moslem world in the eastern Mediterranean. The conquest of Constantinople in 1204 during the Fourth Crusade gave the Venetians virtual control over Byzantine trade, especially in the Black Sea area. By the thirteenth century the efforts of Italian merchants were being reinforced by other traders from coastal cities in France and Spain; collectively they had become the dominant commercial force in Mediterranean trade. Nor were they content with their new commercial sphere of influence; already by 1300 European merchants were exploring trading opportunities in central Asia and China. The lifeblood of this international trade was luxury items, especially spices and fine cloth.

Meanwhile, another window to the East was opened on the northern and eastern fringes of Europe by Viking pirates. Their raiding ventures opened a path through the Baltic Sea and along

the rivers of Russia to the Black Sea and Constantinople. Traders from many areas of northern Europe eventually followed the Vikings along this route, opening a vigorous exchange between the Baltic–North Sea area and Constantinople and the eastern Mediterranean. Eventually this northern trading zone began to develop a commercial life of its own, marking a major expansion of European commercial enterprise. The focal point of this northern trading complex came to be the cities of Flanders.

No less important than international trade was the growth of trade within Europe. In part, that growth was a result of the efforts of aggressive Italian and Flemish merchants to provide increasingly prosperous aristocrats with luxury goods. Their activities created an ever-widening network of routes, especially following the river systems of Europe, that eventually covered most of Europe. During the twelfth century, the chief meeting places of international traders were the fairs of Champagne in France. Here merchants from all over Europe came to display their wares to other merchants, who in turn carried their purchases to local markets and prize customers (see Figure 18.2). By the thirteenth century the fairs were increasingly giving way to permanent markets established in cities.

Complementing the traffic in luxury items was an ever-growing exchange of goods between formerly self-sufficient manors and villages and the growing towns. Local trade in such items as salt, wine, and metals had always existed. From the eleventh century onward, it broadened to provide the growing towns with foodstuffs and raw materials and to carry manufactured products of the towns back to the rural settlements. In volume and number of people involved, the local town-country exchange undoubtedly exceeded international trade.

The expansion of commercial activity in western Europe promoted the growth of manufacturing. By the twelfth century the towns began to offer opportunities for skilled artisans to make a single product for sale to their fellow townspeople and rural buyers or to merchants who distributed them wherever there was a demand. Artisan manufacturing, centered on the workshops of individual craftsmen, long remained a vital element of the town economy and put a vast

Map 18.1 **TRADE ROUTES, TWELFTH AND THIRTEENTH CENTURIES** This map shows the major trade routes developed during the twelfth and thirteenth centuries to link western Europeans with the East and to join major trading centers within western Europe. The crucial centers for the international trade linking East and West were located in northern Italy, especially Venice, Genoa, and Pisa, and in Flanders, especially Bruges and Antwerp. The internal routes, focusing especially in the towns of Champagne, where great international trading fairs were held annually, spread the products of the East from the Italian and Flemish centers over much of western Europe.

quantity of commonplace goods into the exchange system. By the thirteenth century some areas of Europe, particularly Flanders and northern Italy, had developed more complex manufacturing organizations based on the "putting out" system and "cottage" industry, applied to cloth manufacturing. Entrepreneurs purchased bulk quantities of raw wool raised in England by farmers specializing in sheep raising and transported it to Flanders, where it was processed through a series of steps including washing, carding, spinning, weaving, fulling, and dyeing. Each separate operation was performed by specialized laborers, many of them women, who worked for hire in their own homes. The high-quality finished product was distributed on an

FIGURE 18.2 A Medieval Fair In this scene the bishop of Paris is giving his blessing to various merchants who are waiting for the opening of the fair held annually just outside Paris near the monastery of St. Denis. Such fairs provided a major setting for the exchange of goods from far and near. The presence of a figure so important as the bishop of Paris suggests that these fairs were viewed as a vital part of life. (Bibliothèque Nationale, Paris)

international scale by merchants contracted for by the entrepreneur. A comparable system for woolen production developed in such northern Italian cities as Florence.

There is no way to measure accurately what the revival of trade and manufacturing meant to the western European economy in quantitative terms. It seems safe to venture that by the thirteenth century the volume of trade and industry in western Europe surpassed that of the Greco-Roman world, and probably that of the contemporary Byzantine and Moslem economies as well. Agriculture was still the most important economic element, but the wealth from exchange and craftsmanship made a critical difference in the total economy of the West. Moreover, trade and industry increasingly supplied the dynamism that encouraged continued economic growth and diversification.

4. ECONOMIC CONSEQUENCES OF INCREASED PRODUCTION

The wealth generated by the increased agricultural, commercial, and industrial productivity of western Europe manifested itself in a hundred ways: better houses, bigger churches, more elaborate dress, greater quantities and varieties of food, more art and literature, more leisure. But aside from greater wealth, expanded productivity had more specific results that affected the fundamental structures of economic life.

First, economic growth spurred the growth of cities. Towns had never disappeared from western Europe. But between late antiquity and about 1000, they became primarily ecclesiastical, administrative, or defensive centers, sparsely populated and economically dependent on agriculture. Between 1000 and 1300 many of the old urban centers grew dramatically, and many new towns appeared. By 1300 there were European cities of considerable population: Some Italian towns, such as Venice, Milan, Florence, and Genoa, had populations of around 100,000; Paris may have had 80,000 people; and London had 50,000. The vast majority of medieval cities probably had populations of 10,000 or fewer, but these modest figures should not detract from their vitality. Spread widely across the European landscape and closely integrated with the countryside, these modest centers spurred the local agricultural economy and provided an outlet for excess rural population. More significant than their numbers was the fact that most urban residents earned their livelihood from trade and manufacturing, thus making the "new" urban centers quite different from the economically nonproductive towns of the early Middle Ages.

In terms of physical growth, many important towns of the era were simply enlargements of older episcopal, monastic, administrative, or military centers. Merchants and then artisans were attracted to these centers for many reasons: security, favor shown them by ruling authorities, access to rivers and roads, availability of buyers. Often they settled haphazardly outside the walls of the old center, their shops, stalls, and households creating a *suburb* (Latin for "under the city"). As commercial activity increased, the walls were extended to enclose the suburbs. Often the suburban marketplace became the center of urban life. During the central Middle Ages new towns were often established at locations favorable to commerce, and their physical development resembled that of the old centers.

A second consequence of economic expansion was the emergence of a money economy. Money had always circulated in western Europe, but only minimally until the eleventh century. Thereafter, its use rapidly expanded to meet the needs of commercial exchange and then began to affect agricultural production. The impact of the money economy was revolutionary. A whole new form of wealth emerged to challenge the monopoly held by land. Old economic relationships based on services and payment of obligations in kind were replaced by payments in money. By creating a common standard against which all values could be calculated, money

greatly speeded up the exchange process. Money could be accumulated in a way that labor services and produce could not, and such "savings" could be manipulated endlessly to exploit changing economic opportunities. The possession of money allowed people to specialize their economic activities and still have the means to obtain the full range of material goods they needed. In the face of the impact of an expanding money economy, perhaps it is not surprising that conservative moralists of the era warned with increasing frequency that money was the root of all evil.

A third major effect of economic growth was the transformation of agricultural production. The market for surplus food provided by the towns gave manorial lords and peasants alike money incomes with which they could embellish their lives with products from the town markets. This new potential for profit changed the emphasis on the manors from self-sufficiency to surplus production. Under this pressure the traditional system of servile dependency began to dissolve. The dissolution proceeded in two broad directions. In many areas of western Europe, especially in the twelfth century, seigneurs began to break their demesnes into tenancies which were rented to peasants for cash payments. At the same time, they commuted the labor obligations of their serfs and the dues owed them in kind to money payments. Serfs could afford to buy off their obligations because the town market offered them a chance to sell produce and save a little money. But many seigneurs moved in the opposite direction, expanding their demesne and managing its cultivation themselves, often concentrating on a specialized cash crop. Seigneurs who took this course often displaced peasants from their ancient tenancies, forcing them to work for wages or to seek new livelihoods in the towns. In either case, the old manorial system and servile dependence gradually dissolved over much of western Europe. In its place a variety of forms of agricultural exploitation emerged; all were dominated by the concern for profit, an end that could be achieved only by linking the countryside to the towns, their markets, and their money.

A fourth change nurtured by economic growth involved a new attitude as to the purpose of economic endeavor. No longer were producers content with self-sufficiency; they worked and planned to gain more worldly goods. They began to devise strategies and techniques that would increase wealth: lending money for profit, speculating in trading ventures, manipulating land for gain, saving money. A protocapitalist economic mentality was taking shape that prized economic growth rather than stability.

Finally, western Europeans had achieved such economic growth by 1300 that they had seized economic leadership in the vast area surrounding the Mediterranean—a leadership that would eventually be extended to the whole world. No longer did Byzantium and Islam stand as advanced economic centers to a backward western Europe. As we shall see later, political factors helped the advance of the Europeans, but it is beyond question that their enterprise played a vital role in establishing their economic leadership.

5. SOCIAL CHANGE: THE BOURGEOISIE

The economic growth of western Europe during the central Middle Ages brought major changes to the simple social order characteristic of the world of lordship and dependency. Perhaps the most significant change was the emergence of a new social group, the *bourgeoisie*. The shaping of this group resulted from the efforts of traders and artisans living in towns to define a place for themselves in a world lacking legal or social institutions that fitted their situation. In order to pursue their economic interests effectively, they had to seek various "liberties," or, more accurately, special privileges. Their effort slowly created for them a collective status that distinguished them socially from the clergy, noble warriors, and agricultural laborers.

As soon as men and women began to devote full time to commerce and manufacturing, they felt a basic need for personal freedom. Their livelihood depended on their ability to move about in a world that fixed people to fiefs and manors, to dispose of their property at will in a world where property was bound up in an intricate network of obligations, to apply their talents and labor to whatever opportunity arose in a world where long-sanctioned customs dictated how

people spent their time and efforts. And so the merchants and artisans of the towns struggled for personal freedom, using money payments, force, and persuasion to wring concessions of freedom from kings, lords, and bishops. So successful were they that by 1300 merely to breathe the air of a city for a year and a day meant personal freedom.

Although personal freedom was vital, it was not sufficient. Townspeople needed liberties that would allow them to determine their collective destiny, in terms of both defining relationships among themselves and regulating interactions with those outside their urban setting. To gain these added liberties, they sometimes banded together into associations to seek special privileges from those who had political authority over them and over the space their city occupied. Their efforts often resulted in a written document, called a *charter*, which defined their status and rights as a corporate body. Initially, such charters had to be fought for or purchased at a high cost, but acquiring a charter soon grew easier as kings, lords, and bishops realized the profits to be gained by having a thriving town on their domains. Charters varied greatly in content. The typical charter recognized the citizen body of the town as a corporation that could act legally. Usually charters granted personal freedom to the townspeople and defined what they owed to the granting authority. Finally, charters granted some degree of self-governance. In a few cases, especially in Italy, towns gained complete freedom; such towns were called *communes*. More commonly, the townspeople had only limited privileges of self-government.

In shaping political institutions, the townspeople experimented considerably. In most towns there was some degree of popular participation in political life, authority being vested in an elected council. In a typical commune the council usually possessed complete power to legislate, conduct courts, levy taxes, expend money for civic purposes, and negotiate with outside powers. Its only responsibility was to the citizens of the town. Many towns chose a chief administrative official—*mayor, burgomaster, podesta*—who functioned under the supervision of the council. Judicial affairs were entrusted to specially trained judges. Towns with only limited political freedom often had to respect the authority of a royal official, a bishop, or a representative of a feudal lord who exercised many powers in judicial and financial matters. Whatever the form of government, the towns quickly created an elaborate new body of law regulating civic affairs.

A grave problem in every urban center was the regulation of economic activity among merchants and artisans, a problem for which the rest of society had no solution. The usual answer was the establishment of *guilds* within each town. The merchants of a town often organized themselves into a single merchant guild; the artisans formed several craft guilds, one for each trade. The merchant guild existed primarily to protect the interests of merchants from outsiders and to restrain the members from taking unfair advantage of one another and their customers. Each guild enacted rules governing prices to be charged, trading practices to be observed, and the conditions under which trade could be conducted. The craft guilds similarly imposed regulations on their members concerning prices, quality of goods, conditions of labor, and quantity of production. They also controlled the conditions for entering a trade. Boys began as *apprentices* to a master, working from two to seven years under his guidance and living in his household. The apprentice then became a *journeyman* who worked for hire until he could satisfy the guild that he had developed adequate skill to become a *master*. Along with their regulative functions, merchant and craft guilds had social functions. Each usually had its own guildhall, where banquets, pageants, and religious affairs were conducted for the entertainment and edification of the members. Each guild also aided its members when sickness or death struck a family.

Like their rural contemporaries, city dwellers made technical innovations that aided their economic activities. Market facilities were created to allow the display of goods and money-changing operations. Sound coinage systems were established, especially by the Italian towns, whose coins were used in markets all over Europe. Insurance was developed to protect merchants against losses. Bookkeeping systems were devised to keep track of exchange operations and inventories. Merchants created ways to pool their resources for mutual benefit. Partnerships, called *commenda*, were formed in which one or more merchants provided capital to another merchant to conduct a specific trading enterprise in return for a specified share of the profit. Eventually permanent companies were formed in which investors made deposits and received regular dividends paid by those who actually conducted the business enterprise.

Particularly significant as a means of providing capital to promote commercial and industrial growth was the development of a credit system and of an institution specializing in credit services: the bank. Bills of exchange became available, allowing merchants to deposit money in one place in exchange for a receipt that could be used to pay for goods in another place. Moneylending for interest became common. At least in the early stages of commercial growth, the religious establishment strenuously opposed the lending of money for interest (usury) because it allowed people to profit from the misfortunes of others. Gradually, theologians and canon lawyers conceded that lenders who provided funds for investment in speculative activities were entitled to compensation for the risk. By the thirteenth century large-scale lending operations conducted by banks were a vital part of the economy and a source of great profit; among their best customers were high ecclesiastical officials.

The urban environment allowed greater social mobility than did the worlds of nobles and peasants. Trade and industry provided diverse opportunities for merchants and artisans to use their freedom and their talents to increase their wealth and better their social status. Urban political and guild structures created possibilities for individuals to play a part in shaping political decisions and even to achieve major leadership roles. Women also found a wider range of economic opportunities in the towns than were available to noble and peasant women. Aside from assisting their husbands in trading and manufacturing, women could engage in economic ventures independently. Widows of important merchants often continued their former husbands' trading enterprise. Many women were members of craft guilds and apparently practiced their craft alongside men, although often at lower wages. Although urban life permitted social mobility, in the period 1000–1300 bourgeois society tended to become stratified on the basis of wealth. An oligarchy of rich entrepreneurs, usually merchants, increasingly claimed special status and gained control of city governments and guilds. At the other end of the social spectrum from these patricians was a growing number of poor, exploited laborers who sometimes vented their discontent by rioting.

Perhaps the most tragic victims of medieval urban society were western Europe's Jews. Although during the early Middle Ages Jews were viewed as a unique social group and were subject to special legal restrictions, they were allowed and even encouraged to engage in commercial activity. On the basis of this experience Jews were active participants in the early expansion of trade, earning for themselves not only wealth but also a special place in many cities as a self-governing group centered around their synagogues. But by the twelfth century their situation began to deteriorate. As more Christians began to engage in trade and manufacturing, measures were taken to exclude Jews from these activities, driving them to rely on moneylending as a means of livelihood and causing them to be scorned as usurers as well as adherents of a religion increasingly attacked by a variety of Christian intellectual leaders. By the thirteenth century Christian bankers were taking over moneylending operations, devising whatever means they could to exclude their Jewish competitors from this lucrative business. Increasingly forced out of the mainstream of urban economic life, Jews were impoverished, forced into menial occupations, compelled to live in ghettos and wear distinctive clothing, and often savagely persecuted by kings, urban officials, and ecclesiastical authorities.

The urban environment generated its own cultural needs. Commercial and industrial pursuits required literacy, computing skills, and rational planning. The activities of the markets and shops raised a new range of moral problems and special kinds of spiritual longing. The physical circumstances unique to city life encouraged experimentation in architecture, sculpture, and painting. The interaction of people from many parts of Europe and the world beyond made city dwellers aware of cultural differences and raised questions about the validity of local customs. As a result of all these forces, cities became centers of educational, intellectual, and artistic change.

By 1300 the bourgeoisie was still not a very exalted social group; the nobility looked down on merchants and artisans, ecclesiastical leaders disapproved of many of their activities as immoral, and peasants were suspicious of the sharp practices of the "city slicker." Still, the bourgeoisie constituted a dynamic factor in the social order whose members would play an increasingly important role in shaping the future course of Western civilization.

6. SOCIAL CHANGE: THE NOBILITY

Between 1000 and 1300 the nobility remained the dominant social group, its power and influence still defined primarily in terms of lordship and noble dependency. However, changing economic conditions created new circumstances that affected the status and lifestyle of the nobility.

Land remained the basis of aristocratic wealth and high social status. However, in an expanding market economy the value of land depended less on granting it out in return for noble services than on exploiting it as a source of spendable income. In the face of this new reality nobles made significant changes in their use of land. The pressure to keep holdings intact as a source of wealth led to fundamental changes in inheritance patterns and family structures. The earlier practice of shared inheritance among all members of the family, including women, gave way to inheritance restricted to the eldest son. As inheritance patterns changed, the older extended family system in which descent was marked through both parents gave way to a patrilineal family structure in which noble descent was determined through the male line. Such changes solidified male domination over the noble family and constricted the status of younger sons, wives, and daughters. Even though the new inheritance system kept the family patrimony intact, changing economic conditions required new approaches to land exploitation. As noted earlier, some nobles consolidated their holdings into productive units they managed themselves. Many more abandoned the traditional manorial system to become landlords living on money rents paid by peasant tenants. This last course had its risks. In an age of steady inflation many aristocrats made the mistake of agreeing to long-term leases that provided them with fixed returns whose real value declined over time. As a consequence, their families saw their wealth and social status reduced; some even lost their noble status. Some nobles turned to commercial activities to bolster their wealth, either by extracting money payments from town governments in return for privileges or by investing in commercial ventures. Others associated themselves with the increasingly powerful royal governments as a way of enhancing their prestige and protecting lucrative private political jurisdictions. All these factors combined to bring about a more complex stratification of noble society, to limit mobility within that group, and to put greater constraints on the admission of outsiders.

The expanding economy allowed noble society to enjoy a more comfortable material life; in fact, the quest for material goods became an important objective of noble life and the display of material affluence a measure of status. Stone castles featuring more private chambers, fireplaces vented through chimneys, and improved sanitary facilities appeared all over Europe. The adornment of these residences stimulated aesthetic interests, and the urge to use them as places to display status prompted literary patronage; some nobles even became literate. For a price a typical noble could enjoy a much more varied diet than before, including sugar and exotic spices from the East and fine wine from southern France. A greater variety of clothing was available, especially fine woolens and imported silks.

The improved material standard of living was but one aspect of a subtle refinement of noble life. The essence of the new ethos was reflected in the code of *chivalry* that by the twelfth century had emerged to define ideal noble behavior. Chivalry was rooted in the values of the feudal warrior; it stressed loyalty, bravery, generosity, honor, and military prowess. From the eleventh century on, these values acquired new shades of meaning drawn from the changing realities surrounding noble life in a more affluent age and from Christian concepts that—at least in theory—converted the crude, brutal warrior of earlier times into the knight skilled in the practice of courtly manners. Under the code of chivalry the ideal noble was still defined as a warrior who required an elaborate training in the arts of war-

fare before receiving public recognition as a knight. However, chivalry restrained his behavior. He was now expected to treat knights against whom he fought according to rules of honor. In his conduct as a warrior he was obligated to avoid harming noncombatants (clergy, women, children), damaging church property, and disrupting religious activities. The ideal knight fought only for a "good" cause, such as crusading to spread the true faith or punishing evildoers who preyed on the weak. Under the chivalric code the warrior instinct tended to be channeled into carefully arranged engagements, called *tournaments*, where the martial arts were practiced under strict rules and amid a pageantry that featured mannered behavior more than bloodshed and booty taking.

A particularly distinctive feature of the code of chivalry was the role it gave to women. Whereas the old warrior society valued women little except as bearers of children, sources of dowries, and objects of sexual gratification, the code of chivalry made women objects of devotion, loyalty, and sentimental attachment. A true knight was expected to develop a set of manners that would make his presence pleasing to noblewomen. In aristocratic circles an elaborate code of courtly love encouraged unmarried knights to demonstrate their prowess by winning the love of a noble lady. The pursuit of the love of a lady called for patterns of behavior extending far beyond the ability to wield the tools of war, and it placed a higher value on virtues associated with women: graciousness, the capacity to give love, gentleness. In order to respond to the new attention extended to them, noblewomen were expected to develop modes of behavior suited to a more refined world in which males and females mixed in a courtly setting.

The code of chivalry certainly did not totally transform noble behavior. The twelfth- and thirteenth-century record is full of violence and oppression perpetrated by unruly nobles whose excesses could be effectively curbed only by constraints forcefully imposed by superior lords, especially kings. Whether chivalry improved the status of women remains a disputed question. In legal and economic practice their role remained restricted. The emergence of the patrilineal family structure placed them more surely than ever under male domination. The prime objects of

WHERE HISTORIANS DISAGREE

Origins of the Medieval Nobility

During much of this century historians of the Middle Ages have disagreed in explaining the origins of the medieval nobility, the class which dominated political, social, economic, and cultural life.

Early in this century there was general consensus on an interpretation that was given classic expression by the French historian Marc Bloch in his seminal work entitled *Feudal Society*. Reflecting a view of aristocracy rooted in the Ancien Régime in France, Bloch defined "nobility" as a social class enjoying specific hereditary privileges defined by law. He argued that such a class did not emerge until the twelfth century. Before then there had existed a loosely defined aristocracy, the members of which enjoyed social prominence based on their personal association with royalty and on favors—chiefly land grants and offices—flowing from that connection. This social group was destroyed in the tumult following the collapse of the Carolingian empire. Amid that chaos, "new," "self-made" men enjoying a monopoly on military power used that power to carve out a legally sanctioned position of privilege transmitted by blood. In brief, the European nobility was derived from the aggressive, ruthless feudal warriors.

Recent investigations have raised questions about this explanation. Many historians, especially those influenced by concepts of social structures formulated by social scientists, argue that noble status embraces more than inherited legal privileges. They claim that noble status involves factors such as wealth, power over others, lifestyle, and mental perceptions. Any effort to explain the origins of the medieval nobility that focuses on narrow legal concerns without considering these factors is faulted.

Bloch's thesis has been challenged on another ground. He argued that during the tenth and eleventh centuries there was a break in an established order which created an opportunity for "new" men to forge a unique social status for themselves. But recent historians have shown that in many cases there was biological continuity linking Carolingian noble families to noble families of the eleventh and twelfth centuries. It can be demonstrated that some warrior upstarts entered the ranks of nobility during the tenth and eleventh centuries, chiefly by marrying into old noble families. But their social ascent by attaching themselves to existing noble circles does not support the case for a "new" and different nobility in the twelfth century. The issue of the origins of the nobility must involve the study of noble status in the early Middle Ages.

Further complicating our understanding of the origins of the medieval nobility is a changing view of the relationship between noble status and the warrior element in society. It was once nearly axiomatic that by the twelfth century every warrior—every knight—was *ipso facto* a noble. Historians are no longer quite so positive. There is much evidence to suggest that many knights held an inferior social status. What seems to have been more important than simply being a warrior was membership in a new kind of family structure in which the material resources of each family were transmitted from father to eldest son rather than being divided among all members of the family, as had been the ancient Germanic custom. In other words, noble status in the central Middle Ages originated only with the advent of the patrimonial family structure, which permitted the concentration and transmission of wealth in a narrow circle of families.

Their disagreement on the origins of the medieval nobility leaves historians at a loss in explaining a key source of dynamism in the medieval world: the processes which allowed some people to establish a pattern of dominance over society.

marriage remained the improvement of the economic and political status of the family and the rearing of children who would sustain the family status. Some evidence suggests that the new place defined for noblewomen in the chivalric code required them to be sheltered and protected as sex objects unsuited to participate in the world of work and power. What was important about chivalry was its enlargement of the range of activity proper to noble status. That expanded vision served both to distance nobles from the rest of society and to add complexity to the social function served by the nobility.

Taken together, the forces working to transform the conditions of noble life during the central Middle Ages resulted in the definition of the nobility as a leisured class of gentlemen and ladies clearly distinct from the rest of society by birth, wealth, and modes of behavior. The basic elements developed during the central Middle Ages to distinguish this dominant class survived long after the end of the Middle Ages to determine the norms of genteel behavior and to define the privileges enjoyed by those claiming aristocracy.

7. SOCIAL CHANGE: THE PEASANTRY

The peasantry was also affected socially by the currents of economic change. During the twelfth and thirteenth centuries, there was large-scale freeing of serfs, especially in France, England, Flanders, Italy, and western Germany. Some peasants purchased their freedom; some gained it in return for colonizing new lands and others by leaving the manors for the city. A more important cause was the willingness of manorial seigneurs to surrender their rights to a serf's produce and services for money payments. In much of the West the serf was thus becoming a legally free tenant farmer, enjoying whatever benefits freedom brought but also losing the paternalistic protection the manorial lord had extended.

In a general way, the material life of the peasants improved during these centuries. Their incomes increased as results of their greater productivity and the inflationary trends that caused the prices they received for their produce to rise faster than the value of the obligations they owed. As they gained access to local markets, their diet became better, their health and life expectancy improved, and they were able to enjoy a wider range of products. As might be expected, significant gradations in peasant status emerged as turns of fortune allowed some peasants to acquire the use of more land than others and as some proved to be more skillful and intelligent than others.

Some evidence suggests that as serfdom declined the peasants gained a greater degree of self-determination than they had had when most of them were locked into the manorial structure, legally bound to the soil as a dependent population. Most peasants continued to live in small villages and had few contacts with the wider world. In some cases they banded together to gain special privileges from their political superiors, which allowed them to control some aspects of village life, much as town dwellers—the bourgeoisie—were doing. They also sometimes directly influenced the management of the resources of the local church. Free peasants had more opportunity to decide how they would exploit their rented lands and how they would dispose of their crops. They could leave their villages to take up farming where conditions were more favorable, or they could seek their fortunes as traders or artisans in the expanding urban centers.

However, we must not push too far in assessing the improved lot of the peasants, who still remained at the bottom of the social scale. Perhaps they were even further removed from the top because of the increasing complexity, refinement, and class consciousness of the nobility. Peasants became even more the object of scorn by the nobility, whose members assumed that their elevated status and expanding economic needs gave them the right to exploit the peasantry economically. For the most part, peasant life remained hard, poor, limited, and controlled by the dominant aristocracy. As was the case with the nobility and the bourgeoisie, the basic legal and social patterns shaping peasant life became so solidly fixed during the central Middle Ages that they would persist far into the future.

Taken together, the changes just described changed the face of western Europe between 1000 and 1300. It became more populous, richer, more diversified in productive capacity, more complex in social structure, and collectively stronger. These changes put into place fundamental economic and social structures that would endure for centuries to determine how people lived, worked, and interacted with one another.

SUGGESTED READING

Overview of the Central Middle Ages, 1000–1300

Christopher Brooke, *Europe in the Central Middle Ages, 962–1154,* 2nd ed. (1987).

John H. Mundy, *Europe in the High Middle Ages, 1150–1309,* 2nd ed. (1991).

Malcolm Barber, *The Two Cities. Medieval Europe, 1050–1320* (1992).

Taken together, these well-written works will provide excellent coverage of the period covered in Part Four.

R. W. Southern, *The Making of the Middle Ages* (1953). A brilliant essay, concentrating on the "silent" forces affecting society.

Susan Reynolds, *Kingdoms and Communities in Western Europe 900–1300* (1984). A challenging effort to identify collectivities that shaped society in the High Middle Ages.

Economic History

R. H. Bautier, *The Economic Development of Medieval Europe,* trans. Heather Karolyi (1971).

N. J. G. Pounds, *An Economic History of Medieval Europe* (1974).

Two excellent general surveys of economic history.

Georges Duby, *Rural Economy and Country Life in the Medieval West,* trans. Cynthia Postan (1968).

Léopold Genicot, *Rural Communities in the Medieval West* (1990).

Together these two works will provide a good picture of rural life.

Robert S. Lopez, *The Commercial Revolution of the Middle Ages, 950–1350* (1971). A persuasive defense of an interesting thesis.

Jean Gimpel, *The Medieval Machine: The Industrial Revolution of the Middle Ages* (1976).

Social History

Christopher Brooke, *The Structure of Medieval Society* (1971). Describes the general features of the medieval social order.

The following works treat more specialized aspects of medieval society, as indicated by their titles.

Frances Gies and Joseph Gies, *Marriage and the Family in the Middle Ages* (1987).

Christopher Brooke, *The Medieval Idea of Marriage* (1988).

David Herlihy, *Medieval Households* (1985).

Maurice Keen, *Chivalry* (1984).

C. Stephen Jaeger, *The Origins of Courtliness: Civilizing Trends and the Formation of Courtly Ideals, 939–1210* (1985).

Frances Gies and Joseph Gies, *Life in a Medieval Village* (1990).

Shalamith Shahar, *The Fourth Estate. A History of Women in the Middle Ages,* trans. Chaya Galai (1983).

Margaret Wade Labarge, *A Small Sound of the Trumpet: Women in Medieval Life* (1986).

Mary Erler and Maryanne Kowaleski, eds., *Women and Power in the Middle Ages* (1988).

Constance H. Berman et al., *The Worlds of Medieval Women: Creativity, Influence, Imagination* (1985).

Shalamith Shahar, *Childhood in the Middle Ages* (1990).

Michel Mollat, *The Poor in the Middle Ages. An Essay in Social History,* trans. Arthur Goldhammer (1986).

John M. Carter, *Sports and Pastimes of the Middle Ages* (1988).

Joseph Gies and Frances Gies, *Life in a Medieval City* (1969).

CHAPTER 19

The Restoration of Political Order: The Revival of Monarchy, 1000–1300

FIGURE 19.1 A Medieval King's Nightmares These drawings from a manuscript portray a dream of Henry I of England. He dreams that his royal power will not be sufficient to control the major elements of his subjects: the peasants, the nobles, and the clergy. Perhaps because he dreamed what he had to face, Henry I was more successful than most of his contemporaries in winning the support of his diverse subjects. (The President and Fellows of Corpus Christi College, Oxford)

While western Europe's lesser men and women were producing new wealth and rearranging their social relationships, its crowned heads and their agents were successfully engaged in rebuilding political structures capable of controlling much larger political communities than the principalities that had dominated tenth-century western Europe. By 1300 their efforts had produced a level of political order in the West that had not existed since the collapse of the Roman imperial regime. No less important, the major political entities created between 1000 and 1300 marked the origins of states that have persisted until the present. Although state building advanced over all of western Europe, we shall focus attention chiefly on political developments in Germany, Italy, England, and France.

The larger and more effective political entities that developed betweeen 1000 and 1300 emerged from shadowy tenth-century kingdoms ruled by weak monarchs whose power had been assumed by lords exercising private authority on a local level. In expanding their power and creating institutional forms to sustain it, successful rulers of the central Middle Ages drew on a rich tradition that defined the role of the state and its rulers: the distant memory of the Roman Empire; Germanic concepts of warrior kings; the Carolingian ideal of ministerial kingship; political theories derived from biblical history, Greco-Roman philosophy, and Roman law; concepts of lordship and dependence imbedded in feudal practices. But in the final analysis the growth of royal power resulted from the sustained creative efforts of individual rulers to take advantage of contemporary political realities.

1. THE HOLY ROMAN EMPIRE

The earliest effort at political reconstruction during the central Middle Ages involved an entity that later came to be known as the Holy Roman Empire. This state emerged from the combination of parts of the Carolingian kingdoms created by the Treaty of Verdun in 843: the kingdom of the East Franks and the kingdom of Lotharingia and its later subdivisions (see Maps 16.2 and 19.1). During the late ninth and early tenth centuries, royal power declined steadily in these kingdoms as local potentates carved out principalities, imposed their lordship over the local population, and joined hands to replace the Carolingian dynasty with rulers selected from local families. In the Kingdom of the East Franks—Germany—that process resulted in the formation of the virtually independent duchies of Saxony, Bavaria, Franconia, and Swabia, each reflecting pre-Carolingian Germanic tribal groupings whose ethnic ties gave each one internal solidarity and each led by a duke who claimed to exercise the public powers originally bestowed on the ducal office by the Carolingian kings. In Italy an even more chaotic mosaic of local lordships emerged at the expense of royal authority.

In Germany the drift toward localism was reversed by Otto I, the Great (936–973), whose father had been duke of Saxony prior to his election to the royal office. In effect, Otto I sought to restore rulership on the Carolingian model. He successfully compelled the dukes to accept royal overlordship, a struggle that led to the replacement of several ducal families with members of his own family. He earned fame as an effective warrior by inflicting a decisive defeat on Magyar invaders of Germany at the battle of Lechfeld in 955 and by encouraging miltary expansion, colonization, and missionary activity eastward into the Slavic world. His success in these ventures stemmed from his ability to strengthen the institutional base of royal power through an alliance with religious leaders. He made large grants of royal land to bishops and abbots, who became royal vassals, obligated to render to the king the military and political services needed to sustain royal authority. This policy, called *lay investiture*, gave the German ruler virtual control over appointments to ecclesiastical offices and the use of ecclesiastical property.

Once successful in uniting and defending his German kingdom, Otto was drawn into Italian affairs. Although the Carolingian example played a part in shaping this fateful decision, Otto turned south for more immediate reasons. Many Italians, including the popes, were looking for an outsider to curb local disorder and to protect them from Saracen and Magyar attacks. Some of Otto's powerful subjects, especially the dukes of Bavaria, were tempted to fish in those troubled waters in search of a power base from which to defy royal authority. After an initial

Map 19.1 THE MEDIEVAL HOLY ROMAN EMPIRE This map clearly illustrates the vast extent of the Holy Roman Empire at the death of Frederick I Barbarossa in 1190; it was soon enlarged even more when his successor, Henry VI, took control of the Kingdom of the Two Sicilies as a consequence of his marriage to the heiress to that realm. Not only did the size of the empire but also the ethnic and cultural diversity of its population made its governance difficult. After 1200 the major principalities and cities indicated on the map, especially those in Italy, became increasingly independent.

venture into Italy in 951 that resulted in his assumption of the title "king of Italy," Otto returned a decade later to solidify his position. In 962 Pope John XII crowned him "emperor," thus renewing the office Charlemagne had revived in 800. Otto forced his authority on the Italian nobility and entrusted the exercise of royal power to church officials, who became his vassals. In settling affairs in Italy, Otto I was forced to depose John XII, dictate the election of a more pliant successor, and impose the rule that no pope would be selected in the future without the approval of the emperor. This decision, which opened an era of German domination of the papacy, punctuated the fact that the emperor was the head of the Christian community, just as Constantine and Charlemagne had been.

From Otto I's death in 973 until 1056 his policies were continued with considerable success. In both Germany and Italy nobles were made subservient to imperial authority and their efforts to act independently in their local lordships were checked. The religious establishment continued its invaluable service to the emperor. To complement the administrative functions performed by clerical vassals, the emperors developed a corps of secular officials, called *ministeriales*, recruited from the nonfree population under terms that made them totally devoted to royal service. The empire was expanded by the absorption of the old Carolingian subkingdom of Burgundy-Arles. Poland, Bohemia, and Hungary all recognized imperial overlordship. The emperors and their ecclesiastical supporters skillfully wove around the imperial office a theocratic ideology that stressed the sacred role of the emperor as protector of Christendom, a "renewed" (albeit somewhat smaller) Carolingian Empire in the West that was coequal in dignity to the Byzantine Empire in the East (see Figure 19.2).

But the very success of the German emperors provoked opposition from a variety of sources. The nobility remained eager to escape imperial control whenever possible. Aside from the general dislike of foreign domination felt in Italy, the emerging Italian commercial cities were eager to establish their liberty at the expense of imperial control. Rulers in France and the Slavic world were suspicious of imperial designs on their territories. Following ancient Germanic custom, the royal office remained elective, making it constantly vulnerable to political maneuvering by ambitious secular and religious leaders. Moreover, long-established custom dictated that only the pope could bestow the imperial crown, leaving the German rulers vulnerable to challenges to their exalted place in Christendom. That matter became crucial when the Holy Roman Empire became the focus of attack by leaders of a powerful religious reform movement sweeping over western Europe (see Chapter 21).

By the middle of the eleventh century that reform movement found its leadership in the papacy, which for the previous century had been controlled by the emperors. The turning point came when Emperor Henry III (1039–1056), himself an advocate of religious reform, installed a German bishop, Leo IX (1049–1054), as pope. Under Leo's leadership, a circle of reformers, spearheaded by a monk named Hildebrand (later Pope Gregory VII), articulated the ideological and practical goals of reform. In ideological terms this group rediscovered the ancient tradi-

FIGURE 19.2 The Holy Roman Emperor as "Agent of Christ" This tenth-century ivory plaque shows Emperor Otto I offering a model of the cathedral church of Magdeburg to Christ, who is seated in majesty. It reflects the convictions not only that the emperor controlled the Church but also that he was the intercessor between Christ and the faithful Christians on earth. (The Metropolitan Museum of Art, Gift of George Blumenthal, 1941)

tion that insisted that the Christian community— the Church—is an earthly corporate body that must have its own head, its own law, its own resources, and its own liberty in order to fulfill its divine mission of leading humanity to salvation. By implication secular rulers were denied a role as divinely ordained directors of Christian life; at best, princes were agents of the Church, commissioned by ecclesiastical authorities to assist in directing Christian society and subject to priestly judgment in serving their role. In practical terms, the papal reformers proclaimed the need to purify the religious establishment of whatever impeded its freedom of action, including lay control over ecclesiastical offices and property, and to purge from the ranks of the clergy those who had attained office by lay appointment and who exploited religious offices, property, and services for unholy purposes. Although this radical reform program threatened many secular and ecclesiastical leaders, especially vulnerable was the Holy Roman emperor, who not only manipulated ecclesiastical property and offices to create subservient clergymen who sustained his power but also claimed, by virtue of his exalted office, the God-given right to direct the destiny of Christian society.

During Leo IX's pontificate, the papacy turned reforming ideology into a practical reform program that impinged directly on the existing political and ecclesiastical establishment. The role of the bishop of Rome, the successor of St. Peter as Christ's vicar on earth, as head of the Christian community was vigorously propagated throughout the West, often backed up by papal agents sent to intervene in local ecclesiastical affairs. In 1059 a papal decree provided that henceforth popes would be chosen by the College of Cardinals, a body of ecclesiastical officials centered in Rome who assisted the pope in carrying out papal administration; the emperor was deprived of any voice in papal elections except to approve what the cardinals decided. In that same year the papacy formed an alliance with the Normans, a new political force emerging in southern Italy and Sicily (see Chapter 20), thereby gaining a protector that could serve as a foil to the emperor. The papacy issued a steady flow of legislation seeking to eliminate immorality and corruption afflicting the clergy, a cause that was taken up by papally sponsored local church councils all over the West. That legislative program culminated in 1075, when Pope Gregory VII (1073–1085) decreed that lay investiture—that is, control by lay authorities over the election and installation of ecclesiastical officials and over the property associated with these offices—was illegal; henceforth these matters crucial to the liberty of the religious establishment would be decided from within that establishment. This act put the papacy onto a collision course with most of the kings and lords of western Europe, and especially the Holy Roman emperor, in a contest known as the *investiture struggle.*

Confronted with Gregory's prohibition of lay investiture, the reigning German king, Henry IV (1056–1106), chose to act as his predecessors had

in dealing with the religious establishment. In 1075 he filled the vacant episcopal office of the key Italian city of Milan with a candidate of his choice and then defied papal efforts to undo his action. Whereupon in 1076 Gregory VII excommunicated the king, suspended him from office, and invited the Germans to elect a new king. A coalition of German nobles and bishops immediately informed Henry that unless he cleared himself of excommunication before the meeting of an assembly to be held in early 1077, he would be deposed; Gregory was invited to preside over the assembly. Henry's response was tactically brilliant. He went to Italy, where at Canossa he intercepted Gregory, already en route to Germany, and in the garb of a penitent begged the pope's forgiveness. After keeping the king waiting in the snow for three days, Gregory met his priestly responsibility by absolving the repentant sinner. Although the pope had won a moral victory, his action freed Henry to counterattack. During the next few years Henry neutralized his enemies in Germany, captured Rome, forced Gregory into exile, and in 1084 had himself crowned emperor by a pope he installed to replace Gregory.

But Henry's victory was a hollow one. Before his death in 1106 he lost control of Rome to the Normans, saw the reforming party resume control of the papal office, and suffered serious setbacks at the hands of the German nobility. Under his three successors, who ruled until 1152, imperial control in Italy virtually disappeared, usurped by independent towns, nobles, and the papacy. In Germany the royal office became a pawn of warring noble factions that demanded political concessions in return for their support of any candidate for the crown. In 1122 Emperor Henry V did settle the issue of lay investiture by joining the pope in accepting the Concordat of Worms, which provided that the ecclesiastical establishment would control election to church offices and the bestowal of the spiritual powers of those offices while the lands and secular powers associated with such offices would be invested by the king. While this compromise left German rulers with an important role in filling ecclesiastical offices, it deprived them of absolute control over what had long been a mainstay of their power, a subservient clergy willing to serve the ruler's political needs.

More significantly, the long struggle between popes and emperors led to a fundamental change in the power structure of the Holy Roman Empire. The incessant civil strife resulting from challenges to the emperor's authority by the papacy and its supporters created an opportunity for powerful noble families and ecclesiastical leaders to create local lordships over which the royal government had only vague claims of authority and little means of exercising effective control. This development undermined the Ottonian system of royal government, in which royal authority was based on the ruler's claim of being the God-ordained head of the Christian community. Having claimed its liberty, the religious establishment, led by the bishops of Rome, now claimed headship of Christian society, leaving the ministerial king with little upon which to base his right to direct the lordships being shaped in the Holy Roman Empire.

Despite the adverse impact of the investiture struggle, the Holy Roman Empire survived. At mid–twelfth century a new dynasty, the Hohenstaufens, undertook to rebuild imperial government. The first notable Hohenstaufen, Frederick I, Barbarossa ("Red Beard," 1152–1190), charted the new course. To establish an independent material base for royal power, he increased the royal domain, that is, the territory under direct control of the king, and entrusted its administration to nonnoble civil servants who owed their position and loyalty to the king. He also curried the support of Germany's growing cities by conceding liberties in return for financial support. He sought to use these resources as a means of enforcing specific rights over his subjects that he claimed belonged to him by virtue of his office as king and emperor. In general, Frederick's concept of regalian rights was based less on theocratic principles than on secular principles grounded in Roman law and in customs defining lordship and dependency.

Frederick's effort to assert his regalian rights led to a prolonged conflict with a variety of foes. In Germany he sought to collaborate with a few great noble families willing to become royal vassals in exchange for concessions that allowed them considerable power to dominate the lesser nobles in their extensive principalities. But a faction of these nobles, called the Welfs, constantly opposed the king, forcing him finally to break up the large principalities and grant territory to many lesser nobles willing to serve as royal vassals. In Italy an even more potent array of foes, called the Guelfs, faced Frederick. He initially enjoyed the support of the papacy, which granted him the imperial title in 1155, but that relationship soon turned hostile, chiefly because Frederick steadfastly insisted on asserting control over ecclesiastical appointments and property on the basis of rights he claimed adhered to his office. The result was a long battle between emperor and pope, marked by the emperor's attempt to select a pope favorable to imperial interests to replace Pope Alexander III (1159–1181), a true heir of Gregory VII in terms of protecting the liberties of the religious establishment; in 1177 Frederick finally recognized the legitimacy of Alexander, in effect conceding that his imperial office did not entitle him to control the papacy. Throughout this struggle the papacy was supported by the Norman kingdom of Sicily, which remained a constant threat to Frederick's position in Italy until 1186, when he arranged a marriage between his son and the heiress to that kingdom. Especially dangerous to Frederick's position were the rich commercial cities of northern Italy, whose wealth and independence were threatened by Frederick's aggressive efforts to reclaim rights in their governance which he claimed they had usurped. The cities responded by forming the Lombard League, which in 1176 inflicted a serious defeat on the imperial army. Finally, in 1183, Frederick and the Lombard League agreed on the Peace of Constance, which provided that the Italian cities would recognize Frederick's overlordship in return for his concession of specific rights that ensured their control over their internal affairs.

Despite his setbacks and compromises, when Frederick Barbarossa drowned in 1190 while leading the Third Crusade, he left behind the framework for a political system that had the potential to establish effective royal government over his sprawling empire. However, his successors were unable to sustain his program. His son, Henry VI (1190–1197), began his reign auspiciously by successfully claiming the throne of the kingdom of Sicily, acting decisively to check papal attempts to undermine Hohenstaufen power in Italy, and pursuing an aggressive policy that expanded Hohenstaufen influence in the eastern

Mediterranean. However, Henry's early death cut short his ambitious program and plunged the empire into an extended crisis centering around the issue of succession. His only heir was an infant son, Frederick, too young to succeed to his father. Rival candidates representing Hohenstaufen and Welf factions emerged in Germany to claim Henry's inheritance; their rivalry divided Germany into warring camps. The struggle there was complicated by the intervention of Pope Innocent III, King John of England, and King Philip II of France. The northern Italian cities sought to use this tumult to expand their independence from imperial control. As legal guardian of the young Frederick, Pope Innocent III assumed virtual control over the kingdom of Sicily. This complex and prolonged struggle was finally resolved in 1212, when Innocent's ward, Frederick, aided by Philip II of France and by Innocent, won the upper hand in Germany. His victory led to his election as king of Germany and soon after as Holy Roman emperor. Because of the disturbances affecting the empire during the years since his father's death, Frederick II faced a formidable task.

A gifted, educated, cosmopolitan figure whose talents caused some of his contemporaries to hail him as a wonder of the world (*stupor mundi*) while others branded him as irreligious, immoral, the Antichrist, Frederick II took a new approach to his imperial office. Almost immediately after his election in 1212, he made sweeping concessions that gave the papacy control over the German ecclesiastical establishment and assured German princes of extensive rights of government over their lordships. As he progressively disengaged himself from direct rulership over Germany, Frederick turned his energies toward creating in his homeland, the Kingdom of Sicily, a centralized, bureacratic state where the ruler would be absolute. His program for this regime was spelled out in a code of law, called the Constitutions of Melfi, issued in 1231. This document, strongly influenced by concepts drawn from Roman law and by the model of the Byzantine Empire, gave the king supreme authority as lawgiver and judge, set up a bureaucracy to control local affairs, and abolished privileges enjoyed by nobles, towns, and ecclesiastical officials. Frederick then attempted to impose a comparable regime on Italy, a move that again activated the ancient enemies of the Hohenstaufens: the papacy and the Italian cities. Frederick battled this coalition with skill and flair for twenty years but was unable to establish control over Italy. During that interval imperial power in Germany practically vanished to the great advantage of local princes, high ecclesiastical officials, and towns. When Frederick II died in 1250, the prospects were indeed dim for the realization of one of the cherished ideals of medieval society—a Christian empire in which people who held one faith would enjoy one ruler and one law to guide them in the struggle for salvation. But what lay in the future must not obscure the fact that for three centuries prior to 1250 the Holy Roman Empire was the most prominent state in western Europe and that its rulers exercised an authority that provided stability to a large population occupying a considerable part of western Europe.

2. ENGLAND

While the German rulers struggled to govern their extensive empire, political consolidation progressed more effectively in England. During the first half of the eleventh century the effective monarchy established by Alfred and his successors (see Chapter 16) began to falter in the face of efforts by powerful nobles to create private lordships and new threats by Scandinavian invaders. When the last Anglo-Saxon king, Edward the Confessor (1042–1066), died without an heir, a struggle to decide the succession ensued that changed the course of England's history. The victor, a claimant from the Continent, William, duke of Normandy, led an invading army that defeated a rival Anglo-Saxon candidate, Harold, at the battle of Hastings in 1066 (see Color Plate 9). William's victory allowed the Conqueror to claim not only the royal title but also control over England.

From the beginning of his reign William I (1066–1089) based his authority on the powers claimed by his Anglo-Saxon predecessors. To ensure the resources needed to assert those powers and to establish his Norman followers as a new ruling elite in England, he adapted usages borrowed from the system of lordship prevailing in his continental duchy of Normandy to suit his situation in England. Claiming a large portion of England by right of conquest, he set aside extensive lands as a royal domain and then granted the rest to his Norman followers as fiefs. In return they became his direct vassals (called *tenants-in-chief* or *barons*), owing him services, chiefly military, in proportion to the size of their fiefs. Although his tenants-in-chief were allowed to subinfeudate their holdings and acquire their own vassals, William insisted that all subvassals owed first allegiance to the king. Through this arrangement the new king secured a substantial domain from which he derived significant income, the military service of about five thousand knights, and rights of lordship over the newly installed Norman nobility.

Working from this solid power base, William I laid the foundations for a government capable of asserting royal authority throughout his realm. The Anglo-Saxon Witan was replaced by the *Curia Regis* (the court of the king), to which tenants-in-chief and ecclesiastical leaders were summoned to fulfill their obligation as vassals to give counsel to their royal lord and to judge cases involving the king-lord and his vassals. The Anglo-Saxon units of local administration, the shires and hundreds, continued to operate as agencies through which the king kept in direct touch with the English populace in matters of justice, peacekeeping, and taxation. To complement the income from the royal domain, William continued to impose direct taxes on his subjects and to collect dues associated with vassalage. The king's zeal in this matter was demonstrated by the Domesday Book, a compilation drawn up in 1086 to record the results of a survey conducted by royal agents to ascertain fief by fief what the king's subjects possessed and how much they owed the king. The ecclesiastical establishment was drawn into support of the monarchy. William played a key role in filling high religious offices and extracting dues from church property. Such practices risked bringing down the wrath of the reformers who caused so much trouble for his contemporary, Emperor Henry IV. William avoided this danger by making generous gifts to the religious establishment, by respecting the liberty of church officials in con-

ducting religious courts, and especially by championing religious reform in England, a cause pushed with special vigor by Lanfranc, a Norman reformer installed by William as archbishop of Canterbury.

The Norman conquest thus marked a watershed in English history. Aside from giving new vitality to the English monarchy, the coming of the Normans drew England into the vigorous economic, religious, and cultural movements that were revitalizing society on the Continent. To be sure, many of the unique aspects of traditional Anglo-Saxon society were slowly effaced during the next century, a development lamented by many in England then and later. But on the whole England benefited greatly from closer contacts with continental Europe.

During the century following William I's death, his successors (known as the Norman-Angevin dynasty) were energetic, capable kings who worked hard to expand royal power: the rough, brutal William II (1087–1100); the quiet, prudent, avaricious Henry I (1100–1135); the ambitious, tempestuous Henry II (1154–1189); and the colorful, romantic knight Richard I, the Lion-Hearted (1189–1199). Although these kings devoted considerable energy to protecting and managing their extensive continental holdings (see pp. 262–263 and Map 19.2), we shall concentrate here on their efforts to create a strong monarchy capable of ruling a unified state (see Figure 19.1).

Never far from the minds of any of these kings were the protection and expansion of the material and military resources upon which royal power depended. They were avid—too avid, many thought—in exploiting the royal domain, still a major source of royal income, collecting every possible due owed by royal vassals, and discovering new sources of income, especially customs duties on the expanding trade and direct taxes on property. Their military support depended primarily on the services rendered the king by his tenants-in-chief. However, the kings still maintained the ancient royal right to summon the *fyrd*, the army of all freemen in the realm. Toward the end of the twelfth century the kings began to allow those who owed them military service to make money payments, called *scutage* or shield money, in lieu of personal ser-

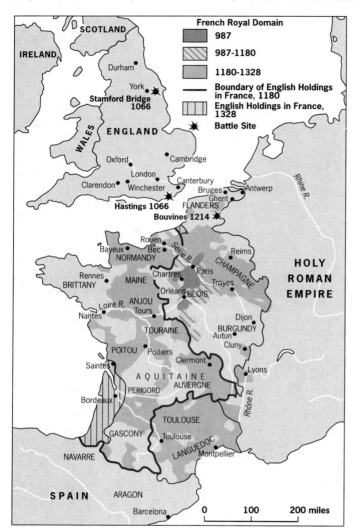

Map 19.2 MEDIEVAL FRANCE AND ENGLAND During the central Middle Ages it was in France and England that the greatest advances were made in consolidating power in royal hands. As the map suggests, England was not plagued with many deeply rooted local political entities, as was France. The map points up two trends that had a vital effect on the political destinies of France and England. First, it illustrates the steady shrinking of English holdings on the Continent. Second, it shows the success of the French kings in bringing much of that territory under direct royal control, thereby creating the territorial basis for a unified French kingdom.

vice; this income was used to hire mercenary troops. By the end of the twelfth century these efforts ensured that the English kings enjoyed a stronger financial and military base for their power than did any other rulers in Europe.

More innovative were steps taken by the twelfth-century English kings, especially Henry I and Henry II, to develop a royal administrative system capable of asserting the royal will, an effort given special impetus by the quest for financial resources. Drawing on the services of the personnel associated with the royal household and the Curia Regis, in which the king's tenants-in-chief were obliged to serve as part of their obligation to their royal overlord, the kings began to gather at their court a corps of individuals who devoted increasing amounts of time to administrative functions. The activities of these semipermanent royal servants soon began to focus on specialized administrative functions. As a result of this process four specialized departments of administration began to take shape during the twelfth century: the *Exchequer*, for collecting moneys due the king; the *Treasury*, for guarding and dispensing royal funds; the *Chancery*, for issuing royal orders and composing royal correspondence; and *royal courts of justice*. The routine business associated with these activities was increasingly performed by literate, non-noble civil servants whose livelihood and status depended on service to the king. A major responsibility of the central administrative apparatus was the supervision of the sheriffs, the royal officials charged with exercising the king's authority in the counties or shires that served as the local units of administration. This professionalized administrative system not only ensured that the bulk of the population became aware of royal authority but also placed increasingly insurmountable obstacles in the way of anyone with ambitions to carve out a private sphere of power.

Of particular significance in expanding royal power during the twelfth century was the development of a royal system of justice which provided one of the positive benefits of effective royal government. The expansion of royal justice was in large part a response to the confusion surrounding the existing system of justice under which various courts—shire, baronial, manorial, ecclesiastical, town—were conducted by judges of diverse competencies who applied different systems of law, procedures, and penalties. The kings' advisers sought to diminish this diversity by expanding the basic royal right to give justice in ways that would provide a system of justice common to all royal subjects, a step that had the added attraction of increasing the royal income derived from fees for court costs and fines.

The expansion of the royal system of justice advanced on many levels. The judicial functions previously performed by the barons acting in the Curia Regis began to be taken over by central judicial bodies directed by professional judges who held sessions at the royal court. The number of royal judges was increased by the introduction of a *circuit court system* under which itinerant judges were sent into the shires at set intervals to try cases in the name of the king. By comparing notes on their individual decisions and by following the guidance provided by judges serving the central courts, these itinerant judges began to shape a *common law* based on precedent that could guide them in deciding new cases. Royal judges sought to expand their jurisdictions

by intruding into judicial realms heretofore controlled by baronial, manorial, ecclesiastical, and town courts. Royal jurisdiction over criminal matters was expanded by legislation defining new crimes against the royal peace. Insisting that no person should lose property unjustly, the kings provided dissatisfied litigants involved in civil cases in the traditional courts an opportunity to purchase *writs* ordering a royal court to inquire into their cases. In effect, purchasing a writ amounted to transferring a civil dispute from the baronial, manorial, and town courts to the royal courts.

To encourage the use of royal courts, important innovations were made to ensure speedier and more efficient judicial processes: regularly scheduled court sessions, clearly fixed court fees, utilization of trained judges, uniform punishments. Significant in this respect was the introduction of the jury system. Building on an earlier practice of requiring subjects to tell under oath what they knew about some matter of public interest, Henry II ordered sheriffs to summon within their shires a *presentment* or *grand jury* made up of knowledgeable local residents who were required under oath to bring charges against those who had committed crimes in that area. On the basis of such testimony, the sheriffs could proceed to bring suspected criminals to trial. After trial by ordeal (see Chapter 13) was outlawed at the Fourth Lateran Council in 1215, comparable groups known as *petit* (little) juries began to be used to decide on the basis of evidence presented to them the guilt or innocence of those accused of violating the law.

The growth of royal power during the twelfth century occasionally brought the monarchs into conflict with the religious establishment. During the reign of William II, the clergy, led by Anselm, archbishop of Canterbury, challenged the monarch's right to appoint ecclesiastical officials; this quarrel was resolved by the Compromise of Bec in 1107, which allowed the church to elect its own officials but gave the king the privilege of investing these officials with the lands attached to their offices. A more serious clash arose in 1164, when Henry II issued his Constitutions of Clarendon, which sought to impose serious restrictions on the jurisdiction of ecclesiastical courts. The archbishop of Canterbury, Thomas à Becket, resisted what he considered to be an infringement on the liberty of the religious establishment and was murdered under circumstances that made it seem that Henry was responsible (see Figure 19.3). During the ensuing uproar Henry was forced to concede certain liberties to ecclesiastical courts. However, despite these challenges the English kings exercised considerable control over religious affairs, and the religious establishment gave its support to the monarchy. Unlike the Holy Roman Empire, England was spared the disruptive impact of a struggle with the clerical establishment.

During the twelfth century the English kings enjoyed remarkable success in expanding royal authority without encountering sustained resistance. However, implicit in the structure of the political system they created was a principle that eventually had to be confronted. Among other things, the English kings were lords whose dependent vassals—especially the great barons—had rights implicit in their status as vassals that must be respected. During the thirteenth century the kings were increasingly called upon to honor those rights, with the result that limits were imposed on the growth of royal power.

King John (1199–1216) was the first to be challenged. Inclined toward rashness and arbitrary action, he managed to suffer defeats at the hands of powerful enemies under circumstances that emboldened some of his subjects to challenge his authority. He became involved in a long struggle with King Philip II of France (see pp. 262–263) that forced him to impose a heavy burden on his subjects but that ended in a disastrous defeat that cost him most of his possessions in France. His situation was complicated when his effort to appoint an archbishop of Canterbury caused Pope Innocent III to suspend all religious services in England until the king bowed before papal authority. These setbacks finally goaded powerful nobles and clergy to meet in 1214 with the express purpose of organizing a rebellion aimed at curbing the king's tyrannical actions. John extricted himself from this crisis by signing the Magna Carta in 1215. Later celebrated as a charter of liberty, the Great Charter basically affirmed the traditional liberties of nobles, clergy, and townspeople. Its framers had no thought of destroying effective royal government; rather, they insisted on the principle that certain of the king's subjects had rights, defined by law, custom, and

FIGURE 19.3 Murder in the Cathedral: The Making of a Martyr This manuscript illustration shows agents of King Henry II murdering Archbishop Thomas à Becket in the cathedral at Canterbury. (The Walters Art Gallery, Baltimore)

contract, which the king must respect. But in doing so they began to define broad principles that curbed royal power in certain crucial areas, especially in taxation without the consent of those taxed and in arbitrary administration of justice without respect for the law.

The clash between the king and the privileged over the extent and limits of royal power continued throughout the reign of John's son,

Henry III (1216–1272). His costly foreign ventures and inept conduct of royal business caused exasperated nobles to resist him in several ways: They forced him to reissue the Magna Carta, compelled him to dismiss the foreigners who served him as advisers, formed a council of nobles to supervise the operation of the royal government, and finally incited a major rebellion. These efforts were ultimately thwarted by the inability of the king's opponents to agree on a course of action and by military measures taken against the rebels. In fact, these clashes hid a more fundamental development upon which Henry's successor, Edward I (1272–1307), capitalized to bring medieval English monarchy to its fullest development. Even during the troubled times of John and Henry III, royal government continued to grow in complexity and effectiveness to the point where many nobles, clergy, and townspeople began to share a sense of its vital importance to their interests. What modern historians have called a *community of the realm* was emerging, comprising powerful elements who shared a consciousness of belonging to a larger entity, a nation, and a concern that the king and his officials govern that realm in a way that would take their collective interests into account.

Edward I's reign represented an effort to solidify the position of the central government in such a way. He introduced administrative reforms intended to correct abuses of power by royal officials that led to complaints from the powerful interests those officials served. He took the initiative in enacting a series of fundamental laws which defined in more precise terms the rights and powers of the king and the manner in which these should be exercised. In pursuing this course of action, which on the whole strengthened royal government at the expense of the nobility, the religious establishment, and the towns, Edward made regular use of *Parliament* as an instrumentality through which the community of the realm could express its political concerns. The roots of this institution lay in advisory bodies, such as the Witan and its successor, the Curia Regis, to which kings had traditionally summoned their tenants-in-chief and high church officials to provide counsel in matters of state. By the thirteenth century it became the practice to add to such advisory bodies representatives who could speak for a broader spectrum of England's free population, a precedent that Edward I sanctioned in his Model Parliament of 1295, to which he summoned two knights from each shire and two burghers from each town to join the feudal barons and clergy in taking counsel with the king. Edward called meetings of Parliament primarily to serve his own purposes, especially to gain approval for additional taxes and for new legislation expanding royal power. However, Parliament did provide an institutional setting in which complaints against royal government could be voiced and suggestions for change proposed; from such pleas emerged the right of Parliament to initiate legislation binding on the king and the entire realm. Although its organization and powers still remained vague during Edward I's reign, its very existence reflected an essential feature of medieval England's political system: The king had to rule in a fashion that took into account the concerns and rights of at least some of his subjects. The sophisticated administrative, judicial, fiscal, and military apparatus that had evolved over three centuries allowed the king a wide latitude to act in ways that brought peace and order to the English populace, but there were "constitutional" limits beyond which royal power could not extend.

3. FRANCE

The emergence of effective monarchy proceeded more slowly in France than in England and under different circumstances. The medieval French state had its origins in one of the subdivisions of the Carolingian Empire created by the Treaty of Verdun in 843 (see Map 16.2), the Kingdom of the West Franks, over which, except for brief intervals, members of the Carolingian family ruled until 987. Under the last Carolingians royal power declined steadily, and the kingdom was fragmented into numerous small principalities controlled by powerful local lords. In 987 these lords, joined by the clergy, finally ended the Carolingian dynasty by electing as their king one of their own, Hugh Capet, count of Paris, whose descendants, called the Capetians, ruled France until 1328. The first four Capetians, who reigned from 987 to 1108, exercised almost no power outside their own domain, a modest territory around Paris (see Map 19.2). Throughout the rest of the kingdom powerful lords did as they pleased in their own principalities. The first Capetians did manage to establish a hereditary claim to the throne and to maintain the fiction inherited from the Carolingian world that the royal office was surrounded by a sacral quality which elevated its holder above all who were his subjects. The kings also claimed lordship over many local potentates, who were considered to be vassals owing services to their royal lord in return for the fiefs that made up their principalities.

For a long time these royal claims meant little in reality. Between 843 and 1108 the history of the Kingdom of France, which can be told only in terms of the history of each of the lordships into which it was divided (see Map 19.2), is primarily a study in political fragmentation. However, by the eleventh century a subtle change began to emerge. Local lords—dukes, counts, viscounts, castellans—began to establish more effective control over their principalities by a rigorous assertion of their rights of lordship. They exploited those rights to shape institutions that permitted them to amass sufficient military and fiscal resources to compel the obedience of their noble and servile dependents, to assume control over the administration of justice, and to command the support of the local religious establishment. This consolidation of local lordships was most notable in the great royal fiefs of northern France, especially Normandy, Flanders, Anjou, Maine, Champagne, Burgundy, and Blois. The effectiveness of such lords was exemplified by William, duke of Normandy, who was able to muster sufficient resources to conquer England. In southern France the royal fiefs such as Aquitaine, Gascony, and Toulouse remained more fragmented.

Until the early twelfth century the Capetian kings of France played no significant role in the process of local consolidation, but then the situation began to change. Louis VI (1108–1137) was able to establish effective control over his vassals in the royal domain and to create an administrative machinery that provided him sufficient resources to exercise the rights of lordship he claimed over vassals holding fiefs once granted by the king. With increasing frequency he acted as judge in cases involving his vassals, protected weaker ones against stronger, controlled the succession of fiefs, and annexed disputed territories to the royal domain. Illustrative of his expanding strength was the decision of the dying duke of Aquitaine to entrust his daughter and heiress, Eleanor, to the protection of his overlord, the king of France. Louis VI promptly arranged for the marriage of his ward to his own son, setting the stage for the annexation of Aquitaine to the royal domain.

The modest progress made by Louis VI in expanding royal influence was threatened by a major crisis that emerged under his successor, Louis VII (1137–1180). In part the crisis resulted from Louis VII's political ineptitude, exemplified by the fate of his marriage to Eleanor. Not only did this patroness of troubadour poets and devotee of the ideals of courtly love fail to produce a male heir, it was also rumored that she had been unfaithful to the king when she accompanied him on the Second Crusade. Perhaps her behavior resulted from her own frustration, for she is alleged to have said that she had discovered she had married a monk instead of a king. As a result, the pious Louis divorced her and was forced to surrender her dowry, the duchy of Aquitaine. But the hapless king's major difficulty did not stem from his political and marital ineptitude. During his reign a sequence of events unfolded to create what historians call the Angevin "empire," comprising several major royal fiefs in France joined together in the hands of a single royal vassal. The architects of this conglomeration were the counts of Anjou, who through inheritance, conquest, and marriage alliances managed to establish hereditary claim to a substantial territory, including Normandy, Anjou, Brittany, Maine, and the Touraine (see Map 19.2). In 1151, by the accidents of inheritance, all these possession fell into the hands of a single family member, Henry. In 1152 that same Henry married the recently divorced Eleanor and acquired Aquitaine as her dowry. For all these territories Henry was vassal of Louis VII. Then in 1154, the already well endowed Angevin heir became Henry II, king of England. Obviously, his "empire" provided him with resources far exceeding those of his lord, the king of France, whose power was in serious jeopardy.

It remained for Philip II Augustus (1180–

1223) to respond to the challenge posed by the Angevin "empire"; he did so in a fashion that marked a turning point in the history of the medieval French monarchy. During the first two decades of his reign he maneuvered successfully to prevent his vassals, the English kings Henry II and Richard I, from solidifying their hold on their continental possessions. With the accession of John came an opportunity for more decisive action. When John allegedly violated the rights of one of his vassals on the Continent, Philip II exercised his right as John's overlord to summon his vassal to stand judgment for his conduct as a vassal, found the English king guilty of being an unfaithful vassal, and confiscated his fiefs. To carry out his sentence, Philip proceeded by force of arms to annex Normandy, Anjou, Maine, the Touraine, and parts of northern Aquitaine to the royal domain, a task made easier by John's troubles with his English subjects and with Philip's ally, Pope Innocent III. Philip's control of these territories was ensured by a victory in 1214 at the battle of Bouvines, where he crushed the forces of John and his anti-Hohenstaufen allies from the Holy Roman Empire. Philip II's victory provided the power base that allowed his successors to continue to bring territory under direct royal control as part of the royal domain. They employed various means of claiming territory: marriage alliances that permitted the Capetian family to inherit fiefs; confiscation of fiefs held by vassals judged unfaithful; recovery of fiefs held by vassals who died without heirs; purchase; conquest. King Henry III of England sought to thwart the expansion of the French royal domain by recapturing the fiefs lost to Philip II, but eventually, in 1259, was forced to agree to a treaty giving up his claims in France except for a small territory in Gascony. When the Capetian dynasty finally ended in 1328, the king or a close member of the royal family exercised direct control over most of the principalities that had once enjoyed virtual independence. What had been a political mosaic had become a consolidated kingdom.

More than territorial consolidation was involved in creating medieval France. The later Capetians, especially Philip II, Louis IX (1226–1270), and Philip IV, the Fair (1285–1314), worked vigorously to develop institutions that would allow them to govern their expanding realm effectively. To create an effective central administration at their capital in Paris, they adapted and expanded primitive institutions inherited from the early Capetians: the Curia Regis, a court of the king's vassals; the royal household (*hôtel*), made up of officials who looked after the personal needs of the royal family; and the *provosts*, agents who managed the royal estates. Out of these institutions gradually emerged an extensive central court staffed by full-time royal agents, often trained as lawyers, serving in specialized departments devoted to financial matters, administration of justice, and record keeping. The jurisdiction claimed by this central administration was constantly expanded by royal ordinances which drew on feudal practice, Roman law, classical political theory, and Christian ideology for precedents justifying the expansion of royal authority. By the reign of Philip IV the central administration had become a fully professionalized body of officials devoted to enhancing royal power and capable of asserting a collective force that guaranteed obedience to the royal will. Perhaps its power even exceeded that of the central government that served the English kings.

As the royal domain grew, the kings were faced with the monumental task of devising a system of local government. Unlike the situation in England, where kings were served by the ancient system of shires and sheriffs that allowed them to intervene directly in local affairs, the early Capetians had no means of exercising authority across most of their kingdom; local government was the monopoly of local lords. Philip II attacked this problem by creating special officials known as *baillis* (bailiffs), whose numbers and powers were increased by his successors. Usually selected from nonnoble personnel drawn from the royal court, these officials were assigned to specific territories within the royal domain to hold courts, collect taxes, and keep order in the name of the king; their enthusiasm for such pursuits was increased by the fact that their reward depended on what they exacted from the king's subjects. Louis IX established special officers called *enquêteurs* (investigators) to check on the conduct of the bailiffs and to report misdeeds to the central government. Although the local nobility continued to perform many political functions and to resist royal intrusion, the bailiffs, acting in the name of the kings, steadily assumed political functions once monopolized by local lords. Their efforts slowly imposed a common administration on France.

The broadening range of royal activities, especially waging war to expand and protect the royal domain and supporting the expanding royal administration, placed a heavy financial burden on the kings. A significant part of the royal income continued to be derived from royal lands, but other sources of revenue had to be found. Aside from feudal dues, fines, and fees for royal services, the royal government had few sources of regular income. As a result, the kings often had to resort to arbitrary exactions from any source possible: towns, the religious establishment, Jews, foreign bankers and merchants, nobles who fell out of royal favor. Especially during the reign of Philip IV, the measures used to satisfy the ravenous royal appetite for money produced complaints of royal tyranny and aroused widespread resistance.

Partly in reponse to their need for revenues, the Capetians instituted another practice that strengthened their authority. Expanding on the ancient practice of seeking counsel by callinng their vassals to the Curia Regis, they began in the fourteenth century to summon representatives of the three major social groupings (*estates*)—the nobles, the clergy, and the townspeople—to advise them and approve their policies. Philip IV convoked three of these *Estates General* to approve policies that extended his authority, thereby giving the impression that the entire nation supported his policy. The Estates General was much more a tool of the French monarchs than the English Parliament was, chiefly because the major power groups in France, especially the nobility, failed to develop a sense of shared interest in and concern for the affairs of the entire realm.

Throughout most of the long period during which the Capetians were consolidating their hold on France, they drew invaluable aid from both the papacy and the higher clergy in France. The kings bestowed wealth on the religious establishment, supported reform, took the side of the papacy in the investiture struggle, and respected religious liberties. In return, high church officials supported the royal claims to greater power and lent their wealth and talent to royal service. This fruitful relationship did not end until the reign of Philip IV, who became embroiled in a bitter struggle with Pope Boniface VIII (1294–1303) over the extent of the king's power to tax ecclesiastical property and judge the clergy. As we shall see (Chapter 24), Philip IV won a stunning victory over the mighty head of Christendom, so long successful in thwarting the Holy Roman emperors. The explanation is clear: By the early fourteenth century the king of France possessed a power base that even the pope could not dissolve by simple command.

Amid both their travails and their successes the Capetians managed one more achievement: They endowed their royal office with an aura that made it seem to many a reflection of kingship at its best. The prestige of the Capetians is best exemplified by Louis IX, eventually recognized as a saint. In no small part because of his actual accomplishments, Louis was hailed in his own time as a lover of justice, model Christian, gallant knight, crusader, peacemaker, promoter of morality, ideal son, husband, and father—in short, the ideal Christian prince (see Figures 19.4 and 20.1). Although not all were endowed with Louis' talents, most of the Capetians shared at least some of that aura of excellence, proving them to be as skillful in fashioning an image as in shaping effective political institutions. That image did much to enhance their real power in France and throughout Europe.

Between 1000 and 1300 the political face of western Europe was certainly changed in ways that prefigured the future by political leaders seeking a solution to a problem that had persisted since the dissolution of the Roman Empire—how to create a stable political order capable of binding men and women into a large-scale community that promoted the common goals of its members. A succession of German rulers sought with some success to unite Germany and Italy into a single state guided by principles defined by Christian universalism; that effort ultimately failed, leaving in its wake a fragmented political order in Germany and Italy that would prevail far into the future and a dream of somehow finding a way to create a single European political community. In England and France equally resourceful leaders fashioned

FIGURE 19.4 A Queen at Work This manuscript illustration shows Queen Blanche of Castile, wife of King Louis VIII (1223–1226), keeping close watch over the education of her son, King Louis IX (1226–1270). Even while she was asserting her role as a mother, she was acting as regent for a kingdom that Louis IX inherited when he was an infant. Her son became a great king and a saint. (Bibliothèque Nationale, Paris, ms. fr. 5716)

institutions that allowed them to exercise sufficient authority over their subjects to ensure peace and order within a limited geographical area, but with constraints that left privileged groups sufficient liberty to ensure their role as partners in the task of governance; these rulers had laid the basis for nation-states as a prime factor in western Europe's political future.

SUGGESTED READING

The Holy Roman Empire

K. J. Leyser, *Medieval Germany and Its Neighbors, 900–1250* (1982). The best general history.

Josef Fleckenstein, *Early Medieval Germany*, trans. Bernard S. Smith (1978).

Timothy Reuter, *Germany in the Early Middle Ages, c. 800–1056* (1991).

Two excellent works on the origin of the Holy Roman Empire.

Horst Fuhrmann, *Germany in the High Middle Ages, c. 1050–1200*, trans. Timothy Reuter (1986).

Albert Haverkamp, *Medieval Germany, 1056–1273*, trans. Helga Brown and Richard Mortimer (1988).

Either of these works provides a sound treatment of the

crucial period in the history of the Holy Roman Empire.

J. K. Hyde, *Society and Politics in Medieval Italy: The Evolution of the Civil Life, 1000–1350* (1973). Effective survey of the complex history of medieval Italy.

Benjamin Arnold, *Princes and Territories in Medieval Germany* (1991). Helpful on medieval Germany's complex internal history.

R. Folz, *The Concept of Empire in Western Europe from the Fifth to the Fourteenth Century*, trans. Sheila Ann Ogilvie (1969). Treats the concepts undergirding the medieval ideal of universal empire.

Uta-Renate Blumenthal, *The Investiture Controversy: Church and Monarchy from the Ninth to the Twelfth Century* (1988). Reflects modern scholarship on a much-disputed problem.

England

Christopher Brooke, *From Alfred to Henry III, 871–1272* (1961). A brief, well-written survey.

Robin Frame, *The Political Development of the British Isles, 1100–1400* (1990).

M. T. Clanchy, *England and Its Rulers, 1066–1272: Foreign Lordship and National Identity* (1983).

Two fuller accounts stressing the evolution of political institutions.

Doris M. Stenton, *English Society in the Early Middle Ages (1066–1307)*, 4th ed. (1965). Particularly strong in relating economic, social, and cultural factors to political history.

R. Allen Brown, *The Normans and the Norman Conquest*, 2nd ed. (1985). Excellent treatment of Norman expansionism.

W. L. Warren, *The Governance of Norman and Angevin England, 1086–1272* (1987). A fine synthesis.

J. C. Holt, *Magna Carta*, 2nd ed. (1992). A fine analysis.

France

Elizabeth M. Hallam, *Capetian France, 987–1328* (1980).

Georges Duby, *France in the Middle Ages 987–1460: From Hugh Capet to Joan of Arc*, trans. Juliet Vale (1991).

Two excellent general surveys of the growth of the kingdom.

Jean Dunbabin, *France in the Making 843–1180* (1985). Especially good in its treatment of France's principalities.

Biographies

Peter Munz, *Frederick Barbarossa: A Study in Medieval Politics* (1969).

David Abulafia, *Frederick II. A Medieval Emperor* (1992).

A. J. MacDonald, *Hildebrand: A Life of Gregory VII* (1932).

David C. Douglas, *William the Conqueror: The Norman Impact upon England* (1964).

W. L. Warren, *Henry II* (1973).

Amy Kelly, *Eleanor of Aquitaine and the Four Kings* (1950).

Frank Barlow, *Thomas Becket* (1986).

John Gillingham, *Richard the Lionheart* (1978).

W. L. Warren, *King John*, rev. ed. (1978).

Michael Prestwich, *Edward I* (1988).

Jean Richard, *Saint Louis: Crusader King of France*, trans. Jean Birrell (1992).

CHAPTER 20

The Medieval Expansion of Europe, 1000–1300

FIGURE 20.1 Departure on a Crusade This scene depicts King Louis IX of France leaving Paris on the Seventh Crusade. It captures some of the solemnity surrounding the crusading movement. With their eyes seemingly on their distant goal in the Holy Land, Louis and his knights depart without a look backward at the group of monks blessing them. (The British Museum)

Linked with western Europe's economic and political revival was a decisive change in the relationship between the West and the world beyond. Between 500 and 1000 western Europeans had been almost constantly on the defensive. After 1000 that situation was reversed. During the next three centuries Europeans employed a variety of means to expand their sphere of influence over a wide area. These efforts marked the beginning of an outward thrust by western Europeans that would continue for centuries.

1. MISSIONARY EXPANSION

The expansionist urge that marked Christianity from its beginnings continued vigorously and successfully during the central Middle Ages. A major area of missionary expansion was in Scandinavia. While the first efforts to convert the Scandinavians began in the ninth century, the crucial era in the conversion of Denmark, Norway, Sweden, and Iceland came in the late tenth and eleventh centuries. In most cases the conversion process was initiated by the native rulers, but they received assistance in instructing their people and organizing a religious establishment from missionaries from England and Germany.

Meanwhile, Christianity was carried eastward into the Slavic world. In this area the major impetus for expansion was provided by the rulers of the Holy Roman Empire and their ambitious lay and ecclesiastical vassals. Beginning in the late tenth century, the Bohemians, Poles, and Hungarians were gathered into the Roman Catholic fold. Somewhat later missionaries accompanied the conquering Teutonic Knights, a military order that had originally served the crusading forces in the Holy Land, to convert the Wends, Prussians, Finns, Livonians, and Lithuanians living along the Baltic coast. During this same period missionary forces from the Byzantine Empire were spreading Christianity among the eastern Slavs, especially the Russians.

During the thirteenth century missionaries from the West made efforts to win converts among the Moslems of North Africa and the Near East, and some even ventured as far afield as the Mongol Empire and China. Although these ventures produced no significant results, they opened vast new prospects for the future.

Wherever the missionary effort succeeded—Scandinavia, central Europe, Iceland, the Baltic area—those who brought Christianity introduced their converts to many aspects of western European culture. As a consequence, the lives of people in newly converted areas were decisively changed; they were "Europeanized" in terms of their institutions and their way of thinking.

2. COLONIZATION AND COMMERCIAL EXPANSION

The western Europeans who thrust outward with the cross were often accompanied—and sometimes led—by others driven toward and beyond Europe's old frontiers primarily by economic interests. As we have already seen, one of the great accomplishments of western Europeans during the era from 1000 to 1300 was the opening and colonization of an extensive agricultural frontier on the eastern fringes of Europe—in today's terms, a territory comprising northern Poland, the eastern part of unified Germany, the Czech Republic, Slovakia, and Austria. This Germanic "drive to the east" had the support of the Holy Roman emperors and religious leaders, but mainly it was carried out by landowners and peasants seeking new lands to exploit. Their occupation of this frontier zone was accompanied by the implantation of western European institutions.

Likewise, between 1000 and 1300 merchants reached beyond Europe to establish a western European presence in a much larger world (see Map 18.1). Italian merchants wrested control of the Mediterranean seaways from the Byzantines and Moslems and established trading posts in Constantinople and several Moslem seaports in Syria, Egypt, and North Africa. Northern Europeans, spearheaded by the Vikings, established settlements at Novgorod, Smolensk, and Kiev; from these emerged the Kievan principality, which constituted the first effective state in Russia. After the armies of the Fourth Crusade conquered Constantinople in 1204, western European merchants established bridgeheads around the Black Sea, which opened access to the cities of Central Asia and China. Italian traders roamed across the Asian world, reaping rich profits and reporting the potential of that vast area in travel accounts such as that composed in the late 1200s by the Venetian Marco Polo. A few bold Europeans were finding their way toward the waterways leading eastward to India and the Indies. Simultaneously, Western seafarers were pushing southward along Africa's west coast, drawn chiefly by the fame of the gold mines of Senegal.

3. MILITARY EXPANSION IN SPAIN AND SOUTHERN ITALY

The outward movement of missionaries, colonists, and traders was often supported by military forces impelled by a variety of motives: land hunger, a quest for booty, a lust for adventure, religious zeal. Military expansionism manifested itself around the whole rim of the European heartland, but the thrust was aimed primarily toward the Mediterranean basin and into areas dominated during the early Middle Ages by Byzantines and Moslems.

One of the most important areas of expansion was the Iberian peninsula. When the Moors (as Moslems are called in Spanish history) conquered the Iberian peninsula in the eighth century, they failed to subdue small pockets of Christians in the extreme northwestern part of the peninsula. In the late eighth and early ninth centuries the Carolingians pushed across the Pyrenees to create the Spanish March in northeastern Spain from territory won from the Moors. Prior to 1000 several petty states developed in these Christian enclaves—León, Castile, Navarre, Aragon, and Barcelona. By the early eleventh century these states began to expand southward, generating a movement that soon turned into a war of liberation called the *Reconquista*. The disintegration in the early eleventh century of the once-powerful caliphate of Córdoba and the emergence of numerous warring Moslem principalities made Christian expansion easier. Given this opportunity, the militant Christians turned their energies to a common assault on the Moors. Large numbers of Christian knights from outside Spain, especially from France, joined the fray. Aside from a thirst for land, the warriors involved in the Reconquista were animated by a powerful religious spirit, as is illustrated by two great vernacular literary works written to celebrate the feats of Christian warriors against the Moorish infidels, the *Song of Roland* and *The Cid*. The first phase of the Reconquista culminated in 1085 with the capture of the key city of Toledo. With the aid of Berber reinforcements from northwest Africa, the Moors were able to halt the Christian advance temporarily and by the mid-twelfth century even threatened to reclaim territory lost to the Christians. Shortly thereafter the Christian offensive was renewed, culminating in 1212 at the battle of Las Navas de Tolosa, where the Christian forces won a decisive victory over the combined forces of the Spanish Moors and their Berber allies. By 1300 the Christians had occupied all of the peninsula except a small region in the south called Granada (see Map 20.1).

Three major Iberian kingdoms—Castile (to which León was joined), Aragon, and Portugal—grew out of the territory rewon from the Moslems during the Reconquista. Each developed its own system of government, although all had certain basic similarities. Monarchy was the basic institution, and the kings steadily gained prestige as a result of their leadership of the Reconquista and the support of their cause by religious leaders, especially the papacy. The newly conquered lands gave them a chance to settle people as farmers or town dwellers under conditions that allowed the king to retain his authority. In each kingdom there emerged a powerful nobility, made up of warriors richly rewarded with grants of land in return for their services in the wars against the Moors. Although these nobles were often bound to the king by ties of vassalage, they posed a constant challenge to royal authority. Seeking to take advantage of the superior skills of some of their conquered subjects as traders and artisans, the kings also granted extensive privileges to the Moslem and Jewish communities in conquered Spanish cities. Like their contemporaries in England and France, the Spanish monarchs sought to develop centralized administrations, well-organized financial systems, and effective courts. Several thirteenth-century kings of Aragon and Castile legislated extensively to define royal powers, and they appointed local officials, comparable to the French bailiffs, to represent them. Both the nobles and the townspeople resisted the expansion of royal power and in the long run compelled the kings to accept limitations on their authority. In each kingdom there developed a *Cortes*, a representative body com-

Map 20.1 CHRISTIAN EXPANSION IN IBERIA
This map shows the progress made by Spanish Christian warriors in reconquering the Iberian peninsula from the Moors during the Middle Ages. Three major kingdoms emerged from the Christian victories—Aragon, Castile (to which León was joined), and Portugal.

posed of nobles, ecclesiastical leaders, and townspeople with considerable power to limit royal decisions on a variety of matters, including taxation.

As the Iberian kingdoms developed, the society of each took on many features common to the rest of Christian western Europe. As a consequence, the Iberian world became an integral part of western European civilization. However, Spanish society retained its unique features, by-products of the merging of Christian and Moslem institutions and ideas during the long period of the Reconquista. As a result, Spain played a special role in the medieval West as the channel through which many Moslem influences flowed into the mainstream of western European society.

Another area drawn into the western European sphere of influence by military force was southern Italy and Sicily, long controlled by the Byzantines and the Moslems. Norman warriors from northwest France were the aggressors here, coming first to southern Italy as adventurers who, in return for land, were willing to sell their military services to local rulers competing for power. Especially anxious for their services were Byzantine officials, who sought desperately to retain control over the area in the name of the emperor in Constantinople. Soon, however, these resourceful warriors, constantly reinforced by new adventurers from Normandy, succeeded in establishing dominance over their supposed masters. By the mid–eleventh century the papacy legally recognized a Norman principality in southern Italy; in return, the Normans agreed to support the papacy in its struggle with the Holy Roman emperors. These same aggressive warriors then wrenched Sicily from the Moslems, a victory recognized in 1130 when the papacy sanctioned the creation of the Kingdom of Sicily, embracing southern Italy and Sicily, with a prince of Norman descent, Roger II, as king. A strong monarchy was soon shaped, featuring a mixture of northern European feudal, Byzantine, and Moslem practices. The Kingdom of Sicily passed into Hohenstaufen hands at the end of the twelfth century and reached its apogee under Frederick II (see Chapter 19). Thereafter, the kingdom began to decline, chiefly because it became a pawn in the rivalry among various European states. But it remained in western European hands, a prize of expansion from which flowed political, economic, intellectual, and artistic influences that had an important effect on western Europe.

4. MILITARY EXPANSION: THE CRUSADES

The most dramatic manifestation of medieval western European expansion involved a succession of military campaigns, called the Crusades, that were directed toward the eastern Mediterranean world. Initially undertaken as religious wars against Islam for control of the holy places where Christianity had originated, these campaigns eventually involved a struggle to maintain a western European outpost in the Near East.

In part, the crusading movement began because political developments in the Near East offered western Europeans opportunities and inducements. As early as the ninth century, the vast Abbasid caliphate began to break up into independent caliphates bitterly contending with one another for territory and for the right to represent the true version of Islam. The rivalry was especially keen in Syria and Palestine, where Abbasid dominance was challenged by the aggressive Egypt-based Shiite Fatimid caliphate and the Byzantine Empire, which sought to reclaim territory it had once possessed as heir to the Roman Empire. In an effort to bolster its declining strength, the Abbasid dynasty brought a vigorous new force into the picture: the Seljuk Turks. They were a people of Asiatic origin who had entered the Moslem world in the tenth century, become converts to Islam, and used their military prowess to expand their influence. By the mid–eleventh century, the Seljuks established their dominance over Baghdad and made the Abbasid caliphs their puppets. They then turned their energies westward in an effort to enlarge their sphere of influence. This expansion brought

them into conflict with the Fatimids and the Byzantine Empire and made the eastern Mediterranean world a confusing battleground. The Turkish menace became especially critical about 1070, when the Turks seized Jerusalem from the Fatimids and inflicted a crushing defeat on the Byzantines at the battle of Manzikert (see below). In the midst of this confusion, local Moslem leaders established several small principalities in Syria and Palestine; they were willing to make any arrangements that would thwart the efforts of their major rivals to establish dominance over this crucial territory.

The Byzantine Empire was also undergoing a crisis in the late eleventh century. After reaching its pinnacle under the greatest emperor of the Macedonian dynasty, Basil II (976–1025), the empire began to decline, in part because a succession of ineffectual rulers allowed the aristocracy to exploit the free peasantry that constituted the backbone of the imperial defense system. The Normans, who had already wrested southern Italy from imperial control, posed a growing threat to imperial control in the Balkans. The Italian city-states, especially Venice, challenged the Byzantine sea power. More seriously, in 1071, at the battle of Manzikert, Byzantine forces suffered a crushing blow from the Seljuk Turks, who in succeeding years conquered most of Asia Minor. This deepening crisis finally produced an effective ruler, Alexius Comnenus (1081–1118), who in his effort to recover Asia Minor began to appeal to the pope and the princes of western Europe for military help against the aggressive Turkish infidels, whom the Byzantines portrayed as a threat to all Christendom.

Despite the volatile situation in the east, there would have been no crusading movement without the confluence of various forces affecting western European society. Increasing material wealth provided the means for ambitious military undertakings, and the greater political order curbed local warfare and freed the war-loving aristocracy for foreign ventures. Changing patterns of landholding, which confined inheritance to eldest sons, created a large pool of young warriors seeking ways to make a fortune. The military potency of European society was being demonstrated by victories on the German, Spanish, and Italian frontiers. The Italian cities were eager to advance their commercial interests in the eastern Mediterranean. The long-standing religious animosity toward Islam was sharpened by the wars in Spain and Italy. The wave of religious reform sweeping over western Europe emphasized the idea that Christians must serve God by working through outward, active demonstrations of their piety. One way in which that activist impulse expressed itself was through an increasing interest in pilgrimages. Thousands of people joined organized voyages to holy places all over Europe and increasingly to the Holy Land, where their occasional victimization by warring Moslem factions heightened anti-Moslem feelings. The religious revival had an especially important impact on the chivalric ideal. Increasingly, it emphasized the responsibility of the true warrior to devote his prowess to holy war that would promote the cause of Christianity and scourge its enemies, especially the hated Moslem infidels.

It was Pope Urban II (1088–1099), a dedicated reformer eager to assert papal leadership over Christendom, who translated the opportunities emerging in the east and the forces of militancy surging through western European society into a specific form of military action. In 1095, after discussions with important ecclesiastical and lay leaders, Urban made public his plan in a stirring speech at Clermont in France. He called on Christian knights to put aside their petty quarrels and join forces under papal leadership in an armed pilgrimage to the east to achieve a variety of ends for the good of the true faith. This army would respond to an appeal that Alexius Comnenus made to the pope in the same year for aid in defending the Byzantine Empire against the Moslem Seljuk Turks. In return for this help Urban hoped to gain Byzantine recognition of papal supremacy over the whole Christian world, thus ending the schism that had occurred in 1054, when the pope and the patriarch of Constantinople had excommunicated each other. Finally, this force, aided by the Byzantines, would capture the holy places in Palestine as a supreme act of piety in the service of God. As an inducement to join his crusade, Urban proclaimed measures to protect the property and families of those willing to take up the cross and promised that each would be rewarded in heaven for fighting this holy war.

The pope's appeal at Clermont was greeted with shouts that it was God's will to do what Urban asked. That enthusiasm was soon transmitted over much of Europe by preachers of the crusading ideal. A number of prominent lords (but no kings) began gathering separate armies in various areas. Before these armies of knights could be organized, an undisciplined horde of peasants and artisans, stirred by the appeals of enthusiastic preachers, began what has been called the Peasants' Crusade. After savagely attacking Jewish communities in several German cities, this ragtag mob moved eastward down the Danube Valley and across Hungary and Bulgaria, causing havoc as it advanced. When it finally reached Constantinople, Emperor Alexius Comnenus quickly dispatched it to Asia Minor, where it was immediately annihilated by the Turks.

By the summer of 1096 four major armies, totaling perhaps twenty-five or thirty thousand armed knights accompanied by considerable retinues, began to move toward the east by different routes (see Map 20.2). Their first goal was Constantinople, where they expected to unite their forces for the attack on the Turks and the march to Jerusalem. The leaders of the armies from the west had no common plan of action. Although Urban II had designated a distinguished bishop to direct the crusading effort in the name of the papacy, the doughty nobles leading the various armies were unwilling to accept direction. Alexius Comnenus had expected mercenary contingents that he could simply take into his pay and order to do what he wished; the armies now converging on his capital were anything but soldiers for hire. Thus, Alexius had to negotiate an agreement with each leader. Eventually, by means that increased the distrust of the proud crusaders for the "Greeks" and of the Byzantines for the western "barbarians," Alexius persuaded each of the crusading leaders to swear a personal oath of allegiance to him and to promise to restore to Byzantine control conquered territories that had previously belonged to the empire. In return, he promised to provide supplies and military support.

In the spring of 1097 the crusaders began their march across Asia Minor, brushing aside modest Turkish resistance but paying little heed to their

Map 20.2 THE EARLY CRUSADES This map shows the major land and sea routes taken by various crusading armies during the First, Second, and Third crusades. The leaders of the major armies are also indicated. The distances involved in these military ventures suggest the challenges faced by the crusaders. The First Crusade established the Latin Kingdom of Jerusalem, far removed from where the armies started their trek. Most of the successive crusades were prompted by the need to defend that kingdom from the Moslem forces that surrounded it.

promise to Alexius to liberate Asia Minor. This disregard for Byzantine interests, coupled with Alexius' failure to provide the hard-pressed crusading armies with promised supplies, virtually ended any hope of effective collaboration between the Byzantines and the crusaders. Once in Syria, the crusading force began to split up, chiefly because its leaders were anxious to ensure their private fortunes. One group left the main body to establish control over Edessa and its surrounding territory, while another, led by the Norman prince Bohemond, established an independent principality centered around Antioch. Not until July 1099 was Jerusalem captured by

the remaining crusaders, who vented their fury by slaughtering hundreds of its inhabitants (see Figure 20.2). Their victory, a remarkable feat considering how far the crusading armies had come and the severe tribulations they had faced for three years, made the First Crusade a success in the eyes of western Europeans.

In the wake of their triumph the crusading leaders disregarded both their pledge to Alexius to serve as his vassals and a papal plan to create a state subordinate to Rome. Instead, in 1100 they elected Baldwin of Flanders, count of Edessa, as king of the Latin Kingdom of Jerusalem. Baldwin retained a sizable territory around Jerusalem as

FIGURE 20.2 The Capture of the Holy City, 1099 This manuscript illustration shows the crusaders making their final assault on Jerusalem in 1099 to mark the successful end of the First Crusade. Their victory ended with the slaughter of those shown defending the city. (Snark International/Art Resource)

the royal domain and granted out the principalities of Edessa, Antioch, and Tripoli as fiefs to major crusading leaders, each of whom became a royal vassal and in turn granted fiefs to his own vassals. Although the king claimed lordship over the princes of the major principalities and often acted in concert with them in the common cause of the Christian establishment, the Latin Kingdom of Jerusalem was unstable internally, constantly riven by princely rivalries and by the ambitions of newcomers from the west. A Latin patriarch of Jerusalem was installed, thus subordinating the Christian establishment to Roman authority. The native population was disturbed very little by the newcomers.

Once the Latin Kingdom of Jerusalem had been established, the defense of "Overseas"

(*Outremer,* as western Europeans called their distant outpost) became a major problem. Almost immediately after the capture of Jerusalem, most of the knights from the west returned home, having fulfilled the vow they had taken to liberate the holy places. Those who stayed took various steps to protect themselves. With the aid of Italian navies they seized the chief Mediterranean seaports in Syria and Palestine; this success allowed the Latins to control the sea routes facing the Latin Kingdom, which were of decisive importance in holding their position. They built a series of impregnable castles at strategic locations in the Holy Land. Before 1130 they established two military orders, the Knights Templar and the Knights Hospitaler; a third, the Teutonic Knights, developed somewhat later. These orders, modeled on monastic organizations, recruited members in the west who vowed to serve God by defending Christians living in and coming to the Holy Land and by raising troops and money to support the Christian establishment in the Holy Land. Despite these measures the Christian position remained tenuous, creating an ongoing concern that during the next two centuries repeatedly persuaded western Europeans to go crusading as a way of serving God. Almost every year some western European knights at least temporarily lent their efforts to defending the Latin Kingdom. On occasion, especially at moments of crisis in the Latin Kingdom of Jerusalem, efforts were made in the west to organize more substantial forces to defend the holy places, thus permitting historians to speak of successive ''crusades.''

The Second Crusade (1147–1149) was prompted by the loss of Edessa to the Moslems in 1144. Papal appeals for action attracted two kings as its leaders: Conrad III, Holy Roman emperor, and Louis VII, king of France. Despite such prestigious leadership, the crusading armies were virtually destroyed by the Turks in Asia Minor. When the two rulers did arrive in the Holy Land with remnants of their forces, their misdirected military efforts aided little in the defense of the Latin Kingdom.

During the years following the Second Crusade, more effective leadership began to emerge in the Moslem world surrounding the Christian holdings. The most brilliant of these new leaders was Saladin, whose success in uniting the Moslem forces of Egypt and Syria posed a powerful threat to the Latin Kingdom of Jerusalem. By 1187 he captured almost all the Christian holdings except Tyre, a few isolated castles, and the northern counties. When the news of this disaster reached the West, the pope called for a new crusade and received the promises of Henry II of England, Philip II of France, and Frederick Barbarossa of Germany to lead armies against Saladin. Frederick left first but was drowned en route. Henry II also died before he could begin his march; however, his successor, Richard the Lion-Hearted, stepped into his place. He and Philip, almost always at odds, made their way to the east by 1191. More concerned with undermining Richard's Angevin ''empire'' back in

France than crusading, Philip stayed on the scene only a minimum time. The colorful English king remained for over a year. After several inconclusive engagements with Saladin, Richard finally agreed to a truce that left Jerusalem in Moslem hands and allowed Christians to visit it. Aside from the return of a few coastal cities to Latin control, the Third Crusade did little to improve the Christian position.

The Fourth Crusade was initially prompted by Pope Innocent III. However, the pope soon lost control over the forces that were raised. To ensure transportation to the east, the crusading leaders turned to the Venetians, who invested far more in ships to transport the crusaders than the disappointingly small crusading force was able to collect. To resolve this problem, the Venetians and the crusading leaders agreed to support a claimant to the Byzantine throne in return for trade concessions for Venice and money and troops to help the crusaders attack Egypt. But having ensconced their Byzantine ally in the imperial office, they found him either unwilling or unable to deliver on his promises. The crusaders and the Venetians therefore decided to take Constantinople for themselves. Their attack was successful; the city fell into Western hands in 1204 and was savagely pillaged. The crusaders immediately established a Latin Empire of Constantinople and elected a Flemish noble as emperor and a Venetian cleric as patriarch of the Greek Orthodox church, thus reuniting the eastern and western Christian communities for the moment. Somewhat reluctantly Innocent III gave his sanction to the whole arrangement. The crusading nobles immediately began to carve out rich fiefs for themselves on Byzantine soil. The Venetians assumed control over the chief port cities of the empire, making them the real beneficiaries of the whole undertaking. The Latin Empire of Constantinople survived until 1261, when forces representing the legitimate Byzantine emperor recaptured Constantinople and ousted the usurpers.

By the beginning of the thirteenth century, the crusading movement was beginning to lose its appeal for western Europeans. In the minds of some the attack of Christians on other Christians during the Fourth Crusade made a travesty of the crusading ideal. The exploitation by the papacy of the crusading ideal as a means of rallying forces to attack such papal enemies as the Albigensian heretics (see Chapter 21) or Emperor Frederick II fueled antipathy in many quarters. Growing numbers in the West began to argue that peaceful missionary activity was a better way to convert the infidel Moslems than military force. The attraction of the Near East as a place to make a fortune waned in the face of the tenuous situation of the Christian establishment in the Latin Kingdom of Jerusalem.

Nonetheless, the continued existence of the beleaguered Christian outpost in the east as well as the ambitions of western Europeans seeking to use the crusading movement to promote political ends prompted new crusades during the thirteenth century. Pope Innocent III organized a fifth crusade, but he died before it could get under way in 1217. Seeking to strike the Moslem threat to the Christian position at its source, this crusade was directed toward Egypt, but an attempted expedition up the Nile ended in a resounding defeat. Emperor Frederick II led the next crusade, chiefly because he wanted to secure possession of the Holy Land, to which he had a legal right by virtue of his marriage to the heiress of the Latin Kingdom of Jerusalem. Through diplomacy he arranged a treaty in 1229 with the Moslems which restored Jerusalem to Christian control. But his victory was tainted in the eyes of many because at the time he occupied Jerusalem he was under sentence of excommunication imposed by the pope as punishment for Frederick's refusal to accept papal direction. In 1244 the Moslems again captured the Holy City. This loss prompted Louis IX of France to organize what amounted to the last major crusade (see Figure 20.1). His four-year stay in the Holy Land did little to strengthen the Christian position. In fact, his attempt at an Egyptian campaign increased the danger by providing the occasion for a strong, aggressive Moslem dynasty, the Mamelukes, to establish itself in Egypt.

The increasingly precarious position of the Latin Kingdom of Jerusalem was relieved temporarily in the mid–thirteenth century, when Christians and Moslems allied to save themselves from the Mongol threat. Early in the century a great leader, Genghis Khan, had transformed the Mongol nomads of Central Asia into a potent military force that swept over Eurasia and fashioned a huge empire stretching from China to central Europe. After 1260 the Mongol threat began to lessen, and the old hostilities between Moslems and Christians in the Near East were renewed. In 1291 the Mamelukes took the last Christian strongholds in the Holy Land. After nearly two centuries, the Latins had finally been ousted from Syria and Palestine.

So ended the most overt and dramatic manifestation of medieval western European expansionism. Historians are not unanimous in their assessments of the consequences of the crusading movement, but they agree that at least in some respects the effects were enduring. The Crusades generated an interaction between East and West which "educated" Europeans to new ideas, products, and styles of life. They extended and solidified western European commercial power. They decisively affected the histories of both the Byzantine Empire and the Moslem world, weakening the former and provoking the latter to a new aggressiveness that was to have a significant impact on Europe during the late Middle Ages and well into early modern times. Perhaps the most significant legacy of the crusading movement was the negative image of western Europeans it generated among people in the east: the greedy, faithless, crude warrior; the crafty, grasping merchant; the ambitious, worldly church official—all of whom would do anything to acquire land, wealth, and power. Such images poisoned East-West relationships for centuries.

However one judges the impact of the Crusades, the loss of Outremer should not detract from the importance of medieval expansionism in all its various forms in changing the position of western Europe with respect to the rest of the world. Extensive territories and their inhabitants in northern and central Europe, Spain, and southern Italy had been drawn permanently into the orb of western European civilization. The sphere of influence of Latin Christendom had been greatly enlarged. The commercial boundaries of western Europe had been vastly expanded. Their contacts with a larger world stretched the mental horizons of western Europeans far beyond what they had been in 1000. This outward thrust marked a preliminary step that eventually would lead to a revolutionary transformation of western Europe's position in a global setting.

SUGGESTED READING

Overviews of Medieval Expansion

J. R. S. Phillips, *The Medieval Expansion of Europe* (1988). A good introduction.

Archibald R. Lewis, *Nomads and Crusaders*, A.D. *1000–1368* (1988). Treats medieval European expansion in an intercontinental context.

Expansion in Spain, Southern Italy, and the Baltic

Anwar G. Chejne, *Muslim Spain. Its History and Culture* (1974). A fine introduction to Moslem Spain.

Thomas F. Glick, *Islamic and Christian Spain in the Early Middle Ages* (1979). Treats the interaction of Islamic and Christian societies.

Angus MacKay, *Spain in the Middle Ages: From Frontier to Empire, 1000–1500* (1977). Traces the rise of the Christian kingdoms.

Donald Matthew, *The Norman Kingdom of Sicily* (1992). A fine study of the birth of a new state in the Middle Ages.

The Crusades

P. M. Holt, *The Age of the Crusades. The Near East from the Eleventh Century to 1517* (1986). A helpful overview.

Jonathan Riley-Smith, *What Were the Crusades?* (1977). A stimulating analysis of the nature of the crusading movement.

Carl Erdmann, *The Origin of the Idea of Crusade,* trans. Marshall W. Baldwin and Walter Goffart (1977). A fundamental work stressing ideological factors.

Jonathan Riley-Smith, *The Crusades. A Short History* (1987).

Hans E. Mayer, *The Crusades,* trans. John Gillingham (1972).

Two fine short histories; perhaps the Riley-Smith work is better.

Erick Christiansen, *The Northern Crusades: The Baltic and the Catholic Frontier, 1100–1525* (1980). A full treatment of an overlooked aspect of medieval crusading.

Joshua Prawer, *The Crusaders' Kingdom: European Colonization in the Middle Ages* (1972). Portrays what happened to the Europeans in the Near Eastern environment.

Norman Daniel, *The Arabs and Medieval Europe,* 2nd ed. (1979). Treats European attitudes toward Islam.

Benjamin Z. Kedar, *Crusade and Mission: European Approaches Toward the Muslims* (1984). Examines the interactions between crusading and missionary concepts.

Michael Angold, *The Byzantine Empire, 1025–1204: A Political History* (1984). Will help the reader understand the Byzantine role in the Crusades.

Malcolm Cameron Lyons and D. E. P. Jackson, *Saladin: The Politics of Holy War* (1982). A perceptive study of a great Moslem leader.

CHAPTER 21
Religious Renewal, 1000–1300

FIGURE 21.1 **The Last Judgment** This magnificent scene carved above the main portal of the west façade of the Gothic cathedral at Chartres illustrates a fundamental idea of medieval Christian teaching: the Last Judgment, when Christ will make a final determination of the eternal lot of all people. Christ is surrounded by symbols of his glory and by life-size representations of individuals who played a role in the unfolding of the Christian drama. The scene conveys a powerful message to the faithful who might stray into sin: The time is at hand to enter the church and partake of grace-giving sacraments so that one will be ready to receive Christ's approval at the final hour. (Scala/Art Resource)

Between 1000 and 1300 powerful religious forces surged through western European society to bring about changes that some refer to as a medieval "reformation." The religious revival of the central Middle Ages was complex, involving diverse approaches to the structuring of Christian society and to the attainment of Christian perfection. It challenged many traditional assumptions about religion and society. It called forth a major intellectual effort that sought to discover in the rich Christian tradition guides that would help shape a fuller religious life. Its impact was felt at all levels of society. In its totality the reform movement provided the prime force binding all Europeans into a unified civilization. Thus, in a real sense, the medieval reformation constituted the central "event" in the history of the central Middle Ages.

1. THE ORIGINS OF THE REFORM MOVEMENT

As we have seen (see Chapter 17), in the tenth century religious life in western Europe was beset by serious problems. At the root of those problems was the immersion of the religious establishment in the system of lordship and dependency that dominated the contemporary society. Ecclesiastical property and offices were controlled by lay lords concerned chiefly with acquiring power and wealth, a system that produced religious leaders who shared the same concerns and an ignorant, impoverished, undisciplined lower clergy badly equipped to provide pastoral care for the lay population. Abuses of all kinds enveloped the administration of the religious services upon which the salvation of souls was believed to depend. The level of Christian spiritual life had reached a low point in spite of the power and wealth wielded by the worldly religious establishment.

In the midst of that difficult era signs of religious renewal began to appear. In large part this renewal was generated as a protest against a corrupt religious establishment, but it was also given impetus by men and women who recaptured from Christian tradition visions of perfection that prompted efforts to purify religious life. The first manifestations of renewal came in the monastic world, which for centuries had served as a focal point for those seeking spiritual perfection. During the tenth century monastic reforms were initiated in various parts of western Europe—Burgundy, Lotharingia, Italy, England—each stressing various patterns of renewal: escape from the heavy hand of secular control; denial of the corrupt material world in favor of poverty; a search for moral perfection; intensification of devotional practices; a quest for a better understanding of the Christian heritage. Here and there bishops sought ways to improve the moral lives of the lower clergy under their jurisdiction and to intensify the teaching of their flocks. Pious rulers, and especially their queens, began to patronize reform activities. Feudal potentates gave generous support to reformed monastic houses, became involved in new devotional practices sponsored by reformed monks, and even curbed their conduct as warriors out of respect for efforts to promote Christian peace. Even simple peasants and townspeople felt the pull of reform, as evidenced by their outcries against the wealth and corruption of those who claimed to direct their spiritual lives.

At its beginnings in the late tenth and early eleventh centuries, the quest for spiritual renewal was spontaneous, diffuse, disorganized, and lacking in specific direction. Although elements of spontaneity continued to surround the reforming effort until well into the thirteenth century, from the early eleventh century onward certain major trends dominated the medieval "reformation." One, spearheaded by the Roman popes with the support of some secular rulers and the intellectual establishment, sought to establish the "liberty" of the religious establishment, to perfect its organization, and to impose on the faithful a uniform discipline and doctrine. A second, focused chiefly in the monastic world but also drawing strength from intellectuals, probed for deeper spirituality, moral improvement, and more meaningful ways of worshiping God. A third involved a vibrant upsurge of popular piety that sought ways by which the poor and meek might share the promises of Jesus. In examining each of these major currents of religious reform separately, it must be remembered that they developed concurrently and constantly intersected, sometimes reinforcing each other and sometimes clashing.

2. PAPAL REFORM: THE QUEST FOR ORDER AND UNIFORMITY

The papacy became involved in the medieval religious revival relatively late. During the tenth and early eleventh centuries it had become bogged down in corruption and been dominated first by Roman nobles and then by the Holy Roman emperors. As a consequence, it asserted little influence over the Christian community of western Europe. The situation began to change in the middle of the eleventh century, when a circle of reformers established control over the papacy and spearheaded a movement called the Gregorian reform by later historians after one of its leaders, the monk Hildebrand, later Pope Gregory VII (1073–1085). These reformers were men of deep moral convictions and well schooled in Christian tradition. As we have seen (see Chapter 19), the Gregorian reformers argued that the Christian community should constitute a visible earthly community, a "Church" (*ecclesia*) as they would have put it, within which the attainment of salvation for all members must be the central concern. They believed with a passion that the community needed its own head, its own laws, its own resources, and its own liberty. On the basis of the ancient Petrine theory (see p. 158), they claimed for the bishop of Rome the divinely sanctioned authority to head the Christian community as Christ's earthly vicar. They argued that God entrusted to his vicar two kinds of divinely ordained power, spiritual and temporal. The pope held spiritual authority, which bestowed on him both the right and the duty to direct the activities of all ecclesiastical officials and to supervise all activities related to saving souls. By virtue of their office, lay princes were vested with temporal power to be used to repress the evil forces that impeded the faithful from gaining God's favors on earth and from earning eternal salvation, but always with the understanding that temporal power could be withdrawn if any prince did not use it in ways that served spiritual ends or if a prince went counter to the spiritual authority, which was always superior. Although this ideology was shaped from long-standing traditions, its articulation in the eleventh-century setting had revolutionary implications in terms of the governance of the Christian community. Most revolutionary of all was its challenge to another long-established tradition which had entrusted to Christian princes, such as Constantine, Charlemagne, and Otto I, a God-given responsibility to guide their subjects along the path leading to salvation.

As pope, Gregory VII acted to convert this ideology into a reform program that focused on concentrating authority in papal hands and on using that power to correct the evils that impeded the purification of Christian society. He launched an effort to free the religious establishment from lay control by prohibiting lay investiture of clergymen with their offices and lands, thereby opening a prolonged political struggle with the princes of western Europe, especially the Holy Roman emperors. He initiated a legislative program aimed at using papal authority to eliminate moral abuses among the clergy, especially the selling of church offices and services (simony) and clerical marriage. To ensure that these efforts at reform were observed, he charted a program aimed at centralizing ecclesiastical authority in papal hands. Even before his pontificate, the papal reformers had placed the responsibility of selecting popes in the hands of clergymen, the College of Cardinals, thereby putting the papal office beyond lay control. Gregory took important steps to make that body the nucleus of a papal administrative machine. Papal *decretals* (legislative enactments) were issued with increasing frequency, laying down regulations for church governance and clerical conduct. Papal legates were sent across Europe to enforce this legislation. The papacy encouraged regional church councils to enact measures aimed at correcting abuses wherever they existed in the Christian world. Provisions were made to expedite the appeal of difficult cases to Rome for settlement. Special attention was given to regularizing and increasing papal income so as to ensure independence of action.

Gregory VII did not live to see his program realized, but its basic tenets remained a powerful force in shaping Christian life for the next two centuries. The consolidation of papal power met resistance from many quarters, particularly from bishops and princes who believed that their ancient rights were threatened and from other reformers who saw the advance of papal authority as still another way of the pope's gaining power and wealth. But Gregory's successors, exemplified by popes such as Urban II (1088–1099) and Alexander III (1159–1181), pursued his policy of centralization with skill and persistence. Their efforts were abetted by their willingness to retreat from Gregory's radical position on the supremacy of ecclesiastical over secular power. This compromise led to mutual support between the papacy and secular princes in establishing a more effective ecclesiastical organization; many kings found such an organization useful in supporting their own efforts to curb stubborn nobles and towns. By the thirteenth century such popes as Innocent III (1198–1216), Honorius III (1216–1227), Gregory IX (1227–1241), and Innocent IV (1243–1254) presided over an immense organization capable of directing religious life all over western Europe in minute detail.

These thirteenth-century ecclesiastical monarchs controlled an elaborate central bureaucracy located in Rome called the papal *curia*. This body was divided into specialized departments dealing with finances, correspondence and records, judicial cases, doctrinal issues, and the discipline of sinners. It was staffed by trained clerical specialists who made careers of papal administration. The College of Cardinals, made up of churchmen especially selected by the pope, sat with the pope in special meetings (called *consistories*) to formulate major policies; its members often served as heads of the specialized departments that handled routine administrative matters. From the curia flowed a steady stream of legislation touching on every conceivable aspect of religious life. The papal judicial system handled an ever-increasing volume of cases appealed to Rome from throughout Europe. The Roman curia extended its authority beyond Rome through a system of papal agents, called *legates*, sent from Rome to supervise the enactment of papal orders. The legatine system, coupled with the curia's extensive correspondence and judicial appeals to Rome, kept the popes well informed about local affairs throughout Europe. A constantly increasing income—derived from papal property, gifts, fees for judicial services, payments for dispensations from papal regulations, and assessments levied on the lower clergy and the laity—sustained this huge organization.

The authority of St. Peter's vicar was extended downward through the age-old hierarchy of archbishops, bishops, and priests. From Greg-

ory VII's time until 1300 considerable effort was devoted to differentiating the status of the clergy from that of the laity and to defining the exact functions of each level within the clerical hierarchy. In that process papal control over the election and supervision of archbishops and bishops was extended, greatly limiting—although not eliminating—secular domination of the clergy. Each archbishop was entrusted with the supervision of several bishops in his *province*, and each bishop was empowered to direct the activities of the priests and laity residing in his *diocese*. Each of these officials headed a small-scale model of the papal curia, called a *cathedral chapter*, staffed by *canons* who had a voice in episcopal elections, advised their superiors, and carried out provincial and diocesan administration. That administration involved conducting judicial proceedings, collecting and dispensing revenues, managing episcopal property, and supervising parish priests, who were charged with administering the sacraments and preaching to the Christian populace. One of the major accomplishments of the era was the establishment across western Europe of a firm structure of local parishes through which Christian teachings could be delivered to all people. For the most part these territorial units, often coinciding with manors and agricultural villages or with specific quarters in urban centers, were freed from lay control over the appointment of priests and parish income and placed under episcopal direction.

Although by 1300 some were beginning to think otherwise, the inspiration behind this effort at centralization was not merely a quest for power. Popes, bishops, monks, and large segments of the laity genuinely believed that effective ecclesiastical organization was only a means by which a higher end could be realized: guiding the Christian flock toward observance of the one right way of behaving and believing that God had ordained as essential to salvation. As a consequence, a major aspect of the papal reform movement centered on defining and standardizing church law and doctrine to provide those in charge of the care of souls with norms governing Christian life and belief.

By the eleventh century there existed an immense body of law relating to Christian life that had been derived from many sources: scriptural injunctions, the writings of the early Church

Fathers, the acts of a long succession of church councils, the pronouncements of popes and bishops (some of which were forged), and legislation by Christian rulers. Many of the provisions of this body of law were confused and contradictory, and some no longer applied to contemporary realities. Moreover, the issues posed by the reform movement demanded new legal solutions. These problems produced a new breed of specialist to serve the religious establishment: trained lawyers working to create a consistent, organized body of law, called canon law, that would sustain the effort to create an independent religious community governed by its own rules. A decisive figure in the effort to create a "code" of law for the religious establishment was Gratian. In 1140 he published his *Decretum,* which represented an effort to apply the rules of logic to the vast body of past precedents in a way that would remove contradictions and produce a consistent set of laws. Gratian's work immediately became the guide for ecclesiastical administration and discipline. Among many other things, his code defined the powers of each rank of the clergy, the jurisdiction of ecclesiastical courts, crimes against the religious establishment and their punishments, the proper use of ecclesiastical income and property, and the manner of conducting religious ceremonies. Throughout the work ran one predominant idea—the supremacy of the papacy in the governance of Christendom. Subsequent codifications that incorporated new legislation greatly expanded canon law, and extensive commentaries aimed at relating its provisions to the real world greatly facilitated its application. By 1300 a powerful instrument for directing Christian society had been forged.

A comparable movement occurred with respect to doctrine. By 1000 there existed a rich body of teachings derived from diverse sources that dealt with Christian belief. Like the law, this material was disorganized, filled with contradictions, and interpreted in a variety of ways. To cope with this problem, another kind of specialist, the trained theologian, emerged. Operating primarily in the setting of monastic and cathedral schools and then universities, these theologians gradually worked out an approach to doctrinal issues that came to be called scholasticism (see Chapter 22). Working within the parameters provided by revealed truth contained in Scripture, scholastic theologians sought to use human reason to resolve by rules of logic the contradictions imbedded in doctrinal tradition. Beyond that, they sought to compile summaries that would set forth in logical, consistent, and holistic terms what constituted the essence of Christian belief. To achieve this end, the scholastics sought to weave all human knowledge into a theological framework which would provide a single body of truth that would provide an authoritative answer to any issue facing a Christian believer.

At the heart of the system of belief developed during the twelfth and thirteenth centuries stood the doctrines of grace, the sacraments, and good works. According to the theologians, God had created human beings in order that they might enjoy eternal salvation, human life being but a test of worthiness. Since humans were corrupted by original sin, the stain imposed on all by the disobedience of Adam and Eve, men and women needed God's grace to save them. That grace was bestowed through the sacraments instituted by Jesus as an essential part of his mission of redemption (see Figure 21.2). Although the grace that flowed from the sacraments was a gift bestowed by God out of his love for humanity, worthiness for that gift depended on the performance of good works pleasing to God.

At the Fourth Lateran Council, held in 1215 under the direction of Innocent III, the number of sacraments was set at seven. Each drew its efficacy by virtue of the fact that it was administered by duly anointed members of the clergy, without whose services no Christian could expect to be saved. *Baptism,* usually administered at infancy, removed the stain of original sin and initiated its recipients into the Christian community. *Confirmation,* usually received at adolescence, infused into Christians the Holy Spirit, strengthening their faith and fortifying them against the Devil at a particularly critical moment in their lives. *Extreme unction,* administered to those in danger of death, strengthened them at the moment they must face the judgment of the Almighty and removed from their souls the stain of minor (or venial) sins. *Marriage* sanctified the wedded state and family life. *Holy orders,* or *ordination,* conferred on select Christian males the priestly powers that permitted them to act as valid successors of Christ and the apostles in teaching the faith and administering the grace-

FIGURE 21.2 The Sacraments These scenes from a fourteenth-century manuscript illustrate three of the seven sacraments—baptism, the Eucharist, and marriage. According to the Church's teaching, only through participation in the sacraments could a Christian gain salvation. (Bibliothèque Nationale, Paris, ms. n. s. fr. 4509)

giving sacraments, especially the Eucharist and penance. The *Eucharist* was the sacrament by which Christ himself became present to the faithful. Its exact nature was not defined until 1215, when the Fourth Lateran Council pronounced the doctrine of *transubstantiation:* When a priest consecrated bread and wine at Mass, their substance miraculously changed into the body and blood of Christ, although their external attributes (color, shape, taste, etc.) remained the same. Partaking of this sacrament—receiving Communion—infused the grace of Christ's substance into the soul. No punishment was more terrible than excommunication—being cut off from receiving the Eucharist. The last sacrament was *penance,* whereby Christians who confessed their sins to a priest and resolved not to repeat them received God's forgiveness, provided that they made some sacrifice or did some good work assigned by the priest. Since the stain of sin barred one from heaven, Christians constantly needed to resort to a priestly confessor to ensure that their

souls, freed from original sin by baptism, were repurified by the removal of all stains caused by the sins they committed in the course of their lives. The Fourth Lateran Council decreed that the faithful must confess at least once a year.

Embroidered on the sacramental system was a rich set of practices sanctioned by the religious establishment that were counted as good works whose performance served to facilitate winning divine favor beyond the saving grace bestowed by the sacraments. By the thirteenth century Christians could avail themselves of an array of prayers and ritual ceremonies that served in every conceivable situation to invoke the help of God, Jesus, the Virgin Mary, and an army of angels and saints and to frustrate the hordes of demons that schemed under Satan's command to corrupt men and women. Opportunities abounded to offer material donations to churches and monasteries, to perform acts of charity, and to do penitential acts, such as fasting, abstaining from pleasures of the flesh, and venerating the relics of saints—all counted as good works. When coupled with the impresssive rites associated with administering the sacraments, involvement in these adjuncts to the sacramental system added a compelling emotional dimension to religious life that played a major role in making religion a central force in the lives of people from all levels of society.

The major fruits of papal reform—expanded liberty for the religious establishment, the centralized administrative system, the wide-ranging body of canon law, and the theological system that made the clergy essential to the salvation of all—permitted religious leaders to extend their influence into a wide range of matters involved in daily life. For example, it is difficult to treat any aspect of thirteenth-century European political life without encountering the influence of the papacy. Pope Innocent III offers a case in point. We need only recall how he manipulated the election of the Holy Roman emperors, finally arranging for his ward, Frederick II, to assume that office. He took an active role in directing affairs in the Kingdom of Sicily and in shaping the complex political interactions among the numerous Italian city-states. After a long quarrel he compelled Philip II of France to take back a wife he had repudiated. He forced or persuaded John of England and several other rulers to accept the status of vassal of the pope. Innocent was active in promoting the Fourth and Fifth crusades and in organizing a crusade against the heretical Albigensians of southern France, thereby helping the French kings to expand their royal domain. While not all of Innocent's ventures into European politics turned out the way he intended, the papal presence was a crucial factor in determining the political scene. Innocent's story was replicated in the careers of most thirteenth-century popes and, on a smaller scale, in those of countless bishops and priests. In the settings in which the ordinary affairs of people's lives were played out, ecclesiastical influences were everywhere present—in matters pertaining to the administration of justice, land transactions, oath taking, marriages, wills, crime, education, warfare, charity. Papal monarchs and their episcopal and priestly agents used religious weapons to gain political ends and political and economic pressures to advance ecclesiastical interests. Seldom in all history has a religious establishment been able to assert its independent authority so decisively in shaping the conduct of secular society as did the thirteenth-century Church in western Europe.

3. MONASTIC REFORM: SPIRITUAL SEEKING

While the quest for greater order in the organization of the Christian religious establishment and for standardization of its law and theology was advanced by popes, bishops, canon lawyers, and theologians, others sought a deeper spiritual understanding. Although those promoting reform on the papal model were always concerned with spirituality, it was in the monastic world that the urge to deepen the spiritual life found its most fruitful institutional setting; in some cases the spiritual forces that shaped monastic reforms derived from impulses welling up in the world of the laity.

In the year 1000 those interested in expanding their spiritual horizons faced a religious mentality of limited dimensions. Most Christians believed in a God perceived as a stern judge whose wrath might fall on helpless, sin-tainted humans at any time and in any form (see Figure 21.1). Human life was surrounded by constant danger from the Devil and his demons, present everywhere and armed with almost irresistible powers to entice men and women ever deeper into sin, for which God's anger would only be greater. The best humans could hope for was to do something that would be pleasing to God or that would persuade the legions of angels and saints who served the judgmental deity to intercede in their behalf. As a consequence, religious life was highly externalized. Men and women sought to propitiate God by offering their material goods, performing acts of charity, praying, and venerating relics of the saints. They searched for acts of penitence to win forgiveness for their sins. Always uppermost in people's minds was the hope for miracles whereby God or his agents would overturn the natural order to cure sickness, turn sure defeat in war into victory, save the harvest, or confound the Devil in his efforts to trap someone into sin. Building on this religious mentality, monastic spiritual seekers sought to deepen their understanding of God and to discover new ways of linking the human spirit to the divine. At first their prime concern was the enrichment of the spiritual life of the select few living the cloistered life, but eventually they widened their vision to embrace the spiritual condition of all Christians.

During the tenth and eleventh centuries the monastic reform movement was dominated by the Cluniac order. The monastery of Cluny had been founded in 910 by a pious lay prince under terms that freed the new foundation from lay control and dedicated its members to strict observance of the Benedictine rule. Cluny's first abbots sought to extend its influence by founding new houses or reforming corrupted existing houses, all of which were placed under the governance of the abbot of the motherhouse as a means of ensuring continued purity of life. As a consequence of the abbots' reforming zeal, by the eleventh century Cluniac monasteries existed all over Europe as centers of spiritual guidance. Cluniac spirituality emphasized an elaborate daily round of prayer and celebration of sacred rites as the main duty of the monks. The Cluniac liturgy was a splendid model of the kind of externalized religion that the contemporary world found so attractive. Many feudal aristocrats established close ties with Cluniac communities, chiefly to gain assurance that the monastic congregations they supported would include them in their prayers for the dead. As a prime sponsor of the Peace and the Truce of God, the Cluniac order made a notable contribution to curbing feudal warfare and promoting the concept of holy warfare as an act pleasing to God. And as promoters of the cult of saints and pilgrimages, the Cluniac monks provided an important outlet for the widespread urge for penitential actions pleasing to God.

By the end of the eleventh century the Cluniac movement began to lose its appeal, in part because of the excessive wealth of the Cluniacs, but more importantly because spiritual seekers increasingly found the externalized forms of piety promoted by Cluny unduly limited and not attuned to changing concepts of the nature of God, of human capabilities, and of the needs of Christian society, especially as highlighted by the Gregorian reform. These views tempered God's harsh judgmental qualities with a new emphasis on his love for humanity (see Figure 21.3) and

Figure 21.3 A Loving, Caring God This sculpture from Chartres Cathedral shows God creating Adam. This Creator is not the awful judge of the last day (see Figure 21.1). Rather, this scene reflects the new understanding of God that had such a powerful effect on the spirituality of the twelfth and thirteenth centuries. (Archives Photographiques, Paris)

on the human capacity to absorb God's love internally and to progress toward perfection through human powers born of human love toward other humans. The new piety especially extolled the virtue of poverty as a condition for personal perfection, a position that left the existing religious establishment open to criticism. The ideal of poverty led to a revival of hermit life based on the model provided by the desert fathers of the fourth and fifth centuries. Although most hermits of the eleventh and twelfth centuries pursued their search for perfection individually, the hermit ideal did produce the Carthusian order, established in France in the late eleventh century. Imposing on its members a severe regimen of poverty, fasting, and prayer as a means of opening the human heart to divine love, the Carthusian order impressed upon an admiring world a model of denial of the self and the world as a means of preparing to meet God.

The monastic movement that during the twelfth century played the most important role in shaping and projecting a new spiritual vision into the world was the Cistercian order. Founded in 1098 by a Benedictine who felt that the ancient rule was not being properly observed by the then-dominant Cluniacs, the Cistercian movement stressed the needs for separation from the world and for a simple life of prayer and physical labor. Cistercian houses were usually established on remote, uncultivated sites where the Cistercian monks and their lay brothers—peasants who bound themselves to monastic life by oath but followed a less austere life than did full members of the order—employed their labor, managerial skills, and technical ingenuity to create thriving agricultural establishments. Cistercian houses, both male and female, soon sprang up all over Europe, linked together by a unique governance system in which decisions affecting all houses were made collectively by the heads of individual houses meeting on a regular basis.

Especially influential in shaping the Cistercian order and its spiritual message was Bernard of Clairvaux (1090–1153), who entered the order in 1112 and almost immediately became its driving force. Bernard viewed monastic life as a preparation for action in the cause of God. That preparation was aimed at the inner spiritual development of each individual monk rather than at the elaborate, communally organized round of external religious acts that characterized Cluniac practice and that dominated the religious mentality of most contemporary Christians. Monks were now to practice physical deprivation, work, and prayer as a part of their spiritual training. Equally important were contemplation and devotion. Bernard's prescription for individual spiritual development focused attention on a loving God reaching out to unleash the potential of the human soul to participate in holiness. The human spirit could best reach back toward that God by contemplating the human, suffering Jesus and by seeking to share the feelings of Mary, Mother of God, of Jesus' disciples, and of those he taught as all of them lived in the presence of God made human for the salvation of other humans. Bernard was fully confident that the love and understanding flowing from such an approach to God would prepare human beings to go forth to fight sin and spiritual poverty without fear of corruption. In his own life he exemplified this new kind of spiritual activism. During his forty-year career in the Cistercian order, he was involved in many important events in Europe. He was the chief instigator of the Second Crusade, proclaiming that involvement was a manifestation of love for God and of service in the divine cause. He served the papacy doggedly in rooting out corruption in the clergy (he even censured papal conduct on occasion). He was a relentless foe of what he perceived as unorthodox and heretical thinking. He constantly hounded Europe's kings to improve their lives and their governments. He had no peer as a popular preacher and as a promoter of the use in the entire Christian community of the devotional practices that were at the heart of Cistercian spirituality. He and other Cistercians served as industrious soldiers of Christ whose chief armament was their sense of godliness derived from their inner spiritual life. Their target was the souls of individual men and women who possessed but did not properly use the power to make themselves better Christians.

Other developments in the monastic world of the twelfth century contributed to the deepening of religious life and the expansion of monastic influence on society. The number of monastic houses for women—nunneries—increased dramatically. These centers enlarged the visibility of women as models of piety and offered many of them opportunities for education and service. An order called the Augustinian Canons was organized as a means of improving the moral quality of the clerics who served in cathedral chapters. Its rule bound the canons to poverty, prayer, and moral excellence while permitting them to continue their responsibilities as pastors and episcopal administrators. Perhaps the most unusual application of the monastic model was the establishment of the crusading orders—the Templars, the Hospitalers, and the Teutonic Knights. Following a model defined by Bernard of Clairvaux, those who entered these orders took a monastic vow stressing obedience, poverty, and service to God as warriors defending the Christians in the Holy Land. Their activities in the cause of holy war earned these orders not only high respect but also immense wealth, which eventually led to their involvement in landholding, commerce, and moneylending.

The expansion of monastic involvement in the world and the search for new spiritual horizons reached a culmination in the early thirteenth century with the establishment of the *mendicant* (begging) orders, the Dominicans and the Franciscans. These orders were a response to new problems that increasingly challenged the clergy's traditional pastoral activities: the growth of urban life, with its unique institutions and tensions; the emergence of more sophisticated law and theology; the growing criticisms of the wealth and power of the ecclesiastical establishment; and doctrinal heresy. The mendicant movement sought to prepare brothers and sisters to serve God not by retreating to the cloister but by going into the world to address these problems without being burdened by material concerns or the stigma of wealth—which were widely believed to be barriers to spiritual perfection. To achieve this end, the mendicant orders insisted on absolute poverty after the model of Jesus and his disciples; neither the individual monk nor the corporate order was to possess wealth. Material support was to be derived from charity extended by those being served; begging for such charity was a key element of the vocation of the mendicants. Although the mendicants were mindful of the necessity of developing inner spiritual resources, the problems they sought to address as pastors called for the development of intellectual skills. As a consequence, their

preparation for active monastic life stressed an education devoted to mastering the intricacies of canon law and theology and to developing the skills needed for effective propagation of Christian beliefs and practices.

The Dominican order drew its name from its founder, a Spanish canon named Dominic (1170–1221). He was inspired to found a new order as a result of a tour through southern France, where the Albigensian heresy (see pp. 289–290) was rampant despite the efforts of the local bishops and Cistercian monks to curb it. Dominic became convinced that orthodoxy would prevail only if preachers learned in theology and free from all suspicion of wealth mingled intimately with heretics to teach them the true faith. In 1215 Pope Innocent III authorized him to organize a new order dedicated to the destruction of heresy by preaching. The rule provided that Dominic's followers would commit themselves to complete poverty and to preaching; their collective activities would be directed by a master general and his subordinate priors who commanded the provinces into which the order was organized. The rule placed heavy stress on the education of each monk in theology and law. The Black Friars, or Friars Preachers, as the order came to be called, quickly established themselves as a major force across Europe, active in preaching and in controlling the formulation and teaching of theology in the universities. Their involvement in university education allowed them to play a major role in shaping the mentality of religious leadership during the thirteenth century.

The inspiration for the Franciscan order was supplied by one of the most appealing figures in all religious history, Francis of Assisi (1182–1226) (see Figure 21.4). The son of a wealthy Italian merchant, Francis, while still a young man who had previously enjoyed a worldly life, underwent a fundamental spiritual conversion that convinced him that he must imitate Jesus in a most literal sense. As he put it, he married "Lady Poverty" and turned his energy to preaching and performing charitable works. He was especially charismatic as a preacher, exuding joy and a sympathy for all God's creatures, especially unfortunate, suffering human beings. To his followers, he was "God's own troubadour," filled with happiness and love. Almost immediately both men and women began to follow him. They sur-

FIGURE 21.4 Francis of Assisi: "God's Own Troubadour" St. Francis of Assisi, portrayed here in a painting done by Cimabue ca. 1280, was perhaps the most powerful spiritual force in the thirteenth century. His ideas on poverty and love deeply affected many of those searching for religious values in his age. (Alinari/Art Resource)

tured organization and a discipline more formal than the founder's simple command that his followers imitate Jesus. The rule of absolute poverty was modified to allow the order to acquire wealth and to place greater emphasis on formal education as preparation for a preaching career. To many devoted Franciscans these compromises represented a denial of the Franciscan ideal; as a result of these concerns, the order was plagued by bitter internal conflicts. The Friars Minor, or Grey Friars, also met strong opposition from local clergy, who resented their exaltation of poverty and their effective skills as preachers and confessors. Despite these obstacles, the Franciscans asserted a powerful influence on religious life at all levels of society. Together, the Franciscans and the Dominicans became pillars of strength for the thirteenth-century religious establishment in terms of propagating its teachings, containing voices of dissent, and expanding spiritual consciousness.

4. POPULAR REFORM: ENTHUSIASM, DISSENT, HERESY

The highly visible efforts of reformers to impose order on religious life and to expand spiritual vision were accompanied by considerable religious ferment among people of modest social status. Reform of this kind manifested itself in the activities of diverse peoples: simple priests, maverick monks, peasants, merchants, artisans, women, even children. What motivated their efforts at religious renewal is difficult to discern. Perhaps they were stimulated by a deeper understanding of the Christian message brought to them by the priests and monks produced by the papal and monastic reform movements. Perhaps they were introduced to new religious ideas by the slowly expanding number of literate laypersons, especially in towns, who were able to explore sacred literature, especially the Bible, and articulate their own interpretation of its meaning. The social and economic changes affecting society at all levels created new pressures that provoked a rethinking of traditional religious values. In reviewing the evidence, one suspects that many simple, uneducated, illiterate people were able to extract from their limited knowledge of God's ways and of Jesus' message fresh religious

rendered their wealth, worked or begged for a livelihood, and preached a simple message of love for God and humanity. In 1210 Francis asked Innocent III for permission to organize a formal religious order that would practice absolute poverty and dedicate its efforts to preaching and good works. Innocent hesitated, feeling that Francis' demands on his followers were too severe and perhaps concerned that the simple message of love and repentance would breed a troop of dissenters with little regard for the machinery that the organized Church supplied for saving souls. Finally, however, he consented. Between then and 1226, when Francis died, the order grew rapidly, spreading to nearly every part of western Europe. As the order expanded, its governing rule was modified to provide a more struc-insights that made their lives more meaningful. Whatever the source, there can be no question that the period 1000 to 1300 witnessed significant religious stirrings throughout the population.

One manifestation of popular religious ferment was the enthusiastic response of simple people to externalized cult practices aimed at seeking God's favor and doing penance for sins. Such people eagerly participated in the cult of relics and the veneration of saints. Simple people participated in pilgrimages to holy places, whether the holy place be a shrine located a few miles away or the scene of Jesus' earthly life in distant Palestine. The infamous Peasants' Crusade reflects the fervor aroused in the popular mind by the crusading movement; even more bizarre was the Children's Crusade of 1212, during which several thousand children were organized for an expedition to the Holy Land and proceeded as far as Marseilles in southern France before less pious merchants sold them into slavery.

Another manifestation of popular religious enthusiasm was the response given to charismatic preachers. Building their message around Jesus' poverty, humility, and love, these preachers often established bands of followers who shared their wealth, engaged in works of charity, cared for the sick, and worshiped in unique ways that emphasized emotion and intimate companionship. Some of these leaders spiced their exhortations to live like Jesus and his apostles with passionate attacks on the moral flabbiness of the clergy and the wealth of the contemporary religious establishment, thus making anticlericalism a regular part of popular religious reform. On occasion, this anticlericalism led to overt action against the established clergy. For example, between about 1050 and 1070, at the very moment when the Gregorian reform movement was gathering momementum, groups of lower-class dissidents called *patarenes* (ragpickers) by their enemies fiercely resisted the authority of bishops appointed to their office by secular rulers in several Italian cities, protesting episcopal wealth, abuse of power, and immorality. Again, in 1145, an Italian monk, Arnold of Brescia, so aroused the populace of Rome against the wealth and secular power of the papacy that the pope was forced to flee and succeeded in recapturing control of the city only by calling upon Emperor Frederick Barbarossa to use force to capture and execute Arnold.

On occasion such popular reform efforts went beyond what the religious and secular authorities would tolerate as dissent and thus became heresy in the eyes of those authorities. Such was the fate of the Waldensian movement. This group was inspired by Peter Waldo, a rich merchant from Lyons in France. In 1173 he gave away his wealth and took up a life of poverty in imitation of Christ—much as contemporary Carthusian and Cistercian monks were doing and as Francis of Assisi would later do. Soon after he began his preaching, Peter sought papal permission to establish a monastic order based on poverty. The pope denied his request, but Peter and his following continued their activity, gradually becoming more radical. Practicing poverty and a strict moral life reflecting many Cistercian ideas about sobriety, temperance, and simplicity, Waldensian leaders went among the common people, especially in urban centers, preaching and praying in the vernacular language. They condemned the clergy, arguing that all Christians could serve a priestly function, and denied the need for sacraments in gaining salvation. They developed their own ministers, both men and women, and their own ritual practices. Eventually they were accused of heresy, and the religious establishment undertook to suppress the movement. Some Waldensian groups, especially in France, returned to orthodoxy, but in northern Italy the movement withstood persecution and survived as a potent force of dissidence in many cities.

Far more radical were the Cathari (from a Greek word meaning "pure"), also called Albigensians (from Albi, the southern French city where the movement was especially strong). Their fundamental beliefs were rooted in a radical dualism, a concept that had originated in the Near East as early as the fourth century, probably as a result of the mixing of Christian and Zoroastrian ideas. The movement spread slowly westward from the Near East, finally reaching northern Italy and southern France in the tenth century. By 1200 its influence was felt throughout Europe, with its major center of strength in southern France.

The Cathari believed that two powers, good and evil, coexisted and constantly competed in the universe. Only things spiritual, including the human soul, were good. Everything material was evil, including the flesh within which the soul was entrapped and the earth itself. This position caused the Cathari to repudiate the God of the Old Testament, who had created the material world, and to deny the humanity of Jesus and the validity of what had been instituted in his name as instruments of salvation, including the earthly religious establishment, the ordained priesthood, and the sacraments, all of which in some way partook of the evil material world. True Cathari—the "perfect," as they called themselves—sought to liberate their souls by escaping the material world. They refused to marry, holding that human procreation was the greatest of all evils. They ate no meat, milk, or eggs, all of which were the products of sexual union. They owned no property and refused to shed blood. Allowances were made by the Cathari communities for those incapable of the rigorous life imposed on the "perfect." Second-grade Cathari, called "believers," were permitted to indulge in things material more freely, although "believers" hoped someday to join the ranks of the "perfect," who alone would be saved. The Cathari developed their own clergy, their own religious services, and their own rules of conduct. Their fervor and discipline produced communities that were remarkably resourceful in asserting political and economic dominance over the areas in which they lived. But above all else, the Cathari impressed those around them with their austerity and moral earnestness.

Needless to say, the unique beliefs and the material success of the Cathari aroused the ire of those outside their exclusive communities and brought charges of heresy against them. As a consequence, the ecclesiastical authorities moved to suppress the movement. Local bishops attempted to convert them by persuasion; that failing, they then hailed them before ecclesiastical courts to try to punish them under the provisions of canon law that provided death sentences for heresy. As we have noted, first the Cistercians and then the Dominicans tried to persuade the Cathari to return to orthodoxy. However, these measures failed, in part because of the dedication of the Cathari and in part because the movement had the support of many local nobles. Pope Innocent III finally took a more drastic step: He enlisted the support of the French monarchy to mount a "crusade" against the heretics. This ferocious Albigensian Crusade (1209–1229) destroyed the main centers of Cathari power and exterminated many members of the movement. To hunt down those that remained, the papacy utilized a special court, the Inquisition, and empowered it to employ special legal techniques, including secret witnesses and torture, to identify suspected heretics and to bring them to trials that resulted in either their return to orthodoxy or their death. These drastic measures provided a final solution for Catharism, perhaps, however, at the cost of defining the care of souls in terms that irreparably damaged the image of an institution which claimed to serve the religion founded by Jesus.

5. CONSEQUENCES OF THE MEDIEVAL RELIGIOUS REVIVAL

During the thirteenth century there were increasing signs that the reform movement was losing its vitality. Most of the forces that had generated reforming ideas and practices during the eleventh, twelfth, and early thirteenth centuries had been successfully encapsulated into the formal structures of the religious establishment as official parts of its organization, its doctrine, its law, its ritual, its moral code, and its spirituality. Those that could not be assimilated were often eradicated or disregarded. There remains but one question: What were the consequences of all the energy spent trying to elevate the level of religious life? Historians have differed widely in their answers to this question, but perhaps most would accept certain outcomes of the medieval reformation.

First, the medieval reformation certainly strengthened the organization of the religious establishment. In contrast to its position in 1000, that establishment had by 1300 developed structures and processes that allowed the clergy, a group clearly distinguished from the rest of society, to impose one body of belief, one code of conduct, and one set of religious practices on the lay members of the Christian community. Seldom in history has an institution been in a position to direct society so decisively. But that position was not gained by accident; it was a consequence of sustained institution building.

Second, the reformation redefined the relationship between church and state. Whereas in 1000 the religious establishment was subordinated to secular powers whose authority was surrounded by a sacral aura, by 1300 the "Church" as a corporate body had defined for itself an area of liberty into which no other authority could intrude. Acting within this sphere, its officials were able to play a vital role in influencing societal development according to norms defined in religious terms. The existence of separate realms for church and state would powerfully affect Europe's future.

Third, the challenges posed by the effort to renew the religious life unleashed intellectual and artistic talents in ways that stretched the mental capabilities and artistic sensibilities of western Europeans far beyond the boundaries of the mentality existing in the year 1000. In short, the religious renewal sparked a cultural renaissance that might not otherwise have happened except for the troublesome issues raised by the intense search for God and for more effective ways of serving his will.

Fourth, the medieval reformation broadened the range of spiritual possibilities far beyond what had been available to Christians in the early Middle Ages. The probing for the meaning of religious life that occurred between 1000 and 1300 in the monastic world and among simple people produced spiritual concepts that greatly enriched Christian life. Of particular importance for the future of western Christianity was one result of medieval spiritual searching: There was an increasing conviction that within each individual follower of Jesus, whatever his or her social status might be, there existed a spiritual realm of infinite dimensions which each could explore and enrich by exercising powers inherent in human nature.

Finally, it can be argued that the medieval reformation caused as many religious problems as it solved. As its most notable monument, the medieval reformation created a powerful, rich, hierarchically structured institution deeply involved in the affairs of the world. In its theology and its law, that institution had defined a highly formal system of religion that claimed to place the keys to salvation into the hands of a distinctive spiritual elite. It remained to be seen whether society would continue to accept that monolithic system in its entirety. Would kings and princes allow religious leaders to direct many aspects of worldly society according to their own rules? Would men and women find the answers to their spiritual needs in the strictly defined system of belief and worship prescribed by the clergy? Was there any flexibility within this highly centralized, legalistic, formal religious structure to allow adjustment to changing times and ideas? In short, did one productive religious reformation create conditions that would soon demand another?

SUGGESTED READING

General Surveys of Church History

Bernard Hamilton, *Religion in the Medieval West* (1986). A valuable guide to the basic tenets and practices of the medieval Church.

Jeffrey Burton Russell, *A History of Medieval Christianity: Prophecy and Order* (1968).

Joseph H. Lynch, *The Medieval Church: A Brief History* (London and New York, 1992).

Either of these brief surveys will provide an excellent introduction to the major developments in medieval religious history.

Hubert Jedin and John Dolan, eds., *Handbook of Church History*, Vol. 4: *From the High Middle Ages to the Eve of the Reformation*, trans. Anselm Biggs (1970). A detailed history of religious life.

R. W. Southern, *Westsern Society and the Church in the Middle Ages* (1970). Stresses relationships between the Church and the world.

Reform: Papal, Monastic, Popular

Colin Morris, *The Papal Monarchy: The Western Church, 1050–1250* (1989).

I. S. Robinson, *The Papacy, 1073–1198: Continuity and Innovation* (1990).
Two excellent treatments of the development of papal power.
Jaroslav Pelikan, *The Christian Tradition. A History of the Development of Doctrine,* Vol. 3: *The Growth of Medieval Theology (600–1300)* (1978). A challenging treatment of the search for a uniform body of doctrine.
Christopher Brooke, *The Monastic World, 1000–1300* (1974).
C. H. Lawrence, *Medieval Monasticism: Forms of Religious Life in Western Europe in the Middle Ages* (1984).
Two good descriptions of various forms of medieval monasticism.
Rosalind and Christopher Brooke, *Popular Religion in the Middle Ages: Western Europe, 1000–1300* (1984).
A. I. Gurevich, *Medieval Popular Culture. Problems of Belief and Perception* (1988).
Two stimulating studies of the beliefs of common people.
R. I. Moore, *The Origins of European Dissent* (1977).
Malcolm D. Lambert, *Medieval Heresy. Popular Movements from Bogomil to Hus* (1977).

Thorough treatments of dissent and heresy with emphasis on the social factors involved.
R. I. Moore, *The Formation of a Persecuting Society. Power and Deviance in Western Europe, 950–1250* (1987). A brilliant treatment of changing attitudes toward dissent.
Bernard Hamilton, *The Medieval Inquisition* (1981). An objective treatment.
Walter L. Wakefield, *Heresy, Crusade and Inquisition in Southern France, 1100–1250* (1979). Excellent on the Cathari.

Biographies

Helene Tillmann, *Pope Innocent III,* trans. Walter Sax (1980).
Watkin Williams, *Saint Bernard of Clairvaux* (1953).
Adolf Holl, *The Last Christian,* trans. Peter Heinegg (1980). Treats Francis of Assisi.
Pierre Mandonnet, *St. Dominic and His Work,* trans. Mary Benedicta Larkin (1945).

CHAPTER 22
Intellectual and Artistic Revival, 1000–1300

FIGURE 22.1 Gothic Sculpture
These Gothic figures from the south portal of the cathedral at Chartres, France, illustrate the warmth and realism of Gothic sculpture. (Jean Roubier)

As in all other aspects of life, the pace of cultural activity quickened during the years between 1000 and 1300, resulting in an outpouring of creative work in thought, literature, and art. The foundations for this cultural outburst had been painfully shaped during a long apprenticeship culminating in the Carolingian revival; the immediate stimulus was provided by the powerful political, economic, social, and religious changes occurring after 1000. These achievements played an important role in giving western European civilization its unique character and in establishing western European preeminence in a world setting.

The cultural achievement of the central Middle Ages can best be understood by a topical approach concentrating on certain areas of cultural activity that dominated thought and expression. However, it is important to note that the cultural development occurring during the period from 1000 to 1300 had a chronological dimension. In broad terms, cultural change occurred in two phases. The first, which extended from about 1000 to 1170, was marked by vigorous exploration and experimentation that immensely expanded the cultural horizons, skills, and resources of thinkers, writers, and artists. As one American scholar put it, that era witnessed a "renaissance." Toward the end of the twelfth century the cultural climate began to change. The buoyant, questing spirit gave way to a concern for organizing and summarizing the diverse accomplishments of the earlier period. This age of synthesis, which extended across the thirteenth century, produced the most mature expressions of medieval culture, but its accomplishments lacked the freshness and spontaneity characteristic of the "twelfth-century renaissance."

The cultural life of the central Middle Ages was divided into two distinctive spheres. In one, Latin was the vehicle of expression. It was in that language that the prime sources of the Christian faith were enshrined: Scripture, the writings of the Church Fathers, the liturgy, canon law. And that was the language employed to explain the meaning of the faith. Those able to use that language, chiefly members of the clergy, became the "learned" in society, a group accorded high respect because its members had access to the written sources that opened the way to salvation. In the other cultural sphere, the languages of the people, the vernacular tongues, prevailed, first as spoken vehicles of communication and then as written languages devoted chiefly to expressing the interests, tastes, and values of the nobility. Although these two cultural spheres intersected and interacted, each made its own unique contributions to the cultural life of the central Middle Ages. In a real sense, the visual arts played an important role in bridging these two cultural spheres.

1. THE WORLD OF LEARNING: EDUCATION

In the world of the "learned" education was of crucial importance. During the early Middle Ages Latin increasingly became a foreign language that had to be learned by those seeking access to religious truth. This crucial need required schools designed primarily to sustain Latin literacy. What was taught in those schools and how it was taught became a prime factor in shaping the mentality of the learned world. As we have already noted (see Chapters 15 and 16), prior to 1000 educational activity was largely confined to monastic schools, although by 1000 a few modest cathedral schools still survived from Carolingian times, and in Italy some municipal schools continued. A curriculum based on the study of the seven liberal arts had been fixed, and basic textbooks defining the content and methodology of these disciplines had been established, chiefly during the Carolingian period (see p. 216). The monastic schools touched a narrow segment of the population and cultivated a limited range of intellectual interests.

During the eleventh and twelfth centuries the educational system underwent a significant expansion and a fundamental change in character. Part of the stimulus came from intellectual ferment within the monastic world (see Chapter 21). More decisive, however, was a shift in the social value of education. There was a mounting need for literate people able to serve the religious establishment, royal governments, and urban commercial enterprises. Education became the avenue by which increasing numbers could prepare themselves for career opportunities created by that demand. Cathedral and municipal schools were better prepared to meet this challenge than monastic schools were and enjoyed a remarkable growth in both number and size. Especially in the cathedral schools there was a marked intensification and expansion of the study of the seven liberal arts, particularly the *trivium*—grammar, rhetoric, and dialectic (logic). In the municipal schools in Italy, the study of law took on new vigor. Many of the most prominent cathedral schools of the early twelfth century, such as those at Paris, Chartres, Laon, and Reims, owed their fame to individual masters who specialized in one of the liberal arts and were thus able to enrich its content and methodology. In fact, being a master became a career in itself, marking the appearance of the professional intellectual as a key force in the world of learning. Since the content of grammar, rhetoric, and dialectic was derived chiefly from classical Latin models, cathedral schools became centers of more intensive and critical study of the Latin classics. The other four liberal arts (the *quadrivium*)—arithmetic, geometry, astronomy, music—were less important in training literate, articulate people to serve new social roles. Still, their content was constantly expanded, chiefly as a result of the renaissance of classical studies.

Toward the end of the twelfth century the monastic, cathedral, and municipal schools no longer met the needs of the world of learning. Because they were often dependent on a single master teaching a specialized discipline, they lacked continuity and curricular breadth. Also, their masters had opened up intellectual vistas and generated specialized scholarly interests that abbots, bishops, and town councils had little practical interest in fostering. Moreover, during the last half of the twelfth century western Europe was flooded with a huge body of new knowledge coming from the Greek and Moslem worlds. Primarily philosophical and scientific in content, this new knowledge challenged existing religious beliefs and demanded a level of learning well beyond that needed to prepare people for careers. The response was a new institution, the university, that consisted of a community of teachers and learners engaged in a collective effort to expand, organize, and transmit knowledge and intellectual skills.

The earliest universities, those at Bologna and Paris, came into existence about 1200; not long after, others emerged in various urban centers across Europe. Following a pattern already used by urban dwellers and by merchants and craftsmen seeking to establish places for themselves in society, the founders of universities organized themselves into self-governing corporations, or guilds (the general Latin term for "guild" was *universitas*). At Bologna the students, for the most part law students, formed a *universitas* to protect themselves against exploitation by townspeople and to regulate the teaching performance of their masters. At Paris the teachers of the arts in the city's episcopal school broke away from the bishop's control and founded a self-governing body, the faculty of the arts, to control the educational process. A crucial step in establishing a university was gaining legal recognition from a public authority—king, bishop, town council—which allowed the corporation to exercise certain privileges. The privileges claimed were wide-ranging, but one was vital: the right to grant a degree certifying that a learner had completed a specified program of training defined by a faculty. Once a guild of teachers and students had established its legal status, it developed its own internal governance structure and operating rules. This process was often lengthy and beset by fierce struggles within the *universitas*.

The core curriculum of the typical university was based on training in the seven liberal arts conducted by a faculty of masters of arts, each a specialist in one of the arts. For most students university training involved becoming acquainted with all of the arts, a program usually requiring four years of study and resulting in a bachelor of arts degree, which qualified its literate recipients for a variety of careers. Those wishing to teach the arts either in a university or in some other kind of school pursued their studies in one of the arts for another year or two and earned a master's degree. Those who aspired to a teaching career beyond instructing students in the liberal arts or who hoped to serve in high places as authorities on technical disciplines could pursue a doctorate in theology, law, or medicine. This degree required additional years of study, research, and public lecturing. At Paris, for example, the theology doctorate took at least thirteen years of study. Although the ultimate objective of university study was earning a degree, many students spent time at universities without earning degrees; simply having been at a university earned them preferment in advancing their careers.

The basic teaching method at universities focused on acquainting students with authoritative texts in the various disciplines. Usually these texts were works by ancient authors, but occasionally the works of "modern" authorities were added. Since books had to be hand copied, they were expensive and scarce. In the face of this problem, the master read the text (thus the origin of the lecture method, derived from the Latin word for "reading," *lectio*), and the students took notes. As the master read the text, he commented on the issues it raised, often citing the opinions of other authorities on each issue and employing logical argumentation to reconcile differences. The purpose of this enterprise was to convey fundamental truths and to train students in the art of defending those truths through argumentation (*disputatio*)—an art that required acquiring a body of knowledge, developing a capacity for logical thinking, and perfecting skills in oral argumentation. Proof of worthiness for a degree was established by a student's performance in a public examination. Such a test required the student to expound on a text, develop and defend a thesis with respect to it, and respond to challenges to the thesis posed by the examining masters. This method produced minds that held a high respect for established authorities, were adept at textual analysis, were skilled in reconciling contradictory positions by logic, and were inclined to settle differences by argumentation.

The early universities were communities of people rather than physical entities. Most classes were held in rented halls. Students took lodgings in private homes. In time, however, universities did take on a physical presence. Patrons began to endow establishments, called *colleges*, for housing and feeding students. The first such institution was the Sorbonne at Paris, named after its patron, Robert de Sorbon, a rich courtier. Chapels, manuscript-copying services, and libraries were built to serve those engaged in teaching and learning. Thus, a university quarter began to emerge in some medieval cities, usually a welcome—although not always peaceful— adornment to urban life.

University students were almost exclusively male and came from a mixed social background; predominantly they were the offspring of people of modest means—petty nobles, merchants, artisans, even affluent peasants—who saw education as a means of economic and social advancement. They ranged in age from fourteen or fifteen to thirty or thirty-five. Since universities were few, students gathered at each from afar, thus constituting a population of strangers in most university towns. Many were supported by their parents or by patrons—usually inadequately, if we can believe the constant pleas for funds voiced in surviving student letters. These letters, however, seldom talk of student expenditures in taverns and on other frivolous pursuits that are recorded in other surviving documents. Students clashed constantly with townspeople, who viewed them not only as foreigners, idlers, and wastrels but also as targets for exploitation. Since students were legally considered members of the clergy and of a privileged corporation, it was difficult for town governments to exercise legal control over them. Town-gown rivalry, often surrounded by bitter recriminations and even violence, became a regular part of urban life in every university center.

2. THE WORLD OF LEARNING: THE MEDIEVAL "SCIENCES"

The evolution of the medieval educational system promoted the structuring of intellectual activity into what medieval scholars would have called "sciences," by which they meant bodies of interrelated knowledge capable of describing and explaining meaningful segments of the total universe of knowledge. In a sense, each of the seven liberal arts constituted a science in the medieval scheme of things, and medieval scholars and teachers greatly enriched each of them. However, the chief monuments of medieval intellectual activity came in more exalted "sciences": theology (which embraced what we would call philosophy), or the study of God; law, or the study of human society; and nature, or the study of the material order. Aside from the challenging intellectual issues innate in each of these areas, various pressing problems in a changing society forced learned individuals to seek to bring order to what was known about each of these sciences and to try to find out more.

If the liberal arts can be counted among the

sciences in the medieval learned world, then perhaps the monument that marks their place in that world was the rich and varied body of literature written in Latin to serve the increasing number of Latin readers and speakers produced by the schools. That literature was strongly influenced in style and language by the classical Latin texts that provided the models upon which the study of grammar and rhetoric was based. Latin authors of the central Middle Ages demonstrated considerable skill in using these models in innovative ways. The Latin vocabulary was constantly enriched by the infusion of new words and by the redefinition of old meanings, and classical literary forms were modified to permit Latin authors to treat matters that concerned them in creative ways. Between 1000 and 1300 there was a great outpouring of Latin prose literature devoted to history, biography, saints' lives, devotional manuals, letters, and political polemics. Perhaps the most original Latin literature took the form of lyric poetry on religious themes, often composed to serve the needs of the liturgy. But medieval writers were equally adept at nonreligious poetry, as exemplified by many student songs, collectively called Goliardic poetry, celebrating drinking, sensual love, gambling, and other worldly themes. Unless serious attention is given to the vast body of literature written in Latin for an "educated" audience, little can be known about what happened in the medieval world, what people thought about that world, and how they felt about the human scene.

Beyond the active commerce of ideas fostered by Latin belles lettres were the higher realms of truth. The queen of medieval "sciences" was theology, not so much because of the number who mastered it (they were few) but rather because of the weight of the subject with which it dealt. Although it had always engaged Christian thinkers, theology made a quantum leap forward as a field of systematic investigation during the central Middle Ages. That advance was due in part to the urgent need felt by religious leaders seeking to unify and systematize basic religious teachings as an aspect of the effort to reform Christian society. But also stimulating theological activity were new methods of intellectual inquiry and new knowledge.

During the early Middle Ages theological inquiry sought primarily to understand and explain the meaning of certain authoritative texts that contained the divine truth—above all else, Scripture. The approach was primarily literary, seeking by careful reading and meditation to discover the levels of meaning contained in the word of God. In the eleventh century, a subtle change in the approach to sacred texts began to occur, providing the key to the emergence of the medieval "science" of theology. Prompted by their growing awareness of the contradictions in scriptural texts themselves and in the way in which past authorities had interpreted the revealed truth, scholars began to explore the extent to which human reason could be useful in grasping religious truth. In this pursuit they turned to the methodology of dialectic or logic, using the rules of formal thinking to test and demonstrate the validity of religious propositions.

The development of the "new" theology, not unlike the advent of the new "science" of later centuries, was slow and tentative, marked by deep suspicion on the part of advocates of traditional ways of exploring religious truths. A key figure in turning the tide was Anselm (1033–1109), abbot of the monastery of Bec in Normandy and later archbishop of Canterbury. A man of learning and unquestioned orthodoxy, Anselm proclaimed as his central intellectual tenet that faith should seek understanding, by which he meant that one steeped in revealed truth should strive to understand that faith in human terms. To demonstrate his point, he undertook to develop a logical proof of the existence of God, one that could stand on its own without depending on revelation. His famous proof, which has intrigued many generations of thinkers, legitimized human reason as a valid tool in the search to understand what revelation meant.

By the early twelfth century the study of dialectic and its application to various problems became a passion in the schools. A key figure in creating a science of theology based on dialectic was Peter Abélard (1079–1142). Son of a minor Breton noble family, Abélard studied with several leading masters in various cathedral schools in France and then became a successful master himself. His promising ecclesiastical career was disrupted by a love affair with one of his pupils, Héloïse, which led to a pregnancy, a secret marriage, a child, the emasculation of Abélard by

Héloïse's outraged kinsfolk, and the separation of the lovers. These "calamities," as Abélard put it, sent Héloïse to a nunnery and condemned Abélard to a life of wandering from monastery to monastery and school to school—perhaps always haunted by his memory of true love but also driven by an urge to know and understand more fully. Abélard's career was filled with controversy, stemming partly from his prideful, combative personality and partly from the force of his ideas, which posed a revolutionary challenge to traditional theological inquiry.

Superbly skilled as a logician, Abélard made a major contribution to systematizing the use of dialectic as a tool of theological inquiry. In a bold book entitled *Sic et Non* (*Yes and No*), he set down a series of cases in which revered authorities disagreed on fundamental doctrinal questions. His approach implied that only the use of reason could resolve these contradictions. Abélard also developed new insights into how human beings came to know. He maintained that the truth consists of concepts formed in the mind from the study of created things, such concepts being the nearest approximation to the perfect knowledge that is God. A philosopher's task is to organize in a logical fashion all that is known so as to create a mental image of God's universe. Abélard's dialectical approach to theology aroused strong opposition, led by the formidable Bernard of Clairvaux, which eventually resulted in an official condemnation of some of his teachings by a church council. But the opposition was to no avail, and the new theology became predominant. It was given special impetus by one of Abélard's students, Peter Lombard (1100–1160), who used the dialectical methodology as the basis for his *Sentences*. In it Peter employed logic to resolve contradictory positions contained in Scripture and the writings of the Church Fathers on a large number of topics relating to basic Christian doctrine. The result was a unified body of theology, systematically organized. The *Sentences* quickly became the basic text for teaching theology, and its dialectical methodology became standard.

The value of the dialectical approach became even more evident during the late twelfth and thirteenth centuries, when scholars in the West came into possession of a vast body of new knowledge derived from Greek philosophy and scientific knowledge along with the Moslem commentaries on that material. During the early Middle Ages western Europeans had lost contact with almost all of Greek philosophy and science. However, from as early as the ninth century Moslem scholars became deeply interested in this material, translated most of it into Arabic, and commented on it extensively (see Chapter 14). Beginning about 1150, this huge body of knowledge again became available in the West, first as a result of the labors of scholars working chiefly in Spain and Sicily to translate Arabic texts into Latin and then later as a result of translations made directly from Greek texts. The new material included most of Aristotle's writings, and he—the Philosopher, as Western thinkers soon called him—quickly became the leading authority on logical methods as well as philosophical and scientific learning. The new learning posed a serious challenge: Not only did it provide scholars with heretofore unfamiliar knowledge about a wide range of matters, especially the natural world, it also confronted them with logically demonstrated systems of truth that directly contradicted many basic Christian teachings.

The major concerns of thirteenth-century theologians, collectively called the Scholastics, centered on mastering the new knowledge, organizing it into a rational system, and reconciling it with Christian doctrine in a way that met the tests of logic without denying the faith. Their assault on these problems was motivated not only by the intellectual challenges innate in these issues but also by their urge to serve the religious establishment in its quest for doctrinal clarity and uniformity. These concerns, explored most intensely in the universities, evoked a variety of responses, often accompanied by bitter intellectual warfare that belies the notion that the Middle Ages was a time of uniformity and conformity in the realm of ideas.

One especially controversial approach to these fundamental issues was formulated by a group of scholars called the Averroists, after Averroës, a famous Moslem thinker who had commented extensively on Aristotle's works (see Chapter 14). The adherents of this school wholeheartedly accepted Aristotelian rationalism, arguing that reason was capable of defining an order of truth that had its own validity irrespective of the tenets of the faith. At the opposite pole was a school of thought that found Aristotelianism to be of little value in leading to the truth about the faith. This school reasserted the Platonic-Augustinian tradition that had long prevailed as the prime approach to theological wisdom. The most notable figure in this group was Bonaventura (1221–1274), a Franciscan teacher in Paris who later became head of the Franciscan order. Bonaventura argued that reason could not discover the ultimate truth, which must come to the intellect intuitively through an illumination from divine sources beyond the power of human reason. Although Bonaventura did not deny the value of a rational consideration of natural phenomena, he held that no fundamental truth would result; in fact, he was convinced that rationalism would ultimately end in doctrinal error.

But the most representative response to the major issues posed by the new knowledge was formulated by a succession of scholars who tried to reconcile revelation and reason. By far the most influential advocate of this approach was Thomas Aquinas (1225–1274), an Italian Dominican whose active career was divided between teaching at the university in Paris and serving at the papal court. During his career as teacher and scholar he produced a huge body of theological writing. His chief works, the *Summa contra Gentiles* and the unfinished *Summa Theologica,* reflect scholasticism in its most representative form. In all of his works Thomas begins with the assumption that God created the universe in such a way that all its parts fit together and have a single purpose. Every human being has the duty to know God and his works, and each has the ability to achieve that end as a result of powers inherent in human nature. There are two paths to this single, unified order of truth: revelation and reason. The task of the mind is to seek the truth by applying itself to those things that are the proper subjects for reason while accepting on faith those things that can be learned only by revelation. Thomas accepted on faith such doctrines as the Creation, the Trinity, and the Incarnation but applied reason to such problems as the existence of God, immortality, the operation of the natural world, the nature of government, and ethics. He was certain that reason directed to the proper ends and guided by sound methodology would provide the intelligence with an order of truth that fitted into the order of truth contained in revelation. If there is a conflict between revelation and reason, he felt, it results from faulty reasoning.

Following the rules of logic formulated by Aristotle and relying heavily on him for knowledge of subjects proper to human reason, Thomas measured the whole realm of human knowledge item after item with a view toward reconciling that knowledge with the revealed truth. His method consisted of a rigorously applied series of steps: formulating a proposition stating some aspect of the truth, setting forth all possible contrary positions, demonstrating the logical fallacies in these contrary positions, and finally showing the logical validity of the true position. Each single truth in Thomas' system is part of an interlocking structure of thought that relates all things to a perfect truth. The final result of his work—his *summae,* or summations— is a synthesis of all knowledge into one vast structure glorifying God and demonstrating the perfection of his creation in terms comprehensible to the human mind. The Thomistic synthesis perhaps best represents the overall spirit of medieval thought: the quest to integrate existing knowledge, both human and divine, into a single structure. New knowledge was seldom a concern of medieval theologians or philosophers.

Another "science" that developed during the central Middle Ages involved the systematic study of law. Although several universities had faculties of law, the major center of legal studies was at the University of Bologna. By the eleventh century strong pressures were being felt in society, especially in the religious establishment and the royal courts, to develop unified, consistent bodies of law as an instrument to promote order in society. However, the legal systems existing at that time were surrounded with confusion and contradictions. Like the theologians, students of law began to employ dialectic as a tool to resolve this problem. We have already noted the work of Gratian (see p. 282), who in his *Decretum* (1140) created a model compendium of canon law, based on the collection and rational reconciliation of a wide range of discordant precedents. Gratian's work became the basic text used in teaching canon law. A long succession of twelfth- and thirteenth-century canon lawyers continued the work of compilation and commentary; by the thirteenth century their labors had produced a highly sophisticated, consistent body of law essential to the governance of religious life in all its aspects.

The development of canon law was greatly stimulated by a revived interest in the study of Roman law. Except for a few places where written law had remained in use during the early Middle Ages, such as southern France and northern Italy, Roman law had long been neglected in the West. Then, in the eleventh century, its study was taken up with great vigor, mainly because the chief embodiment of Roman law, the Code of Justinian (the *Corpus juris civilis*), provided invaluable guidance in defining political authority. Civil lawyers spent their energies writing commentaries (called *glosses*) on the code to try to elucidate its meaning and relate its principles to existing society. Aside from producing an immense body of legal literature, their work decisively influenced the kind of law administered in the rising monarchies and shaped the concepts defining royal power. The legal concepts set forth by the students of Roman law prompted efforts to codify the confused bodies of customary law existing over much of western Europe. An example was the important treatise on English common law compiled by Henry Bracton in the thirteenth century.

Although a precise "science" of society did not emerge during the central Middle Ages, theologians and lawyers had much to say about the nature of human society and the political order. Discussions on these matters were spurred by a variety of influences: explorations by religious reformers of the ancient Christian concepts of the nature of the state and society; the conflict between church and state; the need to justify the claims of the new monarchies; the revival of Roman law; the recovery of classical Greek and Roman works on political theory (especially Aristotle). Gradually the serious study of political theory led to a new view of the nature of society and the political order. Traditional political thought, derived chiefly from Augustine, viewed the state as an instrument for suppressing the sinful nature of human beings; by filling this negative role, rulers prepared the ground for the spiritual perfection of human beings through the efforts of ecclesiastical leaders. Increasingly during the twelfth and thirteenth centuries the state came to be defined as an integral part of the natural order that asserted a unique and necessary positive force for the full realization of human potential.

Thomas Aquinas played an important role in articulating this view of the state. Strongly influenced by Aristotle, he argued that the state was a part of the natural order and existed to permit human beings to live in an ordered community where each could realize his or her innate potential for good. The proper form of government was a result of rational reflection on human needs. In Thomas' view, the ideal state was one in which various classes performed specific functions under the guidance of a just ruler in the interest of providing for the needs of all. Such a system ensured justice, which was the ultimate objective of government. Upon the ruler of the good state fell the heavy responsibility of discovering and applying the principles of natural law required to regulate human society in accord with the divine order. In discovering a positive role for the state as an instrument shaped by rational human actions for promoting human welfare, the political theorists of the central Middle Ages established the foundations for future study of the state and its functioning in a context which took existing realities into account.

In the "science" of the natural world the achievements of medieval thinkers seem pale by the standards of later ages. However, the central Middle Ages did witness one development of major significance for the study of the natural world. During the early Middle Ages thinkers had adhered to a view of nature rooted in Neoplatonism. This view considered the natural world to be an inferior order of reality that represented an illusory reflection of nonmaterial perfect forms. As this Neoplatonic concept was translated into a Christian idiom, nature came to be viewed as part of the universe corrupted by the Fall, lacking in any inherent order, subject to unpredictable alterations by transcendent forces. Given powerful impetus by a monastic ideal that spurned material things, early medieval thought was biased against serious concern with the study of the natural world in its own right. That view began to change by the twelfth century. The scholastic effort to unite all knowledge into a single truth and the vastly increased knowledge of nature resulting from the rediscovery of Greek and Moslem scientific works generated an effort to study the natural world as a fundamental dimension of God's created cosmos. That study led to the conclusion that the material world was good by virtue of being part of God's creation, that there was order in nature because it was part of God's perfect order, and that the natural world was intelligible to human reason. In short, nature had to be understood if theological and philosophical knowledge was to be complete. This fundamental shift in attitude constituted a prime achievement of the medieval search for truth. The discovery—perhaps rediscovery is a better term—of nature provided the starting point for great advances in knowledge.

The changing perspective on the natural world provided powerful impetus to an activity that was central to medieval natural science and eventually important to later advances in science—the mastery of the vast body of knowledge about the natural world that had been collected over the centuries by Greek, Hellenistic, and Moslem scholars. The preoccupation with accumulated knowledge about the natural world is amply illustrated in the field of medicine, which constituted a separate field of study in some universities, especially at Salerno in Italy. There the curriculum focused primarily on mastering Greek and Moslem medical texts. That same avid interest in accumulated knowledge about the natural world is evident in the writings of such theologians as Albertus Magnus (ca. 1206–1280), Thomas Aquinas' teacher at the University of Paris, whose voluminous writings on theology are filled with information about nature drawn chiefly from Aristotle's scientific works.

Despite this fascination with authority, tentative steps were taken to learn more about the natural world than was contained in the ancient texts. In medicine, for example, new knowledge was slowly added to the old as a result of information gleaned from observation of sick people, dissection of bodies of animals and humans, and study of the medicinal properties of plants. Especially noteworthy in encouraging the quest for new knowledge about nature was a group of scholars, most of them Franciscans, centered at Oxford University in the thirteenth century. Robert Grosseteste (1168–1253) and his pupil Roger Bacon (ca. 1214–1294) were its most distinguished members. These men insisted that the truth about the natural world could be gained only through observation and experimentation. Aside from his own experimentation in optics, Bacon raised questions about the blind trust which contemporaries had put in the scientific theories of ancient authorities, especially Aristotle. Such doubts, soon shared by others, had important implications for the exploration of nature, especially in such fields as astronomy and physics. Working at a somewhat less exalted level to expand knowledge about and control over the natural world were astrologers seeking to predict the future and alchemists trying to convert base metals into gold. And not to be overlooked in assessing the natural sciences in the Middle Ages were the increasing body of knowledge about natural phenomena and the advancing levels of technical expertise being accumulated by artisans and farmers engaged in the routine affairs of life. The ground was being prepared for an explosion of scientific knowledge.

3. BEYOND THE LEARNED WORLD: VERNACULAR LITERATURE

The learned world represented by the medieval schools and the Latin writings of theologians, lawyers, scientists, historians, poets, and polemicists involved a relatively narrow circle whose intellectual activities impinged on the lives of most people only indirectly at best. Beyond that narrow world was a larger circle of men and women who sought instruction and entertainment. During the central Middle Ages that world found its voice in vernacular literature, written in the tongues that people spoke in their daily lives about matters of which heretofore most of them had only spoken, not read. By 1000 the language map of western Europe had become a tower of Babel. That map had emerged slowly during the early Middle Ages out of three basic root languages: classical Latin, which evolved into the Romance tongues, such as French, Provençal, Italian, Spanish, and Catalan; Old German, out of which came German, English, Dutch, and the Scandinavian tongues; and Celtic, which evolved into Irish and Welsh. Each of these basic vernacular languages was further divided into local dialects, and many of them were enriched by extensive borrowings from each other and from Latin. Although how it happened is far from clear, the fact that between 1000 and 1300 writers did develop the capability of using these spoken languages to create literary works expressing unique ideas and feelings marked a major landmark in western European cultural development. Somehow that development must have been rooted in the dynamics of a changing world which created a need for and an interest in literacy other than in Latin. For the most part, those who created vernacular literature wrote for an audience of aristocratic laymen and laywomen, suggesting that it was at that level of society where the need was first felt. However, there is some evidence that their works were known and enjoyed by nonnoble townspeople and perhaps even peasants.

One form of vernacular literature that found wide favor among aristocratic audiences was the epic, a song setting down in writing the deeds of great warriors of the past that had been preserved in oral tradition. The great Anglo-Saxon epic *Beowulf*, composed about 800, recounts the adventures of a warrior living in a pre-Christian Germanic society. The epic genre is also illustrated by the Icelandic sagas, such as the anonymous twelfth-century *Poetic Edda* and the *Prose Edda* compiled in the early thirteenth century by Snorri Sturluson; both of these collections reflect a much earlier Scandinavian world dominated by the violent struggles of mythic heroes and pagan values. The chief Germanic epic, the *Nibelungenlied*, composed about 1200, reflects a tradition dating back to the time of the Germanic invasions and to the awesome deeds and terrible fates of heroic warlords and their formidable women. The chief *chanson de geste* (''song of deeds'') produced in French was the *Song of Roland*, written about 1100 to retell the story of Charlemagne's expedition of 778 against the Moors in Spain, which ended in the defeat of the Frankish forces at Roncesvalles. However, the unknown author adorned his account of this historical event and its hero, Roland, with the ideals and customs characteristic of eleventh-century noble society; particular emphasis is given to Roland's prowess as a warrior, his loyalty to his lord, and his willingness to give his life to defend his faith. The same themes dominate the Spanish

epic *Song of the Cid*, which glorifies the deeds of a famous knight involved in the Reconquista of Spain from the Moors.

The epic genre was soon rivaled by a new vernacular literary form, the lyric poem, which during the twelfth century enjoyed a tremendous vogue in the courtly circles of the chivalric nobility. This poetry developed first in Provence in southern France and soon spread over most of Europe. Its creators, called *troubadours*, were chiefly young noblemen whose lack of great fiefs and firm family ties rooted in proper marriages placed them on the fringes of noble society. Through their poetry they sought to expound their sensual love for a noble lady in a fashion that would earn them honor in her eyes and thus status in the society to which she belonged. The troubadours (called *trouvères* in northern France and *minnesänger* in Germany) projected a new set of values for noble society. Their poetry argued that the emotions associated with love—longing, suffering, anticipation of a lover's favor—had the power to ennoble just as much as did prowess in battle or loyalty to a male feudal lord. The search for self-understanding and the emotional probing associated with the quest for love refined the inner spirit and evoked patterns of behavior that combined to create the gentleman as the epitome of noble existence. The lyric writers thus played a crucial role in transforming the values and behavioral patterns upon which the concept of male excellence was based. They were also instrumental in attributing to women a vital role in shaping nobility, a role based on their sexuality and their power to give pleasure. The impetus for this new morality derived primarily from qualities innate in human nature, qualities having little to do with religious values. For this reason, troubadour poetry was viewed with grave misgivings by many religious leaders; perhaps also for this same reason, it enthralled noble society (see Figure 22.2).

Toward the end of the twelfth century, a third type of vernacular literature, the *romance*, began to rival epic and lyric poetry. Romances were stories combining a love theme with adventure, written chiefly to entertain court society; the immensely popular romances enjoyed the special patronage of high-placed noblewomen, such as Eleanor of Aquitaine. The adventure element in

FIGURE 22.2 Medieval Love This miniature showing a knight and a lady captured by love conveys the sense in which troubadour poetry saw love as a force capable of transforming behavior. (Universität Bibliothek, Heidelberg)

these stories was drawn from sources with vague roots in history, especially materials relating to the legendary King Arthur and his court. The authors of the romances used this "historical" material with complete freedom. The treatment of love in these stories reflected a continued probing of themes contained in troubadour poetry. The most gifted romance writers fashioned works with enduring appeal. Among them was Chrétien de Troyes, a late-twelfth-century French author who skillfully exploited the Arthurian material to create an intriguing picture of the ideal knight struggling to achieve chivalric excellence through pursuit of love and adventure and of the noble lady serving as a prime agent in shaping the consummate knight. Another writer, the thirteenth-century German Gottfried von Strasbourg, in his *Tristan and Isolde,* masterfully reveals the meaning of love in the lives of two who were its prisoners. *Parzival,* written by his countryman Wolfram von Eschenbach, is an appealing picture of a man pursuing an unobtainable ideal, symbolized by the Holy Grail. The

concepts of chivalry found their most mature expression in the romances. The themes and actions treated in them had a powerful impact on the behavior of the nobility for centuries and have continued to intrigue writers and audiences down to the present, influencing poetry, operas, and even modern musicals.

While the epics, lyrics, and romances were being written, sung, and read by nobles, other forms of literature evolved to appeal to the tastes and interests of nonnobles. Especially notable were dramas, *fabliaux,* and saints' lives. Although there was some interest in classical drama during the Middle Ages, as witnessed by the attempts of a tenth-century German nun, Hrotsvitha, to write plays in Latin modeled on Terence, medieval drama owed little to past examples. It began as part of the church liturgy; dramatized parts of services eventually moved outside the church into the marketplace. By the thirteenth century the guilds had taken over the responsibility for producing these dramas during religious festivals. Each guild presented one scene from a connected series of scenes that constituted an entire play. Several types of dramatic production developed: mystery plays, enacting scenes from the Bible; miracle plays, treating the highlights of saints' lives; morality plays, personifying human virtues and vices. The presentation of these serious, sacred dramas was punctuated by earthy language and comical portrayals of the key characters. The *fabliaux* were short tales recited in public squares to entertain the crowds. Whatever the subject—it could be almost anything—the *fabliaux* were always close to city life, representing everyday events in the lives of ordinary people. They were filled with vulgar humor and satire aimed especially at corrupt priests, betrayed husbands, and scheming women effective in getting what they wanted from young men. The most famous collection of *fabliaux* was *The Romance of Reynard the Fox,* made up of stories in which animals symbolize people and human characteristics. The spirit of *fabliaux* is also reflected in some of the tales told by Geoffrey Chaucer (ca. 1340–1400) in his *Canterbury Tales,* a highly entertaining collection of stories supposedly told by a group of pilgrims to entertain one another during their journey. Immensely popular were vernacular versions of stories telling of the heroic and miraculous deeds of the legions of Christian saints.

If one had to select a single author whose writings encapsulate the spirit and the art of medieval vernacular literature, it is likely that the choice would be Dante Alighieri (1265–1321). He was to medieval literature what Thomas Aquinas was to medieval theology. Dante was a product of the vibrant urban life of Florence. In his youth he fell in love with a girl named Beatrice, who later married someone else and died young. Beatrice became for Dante the ideal woman as defined by the code of courtly love. Dante was a learned man who wrote in Latin on a variety of subjects. He was also active in Florentine political life, ultimately suffering expulsion from the city because of his identification with a faction that lost control of the city government. While suffering what he called "an undeserving exile," he wrote his masterpiece, *The Divine Comedy,* in his native Tuscan dialect. Outwardly, it tells of Dante's journey through hell, purgatory, and heaven. Tired, discouraged, and confused at the outset, the pilgrim slowly begins to comprehend the harmony, order, and purpose in the universe; his spirit is progressively uplifted and his soul cured of its discontents. Guided through hell and purgatory by the Latin poet Vergil and through heaven by his beloved Beatrice, he is permitted to see all things from the depths of hell to God himself. Within this framework Dante weaves with dazzling poetic skills a rich tapestry reflecting medieval thought. He is a philosopher, presenting with consummate skill the medieval idea that all things in the universe are ordered by God in a cohesive, intelligible scheme. He is a mystic, yearning to the depths of his soul to catch a glimpse of God so that his human disquiet may be satisfied. He is a love poet; Beatrice, his guide in heaven, is a symbol of human love, a purifying and uplifting emotion. He is a scientist, incorporating into his poem many medieval ideas about the structure of the physical universe. He is an admirer of Greek and Roman writers and thinkers, although he has to condemn them to hell as non-Christians. He is a keen political observer, full of fierce partisanship. On his long journey from the gates of hell to its very pit, where Lucifer chews up three great traitors, Brutus, Cassius, and Judas, Dante discusses with Vergil nearly every kind of sin, showing a deep understanding of human nature and its weaknesses. The ascent from hell through purgatory to the seat of God in heaven offers him an equal chance to discourse on every aspect of virtue. Few artists have grasped human life and human aspirations more fully or written of them with greater artistry.

4. IN ALL WORLDS: THE VISUAL ARTS

During the Middle Ages the visual arts were the media common to all, rich and poor, literate and illiterate, learned and ignorant. The era from 1000 to 1300 marked a decisive epoch in art history during which two major styles, Romanesque and Gothic, were perfected and left a mark on artistic expression in western Europe that still asserts an influence. Both styles were preeminently religious in inspiration, created primarily to provide suitable places of worship, but features of both were adapted for secular purposes. The religious establishment was the prime agency promoting artistic endeavor, but almost all elements of society provided support for artistic undertakings.

The Romanesque and Gothic architectural styles were the fruits of a long evolution. The starting point of medieval church architecture was the Roman basilica, the rectangular meeting hall. The early Christians placed their altars in the semicircular *apse* at the rear and conducted the Mass there. The *nave* provided space for the faithful participating in the sacred rites. Side aisles often flanked the nave. The upper walls of the nave rose above the side aisles and were pierced with windows that allowed light into the nave. A lateral aisle, called the *transept,* sometimes crossed the nave just in front of the apse, so that the early church took the form of a cross. Over the centuries, this basic ground plan of church architecture and the art that decorated it were considerably modified by influences from the Byzantine, Germanic, and Celtic worlds and by new creative forces emerging from daily life. During the central Middle Ages artists finally succeeded in blending these many tributaries into distinctive new styles.

Romanesque Barrel and Groin Vaults

Romanesque architecture first appeared in the late Carolingian period and flourished until well into the twelfth century. Its main features are admirably illustrated by several churches still standing: Notre Dame la Grande in Poitiers, the cathedral of Saint Sernin in Toulouse, the cathedral church of Worms, the Abbey Church of Maria Laach in Germany, the church of Sant' Ambrogio in Milan, and the church of Sainte Madeleine at Vézelay in France (see Figure 22.3). The Romanesque style was characterized both by technical innovations and by a new spirit. The monastic world, especially the Cluniac reformers, played a dominant role in developing and spreading this style. The Cluniac emphasis on elaborate rituals and concern for providing the proper setting for the veneration of relics and for gatherings of pilgrims dictated that churches be large enough to house a number of chapels and accommodate great crowds. Architects also wanted to find a replacement for the traditional wooden roofs, which were so often destroyed by fire. The solution was a capacious church built entirely of stone.

So that liturgical needs could be met, the Romanesque style modified the basic ground plan of the traditional basilican structure. The nave was extended beyond the transept to create a *choir,* a space where the main altar was located and where the clergy and monks could gather for worship. The side aisles were also extended around the choir, creating a passageway or ambulatory that encircled the nave and the choir. A series of chapels was constructed off the side aisles and the choir ambulatory, providing spaces for many simultaneous religious services

Gothic Ribbed Vault

FIGURE 22.3 Romanesque Art These photos of the church of Sainte Madeleine at Vézelay in France illustrate some of the main features of Romanesque art. The nave (top right) features round ribbed arches, heavy columns, and thick walls pierced by small windows. Above the main portal (upper left) is a sculptured complex showing Christ instructing his disciples; comparable scenes over entrances were usual in Romanesque churches. The many capitals atop the pillars (lower left) of the nave and the porch leading to the main entrance provided space for carved scenes illustrating biblical themes. Romanesque sculpture was less concerned with realism than with reminding viewers of a religious truth and with moving their emotions. (Nave, Marburg; portal, Scala/Art Resource; sculpture, Marburg/Art Resource)

and for special shrines to display relics. To replace the wooden roof, architects developed techniques that allowed them to throw a barrel vault made of stone over the full length of the nave and choir and the side aisles. These heavy roofs were supported by massive stone walls. Where openings were needed through these walls—such as passages between the nave and the side aisles—round arches set on heavy pillars were used to support the structure above the opening. Groin vaults, again supported by arches and pillars, were evolved to cover the square or rectangular area where the axis of the nave and the choir was crossed by the transept (see illustration, p. 305). However, the barrel vault system of creating a stone roof was satisfactory only for relatively small structures. As the Romanesque style evolved, architects developed a method of building stone roofs over larger naves and choirs. They begin to break up the long barrel vault with rib arches crossing the nave and choir and resting on pillars on opposite sides of the nave and the choir. This technique created a series of bays, or "squares," marked off by pillars at each of the four corners. Each bay could then be covered with cross vaults. The space between the rib and the cross vaults could be filled in with relatively light stone pieces, reducing the roof weight and concentrating its downward thrust on the pillars at the corners of each bay (see illustration, p. 305). Despite these innovations, the stone vaulting covering the structure remained massive and exerted tremendous downward and outward thrust. For this reason Romanesque churches required heavy walls and massive internal columns; the few windows had to be kept small. Thus the typical Romanesque structure had an atmosphere of muted darkness and mystery that was not dispelled by the decorative paintings on piers, arches, and walls and by the candles that supplied artificial light. Yet this atmosphere was also due to the religious mentality of an age that viewed the church as God's citadel standing against a world filled with evil forces, a sacred fortress where men and women could commune with the God who protected them from the howling demons and the frightening forces of nature that raged outside this holy refuge (see Figure 22.3).

By the mid–twelfth century the European world was changing rapidly, and the new environment produced a new architectural style, the Gothic. It appeared first in Ile de France, the domain of the Capetians; the earliest full-scale Gothic church was the Abbey Church of Saint Denis near Paris, built in 1137–1144 by Abbot Suger, the adviser to kings Louis VI and Louis VII. From here the Gothic style spread over much of Europe.

The Gothic style evolved out of a desire for height and light in churches, a desire derived largely from new intellectual and spiritual concepts that fostered a more rational view of God and saw his chief attributes in terms of reason, light, and proportion. The Gothic church was an attempt to leave behind the mystery-shrouded, awesome world of the Romanesque and to create a setting in which the attention of anyone entering the structure would be drawn upward toward the light and purity of paradise—the paradise Dante pictured in poetry. Among the Gothic structures that achieve this effect magnificently are the cathedrals at Paris (Notre Dame), Chartres, Reims, Amiens (see Figure 23.4), Strasbourg, and Bourges in France; at Lincoln, York, and Salisbury in England; and at Cologne in Germany.

Technically, this transformation was made possible by the pointed arch, which carried thrust downward, and the ribbed vault, used to concentrate the thrust at a few points. Architects were able to combine them to fashion tremendously tall skeletons of stone whose weight flowed to earth through a series of slender pillars (see illustration, p. 305). The outward thrust, greatly reduced by the pointed arches and concentrated by the rib vaults, could be offset by thickened columns at the outside of the building or by flying buttresses, pillars set away from the main structure and joined to it by bracing arches high above the ground. Thin walls, supporting nothing but their own weight, could be filled in between the pillars. More important, light could be let into the structure by great arched windows cut through the thin walls. These windows, often interlaced with delicate decorative stonework, pierced the lofty clerestory and the side aisles, and majestic round windows were placed high above ground level at the ends of the nave, the choir, and the transept. The windows were often filled with many-hued stained-glass figures or scenes that suffused the interior with a breathtaking display of colored light (see Figure 22.4 and Color Plate 10).

Nearly every other visual art was put to work to decorate medieval churches. The exterior of a Romanesque church was generally plain except for the west façade, where the great arches built to provide doorways leading to a nave and side aisles provided a setting for sculpture. As illustrated by the church at Vézelay, these spaces were filled with massive, highly symbolic sculpture done in high relief; they portrayed human figures, animals, and abstract decorative patterns. A favorite subject was the Last Judgment, in which a stern Christ was portrayed relegating men and women to heaven or hell (see Figures 21.1 and 22.3). Within a Romanesque church there was more sculpture, chiefly decorative carving adorning the massive piers. The wall spaces were decorated with frecoes portraying scriptural scenes, particularly those that stressed the suffering of Christ and his judgment on humanity. Romanesque sculpture and painting are somber, with human beings portrayed as small, powerless, and dependent, surrounded by symbols of the terrors that beset spiritual life; they grip the emotions rather than the mind.

Gothic architecture brought about changes in the other arts. The exteriors of Gothic churches provided innumerable places for decorative sculpture, giving stone carvers an opportunity to experiment with a fantastic array of decorative motifs. Statues, sometimes executed in the round as well as in relief, became more realistic and humanistic, concerned more with expressing the human qualities of Jesus, the Virgin, the apostles, and the saints (see Figures 21.3, 22.1, and 22.4). The interior of Gothic churches offered less space for painting and sculpture than Romanesque churches did; decoration was concentrated chiefly on columns and arches. Not images but light fills the Gothic church. The painted walls of the Romanesque church were replaced with stained-glass windows. Their creators drew their themes chiefly from scriptural sources, but in their renditions they reflected the daily activities of medieval people in amazing detail. The stained glass at Chartres and in the beautiful Sainte-Chapelle built by Louis IX in Paris enthrall the viewer.

A variety of minor arts was employed to adorn these structures and to serve in carrying out religious services. Skilled metalwork was used for door handles and hinges, candleholders, chalices and pitchers, reliquaries, and railings to divide the space within the church. Woodwork provided pulpits and highly adorned seats for the celebrants of sacred services. Intricate needlework was employed to create splendid vestments for the clergy and tapestries to cover wall spaces. Skilled copyists and miniature painters fashioned beautiful liturgical books: Bibles, missals, psalters, hymnals. Ivory carvings were used to fashion covers for these books. In all these forms, artists demonstrated highly developed skills and imagination to create works that fitted the grand style dictated by the architecture and that reinforced the atmosphere of sanctity proper to holy places. Attendance at religious services constantly exposed the entire population to a dazzling display of the visual arts.

Another art associated with religious activity, music, also developed significantly during the central Middle Ages. Church music consisted primarily of melodies with verses taken from Scripture (especially the psalms) or composed for liturgical events (such great hymns as *Dies Irae* and *Stabat Mater* came from the Middle Ages). Gregorian chant (its alleged inventor was Pope Gregory I), or *plainsong*, developed as early as the sixth century. At first the singing was in unison, but over the centuries variations worked on plainsong developed into contrapuntal music. By the thirteenth century, complex and moving contrapuntal compositions, rendered by many voices and various instruments, filled the churches with sounds almost as heavenly as the light that poured through the stained-glass windows.

The great Romanesque and Gothic cathedrals and abbey churches commanded the best artistic talent and the bulk of the wealth that medieval society had to devote to art. However, the splendid artistic achievement they represent should not let us forget that there were other lines of artistic pursuit. The landscape was dotted with hundreds of small, simple parish churches, each a monument to the small community through whose efforts it had been built. These structures and their decor usually reflect Romanesque or Gothic styles, but often wonderfully creative local touches make one wish more was known about their creators. Living quarters for bishops

FIGURE 22.4 The Gothic Style The splendid church of Notre Dame at Amiens in France exemplifies the Gothic style. Its lofty nave (top left) is vaulted with pointed arches whose ribs carry weight down to the columns flanking the nave. Note the high arches that lead to aisles on either side of the nave. Above these arches is the clerestory, pierced by huge windows lighting the nave; the expanse can be seen in the apse at the far end of the building. The aerial view of the structure (bottom left) shows the flying buttresses used to offset the outward thrust of the roof on its supporting stone skeleton. Also evident is the transept crossing the nave. The façades of the main structure and the transept were decorated with numerous sculptures. Greeting those who entered the south transept was the "Golden Virgin" (top right), a wonderful example of the warmth and realism of Gothic sculpture. (Aerial view, Aerofilms, England; nave and sculpture, Archives Photographiques, Paris)

and the cathedral clergy and for monastic communities were constructed in both the Romanesque and Gothic styles. Many feudal castles, massive rather than elegant or comfortable, were built in the Romanesque style. In the towns, especially from the thirteenth century onward, beautiful town halls and guildhalls were constructed, putting Gothic principles to new uses. These buildings were decorated with paintings and carvings and furnished with skillfully wrought furniture and utensils for daily living. These structures were impressive signs that the religious system never completely absorbed the inspirations or energies of artists.

5. THE UNDERLYING SPIRIT OF MEDIEVAL CULTURE

Certainly it is not easy to find a common denominator for Thomas Aquinas, Dante, the architects and sculptors who built the churches at Poitiers, Amiens, and Chartres, the troubadours, the romance writers, and the authors of *fabliaux*. However, the more one experiences medieval thought and expression, the more one senses an underlying, unifying spirit.

Medieval thought, literature, and art are permeated by a quest for truth and light beyond the world of human existence. This reaching out of the mind and the imagination sprang from the almost universal belief that God controlled the universe and that it was the duty of mortals to know and worship him. The artist and the writer stood in awe of God and humbly used their talents to serve him. Medieval culture viewed as a whole, therefore, has an atmosphere of otherworldliness and of surrender to a power beyond human understanding.

Yet intertwined with this aspiration toward and submission to the Divine is a warm, sympathetic feeling for humankind. Medieval people believed that a human being was God's finest creation. Artists and writers were never disdainful of human powers and potentialities. They took joy in presenting humanity as it was and wrestled constantly with the problem of understanding human nature more fully.

The medieval genius shines forth most singularly in attempts to synthesize these two outlooks. Thinkers, writers, and artists seldom felt that otherworldliness and secularism, spirituality and humanism were contradictory terms. They respected their own powers enough to believe that they could reach out toward God—by building higher cathedrals or by putting together greater *summae* of knowledge or by flights of poetic fancy. Yet they were filled with a faith great enough to believe that their human quest would lead them to a power infinitely greater than themselves and that an ultimate illumination would allow them to realize their full potential as God's creatures. The best cultural artifacts of the Middle Ages are permeated with an intellectual and emotional tension stemming from an effort to accommodate the divine and the human, the spirit and the flesh, the sacred and the secular, faith and reason. Becoming involved with the medieval attempts to reconcile these dichotomies reminds one that medieval thinkers and artists staked out cultural frontiers that would give shape to cultural activity far into the future.

SUGGESTED READING

General Surveys

John W. Baldwin, *The Scholastic Culture of the Middle Ages, 1000–1300* (1971). A perceptive, brief survey.

Philippe Wolff, *The Cultural Awakening,* trans. Anne Carter (1968).

Robert L. Benson and Giles Constable, eds., *Renaissance and Renewal in the Twelfth Century* (1982).

These two works provide insight into the forces bringing about cultural revival.

Jacques Le Goff, *Medieval Civilization 400–1500,* trans. Julia Barrow (1988). Helpful on the social and mental context within which medieval culture took shape.

W. R. Cook and R. B. Herzman, *The Medieval World View: An Introduction* (1983). Suggestive on a big subject.

The Learned World

Jacques Le Goff, *Intellectuals in the Middle Ages,* trans. Teresa Lavender Fagan (1992).

Alan B. Cobban, *The Medieval Universities: Their Development and Organization* (1975).

Stephen C. Ferruolo, *The Origins of the Univeristy. The Schools of Paris and Their Critics* (1985).

These two works will clarify the origins and the working of medieval universities.

Michael Haren, *Medieval Thought: The Western Intellectual Tradition from Antiquity to the Thirteenth Century* (1985). Especially good in showing continuity between the ancient and medieval worlds.

John Marenbon, *Later Medieval Philosophy (1150–1350): An Introduction* (1987). A clear treatment; should be used with Marenbon's volume on an earlier period cited in Chapter 14.

Etienne Gilson, *History of Christian Philosophy in the Middle Ages* (1955). A classic detailed treatment.

Harold J. Berman, *Law and Revolution: The Formation of the Western Legal Tradition* (1983). A seminal study rich in insight.

A. C. Crombie, *Medieval and Early Modern Science,* 2nd ed., 2 vols. (1959). A good survey.

J. H. Burns, *The Cambridge History of Medieval Political Thought, c. 350–c. 1450* (1988). A detailed treatment.

Literature and Art

W. T. Jackson, *The Literature of the Middle Ages* (1960). A useful survey. More valuable is reading medieval literary works; the works mentioned in this chapter are easily available in excellent translations.

Peter Dronke, *Women Writers of the Middle Ages. A Critical Study of Texts from Perpetua (d. 203) to Marguerite (d. 1310)* (1984). Highlights some unsung individuals.

Joachim Bumke, *Courtly Culture: Literature and Society in the Middle Ages,* trans. Thomas Dunlap (1991). Fascinating details on courtly society.

Marilyn Stokstad, *Medieval Art* (1986). A comprehensive survey.

Henri Focillon, *The Art of the West in the Middle Ages,* 2nd ed., 2 vols., trans. Donald King (1969). A masterful, detailed treatment with excellent illustrations.

Georges Duby, *The Age of the Cathedrals: Art and Society, 980–1240,* trans. Eleanor Levieux and Barbara Thompson (1981). A challenging attempt to interrelate art and social developments.

Christopher Wilson, *The Gothic Cathedral* (1989). A stimulating treatment.

Jean Gimpel, *The Cathedral Builders,* trans. Teresa Waugh (1984). Describes the techniques of medieval builders.

Henry Adams, *Mont-St. Michel and Chartres* (1913). A classic work contrasting the spirits of Romanesque and Gothic art.

Erwin Panofsky, *Gothic Architecture and Scholasticism* (1951). Interrelates the intellectual and artistic worlds.

CHAPTER 23

Transition in Economic, Social, and Political Structures, 1300–1500

FIGURE 23.1 **Medieval Siege Warfare** This scene portrays the siege of an English castle in southern France by French forces during the Hundred Years' War. It illustrates very accurately the main weapons used in warfare. Engagements of this type drained large amounts of resources from both the English and the French royal governments. Providing the needs of the armies in these encounters often resulted in the pillaging of the countryside, which disrupted agricultural production and commercial exchange and caused untold misery to many. (The British Museum)

By about 1300 the forces of growth, expansion, revival, and renewal that had propelled western European society forward during the preceding three centuries showed signs of faltering. As a result that society began to encounter stresses and tensions that laid bare the limitations inherent in the medieval pattern of civilization and that required adjustments in institutions and mentalities in order to cope with problems stemming from those limitations. The fourteenth and fifteenth centuries thus became an age of transition marked by developments in political, economic, social, religious, intellectual, and artistic life which transformed the medieval order in significant ways. What emerged was the early modern European world, whose roots were in the medieval world but whose institutional and ideological configuration was sufficiently different to mark a turning point in the history of western European civilization.

1. ECONOMIC AND SOCIAL TENSIONS AND READJUSTMENTS

Perhaps the most obvious sign of changing times came in economic and social life. By 1300 the long period of economic growth that western Europe had enjoyed since about 1000 (see Chapter 18) was ending. For the next century and a half contraction and depression became the order of the day in many aspects of economic life that had been of crucial importance to the prosperity of the eleventh, twelfth, and thirteenth centuries. Amid the economic dislocation new ways of organizing and conducting economic activity began to emerge that pointed toward early modern times. Economic changes were accompanied by social disequilibrium and adjustment. Although the nature and impact of economic and social dislocation and the responses to the changing scene varied from region to region, certain broad patterns affected western Europe generally.

A powerful engine of economic growth of the period from 1000 to 1300 had been sustained population growth. After 1300 western Europe suffered a dramatic population decline. Surviving evidence suggests that by 1300 the population level had begun to outstrip the food supply. That situation, coupled with unfavorable climatic conditions, produced a succession of famines in the early decades of the fourteenth century that began to reduce the population. Then came a demographic catastrophe in the form of a devastating pestilence: the Black Death, an epidemic of bubonic plague that first spread over Europe with deadly effect between 1347 and 1350 and then returned periodically during the next two centuries. The scourge was brought to Europe from the east by rats infested with fleas whose bites transmitted the bacilli to the human bloodstream. Once the disease was loosed in western Europe, it caused an immense loss of life among a population made vulnerable by malnutrition and primitive sanitation conditions. The best estimates suggest that a third of Europe's population was wiped out between 1347 and 1350. Periodic recurrence of the plague continued the downward spiral of the population, so that by the early fifteenth century western Europe had barely half as many people as it had had in 1300. Such a drastic demographic change had massive effects on levels of production, the demand for goods, the labor supply, prices, social relationships, and mass psychology (see Figure 23.2).

While population decline was a prime force in disturbing established economic patterns, it was only one factor. The economy also suffered from structural limitations rooted in the traditional system of production and from disruptive forces outside the economic system. Especially damaging to economic life during the fourteenth and fifteenth centuries was the reduction of commercial exchange. The population decline drastically reduced demand and limited the productive processes that supplied goods for exchange. Political disturbances in eastern and central Asia ended opportunities to penetrate new areas of commercial opportunity. The rise of the Ottoman Empire disturbed the favored position that Italian merchants had long enjoyed in the eastern Mediterranean. Under the pressure of a depressed economy the merchant guilds that had promoted commercial growth prior to 1300 increasingly imposed restrictions on the flow of goods, chiefly in an effort to create and protect the monopoly they held over local and regional trade. Self-governing cities found it difficult to cooperate for mutual benefit. The most successful effort of this kind was the Hanseatic League, which linked about eighty cities in northern Ger-

FIGURE 23.2 The Plague This painting captures the terror inflicted on the population of a city by the Black Death. Even while shrouding the dead for burial, people were suddenly struck down, as is the man shown falling to the ground. Neither the prayers of the clergy nor the pleas of the saints, represented in this scene by St. Sebastian, could help. (The Walters Art Gallery, Baltimore)

governments in an effort to force wages down and fix prices; they also joined landowners to pressure royal governments to pass legislation to freeze wages, such as the English Statute of Laborers (1351). Craft guilds, which had once promoted industrial production, increasingly enacted restrictive rules limiting the volume of production, setting prices, excluding the products of outsiders, barring technical changes, and limiting entrance into each craft. The general effect of such measures was to depress industrial production and to disrupt established patterns of manufacturing long dominated by independent craft workers. Better able to adapt to new conditions were some large-scale industries, such as the wool industry and mining, where new organizational patterns, technologies, and practices of capital accumulation were applied.

Agricultural production was likewise depressed and dislocated. Widespread and persistent warfare ravaged many lands. Colonizing opportunities had nearly disappeared. Famine and plague decimated the rural labor force and sharply reduced the urban demand for food products, especially cereal grains. Large areas of marginal land were taken out of production, dislocating many agricultural workers. Many landowners responded to the depressed economy by hastening along the dismantlement of the traditional manorial system, a process which had already begun before 1300. Some rented their domains to enterprising peasants eager to gain access to more land. Others enclosed their manors in order to concentrate on specialized crops and livestock raising; these operations increasingly depended on hired labor.

Economic dislocation and contraction led to widespread social tension and disturbances in the later Middle Ages. As we noted earlier, even before 1300 Europe's aristocracy was becoming stratified, chiefly on the basis of wealth. That stratification continued and became even more pronounced during the late Middle Ages. These were tenuous times for the highest nobility, not only because changing economic conditions strained their fortunes but also because the unsettled political situation demanded their involvement in violent factionalism and civil war if they were to retain their positions of prestige and power. Some did not survive the murderous conflicts. However, those aristocratic families

many, Scandinavia, and the Low Countries into a cooperative trading enterprise. But ultimately the League declined, chiefly because its members refused to sacrifice local interests.

Industrial production experienced a comparable constriction. Labor shortages increased labor costs to the point where many kinds of industrial production were unprofitable in a setting where demand for goods was despressed by population decline. To redress this situation, some manufacturers began to manipulate urban that did survive maintained their fortunes and increased their privileges, so that their social position became more distinct than ever. Increasingly, these powerful nobles owed their status to their close connections to the monarchs. The high aristocracy pursued an ever more splendid and exclusive lifestyle; it was based on an exaggerated practice of behavior patterns dictated by the code of chivalry.

Although many lesser nobles were also sorely tested by the agricultural depression, they solidified their position as a country gentry asserting a powerful influence over local life. The key to their success was the careful management of production on their landholdings and the exploitation of the local labor supply. They often strengthened their local position by allying themselves with great nobles and by seeking favors from royal governments. While duly impressed by the lifestyle of the great nobles, the lesser nobles were not able and did not try to imitate it. They began to develop a simpler lifestyle attuned to the activities of the small country estate and the local town. By 1500 this gentry had become a powerful force interested primarily in order and stability and support for their economic interests; they became a source of support for the increasingly strong kings. Thus, by 1500 a powerfully entrenched aristocracy continued to dominate society. However, its inner structure as a class was being altered, and its power base was shifting from the relationships once defined in terms of lordship and noble dependence to those defined by birth, wealth, and royal favor.

The peasant world also underwent significant changes during the late Middle Ages. The last vestiges of servile dependence in western Europe had virtually disappeared. While this development improved the legal status of most peasants, it deprived many of the economic security that had characterized serf status in earlier times. Population decline and the dismantling of manors seriously disrupted community groupings that had been a vital part of peasant life. Economically, peasants were thrown more and more on their own as renters or hired laborers, sometimes with disastrous results in a period of limited economic opportunity. Hard-pressed landlords preyed on peasant misfortunes to force on them added financial obligations, higher rents, and lower wages. Royal taxes fell heavily on the peas-

ants, and the wars that their taxes supported often ravaged their farms. With reduced opportunities in the troubled cities and a vanishing frontier, many peasants were trapped in a position of poverty and oppression. They expressed their discontent by frequent and violent rebellions, typified by the *Jacquerie* in France in 1358 and the Peasants' Revolt in England in 1381 (see Figure 23.3). Most of these rebellions were brutally crushed by kings, nobles, and clergy. Despite the generally grim condition of peasant life in the later Middle Ages, there were peasants who succeeded in increasing their landholdings either by purchase or by renting and who found ways of expanding their productivity and wealth in a volatile economic setting. This element of the peasant class would eventually make important contributions to the agricultural recovery of western Europe (see Color Plate 11).

Equally disadvantaged and discontented were certain elements of the urban population. The depression in manufacturing and exchange reduced many small-scale artisans and shopkeepers to the status of laborers for hire or to the ranks of the unemployed. They were also increasingly deprived of a significant voice in urban government such as they had enjoyed during the twelfth and thirteenth centuries. Dominated by rich entrepreneurs, city governments and the guilds sought to regulate the economic activities and wages of urban laborers more stringently. As their status as full members of the urban bourgeois community disintegrated, this element of the urban population demonstrated their discontent by frequent rioting and rebellion, which usually yielded little more immediate benefit to the urban poor than the peasant revolts did for their propagators.

The social group making the greatest advance in the fourteenth and fifteenth centuries was an elite segment of the bourgeoisie engaged in capitalistic ventures. Their success was exemplified by the Medici and the Bardi in Italy, the Fuggers in southern Germany, Jacques Coeur of France, and some of the entrepreneurs associated with the Hanseatic League. Members of this group amassed huge fortunes in such fields as banking, moneylending, and the wool industry. Pursuing techniques characteristic of early modern capitalism (see Chapter 28), these entrepreneurs increasingly determined the course of economic market. Innovative techniques for accumulating capital and organizing large-scale commercial and manufacturing enterprises were being devised. New technological advances were being made and were being applied more widely— water mills in the textile industry, better mining techniques, printing, improved shipbuilding, the compass, the astrolabe, gunpowder. New frontiers were opening by way of the seas that washed Europe's western shores. All these forces pointed toward new economic growth in western Europe. It was obvious, however, that this growth would be achieved in ways different from those that had prevailed in medieval Europe.

FIGURE 23.3 Peasant Violence Pressed by a variety of miseries, peasants often resorted to violence in the late Middle Ages, as illustrated in this drawing showing peasants attacking a knight with axes and daggers. (Bibliothèque Nationale, Paris, ms. fr. 87)

2. MONARCHY UNDER STRESS: FRANCE, ENGLAND, SPAIN

One of the major achievements of the central Middle Ages was the creation in France, England, and Spain of large political communities ruled by monarchs who devised techniques of governance that increasingly allowed them to compel their subjects to observe common rules in certain spheres of political behavior. Within each of these medieval states monarchs recognized the privileged political status of nobles, religious leaders, and urban corporations by allowing these groups to exercise certain rights of lordship over their dependents. As the fourteenth century progressed, various pressures, some stemming from economic decline and social unrest and others from limitations inherent in the medieval political system, began to upset the delicate balance between the central and local spheres of authority. These tensions combined to disrupt the orderly operation of royal governments temporarily and check the expansion of royal power. However, the political disorder proved to be transitory; eventually the consolidation of central authority as the prime force in political life resumed, leading to the establishment of early modern national states.

During the later Middle Ages the royal governments in both France and England had to face monumental internal problems emerging from the economic depression and social dislocations, the efforts of privileged groups to extend their powers to serve selfish interests, and disruptive

development. They seized political control of most city governments and found favor with kings. Culturally they were able to patronize the learning and art associated with the Renaissance, allowing them to play a decisive role in shaping the cultural environment of western Europe. In a sense, this group now represented the bourgeoisie; others who had formerly been counted in this class—simple artisans and small shopkeepers—were becoming a group apart, a laboring class. The new bourgeoisie was destined to play a major role in the future of the West.

By about 1450 the worst of the economic and social stresses of the late Middle Ages were over, and there were signs of recovery everywhere. The population had begun to grow again. The agricultural system became more productive, chiefly as a result of a more rational management of land and labor in relation to the realities of the clashes over succession to the throne. These challenges were complicated by a prolonged military struggle, called the Hundred Years' War (1337–1453), that placed demands on each monarchy far exceeding its traditional military and financial resources. That struggle was an extension of a conflict that had begun in the twelfth century over possessions held on the continent by English kings as fiefs from the French kings (see Chapter 19). Although the French rulers had reclaimed most of these territories by the early thirteenth century, England still held important possessions in Aquitaine (see Map 23.1) which the French kings constantly sought to recapture. French and English interests also clashed in Flanders, where the English sought to check French expansion in order to protect the Flemish woolen industry, which depended on English raw wool, and in Scotland, where the French supported the efforts of the Scots to win independence from England.

These festering issues were brought to a head when in 1328 the last member of the direct Capetian line died. Although England's Edward III (1327–1377) had the best hereditary claim to the French throne, the Estates General selected as king Philip of Valois, who represented a collateral line of the Capetian family. Philip VI's aggressive policy in Flanders and his confiscation of Aquitaine in 1337 on the grounds that Edward had refused to honor his obligations as a vassal led Edward to assert his claim to the French throne and to undertake a war to make good his claim.

The first phase of the Hundred Years' War, which lasted until 1360, was nearly fatal to France. English armies won two great battles at Crécy (1346) and Poitiers (1356), where English longbowmen clearly bested the flower of the French nobility. At Poitiers, King John of France (1350–1364) was captured and taken to England. An internal crisis ensued in France, marked by an effort by some leaders acting in the name of the Estates General to take control of the government, by a peasant rebellion called the *Jacquerie*, and by the ravaging of a large part of France by bands of unpaid mercenary soldiers upon whose services kings on both sides were increasingly forced to rely. Eventually John bought his release by accepting the Treaty of Brétigny (1360), under which he agreed to pay a huge ransom and to give Edward III full title to Guienne as well as a

small territory in northern France, including the key port of Calais. Edward renounced his claim to the French throne.

The Treaty of Brétigny did not, however, end the ancient rivalry. The next phase of the war, which extended from 1364 to 1415, saw sporadic but indecisive fighting. Effective military action was impeded by serious internal problems in both of the rival kingdoms. France enjoyed a brief recovery under Charles V (1364–1380), who rebuilt French military strength and increased royal income to the point where he seriously threatened England's hold on Guienne. However, these gains were undone during the reign of his pitiful successor, Charles VI (1380–1422). A minor when he became king and later the victim of spells of insanity, Charles VI often required regents to act in his stead. His uncle Philip, duke of Burgundy, and his brother, Louis, duke of Orléans, became bitter rivals to fill that role, each joined by a faction of self-seeking nobles. The rivalry between the Burgundians and the Armagnacs (partisans of Louis) plunged France into internal chaos from which most of the population suffered badly.

England was hardly less troubled during these years. Edward III ruled until 1377 amid deepening trouble. To pay for the increasingly costly war against France, he was forced to turn to Parliament to win approval for new taxes. Its members, who represented the forces of privilege in England, responded by claiming a role in deciding how money was spent, controlling royal officials, and initiating legislation through petitions presented to the king. The advancing power of Parliament became particularly notable in the reign of Richard II (1377–1399). His reign was troubled by economic and social problems that led to the Peasants' Revolt in 1381 and by dissatisfaction among the nobles with the king's allegedly autocratic ways. Eventually, Parliament deposed Richard II and chose in his place Henry IV (1399–1413), whose sole right to rule was based on Parliament's approval. Obviously, that institution had assumed a crucial role in political life. However, Parliament proved neither capable of directing the kingdom nor willing to trust the king to do so. It became a forum for agitation by noble factions aimed at dominating the king in order to gain greater privileges.

Henry V (1413–1422) hastened both England and France on their troubled ways by reopening

Map 23.1 **THE HUNDRED YEARS' WAR** In the Hundred Years' War the English fought to regain their once-extensive possessions in France (see Map 19.2), and the French sought to add these territories to the royal domain. The map shows the ebb and flow of that prolonged struggle. When the war began in 1337, England held only a modest territory in southwest France. At the height of their fortunes in the first half of the fifteenth century, they controlled most of northern France. But not for long. When the war ended in 1453, the French had driven them off the Continent except for the city of Calais.

the Hundred Years' War. In 1415 he invaded France and crushed a French army at Agincourt. With the support of the Burgundian faction, he established control over most of France north of the Loire River. In 1420 he forced the humiliating Treaty of Troyes on Charles VI. By its terms, Henry married Charles' daughter and was made heir to the French throne, thereby disinheriting the legitimate heir to the throne, the dauphin Charles. Generous concesssions were made to the duke of Burgundy for his support of the English. The French kingdom seemed on the verge of dismemberment.

But the English were not to enjoy their triumph for long. After both Henry V and Charles VI died in 1422, leaving the infant Henry VI as king of both nations, the French began to recover from what seemed disaster. The rallying point was the dauphin Charles, whose fortunes took a decisive turn in 1429, when a simple peasant girl, Joan of Arc, came to him claiming that God had revealed to her that Charles must free France of the English and assume the crown that rightly belonged to him. Her message bestirred the dispirited Charles and pumped new confidence into the many royal officials, military captains, nobles, and simple soldiers who were loyal to the house of Valois. Joan herself was with the army that in 1429 defeated an English army besieging the key city of Orléans, a victory that was followed by Charles' coronation as king. These events marked the beginning of a series of French triumphs which Joan did not live to see. In 1430 she was captured by the Burgundians and turned over to the English, who put her on trial before an ecclesiastical court that convicted her of heresy and ordered her burned at the stake in 1431.

Joan's dream of a reborn France soon came to pass. Under Charles VII, royal power made a remarkable recovery. Well served by excellent ministers, Charles was able to build a well-trained army paid for by the king, thus ending his dependence on a feudal army and trouble-making mercenaries. That army won victory after victory against the English, who by 1543 held only Calais. In 1439 the Estates General granted the king power to impose a direct tax, called the *taille*, on his subjects. Although many powerful nobles in France continued to act in their own interest, political life focused more and more on the royal government with its increasing ability to establish order, curb the irresponsible behavior of the princes, and tap the growing sense of pride and shared interest felt by many subjects who increasingly thought of themselves as French. When Charles VII died in 1461, his son, Louis XI (1461–1483), inherited a solid base from which to rule what had become a national state (see Chapter 27).

England was in a less happy state during much of the fifteenth century, chiefly because of a deepening factionalism among a few privileged families seeking control of the government as a means of enhancing their power. Surrounding themselves with private armies, these factions pushed England toward a civil war. That struggle, the War of the Roses, so called because the opposing forces adopted the red and the white rose as their symbols, pitted against each other supporters of two rival families with claims to the throne, the Lancastrians and the Yorkists. While this struggle for the crown raged, the regular processes of orderly government were disrupted. Tyranny, intrigue, murder, confiscation of property, and pursuit of private ends were the order of the day. Finally, in 1485, Henry Tudor, a Lancastrian, defeated his Yorkist rival, King Richard III, in a pitched battle at Bosworth Field and assumed the throne as Henry VII. Although Henry's claim to the crown was extremely tenuous, the nation, weary of civil disorder, was willing to follow anyone who promised to restore peace and security. The desire for order was strong among the lesser nobles, the gentry made up chiefly of rural landowners, the prosperous peasant yeomen, and the well-to-do bourgeoisie. Taken together, these elements constituted a substantial force willing to support effective royal government. The old noble factions were badly discredited as a result of their brutal, self-seeking conduct during the War of the Roses. As a result, the new king had considerable freedom to act as he pleased. Henry used the opportunity to fashion a strong central government that united the English people into a nation (see Chapter 27).

The three major Iberian kingdoms—Aragon, Castile, and Portugal—also had their difficulties during the late Middle Ages. By 1300 the holy war against the Moslems had ceased to be the significant factor in Spanish affairs, for the Moslems had been confined to the narrow territory of Granada (see Map 20.1). The Christian kingdoms then turned on one another, competing bitterly for territory. At the same time almost constant civil strife raged within each kingdom, replicating the struggles in England and France. Castile was plagued by a long series of disputed successions that undermined royal authority. Aragon's internal order was compromised by the aggressive overseas policy pursued by its kings, especially in Italy, a policy seldom favored by the nobility, and by conflict between the landed and commercial interests. These senseless quarrels finally began to abate in 1469 when the heiress of Castile, Isabella, married Ferdinand, the heir of Aragon. In 1479, when this couple had succeeded to both thrones, they quickly took steps to end the strife, unify their lands into a single state, and impose stronger royal control over their subjects (see Chapter 27). The Portuguese kings did not meet such violent resistance as did the other Iberian kings, and their heroic struggle to prevent Castile from absorbing Portugal won them broad internal support. They also promoted commercial ventures throughout the fifteenth century, backing Portuguese merchants who expanded southward along the African coast and found lucrative markets.

Thus, by the end of the fifteenth century the major monarchies formed in western Europe during the central Middle Ages had survived a succession of tests. During the age of transition each faced challenges that created new pressures and fresh opportunities for strengthening central government as the only effective agency capable of addressing the common problems and shared interests that increasingly linked together the lives of large numbers of subjects living in what was perceived as a national political community. Medieval kingdoms were becoming early modern nation-states.

3. THE HOLY ROMAN EMPIRE: THE END OF THE UNIVERSAL STATE

Between 950 and 1250 one of the chief political entities in western Europe had been the Holy Roman Empire. Embracing Germany, Italy, and the western fringes of the Slavic world, this state represented an effort to realize a political ideal—a Christian commonwealth uniting all Christian people under a single Christian prince through whose guidance God's plan could be realized (see Chapter 19). After the death of the last great medieval emperor, Frederick II, in 1250, the ideal of a Christian commonwealth lived on, but in reality the medieval Holy Roman Empire began to fragment into a variety of political entities.

In Germany, after a interval without a ruler (called the Interregnum, 1250–1273), the German nobility exercised its long-established right of election to bestow the imperial crown upon a succession of rulers from three different families—the houses of Hapsburg, Luxembourg, and Bavaria—only to repudiate each family in turn when its elected representative threatened to become too powerful. While demonstrating their unwillingness to accept a ruler with any effective power, the nobles, clergy, and townspeople successfully extended their independence from the central government to constitute a mosaic of territorial entities each determining its own political course. The emerging political structure of Germany was given legal definition by Emperor Charles IV (1347–1378), who in 1356 issued a decree called the Golden Bull. It provided that the German ruler would be chosen by seven princes designated as electors: the archbishops of Cologne, Trier, and Mainz and the princes of Saxony, Brandenburg, the Palatinate, and Bohemia. Each elector was granted almost complete independence within his own territory. Other princes and cities demanded and gained the same kind of independence enjoyed by the electors, making the empire little more than a confederation of hundreds of independent political entities. The emperor could call together the princes, church leaders, and representatives of the towns in meetings called *diets,* but he lacked any means of enforcing decisions; he had no national army, no tax system, and no court system. Within their small principalities, many princes created stable, well-organized political systems—Germany was not a lawless land by any means. But in contrast to what was happening in England, France, and Spain during the late Middle Ages, a unified national state failed to emerge in Germany, a condition that would affect German history far into the future.

In Italy, where imperial authority had always been resisted, the trend toward decentralization was even more pronounced after 1250. In theory the ruler elected by the Germans and crowned emperor by the pope still claimed dominion in Italy, and from time to time some Italians did seek to have him exert his authority. After the early fourteenth century, the emperors seldom even tried to exercise any influence over their Italian realms, and a welter of independent states emerged.

In southern Italy the old Norman-Hohenstaufen state was divided after 1282 into the Kingdom of Naples, ruled by a French prince, and the Kingdom of Sicily, ruled by a member of the royal family of Aragon. Their rivalry and misrule brought steady decline to this once-rich area. Finally, in 1435, the two kingdoms were united under Aragonese rule. In central Italy the Papal States dominated. Papal overlordship was bitterly resisted by the local nobles, and it was badly compromised by the absence of the papacy from Rome during much of the fourteenth century (see Chapter 24). However, during the fifteenth century a succession of able, ruthless popes restored their authority, making the Papal States a major force in Italian political life.

Northern Italy was divided among many city-states which had forced concessions from their political overlord, the Holy Roman emperor, that ensured each its political independence. After the death of Frederick II, they battled one another for land, trading advantages, power, and security. Some of the more powerful of the city-states, especially Milan, Venice, and Florence, were able to impose their rule on smaller neighboring cities to create territorial entities that tended to dominate the political life of northern Italy. These cities provided the setting for a powerful cultural movement, the Renaissance, that played a decisive role in the transition from the medieval to the early modern world (see Chapter 25).

Internally, the political system of most of the city-states tended to move from an order with considerable citizen participation toward a system dominated by a single individual (a *signore*, "lord") or by an oligarchy of the rich. In Milan, for example, first the Visconti family and then after 1447 the Sforzas established a regime of despots under whose direction Milan grew rich and expanded its territories. Florence resisted despotism longer; in fact, through most of the

period Florence retained the façade of a republican form of government that allowed its citizens considerable power to decide public issues. Gradually there emerged a behind-the-scenes power that used patronage, bribery, and personal influence to shape political decisions. After about 1430 that role was played by members of a rich banking family, the Medicis. Although they held no exalted titles, the Medicis in effect ran Florence as if they were despots. Venice always remained subject to an oligarchy of rich merchants whose methods did not differ greatly from those of the despots. The turbulent, strife-filled times promoted a new style of politics, described brilliantly in Machiavelli's *The Prince* (see pp. 344–345), which placed heavy emphasis on the absolute sovereignty of the state, its right to create its own moral sanctions, and its superiority over its subjects. Many historians have seen these developments as prototypes for the powerful national monarchies that came to dominate in western Europe at the beginning of the early modern period. Despite the innovative political practices of the Italian Renaissance states, the fragmentation of the peninsula doomed Italy to weakness and prepared the way for a long era during which the many states of Italy became pawns in the power politics practiced by the national states of early modern Europe.

4. THE CHANGING SCENE IN EASTERN EUROPE AND THE MEDITERRANEAN WORLD

While the internal structures of the western European states were undergoing transformations during the age of transition, other highly significant political changes were unfolding along western Europe's eastern and southeastern frontiers that would alter the relationships that had been established between the West and these eastern areas between 1000 and 1300 (see Map 23.2).

Perhaps the most significant development was the demise of the Byzantine Empire. That long-established fixture on the medieval political map never fully recovered from the attacks of the Seljuk Turks in the late eleventh century and the capture of Constantinople by western Europeans in 1204 during the Fourth Crusade. After

ARCTIC OCEAN

0 100 200 300 miles

FINLAND

L. Onega

Ob R.

KINGDOM OF SWEDEN

L. Ladoga

Stockholm

Novgorod

Moscow

BALTIC SEA

TEUTONIC ORDER

Riga

Königsberg

Vilna

Smolensk

Danzig

DUCHY OF PRUSSIA

Oder R.

Vistula R.

Warsaw

GRAND DUCHY OF LITHUANIA

Kiev

Volga R.

Ural R.

KHANATE OF THE GOLDEN HORDE (TARTARS)

ARAL SEA

HOLY ROMAN EMPIRE

KINGDOM OF POLAND

Dnieper R.

Don R.

Astrakhan

Vienna

UKRAINE

Dniester R.

CASPIAN SEA

Budapest

MOLDAVIA

Pruth R.

SEA OF AZOV

KINGDOM OF HUNGARY

WALLACHIA

BLACK SEA

Belgrade

Danube R.

ADRIATIC SEA

BOSNIA

SERBIA

BULGARIA

Varna

Trebizond

Kossovo

Sofia

Nicopolis

MACEDONIA

Constantinople

Thessalonica

AEGEAN SEA

RHODES

MEDITERRANEAN SEA

CYPRUS

CRETE

MAMELUKES

Note: Crete, to Venice, 1204-1669;
Cyprus, Crusader Kingdom to 1489, then to Venice until 1571;
Rhodes to Knights Hospitallers, 1309-1523

Ottoman Possessions, ca. 1355

Byzantine Possessions, ca. 1355

Ottoman Possessions, ca. 1481

Grand Principality of Moscow, ca. 1300-1505

Boundary of Holy Roman Empire

Western Boundary of Mongol Expansion, 13th Century

the Europeans were finally ousted in 1261, a fatal illness afflicted the empire. Civil strife slowly sapped the strength of its government. The Italian city-states, led by Venice, deprived the empire of much of its trade, and bit by bit its territory was pared away, first by Slavic princes in the Balkans and then by the Ottoman Turks. The emperors of the fourteenth and fifteenth centuries appealed desperately to the West for help but received little. Finally, in 1453, the Ottomans captured Constantinople and made the city their capital under the name Istanbul. The fall of Constantinople ended forever the Christian power that had so long shielded western Europe from the threat of the Moslems and had contributed so much to spreading civilized life to central and eastern Europe.

The Ottoman victory marked a renewal of the threat of Moslem aggression against the West, a danger that western Europeans had not faced for centuries. The Ottoman Turks were originally Asiatic nomads who had been uprooted and pushed westward by Mongol expansion in the thirteenth century. They had settled in Asia Minor and accepted Islam. Under their first great ruler, Osman (or Othman, whence the term Ottoman) (1290–1326), the new state began to expand in Asia Minor and then into the Balkans, largely at the expense of the Byzantine Empire. Early in the fifteenth century, Ottoman power was nearly destroyed by Tamerlane, a Mongol warrior who sought to reconstruct the empire of Genghis Khan (see Chapter 20). The collapse of Tamerlane's empire soon after his death in 1405 allowed the Ottomans to resume their expansion. They completed the conquest of the Byzantine Empire by 1453. Early in the sixteenth century, they conquered Syria, Palestine, and Egypt. As the Middle Ages ended, their vast empire loomed as a major threat to the West.

As the Ottoman Turks extended their territorial sway, they fashioned political institutions that gave their empire strength and stability. The Ottomans constituted an elite claiming supremacy over their subjects, many of them Christians, by right of conquest. They retained a strong sense of community based on their ethnic identity and their religion. The Ottoman state was headed by the *sultan*, whose extensive power over all aspects of life was based on his claim to be the successor of Muhammad and empowered to interpret the Moslem law that all followers of Allah were required to obey. A well-organized bureaucracy developed, modeled on both Byzantine and Abbasid models. Local units of government were developed across the empire to carry out the sultan's policies, collect taxes, and administer justice. In practice, the Ottoman regime allowed local communities broad authority to regulate their own affairs as long as they did not disrupt internal peace or challenge the sultan's supreme power. Aside from taxes, the Ottomans extracted human resources from their subject population to sustain their regime. Young boys, often of Christian or Jewish origin, were taken as slaves, converted to Islam, and trained for specialized duties in the civil service or the army. The military corps created from these slaves, called the Janissaries, developed into a highly professional, dedicated force that played a key role in Ottoman expansion and in maintaining Ottoman domination over the large empire. Young girls were also enslaved to serve in Ottoman harems, including that of the sultan, from which successors to the throne were selected.

Central and eastern Europe began to assume a modern shape in the wake of the decline of the Holy Roman and Byzantine empires. The south coast of the Baltic Sea was dominated by Germans, an expansion spearheaded by the crusading order of the Teutonic Knights, who brought traders, missionaries, and agricultural colonists in their wake. Their presence filled the Slavs of central Europe with an abiding distrust and fear of the Germans. The Germanic threat resulted in a union of the ruling houses of Poland and Lithuania under the Lithuanian prince Jagiello, who married a Polish princess and governed both

Map 23.2 CENTRAL EUROPE AND WESTERN ASIA, CA. 1500 This map shows the major political entities in central Europe and western Asia about 1500. Especially threatening to Poland, Lithuania, and Hungary—and to western Europe in general—were two rapidly expanding powers: the Ottoman Empire and the Grand Principality of Moscow (the future Russia).

states as King Ladislas II (1386–1434). The house of Jagiello exerted strong military pressure on the Baltic Germans and the Russian states to the east during much of the fifteenth century, but it never succeeded in creating an effective government for its huge kingdom. To the south, Hungary continued to develop, but its energies were increasingly absorbed in defending itself against the Ottoman Turks and holding back ambitious German nobles bent on taking the Hungarian throne. Until the Ottomans seized control of the Balkans at the end of the fourteenth century, a flourishing Serbian kingdom, created at the expense of the declining Byzantine Empire, dominated that area; after its destruction by the Ottomans, the Hungarians stood as western Europe's outpost against the Turks. Farther east a vigorous Russian state was emerging. We shall return to the story of its development later (see Chapter 32). Suffice it to say here that by 1500 Russia, whose ruler took the title *tsar* (*"caesar"*) to befit his claim that his realm was the "third Rome," was beginning to play an important role in determining the fate of eastern Europe.

SUGGESTED READING

Overview of the Period 1300–1500

Robert Fossier, ed., *The Cambridge Illustrated History of the Middle Ages,* Vol. 3: *1250–1520,* trans. Sarah Hanbury Tenison (1986).

Denys Hay, *Europe in the Fourteenth and Fifteenth Centuries,* 2nd ed. (1989).

George Holmes, *Europe: Hierarchy and Revolt, 1320–1450* (1975).

Any of these three works will provide an excellent overview of the major developments during the period.

Western European Political Development

George Holmes, *The Later Middle Ages, 1272–1485* (1962).

Trevor Rowley, *The High Middle Ages* (1986).

Either of these two works will provide a clear picture of political developments in late medieval England.

John A. F. Thompson, *The Transformation of Medieval England, 1370–1529* (1983). A good picture of social change.

John Gillingham, *The War of the Roses: Peace and Conflict in Fifteenth-Century England* (1981). Stresses the political and military aspect of England's internal strife.

P. S. Lewis, *Later Medieval France: The Polity* (1968). Good on political institutions; see also the study by Duby cited in Chapter 19.

Christopher Allmond, *The Hundred Years' War: England and France at War c. 1300–c. 1450* (1988). A well-done treatment stressing the effects of the war.

F. R. H. DuBoulay, *Germany in the Later Middle Ages* (1983).

Joachim Leuscher, *Germany in the Late Middle Ages,* trans. Sabine MacCormack (1980).

Either of these two works will provide a good overview.

Giovanni Tabacco, *The Struggle for Power in Medieval Italy:* *Structures of Political Rule,* trans. Rosalind Brown Jensen (1989). A difficult but rewarding study.

Bernard Guenée, *States and Rulers in Later Medieval Europe,* trans. Juliet Vale (1985). A comparative study of late medieval political institutions.

Richard W. Kaeuper, *War, Justice and Public Order in England and France in the Later Middle Ages* (1988). A challenging analysis of political change in the later Middle Ages.

Eastern European Political Developments

Donald M. Nicol, *The Last Centuries of Byzantium, 1261–1453* (1972). A clearly presented account.

Halil Inalick, *The Ottoman Empire: The Classical Age, 1300–1600,* trans. Norman Itzkowitz and Colin Imber (1973). The best treatment of a subject not always given an objective evaluation.

John V. A. Fine, Jr., *The Late Medieval Balkans. A Critical Survey from the Late Twelfth Century to the Ottoman Conquest* (1987). A fine treatment of a neglected subject.

Robert O. Crummey, *The Formation of Muscovy 1304–1613* (1987). A good synthesis of a difficult period in Russian history.

David Morgan, *The Mongols* (1986).

Economic and Social History

C. M. Cipolla, *Before the Industrial Revolution: European Society and Economy, 1000–1700* (1976). Effectively places late medieval economic and social history in a larger context.

Harry A. Miskimin, *The Economy of Early Renaissance Europe, 1300–1460* (1969). A detailed study; more general treatments can be found in the works of Bautier and Pounds, cited in Chapter 18.

Specialized aspects of late medieval economic and social history are treated in the following works.

Johannes Schildhauer, *The Hansa: History and Culture,* trans. Katherine Vanovitch (1985).

Robert S. Gottfried, *The Black Death: Natural and Human Disaster in Medieval Europe* (1983).

Graham Twigg, *The Black Death: A Biological Reappraisal* (1984).

Joel T. Rosenthal, *Nobles and Noble Life, 1295–1500* (1976).

Michel Mollat and Philippe Wolff, *The Popular Revolutions of the Late Middle Ages,* trans. A. L. Lytton-Sells (1973).

Biographies

Marina Warner, *Joan of Arc: The Image of Female Heroism* (1981).

Anne Barstow, *Joan of Arc: Heretic, Mystic, Shaman* (1986).

CHAPTER 24

Transition in Religion and Thought, 1300–1500

FIGURE 24.1 Pope Boniface VIII This fresco from the Church of St. John Lateran in Rome shows Pope Boniface VIII proclaiming the great jubilee held in Rome in 1300. The artist, perhaps Giotto, catches something of the autocratic spirit of the proud pontiff whose efforts to assert papal authority led to deep trouble for the Church. (Alinari/Art Resource)

The tensions that beset and transformed western European economic, social, and political structures during the fourteenth and fifteenth centuries were also felt in religious life. After 1300 the religious establishment, which had earlier decisively influenced all aspects of human activity, encountered increasing difficulties in asserting its traditional leadership role. Its leaders, its system of government, and its teachings were challenged on many fronts. From one perspective many of these challenges represented a continuation of the reforming spirit that had characterized religious life between 1000 and 1300. However, others stemmed from new forces unleashed by the troubled times marking the late medieval age of transition. Increasingly, the directive forces in the religious establishment failed to discover effective ways to respond to the mounting challenges.

1. THE CRISIS IN RELIGIOUS LEADERSHIP

One of the major results of the reform movement of the central Middle Ages had been the creation of a centralized system of church governance. By 1300 that system consisted of a hierarchy of ecclesiastical officials, headed by the bishop of Rome, that claimed for itself an independent sphere of authority that allowed it to define and control belief and discipline for the entire Christian community of western Europe. As that structure evolved, it met resistance in many quarters, centering especially on what the limits of ecclesiastical authority were and how religious officials should use their power. During the late Middle Ages that resistance stiffened to the point of creating a crisis in religious governance.

The most dramatic challenge to that system focused on its very center: the papacy. The authority of the papal office was brought to its apogee by the talented popes of the thirteenth century who claimed for themselves a God-given right to exercise "the fullness of power" over all Christians, by which they meant they had the right to make final decisions affecting any aspect of Christian society. When Pope Boniface VIII (1294–1303), a vain, ambitious figure described by Dante as "prince of the new Pharisees" (see Figure 24.1), sought to impose that claim, he en-

countered vigorous resistance from the kings of England and France. The resultant struggle opened a long sequence of events that eventually weakened not only papal authority but also the medieval system of religious governance.

Boniface clashed with these kings over issues that had long been bones of contention between the papacy and the civil authorities. His first setback came when he attempted to stop Edward I of England and Philip IV of France from imposing new taxes on the clergy and church property in their realms to help finance their wars against each other. In a pronouncement (called a *papal bull*) entitled *Clericis laicos*, which was intended to be binding on all Christians, Boniface forcefully maintained that taxes could be laid upon the religious establishment only with papal consent; his case was based on the "liberties" of the ecclesiastical establishment and the right of the head of that establishment to command the obedience of secular rulers. Edward and Philip responded by cutting off revenues from their kingdoms to Rome, forcing Boniface to retreat from his position. Before long Boniface and Philip again clashed, this time over the question of whether the king had jurisdiction in legal cases involving the clergy. Again the strong-minded pope stated his case unequivocally. In a bull entitled *Unam sanctam* (see Historians' Sources, p. 329) he not only claimed the exemption of the clergy from secular justice but also insisted that kings and all other Christians must subject themselves to the pope to be saved. Philip countered with a masterful propaganda campaign which discredited the pope in the eyes of the French public, including many French clergymen. He capped that campaign by sending his agents to Italy to capture Boniface. They were successful, and the pope escaped what might have been an even more painful defeat by dying. St. Peter's vicar had suffered a humiliating defeat at the hands of strong kings intent on asserting greater control over the ecclesiastical establishment in their realms.

Philip IV capitalized on his victory by using his influence over the College of Cardinals to ensure the election of a French bishop as Boniface's successor. In 1309, aware that he would be unwelcome in the turbulent Papal States, the new pope took up residence at Avignon, a city located on the east bank of the Rhone River, just outside

French territory. Until 1377 this city remained the residence of the papacy. During these years of what the Italian writer Petrarch called the "Babylonian Captivity"—referring to the episode in Jewish history when God's chosen people were held captive in Babylon by the sinful Chaldeans, now equated with the French monarchy—the prestige of the papacy suffered badly. The king of England and the Holy Roman emperor used the excuse that the popes were pawns of the French kings to expand their control over ecclesiastical affairs in their realms. Many Christians were troubled by the fact that the pope's claim to power was based on succession to St. Peter as bishop of Rome, not Avignon. These critics were not impressed by the plea of the papacy that Rome was not safe; neither had it been for Peter nor for many earlier popes. The Babylonian Captivity caused scholars and writers to raise major questions regarding church government and to arrive at answers that challenged papal supremacy.

The Avignon popes were extremely active in pursuing policies intended to strengthen papal control over the ecclesiastical organization. Several of the Avignon popes were highly skilled administrators whose efforts brought the long-standing trend toward centralization of religious organization to a culmination. Their most pressing concerns were financial. Affected by the economic despression gripping all of western Europe and cut off from the traditional revenues from their control of the Papal States in Italy, the Avignon popes worked hard to exploit old sources of revenue from all across Europe and to develop new forms of income. Among other things, they resorted to increasing assessments on local churches; "reserving" for themselves the right to fill major ecclesiastical offices in return for payment of a price; granting dispensations from the regulations of canon law in return for fees; selling indulgences which allowed sinners to do penance by making payments in money; and requiring adjudication of cases involving violation of canon law in papal courts for which fees and fines were collected. The concern with expanding financial resources and judicial activities required a huge expansion of the bureaucracy of the papal curia. In terms of revenues, subordinates, and business transactions, the Avignon popes were actually more powerful than even their thirteenth-century predecessors.

This emphasis on organizational affairs posed serious threats to papal prestige. The papal bureaucracy was increasingly open to charges of corruption involving the sale of offices and acceptance of bribes to ensure the desired outcome of requests for papal favors or judicial cases tried in papal courts. With increasing frequency, major ecclesiastical offices were sold to people who never occupied them or who purchased more than one; absenteeism and pluralism led to widespread neglect of the responsibilities attached to key religious offices. Bishops and abbots in all parts of Europe resented the growing papal interference in local religious affairs and tried to escape papal control, often by turning to their kings, who gladly protected them—for a price. Papal taxation aroused bitterness and resistance everywhere. Edward III of England reflected the dislike of the money-grubbing popes when he said "The successor of the Apostles was ordered to lead the Lord's sheep to the pasture, not to fleece them." The officials of the papal curia spent much of this wealth on luxurious living; a symbol of their luxury was the splendid papal palace built in Avignon. The ecclesiastical lifestyle of the city, which Petrarch called "the sewer of the world," aroused the bitter anger of many in Europe whose lot was poverty and suffering in the wake of the Black Death and widespread economic depression. The Avignon popes seemed powerless to curb these excesses and thus suffered the blame.

The Babylonian Captivity finally ended in 1377 with the return of the reigning pope to Rome. However, when he died in 1378, the complex maneuvers of the College of Cardinals to replace him ended with two popes, one in Rome and another in Avignon. Thus began the Great Schism, forty years during which the Christian community was headed by two popes directing two administrations, two tax systems, two sets of Church courts. All western Christendom wondered who was in charge of the keys to the heavenly kingdom. Those who were not confused sought to take advantage of the situation; their efforts were abetted by the politicking of rival popes seeking to gain sufficient allies to oust what each called the anti-pope. Many princes thought in terms of supporting the pope who offered the most advantageous concessions in terms of controlling the ecclesiastical establishments within their realms. Few took seriously the

HISTORIANS' SOURCES

Boniface the VIII: "Unam Sanctam"

In 1302 Pope Boniface VIII issued the following official pronouncement (called a bull) entitled "Unam Sanctam" as a response to claims made by the French king, Philip IV, to try in a royal court a French bishop charged with treason. From it the historian can gain a sense of what medieval popes meant by "fullness of power" and why secular rulers felt that their authority was threatened.

The true faith compels us to believe that there is one holy catholic apostolic church, and this we firmly believe and plainly confess. And outside of her there is no salvation or remission of sins. . . . In this church there is "one Lord, one faith, one baptism" (Eph. 4:5). For in the time of the flood there was only one ark, that of Noah, prefiguring the one church, and it. . . . had but one helmsman and master, namely, Noah. . . . Therefore there is one body of the one and only church, and one head, not two heads, as if the church were a monster. And this head is Christ and his vicar, Peter and his successor; for the Lord himself said to Peter: "Feed my sheep" (John 21:16). And he said "my sheep," in general, not these or those sheep in particular; from which it is clear that all were committed to him. If therefore Greeks or anyone else say that they are not subject to Peter and his successors, they thereby necessarily confess that they are not of the sheep of Christ. For the Lord says in the Gospel of John, that there is one fold and only one shepherd (John 10:16). By the words of the gospel we are taught that the two swords, namely, the spiritual authority and the temporal are in the power of the church. . . . Whoever denies that the temporal sword is in the power of Peter does not properly understand the word of the Lord when he said: "Put up thy sword into the sheath" (John 18:11). Both swords, there-

fore, the spiritual and the temporal, are in the power of the church. The former is to be used by the church, the latter for the church; the one by the hand of the priest, the other by the hand of kings and knights, but at the command and permission of the priest. Moreover, it is necessary for one sword to be under the other, and the temporal authority to be subjected to the spiritual. . . . According to the law of the universe all things are not equally and directly reduced to order, but the lowest are fitted into their order through the intermediate, and the lower through the higher. And we must necessarily admit that the spiritual power surpasses any earthly power in dignity and honor, because spiritual things surpass temporal things. We clearly see that this is true from the paying of tithes, from the benediction, from the sanctification, from the receiving of the power, and from the governing of these things. For the truth itself declares that the spiritual power must establish the temporal power and pass judgment on it if it is not good. . . . Therefore if the temporal power errs, it will be judged by the spiritual power, and if the lower spiritual power errs, it will be judged by its superior. But if the highest spiritual power errs, it can not be judged by men, but by God alone. For the apostle says: "But he that is spiritual judgeth all things, yet he himself is judged of no man" (1 Cor. 2:15). Now this authority, although it is given to man and exercised through man, is not human, but divine. For it was given by the word of the Lord to Peter, and the rock was made firm to him and his successors, in Christ himself, whom he had confessed. For the Lord said to Peter: "Whatsoever thou shalt bind on earth shall be bound in heaven: and whatsoever thou shalt loose on earth shall be loosed in heaven" (Matt. 16:19). Therefore whosoever resisteth this power thus ordained of God, resisteth the ordinance of God (Rom. 13:2). . . . We therefore declare, say, and affirm that submission on the part of every man to the bishop of Rome is altogether necessary for his salvation.

SOURCE: Oliver J. Thatcher and Edgar Holmes McNeal, *A Source Book of Medieval History. Selected Documents Illustrating the History of Europe in the Middle Ages* (New York: Charles Scribner's Sons, 1905), pp. 314–317.

claim of either pope to be spiritual leader of Europe; popes who competed with each other and encouraged the division of Christendom seemed little better than greedy politicians.

As a result of the schism and the increasing corruption, many leaders—bishops, canon lawyers, theologians, and even princes—began to search for ways of ending what seemed a scandalous situation. Their search eventually focused on an institution that had played a major role in the early history of the Christian establishment: a general council. The advocates of the conciliar theory argued that an ecumenical assembly of bishops possessed an authority superior even to that of the pope and thus provided a legitimate means of healing the schism and reforming the clergy. As a result of conciliar agitation four general councils were held between 1409 and 1449, each a stormy affair marked by limited results. The Council of Pisa (1409) addressed the issue of the schism but ended with the installation of a third pope to further complicate that problem. The Council of Constance (1414–1418) finally succeeded in restoring a single pope and articulating the principle of the supreme authority of councils in ecclesiastical governance. In the subsequent two councils the popes devoted singular attention to disarming this dangerous threat to papal authority, a task made easier by disagreements among ecclesiastical leaders representing different nations. A major tactic used by the popes to curb the claims of the conciliarists to supremacy in religious affairs was to seek support for papal authority from secular rulers by making concessions extending their control over the clergy and ecclesiastical income. These concessions limited papal power and hastened a trend toward the creation of "national" churches.

Probably the greatest failure of the conciliar movement was its inability to institute meaningful reform. Despite numerous attempts to enact legislation aimed at curing many of the ills afflicting the ecclesiastical establishment and religious life, the members of the councils were never able to agree on a practical reform program. A major obstacle to reform stemmed from the fact that the councils were dominated by clergymen whose conduct would have made many of them the chief target of reform. When the last council disbanded in 1449, most people had lost confidence in this means of revitalizing the religious system. The greatest influence of the conciliar movement was indirect: It raised fundamental questions about the traditional religious organization and caused many to conclude that the pope's claim to the "fullness of power" was not divinely ordained.

The popes of the last half of the fifteenth century concentrated on strengthening their control over the Papal States in Italy and on making their state a decisive force in the many power struggles raging in Italy in this period. On the whole, they were successful in establishing the Papal States as a preeminent power in Italian affairs. But the methods they employed led many to view the pope as nothing more than a secular prince, scheming, bribing, and brawling to get what he desired for himself, his family, and his friends. That impression was given greater credence by the role the papacy played as patron of Renaissance cultural activity, a role that immersed the papal court in a wide range of worldly activities that seemed to have little to do with the vicarship of Christ. With increasing frequency the popes conceded control of the religious establishment outside Rome and Italy to secular princes in return for nominal recognition of papal supremacy. These developments combined to deprive the papacy of the moral authority that had been its chief source of influence in the thirteenth century, and without that authority the papacy was in no position to command the respect and veneration of large numbers of Christians, as the beginning of the Protestant Reformation soon made evident.

The disarray in church governance resulting from the problems besetting the papacy and the decay of papal prestige was compounded by a steady deterioration of the effectiveness of the entire body of the clergy in the performance of pastoral and administrative responsibilities. A variety of factors combined to distract the secular clergy, charged with everyday ministry to the Christian populace, from its central function and to provide a basis for charges of corruptness and moral laxness against its members. The tone guiding the behavior of the upper clergy was set by popes and the powerful officials of the papal curia, especially the cardinals, whose vast entourages, immense wealth, and talent for political machinations indeed made them "princes of the Church" and targets of criticism. Following the

FIGURE 24.2 Misconduct of Monks Some of the most savage criticism of the late medieval church was aimed at the monastic establishments. These scenes reflect some of the causes of that criticism. Left, a monk and his mistress are held in stocks for passersby to jeer at. Right, a monk drinks excessively. (The British Library)

model of the cardinals, many bishops found the lure of political and social life surrounding the courts of kings and great nobles irresistible. In the face of the fiscal pressures resulting from a declining income in an era of depression, the price demanded by popes and kings to secure appointment to their office, and heavy papal and royal taxes, most bishops were left with little choice except to wring money from their flocks. Some bishops were tempted to meet these demands by requiring payment from the faithful for religious services and by offering lower ecclesiastical offices for sale. Ordinary priests who paid for their offices tried to recoup their costs by similar tactics. Both bishops and priests sought to hold several ecclesiastical offices at once; pluralism led to absenteeism. Absentee clergy often turned religious duties over to poorly trained, poorly paid clerks little suited to guide spiritual life. Divine services, instruction, confessions, preaching, and counseling were slighted, leaving Christians who had religious problems lost, unhappy, and even angry.

Monasticism, long a source of spiritual searching and religious renewal, also suffered stagnation. Between 1300 and 1500 not a single new monastic order of any importance was established, and many of the established orders failed to provide effective spiritual leadership. The Franciscans and the Dominicans were the most powerful and active orders during the later Middle Ages, continuing their work as preach-ers, confessors, and educational leaders. However, both orders attained increasing wealth and became engaged in a quest for power both within the religious establishment and in secular society. In the older Benedictine and Cistercian orders monks and nuns were lax in observing the rules governing discipline and morality. Little attention was paid to the quality of recruits entering monasteries and nunneries; many were aristocratic ladies who could not find husbands, landless younger sons of noble families, and commoners who sought to escape the hardships of life. Absentee abbots thought more about garnering income from monastic properties than about directing the spiritual lives of their charges. As the late medieval age of transition progressed, monastic life increasingly came to be held in low repute. Its bad reputation was mirrored with special force in late medieval literature, such as Boccaccio's *Decameron* and Chaucer's *Canterbury Tales*, both of which equate monastic life with greed, immorality, and hypocrisy (see Figure 24.2).

The combination of challenges to its authority and its own mismangement of the internal governance of the religious establishment led to increasing criticism of the religious leadership by many Christians. In their minds the institutional establishment that claimed the right to direct Christian life was too rich, too powerful, too bloated with self-serving officials. The ecclesiastical establishment had become concerned chiefly with sustaining its power and wealth at the expense of a vast community of faithful already deeply troubled by a variety of economic, social, and political dislocations and disturbed by deep spiritual concerns. One of the most impressive creations of the central Middle Ages was in need of an overhaul.

2. SPIRITUAL DISQUIET

While its system of governance was encountering difficulties that increasingly limited its ability to control the Christian community, the religious establishment was confronted with numerous signs of religious discontent welling up in the tension-filled society of the age of transition. Chiefly as a result of the intense effort by the ecclesiastical hierarchy and the intellectual establishment to impose uniformity of belief and practice on religious life during the central Middle Ages, Roman Catholicism had by 1300 become a highly formalistic religion in which piety was equated with participating in prescribed rituals, receiving the sacraments, and conforming to regulations governing behavior prescribed by canon law. There had, of course, been Christians before 1300 whose spiritual needs were not fully satisfied with that kind of religious experience; their efforts at "reform" had played an important part in the religious revival of the central Middle Ages. Such searching continued in the later Middle Ages, intensified and reshaped by the changing social setting.

Spiritual searching and dissatisfaction took many forms. One of the most important was an increase in the number of mystics, that is, persons who believed they could experience and know God directly without mediation by other persons or institutions. Mysticism was present throughout the Middle Ages; St. Bernard and St. Francis of Assisi were mystics. But the fourteenth and fifteenth centuries produced an especially large number of people who sought ways to experience a personal vision of God. Many of the most influential were simple men and women who never wore clerical garb, like Joan of Arc. None was more prominent than Catherine of Siena (1347–1380). On the basis of visions of Christ she claimed to have experienced, she proclaimed an intensely personal kind of spirituality which she not only shared with others by word of mouth during her extended travels and numerous letters that circulated all over Europe but which she also put into practice through her efforts to help the poor, the sick, criminals, and the downtroddden. So great was her fame that she earned a reputation as a saint in her own lifetime. Although she, as well as many like her, was never seriously at odds with the religious establishment, Catherine practiced a kind of Christianity unfamiliar to contemporary religious officials.

The activities of mystics sometimes resulted in the formation of communal movements that operated almost independently of the established religious system. A prime example was the Brethren of the Common Life (and its female counterpart, the Sisters of the Common Life), founded by a lay preacher named Gerard Groote (1340–1384), who was one of the many spiritual heirs of the great German mystic Meister Eckhart (1260–1327). This loosely knit movement was a product of a new kind of piety called the *devotio moderna*, which stressed prayer, love, and direct communion with God. Devotees of the new piety joined together as brothers and sisters in communities in which they shared their worldly goods, joined in common worship, confessed their sins to one another, devoted themselves to works of charity, sought to educate members of the community, and even produced their own devotional literature. One of the best examples of that literature, still read today as a spiritual guide, is Thomas à Kempis' *Imitation of Christ*. The many communities of the Brethren seldom strayed into heresy, but their piety, their puritanical life, and their mysticism set them apart. Not surprisingly, the Brethren were often attacked for spreading dangerous ideas; perhaps there was some substance to this charge in view of the fact that such important later reformers as Erasmus and Martin Luther were educated in their schools. Akin to the Brethren were the Beguines, associations of laywomen who led a common life, committed themselves to chastity and good works, and supported themselves by working or begging. Similar communities of men, called Beghards, were also established. More radical were the Brethren of the Free Spirit, who among other things denied the existence of sin on the basis of their belief that God existed in all things, an idea that resulted in their condemnation.

The fourteenth and fifteenth centuries produced a hardier crowd of critics—usually condemned as heretics—who voiced ideas that called for radical changes in the religious establishment. Some were intellectual figures, such as Marsiglio of Padua, whose book, *The Defender of the Peace* (1324), mounted a devastating attack on the claim of the religious establishment to exercise superior authority over society. Marsiglio argued that ultimate authority in any community derives not from God but from the will of the members making up that community. The will of the community expresses itself through the state, whose authority is sovereign. Any claim of the religious authorities to independent authority is thus a fiction. Marsiglio advocated that the religious establishment be deprived of its wealth and privileges and be made a branch of government, subservient to the ruler in whom authority was vested by the will of the political community. He argued that the "Church" as a community of all Christians should be ruled by a council representing all elements in Christian society, not by a clerical hierarchy headed by the pope. He denied that the papal office had divine sanction; the pope was simply an ecclesiastical administrator whose powers were defined by the Christian community and who could be limited in any way that community wished. Not surprisingly, Marsiglio was excommunicated by the papacy and his book was condemned.

Somewhat later, John Wycliffe (1320–1384), a teacher and scholar at Oxford, raised equally serious issues about the prevailing practice of Christianity. Wycliffe's critique of the religious establishment stemmed not only from his reflections on matters of faith but also from his sympathy with the growing tide of anticlericalism and antipapalism emerging in an England troubled by the Avignon papacy, the burdens of the Hundred Years' War, and internal political and economic stresses. He first voiced his concerns about the ecclesiastical system by arguing that it had abused its right to hold property and that all Church property should be confiscated by the state. Later he advocated the destruction of the whole clerical hierarchy on the ground that salvation depended not on the clergy but on grace flowing from God; every person was his or her own priest in terms of establishing a relationship with the divine. Here, of course, he was striking a blow at a key idea on which the medieval religious establishment based its institutional po-

sition: the idea that salvation depended on the ministry of a clergy set apart from and above the laity by the sacrament of ordination. Wycliffe also attacked many of the religious practices currently in use—elaborate rituals, prayers to saints, veneration of relics, pilgrimages, and the like. He even questioned the validity of the sacraments as necessary to salvation. He argued that Scripture alone must be the authority for Christian doctrine and began to translate the Bible into English so that all could read it. Although Wycliffe was soon condemned as a heretic and forced to leave Oxford, his teachings attracted many followers, known as the Lollards, and for many years Lollard preachers and writers spread their master's ideas in England. In time, however, they came to challenge all authority; with the support of Parliament the English kings joined the clergy in destroying the movement.

Wycliffe's ideas had their most significant effect not in England but in Bohemia. The leading disciple there was John Huss (ca. 1373–1415), a priest who taught at the University of Prague. When his preaching of Wycliffe's precepts raised a protest from the clergy and ruling faction, most of whom were German and were passionately hated by the native Czechs, Huss became a national hero in Bohemia. Like Wycliffe, he too was excommunicated. Eventually, Huss sought and received permission to appear before the Council of Constance to defend his teaching. Once in Constance, however, Huss was imprisoned, tried, and executed as a heretic in 1415. A rebellion immediately broke out in Bohemia and raged until 1436. Crusade after crusade was preached by the papacy against the Hussites; several German armies, led by an emperor who was anxious to reclaim Bohemia, were soundly thrashed by the aroused Bohemians. Eventually peace was restored when certain religious concessions were granted to the Hussites. However, a faction of the followers of Huss and Wycliffe, called Taborites, was not satisfied by these concessions and became practically a church apart in Bohemia during the last years of the Middle Ages.

Manifestations of religious ferment and frustration took many other forms during the fourteenth and fifteenth centuries. Any number of fiery preachers proclaimed the end of the world and the coming of God's wrathful final judgment. Wildly emotional cults, such as the Flagellants, who whipped one another to atone for the world's sins, preyed on people's religious sensibilities, especially in times of great crises such as the Black Death. Brutal massacres of the Jews in the name of Christian righteousness marred the histories of many cities. A fear of witches flourished on an unprecedented scale, accompanied by numerous trials of those suspected of witchcraft. Increasingly, people sought assurances of salvation by purchasing indulgences, which they believed would ensure that the punishment due for sins would be removed. Never were relics more appealing or more brazenly manipulated, as illustrated by Chaucer's pardoner, always equipped with his bag full of "pigs' bones" for sale to gullible sinners. Literature, art, and sermons were preoccupied with death in particularly horrible forms. All of these unusual forms of religious expression reflected a psychology of fear and uncertainty that sometimes reached the proportions of mass hysteria.

Of course, amid this ferment religious life went on in conventional ways. The established structures of ecclesiastical governance continued to operate, people attended Mass, received the sacraments, prayed, tried to observe church law, sinned, and were forgiven. However, the intensity and variety of discontent pointed toward an emerging religious crisis. Neither the gentle mystics nor the fiery-tongued rebels, neither the adherents of the occult nor the victims of hysteria, were completely at home in the Roman Catholic church. People were striking out in all directions, questioning ritual, organization, and dogma. But the institution that claimed to care for the souls of the disturbed and the dissatisfied either ignored the quest for religious satisfaction or ruthlessly crushed the discontent. It was failing its central mission: to meet the basic religious needs of its vast flock. More important, it seemed unable to discover ways of restoring its power to cure souls.

3. INTELLECTUAL FERMENT AND RELIGIOUS VALUES

The influence exercised by the religious establishment over medieval society was further weakened by fundamental shifts in intellectual life in the late medieval age of transition. Between 1000 and 1300 ecclesiastical leaders seeking to shape society according to Christian concepts received powerful support from an intellectual establishment working to define law and doctrine in terms that would apply universally to a united Christian community and to merge all knowledge into one order of truth which would sustain the Christian worldview. After 1300 intellectuals began to pursue lines of thought that challenged the worldview upon which the authority of the religious establishment was founded and to formulate new interpretations of what constituted truth and right values. Although this transformation was not dramatic, it marked a significant step in the transition to the modern world.

Outwardly, the life of learning continued down familiar paths. The universities remained the focal points of scholarship and teaching in the liberal arts, theology, law, medicine, and science, and most intellectuals continued to pursue knowledge and truth within the institutional framework of the university system. The scholastic method, which since the twelfth century had been employed to establish knowledge and understanding through the application of logical tests to propositions concerning the divine, humanity, and nature, continued to dominate theological and philosophical inquiry. But the emphasis and objective of intellectual endeavor underwent subtle changes. The quest, exemplified by the works of Thomas Aquinas, to synthesize divine and human knowledge, to reconcile revelation and reason in a fashion that would produce a single, all-embracing, consistent order of truth failed to establish dominance over theological and philosophical discourse. For some intellectuals Aquinas' approach raised so many problems that they despaired of reconciling revelation and reason into one complete order of truth. Still others began to attack the basic proposition that faith and reason were compatible. Thus, by 1300 analysis began to take precedence over synthesis and became the keynote to intellectual inquiry during the late Middle Ages.

Not long after Aquinas' death in 1274, such issues led to the formulation of approaches that redirected theological and philosophical inquiry. The Franciscan scholar John Duns Scotus (ca. 1266–1308) argued with great force that God's freedom and power were so exalted that all attempts to describe his attributes rationally imposed untenable limits on divine power. In effect, Duns Scotus was saying that theology was not a proper matter for rational speculation. This trend of thought was expanded by William of Ockham (ca. 1300–1349), an English Franciscan who taught at Oxford. A skilled logician, Ockham assailed the basic rational supports of Thomistic theology. In his mind knowledge of such things as the existence of God and the immortality of the soul came only by intuition and mystical experience. Theology and philosophy thus became separate "sciences," incapable of reconciliation. In defining the realm of reason, Ockham argued that only by sense perception of individual objects could humans know; in this respect he was a philosophical *nominalist,* repudiating the long tradition that ideas constituted the ultimate reality (philosophical *realism*). Duns Scotus and William of Ockham gained powerful disciples who followed up the assault on Thomism. Their attacks shattered the thirteenth-century confidence in establishing one all-embracing truth and with it a powerful prop of the religious establishment.

These challenges to Thomism led thinkers to explore a variety of new issues in new ways. Since reason was distinct from faith, political theorists like Marsiglio of Padua constructed new concepts of the governance of church and state that were especially destructive to theologically based justifications of ecclesiastical power over the social order. The attack on rational theology nourished mysticism and opened the way for the radical theological concepts of Wycliffe and Huss. Many intellectuals, disillusioned by the barren exercises of late medieval scholasticism, found intellectual sustenance in classical literature and philosophy, drawing from these sources a secular, humanistic worldview and value system. Especially pregnant for the future was the growing interest in the material world. Following Ockham's argument that rational inquiry must confine itself to tangible objects, scholars, especially at the universities of Paris and Oxford, produced a considerable body of scientific knowledge and provided significant corrections to Greco-Arabic scientific generalizations. Their efforts laid the groundwork for the revolutionary scientific discoveries of Copernicus, Galileo, and others in the sixteenth and seventeenth centuries.

As intellectual life became more pluralistic and more oriented to worldly, secular concerns, the potential for criticism of the ecclesiastical establishment increased, and that establishment's ability to control intellectual activity for its own benefit decreased.

4. NEW FORCES AND THE RELIGIOUS ESTABLISHMENT

While the religious establishment encountered deepening difficulties in managing its internal affairs and containing religious and intellectual currents that challenged its position, it had to contend with powerful forces outside the sphere of religion that threatened its leadership and depleted its following. Many of these forces portended a new era in western European history; they will receive fuller treatment later. Here, it is important that they be noted as threats to the ecclesiastical dominance.

The aggressive national states beginning to take shape in the fifteenth century represented one such force. Although still observant, even enthusiastic, Christians, ambitious rulers sought to limit and dominate the religious establishment in their realms. Their ambitions were given impetus by a widespread perception of corruption in the religious establishment and by intellectual currents that argued for secular direction of earthly society. In England kings and Parliament joined in enacting laws to prevent the papacy from taxing church property and controlling ecclesiastical appointments. In France the royal government worked steadily, often with the help of the French clergy, to establish a "Gallic" church independent of the papacy and subservient to the crown. In Spain, late in the fifteenth century, the monarchs even undertook to reform the religious life independently of the papacy. These cases were all clear indications that as 1500 approached, "national churches" were becoming a reality at the expense of the "universal Church" of the Middle Ages.

Equally threatening to the domination of society by the religious establishment and a religious mentality was the capitalistic ethos that was emerging in economic life, especially among urban patricians but also among members of the rural gentry and affluent peasants. Challenging the ancient Christian distrust of wealth and materialism, this new ethos viewed wealth and its acquisition as a positive force in society. Its adherents would have liked to see the wealth held by the ecclesiastical establishment put to new uses. Most of them paid little heed to religious arguments condemning the charging of interest, price manipulation, and profit seeking. Implicit in the capitalist ethos was a mentality oriented toward competition, worldliness, individualism, pragmatism, and a work ethic—all values that did not fit easily into the traditional concept of how the drama of salvation should be played out.

Finally, a new breed of thinkers, writers, and artists, sometimes collectively called *humanists,* was emerging to criticize many teachings and practices supported by the medieval religious establishment. The new humanism, developing first and most vigorously in Italy and then spreading to other parts of western Europe, found its intellectual sustenance and its aesthetic values in classical rather than medieval models. While not anti-Christian, humanism nurtured a worldview that gave greater prominence to human life in a worldly setting than did the view long promoted by the religious leaders in the name of Christian truth.

The stressful internal difficulties and the challenging outside forces that combined to undermine the authority of the religious establishment in the later Middle Ages provided the surest indication that an epoch was ending. Admittedly the stresses and strains affecting political, economic, and social institutions all pointed toward the transformation of the basic structures characteristic of medieval western European civilization. However, for centuries the religious establishment—the Church—had been the main force giving that civilization its cohesion, its direction, and its distinctive features. The faltering of that establishment truly heralded the end of an epoch in western European history.

SUGGESTED READING

Problems of Religious Organization

Francis Oakley, *The Western Church in the Later Middle Ages* (1979).

Steven Ozment, *The Age of Reform (1250–1530). An Intellectual and Religious History of Late Medieval and Reformation Europe* (1980).

Two excellent treatments of all aspects of religious history.

John Bossy, *Christianity in the West, 1400–1700* (1985). A stimulating interpretation of religious change.

Yves Renouard, *The Avignon Papacy, 1305–1403,* trans. Denis Bethell (1970). A concise survey.

Walter Ullmann, *The Origins of the Great Schism: A Study in Fourteenth-Century Ecclesiastical History* (1948). A careful analysis of the factors that produced the Great Schism.

Brian Tierney, *Foundations of the Conciliar Theory: The Contributions of the Medieval Canonists from Gratian to the Great Schism* (1955). Stresses the legal basis for conciliar ideas.

Antony Black, *Council and Commune: The Conciliar Movement and the Fifteenth-Century Heritage* (1979). Discusses the ideas of the conciliarists in the context of history and theology.

New Religious Movements

Rufus M. Jones, *The Flowering of Mysticism: The Friends of God in the Fourteenth Century* (1939).

James M. Clark, *The Great German Mystics: Eckhart, Tauler, and Suso* (1949).

Anne Bancroft, *The Luminous Vision: Six Medieval Mystics and Their Teachings* (1982).

Any of these three titles will help the reader to understand the nature and influence of late medieval mysticism.

Albert Hyma, *The Christian Renaissance: A History of "Devotio Moderna,"* 2nd ed. (1965). A full treatment of a movement that deeply affected late medieval religious life.

Richard Kieckhefer, *Unquiet Souls: Fourteenth-Century Saints and Their Religious Milieu* (1984). Rich in insights into the nature and causes of religious "unquiet" in the fourteenth century.

Norman Cohn, *The Pursuit of the Millennium: Revolutionary Millenarians and Mystical Anarchists of the Middle Ages,* rev. ed. (1970). A brilliant description of aberrant religious movements in the later Middle Ages.

Malcolm Lambert, *Medieval Heresy: Popular Movements from Bogomil to Huss* (1977). An excellent synthesis.

Intellectual Movements

Georges Duby, *Foundations of a New Humanism, 1280–1440*, trans. Peter Price (1966). A remarkable synthesis linking many aspects of late medieval cultural history.

Gordon Leff, *The Dissolution of the Medieval Outlook: An Essay on Intellectual and Spiritual Change in the Four-teenth Century* (1976). A perceptive but challenging interpretation of late medieval intellectual development.

Alistar McGrath, *The Intellectual Origins of the European Reformation* (1987). A good analysis of theological trends in the later Middle Ages.

RETROSPECT

The era from 1000 to 1500 was of decisive importance in shaping the essential features of western European civilization. The first three centuries of that period were marked by remarkable developments that changed every aspect of the "backward" society that had been so painfully pieced together during the five hundred years immediately following the collapse of the Roman order. The fruits of that sustained, creative activity were abundant: increased material wealth; larger, more stable political communities; a more complex social structure; expanded mental and spiritual horizons; a deepened understanding of the human condition; and enlarged capabilities for expression. Many of the creations of medieval society would remain essential features of western European society almost to the present: national states; urban complexes; agricultural and commercial organization; representative government; legal systems; a centralized religious establishment; vernacular languages; Romanesque and Gothic art; universities; commercial and agricultural technologies. And the era had another equally important dimension: While gathering strength internally, western European society began to thrust outward into the world beyond its boundaries, taking the first decisive steps toward the establishment of western European preeminence on the world scene. Any attempt to understand either subsequent western European or world history must take into account the achievements of the Middle Ages; such an effort will dispel the long-held view that that was a "dark age."

By 1300 the dynamism that had produced the great leap forward of western European society began to diminish, leading to an era of stressful transition. In part the troubles of the late medieval era stemmed from a series of unpredictable events: a demographic catastrophe that caused massive economic, social, and psychological dislocations; dynastic crises that disrupted the orderly succession of rulers and produced singularly incompetent rulers; misguided political ambitions that led to prolonged, destructive wars; overblown claims to authority in the name of religion; shifts in the power structure in lands lying to the east of Europe's frontiers. Effective responses to the disruptions caused by these events were made difficult by conflicting positions inherent in the institutional structures, thought patterns, and value systems shaped prior to 1300. In fact, those dichotomies were themselves sources of deepening tensions during the later Middle Ages. The medieval ideal of a Christian commonwealth produced sharp disagreement about the leadership of that commonwealth and threats to deep-seated localism. Progress toward the formation of nation-states led to conflicts between royal authority and private privilege. The monolithic religious establishment encountered difficulty in containing the ferment that sought new ways of understanding and living the Christian life. The international, profit-seeking, individualistic enterprises at the cutting edge of economic development were impeded by localistic, monopolistic, self-sufficient economic structures. Faith and reason, Latin and vernacular cultures, religious and secular values vied for people's minds.

However, despite the severity of the crises afflicting western Europe between 1300 and 1500 and the grim prophecies of impending doom uttered by some late medieval millenarians, the end of a civilizational order was not at hand. The institutional patterns and value system fashioned during the central Middle Ages showed remarkable resiliency under pressure. By 1500 it was becoming clear that that system had potential for further development. What we call "modern" Europe was the product of a new burst of creativity which shaped a society with its own distinctive features but with its roots in the Middle Ages. The history of modern Europe is inexplicable and unintelligible without a knowledge of those roots.

PART FIVE

EARLY MODERN TIMES: THE RENAISSANCE TO THE EIGHTEENTH CENTURY

During the second half of the fifteenth century, new developments began to sweep over Europe. What historians call the Middle Ages was ending and early modern times were beginning.

The precursor of change was the Renaissance, which was born in the urban societies of northern Italy during the fourteenth and fifteenth centuries. With roots in classical and medieval civilizations, Renaissance culture developed thought, art, and values that would characterize early modern times.

Several striking changes followed that would alter the course of European history. First, new monarchs succeeded in taking major steps toward creating national states with strong central governments. Second, Europe expanded dramatically as these national states supported the establishment of empires around the globe. Third, the Reformation of the sixteenth century permanently destroyed the unity of the western Christian Church and entwined religion, politics, and violence in new ways.

Other changes proceeded more slowly but no less importantly. Most people remained tied to agriculture and their small villages. However Europe's medieval economy increasingly gave way to commercial capitalism, and during the eighteenth century the agricultural revolution and the spread of cottage industry foreshadowed the greater changes that were to come. The landed aristocracy generally retained its power but was forced to absorb new members into its ranks and face growing challenges from middle-class merchants and entrepreneurs. The dominant cultural trends continued to reflect the tastes of the elite classes.

Finally, the scientific revolution and the Enlightenment of the seventeenth and eighteenth centuries would eventually help undermine the traditional order of early modern Europe and provide an intellectual foundation for the modern society of the nineteenth and twentieth centuries.

CHAPTER 25
The Renaissance: Italy

FIGURE 25.1 Leonardo da Vinci, *The Virgin of the Rocks,* ca. 1485 With Leonardo da Vinci (1452–1519), Renaissance painting, with its emphasis on humanism, reached its peak. In this painting, the Virgin is a beautiful woman and the Christ child is a playful, cuddly little boy. The rock formation is authentic, and the plants are identifiable specimens. (Archives Photographiques, Paris)

While most of European society during the fourteenth century was still medieval, Italian society was already changing, developing some of the characteristics that would become common during the early modern period. Most important, Italian society produced a new culture with roots in both the medieval Christian civilization and the classical Greek and Roman civilizations. This culture, called the Renaissance, would continue to grow in Italy during the fifteenth century and then spread throughout Europe. The Renaissance became a basis upon which thought, literature, and art during the early modern period rested.

1. ITALIAN ORIGINS

Although historians have debated the causes for the rise of the Renaissance in Italy, they usually point to a few factors that distinguish Italy, and particularly northern Italy where the Renaissance was centered, from the rest of Europe.

Above all, northern Italy was unusually urbanized—there were more and larger cities than in most other areas of Europe. The first and most important Renaissance city was Florence, but other cities such as Venice, Pisa, and Milan also became centers of the Italian Renaissance. By the fourteenth century these cities had gained economic prosperity from long-distance trade, commerce, industry, banking, and particularly the production of luxury goods.

These cities marshaled their economic strength to expand and gain power over surrounding lands once controlled by the landed aristocracy. They also took advantage of the exhausting struggles between the Holy Roman emperor and the papacy, two powers that might have been strong enough to hinder the growing political independence of the cities. Political life within the cities became dynamic, often chaotic, but most of the time it was controlled by the new commercial elite.

The society of these large, commercial cities became more fluid as position began to be determined more by wealth than by blood. Medieval aristocratic strictures were weakened. The urban elite, continually infused with new members of the wealthy bourgeoisie and outside talent attracted to the vibrant cities, participated in commercial and industrial exploits—activities usually rejected as inappropriate to the aristocracy elsewhere in Europe. Wealthy leaders of the guilds that dominated commercial and industrial life gained new standing and power. Within the elite there were a large number of relatively young people, more aggressive and individualistic than traditional groups elsewhere.

This urban elite needed to be literate and well educated in practical matters. Schools arose to serve them and taught a curriculum appropriate to their practical interests. The elite also had great wealth to spend, and they turned to culture in general and art in particular. They may have wanted art as an investment, as a means of promoting their own political and social ambitions, or as a matter of civic pride. In any case they became patrons of the arts. Now art was being produced not only for clerical and traditional aristocratic patrons but also for rich, middle-class, and urbanized aristocratic patrons who had different outlooks.

As the demand for art grew, so did the prestige of the artist. In medieval society artists had been little more than low-paid artisans. In Renaissance society they became well-paid professionals and part of a respected intellectual elite that included writers and philosophers.

Finally, the physical and human environment of the Italian cities included advantages not present elsewhere in Europe. The remains and traditions of Greco-Roman civilization were still evident in Italy and its cities. Moreover, these cities, thanks to their proximity to the Near East and their commercial and political ties to the Byzantine lands, often came into contact with the sophisticated Byzantine culture.

Thus the thriving Italian urban society—with its commercial wealth, its political independence, its social fluidity, its schools, its artists, its intellectual elite, and its cultural environment—was the fertile ground in which the Renaissance first grew.

2. GENERAL NATURE

The term *renaissance* means "rebirth." One of the central characteristics of the Renaissance was the self-conscious revival of classical civilization and the sense of creating something different from medieval civilization. Renaissance scholars rejoiced in discovering, mastering, and making available the cultural products of Greece and Rome. At the same time they criticized medieval Scholasticism and medieval culture in general. They envisioned themselves as being part of a new civilization based on a revival of classical civilization intertwined with the purest elements of Christian civilization.

The emphasis on reviving classical civilization reflected a greater concern with secular life. The medieval focus on theology—concern with the spiritual world and formal religious doctrines—changed toward a focus on human beings, their nature and their actions. Medieval Christian theologians had distrusted the flesh as an enemy of the spirit and human wisdom as unable to perceive divine truth by rational processes unless guided by Christian inspiration. Renaissance scholars and artists glorified the human form as beautiful and the human intellect as capable of discovering all truth worth knowing. They viewed human beings as three-dimensional, part of an immediate, concrete, recognizable physical environment.

However, care must be taken in characterizing Renaissance culture as secular. The Renaissance was not antireligious; there was no fundamental questioning of Christian beliefs in this still-religious age. Much of the secularism of the Renaissance was in a Christian and even a pious context. Part of the concern with reviving secular classical civilization stemmed from a desire to better understand early Christianity and Christian principles. Moreover, the secularism of the Italian Renaissance was not a sharp, sudden break with the immediate past. Secular interests had never completely died out, even at the peak of the Church's prestige in the Middle Ages. The twelfth century had already witnessed a revival of interest in classical civilization. It would be better to say that during the Italian Renaissance there was a significant intensification of the secular spirit in thought, literature, and art, all still within a fundamentally Christian environment.

Individualism was another important facet of the Renaissance spirit. In this respect, the difference between the medieval and Renaissance spirits was primarily one of degree. Christianity did much to elevate the dignity of the individual soul and the individual personality. But the medieval clergy had feared pride as a sin. They had taught that the individual ego must be carefully held in check. Medieval monasticism had attempted to suppress the individual ego and submerge it in the group. In practice, then, medieval Christianity had tended to be collectivist. Church artists and writers usually had not signed their names to their work, which was supposed to contribute only to the greater glory of God. Renaissance individualism was prideful, even lusty. People of accomplishment were self-consciously confident, even boastful. They wanted the glory that their work would bring them. People such as Boccaccio (1313–1375), Alberti (1404–1472), Machiavelli (1469–1527), and Cellini (1500–1571) were proud of their identity and uniqueness.

Many of these great scholars and artists displayed another element of the Renaissance ideal—versatility. The educated person of the Middle Ages had usually been a specialist—a theologian or church artist or administrator. But the most renowned Renaissance schoolteachers taught many subjects in addition to the traditional formal ones—dancing, fencing, poetry, and vernacular languages, to mention a few. Many of the Renaissance schools broadened the old theology-oriented seven liberal arts and made much greater use of pagan classical literature and philosophy in the curriculum. One of the most popular books in Europe in the sixteenth century was Castiglione's *Book of the Courtier*. The ideal courtier, said Castiglione, is not only a gentleman and a scholar but also a man of action—a soldier and an athlete. Probably the best illustration of versatility in any age is Leonardo da Vinci (1452–1519). This revered Renaissance figure, one of the most celebrated painters of all time, was also an able sculptor, architect, mathematician, philosopher, inventor, botanist, anatomist, geologist, and engineer.

Finally, the Renaissance was urban and socially limited. While many products of the Renaissance were public and even unavoidable in Italian cities, only an elite participated in or directly supported the Renaissance. The majority of the urban population was made up of wage earners, day laborers, domestic servants, and unemployed people. They lived near or below subsistence level and often depended on charity to survive. Most who were somewhat better off—skilled workers and small merchants—lacked formal education and were far from wealthy. In the countryside access to the culture of the Renaissance was even more limited. Despite Italy's relatively urban environment, most people remained tied to the land. There only a few had enough for more than a minimum of needs and even fewer had the time or money for a formal education. In short, the Renaissance scarcely touched most people in the cities and was unheard of in the countryside.

The Renaissance was also of different significance for women than men, even among the elite. On the one hand, women often participated with men in the new urban schools and played a growing role within the household. Indeed, marriage patterns often resulted in widowed women retaining the family's wealth while not remarrying, giving them considerable economic freedom. Some women did manage to become Renaissance humanists and artists, a few of whom, such as the writer Vittoria Colonna (1492–1547) of Marino and the sculptor Properzia Rossi (ca. 1490–1530) of Bologna, became well known and celebrated in circles of humanists and artists. Perhaps the most famous Renaissance woman was Christine de Pisan (ca. 1364–ca. 1431), who was born in Venice but lived in France. She wrote several poems and books, the most widely read of which was *The City of Ladies*. On the other hand, women during the Renaissance were losing some of the status and public position they had held during the Middle Ages. More than before, they were relegated to domestic life, where they played a supportive, decorous, and sexually inferior role to their husbands. This changing status was particularly evident within the rising middle class, but even noblewomen lost power and the independence they had enjoyed when medieval courtly manners and love had held sway. Women were generally excluded from active, public participation in the culture and society of the Renaissance.

3. HUMANISM

During the fourteenth century, Italy witnessed the rise of humanism. Historians have debated the exact meaning of Italian humanism. Narrowly defined, it means classical scholarship—the study of original Latin or Greek manuscripts.

Broadly defined, it means the recovery of classical manuscripts, educational reform to include greater emphasis on classical scholarship, a rejection of medieval Scholasticism and professionalism, and an optimistic emphasis on human beings—on their capabilities as powerful, rational Christian and secular beings on this earth. Understood in this broad sense, humanism encompasses in its literature, its educational reforms, and its philosophy the main characteristics of the Italian Renaissance.

Literature

The characteristics of Renaissance humanism are richly illustrated by the Italian literature of the fourteenth century. The best of that literature was produced by the Tuscan Triumvirate—so called because it consisted of three men who lived in Florence in the old Etruscan province of Tuscany. The first was Dante Alighieri (1265–1321). In an earlier section (see Chapter 22) we discussed Dante as the greatest of the late medieval writers. His masterpiece, *The Divine Comedy*, is so full of medieval Christian lore and theology that it has been called a *Summa Theologiae* in poetry. Nevertheless, there is so much of the humanistic spirit in *The Divine Comedy* and in Dante's other writings that he also belongs to the Renaissance. In the "Inferno" of *The Divine Comedy*, Dante paints vivid, sensuous word pictures that seem to characterize this world rather than the next. The blazing fires and sulfurous fumes of hell, the cries of lament and curses of the damned come alive in our imagination. Furthermore, the author venerates such pagan classical writers as Vergil and Cicero to a much greater degree than had the medievalists (although a number of medieval writers had tried to make Vergil a Christian).

Dante's other major writings are even more humanistic. His love lyrics, written in his native Tuscan vernacular and addressed to Beatrice, are among the most beautiful in any language. In fact, Dante's writings greatly enriched the Florentine dialect and eventually raised it to the status of the national language of Italy.

Dante was also versatile; he was a man of public affairs as well as of letters. An active participant in the turbulent politics of Renaissance Italy, he was exiled from his native Florence when his faction lost. Dante even went so far as to fill hell in *The Divine Comedy* with his political enemies.

Petrarch (1304–1374), the second of the Tuscan Triumvirate, is often considered the father of Italian humanism. In both his writing and his life he rejected medieval Scholasticism and culture as inferior to classical culture. He argued for the recovery of classical manuscripts, the mastering of Latin, and educational reform. He is best known for his superbly crafted letters to great figures of the past, such as Cicero, Vergil, Livy, and St. Augustine, and for his love sonnets in the Tuscan vernacular to Laura, a married woman whom he saw at Mass and loved from afar.

Boccaccio (1313–1375) did for Italian prose what Dante and Petrarch did for Italian poetry. In his *Decameron*, a collection of one hundred tales or novelettes, Boccaccio exhibits little Christian restraint. He relates bawdy romances with skill and grace, condoning and even glorifying the seamy side of human nature.

Classical Manuscripts

The passionate quest for Latin and Greek literary manuscripts sometimes conflicted with the creation of original Italian literature by siphoning off the interest and energy of the writers. This conflict is illustrated by Petrarch, who rather early in life ceased writing what he called his "worthless" lyrics in order to discover lost classical manuscripts and to copy their style. He did succeed in bringing to light many priceless classical literary gems, but his epic *Africa* (relating the exploits of Scipio Africanus), written in Latin after the style of Vergil's *Aeneid*, lacks spontaneity and is all but forgotten.

Petrarch interested Boccaccio in the recovery of Greek and Latin manuscripts, and the search soon spread. Popes, princes, rich merchants, and bankers subsidized the humanists. In the fifteenth century, Italy was busy with professional humanists hunting for, copying, translating, and editing ancient manuscripts.

Educational Reform

Working with classical manuscripts was related to a broader educational reform encompassed in the humanist movement. Humanists such as Petrarch argued that medieval schooling had been too narrow, that the goal of education should be to produce more rounded, eloquent, virtuous individuals who were able to pursue the good life. Classical literature became a larger part of an educational curriculum that increasingly stressed practical learning. Educational reformers such as Pietro Paolo Vergerio (1349–1420) and Vittorino da Feltre (1378–1446) modified the Scholastic tradition and infused the curriculum with physical exercises, music, philosophy, Latin, and Greek as well as classical literature.

Philosophy

The study of classical masterpieces led to a variety of philosophical inquiries. This phase of humanism had many facets, including a new stress on the rational capabilities of humans, the development of a critical attitude, and a change in the concept of politics.

In 1396 Manuel Chrysoloras, a Byzantine scholar from Constantinople, was invited to Florence. He and other Greek scholars stimulated the study of Greek manuscripts during the fifteenth century. This study led to a revival of interest in Platonism and the establishment of the Platonic Academy in Florence under Marsilio Ficino (1433–1499) and Pico della Mirandola (1463–1494). They believed that, properly understood, Platonic philosophy and Christianity were compatible. They argued that human beings had great freedom and abilities, above all an ability to use will and reason to strive for the good life.

Another element of the humanistic view of life was the development of an analytic attitude. When Lorenzo Valla (1407–1457) proved by linguistics that the Donation of Constantine was a forgery, the scholarly and secular-minded pope raised no objections, although this was one of the documents upon which the papacy had based its claims to temporal power in the West. In fact, Pope Nicholas V made Valla his secretary. By making this discovery, Valla established himself as the father of modern critical historical scholarship.

The Florentine Niccolò Machiavelli (1469–1527), in his celebrated *The Prince*, suggested that Christian morals have little to do with the actual practice of politics (see p. 321). To acquire and maintain political power, the prince (or ruler or governing officials) must be willing to use both amoral and ruthless means. Since politicians, like all human beings, are self-seeking animals, the prince should assume that all rival princes and even his own lieutenants are conspiring for his power. Therefore, the prince should be willing to set his own chief subjects against each other and maneuver them into impotence. A wise prince deceives and treacherously attacks his foreign rivals at the most favorable moment before they can do the same. While Machiavelli was trying to remedy the deplorable reality of a divided Italy overrun and pillaged by more powerful foreign enemies, he also reflected the reality of secular attitudes and politics in fifteenth- and sixteenth-century Italy. His was a political theory that separated politics from ethics, stressing how people behaved rather than how they ought to behave. Few books have had more influence on, or been more descriptive of, modern political thought and practice.

4. FINE ARTS

Several characteristics of the Italian Renaissance are vividly illustrated in the Italian fine arts of the fourteenth, fifteenth, and sixteenth centuries.

Painting

Medieval painting in Europe had been closely allied with the Church. Painters deliberately penalized human flesh in order that the spirit might shine forth unimpeded. The figures, nearly always saints, were stiff, haggard, flat, and elongated. The physical world too was blanked out with solid gold backgrounds. The styles were stereotyped.

In the early fourteenth century Giotto, a contemporary of Dante, began to break this medieval mold of artistic custom by humanizing his figures and painting functional landscape backgrounds. Giotto's subject matter was almost entirely religious, but his treatment of it was such that the humanistic spirit made definite advances at the expense of the medieval. In the early fifteenth century Masaccio greatly developed the trend begun by Giotto a century earlier. He increased the illusion of depth by introducing atmospheric perspective and by further developing linear perspective. He also introduced the principle of the known light source, which thereafter replaced diffused light in painting. His nude human forms were further rounded and humanized (see Figure 25.2). His landscape backgrounds were realistic and detailed. With Masaccio and later painters such as Giovanni Bellini (see Color Plate 12) and Botticelli (see Figure 25.3), the transition from medieval to Renaissance painting was completed and the stage set for such towering geniuses of the Italian High Renaissance as Leonardo da Vinci, Michelangelo, Raphael, and Titian.

It would be difficult to find a more representative figure of the Italian Renaissance than Leonardo da Vinci (1452–1519). All the colorful facets of the Renaissance spirit are richly illustrated by the career and work of this versatile genius. Leonardo was an illegitimate child, as were a number of the famous figures of the Renaissance. He was born near Florence and began his career there, but some of his most productive years were spent in the employ of the duke of Milan. He finally followed King Francis I to France, where he died. Like most Renaissance artists, Leonardo dealt primarily with religious subject matter; but, also like the others, his treatment of it was more secular and human. In his *Virgin of the Rocks* (see Figure 25.1), for instance, Leonardo creates with exquisite grace and beauty the Virgin Mary and the Christ child. The Virgin, however, is the loveliest of women, and the Christ child is a plump and playful baby boy. The characters are human, not divine. The background is a strange rock formation, naturalistic enough to reveal a keen interest in this material earth and yet arrestingly abnormal. The plant forms in the background are actually identifiable. Leonardo's *Last Supper* depicts the reactions of the twelve disciples to Christ's words, "One of you shall betray me." This celebrated fresco, exhibiting the artist's complete mastery of technique and draftsmanship, is essentially a study in human psychology—a subject in which Leonardo showed a special interest. The famous *Mona Lisa* is not religious in subject matter; it is the portrait of a real woman. The mysterious half smile—the mouth smiles but the eyes do not—so captivates the viewer that one is likely to overlook other features of the picture, including the hands, which are said to be the most sensitive ever painted.

Michelangelo (1475–1564) is second only to Leonardo da Vinci as a versatile Italian High Renaissance genius. Since Michelangelo was primarily a sculptor, his painting is sometimes called "painted sculpture." Although a Florentine, much of his life was spent in Rome, where he labored in the service of the popes. His greatest painting was the ceiling fresco in the Vatican Sistine Chapel. The hundreds of individual figures, representing nine scenes from the book of Genesis, marvelously blend together into one harmonious whole. Later Michelangelo painted *The Last Judgment* as an altarpiece for the same chapel. The Christ in this picture is more like a pagan giant than the Jesus of medieval Christianity.

Some critics believe Raphael (1483–1520) to be the greatest painter of all time; others say that he merely synthesized the original work of others. The output during his brief life was enormous. His favorite subjects were religious, but his Madonnas were feminine, gracious women and his Christ child pudgy and mischievous. His best-known paintings, the *Sistine Madonna* and the *Madonna of the Chair*, both in oil, well illustrate this secular treatment of a sacred theme. Many of his vivid portraits are of lay princes and tycoons (see Color Plate 13). His monumental fresco *The School of Athens* reveals the veneration felt for the glory of Greece during the Renaissance.

The fourth of the great painters of the Italian High Renaissance was Titian (1477–1576). A citizen of Venice, the most powerful commercial city of the fifteenth and early sixteenth centuries, Titian reflected the humanistic spirit of the Renaissance to an even greater degree than his three renowned contemporaries. Although a

---

FIGURE 25.2 Masaccio, *Expulsion of Adam and Eve* Masaccio, early in the fifteenth century, developed still further the trend toward humanism and naturalism begun a century earlier by Giotto. His *Expulsion of Adam and Eve from the Garden of Eden* depicts a religious subject in a human, realistic, and detailed manner. The nude figures are rounded and individualized. (Alinari/Scala Art Resource)

FIGURE 25.3 Botticelli, *Adoration of the Magi,* ca. 1477 The theme of this painting is religious, with the Christ child in the center. However, the human figures are depicted with individualism, and the models (Lorenzo de Medici kneeling next to the Christ child; the artist, Botticelli, standing proudly to the far left) are secular and contemporary. (Uffizi/Art Resource)

considerable portion of his painting was of religious subjects, his focus was nearly always the pomp and pageantry of the Church rather than its teachings. But a large part of his subject matter was more secular. The wealth and brilliance of Venice, overflowing with cargoes of luxurious fabrics, tapestries, and gems from the east, provided a challenging array of sensuous and colorful material for the artist to depict. And in the use of color, particularly vivid yellows, reds, and blues, Titian had no peer. He painted the hair of his women a reddish gold hue that has come to be called titian. His portraits of some of the great lay personages of the sixteenth century, such as Francis I of France, Emperor Charles V, and Philip II of Spain, are masterful character studies. With Titian, the break with medieval painting begun by Giotto and Masaccio and widened by Leonardo, Michelangelo, Raphael, and many other great Italian painters was completed.

Niccolò Machiavelli: *The Prince*

The Italian Renaissance developed in an environment in which politics took on an increasingly competitive, secular tone. Within each Italian state, parties fought for power while at the same time the states fought one another for advantage. After 1492 Italy was invaded numerous times by Spain, France, and the Holy Roman Empire. These developments are reflected in the life and work of the great Renaissance political theorist Niccolò Machiavelli (1469–1527).

Machiavelli initiated his career in the Florentine civil service in 1498. He rose to important diplomatic posts within the government but was forced into retirement when the Medici family came back to power in 1512. He never gave up hope of returning to favor, and he wrote his most famous work, The Prince *(1513), in part as an application to the Medici rulers for a job in the Florentine government. The book has since become a classic treatise in political theory, above all for the way that it divorces politics from theology and metaphysics. The following selections from* The Prince *illustrate its style and main themes.*

It now remains to be seen what are the methods and rules for a prince as regards his subjects and friends. And as I know that many have written of this, I fear that my writing about it may be deemed presumptuous, differing as I do, especially in this matter, from the opinions of others. But my intention being to write something of use to those who understand, it appears to me more proper to go to the real truth of the matter than to its imagination; and many have imagined republics and principalities which have never been seen or known to exist in reality; for how we live is so far removed from how we ought to live, that he who abandons what is done for what ought to be done, will rather learn to bring about his own ruin than his preservation. A man who wishes to make a profession of goodness in everything must necessarily come to grief among so many who are not good. Therefore it is necessary for a prince, who wishes to maintain

himself, to learn how not to be good, and to use this knowledge and not use it, according to the necessity of the case. . . .

It is not, therefore, necessary for a prince to have all the above-named qualities, but it is very necessary to seem to have them. I would even be bold to say that to possess them and always to observe them is dangerous, but to appear to possess them is useful. Thus it is well to seem merciful, faithful, humane, sincere, religious, and also to be so; but you must have the mind so disposed that when it is needful to be otherwise you may be able to change to the opposite qualities. And it must be understood that a prince, and especially a new prince, cannot observe all those things which are considered good in men, being often obliged, in order to maintain the state, to act against faith, against charity, against humanity, and against religion. And, therefore, he must have a mind disposed to adapt itself according to the wind, and as the variations of fortune dictate, and, as I said before, not deviate from what is good, if possible, but be able to do evil if constrained.

A prince must take great care that nothing goes out of his mouth which is not full of the above-named five qualities, and, to see and hear him, he should seem to be all mercy, faith, integrity, humanity, and religion. And nothing is more necessary than to seem to have this last quality, for men in general judge more by the eyes than by the hands, for every one can see, but very few have to feel. Everybody sees what you appear to be, few feel what you are, and those few will not dare to oppose themselves to the many, who have the majesty of the state to defend them; and in the actions of men, and especially of princes, from which there is no appeal, the end justifies the means. Let a prince therefore aim at conquering and maintaining the state, and the means will always be judged honourable and praised by every one, for the vulgar is always taken by appearances and the issue of the event; and the world consists only of the vulgar, and the few who are not vulgar are isolated when the many have a rallying point in the prince.

Source: From *The Prince and the Discourses* by Niccolò Machiavelli, translated by Luigi Ricci and revised by E. R. P. Vincent (1935), pp. 56, 65–66, by permission of Oxford University Press.

Sculpture

In sculpture, the artist without peer in any age is Michelangelo. It is true that he had Roman copies of the sculpture of Hellenic Greek masters such as Praxiteles and Scopas to guide and inspire him. But the gifted Florentine was no mere copier. The Greek masterpieces, for all their beauty and grace, were idealized types—half human, half divine. Michelangelo and his lesser-known immediate predecessors and contemporaries added a typically Renaissance characteristic to sculpture: individuality. The statues of the Italian Renaissance are not only human beings but also human individuals. Even Michelangelo's *Pietà*, which represents the mother of Jesus holding the dead body of her son as she looks down piteously, is a study in human emotions. The helplessness and hopelessness of the huge, all-engulfing mother display human resignation at the finality of death—not the Christian hope of resurrection and eternal life. His *Moses* portrays the fierce and rugged strength of man, not God. Moses' beard, as crude as icicles beneath a water tank in the month of January, displays the sculptor's ability to distort deliberately for effect. The three-dimensional medium of marble enabled Michelangelo to exploit to the full his favorite subject, the masculine nude. Numerous statues of David are used to convey not only the virile muscular power but also the agile grace of the male animal. His *Dying Slave* (see Figure 25.4) is a sublime portrayal of both the human form and the human spirit struggling to free themselves from bondage. Some critics think that the great sculptor's finest genius is displayed in the companion statues of two members of the Medici family—Lorenzo, the contemplative type, and Giuliano, the man of action. In these two pieces the master craftsman and artist exhibits every technique of sculpture. The work of Michelangelo is probably our best example of the Renaissance glorification of the human being.

The subject of Renaissance sculpture cannot be dismissed without brief mention of the work of Benvenuto Cellini. His work in gold and silver was of an exquisite delicacy that has never been equaled. His most famous larger work is the bronze statue of Perseus holding up the Gorgon's head. In this amazing conglomeration of unrealities, Cellini showed complete disregard of all accepted traditions and standards, yet with

FIGURE 25.4 Michelangelo, *The Dying Slave* The genius of Michelangelo, master sculptor of the Renaissance, is exemplified in this work, *The Dying Slave,* now in the Louvre, which glorifies both the human form and the human spirit. (Courtesy Michigan State University)

happy results. Such bold and original pioneering was typical of the self-confident, secular nature of the Renaissance mind.

Architecture

Renaissance architecture, like Renaissance sculpture, drew heavily from Greek and Roman sources (see Figure 25.5). From Greece by way of Rome came columns (now merely decorative) and horizontal lines; from Rome came the dome, the arches, and the massiveness that character-

FIGURE 25.5 Circle of Piero Della Francesca: An Ideal Town This mid–fifteenth-century townscape painting expresses ideals of Italian Renaissance architecture: geometry, logic, individuality with order, lightness, and spaciousness. (Anderson/Art Reference Bureau)

ized Renaissance buildings. All of these features (except massiveness) represented a revolt against the Gothic architecture of the later Middle Ages, although the Gothic style had never gained much of a foothold in Italy.

The two greatest monuments of Italian Renaissance architecture are the dome of the cathedral in Florence and St. Peter's Basilica in Rome. The Florentine cathedral is essentially Tuscan Gothic. Its ornate rectangular façade and bell tower reflect both Byzantine and Islamic influences. But its most distinguishing feature is its gigantic octagonal dome, designed and constructed by Brunelleschi in the early fifteenth century. This symbol of the grandeur of ancient Rome served as a model for such later great domes as St. Peter's in Rome, St. Paul's in London, and the Capitol building in Washington, D.C.

But the most grandiose achievement of Renaissance architecture is St. Peter's. This magnificent structure was to the Renaissance era what the Pyramids, the Parthenon, the Colosseum, and the Gothic cathedrals were to their respective epochs. It was built by the popes during the sixteenth and early seventeenth centuries at a cost that shook all western Europe religiously and politically. Its numerous architects drew primarily on classical Greek and Roman sources for their inspiration. Even seventeenth-century baroque features eventually entered into its design. Raphael served for a time as chief architect, and Michelangelo designed the dome. One has to

step inside St. Peter's to appreciate the breathtaking grandeur of this awesome structure. Its lofty proportions and gigantic pillars, its brilliant paintings and sculptures, its gold, marble, and mosaic decorations all glorify the material things of this world as well as the spiritual aspects of this world and the next.

Music

Music was another field of art in which many original contributions were made during the Renaissance period, particularly the sixteenth century. Although most of these developments occurred in northern Europe, especially the Netherlands, Italy was a scene of some importance. Instrumental music became popular, and great improvements were made in the instruments. The harpsichord and the violin family of instruments came into existence. Musical techniques such as major and minor modes, counterpoint (the blending of two contrasting melodies), and polyphony (the interweaving of several melodic lines) rapidly developed. The most illustrious musician of the sixteenth century was Palestrina, chief musician to the pope and probably the greatest master of polyphonic music of all time. Although most of the music of the Renaissance still centered about the Church, it was now more sensuous and versatile. Moreover, new secular forms appeared. The madrigal, popular throughout Europe in the late sixteenth century, was a musical rendition of stanzas of secular lyrical poetry. Renaissance musicians laid the foundations for modern classical music in all its major forms—concerto, symphony, sonata, oratorio, and opera.

5. DECLINE

During the sixteenth century, the Italian Renaissance lost some of its vigor and originality. Certainly this loss did not occur overnight. For decades, and even into the seventeenth century, Italy was recognized as a center of the fine arts and cultural sophistication. Italian art, heavily patronized by the Church, retained much of its momentum. However, the center of Renaissance activity was shifting from Italy to northern Europe, paralleling the shift of commerce from the Mediterranean to the Atlantic. When Venice, Florence, and Milan were the most prosperous commercial and banking centers in Europe, they were the most vigorous seats of Renaissance culture. With the shifting of the trade routes to the west, their cultural vigor declined.

Other sixteenth-century developments probably played a role in the decline of the Italian Renaissance. The invasions of Italy by the French, Spanish, and German armies and the general military and political instability of the sixteenth century seem to have contributed to the decline. The flowering of culture and relative political stability in other parts of Europe may have made Italy a less important or attractive cultural center. In any case, cultural momentum shifted northward as the Renaissance spread outside of Italy.

SUGGESTED READING

General

G. A. Brucker, *Renaissance Florence,* rev. ed. (1983). A useful book on Renaissance Florence.

J. Burckhardt, *The Civilization of the Renaissance in Italy* (1867, 1983). A classic that has influenced all subsequent studies of the subject.

P. Burke, *The Italian Renaissance* (1986). A recent interpretation.

J. R. Hale, *Renaissance Europe: The Individual and Society, 1480–1520* (1978). Strong on individualism.

C. Klapiche-Zuber, *Women, Family, and Ritual in Renaissance Italy* (1985). Useful essays on social life and women.

I. Maclean, *The Renaissance Notion of Women* (1980). Assumptions about women by Renaissance intellectuals.

L. Martines, *Power and Imagination: City-States in Renaissance Italy* (1980). A highly respected recent study.

Humanism

Paul O. Kristeller, *Renaissance Thought: The Classic, Scholastic, and Humanistic Strains* (1961). A highly respected study of Renaissance thought.

A. Rabil, ed., *Renaissance Humanism* (1988). A multivolume collection of essays on all aspects of humanism.

Q. Skinner, *Machiavelli* (1981). A solid, well-written account.

C. Trinkaus, *The Scope of Renaissance Humanism* (1983). A detailed survey.

The Fine Arts

James Beck, *Italian Painting of the Renaissance* (1981). A good recent study.

Bernard Berenson, *The Italian Painters of the Renaissance* (1968). A classic.

Sources

B. Castiglione, *The Book of the Courtier* (1976). Contemporary textbook for gentlemanly behavior.

B. Cellini, *Autobiography* (1956). The artist's own account of an adventuresome life.

N. Machiavelli, *The Prince* (1961). A classic of political theory.

P. Taylor, *The Notebooks of Leonardo da Vinci: A New Selection.* Well illustrated.

CHAPTER 26

The Renaissance: The North

FIGURE 26.1 Albrecht Dürer, *The Four Horsemen of the Apocalypse,* ca. 1497–1498 In this woodcut the great German artist Albrecht Dürer exhibits a skill in his engraving and woodcutting that matched the painting genius of his Italian contemporaries Leonardo and Michelangelo. His painting of this apocalyptic scene reveals the piety, mysticism, and concern with death that were important elements of the northern Renaissance. (The Art Museum, Princeton University)

The northern Renaissance occurred later than the Italian Renaissance and was in large measure imported from Italy. Although northern scholars such as Chaucer visited Italy as early as the fourteenth century, it wasn't until the late fifteenth century, when journeys by scholars, students, and merchants to Italy were commonplace, that the Renaissance flowered in the north. The northern Renaissance also had its own roots and characteristics. It was located more in the courts and universities than in large commercial cities. Northern humanism was more intertwined with Christian pietism than in Italy. In a broad sense, the northern Renaissance sought to humanize Christianity, to reconcile the sacred and the secular.

1. NORTHERN HUMANISM

The trend toward humanism as a basic attitude toward life began in earnest in northern Europe in the late fifteenth century. One of the central figures of northern humanism was Johann Reuchlin (1455–1522), a German scholar. After a sojourn in Italy during which he became imbued with the ideas of the Italian humanists, Reuchlin undertook to introduce the new classical learning into Germany. Specifically, he sought to broaden and enrich the university curriculum by establishing the study of the ''un-Christian'' Hebrew and Greek languages and literature. The Church and university interests vested in the medieval order of things attempted to thwart him, invoking the Inquisition to try him on grounds of heresy. Reuchlin fought back courageously and enlisted a large and enthusiastic following. Eventually the pope condemned him to silence. However, the victory really lay with Reuchlin and his humanist supporters. During the first few decades of the sixteenth century the new humanistic curriculum became established in all the major universities of Germany.

Meanwhile, in England a group of Oxford professors was accomplishing with less opposition what Reuchlin had fought for in Germany. John Colet (1467–1519) was the most prominent member of this group. He, too, visited Renaissance Italy. In true northern humanistic fashion he gave a critical and rational slant to his preach-

ing and teaching of the Scriptures at Oxford. Probably the greatest of Colet's contributions to the new learning was the founding of St. Paul's grammar school in London, with a largely classical curriculum. To guarantee its humanistic orientation, he chose as trustees a guild of London merchants. St. Paul's soon became a model for many other such schools throughout England.

The most famous of the early-sixteenth-century English humanists was Sir Thomas More (1478–1535), Lord Chancellor of the Realm. More's *Utopia*, like Plato's *Republic*, blueprinted an earthly, not a heavenly, paradise. In picturing his ideal commonwealth, More indicted the social, religious, and political events of his own time. Utopia was a society in which private property and profits were unknown. Much attention was given to public health and education. The economy was planned and cooperative. War was outlawed except in self-defense. Religious freedom was granted to all but atheists. Although More eventually was to accept death by beheading rather than recognize Henry VIII as head of the English church in place of the pope, his ideal society was ethical and secular. Humans through their own wisdom, he believed, could create their own perfect world here on earth.

Towering above all the other northern humanists was Desiderius Erasmus (1466–1536). Erasmus was born in Rotterdam in the Netherlands, the illegitimate son of a priest. Reared as an orphan, he was educated in a school run by the Brethren of the Common Life, a pietistic order of laymen that taught the Greek and Latin classics and emphasized simple inner piety rather than ritual and formal creed (see Chapter 24). (Martin Luther, the great contemporary and adversary of Erasmus, also attended a school of the Brethren of the Common Life.) At the age of twenty-one Erasmus entered an Augustinian monastery (again like Luther) and was eventually ordained. Instead of serving as a priest, however, he studied his beloved classics—a pursuit he was to continue at the Sorbonne and for the rest of his life.

Erasmus' vast erudition combined with his great personal charm made him a much-sought-after man. His first book was *Adages*, a collection of wise sayings of the Greeks and Romans with his own comments. It was an immediate success, and other books soon followed. His greatest work was *The Praise of Folly*, in which he ridiculed with subtle humor and delightful satire the ignorance, superstition, credulity, and current practices of his day, particularly those connected with the Church. The folly that he praised was a very human lightheartedness, a sense of humor. Wherever Erasmus went—France, England, Italy, Switzerland, Germany, the Netherlands—he was received with admiration and awe. No other individual so advanced the cause of northern humanism by popularizing the study of the Greek and Latin classics.

In addition to popularizing the new humanistic learning north of the Alps, Erasmus is significant in history for at least two other reasons—his influence on religious and social reform and his efforts to humanize and intellectualize Christianity. He was at his best when laughing to scorn the abuses and superstitious practices of the Roman Catholic church. The taking of money from the poor and ignorant masses by wealthy and corrupt clergy, the veneration of relics, and unquestioning belief in the miraculous were in the eyes of Erasmus beneath the contempt of enlightened men and women. But he was clever enough to sheathe his barbs with humor, thus making them more subtle and effective. Erasmus, however, was no Protestant. When Martin Luther first began his attacks on the Roman Catholic church, Erasmus thought that he was merely seeking to correct glaring abuses and hailed him as a fellow spirit. But when Erasmus discovered that the German reformer was primarily interested in doctrinal reform and that the Protestants were as dogmatic as the Roman Catholics, Erasmus would have nothing more to do with him. Nevertheless, Erasmus' incessant attacks on the abuses of organized Christianity undoubtedly encouraged both Protestant and Roman Catholic reformers.

Erasmus made great efforts to humanize Christianity. Although he never did specifically say so, the implication running through his writings is that Jesus was also a human being—a person to emulate. Erasmus would bypass formal creed, dogma, ritual, organization, and seek the "historical" Christ. Erasmus attempted to steer Christianity into a practice of following the example of a humanized Christ, stressing love, piety, civic virtue, and the best of classical values.

2. LITERATURE

During the late fifteenth and early sixteenth centuries Renaissance literature in the North was closely connected to the spirit of northern humanism with its stress on combining classical scholarship and Christian concerns. Scholars and educators such as Ulrich von Hutten (1488–1523) in Germany, Jacques Lefèvre d'Étaples (1454–1536) in France, Francisco Jiménez de Cisneros (1436–1517) in Spain, and William Grocyn (ca.1446–1519) in England helped establish traditions of literary humanism in their countries. During the middle of the sixteenth century Renaissance literature in the north became more distinctly secular. The most important literary developments in the decades from the mid–sixteenth to the early seventeenth centuries were in England, France, and Spain.

The reign of Elizabeth I (1558–1603) was a period of great energy and optimism in England. Elizabeth herself, like a few other elite women of the period, was educated according to the precepts of the Renaissance. All this was reflected in the literary outpourings of the period. England became "a nest of singing birds" such as the world had never seen or heard. Edmund Spenser's *Faerie Queen* (1590) glorified the versatile individual of the Italian humanists, particularly the ideal set forth by Castiglione in his *Book of the Courtier*. Christopher Marlowe (1564–1593) in his brief life wrote human-centered plays of such caliber that some critics think he would have achieved the stature of Shakespeare had he lived. His *Tamburlaine the Great* and *Edward II* treat the worldly drama of royal ambition. The central figure in *The Jew of Malta*, a forerunner of Shylock, is a product of the revived commercial capitalism. *Doctor Faustus* dramatizes the theme, later immortalized by Goethe, of the intellectual who in true Renaissance fashion sold his soul to the devil in return for earthly knowledge and pleasure.

Mightiest of all the writers of the English Renaissance was William Shakespeare (1564–1616). Although his lyrical poetry was beautiful, his most important work was in drama. Here he was heavily indebted to his contemporary, Christopher Marlowe, as well as to the ancient Greek and Roman dramatists. Marlowe developed the blank verse form, which Shakespeare perfected. In plays such as *Hamlet, Macbeth, Othello, King Lear, The Merchant of Venice, As You Like It, Henry IV, Romeo and Juliet*, and *Julius Caesar*, Shakespeare displayed a mastery of every known technique of the dramatic art.

More important for the student of history, he exemplified and dramatized the secular spirit of the Renaissance. The individual is Shakespeare's subject matter. Rugged, distinctive human personalities are the heroes and villains of his plays. No human emotion, aspiration, or psychological conflict escapes his eye. On the whole, Shakespeare, unlike the Greek dramatists, makes each person the master of his or her own fate. Admiration for Greece and Rome, a keen interest in newfound lands, the first stirrings of modern natural science, the commercial revolution and social problems arising from the emergence of the capitalistic middle class, the rise of national monarchy and a national patriotic spirit—all enter into the fabric of the plays.

The two chief figures in French Renaissance literature were François Rabelais (1494–1553) and Michel de Montaigne (1533–1592). Rabelais was a renegade priest, bored physician, and loving student of the classics. Although he stumbled quite by accident and late in life upon his gift for writing, he turned out to be one of the great creative geniuses in the history of literature. His masterpieces are *Pantagruel* and *Gargantua*. They are fantasies about two completely unrestrained giants who wallow and revel unashamedly in sensual pleasures. These works are an open assault on Christian moral standards and restraints. The wit is coarse and lewd and sympathetic toward the frailties of human nature. Rabelais' rich imagery, his marvelous gift of expression, and his graceful artistry combine to make him one of the founders of modern French prose.

Montaigne was a prodigy born of a wealthy family. Like Rabelais, he was an ardent lover of the classics. The result of his life of study and reflection was his *Essays*. Montaigne was a skeptic. To arrive at reliable truth, he believed, one must rid oneself of all religious prejudice. He was a moral and spiritual relativist, rejecting all absolutes. Unlike his successors of the eighteenth-century Enlightenment, he distrusted the authority of human reason. Unable to replace the authority of Christian dogma with any other firm conviction, Montaigne was nearly always negative in his conclusions. But he immensely enjoyed this game of intellectual hide-and-seek. In fact, Montaigne believed that the chief purpose of life is pleasure—not the "eat, drink, and be merry" pleasure of Rabelais, but urbane, sophisticated, restrained, intellectual pleasure. The influence of Montaigne has been enormous—obviously on essayists from Bacon to Emerson and later, but also on the development of modern rationalism in general.

Standing out above all others in Spanish Renaissance literature are Miguel de Cervantes (1547–1616) and Lope de Vega (1562–1635). Cervantes was a contemporary of Shakespeare, the two dying within a few days of each other in 1616. Cervantes' early life, like Shakespeare's, is obscure. In time he became a soldier of fortune, fought heroically and was wounded in the great naval battle of Lepanto with the Turks, suffered a five-year imprisonment in Algeria, and finally served as a quartermaster for Spain's Invincible Armada. In poverty-stricken later life he settled down to write his famous novel *Don Quixote*. This masterpiece of Spanish literature relates with urbane grace and humor the adventures of a confused knight who filled his noble head too full of the lore of chivalry and his groom, Sancho Panza. Sancho, a squat plebeian on a donkey, and Don Quixote, an emaciated knight on a tall, lean horse, go about Spain from one delightfully charming adventure to another. Cervantes' most immediate purpose was to satirize what was left of medieval chivalry. At a deeper level he probes the balance between the idealism of Don Quixote and the realism of Sancho Panza, revealing that there is some of each in all of us. Finally, since all types and classes of people throughout Spain are lucidly portrayed, *Don Quixote* is a valuable historical source for descriptions of life in sixteenth-century Spain.

Lope de Vega wrote a fabulous number of works in practically every known genre. His plays alone exceed in number those of any other writer, whether we accept the writer's own claim to at least eighteen hundred or recognize only the five-hundred-odd plays that can be accounted for today. The secular person, pictured in every conceivable dramatic situation, is the hero of the great Spanish playwright.

FIGURE 26.2 The Gutenberg Bible An illuminated page from the Gutenberg Bible, after a facsimile. This forty-two-line Bible, printed by Johannes Gutenberg in about 1456, is the earliest known book printed by movable type in the Western world. The craftsmanship exhibited by this illustration is remarkable. Gutenberg's invention launched a revolution in communications. (Rare Book Division, New York Public Library, Astor, Lennox and Tilden Foundations)

Thus the writers of the northern Renaissance had much in common. Their chief interests were contemporary human beings and the exciting, rapidly expanding material world around them. They were inspired by the classical literature of Greece and Rome. They were on the whole nationalistic and wrote in the new national vernaculars.

3. PRINTING WITH MOVABLE TYPE

The spread of humanism and literature in general was stimulated by the invention of printing on paper with movable type. In ancient and medieval times manuscripts had been written and copied in longhand on parchment or papyrus, a slow and costly process that greatly retarded the dissemination of knowledge. In the fourteenth century printing from carved wooden blocks came to western Europe from China by way of the Moslem world and Spain. This process too was tedious, costly, and limited. Also from China came paper made of various fibers—silk, cotton, or flax. Paper was a great improvement over parchment or papyrus for purposes of mass production. (Even the art of printing by movable type itself was a Chinese [Korean] invention, although this is not believed to have influenced its invention in the Western world.)

Johannes Gutenberg set up the first practical printing press using movable type in Europe at

FIGURE 26.3 Matthias Grünewald, *The Crucifixion*, ca. 1510–1515 This northern Renaissance painting from the Isenheim Altarpiece by the German artist Grünewald combines a deeply pious subject matter reminiscent of late Gothic traditions with Renaissance perspective and individualism. (Musée Unterlinden, Colmar)

Mainz in western Germany. The Gutenberg forty-two-line Bible printed in about 1456 is the earliest known book to be printed by the new process (see Figure 26.2). The invention was an immediate success and spread quickly to all the other countries of western Europe. It is estimated that by the end of the fifteenth century more than twenty-five thousand separate editions and nearly 10 million individual books had been printed. Printing was now much cheaper, quicker, and more accurate.

Its effects spread beyond a greater access to religious and secular literature. The printing press encouraged the growth of literacy and made the spread of political and commercial documents easier. Cheaply produced pamphlets and books became a medium for social, religious, and political debate. The new availability of written materials made a variety of studies available to women otherwise hindered from formal training. News sheets would make events much more current to readers in the seventeenth and eigh-

teenth centuries. The printing press would prove crucial to the spread of ideas during the scientific revolution and Enlightenment (see Chapters 35 and 36).

4. ART, ARCHITECTURE, AND MUSIC

Northern Renaissance art was influenced by Italian art and shared many of its characteristics, but it had stronger roots in the Christian, pietistic culture of the late Middle Ages. In general the subject matter of paintings was less secular than that of Italian Renaissance paintings. Northern artists tried to bring the concrete details of Christian life into immediate focus and with great emotional impact (see Figure 26.3).

The most noteworthy fifteenth- and sixteenth-century painters in the north were the Flemings (Belgians) and the Germans. The Van Eyck brothers, Hubert and Jan, lived in Ghent in

FIGURE 26.4 Jan van Eyck, *The Virgin and Chancellor Rolin* The van Eyck brothers, Hubert and Jan, of Ghent in the Netherlands, were fifteenth-century contemporaries of Masaccio. This painting illustrates the clear, naturalistic perspective, the precision of line and detail, and the religious theme that were characteristic of northern Renaissance painting. (Scala/Art Resource)

the Flemish Netherlands in the fifteenth century. Like Masaccio, their Italian contemporary, they brought to near completion the transition from medieval to Renaissance painting (see Figure 26.4). Their greatest joint work is *Adoration of the Mystic Lamb*. Not the least of their contributions to painting was the development of oil as a medium. It was from them that Leonardo da Vinci learned to work in this medium, which he perfected in such masterworks as *Mona Lisa* and *Virgin of the Rocks*.

In sixteenth-century Germany, Albrecht Dürer of Nuremberg and Hans Holbein the Younger of Augsburg were the leading painters. Dürer was a master craftsman of delicate and graceful line. Probably for this reason, his woodcuts and engravings are better than his paintings, and in these media he is without peer in any age (see Figure 26.1). Holbein was a skillful sketcher and woodcutter, but he made his greatest contributions in the field of portrait painting. He painted several portraits of Erasmus and illustrated Erasmus' *Praise of Folly* with pen-and-ink drawings. Many of his most productive years were spent in England in the employ of Henry VIII. Among his greatest portraits are those of Henry VIII (see Figure 27.1), Edward VI, Mary Tudor, and Sir Thomas More.

Renaissance architecture was less prominent in the north. The largest Renaissance structure outside Italy is the vast Escorial near Madrid, which Philip II of Spain built as a royal palace and mausoleum. Its rugged massiveness, rectangular shape, and horizontal lines typify the Renaissance style. Some of the best examples of northern Renaissance architecture are the Renaissance wing of the Louvre in Paris and some of the largest châteaux along France's Loire River. This architecture was essentially derivative; the French Renaissance châteaux were really fortresses being played with.

The music capital of the Western world during the Renaissance period was the Netherlands. It was from the Flemings that the Italian Renaissance musicians, including Palestrina, derived much of their knowledge and inspiration (see p. 350).

5. SIGNIFICANCE OF THE RENAISSANCE IN HISTORY

In retrospect, then, it is apparent that the Renaissance was part of a transition from the Middle Ages to the early modern period. In some measure it was a rebirth of the classical civilizations of Greece and Rome, but it was not merely that. There was much in the Renaissance that was fresh and original, and there was a self-consciousness among Renaissance scholars, writers, and artists that they were part of something new.

In some ways the Renaissance represented a new emphasis on secularism and a rejection of the scholastic Christian culture of the Middle Ages, particularly in Italy. Yet in other ways it remained fundamentally a Christian civilization and an era that, in our terms, was quite religious. Indeed, the depth of religious sentiment during the Renaissance, particularly in the north, is revealed by the Reformation.

The intellectual and cultural themes established during the Renaissance would continue to grow throughout the early modern period. As we shall see, their effects would be felt in the politics, the commerce, and the society of Europeans during the sixteenth, seventeenth, and eighteenth centuries.

SUGGESTED READING

General

J. Huizinga, *The Waning of the Middle Ages* (1954). A superb interpretation important for an understanding of the early northern Renaissance. (See also items at the end of Chapter 25.)

Northern Humanism

E. H. Harbison, *The Christian Scholar in the Age of the Reformation* (1956). By a leading scholar in the field.

J. Huizinga, *Erasmus and the Age of the Reformation* (1957). Probably the best single volume on Erasmus.

R. Marius, *Thomas More: A Biography* (1984). A recent study.

M. M. Philips, *Erasmus and the Northern Renaissance,* 2nd ed. (1981). A good general study.

England, France, and Germany

M. Dowling, *Humanism in the Age of Henry VIII* (1986). An informative history of English humanism.

L. Febvre, *Life in Renaissance France* (1977). A highly respected account.

Werner L. Gundersheimer, ed., *French Humanism 1470–1600* (1969). A solid collection of essays.

J. H. Overfield, *Humanism and Scholasticism in Late Medieval Germany* (1984). Focuses on universities.

Lewis Spitz, *The Religious Renaissance of the German Humanists* (1963). Broad and well written.

Art and Printing

Elizabeth Eisenstein, *The Printing Press as an Agent of Change* (1978). A superb, exhaustive interpretive study.

W. Stechow, *Northern Renaissance Art: 1400–1600* (1966). A useful survey.

CHAPTER 27
The Rise of National States

FIGURE 27.1 Hans Holbein the Younger, *Portrait of Henry VIII,* **1540** Henry VIII and his father, Henry VII, were two of the most forceful of the new monarchs who arose in Europe between 1450 and 1550. These monarchs increased the power of the central government as well as their own personal power. (Alinari/Art Resource)

In the fifteenth and sixteenth centuries, monarchs in western Europe succeeded in creating powerful national states. These monarchs, often referred to by historians as the "new monarchs," aggressively built their dynastic power in three main ways. First, they undermined their competitors, above all the feudal barons. Monarchs turned to members of the lesser nobility and the middle class for backing. Second, they developed new methods of financial and administrative support. National taxes gave monarchs new, independent sources of income, and expanding governmental bureaucracies staffed by officials who owed allegiance to the monarchs extended royal authority throughout the land. Third, they brought the Church more under their command. In some cases they gained the right to appoint church officers within their lands; in other cases they actually established new official churches.

The new monarchs used other methods as well and took advantage of developments occurring at that time. Applying principles of dynastic succession, they married to expand and unify their lands. They increased their income by promoting and tapping into reviving commerce, which brought with it a moneyed economy and a prosperous middle class. With their greater financial resources, new monarchs established standing professional armies that could use the new military tactics and technology that were lessening the importance of the independent mounted armored knight. They suppressed internal violence and made law enforcement more the responsibility of their own agents. To legalize their growing power, the monarchs utilized the principles of Roman law, which considered kings to be sovereigns in whose hands the welfare of all the people was placed.

The most important of these new monarchs arose in Spain, France, and England. Although other factors retarded unification in Italy and Germany until the nineteenth century, Spain, France, and England were already well on their way to becoming powerful national states in the late fifteenth century.

1. SPAIN

Spain became the most powerful and influential of the new states at the opening of the early modern era. The energy and enthusiasm that Spain displayed at this time may be attributed in part, at least, to her long and finally successful struggle against the Moors. By the middle of the thirteenth century the Moors had been driven out of the entire Iberian peninsula except for the southernmost province of Granada. Furthermore, the numerous medieval feudal holdings in what is now Spain had been consolidated into four large kingdoms—Castile, Aragon, Granada, and Navarre (south of the Pyrenees). The marriage of Ferdinand of Aragon and Isabella of Castile in 1469 united to some extent the two largest kingdoms. During their reign (1474–1516)[1] Granada and Navarre were conquered and ties between their lands were strengthened. Thus, within a forty-seven-year span from 1469 to 1516 the Spanish national state was created.

Ferdinand and Isabella strove for political and religious unity. In order to suppress the jealous nobility further, they allied themselves with *hidalgos*—members of the lesser nobility—and the middle class, leaning heavily on them for financial and administrative assistance. In return, the joint sovereigns did everything in their power to advance their fortunes. Vigorous enforcement of law and order, stabilization of the currency, building of roads and bridges, tariff protection of home industries—all served to advance the economic prosperity of Spain in general and the middle class in particular. This commercial expansion was greatly enhanced in 1492 with the "discovery" of the New World in the name of Spain. The ensuing profits and loot further strengthened the hands of the Spanish sovereigns by freeing them from dependence on the Cortes (the representative bodies dominated by the nobility) for funds.

In religious affairs, also, Ferdinand and Isabella gained power over the Church and unified their country. They acquired the right to appoint bishops, reformed the Church, and gained access to some of its wealth. By the end of their reign, the Church in Spain was in effect at the command of the Spanish state. Against the two non-Christian groups in their realm, the Jews and the Moslems, the "Catholic sovereigns" waged a cam-

---

[1]Isabella ruled Castile from 1474 to 1504, and Ferdinand ruled Aragon from 1479 to 1516.

paign of conversion or expulsion. The Jews had long been objects of hatred and persecution in Christian Europe. In part this hatred derived from religious differences, but there was also an economic factor. Church laws against usury had given the Jews a monopoly on moneylending, a precarious but often profitable activity. The envy and hatred of the Christians led to periodic outbreaks of violence. In the late fourteenth century, an outbreak of unusual severity forced many Spanish Jews to seek safety in outward conversion. But these Marranos, as the pseudoconverts were called, were the object of increasing suspicion. Finally, Ferdinand and Isabella, despite some reluctance, introduced the Inquisition into Spain. At the mercy of this court, the Marranos were terrorized by imprisonment, torture, and loss of life and property. In 1492 the remaining Jews were ordered to leave the country. The exiles thus banished (estimated to be in the neighborhood of one hundred fifty thousand) took much of their wealth and all their economic energy and skills with them.[2]

Shortly afterward the Moslems suffered a similar fate. Upon surrendering their last stronghold in Granada, in 1492, they had been promised religious freedom in return for submission to the political authority of the Spanish crown. However, again the "Catholic sovereigns" yielded to the increasing pressure of religious intolerance, and in 1502 the Moslems were ordered to accept Christianity or leave Spain. Although thousands did leave, even more thousands remained and went through the farce of outward conversion. But these "converts," called Moriscos, only delayed their fate. In the two succeeding reigns they too were persecuted and expelled.

Spain, then, was unified religiously under the crown, but at an economic and intellectual cost. Nevertheless, territorially consolidated and politically unified by Ferdinand and Isabella and their successor, Charles V (see p. 368), enriched by the wealth of the New World, and inspired by the crusading zeal of a purified and triumphant religion, Spain was to be the most powerful and influential of the new national states

during the first century of the early modern era (see Figure 27.2 and Map 27.2).

2. FRANCE

The reign of Louis XI (1461–1483), known as the "Spider King," may be said to mark the beginning of France as a modern national state. Louis came to the throne of France eight years after the end of the Hundred Years' War with England. His predecessor, Charles VII, had used the war emergency to obtain powers over taxation (*taille*) and a standing army for the crown. During the last phase of the war a great upsurge of French national spirit, aided by the exploits of Joan of Arc, made possible, at long last, the expulsion of the English invaders. Louis XI put these inherited advantages to clever use. First of all, he set out to crush the power of the feudal nobility who had taken advantage of the royal distress during the Hundred Years' War to assert their virtual independence of the crown. By craft and direct military force he broke up the league the insubordinate nobility had formed against him and reduced the individual nobles to submission. In order to achieve this goal, Louis utilized the rising middle class. In return for its support he placed many members of this class in his councils and in key administrative posts, enabling some to enter the nobility. He also did what he could to foster commerce and industry. Roads, harbors, and waterways were improved. Shipbuilding, commerce, and industry were encouraged by royal subsidies and protective regulation.

Louis XI virtually completed the territorial consolidation of what would become the French national state (see Map 27.1). He brought province after province under direct royal control, until by the end of his reign France had acquired most of its modern territory. This expansive movement brought Louis XI into conflict with Charles the Bold of Burgundy. Charles the Bold (perhaps "the Rash" would have been a more accurate title) had inherited rich and strategically located territories that included the Netherlands, the duchy of Burgundy, and the free county of Burgundy. These he hoped to consolidate into a great national state—the old Middle Kingdom of Charlemagne's grandson Lothair—between France and Germany. Had he succeeded in doing

---

[2]The Jews had earlier been expelled from England, France, and the German states.

FIGURE 27.2 Ferdinand and Isabella A coin of Ferdinand and Isabella, sovereigns of Spain. Spain was the most powerful of the new national monarchies and her coins enjoyed wide circulation in Europe and predominance in the Spanish and English empires in North and South America during the sixteenth, seventeenth, and eighteenth centuries. The Spanish piece-of-eight was commonly called the "dollar," and in 1787 the dollar was adopted by the United States as its standard unit of value. (American Numismatic Society)

so, the course of history might have been changed significantly. However, Charles the Bold was killed battling the Swiss, and his successor, Mary, was unable to prevent Louis XI from seizing the duchy of Burgundy, Picardy, and part of Flanders. (The abortive Burgundian "Middle Kingdom" has been a battleground between France and Germany throughout much of the modern period.) Thus consolidated and enlarged, France was to play a dominant role in European affairs in the centuries that followed.

Louis XI's schemes, however, did not include the betterment of the condition of the lower classes. Having paid for his ambitious programs with heavy taxes but having received little in return, the lower classes remained disaffected and discontented.

3. ENGLAND

Early modern times, so far as English history is concerned, may be said to have begun with the reign of Henry VII (1485–1509), the first of the Tudor dynasty. The political unity of the English national state had been brought about as early as 1066 by William the Conqueror (aided to a considerable degree by geography). However, the feudal system, with its decentralization of administration and society, the Hundred Years' War with France (1337–1453), and the Wars of the Roses (1455–1484) between the rival houses of Lancaster and York, had by the last quarter of the fifteenth century brought England to a state of turmoil bordering on anarchy. Henry Tudor acquired the English throne by victory on the battlefield over the Yorkist King Richard III, who was slain. Himself a member of the Lancastrian family, Henry ended the bloody dynastic feud by marrying Elizabeth of York.

The most pressing task confronting the strongwilled new monarch was the suppression of the turbulent nobility. The great feudal barons had taken advantage of the decades of civil war and the long rule of a weak king prior to the war to defy royal authority. They retained their own private armies and overawed the local courts. At once and with great vigor Henry VII proceeded

Map 27.1 **THE UNIFICATION OF FRANCE, 1461–1527** During the first half of the fifteenth century, France was divided and the monarchy was weak. As indicated by this map, between 1461 and 1527 French monarchs succeeded in bringing most of modern France under their control.

Map 27.2 EUROPE, 1526 This map indicates how widespread the Hapsburg dominions were under Charles V. In addition, Charles V exercised some indirect control over most of the territory within the Holy Roman Empire as its selected emperor. As the Spanish monarch, his lands included Spanish holdings in the New World. The map also shows France nearly surrounded by its Hapsburg rivals and the Islamic Ottoman Empire was a threat to Christian Europe.

to enforce the laws against livery and maintenance,[3] thereby destroying the illegal feudal armies. Since the regular local courts were too weak to proceed against the nobility, Henry set up his own Court of Star Chamber, which, backed by the royal army, was able to overawe the most powerful barons and bring them to justice and to submission to the crown.

In these undertakings Henry VII had the support of the lesser gentry and the middle and lower classes, all of whom yearned for peace and order. The middle class, particularly, desired stability for the sake of its growing business activi-

---

[3]So called from the practice of the peasantry's wearing the lord's badge or livery, signifying membership in his private army, in return for the lord's promise to maintain (support) them in courts of justice.

ties, and it was with this class that the Tudors allied themselves. Henry selected many of his counselors and administrators from the ranks of the bourgeoisie. He made favorable commercial treaties with the Netherlands, Denmark, and even Venice, the jealous queen of the rich eastern Mediterranean trade. Navigation acts were passed to protect English shippers. Henry's frugality and careful collection and handling of revenues not only were good business but also freed the king of dependence upon Parliament for funds.

Henry VII died in 1509, but he passed along to his glamorous son, Henry VIII (see Figure 27.1), a united and orderly national state and a well-filled treasury. And under his granddaughter, Elizabeth, England rose to a position of first-rate importance in European affairs.

4. ITALY, GERMANY, AND THE HOLY ROMAN EMPIRE

Italian- and German-speaking people have played a vital role in European history, particularly in making important contributions to the arts and sciences. However, they did not achieve political unity at the opening of the early modern period, and that disunity created political problems that persisted into the nineteenth and twentieth centuries.

At the opening of the early modern period the Italian peninsula was divided into five major independent states: the Kingdom of Naples, the Papal States, Florence (Tuscany), Venice, and Milan. The Kingdom of Naples, the poorest of the Italian states, occupied the southern third of the peninsula and at times the large island of Sicily (see Map 27.3). During the fifteenth and sixteenth centuries it was a bone of contention over which France and Spain repeatedly fought. The Papal States occupied the central portion of the peninsula. These states were ruled by the pope not only as a supreme pontiff but also as political head. Florence and Venice, republics in name, were dominated by rich banking and commercial families. Milan, another thriving center of commerce, was ruled by an autocratic duke.

The main reason for Italian disunity in the early modern era was the long tradition of independence among the city-states. There the spirit of local rather than national pride and loyalty prevailed. Instead of forging common bonds, the major Italian city-states such as Florence, Venice, and Milan competed with one another for control over the smaller ones, such as Ferrara, Modena, and Mantua. Possibilities of unification under the papacy or the Holy Roman emperor were undermined by a long history of struggles between these two powers. For a while, the Treaty of Lodi (1454–1455), which allied Florence, Milan, and Naples, and alliances between Venice and the Papal States created a balance of power and some stability on the Italian peninsula. But this stability broke down in 1494. In the following decades Italy was repeatedly invaded by France and the Holy Roman Empire. The political division of the Italians in an age of powerful national states continued to be a standing invitation to aggression against them.

During the fifteenth century German-speaking peoples remained split up into more than three hundred virtually independent units. The only political bond among them was the impotent government of the Holy Roman Empire. This ramshackle institution—a survival of the organization set up by Charlemagne in 800 and revived by Otto the Great in 962—purported to be a restoration of the old Roman Empire, but it never was. In the Middle Ages, when the Spanish, French, and English sovereigns had been consolidating their territories and their authority, the German emperors had been frittering away their time and energy trying to bring Italy under their control. While they were away from Germany on these quixotic ventures, the local feudal barons had conspired against them, consolidated their own power, and built up hereditary states of their own within the empire. Meanwhile, territory after territory had slipped from under the emperor's control, until by the opening of the early modern period the Holy Roman Empire included for all practical purposes only the German-speaking states plus Czech-speaking Bohemia.

Eventually seven of the emperor's most prominent subjects gained the right to elect him. This elective feature not only diminished the prestige of the emperor but also forced candidates to bribe the electors and bargain and promise away any chance of strengthening the imperial office. Since the emperor had no sure income,

THE FIVE GREAT POWERS

Republic of Florence
Duchy of Milan
Kingdom of Naples
Papal States
Venetian Republic

Map 27.3 ITALY, 1454 Italy was unable to overcome her political divisions, with the large but weak Kingdom of Naples controlled by outside powers, the center controlled by popes opposed to national unification, and the rich, urbanized north divided among competing states.

he had no military force with which to enforce his will. Even to defend the empire, he was forced to call upon his subject princes to furnish troops. The lawmaking and taxing powers lay in the hands of the Diet, which was composed of three houses: the house of electors, the house of lesser princes, and the house of representatives of the free imperial cities. The Diet had no regular time or place of meeting and was seldom able to reach agreement on any important question. In the late fifteenth century an imperial court was set up to settle disputes between member states. However, lacking any means of enforcing its decisions, this instrument too proved ineffective.

The one factor that gave any semblance of vitality to the Holy Roman Empire was the Hapsburg family. A Hapsburg was first elected em-

peror in 1273. After 1438, with only one brief exception, no one but a Hapsburg was elected until the empire finally died at the hands of Napoleon in 1806. By marriage and diplomacy, the Hapsburgs expanded their original Austrian lands until at the opening of the early modern period they possessed one of the largest and richest dynastic estates in Europe. Although, therefore, the Holy Roman emperor as emperor was virtually powerless, as head of the house of Hapsburg he was one of the most influential of monarchs. Nevertheless, all efforts of the Hapsburgs to strengthen the central government of the empire foundered on the rocks of German particularism—the local interests of the jealous princes.

During most of the first half of the sixteenth century the house of Hapsburg was headed by

FIGURE 27.3 Emperor Charles V This sixteenth-century engraving by Sichem shows Emperor Charles V with symbols of the Holy Roman Empire: sword and crossed globe. (The Bettmann Archive)

Emperor Charles V (see Figure 27.3). Charles V inherited from his parents and four grandparents a vast array of territories and claims. From his grandfather Maximilian he inherited the Hapsburg provinces generally spoken of as Austria, to which were added in Charles' lifetime Hungary, Bohemia, Moravia, and Silesia. As a Hapsburg, he also inherited a good claim to the imperial crown of the Holy Roman Empire. From his grandmother Mary he inherited the Burgundian lands: the free county of Burgundy (Franche-Comté), the Netherlands, Luxembourg, Flanders, Artois, and claims to the duchy of Burgundy and Picardy, which had been seized by Louis XI. From his grandfather Ferdinand he received Aragon, the Kingdom of Naples, and numerous islands in the Mediterranean. From his grandmother Isabella he received Castile and a claim to the entire Western Hemisphere based on the papal Line of Demarcation (1493) and the Treaty of Tordesillas (1494). And from Ferdinand and Isabella jointly, he inherited Granada and Spanish Navarre.

The very size of Charles V's far-flung holdings spelled perpetual trouble (see Map 27.2). The language problem alone was appalling. To this were added differences in local customs, tastes, and eventually religion. Moreover, Charles V was sure to become involved in all the major international conflicts of Europe. Born and reared in the Netherlands, Charles was accepted in Spain only after a serious opposition and open revolt. His efforts to strengthen the government of the Holy Roman Empire and to raise money and troops there were frustrated by the local German princes. Finally, the Lutheran revolt further split the empire and completely shattered the personal power of Charles in Germany.

5. INTERNATIONAL RIVALRIES, 1516–1559

The rise of national states failed to bring peace to Europe. The national monarchs, supported by the bourgeoisie, had justified their own aggrandizement on the grounds that it was necessary to end the interminable feudal wars, and they had in fact established a large measure of internal law and order. However, the little feudal wars were followed by big national and dynastic wars. Although these monarchs established modern diplomatic institutions (earlier developed by the Italians in the fifteenth century), such as permanent ambassadors, they also utilized larger armies and new military technology in their wars.

Throughout the sixteenth century international strife revolved around the house of Hapsburg. Charles V found himself almost continually at war with Francis I of France. Each feared the other's power. Francis I had continued the process initiated by his predecessors of increasing the power of the French monarchy, above all by securing new revenues through the sale of governmental offices, by swelling the state bureaucracy, and by gaining the right to appoint France's bishops and abbots. Francis vigorously contested Charles' election as Holy Roman Emperor. They fought over conflicting territorial claims in Italy and the Burgundian lands and along the French-Spanish border. Charles won nearly all the battles, but he was never able to make his victories permanent.

The relations between Charles of Hapsburg and England were limited to a personal family quarrel. When Henry VIII sought an annulment of his marriage to Catherine of Aragon, the aunt of Charles V, Charles used his influence with the pope to block the proceedings, thus touching off a chain of events that ended with Henry taking over the Church in England and separating it from the Roman Catholic church. It was under Charles' son, Philip II, that conflict between Spain and England was brought to a climax.

Among Charles V's more concrete achievements were his marriage to Isabella of Portugal, which brought about a brief union of Spain and Portugal under Philip II, and his repulse of the Ottoman Turks. The Ottoman Turks had migrated to Asia Minor from Central Asia in the thirteenth century, converted to Islam, and by the beginning of the sixteenth century had built an empire that extended from Egypt to the Danube. Under Suleiman the Magnificent (1520–1566), their ablest ruler, they crushed the Hungarians at Mohacs (1526), swept across Hungary, and in 1529 laid seige to Vienna, the capital city of Hapsburg Austria. At the same time they con-quered all of North Africa as far west as Morocco, and their fleets dominated the Mediterranean. It was feared that all western Christendom might fall to the Moslems. At this point, Charles V rallied the forces of the empire and the Hapsburg provinces and drove the Turks back into Hungary. His captains also administered some defeats to the Moslem Barbary pirates in the western Mediterranean.

In 1555 Charles V began to divide his holdings between his son, Philip II, and his brother, Ferdinand. To Philip he gave the Burgundian provinces and Spain, with its appanages in Italy, the Mediterranean, and the New World. To Ferdinand he gave the Austrian provinces and successfully promoted Ferdinand's candidacy to the crown of the Holy Roman Empire. Henceforth there were two branches of the Hapsburg dynasty—Austrian and Spanish—both of which would long continue to play important roles in European and world history.

In 1559 the Treaty of Cateau-Cambrésis ended the dynastic wars between the Hapsburgs and the French Valois kings. Spain gained dominance in Italy, the center of power in Europe shifted to Spain, and a new era of revolts and wars entwining religion and politics unfolded.

SUGGESTED READING

General—The Fifteenth and Sixteenth Centuries

B. Guenée, *States and Rulers in Later Medieval Europe* (1985). Analyzes the forces underlying Europe's state system.

De Lamar Jensen, *Renaissance Europe: Age of Recovery and Reconciliation* (1981). A good recent treatment.

Eugene F. Rice, Jr., *The Foundations of Early Modern Europe, 1460–1559* (1970). The best general survey of the period, with an excellent bibliography.

The New National Monarchies

M. V. C. Alexander, *The First of the Tudors: A Study of Henry VII and His Reign* (1980). A good biography.

J. H. Elliott, *Imperial Spain, 1469–1716* (1964). An excellent account of Spanish history during this period.

A. Goodman, *The New Monarchy: England, 1471–1534* (1988). Brief and insightful on the Tudor monarchy.

H. Kamen, *Spain 1469–1714* (1983). A useful survey.

R. J. Knect, *Francis I* (1982). An authoritative study.

J. H. Shennan, *The Origins of the Modern European State* (1974). An excellent brief analysis.

Italy, Germany, and the Holy Roman Empire

M. F. Alvarez, *Charles V* (1975). A well-written biography of this outstanding figure.

G. Benecke, *Society and Politics in Germany, 1500–1750* (1974). Early chapters cover the period well.

D. Hay and J. Law, *Italy in the Age of the Renaissance* (1989). A good recent survey.

H. B. Koenigsberger, *The Hapsburgs and Europe: 1516–1660* (1971). A solid account of Hapsburg rule.

International Rivalries

J. R. Hale, *War and Society in Renaissance Europe* (1986). Relates war to political and social developments of the period.

CHAPTER 28

European Expansion, Commercial Capitalism, and Social Change

FIGURE 28.1 Columbus Discovers the New World This illustration is from a letter of Columbus to the treasurer of the king of Spain, published in Basel a year after his first voyage. Here the Spaniards are offering the Indians gifts as they approach the West Indian island. The Indians are portrayed as naked and perhaps even childlike, emphasizing the European perception of them as lesser, uncivilized beings. Pictures such as this excited the wonder and greed of many Europeans. (NYPL Picture Collection)

The rise of national states was closely associated with the expansion of Europe and new economic development. The monarchs who created national states supported voyages of discovery and the overseas conquests that resulted. They took advantage of the wealth that poured in to finance their growing governments and their wars. They also allied themselves with the rising middle class against the feudal aristocracy. The strength of this middle class lay in its commercial wealth and its use of capitalistic methods to gain that wealth. Together, this European expansion and economic development represented a new level of power and wealth that would make Europe dominant over large parts of the globe.

1. THE AGE OF DISCOVERY

In the late fifteenth and early sixteenth centuries European mariners made a series of daring voyages in which they "discovered" not only the New World but also new and much better routes to the East (see Map 28.1). These voyages were made possible by a number of recent developments. Important improvements in the technology of shipping and navigation were being made. New armaments and military tactics gave Europeans advantages over those resisting them. Commercial and organizational skills increased the chances of success for these risky voyages. The governments of the national states along the Atlantic coast promoted these voyages and provided needed financial support. Their principal motive was a desire to bypass the Venetians, the Moslems, and the land barriers that separated them from the riches of the East. But there was also a powerful outward impetus in the spirit of inquiry and adventure kindled by the Renaissance interest in the secular world and in the Christian missionary zeal that had always been a spur to expansion.

The first to begin these voyages in the fifteenth century were the Portuguese. During the first half of the fifteenth century, Prince Henry the Navigator (1394–1460) established a school of navigation and base of operations on the southwestern tip of Portugal from which he sent expeditions down the west coast of Africa. In addition to curiosity, his motives were mercenary and religious: He wanted to capture the gold trade in western Africa and hoped to find the legendary Christian kingdom of Prester John. A broader goal of this Portuguese effort was to find a new route around Africa to India. Pushing steadily down the coast of West Africa, the Portuguese developed a lucrative trade in gold, ivory, sugar, and slaves. In 1488 Portuguese explorers rounded the Cape of Good Hope. In 1498 Vasco da Gama, in what was probably the greatest voyage in the history of navigation, reached India, the object of the quest. Vasco da Gama was out of sight of land ninety-three days—three times as long as Columbus on his voyage to the New World. That the Portuguese knew what they were up to is proved by the fact that Vasco da Gama's return cargo sold for sixty times the cost of the expedition. These glad tidings sent a host of Portuguese adventurers hurrying to the East Indies, where they carved out a huge commercial and political empire. One of these adventurers, Pedro Cabral, swinging too far westward, touched the eastern bulge of South America, thus laying the basis for Portugal's claim to Brazil. With their discovery of this all-water route to the East, the Portuguese broke the Arab and Venetian monopoly over the spice trade. From that point on, the center of commercial activity shifted westward toward the Atlantic seaboard.

Meanwhile, Spain was sending its mariners westward, for by the late fifteenth century most educated people in western Europe assumed that the earth was round, although they greatly underestimated its size. Many navigators therefore believed that the East Indies could be reached by sailing west. The first European to attempt it was Christopher Columbus. (Nothing had come of the tenth-century voyages to Greenland and northern America of the roving Norsemen Eric the Red and Leif Ericson.) Columbus was born in Genoa but moved to Portugal. When, however, Portugal failed to support his proposed westward voyage, he turned to Queen Isabella of Castile, who gave him the necessary backing. His three ships touched a West Indian island on October 12, 1492 (see Figure 28.1). Thinking that the West Indies were islands off the east coast of Asia, Columbus made three further voyages in the hope of bypassing these barriers and sailing on to his real goal, the East Indies. Instead, he

Map 28.1 EXPLORATION AND CONQUEST, FIFTEENTH AND SIXTEENTH CENTURIES This map shows the routes taken by some of the early explorers. It indicates some of the distinctions between the Portuguese and Spanish empires—the Portuguese concentrated in Africa and the East and focused primarily on sea power and trading posts; the Spanish concentrated in the New World and focused primarily on conquest and colonization. Early English and French efforts were more limited and farther north.

was turned back by the South and Central American mainlands and died disappointed, not having realized the magnitude of his discovery.

But others soon realized it, and in the first half of the sixteenth century Spanish expeditions to the New World multiplied. In 1493 the pope drew a line of demarcation dividing the non-Christian world between Spain and Portugal. This line was somewhat altered in favor of Portugal the following year by the Treaty of Tordesillas. Since all of North and South America except the eastern part of Brazil and most of Greenland fell to Spain, the Spanish sailors continued to move westward. Juan Ponce de León,

Hernando de Soto, and Juan Vásquez Coronado explored the southern part of what is now the United States. Balboa crossed the Isthmus of Panama and looked out upon the Pacific Ocean. In 1519 Ferdinand Magellan set out around the world by way of the Strait of Magellan. Although he himself was killed in the Philippines, in 1522 one of his ships completed the circuit. Also in 1519 Hernando Cortez began the conquest of the Aztec Empire in Mexico. In 1531–1532 Francisco Pizarro conquered the Inca Indians in Peru.

The other two national states, England and France, were relatively inactive in discovery and exploration during the fifteenth and early sixteenth centuries. The English crown did, however, sponsor voyages to northern North America by the Italian mariner John Cabot in 1497–1498. These voyages became the basis for England's claims to North America, where England later built a great empire. The French government sponsored Jacques Cartier, who in 1535 sailed up the St. Lawrence to what is now Montreal and claimed Canada for France. Nonetheless, it was not until the seventeenth century that Spain and Portugal were replaced as the world's leading imperial powers.

2. THE FOUNDING OF THE SPANISH NEW WORLD EMPIRE

Although much of the Western Hemisphere at the beginning of the sixteenth century was sparsely inhabited by native or "Indian" tribes, the Spaniards encountered two highly organized societies: those of the Aztecs in Mexico and the Incas in Peru.

The first inhabitants of the Western Hemisphere are generally believed to have immigrated from Asia across the Bering Strait some 10,000–20,000 years ago and perhaps much earlier. They organized into numerous tribes throughout North, Central, and South America.

The first of these tribes to build a highly organized society were probably the Olmecs, who flourished between 1200 B.C. and 400 B.C. in southeastern Mexico, but little is known of this civilization. Other societies developed, but perhaps the best known of these early civilizations was the Maya in southeastern Mexico and Central America. Between A.D. 300 and 900, the Maya developed large urban religious centers. Their writing was a combination of pictures and ideographs. Their best art was brightly colored pottery, gems, gold and silverware, and sculpture. Probably their most remarkable creations were a system of mathematics based on the decimal (actually vigesimal) system and a calendar based on astronomy, both of which were in advance of those used in contemporary Europe. Their massively walled stone cities were connected by elaborately paved roads. Between about A.D. 700 and 900 the Mayan civilization collapsed, perhaps because of a combination of increasing warfare and agricultural exhaustion—the reasons

are unclear. Between 950 and 1200 the Toltecs gained control over what had been some Mayan territory and lands further north.

In the fourteenth century the warlike Aztecs came down from the north and founded a city on an island in Lake Tezcoco—the present Mexico City. From this base they formed alliances that enabled them to conquer and organize a military empire or confederacy comprising most of what is now southern and central Mexico. Theirs was the gift of military and political organization. They developed an elaborate, though stern, system of justice. The Aztecs borrowed many aspects of their culture and religion from previous civilizations. Their religion was important and highly organized. Several thousand priests, both regular and secular, tended the impressive temple and supervised education and morals. The numerous gods were headed by the terrible war god, who demanded human sacrifice, usually prisoners of war. And yet the rank-and-file Aztecs were gentle lovers of poetry and art. Flourishing commerce, agriculture, and mining added to the wealth obtained by conquest.

An even more colorful civilization was that of the Incas on the Andean Plateau of South America. In the fourteenth century the Inca Indians began to extend their sway over their neighbors until their empire covered an area fifteen hundred miles long and three hundred miles wide—including present-day Ecuador, Peru, and parts of Bolivia and Chile. An elaborate system of roads and communications tied this vast and lofty empire together. The all-powerful Inca ruler was treated as a god. However, he had a body of advisers and administrators chosen from the upper classes. The state claimed control over all land and production. The regimented lower classes did all the work under close supervision and shared from the common stores. A high degree of specialization was practiced. Agriculture was well advanced, and huge terracing and irrigation projects had been developed to overcome the difficulties of the Andean terrain. Religious worship, particularly of the sun god, was an important feature of national life. Outstanding were Incan pottery, architecture, textiles, and gold and silver ornamental objects.

The native American civilizations were no match for the marauding Europeans. Spanish military men, particularly those of the lesser no-

FIGURE 28.2 The Aztec Perception of the Spanish Although there are many Spanish records of the Spaniards' arrival and explorations in the New World, this Aztec manuscript (ca. 1519–1522) is one of the few surviving Indian versions of the coming of the Europeans. This illustration shows Cortez arriving in Mexico. Note the depiction of some of the crucial elements of Cortez' conquest: the sword, the horse, the flag, and the cross. (Biblioteca Apostolica Vaticana, Rome)

bility (*hidalgos*), were part of a centuries-old tradition of crusading for Church, crown, and profit. Cortez, with a band of some six hundred soldiers and eighteen horses, overcame the Aztecs by a combination of alliances, treachery, tactics, weapons, and determination. He took advantage of divisions and hostilities between the Aztecs and the subject tribes as well as the Aztec belief that the Spaniards were ancient gods whose return had long been expected. Once inside the capital city, the Spaniards were too strong to be expelled. They slaughtered and looted the poorly armed Aztecs without mercy (see Figure 28.2).

Even more spectacular was the conquest of the Incas. Like Cortez, Pizarro used disunity within the Incan Empire as well as trickery and brutality to defeat the Incas. At one point, Pizarro enticed the Incan emperor into a conference. At a given signal Pizarro's small but well-armed band of Spanish soldiers fell upon the splendidly dressed but primitively armed Incan troops and slew them by the thousands. Pizarro promised to free the Incan chieftain in return for a ransom of gold objects sufficient to fill a room seventeen by twenty-two feet to a height of nine feet, plus a larger amount of silver. This ransom was collected and paid, but Pizarro, who had never really intended to free the emperor, had him put to death anyway.

Spanish administrators soon replaced these conquerors, and throughout the sixteenth century Spaniards flocked to the New World. By 1607, when the first permanent English colony was founded in North America, a quarter of a million Spaniards had settled in the vast Spanish Empire stretching from what is now Arizona to Cape Horn. A number of distinguished missions and cathedrals had been erected, and several thriving universities had been founded. The native civilizations had been almost wholly destroyed and replaced by the Christian civilization of Spain.

3. CAPITALISM AND THE COMMERCIAL REVOLUTION

The discovery of the New World and of all-water routes to the Far East fueled an expansion of European commerce that was already under way. A crucial aspect of this expansion was the development of capitalistic methods. The use of capitalistic methods and the scale of commercial growth was so great that the term *commercial revolution* is used to describe it.

The term *capitalism*, stripped to its barest essentials, means a system whereby private individuals put money to work to make more money. Individuals, competing in a market to maximize their profits, determine what to produce, how to produce it, and what price to charge. It involves, among other things, private property, the profit motive, a substantial amount of free enterprise, the hiring of labor for wages, and the lending of money for interest.

Elements of capitalism had been in existence for centuries, but to a lesser degree and in much more limited form than during the sixteenth century. During most of the Middle Ages agriculture operated at only a subsistence level and was carried out under feudal restrictions. Commerce was a trickle of luxuries for the rich and necessities such as iron, implements, and salt. Guilds hampered commercial and industrial enterprises. The Church supported the concept of the "fair price" rather than competitive pricing and frowned on the lending of money for interest (usury).

During the eleventh century, commercial activities began to revive, and by the thirteenth century a pronounced recovery was under way. The Crusades contributed to this revival. The huge movement of men and supplies from western Europe to the Holy Land enriched the merchants and shippers of Venice and other Italian cities. Some of them set up permanent trading posts in the Near East and introduced the luxuries of the materially more advanced Moslem and Byzantine worlds to western Europe. The Fourth Crusade, which the Venetians diverted to the looting of Constantinople, was particularly fruitful. The Venetians seized not only a great hoard of gold and silver in the stricken eastern imperial capital but also a large part of the territory of the Byzantine Empire itself. This wealth flowed into the stream of western European commerce.

Foremost among the centers of this newly revived commerce and capitalism were the city-states of northern Italy, such as Venice, Genoa, Florence, and Milan. Venice was the queen of the Mediterranean in the thirteenth, fourteenth, and fifteenth centuries. After crushing the sea power of her chief rival, Genoa, in the fourteenth century, Venice enjoyed a virtual monopoly over the lucrative trade with the East. At the peak of its prosperity, Venice's merchant marine numbered some thirty thousand sailors. Milan was the starting point of the overland traffic across the Alps to northern Europe. In the late fourteenth century Milan gained control of the port city of Genoa. Florence manufactured large quantities of fine woolen textiles on a capitalistic basis, and in the fourteenth and fifteenth centuries it was the banking capital of the Western world. The Medici family alone at one time possessed dozens of branch banks scattered throughout western and central Europe.

In northern Europe, the Hanseatic League, composed of some eighty German Baltic and North Sea cities, enjoyed a brisk trade in such commodities as fish, furs, grain, and timber. In southern Germany and the Rhine Valley, numerous trading centers such as Augsburg, Nuremberg, and Cologne sprang up along the overland route between Italy and northern Europe. Finally, the Netherlands, Paris, and London shared in this early period of revived commercialism.

As the main trade routes shifted from the

Mediterranean to the Atlantic during the fifteenth and sixteenth centuries, new commercial centers to the west began to flourish. Contrary to what one might have expected, Spain, surfeited with gold and silver from Mexico and Peru, never developed a thriving commercial capitalism. And although Lisbon became the first great terminus of goods pouring in from the East, the Portuguese, like the Spanish, were so preoccupied with their vast overseas empire that they neglected the marketing opportunities in Europe itself.

These lucrative opportunities were first seized by the Dutch. Enterprising Dutch merchants purchased the goods in Lisbon, shipped them to the Netherlands, and sold them at a nice profit throughout northern and western Europe (see Figure 28.3). In the sixteenth century Antwerp, with its excellent harbor and location, was the leading commercial center in Europe. In the seventeenth century, following the sack of Antwerp in 1585 by Spanish troops, Amsterdam and London led the commercial world. The Dutch even took advantage of their newly won independence from Spain and of Portugal's temporary conquest by Spain in 1580 to seize the best part of Portugal's eastern empire, the area of present-day Indonesia.

Another phase of the commercial revolution was the advent of more bounteous supplies of commodities. Spices, coffee, tea, sugar, dyes, tropical fruits, fine textiles, tapestries, and precious stones, long known but in scarce supply and too expensive for all but the very rich, now came into Europe in ever-increasing volume. From the New World came potatoes, corn, tobacco, and chocolate (all of which had previously been unknown to Europe), new dyes and medicines, gold and silver.

The trade in slaves also swelled the rising stream of commerce. This early modern traffic in human beings was carried out in the later fifteenth century by the men of Portugal's Prince Henry the Navigator. It was later taken over by the Spaniards to supply labor for their empire in the New World. The native Indian populations were decimated by disease and the harsh conditions imposed by the Spaniards. Those who survived proved to be poor slave laborers. The Spaniards thus turned to tropical Africa to supply slaves for their mines and plantations. Thou-

FIGURE 28.3 Jan Gossaert, *Portrait of a Merchant,* ca. 1530 This portrayal of a banker by the Flemish painter Gossaert reflects the spirit of commercial capitalism. This serious, self-assured banker works with pen in hand and business letters in the background. His clothes and rings reveal controlled wealth. (National Gallery of Art, Washington, D.C.; Alisa Mellon Bruce Fund)

sands of Africans were bought from local chieftains and crowded into the holds of ships. Many of them died during the crossings, but the survivors were sold like cattle for a high price in the New World markets. So heavy was this immensely profitable traffic that the racial and social complex of New World society was drastically altered.

New types of business organizations were developed to accommodate the expanding volume of commerce. *Chartered companies* were organized to bypass the medieval guilds, which were unable or unwilling to meet the new demands. The most efficient type of chartered company proved to be the joint stock company. The members of a joint stock company pooled their resources, hired or elected their management, and shared in the profits in proportion to the amount of stock owned. In this way permanence was achieved, since the stock of any individual member could be bought or sold while the company remained intact.

Two of the earliest joint stock companies were the British East India Company, founded in 1600, and the Dutch East India Company, founded two years later. The British company was given not only a trading monopoly over British India but political control of the area as well. The Dutch company was given a monopoly over all Dutch trade east of the Cape of Good Hope. Annual profits of 300 percent were not uncommon for these giant companies. The annual profits of the Dutch East India Company never fell below 12 percent over a period of two hundred years.

Banking expanded in proportion to commerce. In the sixteenth century the Fugger family of Augsburg occupied the place in the financial world that the Medicis of Florence had held in the fifteenth. Jacob (the Rich) Fugger loaned Charles V the money with which he bribed his way to the emperorship of the Holy Roman Empire. In the seventeenth century the Bank of Amsterdam and the Bank of England were founded on a seminational basis. Both of these banks were really private joint stock companies, but in return for certain monopolies, such as the handling of government funds and the issuance of currency, they were obliged to accept a degree of government regulation. Banks of this size were able to mobilize sums of money and credit sufficient not only to launch and control large-scale commercial ventures but to influence government as well.

The commercialization of agriculture was of especially great significance. In some areas, particularly England, it sped up the process of combining smaller plots of land oriented toward subsistence farming into larger plots of land specializing in certain crops or herding for export. The commons—land available for the use of poor tenants—was taken away by large commercial landlords. Increasingly, small farmers were turned into wage laborers, either on the lands of commercial farmers or in the cities. The ranks of the landless poor swelled, while the productive commercial farmers gained wealth.

Industrial activity expanded in this period, particularly mining, shipbuilding, printing, armaments, and textiles, but guilds and governmental restrictions hindered the spread of capitalistic methods in these industries. The greatest expansion of capitalistic practices came with the growth of the domestic, or "putting-out" system. Merchants or entrepreneurs would purchase raw materials and distribute them to artisans, who would do the piecework in their cottages. Then the entrepreneur would collect the finished products, pay the cottagers for their work, and market the goods at a profit. While this system had certain advantages, it limited the volume of production. Until the coming of the machine and the factory system in the late eighteenth and early nineteenth centuries, therefore, large-scale capitalism was to remain commercial rather than industrial.

Part of this commercial revolution was fueled by the extraordinary rise in prices during the sixteenth century. This price inflation was probably related to the dramatic influx of gold and silver from the New World into Europe. However, historians now point to other causes for the price inflation that were perhaps more important. Population grew rapidly during the sixteenth century, particularly in western Europe and in urban areas. Many areas experienced a more than 50 percent increase. England's population almost doubled, while London's population grew by over 400 percent. All these people were competing for goods with each other and with governments. Tempted by the new gold and silver in their hands and pressured by greater expenses, governments spent more and went massively into debt; some governments responded by devaluing their currencies, making matters even worse. All these forces combined to push the demand for goods beyond the available supplies. Traders, merchants, and commercial farmers were in a particularly good position to benefit from the rising prices for commodities, which encouraged them to invest in commercial activities.

4. MERCANTILISM

Governments attempted to exercise some control over economic developments. From the beginning of the Age of Discovery in the late fifteenth century until the end of the eighteenth century, all the governments of western Europe except the Dutch Netherlands pursued a policy that has come to be called *mercantilism*. Mercantilism was, in essence, economic nationalism. While the monarchs of the new national states were consolidating their political power, they were also attempting to unify and centralize their national economies. Efforts were made to standardize national currencies and weights and measures. Internal commerce was encouraged by improving communications and reducing or removing internal tariff barriers. These efforts, however, were only partially successful. More attention was paid to the aggrandizement of each nation's economy at the expense of its neighbors. The basic assumption of mercantilist theory was that gold and silver are the true measure of national prosperity and power. Gold and silver, the mercantilists believed, in addition to being convenient media of exchange, could purchase anything—consumer goods, armies, navies, and administrative personnel. Spain's good luck in Mexico and Peru and its sixteenth-century brilliance and influence undoubtedly strengthened this view.

Spain alone was fortunate enough to come upon the gold and silver directly. All the other states had to devise more roundabout means of acquiring the precious metals. The favorite device was to seek a favorable balance of trade. The importation of expensive manufactured goods was discouraged by high tariffs, whereas the exportation of manufactures was encouraged, if need be, by subsidies. The reverse was true of inexpensive raw materials. The national aim was to buy low and sell high. Colonies were sought as sources of raw materials and markets for manufactured goods. But the colonies were not to be permitted to compete with the manufacturers and shippers of the mother country. Navies were advocated for the protection of the colonies. Sometimes the mercantilists closely regulated a nation's manufactures with a view to maintaining a reputation for high quality abroad. This phase of mercantilism reached its highest development in France in the seventeenth century under Louis XIV's economic minister, Jean-Baptiste Colbert. It was not until the latter part of the eighteenth century that the British economist Adam Smith and the French Physiocrats began to undermine faith in the validity of mercantilist principles and to prepare the way for an era of *laissez-faire*, or free, trade.

5. POLITICAL AND SOCIAL CONSEQUENCES

One immediate political consequence of the rise of commercial capitalism in western Europe was the strengthening of royal absolutism. The monarchs made use of the merchants and bankers in order to increase their own power at the expense of the rival nobility. More money was now available for the royal treasury and the royal army, even if it had to be borrowed. The middle classes, of course, shared the benefits of their alliance with the royal monarchs. Many members of the bourgeoisie were appointed to key positions in the royal administrations. With their increased wealth came increased social and political influence. The strongholds of their influence were the towns and cities whose growth paralleled the expansion of commerce. Western European society was becoming more urban—yet another change from the medieval pattern.

As the power of the national monarchs and the middle class grew, the position of the old nobility weakened. Their wealth and power were based on land, and now money was of growing importance. The inflation of prices further hurt the old nobility in relation to the moneyed bourgeoisie. Not overnight, but slowly and unevenly over decades and centuries, the old nobility of western Europe was losing social and political influence. Money was more easily acquired than blue blood or title. Feudal class lines were weakening, making possible a more fluid social structure and future political change.

Yet in some ways the nobility was not being replaced but was rather being infused with new, though suspect, blood. The successful, wealthy middle class generally dreamed of joining the privileged nobility rather than replacing it as a social class. They did just that by purchasing aristocratic titles, acquiring large estates, and marrying into the nobility. Moreover, various opportunities were grasped by bolder but less established members of the nobility. Many nobles of minor importance in Spain were able to become wealthy and powerful in Spanish lands overseas. In England and the Netherlands many members of the aristocracy openly engaged in business operations, thereby adjusting successfully to changing economic conditions.

The ascendance of the middle class and the changes within the nobility did not bring an immediate improvement in the condition of the lower classes. Indeed, the *nouveaux riches* often proved to be harsher taskmasters than the older aristocracy, who had stronger ties to medieval traditions of social responsibility. The urban wage earners were especially hard hit by the inflation. More were attracted to the cities of western Europe than could be employed, swelling the ranks of the unemployed and forcing many to return to the land as agrarian laborers—the landless poor. Sixteenth-century cities, while increasing in size and number, witnessed an even greater growth of poverty, begging, vagrancy, and crime (see Figure 28.4). As the demand for food overwhelmed the supply toward the end of the century, hunger and starvation spread.

In the countryside, landlords and those wealthier peasants who adapted well to the commercialization of agriculture profited. They were able to sell their surplus crops in cities at inflated prices. More broadly, those peasants in western Europe who had converted their feudal dues to money payments came out ahead, for those payments were fixed despite the rise in prices. But those who profited from the commercialization of agriculture and the rise in prices usually left in their wake large numbers of peasants worse off than before. Landlords who became distressed were likely to pass their hardships along to the peasantry. Peasants who prospered tended to purchase the land of the unfortunate, further dividing the peasantry into the relatively rich and the poor. The number of landless poor grew. Peasant revolts became common throughout Europe in the sixteenth century.

Finally, commercial capitalism probably diminished women's economic status. Most women still worked in traditional occupations—remaining in the countryside, assisting in their husbands' trades, or engaging in typical women's jobs such as domestic service, midwifery, and nursing. In the newer commercial, industrial, or professional occupations stimulated by commercial capitalism, women were usually either excluded or relegated to the lower-status and lower-paid jobs such as carding and spin-

FIGURE 28.4 Cornelius Buys, *Feeding the Hungry*
This early-sixteenth-century painting shows a domestic from a wealthy household distributing bread to the urban poor. Many in the growing cities had to rely on private charity such as this to survive. (Rijksmuseum-Stichting, Amsterdam)

ning wool. As work became increasingly defined as labor for paid wages, the domestic tasks performed by women lost their status as work. Ultimately some women would gain options for greater independence from the spreading commercial capitalism, but they had much to overcome.

6. EUROPEAN DOMINATION OF THE GLOBE

Thus we see that Europe's agricultural, collectivist, "fair price" economy was being transformed into a much more dynamic, urban, competitive, profit-motivated economy. The rise of commerce and capitalism not only changed the nature of European society but also provided much of the explosive force that enabled tiny Europe to dominate most of the rest of the world.

During Europe's Age of Discovery much of the Western Hemisphere, southern Asia, and the coastal areas of Africa were quickly brought under European domination. This amazing expansion continued until by the end of the nineteenth century practically the entire world was dominated by Europe and European civilization. Spanish, Portuguese, English, French, and Dutch colonists, followed later by the nationals of all

the other European countries, flocked to the New World, taking their western Christian culture with them. The brilliant Aztec and Incan civilizations of Mexico and Peru were destroyed. The tribes of American Indians were exterminated, absorbed, or confined to reservations. The Moslem, Hindu, Buddhist, and Confucian civilizations of Asia and Africa were not so quickly or extensively destroyed, but they were clearly affected. The details of European expansion (and eventual contraction) constitute a considerable portion of the history of Western civilization since the sixteenth century.

SUGGESTED READING

The Age of Discovery

C. M. Cipolla, *Guns, Sails, and Empires: Technological Innovation and the Early Phases of European Expansion, 1400–1700* (1965). Stresses the connections between technology and successful expansion.

J. H. Parry, *The Age of Reconnaissance* (1963). A good survey of the causes and consequences of the early voyages.

G. Scammell, *The First Imperial Age: European Overseas Expansion, 1400–1715* (1989). A good recent introduction to the whole period.

V. B. Thompson, *The Making of the African Diaspora in the Americas, 1441–1900* (1988). Informative history covering the Atlantic slave trade and more.

E. R. Wolf, *Europe and the People Without History* (1982). Excellent, providing an alternative perspective on expansion.

Overseas Empires

Charles R. Boxer, *The Portuguese Seaborne Empire* (1970). An excellent study of the Portuguese Empire.

B. Keen and M. Wasserman, *A Short History of Latin America* (1984). A useful recent text.

L. McAlister, *Spain and Portugal in the New World 1492–1700* (1984). A broad survey of the Southern American empires.

K. Sale, *The Conquest of Paradise: Christopher Columbus and*

the Columbian Legacy (1991). A radical reinterpretation with an ecological perspective.

Commercial Capitalism and Social Change

F. Braudel, *Civilization and Capitalism, 15th–18th Century*, trans. S. Reynolds, Vol. 2: *The Wheels of Commerce* (1982). Highly acclaimed and sophisticated.

R. Bridenthal, C. Koonz, and S. Stuard, eds., *Becoming Visible: Women in European History*, Second Edition (1987). Contains good material on this period.

C. M. Cipolla, *Before the Industrial Revolution: European Society and Economy* (1980). Particularly good on demographic and economic change.

Ralph Davis, *The Rise of the Atlantic Economies* (1973). Contains a good survey of sixteenth-century economic history.

H. Kamen, *European Society, 1500–1700* (1984). A general history of social structure and life.

P. Kriedte, *Peasants, Landlords and Merchant Capitalists* (1983). A Marxist interpretation of economic and social change.

A. K. Smith, *Creating a World Economy: Merchant Capital, Colonialism, and World Trade, 1400–1825* (1991). A recent analysis connecting expansion and commercial capitalism.

CHAPTER 29
The Reformation

FIGURE 29.1 Lucas Cranach the Younger, *Protestant Reformers,* **1543**
This painting shows some of the crucial figures of the Protestant Reformation. In the center stands Elector John Frederick of Saxony, whose family protected Luther and other Protestant reformers. Luther is to the far left, his associate Philip Melanchthon is to the far right, and between Melanchthon and Frederick is Huldreich Zwingli, a leading reformer in Zurich. (Toledo Museum of Art, Toledo, Ohio; gift of Edward Drummond Libbey)

Sixteenth-century Europeans were intensely interested in religion. Although Renaissance culture, political developments, and commercial expansion were of great concern, the Church was still at the very center of their lives. The Reformation probably touched more people than any other development of the sixteenth century.

The Protestant Reformation, initiated in the second decade of the sixteenth century by Martin Luther, swept through much of northern Europe. Reform within the Roman Catholic church, often called the Catholic Reformation, followed and included both internal reforms initiated independently of the Protestant Reformation and reforms undertaken to counter Protestantism. In the end, the Reformation split western Europe into hostile religious camps, destroying the medieval unity of the western Christian Church.

1. BACKGROUND

In the late Middle Ages, discontent with the Church grew. Large numbers of people felt spiritually dissatisfied with what the Church offered. Greatly concerned with their own salvation and with leading a more pious life, people looked outside the formal institutions of the Church for guidance and examples. The growth of lay religious organizations such as the Brethren of the Common Life, the popularity of traveling preachers, the continuing search for mystical experiences, and the graphic pious art all testified to widespread and deep spiritual needs that were not being met through the traditional Church. The church hierarchy seemed to have departed too far from the spirit and practices of the apostles and early fathers.

People voiced other complaints about the Church, particularly about many abuses that arose during the fourteenth and fifteenth centuries, when the Church was torn by the Babylonian Captivity, the Great Schism, and the struggles between popes and councils (see pp. 327–332). The lack of education and the worldliness of the clergy, the sale of church offices and services (simony), the favoring of relatives for lucrative church offices (nepotism), and the holding by one man of more offices than he could adequately serve (pluralism)—all were subjects of loud and growing complaint. Many of the higher clergy, even the popes, became preoccupied with their own secular concerns and Renaissance culture. Those who recognized a need to remedy these problems were unable to do enough until it was too late. Eventually the church hierarchy took steps to remedy abuses, but not until much of western Christendom had already left the Roman Catholic fold.

In addition to these spiritual dissatisfactions and complaints about abuses within the Church, other developments made certain areas of Europe fertile for the growth of reform movements. In Germany the Holy Roman Empire lacked the political unity that had helped national monarchs in Spain, England, and France gain control over their national clergy and access to the accumulated wealth of the Church. Local governments grew jealous of the immunity from civil laws and taxation enjoyed by the clergy. People resented the drain of wealth to the clergy and the institutions of the Church outside their territories, especially in Italy. These localities supported lay preachers, who gave numerous popular sermons throughout the year. In some of these same areas, particularly in university towns, Christian humanism took hold. Thanks to the printing press, criticisms of the Church by Erasmus, Ulrich von Hutten, and other humanists became widespread.

For the most part, this growing dissatisfaction with the Church was not revolutionary and did not yet challenge the fundamental doctrines of the Church. There was no widespread sense that the Church was about to be torn apart or that the only alternative was to make a complete break from it. On the other hand, the depth of the problems facing the Church is indicated by the radical reform movements occurring prior to the sixteenth century. As early as the fourteenth century reformers such as John Wycliffe in England and Jan Huss in Bohemia had voiced their protests against the Church. These protests turned into threatening movements of heretical dissent and social revolt, and authorities put them down only with great difficulty. When movements of dissent and revolt against the Church arose in the sixteenth century, they proved to be too powerful and well supported to be suppressed.

2. LUTHERANISM

The Protestant Reformation was composed of four major distinct but related movements—Lutheranism, Calvinism, Anglicanism, and Anabaptism. From these four main stems have sprung the hundreds of Protestant denominations that exist today. The Lutheran revolt was first in point of time.

Martin Luther (1483–1546) was the son of an ambitious miner living in central Germany (see Figure 29.2). At a boarding school run by the pietistic Brethren of the Common Life he, like his contemporary Erasmus, was introduced to a type of Christianity that emphasized simple piety rather than dogma and ritual. Later, at Erfurt University, he received a traditional liberal arts education. He was an excellent student. However, upon the completion of his undergraduate course and just as he was ready to begin study of the law, he suddenly renounced the world and entered an Augustinian monastery. This decision was no passing whim. As a child, Luther had been much concerned about the fate of his soul, and throughout his university days, his religious yearning had increased.

But the young friar found no satisfaction in the monastic life of the sixteenth-century Church. He scourged himself, donned beggar's garb, and went out among his former fellow students with sunken cheeks and gleaming, feverish eyes. It was not until, on the advice of a perceptive supervisor of his monastic order, he began to read the writings of St. Augustine and St. Paul that Brother Martin found the answer to his lifelong quest. On reading in Paul's Letter to the Romans (1:17) "the just shall live by faith," he concluded that here was the true means of salvation—not good works, sacraments, and rituals, but simple faith in Christ. Over a period of years he developed a theology based on the fundamental concept that righteousness is a gift of grace from God attained by faith in Christ's righteousness—justification by faith alone.

In the meantime Luther had become a member of the faculty of the newly founded University of Wittenberg in Saxony. For several years he taught philosophy and theology, quite unaware that his belief in salvation by faith alone was in fundamental conflict with the dogma of

FIGURE 29.2 Lucas Cranach the Elder, *Martin Luther*, 1521 Martin Luther often referred to himself as "a peasant, the son of a peasant." His father, though of peasant stock, was an ambitious miner who moved into the ranks of the bourgeoisie. A complex character, Luther had the brilliant mind and personal force of one of the great leaders and movers of history. (Culver Pictures)

his church. Students flocked from afar to listen to him.

In 1517 a friar named Johann Tetzel came into the vicinity of Wittenberg, selling indulgences on behalf of the pope and Prince Albert of Brandenberg. According to the doctrine of indulgences, which had arisen in the late Middle Ages, Christ and the saints, by their good works while on earth, had accumulated in heaven a treasury of excess merit that the pope could apply to the credit of penitent sinners. People came to believe that the purchase of indulgences would shorten or eliminate a stay in purgatory for them or their loved ones. By the opening of the sixteenth century the dispensing of this vague, extrasacramental means of grace had become hardly more than a money-making venture. Huge sums from all over Europe were taken to Rome for the construction of St. Peter's or for other costly papal projects.

On October 31, 1517, Martin Luther posted on the church door in Wittenberg his Ninety-Five Theses, or propositions, concerning the doctrine of indulgences, which he proposed to be debated publicly. It did not occur to him that this event would mark the beginning of an upheaval to subside only after nearly half of western Christendom had broken away from the Roman Catholic church. He was astonished and at first dismayed to find himself suddenly the national hero of all the various disgruntled elements throughout Germany. When, however, two years later in a public debate at Leipzig Luther finally realized that his position was hopelessly at odds with that of the Church, he lost no time in making the break clean. He published a series of pamphlets in which he violently denounced the pope and his organization and called on the German princes to seize the property of the Church and make themselves the heads of the Christian church in Germany.

A papal bull of excommunication (which Luther publicly burned) soon followed. A few months later Emperor Charles V called the troublesome monk to appear before the Diet of the Holy Roman Empire at Worms (1521). There Luther boldly refused to recant and was outlawed by the highest civil authority in Germany. Although Luther remained under this death sentence with a price on his head for the rest of his life, he was protected by his prince, the elector of Saxony, and German public opinion (see Figure 29.1).

By this time all Germany was in religious and social turmoil. Nearly everyone with a grievance of any kind was looking to Luther for leadership. Religious zealots, such as the Anabaptists, began preaching individualistic and more radical doctrines in his name, and he found it necessary to repudiate them. Taking a somewhat more conservative stand, he decided that only those features of the Roman Catholic church that were opposed to the Scriptures ought to be rejected. In the early stages of the conflict Erasmus and many other humanists thought they saw in Luther a kindred spirit, but this alliance was short-lived. Erasmus soon found Luther to be as dogmatic and uncompromising in matters of doctrine as the Roman Catholic theologians, if not more so. Moreover, Luther's rebellion against the Catholic church did not make him more tolerant of those outside the Christian fold. He favored deporting Jews and burning their synagogues.

Luther also found it necessary to break with a group of rebellious peasants in south Germany. The condition of the peasants was bad and growing worse. The landed aristocracy, themselves losing ground to the rising middle classes, were depriving their peasants of long-established manorial rights such as free use of meadows and woodlands. In 1524 widespread disturbances broke out in southwestern Germany. The next year the peasants published a list of demands, including an end to serfdom, elimination of certain taxes, confiscation of church property, and reform of the clergy. When these were refused, the peasants rebelled in the name of Luther, whom they believed to be against all oppressive authority. Luther was sympathetic with some of their demands, particularly the confiscation of church property and reform of the clergy, but otherwise he proved to be socially and politically too conservative. He rejected their attack on authority as too broad and pleaded with them to refrain from violence. When the rebellious peasants did not follow Luther's advice and continued their violent uprisings in Luther's name, he repudiated them and called on the civil authorities to suppress the revolt by force. The armed authorities did so with a vengeance.

Luther's message, and Protestant reform in general, appealed to many others for a variety of reasons. Governments were interested in breaking the papacy's control over churches—and the revenues controlled by those churches—in their territories. Princes and independent cities could thereby benefit politically and economically from reform. Merchants and artisans resented the freedom from taxation enjoyed by Catholic religious orders and the privileged position of priests. Lutheranism spread most rapidly in the cities and towns of Germany. Certain noblewomen in Catholic areas became powerful supporters of the reform movement. Leaders such as Marguerite of Navarre (1492–1549), sister of Francis I of

France, and Mary of Hungary (1505–1558), queen of Hungary and regent of the Netherlands, used their positions to protect both reformers and humanists.

Luther's new religion, as he eventually formulated it, made the Scriptures the sole authoritative source of Christian dogma. That all might have access to the Bible, he translated it into German.[1] He conceived of the Church as the whole body of believers in Christ, not the Roman Catholic church or any other specific organization. He abolished the hierarchy of pope, cardinals, and bishops, and he reduced the importance of the clergy in general, proclaiming the priesthood of all believers. The ritual of worship was made much simpler. Of the seven sacraments of the Roman Catholic church, Luther kept only the two he found mentioned as sacraments in the Bible: baptism and the Eucharist. He rejected the Roman Catholic doctrine known as transubstantiation (see p. 283). Luther interpreted the scriptural passages that refer to the Holy Eucharist, or Lord's Supper, to mean that during the administration of the sacrament Christ's body somehow enters into the bread and the wine, but the bread and wine remain—consubstantiation. He denied the Roman Catholic belief that a sacrifice is involved. He abolished monasteries and the celibacy of the clergy. Luther himself married a former nun. Although Luther refused to allow women formal roles as preachers or teachers, some women such as Elizabeth of Braunschweig and Argula von Grumbach played important roles in spreading Lutheranism. In general, he sharply distinguished religious matters from political and social matters, leaving the believer spiritually free and the secular rulers in charge of political and social matters.

The Emperor Charles V was greatly distressed by this religious revolution, which further divided his scattered and chaotic empire. Many German princes saw in Lutheranism a chance to increase their own political and financial independence from Charles V and the Italian papacy. Although determined to suppress the Protestants, Charles V was too busy with his

wars against the French and the Turks to make much headway. Years of indecisive fighting between the Roman Catholics under Charles V and the Protestants ended in 1555 with the compromise Peace of Augsburg. Each of the more than three hundred German princes was left free to choose between Lutheranism and Roman Catholicism; his subjects were to abide by his choice. Luther himself died in 1546, just before the fighting began. By this time, Lutheranism had triumphed in the northern half of Germany and soon had spread, under the leadership of the Scandinavian monarchs, to Denmark, Norway, Sweden, and most of the Baltic provinces (now Latvia, Estonia, and Finland), which were then under Swedish control. In addition, Lutheranism heavily influenced all later Protestant movements, the most important of which was Calvinism.

3. CALVINISM

John Calvin shares with Luther the position of first importance in the founding of Protestant Christianity. Born in France in 1509, John Calvin was twenty-six years younger than Luther. He was the son of a lawyer who was secretary to the bishop of Noyon in Picardy. Young Calvin had a radiant personality that made for warm friendships. Long association with aristocratic friends probably accounted for his elegant manners. His father sent him first to the University of Paris for a thorough grounding in the humanities and theology and then to the best law schools in France. Upon finishing his legal training, he entered a humanistic literary career. Suddenly, at the age of twenty-four, after reading Luther's writings and having an intensely personal religious experience, Calvin converted to Protestant Christianity.

The zealous young reformer soon aroused the ire of both Roman Catholic authorities in France and the French government and was forced to flee for his life. Calvin then spent the next two years in hiding writing the first edition of *The Institutes of the Christian Religion.* Published in Basel, Switzerland, when Calvin was only twenty-six, this theological treatise was to become the most influential writing in the history of Protestantism. Its precise, forceful logic reveals

---

[1]Luther's translation was in such excellent German that it had great influence on the standardization of the modern literary German language.

the fine legal training and powerful intellect of the author. Its lucid, facile style influenced the formulation of modern literary French. It immediately made Calvin an important name in literary and theological circles.

Probably Calvin's most significant contribution to Christian theology is his sublime concept of the majesty of God. To the author of the *Institutes*, the Divine Creator is so majestic and awe inspiring, and human beings so insignificant by comparison, that salvation by election, or *predestination*, as it is more often called, seems to follow logically. According to Calvin, God in the beginning planned the whole universe to the end of time. For unfathomable reasons of his own, God selected those human beings who would be saved and those who would be damned. He planted in the minds of the elect a saving faith in Christ and an insatiable desire to live the Christian life and to bring about the Kingdom of God on earth. In no other way could one acquire this faith and this desire. Calvin based this doctrine on the Scriptures (particularly the writings of St. Paul), which he considered to be the sole authoritative source for Christian theology. St. Augustine, the most influential of the early Church Fathers, and Luther also believed in salvation by election, but neither they nor anyone else had ever spelled out the doctrine so precisely.

Shortly after the publication of the *Institutes*, Calvin went to Geneva. That city, like most of the rest of Switzerland, was in the throes of a religious and political revolt brought on partly by the influence of Luther and the native Swiss reformer Huldreich Zwingli (1484–1531). At first accepted by Protestant leaders, then rejected, Calvin finally returned in 1540 to try to make Geneva a model city of God on earth. Calvin, by sheer force of personality and intellect, soon rose to a position of great power in the city. He brought the town council, which was remarkably democratic and representative for the sixteenth century, under the dominance of a consistory composed of Protestant pastors and laity. Under Calvin's leadership the town council and the consistory set up a strict system of blue laws. Churchgoing was compulsory. Dancing, card-playing, theatergoing, drinking, gambling, and swearing—all were forbidden. Enforcement was vigorous and penalties severe, even for the six-

teenth century. The most famous penalty was the burning of Michael Servetus, an eccentric amateur scientist and theologian whom the Roman Catholic church had already condemned to death for heresy.[2] Servetus escaped his Catholic persecutors in Lyon and went to Geneva. When he arrived, he was seized, tried, convicted, and burned at the stake.

Calvinist ritual was even simpler than that of the Lutherans. The worship service consisted of preaching, praying, and psalm singing. Like Luther, Calvin retained only two of the seven sacraments—baptism and the Holy Eucharist, or Lord's Supper. But to Calvin, Christ was present only in spirit in the bread and wine and only for the elect. Calvin patterned his system of church government after that of the very earliest church as described in the Bible (Acts of the Apostles). The local churches were governed by laymen called *elders* who were elected by the congregations. A measure of unity in faith and practices was maintained by means of a hierarchy of representative assemblies.

During the second half of the sixteenth century it was Calvinism rather than Lutheranism that became the most dynamic force in Protestantism. Protestant Christians came from many countries to sit at the feet of Calvin and to study at the University of Geneva, which he founded. John Knox, who came from Scotland to study under Calvin, called the Genevan theocracy "the most perfect school of life that was ever on earth since the days of the apostles." Calvinists combined vigorous evangelical appeals with a systematic theology and a well-organized church. The Calvinist ethic of "the calling" to one's station on earth, no matter what it was, dignified striving and hard work.

Calvinism became dominant in most of Switzerland (Swiss Reformed), the Dutch Netherlands (Dutch Reformed), Scotland (Presbyterian), and the German Palatinate. It also had a strong minority following in England (the Puritans) and a smaller but vigorous following in France (the Huguenots), Bohemia, Hungary, and Poland. The Calvinists played an important part

---

[2]The most serious of Servetus' heretical views were his denial of the Trinity, which cast doubt on the divinity of Christ, and his rejection of childhood baptism.

in the founding of the United States, particularly the Puritans in New England, the Dutch Reformed in New York, and the Scotch-Irish Presbyterians along the frontiers of all the original states. Such well-known denominations in present-day America as the Congregationalists, the Presbyterians, and the Baptists are Calvinist in origin.

4. ANGLICANISM

The foundations of the Reformation in England had been developing for many years before it was actually initiated by the actions of King Henry VIII (1509–1547). Lollardy, a movement of religious and social dissent stretching back over a hundred years, persisted as an underground movement into the sixteenth century. Humanism and anticlerical sentiments were gaining in strength. In 1525 William Tyndale (1494–1536), influenced by Luther, started printing an English translation of the Bible. However, the occasion of the beginning of the Reformation in England was the desire of Henry VIII for a new wife and a male heir. Catherine of Aragon, to whom he had been married for eighteen years, had given him only a daughter, Mary. When it became apparent that Catherine would have no more children, Henry decided to ask the pope to annul the marriage. The pope, however, was in no position to grant the annulment. Catherine was the aunt of Emperor Charles V, whose troops were at that very moment in control of the city of Rome. When Henry finally realized the pope was not going to accommodate him, he took matters into his own hands. At his bidding a subservient Parliament passed the Act of Supremacy (1534), making the king of England, not the pope, head of the Church in England. Later the monasteries, strongholds of papal influence, were dissolved and their holdings confiscated by the Crown. Meanwhile, Thomas Cranmer, whom Henry made archbishop of Canterbury, had arranged the annulment, and Henry had married Anne Boleyn. (He was to marry six times in all.) Henry was, of course, excommunicated by the pope.

But Henry VIII was no Protestant. In the days before the annulment controversy the pope had given him the title "Defender of the Faith" for his anti-Lutheran writings. Now he had Parliament pass the Six Articles reaffirming the Catholic position on all controversial doctrinal points except that of papal supremacy. Protestants, on the one hand, and Roman Catholics who refused to acknowledge the headship of Henry VIII in place of the pope were persecuted with equal severity.

It was during the reign of Henry VIII's young son, Edward VI (1547–1553), that the Anglican church first became Protestant. Archbishop Cranmer drew up a Book of Common Prayer and Forty-two Articles of Faith that were definitely Calvinist in flavor. Edward VI was succeeded by his elder sister, Mary (1553–1558), who was the daughter of Catherine of Aragon and a devout Roman Catholic. Mary's ambition was to restore her kingdom to the Roman Catholic fold. Her first step was to marry her cousin, Philip II of Spain, the most powerful champion of resurgent Roman Catholicism in all Europe. Next she asked and received papal forgiveness for her wayward people. Finally, "Bloody Mary" burned at the stake some three hundred Protestants, including Archbishop Cranmer. But Mary's marriage to a man soon to be king of Spain, England's most dangerous rival, and her persecutions were extremely unpopular in England; in the long run her policies hurt rather than helped the Roman Catholic cause there.

Elizabeth I (1558–1603), the Protestant daughter of Anne Boleyn, followed Mary on the English throne. This high-spirited, cynical, and politically minded queen found theology tiresome. Her chief interest was to find a satisfactory compromise that would unify her people. During the course of her long reign the Anglican church became definitely, but conservatively, Protestant. Cranmer's Book of Common Prayer was readopted with slight alterations. The Forty-two Articles were changed to the Thirty-nine. Some of the more controversial doctrinal points that seemed to prevent the various Protestant sects from uniting were reworded. Although celibacy of the clergy was abandoned, the episcopal system (government of the church by bishops) was retained. A rather elaborate ritual was adopted. Two of the sacraments, baptism and the Eucharist, were retained.

Although the great majority of the English people appeared to have accepted Elizabeth's compromise settlement, two groups remained dissatisfied. One was an extreme Calvinist element that sought to "purify" the Anglican church of all remaining traces of Roman Catholicism. These Puritans were to increase in strength until, under Oliver Cromwell's leadership in the next century, they gained temporary control of the country. The Roman Catholic minority, on the other hand, lost steadily in numbers. The support that some Roman Catholics gave to Philip II's attempt to conquer England and to the effort of Mary, Queen of Scots (a Roman Catholic), to overthrow Elizabeth (see Chapter 30) tainted all of them with the suspicion of treason and played into Elizabeth's hands. By the end of her reign, England was one of the Protestant countries of Europe.

5. THE ANABAPTISTS

Some reformers believed that Luther, Calvin, and the Anglican leaders had not gone far enough. They would break more sharply with all the existing institutions of the early sixteenth century—political, economic, and social as well as religious. Hence the term *radical* is often applied to them. Since these "radicals" were highly individualistic in their approach to religion, it is difficult to generalize about the many sects with their widely differing views and points of emphasis.

Generally, these sects tended to emphasize the evilness of the world, the mystical communion with God, the Second Coming of Christ, and the righteousness of the poor in their struggle against the rich. In some cases, religious reform became a means of social reform—a revolt of the poor against the rich.

These sects commonly rejected the doctrine of infant baptism. The true Christian, they believed, was one who was "born again" and baptized as an adult according to Scripture. Those who had been baptized as infants must be rebaptized. Anabaptism means *re*baptism. The Anabaptists believed that the true church of Christ on earth is a gathered church composed only of born-again Christians. The Anabaptists attempted to live lives of uncompromising holiness as dictated by the Bible or by the Holy Spirit speaking directly to each individual. These sects refused to recognize or participate in civil government, take oaths of allegiance, recognize titles, or serve in armed forces. Some practiced a shared economy. Most of them were poor. They were feared and persecuted by Roman Catholics, Lutherans, Calvinists, Anglicans, and secular leaders alike.

A few of the early Anabaptist leaders were violent activists, such as Thomas Müntzer, who inflamed the peasant rebels of southwest Germany, and John of Leyden, who set up a violent dictatorship in Münster in northwest Germany. This bizarre "heavenly Jerusalem" held out for more than a year against besieging Lutheran and Roman Catholic armies. The leaders were then tortured to death and their bodies hung in iron baskets from a church tower as a warning to radical dissenters. But the great majority of the Anabaptist leaders were pious and gentle—in fact, pacifists. Conrad Grebel, the first prominent Anabaptist leader, was a humanist from an upper-class family of Zurich, Switzerland. Probably the most successful and influential of all the Anabaptist leaders was the convert Menno Simons, a gentle former Roman Catholic priest from the Dutch Netherlands. His followers, the Mennonites, spread throughout much of western Europe and later the United States. Also in the Anabaptist tradition was the Society of Friends, commonly known as Quakers. Founded by George Fox in England in the mid–seventeenth century, this pietistic and pacifistic sect has spread to many parts of the world.

6. CATHOLIC REFORM

The rise of Protestantism touched off an aggressive Catholic reform movement during the 1530s and 1540s, but even before this movement some efforts to revitalize Roman Catholicism had already taken place. In Spain, around the turn of the sixteenth century, Cardinal Ximenes had forestalled a possible protest movement by enforcing strict discipline on the clergy and waging bitter warfare against heresy. During the first few decades of the sixteenth century several religious orders such as the Theatines, the Capuchins, the Barnabites, and the Ursulines were founded and dedicated themselves to clerical reform and education within the Catholic church. Even before the revolt of Luther and Calvin, Catholic leaders from several countries pushed for the calling of a general council to authoritatively enact badly needed reforms. However, the secular interests of the Renaissance popes and the popes' fears that an assertive reform council might again challenge the absolute authority of the papacy prevented a coordinated European-wide reform. The last council to meet before the Reformation, the Fifth Lateran Council (1513–1517), bowed to the pope's control and enacted no major reforms.

After the 1520s and 1530s, with area after area becoming Protestant, countermeasures of a rather drastic nature became imperative. There were two schools of thought concerning the proper course of action. One, led by the liberal Cardinal Contarini of Venice, advocated compromise and conciliation. Contarini eventually went so far as to meet with Melanchthon, a close friend of Luther and an important figure in the Lutheran revolt, in earnest quest of an acceptable compromise. They were unsuccessful; the two religions appeared to be incompatible. The other school of thought was led by the conservative Cardinal Caraffa of Naples. Caraffa believed that many corrupt practices in the Church needed to be reformed but that no compromise whatever should be made in the dogma. He believed that the Protestants were heretics and could reunite with the Roman Catholic church only by recanting and submitting to the pope. This is the school of thought that triumphed, and Caraffa became Pope Paul IV. The upshot of this line of thinking was the calling of a Church council at Trent, an imperial city in northern Italy.

The Council of Trent

The Council of Trent, which was in session off and on for eighteen years from 1545 to 1563, was probably the most important council in the history of the Roman Catholic church. The popes skillfully controlled its membership and voting procedure. The ultimate decisions of the council were in two categories: dogmatic and reformatory. In matters of faith or dogma, all the traditional doctrines of the Church were reaffirmed and redefined, especially controversial ones such as the sacraments, transubstantiation, auricular confession, celibacy of the clergy, monasticism, purgatory, invocation of the saints, veneration of relics, and indulgences. The dogmatic canons

and decrees of the council concluded: "Anathema to [accursed be] all heretics! Anathema! Anathema! Anathema!" The council also took stern measures to stop corrupt practices. Simony, nepotism, pluralism, and immorality and ignorance among the clergy were condemned. Schools for the education of the clergy were advocated. Bishops were admonished to exercise closer supervision and discipline over the lower clergy. To implement its canons and decrees, the council endorsed the Inquisition, which had recently been set up in Rome to combat heresy, and inaugurated the Index of Forbidden Books to prevent the reading of heretical literature except by authorized persons. Both instruments were placed under papal control and supervision.

Thus the Roman Catholic church at last spoke out, selected its weapons, and girded itself for more effective battle against the Protestants. At its service was the militant new Society of Jesus.

The Society of Jesus

The founder of the Society of Jesus, Ignatius Loyola (1491–1556), was a member of the Spanish lesser nobility, and until early middle life he was an obscure soldier (see Figure 29.3). In a battle with the French his leg was crushed by a cannonball. During the months of agony and convalescence Loyola read lives of the Christian saints and underwent a deep spiritual conversion. He determined to devote his tremendous energies and latent talents to the service of the Roman Catholic church—to become a soldier of Christ, the Virgin Mary, and the pope. He set off for the University of Paris to begin his education. Loyola was, however, neither a scholar nor a theologian but a man of action. He soon began to attract a band of followers, with whom he organized the Society of Jesus.

The Jesuit order, as the Society of Jesus was commonly known, was founded along military lines. Absolute and unquestioning obedience was the first requirement. Loyola admonished his followers, ". . . if she [the Church] shall have defined anything to be black which to our eyes appears to be white, we ought in like manner to pronounce it to be black." Applicants for membership were carefully selected and trained. For the spiritual guidance and inspiration of the

WHERE HISTORIANS DISAGREE

The Meaning of the Reformation

Most historians agree that the Reformation was of major significance, but when they address the more difficult questions of its exact causes and nature, agreement ends.

Before the twentieth century, historians often confused their own religious preferences with historical analysis, becoming more interested in assigning blame or praise. Protestant scholars focused on the corruption of the Roman Catholic church, the heroic piety of Protestant figures, and the positive force of the Protestant Reformation in the modern world. Catholic scholars contended just the opposite, arguing that there had been no crying need for doctrinal reform, that the Protestant leaders were self-centered and ignorant theologians, and that the Protestant Reformation was to blame for the flood of secularization in the West.

Most twentieth-century historians look at the Reformation in more complex terms. Many favor sophisticated religious and cultural interpretations of the Reformation. These historians argue that the Reformation grew out of deep and widespread spiritual longing and dissatisfaction with the practices of the Catholic church. They emphasize that whatever other qualities Protestant leaders may have had, they were deeply religious people whose reforming doctrines and practices appealed to the spiritual and cultural needs of many. These historians also stress the spiritual concerns revealed in Catholic reform. To these historians, the sixteenth century was an age of religious reform.

Other historians think of the Protestant Reformation in primarily political terms. They stress that the time was ripe for the Reformation not only because of religious tensions but also because secular authorities favored it. They emphasize that vast numbers of people became Protestant or remained Catholic (or reconverted) because their political leaders demanded it. They view the various religious movements of the sixteenth century as associated with nationalism. They believe it to be significant that the Protestant Reformation began in Germany, where there was no strong central government and where Luther strongly and openly appealed to German nationalism against Rome. By contrast, the strong rulers of France and Spain were able to extract such concessions from the pope as to create what amounted to a Gallican church and Spanish Catholic church, while successfully withstanding the Protestant challenge. The various Calvinistic churches were generally set up along national lines, such as the Swiss, Dutch, German, and Scottish Reformed churches. And of course the Anglican church was a national church.

Still other historians interpret the Reformation from an economic perspective. They point out the hunger for the rich lands held by the Roman Catholic church, the resentment over the tax exemption of these lands and the draining away of money to Rome, and the opposition of the commercial class to the Church's ban on usury. Related to these points is the "Weber thesis." Max Weber and other scholars have argued that the hard work and asceticism which Calvinism stressed fit well with the emerging spirit of capitalism, which emphasized hard work, saving, and reinvestment. Thus Calvinism appealed particularly to people in commercial centers in Holland, England, Switzerland, and New England. From this perspective, then, Protestantism helped solve various economic problems of the era.

The long history and depth of these controversies over the meaning of the Reformation reveal how difficult the evaluation of major religious change can be.

FIGURE 29.3 Ignatius Loyola (1491–1556) Ignatius Loyola, by founding the Society of Jesus (the Jesuits), played a key role in the Catholic Reformation. Although not as scholarly as Luther or Calvin, he was a superb organizer and leader. (Culver Pictures)

members of the Society, Loyola wrote the *Spiritual Exercises*. The *Exercises* guide the member through a solid month of concentrated meditation, a week each on the horrors of sin, the life of Christ to Palm Sunday, his suffering and crucifixion, and his resurrection and ascension. This remarkable work has proved to be a powerful tool for training and rededication. Jesuits served as priests, teachers, medics, diplomats, or in almost any other capacity suitable to their talents and training—but always with the interests of the Catholic church in mind. After years of service a few of the most outstanding were admitted to the highest circle of officers, who, under a general elected for life and residing in Rome, governed the order.

Loyola's high standards, far from deterring applicants, served as both a challenge and an attraction. The Society of Jesus grew rapidly. As priests, the Jesuits were nearly always the best trained, the most popular, and the most influential. As teachers, they were usually more highly educated, devoted, and attractive than their competitors. They have always been keenly aware of the power of education, especially for the very young. "Give me the child, and I care not who has the man." The Jesuits soon gained control of education in most Roman Catholic countries.

These dedicated soldiers of Christ also made the best missionaries. In North and South America the dauntless Jesuits went among the Indians and converted most of them to Roman Catholic Christianity. In the Far East, Francis Xavier, second only to Loyola himself in Jesuit history, converted tens of thousands.

Not the least important of Jesuit activities was that of gaining the confidence of kings, princes, and other political personages, and thereby influencing state policy. This militantly zealous order was a powerful stimulant to the wavering cause of Roman Catholicism. In Italy, Spain, Portugal, and Ireland, where Protestantism had only a weak foothold, the Jesuits helped stamp it out altogether. In France and Belgium they helped to turn the tide against the Protestants. In southern Germany, Poland, and the Austrian Hapsburg lands, all of which seemed to be on the verge of going Protestant, the Jesuits reversed the trend and helped make those lands strongholds of Roman Catholicism.

7. WOMEN AND THE REFORMATION

As with the Renaissance, scholars question whether the Reformation benefited women socially or in any aspect of public life. Although Luther may have encouraged greater sharing within the household—the ideal of the companionate marriage—and acceptance of sexuality within the marriage, it is difficult to argue that his reforming ideas greatly improved the condition of women. In his eyes, women were expected to be satisfied to be pious wives, mothers, and household managers, remaining clearly under the authority of their husbands. Despite some advocacy of mutual cooperation within the

FIGURE 29.4 Angela Merici (1474–1540) Catholic reform was supported by the growth of women's organizations such as the Ursulines. Here the founder of the Ursulines, Angela Merici (1474–1540), is shown on her deathbed. (Ursuline Provincialate)

voted to teaching girls, and the Carmelites, under the leadership of the influential Saint Teresa of Avila (1515–1582), gave women some opportunity to play a more active role within the Church.

If the direct effect of the Reformation on women is uncertain, it is clear that women during that era suffered from an explosion of witch-hunts and prosecutions for infanticide. The belief in witchcraft dated back for centuries, but it was not until the sixteenth century that large numbers of women were actually prosecuted and put to death on charges of witchcraft. Protestants and Catholics alike charged women, usually older, lower-class women living in rural villages, with the heretical crime of making a pact with the devil and causing harm to their enemies. Tens of thousands of women were tried for witchcraft, and perhaps a third of them were put to death.

Concurrent with these witchcraft hunts of the Reformation era came a flood of prosecutions for infanticide. While authorities prosecuted far fewer women for infanticide than for witchcraft, those prosecuted were more likely to be found guilty and executed. Usually the objects of these prosecutions were poor, unmarried younger women living in cities.

How much the Reformation itself had to do with this wave of lethal prosecutions of women is unknown. Perhaps more important were the growing efforts by the state to regulate behavior, the environment of fear during this period, and the general suspicion of women outside the norm in this male-dominated society. In any case, during the sixteenth and seventeenth centuries both Catholic and Protestant authorities, whether religious or secular, found sufficient theological and civil justifications to carry out these prosecutions that cost so many women their lives.

8. SUMMARY

Protestantism grew out of a widespread desire for greater spiritual satisfaction and correction of abuses within the western Christian Church. Political and economic factors soon came into play to broaden the appeal and strength of the Protestant Reformation. Towns, princes, and kings saw the advantages of acquiring control over religious institutions and the tremendous wealth

marriage, Calvin also rejected female independence and placed the husband at the head of the household.

The Protestant abolition of monasteries included women's religious orders, thereby eliminating one of the few occupational outlets available to sixteenth-century women. Protestantism offered no comparable alternative for the thousands of women who left the often socially prestigious Catholic convents. Only well into the seventeenth century and in certain Protestant sects such as the Quakers did women start to play a public role as preachers.

Catholic reform also resulted in few if any significant changes for women. Only the growth of pious Catholic women's organizations, such as the Ursulines (see Figure 29.4), who were de-

FIGURE 29.5 Adriaen van de Velde, *Fishing for Souls,* 1614 This allegory of the religious struggle during the Reformation shows Protestants on the left and Catholics on the right competing for souls in the waters that divide western Christendom. Above the fray, God's rainbow unites them all. (Rijksmuseum-Stichting, Amsterdam)

controlled by these institutions. This wealth and control served to strengthen their own political power. Since religious affiliation was viewed as integral to political and social order, conversion of political leaders eventually meant conversion of most of their people.

Initially Lutheranism was the dominant Protestant denomination, but in the second half of the century Calvinism became the most dynamic. By the end of the third quarter of the sixteenth century, Protestantism had triumphed in the northern half of the Germanies, in Scandinavia, in most of the Baltic provinces, in most of Switzerland, in the Dutch Netherlands, in Scotland, and in England. In addition, it had gained a strong minority following in France, Poland, Bohemia, and Hungary.

No matter how much the various Protestant denominations disagreed among themselves, most shared beliefs that put them at odds with the Roman Catholic church. They believed in justification by faith alone. They believed that the Roman Catholic church had departed so far from

the spirit and practices of the apostles and early Fathers that it could no longer be considered God's appointed custodian of the Christian religion. Scripture alone, not the decisions and traditions of the Roman Catholic church, was their sole authoritative source for Christian dogma. They emphasized the direct relationship between human beings and God. They thought of the Church as a priesthood of all believers. They rejected papal supremacy, the divine sanction of the Roman Catholic church, the celibacy and indelible character of the priesthood, monasticism, and such other characteristic Roman Catholic doctrines as purgatory, transubstantiation, invocation of saints, and veneration of relics.

The Roman Catholic church was not impotent in the face of these challenges. It had already initiated some internal reform efforts of its own prior to the outbreak of Protestantism, and those reform efforts grew throughout the sixteenth century. It also initiated a broad-based counter-Reformation to strengthen its hold in areas that remained Roman Catholic and to try to regain areas lost to Protestants. Despite some successes, however, it was never able to reconquer or re-convert the territories in which Protestants had gained a clear majority (see Figure 29.5, p. 393).

The Reformation definitively split western Christendom into hostile religious camps, and this religious hostility would spill over into decades of bloody wars and revolts.

SUGGESTED READING

General

De Lamar Jensen, *Reformation Europe, Age of Reform and Revolution* (1981). A very good work.

H. Koenigsberger and G. Mosse, *Europe in the Sixteenth Century* (1987). A broad survey with bibliography.

R. L. de Molen, *Leaders of the Reformation* (1984). Portraits of key figures.

S. Ozment, *The Age of Reform, 1250–1550* (1980). A broad, respected interpretation.

L. W. Spitz, *The Protestant Reformation* (1985). A solid, recent survey.

Lutheranism

E. Erikson, *Young Man Luther: A Study in Psychoanalysis and History* (1962). A highly important and influential interpretation.

H. G. Haile, *Luther: An Experiment in Biography* (1980). A modern treatment.

R. W. Scribner, *The German Reformation* (1986). A balanced treatment of Luther and the German Reformation.

Calvinism

W. Bousma, *John Calvin: A Biography* (1987). Calvin in his historical context.

W. E. Monter, *Calvin's Geneva* (1967). A fine study of the Reformation in Geneva.

Anglicanism

A. G. Dickens, *The English Reformation* (1974). The best survey.

J. J. Scarisbrick, *The Reformation and the English People* (1985). A short survey.

The Anabaptists

C. Clasen, *Anabaptism, A Social History, 1525–1618* (1972). Connects religious and social history.

M. Mullett, *Radical Religious Movements in Early Modern Europe* (1980). An excellent survey.

Catholic Reform

N. Davidson, *The Counter-Reformation* (1987). A solid, brief survey.

J. Delumeau, *Catholicism Between Luther and Voltaire* (1977). A respected interpretation of Catholic reform.

J. C. Olin, *The Autobiography of St. Ignatius Loyola* (1974). The life and ideas of the founder of the Jesuits.

Women and the Reformation

M. J. Boxer and J. H. Quataert, eds., *Connecting Spheres: Women in the Western World, 1500 to the Present* (1987). Includes useful material on the period.

R. Bridenthal, C. Koonz, and S. Stuard, eds., *Becoming Visible: Women in European History, Second Edition* (1987). Includes a good chapter on this period.

B. Levack, *The Witch-Hunt in Early Modern Europe* (1987). An excellent analysis with focus on causes.

CHAPTER 30
Politics and the Wars of Religion

FIGURE 30.1 François Dubois, *St. Bartholomew's Day Massacre* This painting of the St. Bartholomew's Day Massacre in 1572 by François Dubois, a contemporary Protestant painter, shows soldiers indiscriminately killing Huguenots in Paris. (Musée Cantonal des Beaux-Arts, Lausanne)

The Peace of Augsburg in 1555 brought an end to war between Catholics and Lutherans in Germany, and the Treaty of Cateau-Cambrésis in 1559 ended the Hapsburg-Valois wars. But these halts to long conflicts did not bring an end to the bloodshed. On the contrary, the period between 1560 and 1648 witnessed an outbreak of revolts, massacres, civil wars, and international wars that was unprecedented. While people in several areas suffered, the most intense and extended fighting occurred within the boundaries of the Holy Roman Empire. By the end of the Thirty Years' War in 1648, probably a third of the German population had died from the war.

Certainly religious differences were involved in these conflicts and accounted for the ferocity of the struggles (see Map 30.1). But politics and greed were also intertwined, with leaders vying for political gain and mercenaries thirsty for loot. Both crossed religious lines to make war for their own purposes.

1. THE CRUSADE OF CATHOLIC SPAIN

Emperor Charles V had bequeathed the greater part of his vast empire to his son Philip II (1556–1598) (see Figure 30.2). In addition to Spain, Philip's inheritance included the Netherlands, Franche-Comté, Milan, the Kingdom of Naples, Sardinia, and the Spanish Empire overseas. In 1580 Philip conquered Portugal in the name of his Portuguese mother and became master (at least in name) of Portugal's huge eastern empire.

Philip II, unlike his father, was a native Spaniard. He utilized the gold and silver flowing in a steady stream from the New World and the lucrative commerce of the East Indies and the busy Netherlands in the interests of Spain. Ignoring the Cortes and the local rights of Aragon and tending personally to the myriad details of government, the meticulous and stubborn Philip brought Spain under his sway to an extent that Ferdinand and Isabella and Charles V had never been able to do. With the best army in Europe and the will to use it, there is little wonder that the king of Spain was the most feared man in western Christendom.

The Roman Catholic church was of great importance to Philip II. He conceived it to be his chief mission in life to use the great wealth and power of Spain to restore the dominion of the Roman Catholic church over all of western Christendom. In the Netherlands, in England, and in France, Philip II threw the might of Spain on the side of the Roman Catholics in their counteroffensive against the Protestants.

Revolt in the Netherlands

Unlike his father, Philip II was considered by the Netherlanders to be an unsympathetic foreigner who taxed their prosperous commerce and industry for the benefit of Spain. The absolutist monarch and his Spanish administrators also overrode the traditional political privileges of the nobles and the cities in the Netherlands. Nonetheless, religion was the foremost cause of dissension. By the mid–sixteenth century, nearly half the people in the Netherlands had become Protestant. Most were Calvinists, but a considerable number were Anabaptists. Philip II, who would tolerate no heresy in his empire, took stern measures to stamp out Protestantism. The Inquisition was used to enforce the laws against heresy. In 1566, bands of outraged Protestants began to deface Roman Catholic churches. Philip thereupon dispatched Spanish troops under the duke of Alva to reduce the Netherlands to submission. A six-year reign of terror followed, during which thousands were put to death.

Far from being cowed, however, the Netherlanders resisted fiercely. They found a brilliant leader in William of Orange, or William the Silent, as he came to be known. They took to the sea, playing havoc with Spanish commerce and communications. When, in 1580, Philip conquered and annexed Portugal, the hardy Dutch "Sea Beggars" seized the richest parts of the Portuguese Empire in the East Indies. The Spanish infantry quickly overran the ten southern (Belgian) provinces, but against the seven northern (Dutch) provinces, made up largely of islands and peninsulas and skillfully defended by the Dutch fleet, Spain's armies could make little headway. Most of the Protestants soon fled north from the Spanish-occupied southern provinces. Likewise, most of the Roman Catholics fled south from the Protestant-dominated north. In 1579 the ten Roman Catholic southern provinces (now Belgium), fearful of the growing power of the

Map 30.1 **RELIGIOUS MAP OF EUROPE, CA. 1560** This map indicates the religious divisions in Europe during the Reformation. In the turmoil between 1560 and 1648, most of those areas that had already turned Lutheran or had established Calvinist churches would remain Protestant. Those areas in which Protestant groups were in the minority would be subject to pressures and change.

Protestant northern provinces (which also spoke a different language), submitted to the Spanish yoke. The seven northern provinces, however, banded together in the Union of Utrecht and continued the struggle for independence. When in 1584 William the Silent was assassinated by a hireling of Philip II, other able leaders arose to take his place. Finally in 1609, eleven years after Philip's own death, Spain agreed to a twelve-year truce, and in 1648 Spain recognized the complete independence of the Dutch Netherlands, as the seven northern provinces are commonly called. In the seventeenth century the little Dutch republic led the world in commerce, bank-

FIGURE 30.2 Philip II Philip II of Spain was the most feared monarch in the Western world during the second half of the sixteenth century. A meticulous and stubborn ruler, he struggled to extend his own power and the dominance of the Roman Catholic church over Protestantism. (Alinari/Scala/Art Resource)

ing, and painting and was second to none in science and philosophy.

Thus Philip II's crusade in the Netherlands was only partly successful. He saved the southern provinces for Spain for another century, and for the Roman Catholic church, but the Dutch provinces, the richest in his empire, were lost both to Spain and to the Church.

Struggles with England

Most grandiose of all Philip II's crusading efforts was his attempt to restore wayward England to the Roman Catholic fold. His first move was to marry England's Roman Catholic queen, Mary Tudor. They wed in 1554, two years before his own rule over the Spanish Empire began. However, Mary's marriage to the king of a feared and hated rival power and her persecution of English Protestants only increased her own unpopularity and that of the Roman Catholic cause in England. Moreover, the marriage failed to produce an heir. When Mary died in 1558, Philip sought to continue his influence in England by trying to marry her successor, Elizabeth. But Elizabeth, a Protestant and high-spirited English patriot, refused.

Elizabeth proved to be one of England's ablest monarchs (see Figure 30.3). In style and policy, she was a *politique*—a ruler who avoided strong religious stands and emphasized moderation, pragmatism, tolerance, or avoidance in religious matters. For her, like other *politiques* such as William of Orange, religious concerns were subordinated to the need for political unity. She guided the Anglican church to a moderate Protestant position.

Spain's military successes led Elizabeth to support Spain's opponents. In the 1570s and 1580s she signed an alliance with France and aided the Dutch Protestant rebels. She also encouraged English sea dogs to plunder Spain's treasure ships sailing from its New World colonies—indeed, to plunder the colonies themselves. When in 1587 Spanish plots against Elizabeth clearly implicated Mary, Queen of Scots (a Catholic), Elizabeth was forced to execute her. It was then clear that England would not peacefully rejoin the Catholic fold.

Philip II tried to conquer England by direct military action. In 1588 his "Invincible" Armada sailed forth—130 ships, many of them great galleons. Aboard was a formidable Spanish army. The Armada was to go first to the Netherlands and pick up additional soldiers. In the English Channel it met the somewhat larger English fleet, composed mostly of smaller but swifter and more heavily armed ships. The Spaniards fought well until finally their formation was broken by English fire ships sent into their midst. Once scattered, the Spanish ships were no match for the English fleet. Storms played a major role in the loss of Spanish ships, and only about half the ships ever reached Spain. It was at this point that England began to wrest control of the seas from

FIGURE 30.3 Marcus Gheeraert, *Queen Elizabeth I* Marcus Gheeraert's portrait of Queen Elizabeth I shows this monarch at the height of her power (a picture of her victory over the Spanish Armada in the background, the crown to her right, her right hand on the globe) and wealth (her jewel-laden attire). (Cooper-Bridgeman Library)

Spain. Not only had Philip II failed to exterminate Protestantism in England, but the Roman Catholic cause there was now tainted with treason, and Protestantism was stronger than ever.

Confronting the Ottoman Turks

In the sixteenth century, the Ottoman Empire under Suleiman had grown in power to its greatest extent. Victories over Christian troops in Hungary had threatened central Europe. Ottoman fleets dominated large parts of the Mediterranean. The Hapsburgs had traditionally led in the struggle against the Ottomans and Islam in general, and Philip II took up the challenge with vigor. Under the urging of the pope, Venice, Genoa, and Spain amassed a fleet of more than two hundred vessels under the command of Philip's illegitimate half brother, Don Juan. In 1571 this fleet caught and annihilated the somewhat larger Turkish fleet off Lepanto on the coast of Greece. This was one of the few clear-cut successes of Philip's career. Lepanto greatly diminished the Turkish menace to Christendom by sea.

2. THE RELIGIOUS WARS IN FRANCE

In France and Germany during the late sixteenth and first half of the seventeenth centuries, struggles between Protestants and Catholics combined with conflicts between different political factions to break out into bitter wars, usually called the Wars of Religion.

In France Calvinism had made slow but steady progress during the reigns of Francis I (1515–1547) and Henry II (1547–1559) in spite of vigorous persecution by those Roman Catholic monarchs. By 1559 the Huguenots, as the French Calvinists were called, numbered possibly a twelfth of the total population. However, since their ranks included many of the prosperous bourgeoisie and some of the greatest noble families of France, their influence was far greater than their numbers would indicate. Enmity between the Huguenots and the Roman Catholics, which had smoldered under the strong rule of Francis I and Henry II, broke into open and consuming flame under Henry II's three ineffective sons, who ruled in succession from 1559 to 1589. All three were dominated by their powerful and ambitious mother, Catherine de Médicis. This situation invited political as well as religious faction and intrigue, and in the civil wars that followed politics and religion were intertwined.

The leadership of the Roman Catholic faction was assumed by the powerful Guise family; that of the Protestants by the influential Bourbon family, who were related to the royal line. The first eight years of fighting were ended in 1570 by an uneasy truce. However, Catherine de Médicis became fearful of the growing influence of the Huguenots. She turned for support to the Catholic Guises, and under their influence she agreed to a plan to massacre the Huguenots. At a given signal at midnight, August 24, 1572 (St. Bartholomew's Day), the Roman Catholics in Paris fell to slaughtering the Protestants (see Figure 30.1). The massacre soon spread to the provinces and went on for a number of weeks. Thousands of Huguenots were slain.

The ablest of the Huguenot leaders, young Henry (Bourbon) of Navarre, escaped and rallied the remaining Protestant forces for the war that was now renewed in earnest. The wealth and energy of the numerous bourgeois and noble members of the Huguenot faction, plus the brilliance of their dashing young leader, offset the superior numbers of the Roman Catholics. Eventually Henry III, the third son of Catherine de Médicis to rule France, organized a moderate Roman Catholic faction to stand between the uncompromising Guise faction and the Protestants. The struggle now became a three-cornered "War of the Three Henrys" (Henry, duke of Guise, Henry of Navarre, and Henry III, king of France). Philip II of Spain threw his support to Henry, duke of Guise. Henry III, now regarding Henry, duke of Guise, as the greater menace to his own royal authority, had him assassinated in 1588. The next year an agent of the Guises assassinated Henry III. This left Protestant Henry of Navarre, by right of succession, King Henry IV of France. However, it was only when he abjured Protestantism four years later and went through the formality of becoming a Roman Catholic that the great majority of his subjects, who were Roman Catholics, allowed him to enter Paris and be legally crowned. "Paris is worth a Mass," he is alleged to have remarked. Five years later (1598) he issued his famous Edict of Nantes, which, by granting tolerance to the Protestant minority, ended religious strife in France for nearly a century.[1] By these acts, Henry revealed himself as a *politique,* favoring national unity over religious concerns. He enjoyed some of the same success and popularity as other *politiques,* such as Elizabeth I in England and William of Orange in the Netherlands.

3. THE THIRTY YEARS' WAR IN GERMANY

The Peace of Augsburg (1555), which had brought to a close the first armed conflict in Germany between the Roman Catholics and the Lutherans, proved to be only an uneasy truce. Since the signing of the treaty, which recognized only Roman Catholics and Lutherans, the Calvinists had made strong headway in several states of the Holy Roman Empire and demanded equal

---

[1]The Huguenots rose up in a brief rebellion (1627–1629) against Cardinal Richelieu when he removed their military and political privileges.

FIGURE 30.4 The Thirty Years' War This print shows Magdeburg, where in 1631 one of the battles of the Thirty Years' War was fought. The last and the bloodiest of the religious wars that accompanied the Reformation, the Thirty Years' War devastated much of Germany and exhausted its participants. (NYPL Picture Collection)

recognition. Furthermore, lands of the Roman Catholic church were constantly being secularized in Protestant areas in violation of the treaty. On the other hand, the Roman Catholics, being more aggressive as a result of the clarification of their position by the Council of Trent and the activities of the militant Jesuits, talked of exterminating Protestantism in the Holy Roman Empire and recovering all their lost lands and souls. In alarm, the Protestants formed a defensive league. The Roman Catholics countered by forming a league of their own.

The increasing tension finally erupted into the Thirty Years' War (1618–1648) (see Figure 30.4). In this war the religious issue was complicated and often confused by political and dynastic issues. The individual princes of the empire were struggling to maintain or even increase their independence from the emperor. The Hapsburg dynasty, both Austrian and Spanish, threatened to become so powerful that the apprehensive Bourbons of France entered the war against them. The upshot was that eventually the Roman Catholics, the Holy Roman emperor, and the

Hapsburg dynasty (the emperor was an Austrian Hapsburg) formed one faction against which were arrayed the Protestants, most of the individual princes of the empire, and the Bourbons.

The long-brewing Thirty Years' War began in 1618 when a group of Bohemian nobles, mostly Calvinists and fearful of losing both their religious and their political rights, declared their Hapsburg ruler deposed and chose the Calvinist elector of the Palatinate as their king. The Hapsburg Holy Roman emperor, aided by the Roman Catholic League and by Hapsburg and Roman Catholic Spain, took the field and easily crushed both Bohemia and the Palatinate. Hundreds of Calvinist Bohemian nobles were executed and their property confiscated. Protestantism was outlawed in Bohemia. The Calvinist Palatinate was annexed to Roman Catholic Bavaria. This quick, crushing victory by Roman Catholic and imperial forces frightened not only the Protestant princes of northern Germany, but also the Protestant neighboring states.

In 1625 Lutheran King Christian IV of Denmark, who held numerous bishoprics in Germany that had been illegally secularized, entered the war against the Roman Catholic and imperial forces. Christian IV was aided by English subsidies and numerous German Protestant princes. At this critical juncture a brilliant soldier of fortune, Albrecht von Wallenstein, offered his services to the emperor. This military genius raised a volunteer army of fifty thousand adventurers of various nationalities. Wallenstein's army, together with the regular imperial and Roman Catholic forces, defeated Christian IV and drove him out of Germany. The Danish king was deprived of nearly all his German holdings. Upon the conclusion of this phase of the war in 1629, the victorious emperor issued the Edict of Restitution, restoring to the Roman Catholic church all the lands illegally secularized since the Peace of Augsburg—more than a hundred tracts, large and small.

The whole Protestant world was now genuinely alarmed at the resurgent power of the Roman Catholics. The German princes were faced with the loss of their powers to the Holy Roman emperor. The French Bourbons were concerned about the rapidly growing strength of the Hapsburgs. At this juncture another Protestant champion stepped forward—Gustavus Adolphus of Sweden. This Lutheran "Lion of the North" was a military leader of great ability. Furthermore, he was well backed by French gold. Gustavus Adolphus led his army victoriously through the Germanies, gaining allies among the Protestant princes as he went. The Hapsburg emperor hastily recalled the ambitious Wallenstein, whom he had dismissed upon the conclusion of the Danish phase of the war. Two of the ablest military commanders of early modern times now faced each other. In the battle of Lützen (1632) Wallenstein was defeated, but Gustavus Adolphus had been killed and the victory was far from decisive. Fortunately for the Protestants, Wallenstein was dismissed and two years later was assassinated. Since Sweden had failed to turn the tide of the war, the Bourbon king of France in 1635 threw the full weight of his military might directly into the fray. For thirteen more years the war dragged on until all participants were exhausted. The Treaty of Westphalia in 1648 finally brought the struggle to a close (see Map 30.2).

In general, thanks largely to the intervention of France, the Roman Catholics, the Holy Roman emperor, and the Hapsburgs suffered a setback. Not only were the Roman Catholics thwarted in their efforts to exterminate Protestantism in Germany, but the Calvinists now gained equal status with the Lutherans and Roman Catholics in the Holy Roman Empire. The Holy Roman Empire practically fell apart. According to the terms of the Treaty of Westphalia, each of the more than three hundred individual princes could now make his own treaties. Three of the most important princes, the rulers of Brandenburg, Bavaria, and Saxony, made sizable additions to their territories. Sweden gained strategic territories along the German Baltic and North Sea coasts. France gained the important bishoprics and fortress cities of Metz, Toul, and Verdun and the province of Alsace except for the free city of Strasbourg. The complete independence of Switzerland and the Dutch Netherlands was officially recognized. The Austrian Hapsburgs retained their hereditary possessions but lost prestige as emperors of a disintegrating Holy Roman Empire. Also, their relative position declined as that of France rose. The Spanish Hapsburgs fared worse. After eleven more years of fighting with France they yielded a strip of the Spanish Netherlands and another strip along the Spanish border to France. Spain's days of greatness were finished.

The immediate effect of the Thirty Years' War on Germany was disastrous. For three decades hostile German and foreign armies had tramped back and forth across Germany, killing, raping, and looting the defenseless inhabitants. In the wake of Wallenstein's army of fifty thousand, for instance, swarmed one hundred fifty thousand camp followers bent on plunder. To the usual horrors of war was added religious fanaticism. Some 30 to 40 percent of Germany's inhabitants lost their lives from this war. Many years would be required for Germany to recover from these wounds.

The Thirty Years' War was the last and the bloodiest of the religious wars that accompanied the Reformation. Although there would still be much religious strife and controversy, the religious map of Europe would henceforth change very little. After 1648 political rather than religious affairs would occupy center stage in the Western world.

Map 30.2 EUROPE, 1648 This map of Europe after the Treaty of Westphalia in 1648 shows that what would eventually become unified into Germany during the nineteenth century was still greatly divided within a Holy Roman Empire that was weaker than ever. With the rapid decline of Spain, most political conflict in the century after 1648 would be among France, England, Austria-Hungary, and Brandenburg-Prussia.

SUGGESTED READING

General

R. Dunn, *The Age of Religious Wars, 1559–1689* (1979). A good, brief survey.

G. Parker, *Europe in Crisis, 1598–1648* (1979). A survey and interpretation of this period as one of general crisis.

T. Rabb, *The Struggle for Stability in Early Modern Europe* (1975). Analyzes the ''crisis'' interpretation.

The Crusade of Catholic Spain

W. T. MacCaffrey, *Queen Elizabeth and the Making of Policy, 1572–1588* (1982). A good recent analysis.

C. Martin and N. Parker, *The Spanish Armada* (1988). Provides some new insights.

G. Mattingly, *The Armada* (1959). Brilliantly shows the impact of the Armada's failure on all of Europe.

Geoffrey Parker, *Spain and the Netherlands, 1559–1659* (1979). A clear introduction.

P. Pierson, *Philip II of Spain* (1975). A well-written biography.

J. Ridley, *Elizabeth I* (1988). A good recent biography.

Religious Wars in France

M. Greengrass, *France in the Age of Henri IV* (1984). A fine recent history of this crucial period.

J. H. M. Salmon, *Society in Crisis: France in the Sixteenth Century* (1975). Focuses on French institutions.

The Thirty Years' War

P. Limm, *The Thirty Years' War* (1984). A brief survey with accompanying documents.

T. K. Rabb, ed., *The Thirty Years' War* (1981). A collection of differing interpretations of the war and its significance.

CHAPTER 31

Society, Faith, and Culture in the Seventeenth and Eighteenth Centuries

FIGURE 31.1 Thomas Gainsborough, *Miss Catherine Tatton* Although the middle class was growing during the early modern era, the culture of the period was still dominated by the aristocracy. This portrait of an aristocratic lady by Thomas Gainsborough (1727–1788) reflects the luxury and tastes of the eighteenth-century aristocracy, which commissioned many such paintings. (Scala/Art Resource)

For most people the structure of society, the way of life, and the relevant social institutions changed only slowly throughout most of the seventeenth and early eighteenth centuries. More rapid change occurred thereafter, but it was usually concentrated in certain areas and classes. Despite the continued rise of the bourgeoisie and considerable political change, the aristocracy remained socially dominant and governments headed by kings generally continued to centralize their power. Religious faith remained of great importance to most people, but after the middle of the seventeenth century new religious movements such as pietism were no longer the revolutionary force they had been during the previous century. The literature and arts of the period reflected the spirit of royal absolutism and the values of the aristocracy, with their exaltation of kings, princes, and nobility and also their concern for order and form.

1. SOCIETY

Population Growth

One of the greatest sources of change in Western society has been population growth. As we have seen (see pp. 377–380), European population grew substantially during the sixteenth century, putting pressure on economic life, adding to social turmoil, and creating changes in the quality of life for different classes of people. This population growth leveled out during the first two decades of the seventeenth century. On the whole, during the seventeenth century Europe's population was able only to maintain itself or grow slightly. In some areas population declined markedly. The typical enemies of population growth were poverty, disease, famine, and war. Most people lived close to the subsistence level. Any disturbance—a poor harvest, a natural catastrophe, a war—quickly used up their meager reserves of food and opened the door to hunger, declining health, disease, and famine. The Thirty Years' War was particularly devastating, leading to a decline in the German population of some 40 percent during the first half of the seventeenth century. The relatively late age of marriage—late twenties for men, mid-twenties for women—also helped keep down the number of births in a society in which life expectancy was short and only about half of the babies born would reach maturity.

During the eighteenth century, particularly after the 1730s, the European population grew sharply—from approximately 110 million in 1700 to 190 million in 1800. Although the causes are unclear, it seems that an increasing birthrate and declining death rate were achieved by earlier marriages, better and more regular nutrition, fewer plagues, and less devastating wars. Agricultural and commercial prosperity, along with continuing improvements in transportation facilities, diminished the periodic famines in many areas. In particular, historians credit the introduction of the potato from the New World and its widespread cultivation in eighteenth-century Europe with crucially increasing supplies of nutritious food. More effective urban sanitation and increased use of quarantines probably improved health. Medical practices were not one of the causes of population growth. Certainly some progress was made in medical knowledge and there were a few better hospitals in eighteenth-century Europe than before. But with the exception of developing smallpox inoculation, which was little used outside England until the nineteenth century, eighteenth-century doctors, hospitals, and medicines probably caused more deaths than they prevented.

There was an ironic price to pay for this eighteenth-century increase in population. Greater competition for food drove prices up while that same competition for jobs usually drove wages down. At the same time that more people were able to survive, more experienced hunger and poverty. The poor were forced to wander and migrate more than ever.

Social Structure

Seventeenth- and eighteenth-century people viewed their society as divided—into different occupational groups and classes—and hierarchically ordered—the different groups and classes ranked from high to low status by birth, office, wealth, or education. Mobility between these ranked orders of society was viewed as the exception. People considered the social order to be relatively rigid and correct. In fact, however, mobility and change occurred. Wealth, education,

FIGURE 31.2 Louis le Nain, *The Cart,* 1641 In contrast to most seventeenth-century artists, le Nain shows the life of the French peasantry. This farmyard scene (notice the mixture of ages), so typical of the countryside, contrasts sharply with the life of the aristocracy. (The Louvre, Paris)

and new opportunities for governmental service opened avenues for middle-class merchants, bankers, and professionals as well as the gentry to move into the ranks of the aristocracy. Nevertheless, social mobility was never the option for many, as it would become during the nineteenth and twentieth centuries.

As in previous centuries, the aristocracy enjoyed the highest status and the greatest number of privileges. Their position was defined not by wealth but by title and blood. Some were fabulously rich, but others were relatively impoverished. However, an aristocrat was expected to have enough wealth to fulfill costly political, social, and military functions. Usually that wealth derived from the lands they owned, and most of it was protected by numerous exemptions from taxes.

Below the aristocrats were the clergy and commoners. In these groups there were ordered ranks as well. In the cities the wealthiest merchants, particularly those from "old families," were on top. They enjoyed some of the distinctions of rank and power that aristocrats had, and some were granted aristoratic status. Below them were guild members, followed by artisans and unskilled workers. In the countryside the ownership of land usually determined status. The

wealthiest landowners, often called the gentry, performed many of the functions of the landed aristocracy. Below them, landowning peasants enjoyed some position, leaving the landless peasants toward the bottom—though even they were in a higher position than those who were still serfs and bound to their masters.

Within this social structure, it was the group rather than the individual that was supposed to be of primary importance. First came the family and the household, then the local community, finally the larger social order with its various orders and hierarchies. In our sense of the term, national identity was still of secondary importance for most people.

Rural Life

Seventeenth- and eighteenth-century Europeans lived predominantly in rural settings. In western Europe approximately 80 percent still lived in the countryside; in the less urbanized eastern Europe the percentage was even higher. In rural areas life was centered on the traditional village (see Figure 31.2). Most villages were small, ranging in size from a few families to little over a hundred families. There life was communally oriented: villagers knew each other, strangers stood out, and almost all effective authority was local. Community pressures limited what we today would consider the rights of dissent and privacy. The local church or manor served as a center of communal activities. Still relatively isolated, villages had to be self-sufficient. When bad harvests occurred, as they did on a regular basis, help from outside was rarely available.

Most people were relatively poor, living in small, crowded structures. Inside there few furnishings or possessions. At one end was a stone hearth for light, cooking, and heat, but shortages of fuel (wood and peat) meant people suffered from the cold. Bread and grain products made up most of their meals, though in various areas meat, vegetables, fruits, and dairy products supplemented their diets. If they owned or had rights to land, they could raise their own food. Even this was of little help when the crops failed.

During this period the traditional pattern of rural life was slowly being altered. The traditional village was experiencing intrusion from the outside, change in its age-old pattern of life, and loss of people to the growing cities. The political isolation of the village was being broken by the increased presence of officials from the growing central governments, by the growing absence of the local nobility (who were attracted to the courts and capital cities), and by the decline of communal political institutions. Above all, economic life was being changed by the agricultural revolution and the spread of cottage industry—both of these facilitated by improving means of transportation.

The Agricultural Revolution At the beginning of the seventeenth century, crops and animals were raised in western Europe much as they had been since the Middle Ages. Most fields were open and divided into various strips of land. Crops were rotated and land allowed to lie fallow (unplanted) one out of every two or three years to keep the soil fertile. Large strips of land were set aside as "commons"—open areas where villagers grazed their animals and gathered food and hay. Decisions about crops, animals, and land use were usually determined by tradition and the practices of the community.

During the seventeenth and eighteenth centuries, changes in agricultural production initiated in Holland spread to England and then to other areas of western Europe. These changes were so important that they have been called an agricultural revolution. New crops such as potatoes, turnips, and clover were introduced. New methods of rotating crops, such as from grains to tubers (potatoes and turnips) to hay (grasses for animal fodder), were developed. Fertilization of the soil was increased by using manure from larger animal herds. These changes enabled farmers to eliminate fallow land. In addition, Dutch innovators developed methods of draining wetlands so that new crops and methods could easily be introduced. They also experimented with breeding to create new strains of more productive cattle.

In the early eighteenth century, the new crops and methods spread to England. Charles "Turnip" Townsend experimented with crop rotation and the use of turnips and clover. His contemporary and compatriot, Jethro Tull, advocated the use of a seed drill, which made planting more efficient and productive. Another Englishman, Robert Bakewell, improved the existing types of sheep and cattle by selective breeding.

These changes were sometimes connected to the enclosure of open fields and commons, particularly in England. The consolidation and enclosure of scattered strips and farms allowed larger landowners the freedom to apply new agricultural methods. Enclosures had been used in Great Britain since the sixteenth century, but the profits that could be made in commercial agriculture employing new crops and methods stimulated numerous landlords to seek enclosures during the eighteenth century. After 1750 Parliament authorized a wave of enclosures that transformed the British countryside. While these enclosures hastened the agricultural revolution, they left large numbers of rural poor unable to survive as small farmers. Many of them were forced into the ranks of rural or urban workers.

Cottage Industry During the seventeenth and eighteenth centuries, "cottage industry," or the "putting-out system," expanded greatly in rural areas. According to this system, a merchant-capitalist provided raw materials (usually for production of textiles such as wool or linen) and sometimes equipment (such as a handloom or spinning wheel) to peasants. Peasants, working in their cottages, turned these raw materials into

FIGURE 31.3 Cottage Industry Most cottage industry was in textiles. Here the various members of a rural household in Ireland work together, beating and combing flax into linen, which will be spun and woven. (The Mansell Collection)

finished products—spinning and weaving wool into cloth (see Figure 31.3). The merchant periodically returned, paid for the peasants' labor by the piece, and distributed the finished products to distant markets. The pay was low, lower than that offered in cities, but it was enough to help large numbers of peasants and rural workers to survive. The growth of cottage industry during the eighteenth century, particularly in Great Britain and parts of France and Germany, helps explain how so many people could remain in rural areas.

Urban Life

Cities grew during the seventeenth and eighteenth centuries, but unevenly. Until the middle of the eighteenth century, most of the growth was in the capital and port cities, particularly in northern and western Europe. These cities swelled with the growth of central governments and commerce. After the 1750s new cities arose and small cities grew, reflecting the general population growth and new concentrations of agricultural and industrial activity, particularly in Great Britain.

This urban growth meant greater prosperity for some, but a large percentage of the urban masses were not beneficiaries. They continued to live precariously at little more than a subsistence level. The poorest were the hardest hit by the surplus of labor, inflation, and disasters such as war, disease, and failed harvests. In bad times, food riots were common. As traditional ways of aiding the poor—through the Church or private charity—were overwhelmed, cities tried to control begging and enact various sorts of poor relief. Legislation, such as the English Poor Laws, required the impoverished to work on public projects or in workhouses and provided some training, but laws such as these were often not carried out or were used more to control and discipline the poor than to help them.

However, there were more kinds of food, more goods, and more opportunities in cities. Artisans and skilled workers lived relatively comfortable lives. Those who found regular unskilled jobs as haulers or domestic servants were probably better off than the rural poor. Many worked or supplemented their income on small plots of land within or just outside the city; some cities owned large tracts of land and hired people to farm them.

Those who benefited most from improvements in the standard of living were the middle and aristocratic classes, particularly those taking advantage of the opportunities in commerce and industry and in the expanding governmental bureaucracies. A growing class of urban professionals attended institutions of higher education. In an expanding number of colleges they joined young aristocrats sent by families who felt that more education and culture were appropriate to members of the aristocracy. The middle classes continued to use their wealth to enter the aristocracy through the purchase of titles and offices, the acquisition of large estates, and judicious marriages.

The Family

The family, so central to social life and the socialization of future generations, is usually one of our most conservative institutions, evolving only gradually over time. This pattern of subtle, slow change held true for most of the seventeenth and eighteenth centuries.

The family functioned as both a social and an economic unit. In this household economy (or family economy), everyone who could worked for the good of the household. Husband, wife, children, servants, and apprentices were part of this unit of production and consumption. Even those who earned wages elsewhere usually sent part of their earnings back to the family. Children were often sent away to other households when they could earn more outside their own family.

Child rearing and attitudes toward children were strikingly different from those of today. Children were generally not at the center of family life nor of primary concern. Girls were less valued than boys, reflecting women's subordination to men. Infanticide, though illegal, was not unknown, abandonment was a common practice, and what we would consider neglect was more often the rule than the exception. Much of this behavior may be explained by the high rate of infant mortality (some 30 to 50 percent of children died within the first five years of life), the generally precarious state of the household economy, and simple poverty. Certainly the lack of birth control may have played a role: Modern methods were unknown, the unreliable method of withdrawal was discouraged or condemned, and abortion was dangerous. Parents usually had to view those children who survived not only as family members but as assets or liabilities in the survival of the family. With life so precarious for their children, any great emotional involvement with them was risky.

It was once thought that most people lived in extended families—more than one married couple and their children in the same household; however, most historians now agree that as a rule people lived in a nuclear family household consisting of one couple and their children. Nevertheless, the typical family household during the sixteenth, seventeenth, and most of the eighteenth centuries was a much more populated, public place than the household of a modern nineteenth- or twentieth-century nuclear family. At various times a variety of relatives lived in or moved through the household, as did domestics and laborers. The household was far more open to members of the community and pressures from the community at large. The father, older children, other relatives, and community adults in general participated with the mother in raising and socializing young children.

Marriages continued to be entered into for primarily economic and social reasons. The land, wealth, skills, and position one held were the most important considerations in contemplating marriage; sentiment, particularly being in love, played a secondary role. Children were the expected product of a successful marriage. Typically, a married woman gave birth to more than five children, though the odds were that many of those would fail to reach adulthood or even get beyond the first few years of childhood. Marriages whether happy or not, were expected to last. Divorce, though permitted in Protestant communities, was in most cases difficult if not impossible. Separation was more accepted, but death, which often struck people at a relatively young age, was usually the only way out of an unsuccessful marriage.

Within the middle and upper classes, a significant change came during the second half of the eighteenth century. Sentiment became more important as a motivation for marriage; economic and social considerations, while still important, were not quite as dominant as before. Premarital sex and sex outside of marriage were on the increase, as evidenced by the growing number of births registered within a few months of marriage and by the rising rates of illegitimacy. People were marrying at an earlier age and moving around more. Child rearing and homemaking were being turned into a woman's profession in middle-class households. Along with the rising likelihood that most babies born would survive came a changing perception of children as more special, precious, and loved— not miniature adults to be used, as they had more often been perceived in the sixteenth and seventeenth centuries. Indeed, what was happening during the second half of the eighteenth century was a slow transformation to the modern family, which would come into bloom with the spread of industry and the dominance of the middle class during the nineteenth century.

Women

Women, while continuing to play a subordinate role to men, were central to the economic well-being of the family among the lower classes. Their work started when they were children, helping with the lighter tasks of farming or cottage industry. In her early teens, a girl often left home to work as a servant, trying to gain skills and money for her future marriage and the establishment of a new household. As a married woman, she could expect to spend much of her time pregnant (five or more pregnancies were not unusual) and involved with child care. But her tasks as childbearer and child rearer were no more important than her other economic and social functions. In addition to the standard household chores, women were expected to work as much as possible. Women participated in the collecting and threshing of grain, took primary responsibility for gardening, raised poultry, supervised and processed dairy production, and shared in the manufacture of household items and products for commerce (particularly spinning) as the putting-out system spread. When women worked in wage-earning occupations, it was generally at less pay and in lower-status positions than men. The line between acceptable "women's work" and "men's work" widened as the emphasis on women's domestic responsibilities grew. Within the household women were legally subordinate to their husbands and generally expected to be subject to his authority. Outside a household, women were particularly vulnerable. They lacked many legal rights and were denied most alternatives for independent employment. There were some occupations open to women, such as glove making, spinning yarn, midwifery, and nursing, but the status and pay of these occupations were often diminished because of their association with women.

Middle- and upper-class women had fewer opportunities for participation in economic life. Respectable careers open to unmarried middle-class women were limited to those of governess or lady-in-waiting. Once married, the middle-class woman was at the center of the family, but for any real economic independence she had to wait for the death of her husband. More than lower-class women, middle-class women were increasingly seen as responsible for upholding standards and supervising the help within the home. Most aristocratic women were similarly limited in the economic roles they played, but they could turn to influential social and cultural roles (see Chapter 36). Some, such as Queen Christina in seventeenth-century Sweden, Maria Theresa in eighteenth-century Austria, and Catherine the Great in eighteenth-century Russia, became rulers. Others, such as Maria de Médicis in seventeenth-century France, became surrogate rulers or royal regents. More often, they held privileged positions in royal courts and served as unofficial advisers. As courtiers women could gain position, wealth, and prestigage for themselves and their families.

2. FAITH: THE GROWTH OF PIETISM

After the end of the Wars of Religion in the mid–seventeenth century, a relative status quo existed between Catholicism and Protestantism. While hostility still existed among the believers of different Christian faiths, it no longer broke out into the violence and revolution characteristic of the Reformation era. Religious life remained centered in the local parish. In his church, the priest or pastor conducted services and supervised various charitable and educational activities. Although most people retained an allegiance to the established Catholic or Protestant churches, some new religious movements did arise during the seventeenth and eighteenth centuries. The most important were a number of pietistic sects which stressed the importance of active faith in leading a religious life.

In Germany Philipp Spener (1635–1705) and Count Zinzendorf (1700–1760) became leaders of pietist movements of considerable dimensions. Spener, a Lutheran pastor, recoiled from the formal officiousness that his church had fallen into after the heated religious strife of the sixteenth and early seventeenth centuries. He minimized dogma and external forms in favor of inner piety and holy living. His largely Lutheran following included some of the leading intellects of Germany. Count Zinzendorf, a well-to-do Saxon nobleman, undertook to restore the Bohemian Brethren, the persecuted and scattered followers of the early-fifteenth-century reformer Jan Huss. He called his group the Moravian Brethren. The Moravians, too, shunned intricate dogma and formal ritual. They set up model communities based on brotherly love, frugal living, hard work, and inner piety.

In Lutheran Sweden, Emanuel Swedenborg (1688–1772), a distinguished scientist, inventor, and public servant, founded a movement somewhat like the Moravian Brethren, based on his visions, which he took to be direct revelations of God. Swedenborg wrote several learned theological works stressing inner and outward piety and individual communion with God.

England, however, was the seat of the most widespread and influential pietistic movements of the seventeenth and eighteenth centuries. The first was the Society of Friends, or Quakers, as they were generally called, founded by George Fox (1624–1691). Fox, a man of great energy and stubborn independence, detested formalism in religion as well as in society and government. He believed that true Christianity is an individual matter—a matter of plain, pious living and of private communion with God under the guidance of a divine "inner light." Opposed to war, rank, and intolerance, the Quakers refused military service, the use of titles, and the taking of oaths. In these respects the Quakers were different from most of the other pietists. They were considered dangerous to the established order and were severely persecuted.

A more moderate and popular pietist movement was Methodism. The prime mover in Methodism was John Wesley (1703–1791). John Wesley and his brother, Charles, became converted to a more fervent, evangelical type of Christianity. When the Anglican churches closed their doors to John Wesley, he preached emotional sermons to huge throngs in the streets and fields. George Whitefield, the most eloquent of all the early Methodists, electrified tens of thousands in England and America and converted many to pietistic Christianity. The real founder of Methodism in the American colonies was Francis Asbury (1745–1816), who in many respects duplicated the work of John Wesley in England. In both England and America the Methodists grew rapidly in numbers, mostly among the middle and lower classes.

The various pietist groups were definitely not political revolutionaries. They were intensely interested in social reform—in education, health and sanitation, temperance, penal reform, and abolition of the slave trade. But they hoped to achieve these reforms by private charity rather than political action. They tended to accommodate themselves to the political status quo in the belief that spiritual and social conditions could be improved within that framework of government.

3. CULTURE

The cultural styles of the seventeenth and eighteenth centuries reflected the dominance of royal and aristocratic tastes—particularly in the baroque, classical, and rococo styles. The main exceptions were in the Dutch Netherlands and eighteenth-century England, where paintings and literature often reflected the tastes of the ascending middle class. Bridging the middle and upper classes were the scientific revolution and the Enlightenment, two intellectual and cultural developments of great importance that will be examined on their own in Chapters 35 and 36.

Literature

The reign of Louis XIV (1643–1715) was the golden age of French literature. The elegance, the sense of order, and the formalism of the court of the Grand Monarch were all reflected in the literature of the period, sometimes called the Augustan or classical period of French literature. It was in the field of drama that the French writers attained their greatest success. Corneille wrote elegant tragedies in the style of and often on the same subjects as the ancient Greek tragedies. The struggles of human beings against themselves and against the universe furnish the dramatic conflicts. Corneille's craftsmanship and style are handsomely polished, though often exalted and exaggerated.

Even more exquisitely polished were the perfectly rhymed and metered couplets of Racine's tragedies: *Andromaque* relates the tragic story of Hector's wife after the death of her husband at the hands of Achilles and the ensuing fall of Troy. *Phèdre* is about the wife of the legendary Greek king Theseus who falls in love with her stepson. This story had also been the subject of plays by Euripides, Sophocles, and Seneca.

One of the greatest of all the French dramatists was Molière. In his charming and profound comedies—such as *Tartuffe, Le Misanthrope,* and *Les Femmes Savantes (The Learned Ladies)*—Molière devastatingly portrays and satirizes the false, the stupid, and the pompous: egotists, pedants, social climbers, false priests, quack physicians. The tragic conflicts and personality types of Corneille, Racine, and Molière are universal and eternal.

Perhaps the most popular novel of the period was *Grand Cyrus,* a historical romance by Madeleine de Scudéry. The fact that this book was published under the name of her brother Georges indicates some of the difficulties women faced in cultural pursuits.

Other major French writers of the age of Louis XIV were Blaise Pascal, the scientist and mathematician who also wrote the marvelously styled *Provincial Letters* against the Jesuits and the deeply reflective *Pensées (Thoughts);* Madame de Sévigné, who wrote almost two thousand letters to her daughter, each a work of art; and the duke of Saint-Simon, who spent the latter part of his life writing forty volumes of *Mémoires.* Madame de Sévigné and the duke of Saint-Simon, both of whom were eyewitnesses at the court of Louis XIV, constitute two of the most important sources we have for the history and life of that period.

The common denominator among all these writers is their emphasis on and mastery of elegant and graceful form. In this emphasis they reflect the spirit of royal absolutism at its height. However, form is valued not merely for its own sake but as an artistic clothing for subtle and critical thought. French literature in the late seventeenth century overshadowed that of all other countries of Europe, much as did French military and political influence. The lucid, graceful French language became the fashionable language of most of the royal courts and courtiers on the European continent.

French literature in the eighteenth century continued for the most part in the classical vein. Voltaire wrote dramas and poems carefully tailored to the dictates of classical formalism. His prose works exalted logic and the ideals of Greece and Rome. Only Rousseau among the major eighteenth-century French writers departed from the classical spirit to anticipate the romanticism of a later era.

Next to France, England produced the most important literature in the seventeenth and early eighteenth centuries, and like the French, the English authors generally wrote in the classical vein. The giant of English letters in the mid–seventeenth century was John Milton (1608–1674). This learned Puritan was steeped in the literature of ancient Greece and Rome. His exquisite lyrics *L'Allegro* and *Il Penseroso* and incomparable elegy *Lycidas* are thickly strewn with references to classical mythology. The conscientious Milton contributed much of his great talent and energy to public affairs. During the Puritan Revolution he went blind while working as a pamphleteer for the Puritan cause and secretary for Oliver Cromwell. The chief literary product of this period of his life is *Areopagitica*, probably the noblest defense of freedom of the press ever penned. Milton's masterpiece is *Paradise Lost*, written in his blindness and after the restoration of the Stuart kings had ruined his public career. *Paradise Lost* is a poem of epic proportions based on the Genesis account of the rebellion of Satan against God and the temptation and fall of human beings. This majestic theme is treated in stately blank verse of formal elegance. Even in this deeply religious work, Holy Writ is interwoven with classical pagan myth.

The two greatest poets to succeed Milton were John Dryden in the late seventeenth century and Alexander Pope in the early eighteenth century. Both were satirists, both displayed a massive knowledge of Greek and Roman lore, and both wrote chiefly in the formal rhymed couplets typical of the classical period. In the precision of their form, as in the sharpness of their satire, their appeal was to reason rather than to emotion.

The eighteenth century in English literature was an age of great prose. Following the upheavals of the seventeenth century, the Puritan and Glorious revolutions, it was a time of political and religious bitterness and bickering. In pungent and incisive prose Jonathan Swift, in his *Gulliver's Travels* and political essays, and Richard Sheridan, in his numerous dramas, pilloried the fops, pedants, bigots, and frauds of the day, much as Molière had done a century earlier across the Channel. It was in the eighteenth century that the English novel was born. More than other literary forms, it was aimed at and reflected the tastes of England's rising middle class. Samuel Richardson, in *Clarissa Harlowe*, and Henry Fielding, in *Tom Jones*, used this medium to analyze human personality, emotions, and psychology, just as Corneille and Racine had used the poetic drama in France for the same purpose.

In the eighteenth century several writers—Robert Burns in Great Britain, Rousseau in France, Schiller and Goethe in Germany—anticipated romanticism (see Chapter 41). But the prevailing spirit in eighteenth- as in seventeenth-century literature was classical. Precision, formalism, and ofttimes elegance marked the style. Ancient Greece and Rome furnished the models. The appeal was generally to reason. The royal monarchs and their courts had little to fear from this literature. They could derive comfort from its formal order and laugh with the rest of the world at its satire, which was aimed at humankind in general rather than at the ruling regimes.

Painting and Architecture

If the literature of the seventeenth and eighteenth centuries did not offend the absolutist kings and their aristocratic courtiers, the visual arts of the period usually glorified them (see Color Plate 17). The dominant style of painting and architecture during the seventeenth century was baroque, which used elaborate swirling forms and colors to achieve dramatic, emotional effects. The baroque style was originally associated with the Roman Catholic Reformation and reflected the resurgence of a revitalized Roman Catholic church led by the militant Jesuits. Later its massive and ornamental elegance reflected the wealth and power of the absolutist monarchs and their courts, then at the peak of their affluence.

The most popular of the baroque painters of the early seventeenth century was the Fleming Peter Paul Rubens (1577–1640). After studying the work of the Italian High Renaissance masters, Rubens returned to Antwerp and painted more than two thousand pictures, many of them huge canvases. He operated what amounted to a painting factory, employing dozens of artists who painted in the details designed and sketched by the master. Rubens, a devout Roman Catholic, first painted religious subjects (see Color Plate 14). His later subjects were pagan mythology, court life, and especially voluptuous nude women—all painted in the most brilliant and sensuous colors (see Figure 31.4).

Spain boasted two of the greatest seventeenth-century painters: El Greco and Velásquez. El Greco, whose real name was Domenikos Theotokopoulos, was a native of the Greek island of Crete (hence "The Greek"). After studying the

FIGURE 31.4 Peter Paul Rubens, *Henry IV Receiving the Portrait of Marie de Médicis,* 1621–1625 Rubens was commissioned by Marie de Médicis, widow of King Henry IV of France, to paint this allegorical scene showing Henri IV considering a proposed marriage to Marie de Médicis. The swirling lines, dramatic perspective, rich color, and opulence are typically baroque. (The Louvre, Paris)

Italian Renaissance masters, he settled down in Toledo and developed a style of his own. By deliberate distortion and exaggeration he achieved sensational effects. *View of Toledo, St. Jerome in His Study,* and *Christ at Gethsemane* illustrate his genius. El Greco's favorite subject was the reinvigorated Church of the Roman Catholic Reformation. Considered by his contemporaries to be a madman, he is now regarded as the forerunner of several schools of nineteenth- and twentieth-century painting. Velásquez was a painter of great versatility. Although much of his earlier work was of a religious nature, he also painted genre subjects (depicting the life of the common people) and later portraits. He is considered one of the greatest of portrait painters. As official court painter, he exalted and glorified the Spanish royalty and ruling classes at a time when they had really passed their peak in world affairs.

During the second half of the seventeenth and then the eighteenth century, classicism, with its greater emphasis on control and restraint, gained favor. Good examples of classicism are in the works of the French artists Nicolas Poussin and Claude Lorraine (see Color Plate 15). Poussin spent most of his life in Italy studying the Renaissance masters. Although his biblical and mythological scenes are more vibrant and pulsating than the Italian Renaissance paintings that inspired them, they are much more serene, subtle, and controlled than the works of Rubens and El Greco.

In eighteenth-century Great Britain, Joshua Reynolds, Thomas Gainsborough, George Romney, and Sir Thomas Lawrence vied with one another for commissions to paint the portraits of royalty and aristocracy. The results were plumes, jewels, buckles, silks, brocades, and laces in dripping profusion (see Figure 31.1).

FIGURE 31.5 **The Baroque Style** This photo is of the interior of the basilica St. Andrea della Valle, which was built in the latter part of the seventeenth century. It well illustrates the elaborate, gaudy splendor of the baroque style, the hallmark of the age of royal absolutism and affluence. In this case the royal monarch was the pope, ruler of a Church reinvigorated by the Roman Catholic Reformation. (Alinari/Scala/Art Resource)

In the Dutch Netherlands painting did not reflect royal and aristocratic tastes. Here in the busy ports and marketplaces commerce was king, and the great Dutch painters of the seventeenth century, notably Frans Hals, Jan Vermeer, and Rembrandt van Rijn, portrayed the bourgeoisie and common people (see Color Plate 16). Rembrandt is universally recognized as one of the greatest artistic geniuses of all time. As a portrayer of character he has never been surpassed. His mastery of light and shade (*chiaroscuro*) made it seem as if the very souls of his subjects were illumined. *Syndics of the Cloth Guild*, *The Night Watch*, and *The Anatomy Lesson of Dr. Tulp* (see p. 443) are among his most pow-

erful portrait studies. These three paintings also vividly depict the commercial prosperity, the festive urban life, and the growing interest in natural science in the seventeenth-century Dutch Netherlands.

Baroque architecture, like baroque painting, was an elaboration and ornamentation of the Renaissance and a product of the Roman Catholic Reformation (see Figure 31.5). In the late sixteenth, the seventeenth, and the eighteenth centuries Jesuit churches sprang up all over the Roman Catholic world. The most important and one of the best examples of the baroque style is the Jesuit parent church, Il Gesù, in Rome. Also, like the painting, baroque architecture was later used to represent the gaudy splendor of the seventeenth- and eighteenth-century absolute monarchs and their courts.

Towering over all other monuments of baroque architecture, much as St. Peter's towered over all other Renaissance structures, was the Versailles Palace of Louis XIV (see Figure 32.1). The exterior of Versailles is designed in long, horizontal, classic lines. The interior is lavishly decorated with richly colored marbles, mosaics, inlaid woods, gilt, silver, silk, velvet, and brocade. The salons and halls are lighted with ceiling-to-floor windows and mirrors and crystal chandeliers holding thousands of candles. The palace faces hundreds of acres of groves, walks, pools, terraces, fountains, statues, flower beds, and clipped shrubs—all laid out in formal geometric patterns. So dazzling was this symbol of royal absolutism that many European monarchs attempted to copy it. The most successful attempt was Maria Theresa's Schönbrunn Palace in Vienna.

In England Sir Christopher Wren was the greatest architect of the baroque period. The great fire that destroyed most of the heart of London in 1666 provided Wren with an opportunity to build numerous baroque structures. His masterpiece is St. Paul's Cathedral, with its lofty dome and columns.

In the eighteenth century, architecture tended to become less massive, relying heavily on multiple curves and lacy shell-like ornamentation. This style is usually referred to as rococo. One of the best examples of the rococo style is Frederick the Great's Sans Souci Palace at Potsdam. The rococo style, like the baroque, represented an age of royal and aristocratic affluence.

Music

The classical spirit pervaded the music of the seventeenth and eighteenth centuries as it did the literature and the visual arts; and like the literature and the visual arts, the music was an outgrowth of Renaissance developments.[1] The piano and the violin family of instruments, whose forebears appeared in the sixteenth century, developed rapidly in the seventeenth. In the late seventeenth and early eighteenth centuries, three Italian families, the Amati, the Guarneri, and the Stradivari, fashioned the finest violins ever made. The seventeenth century was also marked by the rise of the opera. Alessandro Scarlatti in Italy, Jean-Baptiste Lully in France, and Henry Purcell in England popularized this grandiose combination of music and drama. The eighteenth was the great century of classical music—the age of Bach, Handel, Haydn, and Mozart.

Johann Sebastian Bach (1685–1750) was a member of a German family long distinguished in music. Noted in his own lifetime chiefly as an organist, he composed a vast array of great music for organ, harpsichord, and clavichord (forerunner of the piano), orchestra, and chorus, much of which has been lost. Most of Bach's compositions were religiously inspired, and he holds the same position in Protestant music that the sixteenth-century Palestrina does in the music of the Roman Catholic church. Bach was not widely appreciated in his own day. It was not until Felix Mendelssohn "discovered" him in the nineteenth century that he became widely known.

George Frederick Handel (1685–1759) was born in central Germany in the same year as Bach and not many miles distant. He studied Italian opera in Germany and Italy and wrote forty-six operas himself. He became court musician of the elector of Hanover. Later he made his home in England, as did the elector, who became King George I of England. Handel wrote an enormous quantity of music, both instrumental and vocal. All of it is marked by dignity, formal elegance, and melodious harmony—fitting for and appreciated in an age of royal splendor. His best-known work is the majestic oratorio *The Messiah*, heard every Christmas season.

Franz Joseph Haydn (1732–1809), unlike Handel, was primarily interested in instrumental music; he was the chief originator of the symphony. During his long career in Vienna, which he helped to make the music capital of the world, he wrote more than a hundred symphonies in addition to scores of compositions of other forms of music, particularly chamber music. It was in his hands that orchestral music really came into its own. All his work is in the formal, classical style. He became a friend and an important source of inspiration for the younger Mozart.

---

[1] Some music historians designate the music of the seventeenth and early eighteenth centuries, including that of Bach and Handel, as baroque, which was a forerunner of classical.

FIGURE 31.6 Pieter Brueghel the Younger, *Flemish Country Festival* This early-seventeenth-century painting shows one of the many typical festivals that took place during the year. Often such festivals were occasioned by religious holidays and celebrations. Here the lines between religion, social life, and popular culture blur as villagers gather and celebrate. (Galleria Sabauda, Turin/Art Resource)

Wolfgang Amadeus Mozart (1756–1791) is regarded by many students as the greatest musical genius of all time. Born in Salzburg, he spent most of his adult life in Vienna. Mozart began composing at the age of five (possibly four), and gave public concerts on the harpsichord at the age of six. At twelve he wrote an opera. Before his untimely death at the age of thirty-five, he wrote more than six hundred compositions in all the known musical forms. Symphonies, chamber music, and piano sonatas and concertos were his favorite forms. His best-known operas are *The Marriage of Figaro, Don Giovanni,* and *The Magic Flute*. In the masterful hands of Mozart the classical style reached the peak of its perfection. Never had music been so clear, melodic, elegant, and graceful.

Popular Culture

The formal literature and the baroque art of the seventeenth and eighteenth centuries reflected the concerns and tastes of the elite classes. However, the lower classes were not without cultural outlets that fit their lives and were available to them.

Numerous festivals and public ceremonies occurred throughout the year (see Figure 31.6). Some reflected the seasons, which were of particular importance to societies so dependent on agriculture, while others reflected events on the Christian calendar, such as Christmas and Easter. Traditional weddings involved a community procession and festivities as well as a religious ceremony. Music, dancing, feasts, game, and play were part of these festivals and community events.

Sports also brought communities together and were often violent. The most popular involved animals, such as cockfighting and dogfighting. Others, such as soccer and cricket, became more organized, sometimes drawing large crowds.

Literacy was growing, thanks to the printing press, the demands of business, and more primary schools. Some 40 to 60 percent of the population in England and France could read by the end of the eighteenth century, and this was reflected in the growth of popular literature. Stirring religious tracts as well as romances of chivalric valor were widely circulated.

Finally, the line between elite and popular culture was not very sharp. Members of all classes could be found at village festivals and sporting events. The middle and upper classes read some of the same popular literature enjoyed by the lower classes, while the lower classes had some access to the plays, art, and architecture that reflected elite tastes.

SUGGESTED READING

General

F. Braudel, *The Structures of Everyday Life: The Limits of the Possible* (1982). A massive, highly respected social history.

H. Kamen, *European Society, 1500–1700* (1985). A solid survey.

I. Woloch, *Eighteenth Century Europe, Tradition and Progress, 1715–1789* (1982). Emphasizes social history and popular culture.

Society

P. Ariés, *Centuries of Childhood: A Social History of Family Life* (1962). A path-breaking work.

J. V. Beckett, *The Aristocracy in England* (1986). A good recent study.

J. Blum, *The End of the Old Order in Rural Europe* (1978). Excellent comparative study.

M. W. Flinn, *The European Demographic System, 1500–1820* (1981). A recent survey.

A. Fraser, *The Weaker Vessel: Woman's Lot in Seventeenth-Century England* (1985). Portraits of seventeenth-century women.

P. Laslett, *The World We Have Lost* (1965). A classic study of English society during the period.

E. Shorter, *The Making of the Modern Family* (1975). Interpretive, controversial, and well written.

L. Stone, *The Family, Sex and Marriage in England, 1500–1800* (1977). A sophisticated interpretation.

L. Tilly and J. Scott, *Women, Work and Family* (1978). A highly respected work.

J. de Vries, *European Urbanization, 1500–1800* (1984). Broad recent survey.

Faith

A. Armstrong, *The Church of England, the Methodists, and Society 1700–1850* (1973). A broad survey.

G. R. Cragg, *The Church and the Age of Reason* (1961). A solid survey.

Culture

A. Adam, *Grandeur and Illusion: French Literature and Society 1600–1715* (1972). A thorough survey of French literature and its relation to seventeenth-century society.

P. Burke, *Popular Culture in Early Modern Europe* (1978). Focuses on ordinary people.

J. Held, *Seventeenth and Eighteenth Century Art: Baroque Painting, Sculpture, Architecture* (1971). A useful general survey.

C. Palisca, *Baroque Music* (1968). Excellent survey.

C. Rosen, *The Classical Style: Haydn, Mozart, Beethoven* (1972). Excellent study.

I. Watt, *The Rise of the Novel: Studies of Defoe, Richardson, and Fielding* (1957). A good introduction.

CHAPTER 32

Royal Absolutism in Western and Eastern Europe

FIGURE 32.1 Pierre Patel the Elder, *Versailles,* 1668 This painting shows Louis XIV's palace and grounds at Versailles in 1668. The scale and order of Versailles reflected the grandeur of the French monarchy at its height. Other European monarchs modeled their palaces after Versailles in an attempt to increase their own prestige. (Lauros-Giraudon/Art Resource)

During the seventeenth and eighteenth centuries, several monarchs in western and eastern Europe increased the power of their central governments and elevated themselves as holders of that power. These monarchs often justified their absolute powers as a divine right and surrounded themselves with advisers and admirers who supported royal absolutism. While in some countries the trend was away from monarchical power, royal absolutism became the dominant political development of this period.

1. ABSOLUTISM IN WESTERN EUROPE: FRANCE

France was the most powerful nation in western Europe throughout most of the seventeenth and eighteenth centuries. Under Louis XIV royal absolutism not only reached its peak in France but also served as a model that other monarchs sought to emulate.

While French monarchs had been gaining power for their central government and themselves since the fifteenth century (see pp. 362–363), the immediate roots of royal absolutism in France go back to the reign of Henry IV (1589–1610).

The Roots of French Absolutism

When Henry IV became king of France in 1589, his country was torn by several decades of bitter religious war. Respect for law and order had broken down. The feudal nobility had in many cases reasserted its own authority. The finances of the central government were in chaos. Roads and bridges were in disrepair. French prestige abroad was at a low ebb; even the city of Paris was garrisoned by the Spanish troops of Philip II.

Henry of Navarre, the first of the Bourbon dynasty to rule France, set out to change all this. The new king, in his prime at the age of thirty-six, was debonair and witty, courageous, generous, and optimistic. His slogan ''A chicken in the pot of every peasant for Sunday dinner'' was more than an idle phrase; it is little wonder that *Henri Quatre* became the most popular monarch in French history. The romantic Henry had in the duke of Sully an able, methodical administrator to serve and steady him. The most urgent task

was to restore the authority of the central government. This Henry set out to do by vigorously suppressing brigandage and enforcing the law. The lesser nobility was brought to heel directly and quickly. The powerful nobility was dealt with more gingerly, but by the end of Henry's reign real headway had been made toward reducing the nobles to obedience to the central government.

Henry and Sully launched a comprehensive program of economic reconstruction. Agriculture and commerce benefited from the increased security of life and property, from the repair of roads, bridges, and harbors, and from the freeing of internal and external commerce from many obstructions and tariff barriers. Marshes were drained for farming. Better breeding methods were introduced. Peasants' livestock and implements were protected against seizure for debt or taxes. New industries producing glass, porcelain, lace, tapestries, and fine leather and textiles were subsidized and protected by the state. Silk culture, which brought vast wealth to France, was introduced. Sully's efficient administration of expenditures resulted in a budget surplus for the first time in many years.

Henry defused the religious turmoil that had weakened France by granting religious toleration to the Huguenot minority. A *politique,* Henry abjured Protestantism in order to gain acceptance as king of an overwhelmingly Roman Catholic nation. The Edict of Nantes, which Henry IV issued in 1598, granted the Huguenots not only complete freedom of conscience and limited public worship but also civil and political equality. Moreover, they were given military control of some two hundred fortified cities and towns as a guarantee against future oppression.

Having laid the foundations for royal supremacy, economic health, and religious toleration, Henry IV in the last years of his reign devoted an increasing amount of attention to foreign affairs. His goal was to make France first secure and then supreme in Europe by weakening the power of the Spanish and Austrian Hapsburgs. In 1610 he readied his armies for a campaign, but just as he was preparing to join them he was assassinated by a fanatic.

After fourteen years of retrogression under Henry IV's Italian wife, Marie de Médicis, and their young and inept son Louis XIII (1610–1643),

Cardinal Richelieu gained active control over the government of France. Although technically a mere servant of the fickle Louis XIII, the masterful cardinal made himself so indispensable that for eighteen years (1624–1642) he held firm control over French affairs. Handsome, arrogant, and calculating, Richelieu was a true Machiavellian. His twofold policy, from which he never veered, was similar to that of Henry IV—to make the royal power supreme in France and France supreme in Europe.

Believing the high nobility and the Huguenots to be the chief threats to royal absolutism, Richelieu crushed them both. With the royal army at his disposal, he boldly destroyed the castles of nobles who remained defiant, disbanded their private armies, and hanged a number of the most recalcitrant. The special military and political privileges that the Huguenots enjoyed under the Edict of Nantes were considered by Richelieu to be intolerable, giving them the status of a state within a state. After a bloody two-year struggle, he stripped the Huguenots of these privileges, although he left their religious and civil liberties intact.

In order to dilute local political influence, which in some provinces was still strong, the dynamic minister divided France into some thirty administrative districts called *généralités,* each of which was placed under the control of an *intendant,*[1] who was an agent of the crown. These *intendants* were chosen from the ranks of the bourgeoisie and were shifted around frequently lest they become too sympathetic with the people over whom they ruled. The royal will was thus further extended throughout France.

Although Richelieu was a cardinal in the Roman Catholic church, he did not hesitate to plunge France into the Thirty Years' War in Germany on the side of the Protestants. His purpose, of course, was to weaken the Hapsburgs, chief rivals of the French Bourbons for European supremacy. When Richelieu died in 1642, he had gone far toward bringing to fruition Henry IV's policies of royal supremacy in France and French supremacy in Europe. Richelieu, however, did not share Henry IV's concern for the common people. Their lot became harder under the imperious and ruthless cardinal, at whose death they rejoiced.

Richelieu was succeeded by his protégé, Cardinal Mazarin. Louis XIII's death in 1643, one year after that of his great minister, left the throne to Louis XIV (1643–1715), a child of five. Mazarin played the same role in the early reign of Louis XIV that Richelieu had played during most of the reign of Louis XIII. From the death of Richelieu in 1642 until his own death in 1661, Mazarin vigorously pursued the policies of his predecessor. The Thirty Years' War was brought to a successful conclusion. Between 1648 and 1652, he put down the *Fronde*—a series of uprisings by disgruntled nobility and townspeople. All who challenged the crown's authority were crushed. When Marazin died in 1661, he passed along to young Louis XIV a royal power that was unprecedented and a national state that was easily the first power of Europe.

Louis XIV and His Government

Louis XIV was twenty-three years old when, in 1661, he stepped forth as the principal actor on the world's gaudiest stage. Young Louis was well fitted for the part. He had a sound body and a regal bearing. His lack of intellectual brilliance and deep learning were more than offset by a large store of common sense, a sharp memory, a sense of responsibility, and a capacity for hard, tedious work. From his Spanish mother, from Mazarin, and from his tutors he had gained the conviction that he was God's appointed deputy for France. In Bishop Bossuet he had the most famous of all theorists and exponents of royal absolutism. Bossuet in numerous writings argued that absolute monarchy is the normal, the most efficient, and the divinely ordained form of government. He contended that, furthermore, the royal monarch, the image of God and directly inspired by God, is above human reproach and accountable to God alone. These ideas as acted out by Louis gained and held the ascendancy throughout the continent of Europe during the late seventeenth and most of the eighteenth centuries.

Absolute though he might consider himself (the words *"L état, c'est moi"* ["I am the state"]

---

[1]The *intendants* had existed before Richelieu's time, but he greatly increased their power and functions.

are often attributed to him), Louis could not possibly perform all the functions of government personally. Actually, the great bulk of the decisions and details of government were handled by a series of councils and bureaus and were administered locally by the *intendants*. Distrusting nobles, Louis appointed members of the middle class to the important offices of his government. As supervised by the industrious Louis XIV, however, the administrative machinery worked smoothly and efficiently. In fact, it was the envy of his fellow monarchs and probably constituted his most constructive achievement. There was no semblance of popular participation in government. The role of the people was to serve and obey; in return, they enjoyed reflected glory and received such benefits as the monarch might be willing and able to bestow on them.

In line with Louis XIV's concept of divine right absolutism, he believed that he should have a palace worthy of God's chief deputy on earth. Hating tumultuous Paris, congested and crowded with vulgar tradespeople, he selected Versailles, eleven miles southwest of the city, to be the new seat of government. There as many as thirty-five thousand workmen toiled for thirty years, turning the marshes and sandy wastes into the world's most splendid court (see Figure 32.1). Around his court Louis XIV gathered the great nobles of France and turned them into court butterflies (see Figure 32.2). He subsidized and brought to Versailles the leading French artists and literacy figures. But this great monument to royal absolutism was not beloved by all. The balls, parades, hunts, and social ritual were not sufficient to absorb the energy of the vivacious and ambitious nobility of France. The court seethed with gossip, scandal, and intrigue. Nor did the hard-toiling, heavily taxed French masses, who were supposed to enjoy the reflected glory of the monarch, always appreciate such extravagant glamour. Indeed, there were increasing expressions of discontent.

Colbert and the French Economy

Louis XIV was fortunate to have at his command during the first half of his reign a prodigious financial manager. Jean-Baptiste Colbert (1619–1683) was an inordinately ambitious social climber who realized that, because of his bourgeois origin, his only means of advancement was through indispensable service to the king. An engine of efficiency, he toiled endlessly, supervising the countless details of the French economy.

Under Colbert, mercantilism reached its peak. French industries were protected by prohibitive tariffs, while exports and new industries were subsidized. Raw materials, however, were strictly husbanded. Imperial and commercial activities in India and North America were vigorously promoted. To protect this growing empire and the commerce it generated, a large navy was built. But Colbert did not stop with these traditional mercantilist practices. In order to gain a worldwide reputation for the uniformly high quality of French products, all manufacturing was subjected to the most minute regulation and supervision. So many threads of such and such quality and color must go into every inch of this textile and that lace. A veritable army of inspectors enforced the regulations. This extreme policy of mercantilism, the economic adjunct to royal absolutism, has come to be called Colbertism. It achieved its immediate end so far as quality and reputation were concerned, but it stifled initiative and retarded future industrial development. That Colbert was able to balance the budget and achieve general economic prosperity in the face of Louis XIV's lavish expenditures, including the building of Versailles, was a remarkable feat. It is well, however, that Colbert died in 1683, for Louis' wars of aggression eventually wrecked most of the great minister's work. Much of Europe copied Colbert's policies and techniques during the latter part of the seventeenth and most of the eighteenth centuries.

Absolutism and Religion

It was virtually inevitable that Louis XIV's concepts of divine right monarchy would have religious repercussions. First, they ran counter to the papal claims of authority over the French clergy. Numerous conflicts between the king and pope resulted in a statement of Gallican Liberties, which greatly freed the French church from Roman domination. Second, Louis' absolutism ran afoul of the Jansenists, an influential group within France's Catholic church that emphasized predestination, inner piety, and the ascetic life.

FIGURE 32.2 Charles Lebrun, *Chancellor Seguier* Chancellor Seguier, a patron of the seventeenth-century French artist Lebrun, is shown here as an ambitious courtier to Louis XIV. In formal robes, this member of France's new nobility (*noblesse de robe*) is attended by pages as if he were a monarch. (The Louvre, Paris)

Eventually the Jesuits persuaded the pope to declare Jansenism heretical and aroused Louis XIV against the Jansenists. He outlawed the sect and destroyed its buildings. Finally, Louis XIV moved against the Huguenots—France's Protestants. In 1685 he revoked the Edict of Nantes and the Protestant religion was outlawed. Although Huguenots were forbidden to emigrate, many—probably a quarter million—succeeded in doing so, taking much of their wealth and all their economic knowledge and skills with them to Protestant areas of Europe and America.

Louis XIV's Wars of Aggression

The Sun King was not content to rule the world's most powerful nation. He wanted to expand France's borders. Louis' war minister, the marquis of Louvois, organized France's huge military establishment on a scientific and business-like basis, replete with supply depots and hospitals. He introduced strict discipline, uniforms, and marching drills. Sébastien de Vauban was one of the great designers of fortifications and of siege operations. It was a common saying that a city defended by Vauban was safe and that a city besieged by Vauban was doomed. Henri-Jules Condé was an able and dashing military leader and the viscount of Turenne a masterly planner of campaigns and battles.

During the last four decades of his seventy-two-year reign Louis XIV fought four wars of aggression, at times unifying most of the other military powers of western Europe against him. By the end of the Dutch War in 1678, Louis XIV had gained some valuable territories. But the tide turned. His final struggle, the War of the Spanish Succession, lasted eleven years (1702–1713) and resulted in a series of defeats. Beaten and exhausted, Louis XIV was forced to accept the Treaty of Utrecht (1713). He was left with little more than he had started with some fifty years earlier.

Louis XIV lived only two years after the signing of the Treaty of Utrecht. He had long outlived his popularity. As the body of the grandest of all the absolute monarchs was drawn through the streets of Paris, some of his abused people cursed in the taverns as the coffin passed.

The Decline of French Absolutism

The French monarchy never again achieved the power it had wielded under Louis XIV. Certainly France remained a first-rank power with a large army, a centralized bureaucracy, and a growing economy. But between 1715 and 1789 the monarchy slowly declined.

Expensive wars and unreformed taxation policies left the treasury depleted after Louis XIV's death. The clergy and nobility retained most of their immunity from taxation despite the efforts of several ministers to break those privileges. The debt grew, and the monarchy was weakened by its inability to reform its finances to lessen the burden of that debt.

Underlying these political and financial problems was a resurgence of the aristocracy. In the decades between 1715 and 1789 the monarchy was faced by an increasingly assertive aristocracy anxious to recapture some of its old political power. Ambitious aristocrats thwarted the kings' efforts to reform taxes. They set themselves up as centers of aristocratic opposition to the monarchy, above all through their control of the *parlements* (law courts).

Thus, by the middle decades of the eighteenth century, the French monarchy had clearly declined from its heights under Louis XIV. When problems came to a head in the 1780s, the king was unable to handle them and the monarchy was toppled by a great revolution.

2. ABSOLUTISM IN EASTERN EUROPE

At the beginning of the seventeenth century eastern Europe exhibited certain characteristics that set it in sharp contrast to western Europe. Economically, the states east of the Elbe River were less commercially developed than those in western Europe. Estate agriculture (large landed estates owned by lords and worked by their serfs) remained the rule. Socially, the landed aristocracy dominated these areas to a greater extent than in western Europe. Indeed, this aristocracy had generally succeeded in reversing the medieval trends toward greater freedom for the peasantry and the growth of towns. During the fifteenth, sixteenth, and seventeenth centuries serfdom was reimposed with greater severity than ever, and the landed aristocracy won in its struggle with competing urban centers. Politically, many areas lacked the strong central government found in the western European states.

The most significant political developments in central and eastern Europe during the seventeenth and eighteenth centuries were the rise of Prussia, the centralization of Austria, and the expansion of Russia, three states that developed strong national governments and powerful monarchies. At the opening of the seventeenth century, the two chief powers in central and eastern Europe were the Ottoman and Hapsburg empires. Although the Islamic Ottoman Turks had been restrained by Hapsburg military power in the sixteenth century on both land and sea, they were about to renew their effort to conquer Christian Europe. The Austrian Hapsburgs, in addition to disputing the control of southeastern Europe with the Turks, dominated the Holy Roman Empire, which included all the German states. In northeastern Europe, Sweden, Prussia, Poland, and Russia competed for hegemony. Among all these powers, Prussia and Russia had hitherto been the least conspicuous in world affairs. During the seventeenth and eighteenth centuries, Prussia and Russia would become major powers and assume an active role in international politics.

The Hohenzollerns and the Hapsburgs

The political history of Prussia is in large measure the history of Hohenzollern family rulers. In 1415 the Hohenzollerns became rulers of Brandenburg (1415), a bleak and thinly populated little province within the Holy Roman Empire. In the centuries that followed until they were finally overthrown at the end of the World War I in 1918, they followed a threefold policy: militarism and territorial aggrandizement, paternal despotism, and centralized bureaucracy. The first to take major steps toward making Brandenburg an important power was Frederick William (1640–1688), the Great Elector. One of the ablest of all the Hohenzollerns, he acquired several new territories at the end of the Thirty Years' War. He centralized and administered the governments of his scattered territories with energy and skill. He won in his struggles with the Estates, the representative assemblies of the realm, gaining the crucial power to collect taxes and eliminating the Estates as a functioning institution. He established and strengthened his standing army. He managed an important compromise with the landed aristocracy, allowing them complete control over their serfs but committing them to his government as members of his bureaucracy and his military officer corps. He protected the native industries, improved communications, and aided agriculture. In a most intolerant age he followed a policy of religious toleration. When Louis XIV revoked the Edict of Nantes in 1685, Frederick William welcomed thousands of industrious Huguenots to Brandenburg. At the death of the Great Elector in 1688, Brandenburg was on the road to becoming a great power.

The next Hohenzollern, Frederick I (1688–1713), acquired the title of king for the dynasty. The Hapsburg Holy Roman emperor in 1701 granted Frederick the title in return for aid against Louis XIV in the War of the Spanish Succession. Frederick I chose Prussia rather than Brandenburg for the name of his kingdom, since Prussia was outside the Holy Roman Empire and a free sovereign state. Hence Brandenburg became Prussia.

From 1713 to 1740 Prussia was ruled by a vigorous militaristic autocrat, Frederick William I (since he was the first Frederick William to be king). Unquestioned absolutism, machinelike centralized bureaucratic administration, and, above all, militarism were his obsessions. He built the Prussian army into the most efficient and one of the largest fighting forces in Europe. And yet Frederick William was so efficient and miserly that he was also able to pass along to his talented son, Frederick II, a well-filled treasury.

In the same year (1740) that Frederick II became King of Prussia, Maria Theresa became archduchess of the Austrian Hapsburg dominions. During the second half of the seventeenth century the Austrian Hapsburgs had successfully carried out a policy of centralizing their power in those lands they directly controlled (rather than the Holy Roman Empire) and expanding to the east. The monarchy improved its administration, established a powerful standing army, gained at least a fragile allegiance of the nobility, and acquired territories at the expense of the Ottoman empire and Poland.

In 1740 Frederick II challenged Maria Theresa's authority by marching his troops into Silesia, one of the richest of the Hapsburg provinces. This Machiavellian act by the young Prussian king plunged most of the major European states into a series of wars for the mastery of central Europe. The War of the Austrian Succession lasted for eight years (1740–1748). Maria Theresa successfully repelled the Bavarians, Saxons, French, and Spaniards, but she was unable to dislodge Frederick II from Silesia. Frederick, on his part, cynically deserted his allies as soon as he had achieved his own purposes.

The Hapsburgs, however, had no intention of being thus despoiled of one of their fairest provinces by the upstart Hohenzollerns. Proud rulers over territories many times the size and population of Prussia and for centuries emperors of the Holy Roman Empire, they viewed the Hohenzollerns with condescension. Maria Theresa's able diplomat, Count Kaunitz, was soon at work lining up allies.

Frederick was not one to wait for his enemies

FIGURE 32.3 Frederick II Before His Troops During the seventeenth and eighteenth centuries, the rulers of Brandenburg-Prussia used their armies to build up the state, making it one of the major powers of eastern and central Europe. Here, Frederick II of Prussia is shown in a characteristic military pose, exemplifying the strong alliance of the monarchy and army. (The Mansell Collection, London)

to strike first. As soon as he became aware of their designs, he opened hostilities by overrunning Saxony (see Figure 32.3). Thus began the Seven Years' War (1756–1763). Frederick, with his slender resources, soon found himself at bay; the four greatest military powers on the continent of Europe were closing in on him from all directions. After tenaciously holding his enemies off for six years, defeat appeared to be near. Then in 1762 the Russian Tsarina Elizabeth, one of his bitterest enemies, died and was succeeded by the ineffective Peter III, who was an ardent admirer of Frederick II and who put Russia's forces at the disposal of Prussia. Although Peter III was soon murdered by a group of his own officers and court nobility and Russia withdrew from the war, the remaining allies had no further stomach for the fight. The Peace of Hubertusburg in 1763 left things as they had been at the beginning of the war, with Prussia retaining the controversial Silesia. In the same year the Treaty of Paris brought to a close the colonial struggle between Great Britain and France in India and North America, leaving Great Britain master of both.

Having so narrowly escaped destruction, Frederick the Great spent the remaining twenty-three years of his life reconstructing his war-ravaged territories. He encouraged agriculture, subsidized and protected industry, and invited immigrants into his well-governed territories. At no time, though, did he neglect his war machine. In 1772 he joined Austria and Russia in the first partition of Poland. Frederick took West Prussia, thus joining East Prussia with the main body of the Prussian state. When Frederick II died in 1786, Prussia had been raised to the status of a great power, sharing the leadership of central Europe equally with Austria. During his reign Prussia's size and population had more than doubled, and its military exploits pointed to a spectacular future (see Map 32.1).

Russia and the Romanovs

While Prussia was becoming a great power in central Europe, Russia was rising to prominence to the east. The first of the grand dukes of Muscovy under whom Russia took on the shape of a modern national state was Ivan III (1462–1505). In 1480 Ivan III defeated the rapidly declining Mongols and limited their power in Russia to the southeastern area. Ivan greatly extended his sway to both the north and the west by military conquest. After his marriage to Sophia Palaeologus, heiress to the now-defunct Byzantine (Eastern Roman) Empire, Ivan declared himself successor to the Eastern Roman Caesars—hence the title "tsar." When he died, the foundations of a Russian national state had been laid (see Map 32.2).

Ivan IV (1533–1584), "the Terrible," added both to the authority of the Russian tsars and to the territories over which they ruled. He destroyed the remaining power of the Mongols in southeastern Russia and annexed most of their territory. It was during Ivan IV's reign that Russia's conquest of Siberia was begun. Half a century later the Russian flag was planted on the shores of the Pacific.

The twenty-nine years following the death of Ivan IV are known as the Time of Troubles (1584–1613). Weak rulers and disputed successions resulted in such anarchy that the Poles were able

Map 32.1 THE GROWTH OF PRUSSIA, 1614–1807 These maps show the growth of Brandenburg-Prussia during the seventeenth and eighteenth centuries. The maps reveal the lack of connections among many of Brandenburg-Prussia's lands; one of Prussia's long-term goals in the eighteenth and nineteenth centuries was to connect those territories it already controlled as well as to expand its holdings.

to capture Moscow and hold it briefly. To end the political chaos, a group of leading nobles in 1613 chose Michael Romanov as tsar.

The early decades of the Romanov dynasty, which was to rule Russia until the Revolution of 1917, were not easy. There were great popular discontent and numerous uprisings between the late 1640s and the early 1670s as the lower classes rebelled against the nobles and the central government, who were making serfdom even more onerous and life for townspeople more difficult. The discontent reached a climax with the revolts led by Stenka Razin in the late 1660s and early 1670s. Razin was finally caught and executed, thus ending that series of threats. During this same period problems within the Russian Orthodox church broke out as many, known as the Old Believers, rejected liturgical changes initiated by the patriarch of Moscow. The effect of this controversy was to drive the Church into greater dependence on the secular government. Nevertheless, by the final decades of the seventeenth century the Romanov tsars had managed to overcome these problems, improve the central administration, and extend their authority. They

gradually established commercial and cultural contacts with the West. Increasing numbers of traders, artisans, and adventurers from central and western Europe, particularly Germany, came to Russia to seek their fortunes. Thus the stage was set for Russia to become more fully involved in European affairs. This involvement became especially important during the reign of Peter the Great.

Peter I (1689–1725) was an unusually large, vigorous, and ambitious individual. At the age of seventeen he seized the reins of government from his elder sister. For the next thirty-six years he devoted his boundless energy to the twofold policy of strengthening his own authority and his military forces and of gaining access to the west on the Baltic and Black seas.

Peter concluded that one of the best ways to increase his own political and military power was to copy Western practices. He traveled in western Europe and learned much about Western customs and techniques, which he proceeded to introduce into Russia. After crushing a revolt of his bodyguard with a ruthlessness that cowed all potential troublemakers, he adopted the bu-

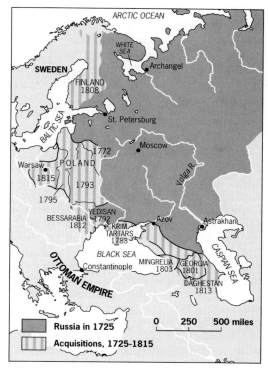

Map 32.2 **THE GROWTH OF RUSSIA IN THE WEST** These maps show the steady expansion of Russia to the west and south, acquiring access on the Baltic and Black seas under Peter the Great and extending its territories further in the course of the eighteenth century.

reaucratic system of western European monarchs in both central and local government to make his authority more absolute. Western technicians were brought to Russia in large numbers, and new industries were subsidized and protected by mercantilist policies. Western, particularly French, social customs were introduced to the upper and middle classes of Russian society. Women were brought out of seclusion, and the long beards and flowing Oriental robes of the men were banned. These reforms hardly touched the peasant masses, who were increasingly tied down in a system of serfdom bordering on slavery—a process that had been going on in Russia throughout the sixteenth and seventeenth centuries. When the patriarch of the Russian Ortho-

dox church opposed the tsar's authority and some of his Westernizing policies, Peter abolished the patriarchate. Henceforth, the Orthodox church was a powerful instrument of the Russian government. But Peter the Great's chief concern was always his military establishment. He built a navy and patterned his conscript army after that of Prussia. By the end of his reign, Russia had one of the major fighting forces of Europe.

When Peter became tsar, Russia had no warm-water access to the west. Sweden held the coveted shores of the Baltic Sea, and the Ottoman Turks occupied the territory north of the Black Sea. Peter's efforts to dislodge the Ottoman Turks were not very successful, but after an extended, costly war with Sweden, in which Peter lost the early battles to his adversary, Charles XII, Peter's efforts were rewarded. By the Treaty of Nystad in 1721, Russia received the Swedish Baltic provinces of Livonia, Estonia, Ingria, and Karelia. On the Neva River near the Baltic, Peter built a new, modern capital, St. Petersburg, facing the west. At his death in 1725, Russia was a great and growing power ready to play a major role in European affairs.

Peter the Great was followed by a succession of weak or mediocre rulers. After an interval of thirty-seven years, Catherine the Great (1762–1796) ascended the Russian throne. Catherine was an obscure princess from one of the little German states. She had been married for political reasons to young Peter III, grandson of Peter the Great, while he was still heir to the Russian crown. After he became tsar, Peter III quickly alienated all classes of his subjects. Less than a year after her husband became tsar, Catherine conspired with a group of aristocratic army officers, who murdered Peter and declared Catherine tsarina of Russia.

The Machiavellian tsarina prided herself on being an enlightened despot, as was fashionable in the late eighteenth century, but few of her enlightened ideas were translated into political or social deeds. Some apparent reforming efforts ended when Russian serfs rose in one of the greatest insurrections in history. In 1773, under the able leadership of a Don Cossack, Pugachev, hundreds of thousands of serfs marched against their masters. The rebellion was put down with difficulty. The cruel repression left Russian serfs almost as slaves to the privileged nobility.

Catherine the Great followed an aggressive foreign policy. Peter the Great had reached the Baltic by despoiling the Swedes. Catherine reached the Black Sea, the Balkan peninsula, and the heart of Europe by defeating the Turks and destroying Poland. When she finally died in 1796, Russia was a nation ominous in size and power and a major factor in European and world affairs.

Poland, Sweden, and the Ottoman Empire

By the end of the eighteenth century, Prussia and Russia were rising, major powers in Europe. Poland, Sweden, and the Ottoman Empire did not fare so well.

Poland, at the opening of the eighteenth century, was the third largest country in Europe, exceeded in size only by Russia and Sweden. In the sixteenth and seventeenth centuries it had appeared that Poland would become a major power. Taking advantage of Russia's Time of Troubles (1584–1613), the Poles had captured Moscow. In the latter part of the century they had saved Vienna from the Turks.

Actually, however, the Polish nation was far from strong. Sprawling over a large area between Russia and the German states, it enjoyed no natural boundaries either to the east or to the west. The eastern half of its territory was inhabited by Russian-speaking people. The northern provinces were peopled largely by Latvians, Lithuanians, and Germans. There were also many Germans in the west. Religious cleavages followed the language lines.

Moreover, there was no strong middle class to vitalize Poland's economy. In the late Middle Ages a sizable overland commerce between the Black and Baltic seas had flowed across Poland. But with the shifting of commercial routes and centers to the west in the early sixteenth century, Poland's commerce had withered. Furthermore, the Polish nobility, jealous of its own power and fearful of an alliance between the bourgeoisie and the king, deliberately penalized commerce with severe restrictions. The great mass of the people were serfs, tilling the soil of the powerful nobility.

In the face of so many divisive forces, only a strong central government could have made Poland into a stable national state. But here lay Poland's greatest weakness. The kingship was elective, and the great nobles who held the elective power saw to it that no strong king ever came to the throne. During the eighteenth century the kings were all foreigners or puppets of foreign powers. The legislative Diet was completely monopolized by the nobility. So that each noble's rights were safeguarded, unanimity was required for the passage of every measure. This system guaranteed virtual political anarchy. National spirit was weak. The all-powerful nobles were far more concerned for their own private interests than for the well-being of the nation.

It would have been surprising had such a power vacuum as eighteenth-century Poland not invited the aggression of its ambitious neighbors.

In 1772 Catherine the Great and Frederick the Great bargained to take slices of Polish territory. The somewhat less greedy Maria Theresa of Austria, fearful of being outdistanced by Russia and Prussia, joined them. This aggression at long last stirred the Poles to action. Sweeping reforms were passed, improving the condition of the peasants and the bourgeoisie and giving the king and the Diet power to act effectively. But it was too late. They were no match for the professional armies of Russia, Prussia, and Austria, who in 1795 divided the remainder of Poland among themselves.

Poland was not the only victim in eastern Europe of the powerful Russian, Prussian, and Austrian armies. Sweden and the Ottoman Empire also declined, both relatively and actually. Sweden had become the dominant military power in northern and eastern Europe under Gustavus Adolphus in the early seventeenth century. At the opening of the eighteenth century Sweden was second only to Russia in size among the nations of Europe, holding large areas east and south of the Baltic in addition to the homeland. However, its population and resources were too small to hold such far-flung territories, which were coveted by the ambitious and growing Prussia and Russia, for very long. Charles XII made a spectacular effort to hold them, but in the end he lost all his trans-Baltic territories except Finland, and he dissipated Sweden's strength in doing so. Sweden has never been a major power since.

The Ottoman Turks, after reaching the gates of Vienna early in the sixteenth century and again late in the seventeenth century, weakened rapidly. The Treaty of Karlowitz in 1699 limited their power in Europe to the Balkan peninsula and a strip of territory north of the Black Sea. Their two serious defeats at the hands of Catherine the Great marked the beginning of the breakup of the Ottoman Empire.

By the end of the eighteenth century, the three dominant powers in central and eastern Europe were the relatively static Austrian Hapsburg Empire and the two rapidly rising states—Prussia and Russia (see Map 32.3). Each of these states, like France in western Europe, had developed strong central governments with standing armies, large bureaucracies, and organized systems of taxation under the monarch's control.

Map 32.3 EASTERN EUROPE, SIXTEENTH–EIGHTEENTH CENTURIES Between the sixteenth and eighteenth centuries, political power in central and eastern Europe shifted fundamentally. The first map shows Sweden, the Holy Roman Empire, Poland, and the Ottoman Empire in the sixteenth and early seventeenth centuries. The second map shows that by the end of the eighteenth century, these powers except for Sweden had all but been replaced by Prussia, the Russian Empire, and the Austrian Empire, and Sweden's holdings had been diminished by Russian Expansion.

SUGGESTED READING

General

P. Anderson, *Lineages of the Absolutist State* (1974). A good Marxist analysis.

R. N. Hatton, *Europe in the Age of Louis XIV* (1979). A well-illustrated survey.

D. McKay and H. Scott, *The Rise of the Great Powers, 1648–1815* (1983). A good survey.

D. Pennington, *Europe in the Seventeenth Century* (1989). A recent introduction.

Absolutism in Western Europe

W. Beik, *Absolutism and Society in Seventeenth-Century France* (1985). A well-written interpretation of French absolutism.

W. F. Church, ed., *Louis XIV in Historical Thought* (1978). Conflicting interpretations of Louis XIV.

P. Goubert, *Louis XIV and Twenty Million Frenchmen* (1970). A respected study of French society and politics.

H. Rowen, *The King's State: Proprietary Dynasticism in Early Modern France* (1980). Analyzes the theory of Louis XIV's rule.

V. L. Tapié, *France in the Age of Louis XIII and Richelieu* (1974). A good survey.

A. Trout, *Jean-Baptiste Colbert* (1978). Analyzes his economic policies.

Absolutism in Eastern Europe

P. Coles, *The Ottoman Impact on Europe, 1350–1699* (1968). A well-written study.

N. Davies, *God's Playground: A History of England*, Vol. 1; *The Origins to 1795*. (1981). A full introduction.

P. Dukes, *The Making of Russian Absolutism: 1613–1801* (1982). A solid survey.

R. J. Evans, *The Making of the Hapsburg Empire, 1550–1770* (1979). A solid, recent account.

H. Holborn, *A History of Modern Germany 1648–1840* (1966). The best on the subject.

H. C. Johnson, *Frederick the Great and His Officials* (1975). Focuses on Prussian administration.

H. W. Koch, *A History of Prussia* (1978). A good analysis of the rise of Prussia.

I. de Madariaga, *Russia in the Age of Catherine the Great* (1981). Highly regarded recent study.

M. Roberts, *Sweden's Age of Greatness* (1973). A good summary of Sweden during this period.

CHAPTER 33

The Challenge to Absolutism: England and the United Netherlands

FIGURE 33.1 **The English Cabinet** This scene shows Robert Walpole, who served as prime minister of England from 1721 to 1742, presiding over a session of the cabinet. Walpole and the other cabinet members shown here were all members of Parliament and belonged to the majority party in that body. In sessions such as this they decided upon the major policies to be followed by the government; their control of Parliament allowed them to enact their decisions. Thus, the cabinet became the effective executive power in Great Britain, a position that it still holds today. The emergence of the cabinet system was one of the major outcomes of the bitter political struggle in seventeenth-century England. (The Bettmann Archive)

While royal absolutism dominated the political scene in France and elsewhere on the Continent, England and the United Netherlands moved toward a form of government that placed limitations on the authority of the executive and the power of the state. In these two nations a constitutional system was emerging that gave a representative body the authority to define the law and sought to create a balance between the power of the state and the rights and liberties of citizens of the state. The constitutional changes made in England and the United Netherlands during the seventeenth century strongly influenced later struggles against absolutism in many parts of the world.

1. EARLY STUART ATTEMPTS AT ABSOLUTISM

The absolutism shaped by the Tudors (see Chapters 27, 29 and 30) was subjected to serious challenges during the seventeenth century. "Good Queen Bess" died in 1603 without a direct heir. She was succeeded by a distant cousin, James Stuart (1603–1625), king of Scotland. He was an avowed absolutist, but he was woefully ignorant of the delicate workings of the Tudor political system and not suited by temperament for the hard work or gifted with the political adroitness needed to keep that system going. His political ineptitude contributed to a progressive breakdown of the Tudor system and to a polarization of political forces.

But not all the troubles of James I's reign were the makings of a king known in his own days as "the wisest fool in Christendom." New problems were facing England that threatened the general satisfaction most people had felt toward Tudor governance. Major economic changes were in process, creating new opportunities for highly profitable investments in agriculture, manufacturing, and trade. Those who benefited most from these changes, the lesser nobility (the gentry) and merchants, were increasingly insistent on having a voice in shaping royal policies affecting their economic interests and on limiting arbitrary royal interference that curbed their freedom of action. These same changes were adversely affecting other groups, especially rural tenants and laborers, thereby fostering popular

discontent. A major realignment of power was taking shape in Europe, marked by the ascendancy of France. This development encouraged the English rulers to seek closer ties with their traditional enemy, Spain, a course that many still basking in the glories of the victory over the Armada viewed as unpatriotic.

The very structure of the Tudor political system lacked key elements required for effective absolutism. Too much depended on the personal qualities of the monarch and a narrow circle of royal advisers. England lacked a well-developed bureaucracy and a well-organized military force to support the ruler's absolute authority. The central government had limited control over local government, which was dominated by the local gentry, the members of which were jealous of their offices and protective of their local interests. The traditional system of common law served to limit arbitrary acts by the royal government. Most serious of all were the limited financial resources of the Crown. It could not manage on the traditional sources of revenue from royal lands, customs duties, and feudal dues. Additional income could be derived only from taxes, which Parliament had long since established its right to approve. If absolutism were to continue, significant political reforms aimed at increasing the power of the monarch would be required. Such changes posed a threat to powerfully entrenched interests in England.

Another increasingly acute source of tension involved religious issues. Many people, including an important segment of the gentry and the merchants, were not satisfied with the Anglican settlement carried out during Elizabeth's reign (see Chapter 30). The major dissenters were the Puritans, who wanted reforms that would make the established religion more "Protestant": simpler ritual, more emphasis on Scripture, less episcopal control over local churches. There also remained many Roman Catholics who hoped to undo the Reformation; their presence was a cause of constant concern for all Protestants.

During James I's reign these issues found their focus in Parliament, especially in the House of Commons, a body that theoretically represented the entire English populace but was actually dominated by the country gentry, merchants, and lawyers. The king was forced to summon Parliament because of the increasing need for funds. Although Parliament usually provided some financial aid, its members constantly raised issues that challenged royal policy. They criticized James I's royal advisers for corruption, favoritism, and incompetence. They questioned his unwavering support of Anglicanism and his lenient policy toward the Catholics. They condemned the alliance he made with Spain early in his reign and his failure to support the Protestant cause when the Thirty Years' War began in 1618. James responded by repeatedly dismissing Parliament. He then tried to utilize other means of raising money, but these efforts were challenged in the courts as contrary to custom and therefore illegal. The king answered by dismissing judges, which led to more parliamentary criticism. Throughout this long series of clashes, Parliament proved itself to be an undisciplined, intemperate body. But its confrontations with the king heightened the fear that the royal government was bent on extending its prerogatives to the point where customary political processes, traditional rights, and the law would be subverted, opening the way to tyranny.

Under James' successor, Charles I (1625–1649), the conflict deepened into civil war. Charles was no less stubborn than James in his insistence on royal supremacy and in his refusal to bend before the claims of Parliament and the courts. The king's major problem continued to be a need for funds, a need made more desperate by a blundering foreign policy that resulted in costly but unsuccessful military ventures in France and Spain. To Charles' requests for additional taxes Parliament responded by continuing to challenge royal policy on a variety of issues. Increasingly, the leaders of Parliament began to make specific their definition of what they meant by royal violation of the traditional system and the law. Their views found particularly forceful expression in the Petition of Rights submitted to the king in 1628. This bold document demanded that the king desist from various illegal acts: imposing martial law in peacetime, levying taxes without Parliament's approval, imprisoning citizens without trial, and quartering soldiers with private citizens. Desperate for money, Charles accepted the Petition of Rights, thereby admitting that he had acted illegally. But when Parliament in its next session, in 1629, insisted that the king respect the petition's provisions on taxation, Charles dismissed it over the bitter protests of its leaders.

For the next eleven years Charles ruled without Parliament. To do so, he was forced to rely on a variety of means of raising funds that pushed royal authority to the limits of legality. Ultimately, it was Charles' religious policy that forced him once again to confront his enemies on their own ground—in Parliament. With Charles' support, his chief religious adviser, William Laud, archbishop of Canterbury, initiated a vigorous "reform" aimed at giving greater emphasis in the Church of England to elaborate rituals, episcopal authority over local churches, and the doctrine of free will. To the Puritans Laud's reforms were detestable, the very opposite of the most fundamental precepts of Calvinistic Protestantism. Many fled to the New World in search of a setting where they would have the freedom to institute real Protestantism. Laud's policies even alarmed some Anglicans, who sensed that England was on a course that would lead it back to Roman Catholicism. But it was the absolute refusal of the Scotch Presbyterians to accept the "beauty of holiness," as Charles called Laud's reforms, that precipitated a crisis. In 1639 they revolted and invaded northern England, creating a military crisis that forced Charles to summon Parliament into session in 1640 in order to raise money to resist the Scottish threat to the kingdom.

The first Parliament of 1640, called the Short Parliament, was dismissed after three weeks because it again challenged royal authority. But the Scots continued to press, and Charles was forced to capitulate. He summoned the Long Parliament, so called because it was to sit for twenty years. With an amazing show of unity Parliament proceeded to legislate the end of Stuart absolutism. It forced Charles to sacrifice his chief ministers, including Laud. It abolished the hated extraordinary courts, including the Star Chamber and the Court of High Commission, which had long been tools used by the Crown to avoid the common law. An act was passed requiring a meeting of Parliament every three years and curbing the power of the king to dismiss Parliament. Severe limitations were placed on the king's power to tax without parliamentary approval. To all of this Charles acceded, chiefly because he needed money to fight the Scots.

Up to this point Parliament had succeeded brilliantly in legislating what amounted to a bloodless revolution that established limited monarchy. But the parliamentary forces then began to divide over the question of how to use Parliament's power. In general, its leadership was forced into directions that caused alarm in many quarters and drove many back toward support of the king, who gave every sign that he would resist being a limited monarch. Suspicion of his intentions caused parliamentary leaders to remove control of the administration and the army from his hands and to impose taxes that seemed as burdensome as those imposed by Charles earlier. Religious opinion in Parliament moved in the direction of ending Anglicanism "root and branch" in favor of some form of Presbyterianism. This mounting extremism caused many influential leaders to believe that Parliament was setting a course that would upset the established order. The division in the parliamentary ranks emboldened Charles to try to restore his control; he went so far in early 1642 as to attempt to arrest the leaders of Parliament. This action was a call to arms, pitting against one another elements of a ruling class that had lost its community of interest, an interest that had long focused on the monarch.

2. CIVIL WAR, COMMONWEALTH, AND PROTECTORATE, 1642–1660

The opening of armed strife divided England along lines that defy easy definition. The opposing forces did not represent clear-cut economic interests or social classes. A considerable following, soon known as the Cavaliers, rallied around Charles, who represented himself as the champion of the established order against the political and religious radicals in Parliament. The backbone of the Cavalier forces came from the great noble families and their clientele among the country gentry living in the more economically backward areas of northern and western England. Although the opposition, called the Roundheads, also had noble supporters, it drew its main strength from lawyers, the gentry of the south and east, and the commercial interests; many from these elements were Puritans. This core was soon reinforced by advocates of radical political and economic changes favoring the poor and oppressed. In the intricate matter of choosing sides there figured complex personal factors—family ties, friendships, personal loyalties—much after the fashion of the American Civil War.

The first phase of the civil war lasted through 1646. While neither side was prepared militarily, for a time the Cavaliers seemed to have the upper hand. But the Roundheads had forces working in their favor: support by the navy, domination of the richest part of England, control over the regular administrative system and Parliament, the power to vote taxation. In 1643 the Roundhead cause was bolstered by an alliance with the Scots. But ultimately the outcome of the struggle was determined by the success of the Roundheads in creating an effective army. The chief architect of the victorious army was a simple farmer with strong Puritan convictions, Oliver Cromwell. He organized a cavalry regiment of disciplined, deeply religious recruits who proved more than a match for the Cavalier forces they faced. His system was soon applied to the entire Roundhead force to create the New Model Army, made up of highly motivated troops paid and equipped in a businesslike fashion. It quickly proved itself superior to the Cavalier army, so that by 1646 the Cavalier army was crushed and Charles was forced to surrender.

However, with victory within their grasp, the Roundheads were unable to work out an acceptable settlement. Moderate leaders in the Roundhead camp wished to establish a limited monarchy and a Presbyterian religious order. Charles remained unwilling to accept such a settlement and raised fears of a renewal of the civil war by fleeing his captors and allying himself with the Scots. More ominous was the increasing prominence of Roundhead leaders who demanded a more radical religious reform favoring the independence of local churches and freedom of conscience. These religious Independents were supported by various political radicals, most notably the Levellers, who advocated the end of monarchy, democratic elections, and the redistribution of wealth. These religious and political radicals dominated the New Model Army, where discontent was fed by the fact that pay was considerably in arrears. Fearful that the radicals would seize complete control, the moderate

Roundheads ordered the army demobilized. They turned back to the king, who suddenly expressed considerable enthusiasm for parliamentary control over the monarchy as well as for Presbyterianism. The Independents, led by Cromwell, would not be denied. They destroyed the hope of Charles and his Scottish army in a single battle in 1648 and, along with it, the cause of the Cavaliers and the moderate Roundheads. Backed by the New Model Army, Cromwell acted decisively to ensure the position of the Independents. He purged the Long Parliament of all members not dedicated to his cause and gave the so-called Rump Parliament chief authority in the land. It immediately legislated out of existence the Anglican church, the House of Lords, and the monarchy. And at Cromwell's urging it decreed the execution of the king in 1649 on the grounds that he was "a tyrant, traitor, and murderer."

For eleven years after Charles I's death Cromwell and his Independents sought to rule England without a king. Always in a minority and dependent on the army, the Cromwellians experimented with various forms of government but ultimately failed to establish an acceptable order. They first sought to create a republican form of government called the Commonwealth. A one-house Parliament was made the supreme authority, with a state council of forty-one members charged with conducting the daily affairs of government. Under Cromwell's guidance this government pursued several positive policies. Considerable toleration was extended to all Protestants, a policy that required curbing political and religious extremists in the army. Effective, albeit severe measures were taken to subdue the rebellious Irish and Scots. An aggressive foreign policy, aimed at promoting English commercial and colonial interests, was undertaken. Navigation acts were passed to ensure that trade within England's emerging empire would be monopolized by England. None of these policies, however, helped to popularize the Commonwealth. The Cromwellians could not shed their image as regicides, Puritan extremists, and political radicals (see Figure 33.2). Resistance to the Commonwealth grew steadily. Cromwell ultimately blamed the failure of the Commonwealth on what he considered the self-serving leaders of Parliament, causing him to take steps to curb its

Oliver seeking God while the K. is murthered by his order.

FIGURE 33.2 A Satire on Cromwell The deep religious fervor of the Puritans and the taint of regicide that lingered throughout the Commonwealth and the Protectorate are satirized here as Oliver Cromwell is shown at prayer while Charles I is being executed. (NYPL Picture Collection)

power and to act without it—a course that convinced many that Cromwell was no less a tyrant than his royal predecessors.

In pursuit of what he called a "healing and settling" course for England, Cromwell tried one more experiment, called the Protectorate. A written constitution was drawn up that entrusted power to a lord protector (Cromwell), who was advised by a Council of State and guided by a one-house Parliament elected by property holders. From the beginning the lord protector and Parliament clashed on most issues, largely because the elected Parliament represented political and religious positions that ran contrary to the convictions of those who alone could assure Cromwell's continued dominance, the "godly" men of the New Model Army. To sustain his power Cromwell was forced to impose a virtual military dictatorship that aroused resistance across a wide spectrum of opinion and bred conspiracies that constantly threatened public order. More and more people began to see the restoration of monarchy as an alternative to Cromwell's regime. In fact, in 1657 Parliament asked Cromwell to become king, an honor he declined; but he did agree to remain lord protector for life. Thus, when he died in 1658, the wheel had come nearly full circle: A man who had led his soldiers to the abolition of monarchy had himself become king without title.

Cromwell was succeeded as lord protector by his son Richard, but this weak figure was soon swept aside by forces favoring the restoration of monarchy. By 1660 elements in the New Model Army joined with people of property and commerce to end the Protectorate. The Long Parliament voted to dissolve itself. A new Parliament was elected and in 1660 invited Charles Stuart, the son of Charles I, to return from exile and assume the crown.

3. THE RESTORATION, 1660–1688

The Restoration that brought the Stuarts back to the throne also saw the reestablishment of both houses of Parliament, the Anglican church, the traditional courts of law, and the old system of local government. However, what seemed outwardly to be a return to the system that had prevailed before the execution of Charles I by no means resolved the basic problems that had divided England since 1603, particularly those involving the relationship between king and Parliament and the religious establishment. Nor did it negate the advancing claims of England's gentry and merchants to a decisive voice in political decision making. Between 1660 and 1688 political tensions continued, although at a less violent level than had been the case in the preceding two decades.

The reign of Charles II (1660–1685) began in a climate of forgiving compromise. The king and Parliament joined in repealing all the acts of the Commonwealth and the Protectorate. Only a few Cromwellians were punished for their part in killing Charles I. Confiscated properties were returned to their original owners. The king was assured of a sizable income on a regular basis, but he was deprived of many ancient rights that had allowed his predecessors to exact taxes without approval of Parliament. Not only was control of taxation reserved to Parliament, but the Triennial Act was passed to ensure that it would meet every three years whether or not the king so wished. However, this settlement did not get to the basic political issue: Where did ultimate authority rest? Even more disconcerting was the religious settlement embodied in a series of parliamentary acts passed in 1661 and 1662 and known as the Clarendon Code after Charles II's chief adviser, the earl of Clarendon. These acts not only reestablished the Anglican church but also made it illegal for nonconformist Protestants, including Independents and Presbyterians, to meet for religious purposes, to conduct services in their own way under the leadership of their own preachers, and to hold local political offices. In brief, the Clarendon Code promised to nonconformists (that is, non-Anglicans) little better than criminal status.

Dissatisfaction stemming from these issues once again surfaced in Parliament. The discontent was intensified by a series of disasters that befell England during the early years of Charles' reign. He involved England in a war with the Dutch that led to a humiliating defeat. In 1665 a plague struck England, followed the next year by a fire that destroyed most of London. Many God-fearing English felt that these misfortunes were divine retribution for the immorality of the royal court, where the model of profligacy was set by the king himself. Parliament reacted to public wrath over religious issues by forcing Clarendon out of office in 1667 and to a failed foreign policy by becoming stingier in approving taxes. Charles paid little heed to the growing opposition, choosing instead to pursue two policies he personally favored: an alliance with France and religious tolerance in England that would permit Roman Catholics to worship freely. In 1670 he signed a secret treaty with Louis XIV by which he agreed, in return for a subsidy, to join France in a war on the Dutch and to promote the Catholic cause in England; when the terms of this treaty became known, anti-Catholic and anti-French sentiment reached fever pitch. In 1672 Charles issued a Declaration of Indulgence, which set aside the laws restricting the practice of Roman Catholicism. An outraged Parliament forced the king to withdraw the Declaration of Indulgence and passed the Test Act (1673), which excluded Catholics from all public offices. And when Charles joined France in another unsuccessful war against the Dutch in 1672–1674, Parliament forced him to seek peace by refusing financial support.

As his reign progressed, Charles showed considerable ingenuity in neutralizing his opponents in Parliament. Increased tax returns resulting from an improving economy coupled with Louis XIV's subsidies minimized Parliament's ability to pressure the Crown by denying taxation. More significantly, Charles skillfully built a political following—an embryonic "party"—devoted to a strong monarchy and Anglicanism. Its members, scornfully dubbed "Tories" (a term used to designate Irish bandits) by the opposition, could often control Parliament in support of the king. An opposing "party," committed to parliamentary supremacy and religious tolerance for all Protestants, was also formed; its members were called "Whigs" (after a term used to designate Scottish horse thieves and murderers). Charles' successes led many to feel that absolutism was returning to England. But one obstacle kept Charles from totally controlling English political life: a rising fear that the king was determined to restore Catholicism.

James II (1685–1688) inherited a strong position from his brother, based in large part on the Tory majority in Parliament, a sound financial position, and the legitimacy of his claim to the throne. But he soon dissipated this strength by his open avowal of Catholicism and attempts to improve the position of Catholics in England, which neither the Tories nor the Whigs would tolerate. When in 1688 a son was born to James and his Catholic wife and baptized in the Catholic faith, ensuring that the Stuart dynasty would be perpetuated by a Catholic successor, Tory and Whig leaders invited James' Protestant daughter, Mary, and her husband, William of Orange, the stadholder of several provinces in the Dutch Netherlands, to assume England's throne. When William invaded England in late 1688, the great

majority of the people rallied to his side; James II fled to France. For a second time, the unhappy Stuarts had been forced off England's throne, but this time the revolution was bloodless.

4. THE GLORIOUS REVOLUTION AND ITS CONSEQUENCES

Unlike the execution of Charles I, the flight of James II did not lead to radical political experimentation. Instead, what the English call a Glorious Revolution was carried through in the form of several fundamental legal enactments that established the basis for England's future constitutional system.

Immediately after the triumph of William and Mary, Parliament declared the throne vacant by reason of James' abdication. It then voted to grant the crown to William III and Mary as co-rulers, thereby establishing Parliament's control of the throne. A Bill of Rights was passed in 1689 that set forth clear limits on royal power. This fundamental charter assured the members of Parliament of the right of free speech and immunity from prosecution for statements made in debate. It forbade a variety of acts that had long been the basis of royal absolutism: taxing without the consent of Parliament, suspending laws passed by Parliament, maintaining a standing army in peacetime, requiring excessive bail, depriving citizens of the right to trial in the regular courts, interfering with jurors, and denying people the right to petition the king. The Bill of Rights implied that government was based on a contract between ruler and ruled, a concept of government increasingly attractive among "enlightened" leaders in western Europe. This theory of government was set forth with special force by John Locke in his *Two Treatises on Civil Government,* published in 1690 (see pp. 464, 468, 473). Locke argued that a government was the product of a contract entered into by rational people in order to establish an authority capable of protecting rights that belonged to all humans by the laws of nature: the rights of life, liberty, and property. Any government that violated these natural rights broke the contract that had brought it into existence; in this event its subjects had a right to correct or even overthrow it. To settle the long-standing religious issue, a Toleration Act was passed that allowed religious freedom to Puritans and Independents but not to non-Protestants. Finally, the Act of Settlement was enacted in 1701 to ensure that none but Protestants could inherit the throne.

The initial settlement marking the Glorious Revolution certainly resolved some fundamental issues that had troubled England for nearly a century. However, there still remained problems to be addressed. Under William's leadership England's foreign policy underwent a basic reorientation which called on the nation to commit its resources to a long, burdensome but eventually successful series of wars in many parts of the globe to prevent France from establishing world dominance (see Chapters 32 and 34). Closer to home the Irish problem was resolved to England's advantage. Early in his reign William led an army into this unhappy land, where discontent had long festered and which now became a center of Stuart intrigue—funded by the French—aimed at recovering the English throne. Having established control by force, William instituted a policy aimed at the suppression of Roman Catholicism and at reducing Ireland to colonial status, a policy that provided expanded opportunity for English landlords to uproot Irish Catholic landowners and take possession of their property. Scotland enjoyed an easier fate in the face of increasing English power. Early in his reign William began negotiations with the Scots that finally bore fruit after his death. In 1707 Parliament passed the Act of Union, which joined the two kingdoms into a single nation henceforth known as the United Kingdom of Great Britain. The settlement gave the Scots a liberal number of seats in Parliament and guaranteed their Presbyterian religious establishment.

A major consequence of the Glorious Revolution was Parliament's increasing involvement in the conduct of affairs of state. Partly this expanded role was a consequence of the fundamental principle established by the settlement of 1688–1689: the need for parliamentary approval of important political decisions. No less important was the royal need for additional funds. Chiefly as a result of the burdens of global war, annual government expenditures had increased threefold between the reign of Charles II and that of William and Mary. To meet these expenditures, the monarchs had to call Parliament nearly every year. These frequent sessions of Parliament required that the royal government pay special attention to the election process in order to gain sufficient votes from qualified voters—chiefly property owners—to secure a majority in Parliament that was willing to support royal policy. Because Parliament was increasingly important, party strife between Whigs and Tories became a decisive feature of political life. Party leaders played an ever-larger role in counseling the rulers and overseeing public affairs. This ever-increasing identification of Parliament with the management of the nation's affairs probably did more than the noble principles of the Bill of Rights to secure parliamentary control of public life.

These developments raised a major constitutional issue: How should the Crown and Parliament interact so that the monarchy could discharge its executive functions in a way acceptable to Parliament? Certainly, the Glorious Revolution in no sense sought to deprive the Crown of the responsibility for administering affairs of state; but just as certainly, that settlement made the traditional executive system inadequate. For centuries English monarchs had relied on powerful ministers of their own choice and responsible to them alone to assist them in conducting government affairs and shaping policy. In the face of the new reality posed by the supremacy of Parliament, that system was no longer workable. The need for a new mechanism of interconnecting Crown and Parliament became especially obvious during the reigns of the first members of the Hanoverian dynasty, George I (1714–1727) and George II (1727–1760), both of whom spoke English poorly and were more interested in affairs in Germany than in England.

The answer was the *cabinet system,* under which royal ministers were increasingly chosen from members of the House of Commons on the basis of their ability to secure parliamentary approval to carry on the affairs of state in the name of the monarch. Since the Commons tended to divide into parties, it was only prudent for the rulers to seek the leaders of the majority party in the House of Commons for appointment as ministers responsible for exercising executive functions. Those chosen to constitute the cabinet of ministers slowly learned to accept mutual responsibility for the formulation and execution of policy and to assert their collective influence in ensuring that their party followers in Parliament supported their program. If the cabinet failed to command a majority in the House of Commons, its members had to surrender their positions as ministers in favor of a new cabinet that did have a parliamentary majority. One member of the cabinet, eventually called the *prime minister,* came to be recognized as the leader and spokesperson of the whole group; a major qualification for this designation was leadership of the majority party in the Commons.

Although Queen Anne (1702–1714) relied heavily on John Churchill, duke of Marlborough, to conduct her government, the key figure in shaping the cabinet system was Robert Walpole (see Figure 33.1). A longtime member of the Commons, he became George I's chief minister in 1721, primarily because of his leadership of the dominant Whig party in the Commons. From then until 1742 he virtually ran England by surrounding himself with fellow ministers who could control votes in Parliament and who would follow his leadership. Walpole proved to be a master at dispensing patronage and manipulating elections as a means of sustaining a Whig majority in Parliament and maintaining discipline among his Whig followers. Not until he lost control of the Commons over a foreign policy issue was he forced to relinquish his position as prime minister. However, the king had little choice but to appoint another prime minister and cabinet that could command a majority in Parliament. Henceforth to the present, the executive functions of government in Great Britain would be carried out in the name of the monarch by a circle of party leaders who could command a majority in the House of Commons but who were likewise required to render account to that body for their conduct of public affairs.

→ The Glorious Revolution marked a turning point in Great Britain's history. Two great decisions had been reached. First, royal absolutism had been repudiated in favor of a limited monarchy in which ultimate authority was entrusted to an elected Parliament. Second, religious uniformity had given way to religious toleration for all Protestants. The resolution of these issues restored Great Britain's internal stability and provided a basis for its rapid advance to the status of world power. However, the "revolution" had its limitations. The right to vote in parliamentary elections and eligibility for election to a seat in the House of Commons were limited to a narrow

circle of men of wealth, chiefly landowners and merchants. The apportionment of seats in the House of Commons had less to do with ensuring that each seat represented the same number of people than with guaranteeing "safe" seats to prominent families. The Glorious Revolution was a victory for a narrow oligarchy of entrepreneurial landowners and merchants who had successfully taken advantage of changing economic conditions to establish themselves as the wealthiest segment of the English population. Until the nineteenth century these "gentlemen" dominated Great Britain in a fashion that served their collective interests.

5. THE UNITED NETHERLANDS

Absolutism was also successfully challenged during the seventeenth century by the Dutch. Their success led to the creation of a new nation in which prevailed a political and social environment that allowed the Dutch to forge themselves a leadership role in European commerce, banking, and intellectual and artistic life. That new nation emerged from the Dutch refusal to accept the absolutist system that Philip II of Spain attempted to force on them (see Chapter 31). Although Philip II was able to impose Spanish rule over the ten southern provinces of the Netherlands (now Belgium; see Map 33.1), the seven northern provinces resisted and by 1609 had established effective independence as the United Provinces of the Netherlands; their independence was officially recognized by the Treaty of Westphalia in 1648.

The new state adopted a republican form of government. Each province, ruled by an elected executive (called the *stadholder*) and a provincial representative assembly, retained extensive control over local affairs. Although most of the stadholders came from the landed aristocracy, especially from the House of Orange, a powerful family that had played a crucial role in the struggle for independence, the provincial governments over which they presided were dominated by commercial and financial leaders who resisted the establishment of a strong central government. The only truly national political institution was the Estates General, made up of delegates from each province who acted only on instructions from the provincial governments. It en-

FRIESLAND

NORTH SEA

GRONINGEN

OVERIJSSEL

ENGLAND

Amsterdam

The Hague
Rotterdam

GELDERLAND

London

ZEELAND

UTRECHT

ENGLISH
CHANNEL

Bruges

BRABANT

Antwerp

UPPER
GELDERLAND

Ghent

FLANDERS

Brussels

LIMBURG

ARTOIS

LIÈGE

HAINAUT

Rhine R.

CAMBRAI

LUXEMBOURG

TO LIÈGE

Luxembourg

GERMAN
STATES

FRANCE

▓ United Provinces

▨ Spanish Netherlands
(Belgium)

0   50   100 miles

Map 33.1 **THE UNITED PROVINCES, 1609** This map illustrates how small a territory the Dutch Republic
occupied in its golden age—no larger than a corner
of England. Yet through the cities of this small area
flowed much of the commerce of the seventeenth
and eighteenth centuries. With that commerce came
a flow of money that made such cities as Amsterdam the financial centers of the world.

joyed limited powers and asserted very little direction over national affairs. The citizens of the
Dutch Netherlands enjoyed considerable freedom to pursue their personal and collective interests. Particularly noteworthy was religious
freedom. The Reformed church, strongly Calvinist in doctrine and practice, was established by
law, but other religious groups, including Roman
Catholics and Jews, were tolerated, a fact that
attracted religious refugees from other European
nations.

The Dutch Netherlands, a nation of only
about a million, made its chief mark on the seventeenth-century world in commerce and finance. That success was based on the seafaring
skills of its people and the entrepreneurship of
its vigorous bourgeoisie. Those talents, developed over many centuries, allowed the Dutch to
become world leaders in commerce. Experienced
Dutch sailors plundered Spanish commerce and

overseas colonies to reap a rich reward. When
Spain temporarily annexed Portugal in 1580, the
Dutch seized most of Portugal's lucrative holdings in the East Indies. The Dutch East India
Company, set up in 1602 to develop trade with
the East Indies, returned huge profits to its stock-
holders during the entire seventeenth century.
The Dutch also established a flourishing colony
in North America. In addition, Dutch traders
took advantage of their favorable geographical
position to gain a near-monopoly on the carrying
trade of Europe. A large proportion of Europe's
ships were built in Dutch shipyards.

The extensive trading activities of the Dutch
produced a huge flow of wealth into the hands
of Dutch merchants. This capital allowed them
to become Europe's leading moneylenders, serving princes, merchants, and landowners willing
to pay for the use of Dutch capital. The financial
activities of the Dutch were institutionalized in
the Bank of Amsterdam, set up in 1609. It became
a model for national banks later established elsewhere in western Europe. Its location in Amsterdam reflected the fact that that city had become
the world's chief commercial and financial center.

The wealth and freedom of Dutch society
generated a vigorous cultural outburst. Some of
the chief intellectuals in Europe found refuge in
the United Provinces, including the philosophers
René Descartes from France, John Locke from
England, and Baruch Spinoza, a Jewish refugee
from Portugal. Among the notable Dutch intellectuals was Hugo Grotius, whose *On the Law of
War and Peace* was the first great treatise on international law and has remained a classic on the
subject ever since. Freedom of the press enabled
the United Provinces to become the leading European center of book publishing. This was also
the golden age of Dutch painters. While baroque
painters in other countries were glorifying royalty and nobility, Jan Vermeer, Franz Hals, and,
above all, Rembrandt van Rijn were celebrating
the spirit of Dutch society by dignifying—sometimes glamorizing—the middle and lower
classes (see Figure 33.3). Dutch scientists played
an important role in advancing the scientific revolution, including the invention of the telescope
and the microscope. All of these activities gave
the Dutch an important role in western European
intellectual and artistic life.

As the seventeenth century drew to a close,

FIGURE 33.3 Rembrandt van Rijn, *Syndics of the Cloth Guild* In the Dutch Netherlands of the seventeenth century, commerce was king. Under the leadership of such men as are shown here, the tiny Dutch Netherlands attained a first-rank position in the world of science, philosophy, and trade. Rembrandt, one of the greatest portrait painters of all time, was probably also the greatest of the baroque painters. (Fotocommissie Rijksmuseum, Amsterdam)

the Dutch preeminence in commerce and banking began to decline, especially in the face of England's sea power and France's land might. But that decline could not efface the notable contributions of the Dutch to seventeenth-century western European civilization, a contribution due at least in part to the freedom enjoyed by Dutch citizens to assert their talents as they chose.

SUGGESTED READING

General Treatments

Barry Coward, *The Stuart Age. A History of England 1603–1714* (1980). A fine overview of Stuart England.

Derek Hirst, *Authority and Conflict: England, 1603–1658* (1986).

J. R. Jones, *Country and Court, England, 1658–1714* (1978). Taken together, these two volumes give a balanced treatment of the period.

Christopher Hill, *A Century of Revolution, 1603–1714,* 2nd ed. (1991). A provocative study from a Marxist perspective.

C. G. A. Clay, *Economic Expansion and Social Change: England, 1500–1700,* 2 vols. (1984). An excellent synthesis, rich in details.

From Civil War to Glorious Revolution

Robert Ashton, *The English Civil War: Conservatism and Revolution, 1603–1649,* 2nd ed. (1989). Good on issues.

Ann Hughes, *The Causes of the English Civil War* (1991). A challenging overview of the causes of the Civil War.

G. E. Aylmer, *Rebellion or Revolution? England, 1640–1660* (1986). A balanced treatment of the civil war and the era of Cromwell.

Ronald Hutton, *The British Republic, 1649–1660* (1990). Excellent on the political affairs of Cromwell's age.

Christopher Hill, *The World Turned Upside Down: Radical Ideas During the English Revolution* (1972). An important work on radicalism.

Patrick Morrah, *Restoration England* (1979). A good social history.

John Miller, *The Glorious Revolution* (1983). A brief, thoughtful description and assessment of the Glorious Revolution.

Lois G. Schwoerer, ed., *The Revolution of 1688–1689: Changing Perspectives* (1992). Presents various views on the nature and significance of the Glorious Revolution.

P. Laslett, *The World We Have Lost,* 2nd ed. (1971). A brilliant evocation of the English society of about 1700.

The Dutch Netherlands

Charles Wilson, *The Dutch Republic and the Civilisation of the Seventeenth Century* (1968).

K. H. D. Haley, *The Dutch in the Seventeenth Century* (1972). Either of these two titles will provide a good overview of Dutch society in its most glorious age.

Jonathan I. Israel, *Dutch Primacy in World Trade, 1585–1740* (1989). An excellent description of Dutch economic activity in a world setting.

Simon Schama, *The Embarrassment of Riches. An Interpretation of Dutch Culture in the Golden Age* (1988). A brilliant portrayal of social life.

Biographies

Pauline Gregg, *King Charles I* (1981).

Antonia Fraser, *Cromwell. The Lord Protector* (1973).

Barry Coward, *Cromwell* (1991).

Antonia Fraser, *Royal Charles: Charles II and the Restoration* (1979).

S. B. Baxter, *William III and the Defense of European Liberty* (1966).

CHAPTER 34

Overseas Colonization and the Competition for Empire

FIGURE 34.1 The Taking of Quebec, 1759 This eighteenth-century engraving shows British forces capturing Quebec from the French in 1759. This victory was a major turning point in the eighteenth-century competition for world empire. (Library of Congress)

During the seventeenth and eighteenth centuries the European nations intensified their competition for overseas possessions and commerce. They were spurred on in large part not only by the riches that flowed to Europe from these possessions but also by a conviction that overseas possessions enhanced the power of nations. Whereas Spain and Portugal had led the way beyond the Atlantic frontier during the sixteenth century, England, France, and the United Netherlands threw themselves vigorously into colonization and commercial expansion during the seventeenth and eighteenth centuries and soon outstripped their older rivals. As large as the world beyond western Europe was, the competition for it led to struggles among the leading European powers which decisively affected the power relationships among the competing nations. And while Europeans colonized, traded, and competed around the globe, European civilization spread with them, impacting with varying results on the native populations encountered by the Europeans. The seventeenth and eighteenth centuries marked a turning point in the establishment of western European domination over much of the world. No less significantly, European expansion laid the basis for a global economy.

1. THE NEW WORLD: THE ENGLISH, THE FRENCH, AND THE DUTCH

One of the areas attracting the English, French, and Dutch was the New World, where all three established colonies during the seventeenth century and soon became embroiled in bitter rivalry for dominance. Spain and Portugal still retained their vast empires in Central and South America and during the seventeenth and eighteenth centuries continued to earn rich returns from their enterprises. Having exhausted the easy hauls of gold and silver, the Spanish and Portuguese turned their energies toward creating large plantations worked by oppressed natives and imported African slaves to produce agricultural products marketable in western Europe. Their presence in South and Central America forced the attention of the English, French, and Dutch toward North America and the Caribbean area.

The English were the most successful colonizers in North America. Although some settlers left England to escape political and religious oppression, most were lured by the prospect of cheap land. Colonizing ventures were organized by joint stock companies chartered by the government or by individuals granted huge tracts of land for the purpose of colonization. Between 1607, when the first English colony was planted at Jamestown, Virginia (see Figure 34.2), and 1733, when the last colony was founded in Georgia, England established control of the Atlantic seaboard from Maine to the Spanish colony in Florida. In the thirteen colonies a stable order soon emerged that had a growing potential to supply England with not only raw materials and agricultural products but also markets for manufactured goods. Before long settlers were pushing westward from England's coastal colonies in search of new lands to occupy. English explorers and traders penetrated into the Hudson Bay area in Canada and claimed for England a huge territory, where a profitable fur trade soon developed. Flourishing English colonies were established in the West Indies, especially in Barbados, Jamaica, and Bermuda. In this area the English concentrated on developing profitable sugar plantations, utilizing African slaves as a labor supply.

France also undertook to colonize in the New World, although not as successfully as England. The first French colony in the New World was established by Samuel de Champlain at Quebec on the St. Lawrence River in 1608. Champlain later explored and claimed for France the entire St. Lawrence Valley from the Atlantic to the Great Lakes. Toward the end of the seventeenth century, during the reign of Louis XIV, the French extended their holdings in North America by exploring and claiming a huge territory called Louisiana, stretching down the Mississippi Basin from the Great Lakes to the Gulf of Mexico. The French also established prosperous colonies in the West Indies, especially on Martinique and Guadeloupe, where sugar production was the major economic activity. Except for the West Indies, settlers were slow to come to France's vast, rich lands in the New World, in part because of governmental policy. France closed its empire to non-Catholics, thus excluding an element so important in populating England's colonies—the religiously dissatisfied. By

FIGURE 34.2 The New World Frontier This representation of the first settlement at Jamestown, Virginia, suggests something of the drastic changes that affected those who left European society—symbolized by the great ship standing at anchor—to face the wilds of the New World. (Culver Pictures)

adopting a policy of land allocation that favored the aristocracy, the French government made it difficult for commoners to obtain land overseas. The opportunities for profit offered by the fur trade also discouraged agricultural settlement. When England seized France's American empire in 1763, perhaps no more than eighty thousand settlers lived in New France, compared with the 2 million inhabitants of the English colonies. But that sparse population left its imprint, especially in the form of Roman Catholicism, the French language, and social practices established by settlers in the St. Lawrence Valley and southern Louisiana—marks that persist to the present.

The Dutch also became involved in the colonization of North America. In 1621 the Dutch West India Company was chartered to undertake colonizing and commerce in the New World. In 1624 a Dutch colony was planted on Manhattan Island, a location especially attractive because of its potential as a center from which trade could be controlled. Soon other Dutch communities were established in the valleys of the Hudson, Connecticut, and Delaware rivers. However, the Dutch did not push their colonizing effort very

seriously. Their interest was chiefly in trading, which led them to concentrate their energies on the more profitable East Indies. In 1664 the English seized New Netherland, ending Dutch colonization in North America.

2. EUROPEAN PENETRATION OF THE FAR EAST AND AFRICA

During the sixteenth century, Portugal was the dominant European power in the Far East. In the seventeenth century, however, the Dutch, English, and French aggressively entered into the area (see Map 34.1). The Dutch were the first. In 1602 all the competing Dutch companies interested in Far Eastern trade were joined into a single Dutch East India Company, to which the Dutch government gave almost complete freedom of action. The company soon drove the Portuguese out of the East Indies and established a trading empire that embraced Sumatra, Java, Borneo, the Moluccas, the Celebes, the Malay peninsula, and Ceylon. The English tried to seize a share of this rich area, but they were rebuffed

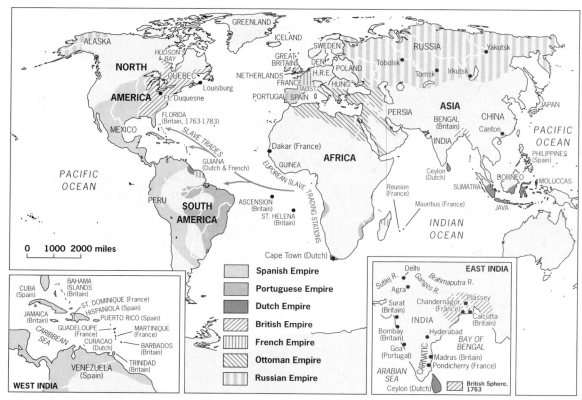

Map 34.1 OVERSEAS POSSESSIONS, 1763. This map shows the extent to which the major European powers had established control over the world by the middle of the eighteenth century. It especially points up the success of England in the quest for overseas possessions. The rich trade flowing between Europe and the overseas possessions had become a vital factor in the economies of these nations. Increasing its overseas possessions and trade was of vital importance to every European state.

by the Dutch as early as 1623. To safeguard the sea route to the Indies, the Dutch established a colony at the Cape of Good Hope in South Africa. Its growth was slow, but the Dutch influence was eventually strong enough to influence the history of South Africa to the present. The Dutch East India Company's interests in the East Indies were represented by a governor-general with headquarters in Java, who in turn set up several other fortified governmental centers throughout the island empire. For years after, the Dutch continued to profit from their holdings in the Indies. They demonstrated remarkable skill in utilizing the native agricultural economy to produce commodities such as spices that were in great demand in western Europe. Consequently, their presence disturbed the existing patterns of life in the area very little. The Dutch also made attempts to penetrate China and Japan but enjoyed only limited success, chiefly because neither the Chinese nor the Japanese welcomed Europeans or their products.

Although shut out of the East Indies by the Dutch, the English soon carved out their own niche in the Far East. An English East India Company was chartered in 1600 and given a monopoly on English trade in the East. This company concentrated chiefly on India, slowly forcing the

FIGURE 34.3 A Refuge in a Foreign World. This drawing shows a European factory, or trading settlement, built in seventeenth-century India. Within the confines of such structures were warehouses, places of residence, market facilities, and even a church. The structure illustrates how the Europeans isolated themselves from the native population in the Far East. (The Bettmann Archive)

Portuguese to let English traders into that rich land. The company founded its own "factories" (trading posts) at key locations—Surat, Madras, Bombay, and Calcutta (see Figure 34.3). For a long time the East India Company was content to exploit the trading opportunities available in these cities; the merchants interfered little with Indian affairs and had little influence on Indian society. Eventually, however, they had to contend with another European rival in India. In 1664, the French organized their own East India Company, which soon established an outpost at Pondicherry. From this center the French company built up an expanding sphere of influence

in India and a prosperous trade that returned large profits.

During the seventeenth and eighteenth centuries, western Europeans made significant inroads into sub-Saharan Africa. Again the Portuguese had been the early leaders, but they were eventually joined by others. It was the establishment of the plantation system in the New World that sparked Europeans' new interest in Africa. The plantations needed labor; African slaves could provide that commodity. Portuguese, Dutch, English, French, and North American traders and adventurers, acting with the support of their governments, established a series of trading posts along the West African coast stretching from modern Senegal to Angola chiefly for the purpose of purchasing slaves to be transported to the New World. The lure of these markets for human beings soon asserted a sinister effect on the native African population far inland from the slave coast.

3. THE IMPACT OF EUROPEAN EXPANSION: NATIVE AMERICANS

The increasing presence of European colonists and traders around the globe during the seventeenth and eighteenth centuries had a significant effect on the native populations of the areas to which Europeans went. In many ways these encounters between Europeans and natives set a pattern that was to impose a bitter heritage on the modern world.

Of all the non-Europeans who felt the impact of the Europeans, the native Americans—American Indians—were perhaps most immediately and drastically affected. Their long-established patterns of life, ranging from the sophisticated civilizations of the Incas in Peru and the Aztecs and Maya in Mexico and Central America to the pastoral and hunting cultures of the North American Indians, were irreparably disrupted by the onslaught of the intruders.

We have already described the destructive impact of the Spanish and Portuguese *conquistadores* on the Aztec, Maya, and Inca civilizations. During the seventeenth and eighteenth centuries, the dislocation continued. The Spanish and the Portuguese had put into place an administrative system that allowed them to dominate political, economic, and social conditions with little regard for the established patterns of native life. Since their fundamental concern was their own enrichment, they viewed the Indians chiefly as laborers on the expanding plantation system and in the mining enterprises from which huge profits could be gleaned. To add to the disruption of native social and economic life, the European masters imported large numbers of black slaves from Africa. Despite their dominance and their disdain for the native Americans, the Europeans in Latin America were never numerous enough to destroy the native American cultures com-

pletely. With passing time their blood and their culture intermingled with those of the native Americans. As a result, significant elements of native American culture were assimilated into the dominant European pattern of life, especially in family structure, agricultural techniques, art motifs, and even religion. Although the ancient Indian civilizations of Central and South America were disrupted forever, enough Indian culture survived to give Latin American society a special hybrid character that has survived to this day.

The Indians of North America suffered a different, and perhaps crueler, fate. In general, the interactions between French settlers and the Indians were not particularly disruptive to Indian society, chiefly because the French were few in number and usually more concerned with trade than land occupation. The English settlers pursued a more ruthless course. From the beginning they were chiefly interested in occupying and exploiting the land, an intention that in the final analysis demanded the displacement of the natives. Although English-Indian relationships were occasionally marked by friendliness and mutual assistance, the English colonial establishment almost from the beginning asserted inexorable pressures on the Indians. As a consequence, the Indians began to disappear from "new" America; their demise was often accompanied by conniving and brutality on the part of the settlers, who began to perceive themselves as the real "Americans." In an effort to protect their land, the Indians fought back savagely. In their struggle for survival they inevitably became embroiled in the mounting rivalry between the English and French for control of North America, a course that made them even more vulnerable. Their resistance nourished a feeling among the colonists that the native Americans were inferior savages whose extermination would best serve everyone's interests. The British government struggled from afar to establish an Indian policy aimed at respecting Indians' rights to their lands and dealing with them honorably in resolving conflicts. But the land-hungry settlers paid little heed and proceeded with the grim business of displacing or exterminating the Indians in the vast Indian stronghold lying between the Appalachians and the Mississippi. The resultant dislocations completely undermined the foundations of native American culture and condemned the Indians to a long-standing inferior status.

4. THE IMPACT OF EUROPEAN EXPANSION: THE FAR EAST

In contrast with the dislocation of native life that marked the coming of the Europeans to the New World, Europeans' impact on the peoples of the Far East was far less disruptive. Few Europeans went to that part of the world; those who did were seeking trading opportunities rather than land upon which to settle. The newcomers isolated themselves in trading depots located in seaboard cities in India and the East Indies, where their contacts with and influence on the natives were slight.

When the Europeans first became involved in India, they encountered a strong state led by other foreigners, the Islamic Moguls, a branch of the Mongol horde of Tamerlane, who early in the sixteenth century had conquered and imposed unity on India. Mogul rule brought prosperity to India's upper classes and created a brilliant chapter in India's already rich cultural history. As the seventeenth century progressed, however, Mogul power began to decline. Political power increasingly fell into the hands of native Indian princes, a development that proceeded rapidly during the eighteenth century. Because this situation aided both the English and the French in establishing their commercial interests in India, the intruders encouraged political localism. Thus, their presence had an impact on the political structure of India but in no sense a determining influence until much later.

Indian society retained both its cohesion and its unique identity despite the presence of the foreigners, be they Islamic Asiatics or Christian Europeans. India's long-established primary social institutions—the family, the village, and the caste system—exercised a decisive role in shaping the lives of most Indians, who were little affected by those who wielded political power. Undergirding these ancient social institutions was a conservative mentality rooted in the religious beliefs and practices embodied in Hinduism and sustained by Hindu priests, called Brahmins, who played a powerful role in directing Indian life. Indians were inclined to accept their situation in the present world because they believed that each individual's lot represented a necessary step in the progression toward ultimate fulfillment in another world. Progress, competition for wealth, and the search for new things did not hold the same attraction for Indians as for Europeans. Indians were not impressed by European civilization. They were convinced that they had reflected as deeply on human problems as the foreigners had and had arrived at superior answers. Indians could point to a remarkable art and literature as proof of the vitality of their way of life. Little the Europeans could offer to India seemed able to improve on Indian institutions and values. The outsiders found that a few hundred soldiers and a few cannon could not shake the Indians' confidence in their village and family life, their caste system, their religion, and their culture. Moreover, the continued existence of the basic pattern of Indian civilization in no way impeded the Europeans from reaping huge profits from their commercial enterprise in India. Only slowly and almost imperceptibly did the European way of life make any significant impression on India. And as time passed, Europeans developed a deep respect for some aspects of Indian civilization.

The Dutch presence in the East Indian world likewise had little influence on native society. In fact, the Dutch found it in their interests to sustain the existing order because it lent itself easily to commercial arrangements favorable to the outsiders.

The other major cultural centers in the Far East—China and Japan—were also little affected by the intrusion of Europeans during the period from 1500 to 1800. Again, this was a consequence of the vitality of the native civilizations. In China the Manchu dynasty established a strong political regime during the seventeenth century that brought internal peace, prosperity, and a revitalization of Chinese social, religious, and cultural life along traditional patterns. Chinese civilization came to be greatly admired in Europe in the eighteenth century. However, the Manchus carefully controlled the activities of Western traders—called "Ocean Devils" by the Chinese—with the consequence that European influences were barely felt in China. Japan also enjoyed internal stability under the rule of the Tokugawa shoguns, who in the early seventeenth century established firm control over Japan's ancient feudal system and encouraged a close adherence to ancient social, cultural, and religious customs and values. The new rulers soon adopted a policy of excluding all Europeans from access to Japan, a policy of isolationism that continued until the nineteenth century and that ensured that European influences would be minimal.

5. THE IMPACT OF EUROPEAN EXPANSION: SUB-SAHARAN AFRICA

European expansion into sub-Saharan Africa during the seventeenth and eighteenth centuries had a decisive effect on the societies existing in that vast territory. The centuries prior to 1500 had witnessed the formation of several prosperous states across a wide belt of territory south of the Sahara from the Atlantic to the Indian oceans and then far southward along the east coast of Africa. These states—Ghana, Mali, Songhay, the kingdoms of Hausaland, and the Swahili city-states on the east coast of Africa—were strongly influenced by the Islamic religion, culture, and technology from North Africa. However, in all of them the imprint of much older native African cultures was also strongly felt, producing an amazingly cosmopolitan culture, especially in the cities that dominated these states. The remarkable affluence of these states depended on a vigorous trans-Saharan and Indian Ocean trade that carried gold, ivory, slaves, and many other products northward to the Islamic and European worlds and eastward to India. In fact, many of these states had been brought into existence by enterprising native chieftains who organized extensive realms so as to control more effectively the trading ventures that brought such great riches. Because their existence depended so heavily on trade and because the techniques their rulers borrowed to assert their power had little impact on the great bulk of the native population, these states tended to be unstable. Nonetheless, their creation and their active intercourse with outside cultures marked an important stage in the development of sub-Saharan Africa and its involvement with the larger world. Farther to the south, beyond the sphere of Islamic influence, the native population continued its agricultural existence according to ancient customs, as yet little touched by developments to the north.

These developments in pre-1500 sub-Saharan Africa created a situation that made Africa particularly susceptible to the onslaught of the western Europeans, chiefly because the destinies of so many African states were tied directly to trade with the outside world. Coming by sea to the Atlantic coastal areas of sub-Saharan Africa, the Europeans very quickly caused a redirection of trade routes. Whereas the traditional trade routes plied by African traders had been oriented northward toward the Mediterranean world and eastward toward the Indian Ocean, attention now shifted toward the Atlantic coasts of Africa that gave access to western Europe and the expanding European empires in the New World and the Far East. The European newcomers made little effort to settle in sub-Saharan Africa, chiefly because they could get what they wanted by doing little more than establishing a few trading posts on the Atlantic shores of Africa. What they wanted were the valuable raw materials of Africa, especially gold, and then before long the Africans themselves—as slaves to perform the arduous labor of creating a rich agricultural establishment in the New World. Throughout the seventeenth and eighteenth centuries massive numbers of black Africans—perhaps as many as 11 or 12 million—were uprooted from their native soil, sold into the hands of English, French, Dutch, Portuguese, Spanish, and American slave traders, packed into ships that transported them under inhuman conditions to the New World, and auctioned off to white masters to toil as chattels on the plantations and in the mines of the New World. This traffic in human beings and the cheap labor it supplied resulted in huge profits that became a major source of capital formation in the western European world. In a real sense, the slave trade and slave labor underpinned the rising level of prosperity enjoyed by many people in both Europe and the New World who were not directly involved in either trading or exploiting slaves.

As the Europeans opened slave stations along the coasts of sub-Saharan Africa, significant new political alignments arose in Africa. African kingdoms along or with access to the West African coast flourished as a result of their domination of the trade flowing from inland Africa into the hands of European traders. Among the most prominent of these kingdoms were Oyo, Benin, Asante, Kongo, and Ngola. Often the ruling elements of these kingdoms became prime agents in supplying slaves to the Europeans, leading them to intervene among inland tribes to find slaves to sell. Native chiefs living inland likewise became caught up in the slave trade. Armed with guns supplied by Europeans, the native tribes began to wage war on one another as a means of procuring slaves. The Europeans asserted subtle influences on the coastal states in order to enhance their own trading interests, thus promoting a slow deterioration of the capability of the Africans to control their own destiny. As the demand for slaves increased and the prices commanded by the African slave suppliers rose, European traders moved farther and farther south along the west coast of Africa to turn the attention of more and more native Africans toward serving European trading interests, especially slavery, with the same disruptive consequences. On the east coast of Africa the European presence was equally disruptive. Here the Portuguese effort to seize control of the trade in gold and copper that flowed from central Africa through the Swahili city-states toward Persia and India brought about a decline of those cities and the brilliant civilization they supported. Only deep in the central part of Africa did the native population remain relatively free of the impact of European intrusion.

On the whole, the development of sub-Saharan Africa was seriously impeded by the encounter of its peoples with the western Europeans during the seventeenth and eighteenth centuries. Africa's human resources were depleted, its natural resources plundered, and its political and social structures disrupted. The Europeans gave little in return, especially when compared with what the Moslems of North Africa had contributed to the enrichment of sub-Saharan Africa prior to 1500. Despite the traumatic consequences of European expansion in this era, the Africans retained many elements of their native tradition, which would reemerge later as a significant aspect of their liberation from European domination. And those who were uprooted from Africa took elements of their native culture with them that helped sustain their miserable lives as slaves and that eventually asserted an influence on the civilization of the New World.

6. THE STRUGGLE FOR OVERSEAS EMPIRE

In spite of the vast lands available in the New World and rich trading opportunities to exploit in the highly civilized East and sub-Saharan Africa, the aggressive European nations could not keep out of one another's way in their overseas expansion. As a consequence, their rivalry became global, and the outcome of their struggles began to determine the destinies of peoples only remotely involved in the affairs of Europe.

During the seventeenth and eighteenth centuries the competition for empire was rooted in two interrelated factors: the essential importance of overseas trade to the expanding economies of the major European nations and the policy of mercantilism practiced by most European powers.

The growing importance of overseas commerce not only to national economies but also to people's daily lives was abundantly clear. New products from abroad—among others, spices, sugar, tobacco, cotton, silk, and tea—were in high demand; some of them even became necessities. So also were some manufactured goods from the Far East, especially cotton textiles and chinaware. Colonists needed the products of European manufacturers. The desire of traders to transport these goods stimulated shipbuilding. The distribution of products from colonial and commercial outposts created new opportunities for merchants. The funding of overseas trading and colonizing ventures stimulated the development of banking and credit. The profits garnered from overseas trading activities not only improved the standard of living of those who earned the profits but also became a prime source of capital for investment in western European agriculture, manufacturing, and commerce. Even governments relied on the gains from overseas trade to provide taxes and loans. In short, Europe's economy had been given a new and vital dimension by its global involvement. Control of that economy was vital to the well-being of each European nation, even to the point of fighting others for a share of the lucrative overseas trade.

The realities of seventeenth- and eighteenth-century economic life found expression in the widely accepted economic policy of mercantilism, which accentuated the importance of overseas trade and colonies to every nation. Mercantilist policy was based on the conviction that the economic well-being of a nation depended on governmental management of exchange operations in a way that would produce a favorable balance of gold and silver coming into the economy. Colonies were viewed as a source of cheap food and raw materials and an outlet for manufactured goods that would return a profit to the mother country. Such a view made the accession and careful management of colonies crucial to each nation that aspired to be rich, and thus powerful. Especially important was the need for each nation to monopolize trade with its own colonies, which placed a premium on developing naval power and regulating economic life in the colonies. Likewise, mercantilism dictated that each nation make every effort to restrict the colonizing ventures of rival nations and to deprive them of their colonial possessions whenever possible. Adherence to mercantilist policy meant that every conflict among the major European nations in the seventeenth and eighteenth centuries was extended to their colonies and that every major peace settlement included a redistribution of overseas possessions.

The competition for the fruits of overseas empires began in the sixteenth century with the English and Dutch assaults on Spanish and Portuguese trading activities and overseas holdings. Initially the Dutch won the advantage, but by the middle of the seventeenth century England began to play a more aggressive role in the competition for empire and trade, a development that was one of the major outcomes of the seventeenth-century political upheaval that put control of the English state into the hands of the country gentry and the merchants. As early as 1651 England passed its first Navigation Act, which provided that all goods coming to and from England and its overseas possessions must be carried in English ships. This policy posed a challenge to the commercial interest of the Dutch, who were especially successful in providing shipping services to other nations. It also encouraged the growth of the English merchant fleet and the navy, which had been badly neglected during the early Stuart period. On three different occasions between 1651 and 1688, England engaged the Dutch in warfare. As a result, Dutch commercial ascendancy began to be undermined while England's commercial power grew. Indicative of the shifting balance was the seizure of the Dutch North American colonies by the English.

Toward the end of the seventeenth century both the English and the Dutch began to see that France was their chief threat, for France too became increasingly committed to expanding its colonial and commercial power. The result was an Anglo-Dutch alliance made by William of Orange when he became king of England in 1689. No longer the major sea power in Europe, the Dutch were increasingly content to keep their already established holdings in the East Indies, to continue their declining but still profitable carrying trade, and to reap great profits as the chief bankers and moneylenders of Europe.

From 1689 to 1763 England and France fought each other regularly in Europe (see Chapter 32 for the European aspect of these wars), and each engagement had its repercussions abroad (see Map 34.1). Several times during the War of the League of Augsburg (1688–1697), English and French forces engaged in North America, where the war was called King William's War. Neither in Europe nor in America was the action decisive, and no changes were made in the holdings of either combatant. England had more success during the War of the Spanish Succession (1702–1713). In North America, where the struggle was called Queen Anne's War, England captured Acadia (Nova Scotia) and received recognition of its claims to Newfoundland and Hudson Bay. From France's ally, Spain, England received Gibraltar and Minorca, ensuring access to the Mediterranean. Spain also granted to England the right to supply Spain's colonies with slaves (the *asiento*) as well as the privilege of sending one ship a year to the Spanish colonies in America. These concessions ended Spain's long effort to close its empire to outsiders and gave England the advantage over other nations in exploiting the trading opportunities provided by the Spanish overseas holdings.

From 1713 to 1740 England and France remained at peace. During this calm neither nation was idle in overseas matters. France, realizing the weakness of its position, was especially active in North America. It tried to protect its holdings from English sea power by building a strong fort at Louisburg at the mouth of the St. Lawrence. The French also began to construct and garrison a series of forts to make its hold on the vast territories it claimed along the St. Lawrence valley through the Great Lakes region and down the Mississippi Valley more secure. England concentrated its efforts on widening the commercial breach it had made in Spain's empire in 1713. However, English colonists in North America were steadily advancing westward beyond the Appalachians toward a confrontation with the French for control of the Ohio Valley, where a powerful coalition of native American nations, the Iroquois Confederacy, still held the balance of power. A new European war in 1740, the War of the Austrian Succession, led to a sharp conflict between England and France in both America (King George's War) and India. At the end of the war in 1748 each power restored its spoils to the other, England giving up Louisburg and France restoring Madras.

An eight-year truce ensued in Europe, each side preparing desperately for the struggle that everyone knew would soon reopen. In North America, the French renewed their effort to build a barrier against the westward expansion of the English colonies, focusing their attention now on the Ohio Valley. The inevitable clash came in 1755, when a British attempt to oust the French from Fort Duquesne, at the present site of Pittsburgh, was defeated. The battle in America was clearly joined; one power must destroy the other. In India a no less dramatic struggle was shaping. Although the French had entered the scene in India later than the English, by 1740 they had created a position of some strength. Between 1740 and 1756 the French and British each sought to take advantage of the deepening political crisis in India that resulted from the decline of Mogul power to wring from native Indian princes and political factions concessions that strengthened its own position. Competition became so vicious that soon an undeclared war was on.

Thus, at the opening of the Seven Years' War (called the French and Indian War in America) in 1756, France and England were pitted against each other on three continents. In that war England, led by William Pitt, threw its chief efforts into the colonial war and won a smashing victory. In North America the French, with considerable support from their native American allies, held their own until 1757. After that the superior British forces, supported by the navy, overpowered the French outposts one by one. The decisive blow came in 1759, when the British captured Quebec, opening all Canada to the British (see Figure 34.1). British naval units captured the chief French holdings in the West Indies. In India, Robert Clive, a resourceful agent of the East India Company, won a decisive victory for the British at the battle of Plassey in 1757 and enlarged England's sphere of influence by conquering several native Indian states.

The Seven Years' War ended in 1763 with the Treaty of Paris. France surrendered Canada and all Louisiana east of the Mississippi (except New Orleans) to England. Spain, which had been an ally of France, ceded Florida to England. By a special treaty France compensated Spain for this loss by giving Spain the rest of Louisiana (west of the Mississippi). All French possessions in the West Indies except Guadeloupe and Martinique also fell to England. France's empire in India likewise went to Britain. The French were permitted to enjoy trading privileges in India and to keep Pondicherry, but Britain controlled the chief centers of trade, ending any hope of a French recovery of power there. The Treaty of Paris closed an era in European expansion. Although the Dutch and Spanish still had extensive holdings abroad, Great Britain had fought its way to supremacy in colonial and commercial affairs. The English could now turn to the exploitation of that empire.

Since Columbus' voyage the Europeans had wrought an important change around the world. Energetic colonizers had planted European civilization on the soil of the New World. Enterprising merchants had begun to tap the wealth of a considerable part of the Far East and sub-Saharan Africa, creating for the first time a global economy in which the level of prosperity in European nations was directly related to their access to the labor and products of peoples all over the earth. European patterns of civilization had begun to alter the lives of peoples who had developed their own cultures long before the Europeans came. For good or bad, the Europeanization of the world had begun. And from then on, European history never ceased to have a global scope.

SUGGESTED READING

European Expansion

J. H. Parry, *Trade and Dominion: The European Overseas Empires in the Eighteenth Century* (1971).

Holden Furber, *Rival Empires of Trade in the Orient, 1600–1800* (1976).

Either of these studies will provide an excellent account of the building of commercial empires.

Alan K. Smith, *Creating a World Economy: Merchant Capital, Colonialism, and World Trade, 1400–1825* (1991). Treats the major factors involved in the emergence of a global economy.

The Impact of European Expansion

Bernard Bailyn, *The Peopling of British North America: An Introduction* (1986).

W. J. Eccles, *France in America,* rev. ed. (1990).

These two works will help the reader understand the occupation of North America by Europeans.

Gary B. Nash, *Red, White, and Black. Peoples of Early America,* 2nd ed. (1982). An interesting study of interactions among different peoples in colonial America.

Wilcomb E. Washburn, *The Indian in America* (1975). A good survey.

Karen Ordahl Kupperman, *Settling with the Indians: The Meeting of English and Indian Cultures in America, 1580–1640* (1980).

James Axtell, *The Invasion Within: The Contest of Cultures in Colonial North America* (1985).

Two excellent studies of the impact of European civilization on native American life.

Richard White, *The Middle Ground: Indians, Empires, and the Republics in the Great Lakes Region, 1615–1815* (1991). A brilliant analysis of what happened to Indians caught between European rivals for power in North America.

James Lockhart and Stuart B. Schwartz, *Early Latin America: A History of Colonial Spanish America and Brazil* (1983).

Mark A. Burkholder, *Colonial Latin America* (1990).

Either of these two excellent surveys will provide information on the fate of Indian civilizations in Latin America.

Stanley Wolpert, *A New History of India,* 4th ed. (1992). The appropriate parts of this work will provide a good introduction to Indian society at the time of the European intrusion.

Roland Oliver and Anthony Atmore, *The African Middle Ages, 1400–1800* (1981). A clear treatment of a complex subject.

James A. Rawley, *The Transatlantic Slave Trade: A History* (1981). A balanced account.

Patrick Manning, *Slavery and African Life: Occidental, Oriental and African Slave Trades* (1990). Excellent on the impact of slave trade on African culture.

Imperial Rivalry

W. L. Dorn, *Competition for Empire, 1740–1763,* rev. ed. (1963). A classic work.

CHAPTER 35
The Scientific Revolution

FIGURE 35.1 Isaac Newton Isaac Newton (1642–1727) became the leading figure of the Scientific Revolution, employing the new methods of science and drawing together discoveries in astronomy and physics to create a systematic explanation of the physical laws of the universe. This portrait suggests his youthful vigor and keenness. He was still in his twenties when he developed some of his greatest theories. (The Bettmann Archive)

Until the seventeenth century even the most learned scholars of Europe agreed with the standard medieval understanding of the physical nature of the earth and the universe. This medieval understanding was based on the views of the fourth-century B.C. Greek Aristotle, as modified by Ptolemy and medieval Christian scholars. According to this Christian medieval understanding the earth was stationary and in the center of the universe. Around it moved the planets, the sun, the stars, and the heavens in an ascending series of spheres. This universe was finite and focused on the earthly center of God's concern. "Scientific" investigation generally took the form of making deductions from accepted, authoritative medieval assumptions about the physical universe. The questions asked were usually the more philosophical or theological ones of ultimate causes for an event—guesses as to why something had occurred.

During the seventeenth century a relatively small number of scholars undermined this medieval understanding of nature and replaced it with a modern scientific view. According to this new scientific view, the earth was a moving body and no longer at the center of the universe. Rather, it, along with the planets, moved around the sun in an infinite universe of other similar bodies. Scientific investigations generally took the form of observing, measuring, experimenting, and coming to reasoned conclusions through the use of sophisticated mathematics. Medieval assumptions about the physical universe were viewed with a skeptical eye. The questions asked were usually the more concrete, pragmatic ones of *how* an event had occurred rather than the ultimate reasons for *why* such an event had occurred. The new scientific synthesis was one of a mechanistic universe of forces acting according to mathematically expressible laws and open to human reason and investigation.

Until the eighteenth century the impact of this modern scientific view, known as the Scientific Revolution, was limited. Nevertheless, it was an intellectual revolution of great significance, for with it Western civilization was making a turn from its medieval assumptions and embarking in a direction unique among the cultures of the world. Science would grow to become one of the main factors distinguishing the West and accounting for its power and dynamism.

1. CAUSES AND SPREAD

There were several causes for the development and spread of the Scientific Revolution, some of which extend back to the late Middle Ages and Renaissance. Medieval universities had been growing for some time and included the study of philosophy and other subjects that would be central to the Scientific Revolution, including astronomy, physics, and mathematics. Certainly the emphasis and the greatest prestige were accorded to theology and nonscientific study in these medieval universities, but nevertheless there were places on the faculty for many of the central figures of the Scientific Revolution, such as Galileo and Newton.

The Renaissance involved a search for classical writings. The discovery of Greek authorities who contradicted Aristotle and the growth of Neoplatonism as an alternative to Aristotelian thought in Renaissance Italy encouraged scholars to question medieval scientific assumptions. The Renaissance stimulated interest in analyzing and describing physical reality, a key concern of the Scientific Revolution. The Renaissance was also an age of commercial and geographic expansion in the West, which created a demand for new instruments and precise measurements, particularly for navigation on open seas. This demand encouraged scientific research, especially in astronomy and mathematics. In turn, the better instruments developed during the Renaissance helped scholars make accurate measurements, something crucial for the new science. During this same period, the printing press was invented, which facilitated the dissemination of the new science, even if initially to only a select few.

The Reformation played a mixed role in the Scientific Revolution. Generally, both Catholics and Protestants criticized the scientific discoveries that so threatened the medieval Christian view of the universe. During the sixteenth century there was perhaps more room within the Catholic church for scientific research than among Protestants, but by the middle of the seventeenth century this was clearly not the case. By then the Counter-Reformation Catholic church had turned into an enemy of much of the new science, while Protestants began to accept it. This was particularly so in England, where the Puritans encouraged the new science and where it took hold most firmly.

During the seventeenth century, governments supported science, in part hoping that scientific inquiry would yield discoveries that would increase the power and prosperity of the state. With governmental support scientific academies were established and played a significant role in the advancement of science. The earliest and most important of these were the Royal Society in England, chartered in 1662 by Charles II, and the Académie des Sciences in France, founded by Colbert four years later. These organizations and others patterned after them furnished laboratories, granted subsidies, brought scientists together to exchange ideas, published their findings, and encouraged scientific achievement generally. They also helped make scientists a more socially acceptable group and contributed to the creation of a new set of values supportive of the new science.

Finally, religious and psychological factors played an important, if difficult to evaluate, role in the development and spread of the Scientific Revolution. Many of the new scientists had strong, though not always traditional, religious motives for their work, particularly a desire to gain insight into the perfection of God's universe.

2. ASTRONOMY AND PHYSICS: FROM COPERNICUS TO NEWTON

The first branches of modern natural science to attract systematic attention were astronomy and physics. Discoveries in these fields would dramatically alter the perception of nature and the earth's place in the universe.

Nicolaus Copernicus

The first steps were taken in the sixteenth century by Nicolaus Copernicus (1473–1543), a Polish clergyman interested in astronomy, astrology, mathematics, and church law. Like so many other northern European scholars in the fifteenth century, he crossed the Alps to study in an Italian university. There he was influenced by the rediscovery of Greek scholarship, particularly Platonic and Pythagorean thought, that differed

from the accepted, mathematically complex Aristotelian-Ptolemaic tradition. This rediscovered Greek thought emphasized the importance of a hidden, simpler, mathematically harmonious reality underlying appearances. With a religious, mystical passion, Copernicus sought a simpler mathematical formulation for how the universe operated. This search convinced him that the earth was not the center of the universe but rather that the sun was the center. Moreover, the earth was not stationary but moved in perfect divine circles around the sun, as did other bodies in the universe. This change from an earth-centered (geocentric) to a sun-centered (heliocentric) universe has come to be known as the Copernican revolution (see Figures 35.2 and 35.3).

Copernicus worked on his heliocentric model of the universe for almost twenty-five years, but, fearing the ridicule of the laity and the ire of the clergy, he did not have it published until 1543, the year of his death. Few knew of his views and even fewer accepted them. Nevertheless, their significance and their threat to the Christian conception of the universe would be recognized and condemned by both Catholic and Protestant authorities, who would denounce the Copernican system as illogical, unbiblical, and unsettling to the Christian faith. Nevertheless, his views would stimulate other scholars investigating the physical nature of the universe.

Tycho Brahe

After Copernicus, the most important astronomer of the sixteenth century was a Danish aristocrat, Tycho Brahe (1546–1601). He persuaded the king of Denmark to support him, and he built the most advanced astronomy laboratory in Europe. There he gathered unusually accurate, detailed information about the planets and stars, even though the telescope had not yet been invented. Particularly important were his discoveries of a new star in 1572 and a comet in 1577, both of which undermined the Aristotelian assumptions about a sky of fixed, unalterable stars moving in crystalline spheres. He did not share Copernicus' belief in a heliocentric universe, nor did he grasp the sophisticated mathematics of the day. He believed that the earth remained the stationary center of the universe, as argued by Aristotle and Ptolemy, but he concluded that the

FIGURE 35.2 The Medieval View of the Universe This woodcut (1559) shows the traditional Ptolemaic conception of the universe. At the center is the earth, surrounded by ascending spheres of air, fire, the sun, the planets, the stars ("firmament"), the crystalline ring, and the "primum mobile." (The British Museum)

FIGURE 35.3 The Copernican Conception of the Universe (Woodcut, 1576) At the center is the sun, surrounded by the circling planets (one of which is the earth), all bounded by an infinity of stars and the heavens. One of the central developments of the Scientific Revolution was the replacement of the Ptolemaic geocentric by the Copernican heliocentric conception of the universe. (The British Museum)

other planets revolved around the sun, which itself moved around the earth and moon. However, the astronomical observations he gathered would be used by other scholars who became convinced that the earth moved around the sun.

Johann Kepler

Tycho Brahe's assistant, Johann Kepler (1571–1630), built upon Brahe's observations while returning to the Copernican heliocentric theory. A German Lutheran from an aristocratic family, Kepler believed there was an underlying mathematical harmony of mystical significance to the physical universe. He sought such a mathematical harmony that would fit with Brahe's observations. His most important findings were the

three laws of planetary motion, proposed between 1609 and 1619: first, that the planets moved in ellipses around the sun; second, that their velocity varied according to their distance from the sun; and third, that there was a physical relationship between the moving planets that could be expressed mathematically. He thus further undermined the Aristotelian universe accepted by medieval thought and provided support for the Copernican revolution. Moreover, he extended the Copernican revolution in ways that would be fully realized by Galileo and Newton.

Galileo Galilei

The Italian astronomer, physicist, and mathematician Galileo Galilei (1564–1642) believed, like Copernicus and Kepler, that there was a hidden harmony to nature. He felt that this harmony could be discovered through experimentation and mathematics. He investigated motion through controlled experiments and demonstrated that motion could be described mathematically. He showed that bodies once set into motion will tend to stay in motion and described the speed of falling bodies mathematically. He thus undermined Aristotelian physics and established rules for experimental physics.

Galileo then moved on to astronomy, using a telescope he built in 1609. The telescope revealed to Galileo that the moon had a rough surface not unlike the earth's, that Jupiter had moons, and that the sun had spots. He confirmed the Copernican hypothesis and provided support for the view that other heavenly bodies were like the earth and imperfect. By implication, this finding meant that the natural universe was ordered and uniform, without the hierarchical distinctions of the accepted medieval view.

Galileo aggressively published and defended his views against detractors, most notably in *Dialogue on the Two Chief Systems of the World*, published in Italian in 1632. This text brought him into conflict with conservative forces in the Catholic church, which condemned his theories at an inquisition in 1633, forcing him to recant.

Isaac Newton

The uphill trail blazed by Copernicus, Brahe, Kepler, and Galileo was continued on to a lofty peak by Isaac Newton (1642–1727) (see Figure 35.1). As a student at Cambridge University, he distinguished himself enough in mathematics to be chosen to stay on as professor after his graduation. Starting in his early twenties, Newton came forth with some of the most important discoveries in the history of science—or indeed of the human intellect. He developed calculus and investigated the nature of light. He formulated and described mathematically three laws of motion: inertia, acceleration, and action/reaction. He is probably best known for the laws of universal attraction, or gravitation. The concept matured and was refined in Newton's mind over a period of years. As it finally appeared in 1687 in his *Principia (The Mathematical Principles of Natural Knowledge)*, the law is stated with marvelous simplicity and precision: "Every particle of matter in the universe attracts every other particle with a force varying inversely as the square of the distance between them and directly proportional to the product of their masses." This law, so simply expressed, applied equally to the movement of a planet and a berry falling from a bush. The secret of the physical universe appeared to have been solved—a universe of perfect stability and precision.

What Newton had done was to synthesize the new findings in astronomy and physics into a systematic explanation of physical laws that were true for earth as well as for the heavens. This Newtonian universe was uniform, mathematically describable, held together by explainable forces, atomic in nature. The universe was essentially matter in motion.

Like most other figures of the Scientific Revolution, Newton was profoundly religious; he believed in God and a God-centered universe, as well as alchemy. By the later years of the seventeenth century and the beginning of the eighteenth century, the new science was becoming more acceptable than it had been for Newton's predecessors, as is illustrated by his career. He became a member of Parliament and served for many years as director of the Royal Mint. He was knighted by Queen Anne. His acceptance, as contrasted with the ridicule and persecution suffered by Copernicus and Galileo, indicates the progress that had been made by the scientific community between the sixteenth and the eighteenth centuries.

3. SCIENTIFIC METHODOLOGY

The scientists who made discoveries in astronomy and physics succeeded in undermining the medieval view of the universe as stable, fixed, and finite, with the earth at its center. They replaced it with a view of the universe as moving and infinite, with the earth merely one of millions of bodies, all subject to the laws of nature. In the process they were also developing and using new methods of discovery, of ascertaining how things worked, and of determining the truth. Indeed, at the heart of the Scientific Revolution was the new methodology of science. According to this new methodology, earlier methods of ascertaining the truth, which primarily involved referring to traditional authorities such as Aristotle, Ptolemy, and the Church and making deductions from their propositions, were unacceptable. The new methodology emphasized systematic skepticism, experimentation, and reasoning based on observed facts and mathematical laws. The two most important philosophers of this new scientific methodology were Francis Bacon and René Descartes.

Francis Bacon

Francis Bacon (1561–1626) was a politician and was once lord chancellor of England under James I. He had a passionate interest in the new science. He rejected reliance on ancient authorities and advocated that scientists should engage in the collection of data without holding preconceived notions. From that information, scientific conclusions could be reached through inductive reasoning—drawing general conclusions on the basis of many particular concrete observations. He thus became a proponent of the empirical method, which was already being used by some of the new scientists. In addition, he argued that true scientific knowledge would be useful knowledge, as opposed to medieval Scholasticism, which he attacked as too abstract. He had faith that scientific discoveries would be applied to commerce and industry and generally improve the human condition by giving human being great power over their environment. He thus became an outstanding propagandist for the new science as well as a proponent of the empirical method (see Figure 35.4). He did not, however, have a good understanding of mathematics and the role it could play in the new science. Descartes did.

René Descartes

René Descartes (1596–1650) was born in France and received training in Scholastic philosophy and mathematics. He spent his most productive years as a mathematician, physicist, and metaphysical philosopher in Holland. In 1619 Descartes perceived connections between geometry and algebra that led him to discover analytic geometry, an important tool for scientists. He expressed his philosophy and scientific methodology in his *Discourse on Method* (1637), a landmark in the rise of the scientific spirit. It was an eloquent defense of the value of abstract reasoning.

FIGURE 35.4 Title Page of Bacon's *Novum Organum* This title page from Francis Bacon's *Novum Organum* (*New Instrument*), published in 1620, shows a ship of discovery sailing out into the unknown. Below is the quotation ''Many shall venture forth and science shall be increased.'' (The Bettmann Archive)

He would question all authority no matter how venerable—be it Aristotle or the Bible. He tried to remove systematically all assumptions about knowledge to the point where he was left with one experiential fact—that he was thinking. ''I think, therefore I am'' he believed to be a safe starting point. From this starting point he followed a rigorous process of deductive reasoning to come to a variety of conclusions, including the existence of God and the reality of the physical world. He argued that the universe could be divided into two kinds of reality: mind, or subjective thinking and experiencing, and body, or objective physical substance. According to this philosophy, known as "Cartesian dualism," the objective physical universe could be understood in terms of extension and motion. "Give me extension and motion," said Descartes, "and I will create the universe." Only the mind was exempt from mechanical laws.

Descartes, like Bacon, rejected Scholastic philosophy as not useful (although his deductive method had similarities to the reasoning used in Scholastic thought). He emphasized the power of the rigorous, reasoning individual mind to discover truths about nature and turn them to human needs. Unlike Bacon, he emphasized mathematical reasoning, not empirical investigation. By challenging all established authority, by accepting as truth only what could be known by reason, and by assuming a purely mechanical, physical universe, Descartes was in dispute with medieval thought and established an influential philosophy and methodology for the new science.

4. OTHER DISCIPLINES

The individuals who made the great discoveries of the Scientific Revolution all used, to varying degrees, the new scientific methodologies promoted by Bacon and Descartes during the first half of the seventeenth century. Clearly astronomy and physics led the way, but important discoveries were made in other sciences as well.

In the sixteenth century Vesalius, a Fleming living in Italy, wrote the first comprehensive textbook on the structure of the human body to be based on careful observation. Because he dissected many human bodies in order to make his observations, he ran into serious opposition from clerical authorities. In disgust he gave up his scientific studies and became the personal physician of Emperor Charles V. In the seventeenth century William Harvey, an Englishman who also studied in Italy, discovered the major principles of the circulatory system, thus making it possible for surgeons to operate on the human body with somewhat less fatal consequences than had previously been the case (see Figure 35.5). Vesalius and Harvey are regarded as the founders of the science of anatomy.

In the seventeenth century, an Irish nobleman, Robert Boyle, laid the foundations for mod-

FIGURE 35.5 Modern Anatomy This illustration from an anatomy book published in 1639 by William Harvey shows the circulation of blood. Harvey's empirical, descriptive approach was typical of the new science. (Art Resource)

ern chemistry by attacking many assumptions inherited from the ancients and by beginning the systematic search for the basic physical elements. He relied on the experimental method and argued that all matter was composed of atoms. He discovered a law of gases that still bears his name.

The language in which science is expressed is mathematics. In the early seventeenth century a Scotsman, Sir John Napier, invented logarithms, by which the process of multiplying and dividing huge numbers is greatly simplified. Shortly afterward the system was applied to the slide rule. About the same time, René Descartes adopted the symbols now used in algebra and devised analytic geometry, a method of combining and interchanging algebra and geometry. In the latter part of the seventeenth century Newton and the German Wilhelm Leibnitz, working independently, invented calculus, upon which many of the most intricate processes of advanced science and engineering are dependent.

During the seventeenth century some of the basic scientific instruments were invented. Both the telescope and the microscope were products of the Dutch Netherlands. However, it was Galileo who first used the telescope in systematic astronomical observations. Antoni van Leeuwenhoek, a Dutchman, was the chief pioneer in the use of the microscope. He discovered bacteria two hundred years before Pasteur learned how to combat them; he also observed the cellular structure of plant and animal tissue, the structure of the blood, and its circulation through the capillary system. Another Dutchman, Christiaan Huygens, invented the pendulum clock, making possible the precise measurement of small intervals of time for the first time in history.

The methods and discoveries of the Scientific Revolution spread to disciplines outside of what are usually considered the sciences. A good example is political theory, with the seminal thought of Thomas Hobbes (1588–1679) and John Locke (1632–1704).

Hobbes gained contact with the new sciences from several quarters. As a young man he served as a secretary to Francis Bacon. While traveling on the continent, he came into contact with Descartes and Galileo. He studied the writings of William Harvey. Hobbes acquired an expertise in both geometry and optics. Toward the middle of his life Hobbes became involved in the political events of his times and turned his attention to political theory. Dismayed by the civil strife raging during the civil war in England, Hobbes developed a political theory justifying absolutism in the name of law and order. In his *Leviathan* (1651), Hobbes started from a very few principles about human nature and rigorously deduced explanations for the founding and proper functioning of the state. He argued that human beings are most concerned with the preservation of their own lives, the avoidance of pain and pursuit of pleasure, and striving for power to protect themselves and get what they want. In the hypothetical state of nature, people are in a continual competitive struggle with one another. Self-interest and reason eventually lead people to exit the state of nature by way of a social contract among themselves. This social contract creates and grants massive powers to a sovereign, who uses those powers as necessary to keep the peace. Hobbes, like other seventeenth-century scientists, assumed a mechanistic, materialistic universe. His reasoning was much like Descartes'— rigorous, mathematical, and deductive. In the end, Hobbes concluded that absolutism was in accordance with natural law, though his method of reasoning pleased neither kings nor aristocrats.

Locke was also heavily influenced by the new seventeenth-century science. He acquired a medical education at college, read the works of leading scientific thinkers such as Francis Bacon and Isaac Newton, and was a friend of Robert Boyle. Like Hobbes, Locke was involved in some of the political events of his times. Locke also started with human beings in a state of nature, made some basic assumptions about the human condition, and traced the exit from the state of nature by way of a social contract. Yet Locke came to some significantly different conclusions. Assuming that human beings were not quite so self-centered and that things in the state of nature were not so bad, Locke argued that the sovereign had far fewer powers than Hobbes had claimed and that individuals retained the right to revolt under certain circumstances. Applying reasoning similar to that of seventeenth-century scientists, Locke concluded that British constitutionalism was in accordance with natural law.

Thus both Hobbes and Locke extended the Scientific Revolution to new fields. While their conclusions differed, they set a new standard for political theory, becoming two of the most influential political theorists of modern times.

5. IMPACT

By the end of the seventeenth century, the Aristotelian medieval world view had been broken and replaced by the Copernican-Newtonian worldview. The methodology of modern science was established. Scientists had created the foundations for the modern sciences of astronomy, physics, mathematics, chemistry, and anatomy, and study in other disciplines was under way.

Although the new scientists' work had gained some acceptance, their ideas were still known to only a few. Only a small group of people actually participated in this revolution in science. Most were men. Certainly some women overcame barriers and did participate. Margaret Cavendish (1623–1673) wrote works on natural philosophy and the scientific method. Maria Sibylla Merian (1647–1717) became a leading entomologist. Other women participated in scientific research. But men were reluctant to recognize them, and women were generally excluded from scientific societies. Moreover, the findings of the new sciences were not used to liberate women from traditional assumptions or roles, but rather to reaffirm notions of women's inferiority.

The impact of science on the masses remained minimal during the seventeenth century. Some members of the wealthy elite supported and were influenced by the new sciences, seeing potential benefits from them. But even they were few in number. It was not until the Enlightenment of the eighteenth century that the ideas of the Scientific Revolution spread widely and were applied in new ways.

SUGGESTED READING

General

J. Ben-David, *The Scientist's Role in Society* (1971). A sophisticated social interpretation.
A. R. Hall, *The Revolution in Science, 1500–1750* (1983). Full of detail.
M. Jacob, *The Cultural Meaning of the Scientific Revolution* (1988). A strong interpretation.
L. Schiebinger, *The Mind Has No Sex? Women in the Origins of Modern Science* (1989). An informative recent study.
A. G. R. Smith, *Science and Society in the Sixteenth and Seventeenth Centuries* (1972).

Astronomy and Physics

S. Drake, *Galileo* (1980). A brief study.
F. Manuel, *A Portrait of Isaac Newton* (1968). Uses a psychoanalytic perspective.
E. Rosen, *Copernicus and the Scientific Revolution* (1984). A good recent study.
R. S. Westfall, *Never at Rest: A Biography of Isaac Newton* (1981). An excellent biography.

Scientific Methodology

T. S. Kuhn, *The Structure of Scientific Revolutions* (1962). An important, influential interpretation of the Scientific Revolution.

Other Disciplines

P. Laslett, *Locke's Two Treatises of Government* (1970). Includes an introductory analysis with the texts.
C. B. MacPherson, *The Political Theory of Possessive Individualism: Hobbes to Locke* (1962). A controversial Marxist interpretation.

Sources

M. B. Hall, ed., *Nature and Nature's Laws: Documents of the Scientific Revolution* (1970). A good collection.

CHAPTER 36
The Enlightenment

FIGURE 36.1 *Madame Geoffrin's Salon,* 1755 Meetings in aristocratic Parisian salons such as this were typical of the Enlightenment. Here thinkers, artists, musicians, writers, and aristocrats exchanged views and helped spread the philosophy of the Enlightenment. (Giraudon/Art Resource)

As a period of intellectual history, the eighteenth century is usually referred to as the Enlightenment, or the Age of Reason. The Enlightenment was initiated toward the end of the seventeenth century by a number of intellectuals who attempted to popularize the ideas of the Scientific Revolution. During the eighteenth century this popularization continued, and new attempts were made to apply the methods of natural sciences to human behavior and social institutions. Western thinkers were speculating on the broader meaning of science—its ethical, political, social, and economic implications. They subjected almost everything to the critical standard of reason. In doing so, Enlightenment thinkers rejected the assumptions of their medieval and Renaissance predecessors, who had looked to the Christian or classical past for guidance. Enlightenment thinkers argued for reform and change. They felt that people were ready to shrug off the shackles of tradition and custom and participate in the progress of civilization; to these optimistic intellectuals, people were ready to become enlightened.

The Enlightenment was limited in some respects. During the eighteenth century the Enlightenment was centered in western Europe. Moreover, Enlightenment thought spread primarily to only the elite of the urban aristocracy and middle classes. Nevertheless, the ideas and attitudes developed during the Enlightenment would come to dominate most parts of Western civilization over the next two centuries.

1. ENLIGHTENMENT CONCEPTS

Although Enlightenment thinkers differed widely among themselves, they shared a belief in certain broad concepts that together make up the philosophy of the Enlightenment. The three most important concepts were reason, nature, and change and progress.

Enlightenment thinkers argued that all assumptions should be subjected to critical and empirical reasoning. Traditional institutions or customs should not be accepted because they have been long-lasting but rather should be examined critically and held up to the standard of reason. True knowledge is gained empirically.

All we know and all we can ever know is what we perceive through our senses and interpret with our reason. There are no such things as innate ideas or revealed truth.

Enlightenment thinkers believed that nature is ordered, functions reasonably, and constitutes a standard for judgment. Nature is governed by a few simple and unchangeable laws. Those who think they can change one of these laws—who think they can, by praying, for instance, bring down rain on parched crops and perchance a neighbor's unroofed house—are dupes of their own egotism. Nature does not act capriciously. Proper empirical analysis will show that nature functions in line with the laws of reason. Nature is good and beautiful in its simplicity. Human beings have corrupted it with their complex political, social, and religious restrictions. A move to nature is a move toward wholesome vigor and freedom.

Most Enlightenment thinkers felt that change and progress work hand in hand as human beings work to perfect themselves and their society. Change should not be viewed with distrust as a deterioration from a previously superior, more perfect state of things. Change, when dictated by reason and in line with nature, liberates individuals and should be pursued. Such change contributes to individual and social progress on earth. Human beings are naturally rational and good, but the proponents of mystic religions have distorted human thinking and prevented proper progress by preaching false doctrines of original sin and divine moral laws. Rid people's minds of these religious hindrances, and they can and will build a more perfect society for themselves.

The concepts of reason, nature, and change and progress worked together in the minds of Enlightenment thinkers and generally formed a structure for their more specific ideas. Enlightenment thinkers used reason and nature to criticize institutions and customs of the past that still dominated their eighteenth-century society. Reason and nature further guided these thinkers as they determined what changes should take place. They felt that as individuals and societies made appropriate changes, human life would become more informed by reason and more compatible with nature. They believed that human beings were on the verge of enlightenment—of great progress—if people would simply open their eyes and become mature, reasoning adults. This progress would take the form of people leading increasingly happier, freer, more moral lives.

2. THE *PHILOSOPHES*

Enlightenment ideas were put forth by a variety of intellectuals who in France came to be known as the *philosophes* (see p. 470). *Philosophes* is French for "philosophers," and in a sense these thinkers were rightly considered philosophers, for the questions they dealt with were philosophical: How do we discover truth? How should life be lived? What is the nature of God? But on the whole the term has a meaning different from the usual meaning of "philosopher." The *philosophes* were intellectuals, often not formally trained or associated with a university. They were usually more literary than scientific. They generally extended, applied, popularized, or propagandized ideas of others rather than originating those ideas themselves. The *philosophes* were more likely to write plays, satires, histories, novels, encyclopedia entries, and short pamphlets or simply participate in verbal exchanges at select gatherings than to write formal philosophical books.

It was the *philosophes* who developed the philosophy of the Enlightenment and spread it to much of the educated elite in western Europe and the American colonies. Although the sources for their philosophy can be traced to the Scientific Revolution in general, the *philosophes* were most influenced by their understanding of Newton, Locke, and English institutions.

The *philosophes* saw Isaac Newton as the great synthesizer of the Scientific Revolution who rightly described the universe as ordered, mechanical, material, and only originally set into motion by God, who since then has remained relatively inactive. Newton's synthesis showed to the *philosophes* that reason and nature were compatible: Nature functioned logically and discernably, and what was natural was also reasonable. Newton exemplified the value of reasoning based on concrete experience. The *philosophes* felt

that his empirical methodology was the correct path to discovering truth.

John Locke (1632–1704) agreed with Newton but went further. This English thinker would not exempt even the mind from the mechanical laws of the material universe. In his *Essay Concerning Human Understanding* (1690), Locke pictured the human brain at birth as a blank sheet of paper on which nothing would ever be written except by sense perception and reason. What human beings become depends on their experiences—on the information received through the senses. Schools and social institutions can therefore play a great role in molding the individual from childhood to adulthood. Human beings were thus by nature far more malleable than had been assumed. This empirical psychology of Locke rejected the notion that human beings were born with innate ideas or that revelation was a reliable source of truth. Locke also enunciated liberal and reformist political ideas in his *Second Treatise on Civil Government* (1690), which influenced the *philosophes*. On the whole Locke's empiricism, psychology, and politics were appealing to the *philosophes*.

England, not coincidentally the country of Newton and Locke, became an admired model for many of the *philosophes*. They tended to idealize it, but England did seem to allow greater individual freedom, tolerate more religious differences, and evidence greater political reform than other countries, especially France. England seemed to have gone furthest in freeing itself from traditional institutions and accepting the new science of the seventeenth century. Moreover, England's approach seemed to work, for England was experiencing relative political stability and prosperity. The *philosophes* wanted to see in their own countries much of what England already seemed to have.

Many *philosophes* reflected the influence of Newton, Locke, and English institutions, but perhaps the most representative in his views was Voltaire (1694–1778) (see Figure 36.2). Of all the leading figures of the Enlightenment, he was the most influential. Voltaire, the son of a Paris lawyer, became the idol of the French intelligentsia while still in his early twenties. His versatile mind was sparkling; his wit was mordant. An outspoken critic, he soon ran afoul of both church

FIGURE 36.2 Frederick the Great with Voltaire Voltaire, seated, talks with Frederick the Great. This picture reveals the image of the great Enlightenment thinker at work with books, papers, and pen and with the international stature sufficient to gain the ear of enlightened despots such as Frederick. Yet Frederick's enlightenment may have been more form than substance. (Bibliothéque Nationale, Paris)

FIGURE 36.3 The Encyclopedia This engraving from one of the many technical articles in the *Encyclopedia* shows workers preparing type for printing, with details of materials used in the process. It reveals the optimistic faith in the ease and practicality of learning that was typical of Enlightenment thought. (French Embassy Press and Information Division)

and state authorities. First he was imprisoned in the Bastille; later he was exiled to England. There he encountered the ideas of Newton and Locke and came to admire English parliamentary government and tolerance. In *Letters on the English* (1733), *Elements of the Philosophy of Newton* (1738), and other writings, he popularized the ideas of Newton and Locke, extolled the virtues of English society, and indirectly criticized French society. Slipping back into France, he was hidden for a time and protected by a wealthy woman who became his mistress. Voltaire's facile mind and pen were never idle. He wrote poetry, drama, history, essays, letters, and scientific treatises—ninety volumes in all. The special targets of his cynical wit were the Catholic church and Christian institutions. Few people in history have dominated their age intellectually as did Voltaire.

The work that best summarizes the philosophy of the Enlightenment is the *Encyclopedia*. The *Encyclopedia* was a collaborative effort by many of the *philosophes* under the editorship of Denis Diderot (1713–1774) and Jean le Rond d'Alembert (1717–1783). This gigantic work undertook to explore the whole world of knowledge from the perspective of the *philosophes*. Its articles on subjects ranging from music to machinery expressed the critical, rationalistic, and empiricist views of the *philosophes* (see Figure 36.3). The practicality of science and knowledge in general was emphasized. One of the work's main messages was that almost anything could be discovered, understood, or clarified through reason. An

The *Philosophes*

Enlightenment thinkers often referred to themselves as "philosophes," which is technically the French word for philosophers. The term had a special meaning bound up with the spirit of the Enlightenment. This is dealt with directly in the following selection, "The Philosopher," from the Encyclopedia. *It has traditionally been assumed that Diderot is the author of "The Philosopher," but it may have been written by another person, perhaps Du Marsais. In any case, it is an authoritative treatment of the topic according to Enlightenment precepts.*

Other men make up their minds to act without thinking, nor are they conscious of the causes which move them, not even knowing that such exist. The philosopher, on the contrary, distinguishes the causes to what extent he may, often anticipates them, and knowingly surrenders himself to them. In this manner he avoids objects that may cause him sensations that are not conducive to his well being or his rational existence, and seeks those which may excite in him affections agreeable with the state in which he finds himself. Reason is in the estimation of the philosopher what grace is to the Christian. Grace determines the Christian's action; reason the philosopher's.

Other men are carried away by their passions, so that the acts which they produce do not proceed from reflection. These are the men who move in darkness; while the philosopher, even in his passions, moves only after reflection. He marches at night, but a torch goes on ahead.

The philosopher forms his principles upon an infinity of individual observations. The people adopt the principle without a thought of the observations which have produced it, believing that the maxim . . . so to speak, of itself; but the philosopher takes the maxim at its source, he examines its origin, he knows its real value, and

only makes use of it, if it seems to him satisfactory.

Truth is not for the philosopher a mistress who vitiates his imagination, and whom he believes to find everywhere. He contents himself with being able to discover it wherever he may chance to find it. He does not confound it with its semblance; but takes for true that which is true, for false that which is false, for doubtful that which is doubtful, and for probable that which is only probable. He does more—and this is the great perfection of philosophy; that when he has no real grounds for passing judgment, he knows how to remain undetermined.

The world is full of persons of understanding, even of much understanding, who always pass judgment. They are guessing always, because it is guessing to pass judgment without knowing when one has proper grounds for judgment. They misjudge the capacity of the human mind; they believe it is possible to know everything, and so they are ashamed not to be prepared to pass judgment, and they imagine that understanding consists in passing judgment. The philosopher believes that it consists in judging well: he is better pleased with himself when he has suspended the faculty of determining, than if he had determined before having acquired proper grounds for his decision. . . .

The philosophic spirit is then a spirit of observation and of exactness, which refers everything to its true principles; but it is not the understanding alone which the philosopher cultivates; he carries further his attention and his labors.

Our philosopher does not believe himself an exile in the world; he does not believe himself in the enemy's country; he wishes to enjoy, like a wise economist, the goods that nature offers him; he wishes to find his pleasure with others; and in order to find it, it is necessary to assist in producing it; so he seeks to harmonize with those with whom chance or his choice has determined he shall live; and he finds at the same time that which suits him: he is an honest man who wishes to please and render himself useful.

SOURCE: Merrick Whitcomb, ed., "French Philosophers of the Eighteenth Century," in *Translations and Reprints from the Original Sources of European History*, Vol. VI, No. 1 (Philadelphia: University of Pennsylvania Press, 1898), pp. 21–23.

underlying current was criticism of the irrational and of whatever stood in the way of the Enlightenment, whether it was religious intolerance or traditional social institutions. The first volume appeared in 1751. Its threat to the status quo was recognized by governmental and church authorities, who censored it, halted its publication, and harassed its editors. Thanks in great part to the persistence of Diderot, who fought the authorities and dealt with a difficult group of contributing authors, the project was completed with the publication of the final volume in 1772. The *Encyclopedia* sold well and played an important role in the penetration of Enlightenment ideas outside the major cities and courts.

By this time the Enlightenment was evolving to a different stage. The *philosophes* were becoming more quarrelsome among themselves. This disagreement reflected a greater acceptance of the fundamental philosophy of the Enlightenment, for the debates tended to center on how far Enlightenment concepts could be extended. Some *philosophes,* such as Baron d'Holbach (1723–1789), verged on atheism in attacks on organized religion. Others, such as Marie-Jean de Condorcet (1743–1794), were so optimistic that they almost made a religion out of progress itself. Enlightenment thinkers were also tending to specialize. Some laid the foundations for the development of the social sciences during the nineteenth century. For example, Cesare Beccaria (1738–1794) contributed works on modern criminology and penology, and Adam Smith (1723–1790) wrote what would be the fundamental text of classical economics. Finally, some Enlightenment thinkers took more challenging positions, often contradicting some of the ideas of the Enlightenment itself and providing a transition to the succeeding intellectual traditions. The most important example of these thinkers is Jean-Jacques Rousseau (1712–1778).

One of the most original thinkers and writers of all time, Rousseau crusaded for a return to nature—beautiful, pure, simple nature. The message struck home in a society weary of arbitrary and often corrupt governmental bureaucracy and an oppressively artificial and elaborate code of social etiquette. Rousseau was lionized. Great ladies, including the queen of France, began playing milkmaid. In his novel *La Nouvelle Hé-*

loïse, Rousseau extolled the beauties of free love and uninhibited emotion. In *Émile* he expounded the "natural" way of rearing and educating children. He would let children do what they like and teach them "practical" knowledge. Rousseau shared much with other *philosophes,* even contributing to the *Encyclopedia,* but after the 1750s he broke from them for personal as well as intellectual reasons. In *The Origin of Inequality among Men* (1753), Rousseau argued that civilization was not necessarily a progressive boon to humanity, that human beings had lost much since their exit from the state of nature. In *The Social Contract,* Rousseau became one of the few *philosophes* to make a fundamental contribution to political theory. Rousseau generally placed greater faith in emotion, feeling, and intuition than in reason. In this he was a forerunner of the romantic spirit and expounded its principles long before that movement reached its peak.

The *philosophes* had a self-conscious sense of a spirit of enlightenment. They felt that they were leading a mission of liberation, that by striking the match of reason the darkness of the past would be dispelled and humanity would quickly and easily liberate itself. By becoming thus enlightened, humanity could move from childhood to adulthood. They attacked war and the military values of the traditional aristocracy. They rejected artificial social distinctions. They lauded most forms of freedom, including freedom of the press, speech, and religious belief. They supported the application of science to economic activity, a view appealing to the middle class and liberal aristocracy. They believed that their eighteenth-century civilization was ready for enlightenment and the great progress that would result. Yet the optimism of most of the *philosophes* was not wild-eyed; indeed, there was an underlying current of pessimism in the works of thinkers such as Diderot, the marquis de Sade, Rousseau, and even Voltaire.

In characterizing the *philosophes,* historians have disagreed. Some view the *philosophes* as shallow, self-concerned dilettantes who had few deep or original ideas and who were afraid of real reform. Most historians, however, argue that the *philosophes* were thoughtful, sincere thinkers who performed an important service by laying the intellectual foundations of modern society.

3. WOMEN AND THE SOCIAL CONTEXT

There were several centers of Enlightenment thought in the cities and courts of Europe, particularly western Europe, but the heart of the Enlightenment was in Paris. Gatherings were regularly held in the salons of several wealthy Parisian patrons, usually women of the aristocracy or upper middle class such as Madame du Deffaud or Madame Geoffrin (see Figure 36.1). There the *philosophes* met with one another and members of the international upper middle class and aristocratic elite. They debated the ideas of the Enlightenment in an environment lush with art, music, and wealth. These gatherings facilitated the spread of Enlightenment ideas among social and intellectual elites and added much to the social respectability of intellectuals.

As patrons and as intellectual contributors to these gatherings, women played an important role in the Enlightenment. Women such as Madame Geoffrin provided essential financial support to several *philosophes*, particularly for the *Encyclopedia*. Other women corresponded by letter with leading intellectual, political, and social figures throughout Europe, using letter writing as an art just as conversation was an art in the salons. The salons were open to women with the right intellectual or social qualifications. The *philosophes* tended to support improving the education and position of women. The Enlightenment emphasis on individualism theoretically and in the long run led toward accepting the idea of political and social equality between men and women. Nevertheless, it cannot be said that the *philosophes* advocated equal rights for women in a modern sense nor that they challenged fundamental assumptions about the subordinate public roles appropriate for women. One of the few people to argue for real change in the condition of women in the eighteenth century was Mary Wollstonecraft (1759–1797). In 1792 she published *Vindication of the Rights of Women,* but generally her plea for equal rights for all human beings fell on deaf ears.

Meetings in Paris salons were paralleled by smaller meetings in other French and foreign cities as well as by less organized meetings in coffeehouses and the homes of the liberal aristocracy. Enlightenment ideas were read and discussed in local academies, Freemason lodges, societies, libraries, and clubs.

4. ENLIGHTENMENT AND RELIGION

The Enlightenment was profoundly secular in character, but religion played an important role. Very few Enlightenment thinkers were either atheists or traditional Christians. Most were skeptics influenced by the arguments of Pierre Bayle (1647–1706). Many believed in some form of deism. They believed that this wonderful mechanism called the universe could not have come into being by accident. Some infinite Divine Being must have created it and set it in motion. However, the finite mind of human beings cannot comprehend the infinite. Therefore, God is unknowable. Furthermore, God, having set his perfect mechanical laws into motion, will never tamper with them or interfere in human affairs. God is impersonal.

It is readily apparent that the beliefs of the *philosophes* were in conflict with the doctrines of the Christian churches—Roman Catholic, Protestant, and Orthodox alike. Christian theologians argued that God remained active in the universe, that God's ways are revealed through religious literature and institutions, and that faith constitutes a valid alternative to reason. Enlightenment thinkers and Christian leaders were soon engaged in debate, spending much time and effort attacking each other. In countries such as France and Italy, where clerics were strongly entrenched in government, they censored the writings of the *philosophes* and sought to interrupt their work. In the long run, however, the ideas of the Enlightenment spread, and the Church probably lost more than it gained by so ardently attacking the *philosophes* and their ideas.

In general the Enlightenment promoted toleration toward religious minorities, whether Christian or otherwise. For example, Enlightenment thinkers such as Locke in England and Baron de Montesquieu in France were among several who attacked discrimination against Jews. While the century did not witness an end to anti-Semitism, monarchs and political leaders influenced by the Enlightenment lessened some dictates against Jews in Austria, France, Prussia, and Portugal.

5. POLITICAL AND ECONOMIC ASPECTS OF THE ENLIGHTENMENT

Enlightenment thinkers devoted much thought to matters of government. If human beings are by nature rational and good, then surely, if given the opportunity, they can devise for themselves efficient and benevolent political institutions. Corrupt tyrannies were no longer tolerable. Of the numerous "enlightened" thinkers in the field of political science, three stand out above the others in influence: Locke, Montesquieu, and Rousseau.

Locke's most eloquent plea was for the natural rights of human beings, which are life, liberty, and property. He theorizes, in his *Two Treatises on Civil Government,* that to safeguard these rights individuals voluntarily contract to surrender a certain amount of their sovereignty to government. The powers of the government, however, whether it be monarchical or popular, are strictly limited. No government may violate the individual's right to life, liberty, and property. If it does, the people who set it up can and should overthrow it. These ideas were fundamental in the thinking of the makers of both the French and the American revolutions. Jefferson wrote many of Locke's ideas into the Declaration of Independence, frequently using his exact words. They likewise appear in the U.S. Constitution and in numerous French declarations of liberty.

Baron de Montesquieu (1689–1755) was less a theorizer than a discerning student of history and shrewd analyst of political systems. His masterpiece is *The Spirit of the Laws.* Although a great admirer of the English government after the Glorious Revolution, Montesquieu came to the conclusion that different types of government are best suited to various conditions. For instance, absolute monarchy is best for countries of vast area, limited monarchy for countries of moderate size like France, and republics for small states like Venice or ancient Athens. Not only did he approve of Locke's doctrine of limited sover-

eignty, but he specified how it can best be secured—by a separation of powers and a system of checks and balances. The powers and functions of government should be equally divided among king, lords, and commons, each one being checked by the other two. This theory was probably Montesquieu's greatest practical contribution to the science of government. The principle was incorporated into the U.S. Constitution—kings, lords, and commons becoming the executive, judicial, and legislative branches of government.

Rousseau offered a more radical political theory. This morbid, erratic genius based the conclusions in his *Social Contract* and his *Second Discourse* upon pure imagination. People in the state of noble savagery were free, equal, and happy. It was only when some began marking off plots of ground, saying "this is mine," that inequality began. In order to restore their lost freedom and happiness, people entered into a compact, each with all the others, surrendering their individual liberty to the whole. Since sovereignty is indivisible, the general will is all-powerful. Although Rousseau never made it clear just how the general will would actually operate in practice, he apparently assumed that the individual would be free by virtue of being part of the general will. Rousseau had great influence on the leaders of the second and more radical phase of the French Revolution.

Some of the eighteenth-century planners of the better life through reason turned their thoughts to economics. Since the late fifteenth century, mercantilism had been the dominant economic theory and practice in western Europe. This system of regulated nationalistic economy reached its peak in the seventeenth century. Only the Dutch Netherlands held out for free trade. But if, according to the fundamental assumptions of the Enlightenment, the universe is run by a few simple mechanical laws, why should there not be a similar natural order in the field of economics? A group of French Physiocrats, led by François Quesnay, personal physician to Louis XV, began to teach that economics has its own set of natural laws, that the most basic of these laws is that of supply and demand, and that these laws operate best when commerce is freed from government regulation. This doctrine came to be known as *laissez-faire* (or free trade and enterprise).

The chief developer of the theory of laissez-faire was Adam Smith, a Scottish professor of philosophy who associated with the Physiocrats while sojourning in France. His *Wealth of Nations,* published in 1776, has remained the bible of laissez-faire economics ever since. The ideas of the French Physiocrats and Adam Smith strongly influenced the leaders of the American and French revolutions.

6. ENLIGHTENED DESPOTISM

While critical and combative, the *philosophes* were not political or social revolutionaries. They hoped for fairly painless change from above rather than a revolutionary transfer of power to the still-unenlightened masses. Many followed Voltaire in believing that enlightened despotism was the form of government that offered the greatest chances for enactment of enlightened reforms. By the middle of the eighteenth century several monarchs found these views attractive, styled themselves as enlightened monarchs, and attempted to enact reforms that at least appeared to fit with Enlightenment thought. These monarchs have been distinguished from their predecessors and termed "enlightened despots." To what extent this is a valid characterization of their rule remains to be seen.

The most sensational of the enlightened despots was Frederick the Great of Prussia (1740–1786). Frederick had from boyhood loved music, poetry, and philosophy. At the end of the Seven Years' War (1756–1763), the second of his two wars of aggression, he settled down as a model enlightened despot and attempted to apply the laws of reason to statecraft. Frederick was an avid reader of the French philosophers. He even invited Voltaire to visit him at Potsdam, but Prussia was not big enough to hold two such egos at once. The two quarreled and, after several years, parted.

Frederick made much of religious toleration. However, he continued to penalize the Jews and never ceased to ridicule Christians of all denominations. He was a strong advocate of public education, although he spent very little on it in comparison with what he spent on his army. The centralized Prussian bureaucracy became the most efficient government in Europe. True to the prevailing thought of the Enlightenment, however, he had no faith in popular self-government. Nor did he make a move to free the serfs or end the feudal system in Prussia. Probably the most lasting of Frederick's contributions to Prussia were his codification of the law and improvements in the administration of justice. In the field of economics, Frederick was a mercantilist, although he did share the Physiocrats' appreciation of the importance of agriculture.

The most sincere of all the enlightened despots was Joseph II of Austria (1780–1790). Unfortunately, he lacked the practical sagacity of Frederick the Great. His well-meaning but ill-conceived efforts to centralize the administration of the far-flung Hapsburg territories, to replace the numerous languages of his subjects with German, to secularize the strongly entrenched Roman Catholic church, and to free the serfs in a society still based on feudalism all backfired.

Other monarchs, such as those of Sweden, Sardinia, Spain, and Portugal, attempted or enacted reforms that could be seen as enlightened. Even in Russia, Catherine the Great made apparent efforts at enlightened reforms, but ultimately she did not put most of those reforms into practice.

Significantly, France alone of the great powers on the Continent failed to produce an even faintly enlightened despot. Upon attaining the French throne in 1774, the well-meaning Louis XVI appointed the Physiocrat Turgot as minister of finance. Turgot, a friend of Voltaire, initiated a program of sweeping reforms that might have forestalled the French Revolution. However, within two years' time the powerfully entrenched vested interests persuaded the weak-willed king to dismiss him.

Whether there was a phenomenon of enlightened despotism occurring during the eighteenth century, remains a debated question among historians. If there was, it was usually a matter more of form than of content. Several eighteenth-century monarchs acted in certain enlightened ways, believed themselves to be enlightened, admired some of the *philosophes,* and were admired in return. Several supported culture, favored a less religious and more rational justification for their rule, and consulted with *philosophes*. Yet most of their "enlightenment" was superficial. Many of the reforms they made were simply an update in the long process of making the central government more effective and powerful. Few tried to enact fundamental social, political, or economic reforms dictated by Enlightenment thought, and even those who tried, such as Joseph II, generally failed to effect those reforms.

7. CONCLUSION

Enlightenment thinkers applied and popularized a secular, rational, reformist way of thinking that undermined the intellectual foundations of traditional society. Their ideas threatened the Church more than any other institution, and one of the legacies of the Enlightenment was a widening gap between religiously influenced ideas and accepted scholarly thought. These thinkers, probably unknowingly, laid the intellectual foundations for the revolutions that swept Europe and America from the last quarter of the eighteenth century to the mid–nineteenth century. Moreover, their way of thinking and the ideas that arose from it would form the intellectual core of the liberal middle-class ideology that was ascendant during the nineteenth century and is still strong in the twentieth century.

SUGGESTED READING

General

C. Becker, *The Heavenly City of the Eighteenth-Century Philosophers* (1932). An influential, thought-provoking classic.

P. Gay, *The Enlightenment: An Interpretation*. Vol. I: *The Rise of Modern Paganism*. Vol. II: *The Science of Freedom* (1969). Detailed treatment by a leading authority.

N. Hampson, *The Enlightenment* (1982). A highly respected survey.

The Philosophes

T. Bestermann, *Voltaire* (1969). A solid biography.

A. M. Wilson, *Diderot* (1972). An excellent biography.

The Social, Political, and Economic Context

L. Krieger, *Kings and Philosophers, 1689–1789* (1970). A broad survey making connections between thought and politics.

H. Payne, *The Philosophes and the People* (1976). Focuses on the gap between the *philosophes* and the people.

P. Quennell, ed., *Affairs of the Mind: The Salon in Europe and America from the 18th to the 20th Century* (1980). Emphasizes the role of women.

S. I. Spencer, ed., *French Women and the Age of Enlightenment* (1984). Covers important aspects of the topic.

Enlightened Despotism

H. Scott, *Enlightened Despotism* (1990). A good recent analysis.

E. Wangermann, *The Austrian Achievement, 1700–1800* (1973). A good study of enlightened monarchs.

Sources

L. G. Crocker, ed., *The Age of Enlightenment* (1969). A good anthology.

P. Gay, ed., *The Enlightenment: A Comprehensive Anthology* (1973). A good selection of documents.

RETROSPECT

During the fourteenth and fifteenth centuries, various tensions and a weakening of social institutions marked the transformation of the medieval world. During the fifteenth and sixteenth centuries, the institutions and developments that would characterize early modern times grew out of the changing medieval system.

The first challenge to the medieval system came in the cities of northern Italy during the fourteenth and fifteenth centuries. There the ideas, values, and culture of the Renaissance arose. Although rooted in the medieval world, scholars, writers, and artists began looking back to classical Greece and Rome for models instead of accepting medieval scholastic authority. Cultural leaders focused more on individual human beings living in a concrete, material, Christian world rather than on medieval theology. The social and cultural elite were becoming more self-centered, proud, versatile, and materialistic. These Renaissance qualities produced new, vibrant literature and art, making northern Italy the cultural center of the West.

During the fifteenth and sixteenth centuries the Renaissance spread from Italy to northern Europe, particularly to the courts of princes and kings and to university towns. There the Renaissance took on a more piously religious character as northern humanists tried to reconcile Christian and classical cultures.

In place of the declining feudal monarchies and empires arose the national or territorial state, which became the dominant political institution of the early modern era. The rise of the national states ended the independence of numerous feudal lords by bringing them under the authority of national monarchs. Talented monarchs such as Ferdinand and Isabella in Spain, Louis XI in France, and Henry VII in England increased their own power and established foundations for the continued growth of national monarchical power. Those areas that did not unify into national states, such as in Germany and Italy, suffered from political weakness.

National monarchs encouraged Europeans to expand into the non-Western world. Voyages of "discovery" soon led to commercial trade, spreading Christianity, and political control. During the fifteenth and early sixteenth centuries, Portugal and Spain led in this expansion of Europe. England, France, and the Netherlands soon followed. By the end of the sixteenth century, large parts of the rest of the world, particularly in the Western Hemisphere, southern Asia, and coastal Africa, had come under European economic and political domination.

The expansion of Europe was also stimulated by new economic developments. Europe's medieval economy, characterized by subsistence agriculture, monopolistic guilds, and localism, slowly gave way to capitalistic practices and institutions. Increasing population and rising prices spurred commerce and created social turmoil, with the poorer peasants suffering the most. The old landed aristocracy was now threatened by newcomers into the class and by a new middle class of aggressive entrepreneurs, merchants, bankers, and lawyers. It is true that the bourgeoisie sought most of all to enter the ranks of the nobility and did so whenever possible, and that the nobility held the upper hand politically and socially for two or three more centuries. But by 1600 class lines had become more fluid.

The fifteenth and sixteenth centuries were marked by a deepening concern for religious matters. During the 1500s the western Christian church, which had monopolized religious life and strongly influenced the intellectual, political, and economic life of Europe during the Middle Ages, was split asunder by the Reformation. Great religious leaders such as Martin Luther and John Calvin broke from the Roman Catholic church and laid the foundations for the various Protestant churches. Much of northern Europe became Protestant. This advance of Protestantism stimulated reform efforts already underway within the Roman Catholic church. Catholic doctrine was forcefully affirmed at the Council of Trent, and new religious orders such as the Jesuits reinvigorated the Church.

The religious struggles of the Reformation combined with political forces to give rise to the

Wars of Religion. From the middle of the sixteenth to the middle of the seventeenth centuries, much of Europe was struck by war and political turmoil that was connected to religious issues. The most devastating of these wars was the Thirty Years' War, which broke out in Germany in 1618 and was not concluded until 1648 with the Peace of Westphalia.

The economy and society—rural, based on agriculture, and with a vast mass of peasantry dominated by the privileged aristocracy—changed only slowly during most of the seventeenth and eighteenth centuries. Gradually the central governments, the growing cities, and the middle classes altered life within the traditional village. The pace of social change quickened in the mid–eighteenth century as population grew, agriculture was revolutionized, and cottage industry spread. Religious affiliations changed little; established Catholic and Protestant churches remained committed to the hierarchical social order and the dominant political systems of their states. Even the numerous pietist and quietist religious sects that arose during this period passively accepted, for the most part, the political authority of the established and usually absolutist governments.

The baroque and classical styles, which prevailed in literature and the arts in western Europe throughout most of the seventeenth and eighteenth centuries, generally harmonized with and often exalted the absolutist monarchs and their courts. These styles stressed a combination of grandeur, richness, and order that appealed to monarchs and the privileged orders, who so often were the patrons of the arts.

The seventeenth and eighteenth centuries were the apogee of royal absolutism as a form of government in the Western world. The clearest example of royal absolutism in western Europe arose in France, where under Henry IV, Richelieu, Mazarin, and Louis XIV, the Bourbon monarchy achieved a degree of control that was unprecedented and a position of dominance in Europe. European history during the years 1661–1715 has been called the age of Louis XIV. Louis and his court were the envy of all other monarchs, who sought to emulate them. France possessed a military strength so great that the major states of western and central Europe working in combination held France in check only with difficulty.

Royal absolutism also dominated the political forms of central and eastern Europe during the seventeenth and eighteenth centuries. There the most important political developments were the rise of two military despotisms—Prussia and Russia. The Hohenzollerns of Prussia, consistently pursuing the policies of royal absolutism, militarism, and territorial aggrandizement, more than doubled their territory and population and challenged Austria for the leadership of the German-speaking world. Russia, under two strong absolutist monarchs, Peter the Great and Catherine the Great, defeated Sweden and the Ottoman Turks and gained valuable territory facing the West. Poland, which failed to develop a strong central government, disappeared from the map, carved up by Russia, Prussia, and Austria.

INDEX

Note: Page numbers followed by the letter *f* or *m* indicate figures or maps, respectively.